Kill Khalid

Also by Paul McGeough

Manhattan to Baghdad: Despatches from the Frontline in the War on Terror

In Baghdad: A Reporter's War

Mission Impossible: The Sheikhs, the U.S. and the Future of Iraq

Kill Khalid

The Failed Mossad Assassination of Khalid Mishal and the Rise of Hamas

PAUL McGEOUGH

THE NEW PRESS

NEW YORK
LONDON

Requests for permission to reproduce selections from this book should be mailed to:
Permissions Department, The New Press,
38 Greene Street, New York, NY 10013.

Published in the United States by The New Press, New York, 2009
Distributed by W. W. Norton & Company, Inc., New York

LIBRARY OF CONGRESS CATALOGING-IN-PUBLICATION DATA
McGeough, Paul, 1954–
Kill Khalid : the failed Mossad assassination of Khalid Mishal and the
rise of Hamas / Paul McGeough.
p.   cm.
Includes bibliographical references and index.
ISBN 978-1-59558-325-3 (hc. : alk. paper)   1. Mash'al, Khalid,
1956—Assassination attempt.   2. Politicians—West Bank.   3. Harakat
al-Muqawamah al-Islamiya.   4. Arab-Israeli conflict.   I. Title.
DS126.6.M375M43   2009
956.95'3044—dc22   2008040455

The New Press was established in 1990 as a not-for-profit alternative to the large,
commercial publishing houses currently dominating the book publishing industry.
The New Press operates in the public interest rather than for private gain, and
is committed to publishing, in innovative ways, works of educational, cultural,
and community value that are often deemed insufficiently profitable.

www.thenewpress.com

Composition by NK Graphics
This book was set in Adobe Caslon
Maps on pp. vi and xvi by Rob Carmichael

Printed in the United States of America

2 4 6 8 10 9 7 5 3 1

For Pam

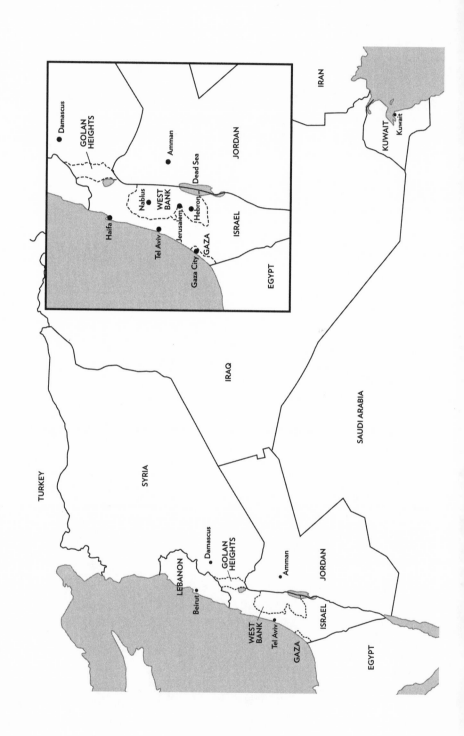

Contents

Acknowledgments   *ix*

Who's Who   *xi*

1: The Tourists   *1*

2: Village of the Sheikhs   *4*

3: The Tap Dancer from Amman   *17*

4: The Education of a Terrorist   *30*

5: "Have You Guys Lost Your Minds?"   *40*

6: Arafat's Circus   *49*

7: The Palestinian Project   *61*

8: The Bearded Engineer in a New York Cell   *78*

9: Violence Is the Only Weapon   *95*

10: A Little Obscurity Is Good   *110*

11: "They Used a Bizarre Instrument"   *129*

12: Mishal Must Not Die   *144*

13: "Who the Hell Is Khalid Mishal?"   *161*

14: Pulling a Rabbit from the King's Threadbare Hat 178

15: The Price Bibi Paid 196

16: The Legendary Image of Mossad 215

17: Brother Against Brother 230

18: Handcuffed and Deported 247

19: Dead Men Walking 267

20: Follow the Money 294

21: Government from the Trenches 312

22: "No Gold Bars Left" 336

23: Everything Is Not as It Seems 349

24: An Eye for an Eye 365

25: Taking the Holy Land to Court 383

26: The Man Who Wouldn't Die 396

Epilogue 415

Chronology 419

Notes 425

Index 457

Acknowledgments

Except where stated otherwise, *Kill Khalid* is based on my interviews with key players and observers of the Middle East crisis. The interviews were conducted in six countries during 2007 and early 2008. Inevitably, there were a few knock-backs and many sources cooperated on condition that I not disclose their identities. I thank them all. One interviewee who set no conditions for my inordinate demands on his time was Khalid Mishal.

Along the way many others gave me more help than I can ever thank them for. In Manhattan, Sally Roth was an enthusiast from the first moment I discussed the idea with her. Without her active support and encouragement, the book might not have gotten off the ground. Marc Favreau, editorial director at The New Press, had the faith and trust to back me. Later in the project, he revealed an exceptionally deft hand in the art of how and where to tweak a complex manuscript as he pushed me to where I needed to be.

In Amman, Ranya Kadri was unstinting with her time, thoughtful analysis, and professional guidance as she cut a swath through cultural, linguistic, and informational barriers that would have defeated ordinary mortals. Randa Habib, too, was incredibly generous with her time and guidance.

In Sydney, Alan Oakley, editor of the *Sydney Morning Herald*, was hugely supportive, both in his enthusiasm for the project and in allowing me to disappear from his newspaper for more than a year. Richard Walsh, of my Australian publisher, Allen & Unwin, was a beacon on dark days. An exacting taskmaster, Richard worked over the manuscript in his energetic and demanding way, with encouragement and clarity when it was most needed.

Maher Mughrabi followed him with lessons not just about the spelling of Arabic names, but also about sensitivities and history.

An army of my colleagues—Arab, Israeli, and foreign journalists and authors—has covered the Middle East for the two decades on which I have focused. I salute them and thank them for the thousands of news reports and feature articles and dozens of books that enriched my understanding of people and places, times and events.

This writing business is unforgiving terrain, so a forgiving wife is a godsend. Pam Williams was patient, caring, and inspiring, even in the face of truculence. She generously does her own informal PhD on whatever the current assignment is. *Kill Khalid* could not have seen the light of day without her multi-skilling—dear wife, loyal friend, incisive colleague, and sound editor.

Paul McGeough
Sydney
October 2008

Who's Who

IN HAMAS

Khalid Abu Hilal—Fatah commander who defected to Hamas in the lead-up to the June 2007 crisis in Gaza

Mohammad Abu Sayf—Khalid Mishal's bodyguard

Mousa Abu Marzook—deputy and former leader of the Hamas Political Bureau

Jawad Abu Sulmiyah and **Saib Dhahab**—first Hamas members killed in clashes with Israeli forces

Isa Al-Najjar—one of the founders of Hamas

Abdel Azziz Al-Rantisi—senior leader in the Gaza Strip

Mahmoud Al-Zahar—senior leader in the Gaza Strip

Yehia Ayyash—master suicide bomber; also known as "The Engineer"

Nadia El-Ashi—wife of Abu Marzook

Ibrahim Ghosheh—Hamas media officer

Ismail Haniyah—appointed prime minister of the Palestinian Authority in 2006

Abu Maher—Mishal's driver

Khalid Mishal—Damascus-based leader of Hamas; also referred to as Abu Walid

Khalid Mishal's family

    Abd Al-Qadir—Mishal's father; also referred to as Mullah Abd Al-Qadir

    Fatima—Mishal's mother

Amal—Mishal's wife

Maher—younger brother of Khalid Mishal

Mohammad Nazzal—member of Hamas Political Bureau

Mohammad Salah—Hamas bagman from Chicago

Said Siam—appointed as interior minister of the Palestinian Authority in 2006

Azzam Tamimi—friend of Mishal since their teenage years and the author of *Hamas: Unwritten Chapters*

Sheikh Ahmad Yassin—spiritual founder of Hamas; assassinated by Israel in 2004

IN JORDAN

King Abdullah II—crowned king of Jordan upon the death of his father, Hussein, in 1999

Abdullah Azzam—Palestinian-born mentor to Khalid Mishal and Osama Bin Laden

General Samih Batikhi—head of General Intelligence Department, also known as the Mukhabarat, in the 1990s

Steve Bennett—first secretary, Canadian Embassy

Hussein Bin Talal—king of the Hashemite Kingdom of Jordan from 1952 until his death in 1999

Wesley Egan—U.S. ambassador to Jordan, 1994–98

Oded Eran—Israeli ambassador to Jordan in 1997

Randa Habib—Amman bureau chief for Agence France-Presse

Prince Hassan—brother of and crown prince to King Hussein; was widely expected to succeed him as king of Jordan

Ranya Kadri—journalist

Saad Na'im Khatib—assisted in the capture of Mossad agents in Amman in 1997

Dave Manners—CIA station chief, Amman

Mike Molloy—Canadian ambassador to Jordan

Nasouh Muheiddin—director of public security in Amman

Samir Mutawi—information minister in the mid-1990s

Queen Noor—fourth wife of King Hussein

Asad Abdul Rahman—lectured Khalid Mishal at university in Kuwait; adviser to Yasser Arafat

Fahd Al-Rimawi—editor and proprietor of the weekly newspaper *Al-Majd*

General Ali Shukri—director of King Hussein's private office
Bassam Akasheh—surgeon and director of Queen Alia Heart Institute at King Hussein Medical City, Amman
Sami Rababa—chief anesthesiologist at Queen Alia Heart Institute
Walter Wilson—director of infectious diseases division, Mayo Clinic, Rochester, Minnesota

IN THE OCCUPIED TERRITORIES

Yasser Arafat (1929–2004)—president of the Palestinian Authority, one of the founders of Fatah; chairman of the executive committee of the Palestine Liberation Organization (PLO)
Mahmoud Abbas—also known as Abu Mazen; prime minister and later president (2004–present) of the Palestinian Authority
Mohammad Dahlan—security director and Fatah leader in Gaza
Keith Dayton—lieutenant general, U.S. Army, U.S.-appointed security coordinator between Israel and the Palestinian Authority
Rajoub brothers—**Jibril** stood as a Fatah candidate and **Nayef** as a Hamas candidate in the 2006 elections
Terje Roed-Larsen—Norwegian diplomat and UN representative to the PLO
Nabil Shaath—Palestinian businessman, minister in the Palestinian Authority, and longtime adviser to Yasser Arafat
Raji Sourani—head of the Gaza Center for Human Rights and Law

IN ISRAEL

Ehud Barak—prime minister, 1999–2001
Nahum Barnea—*Yedioth Ahronoth* journalist
David Berger—Canadian ambassador to Israel, 1995–99
David Boim—son of Joyce and Stanley Boim who died in a Hamas attack near Jerusalem in 1996
Alvaro de Soto—UN envoy to the Middle East Quartet
Levi Eshkol—prime minister, 1963–69
Baruch Goldstein—Jewish-born settler who killed thirty Palestinians in a Hebron mosque in February 1994
Efraim Halevy—diplomat and director of Mossad, 1998–2002

Tzachi Hanegbi—justice minister, 1996–99

Shalom Harari—Israeli Arabist and administration official based in the Gaza Strip in the 1980s

Martin Indyk—U.S. ambassador to Israel, 1995–97, and senior Clinton adviser

Dan Kurtzer—U.S. diplomat stationed in Israel in the mid-1980s

Zvi Malchin—Mossad agent in the 1960s

Benjamin Netanyahu—prime minister, 1996–99

Ehud Olmert—prime minister, 2006–8

Smadar Perry— *Yedioth Ahronoth* journalist

Yitzhak Rabin—prime minister, 1974–77; 1992–95

Ariel Sharon—prime minister, 2001–6

Norman Spector—former Canadian ambassador to Israel, 1992–95

Majali Whbee—adviser to Ariel Sharon

Gilad Shalit—nineteen-year-old corporal in the Israel Defense Forces who was captured by Palestinian militias in June 2006

Danny Yatom—director of Mossad, 1996–98

IN THE UNITED STATES

Elliott Abrams—deputy National Security Council adviser under Bush, appointed 2005

Mufid Abd Al-Qadir—Khalid Mishal's Texas-based brother and a Holy Land Foundation fund-raiser

Shukri Abu Baker—chief executive and president of the Holy Land Foundation

Sandy Berger—Clinton's national security advisor, 1997–2001

George W. Bush—president, 2001–9

Bill Clinton—president, 1993–2001

Stanley L. Cohen—New York lawyer retained by Abu Marzook

Michael T. Dougherty—FBI special agent

A. Joe Fish—presiding judge at the 2007 Holy Land Foundation trial in Dallas

Linda Hamilton—wife of Bernard C. Welch Jr.

Joseph Hummel—FBI special agent

Nathan Lewin—Washington lawyer working in partnership with his daughter **Alyza Lewin**

Denis Lormel—head of the FBI's Terrorist Financing Operations Section

Rob Malley—Clinton adviser on Arab-Israeli affairs

Akram Mishal—cousin of Khalid Mishal employed at the Holy Land Foundation

Colin L. Powell—secretary of state, 2001–5

Condoleezza Rice—secretary of state, 2005–9

Bruce Riedel—Clinton adviser on Near Eastern affairs

Dennis Ross—Middle East envoy and peace negotiator in the George H.W. Bush and Clinton administrations

George Tenet—director of the CIA, 1997–2004

Bernard C. Welch Jr.—convicted for the murder of Dr. Michael Halberstam in 1980

David Welch—assistant secretary for Near Eastern affairs, 2005–9

Robert Wright—FBI agent working on Hamas investigations in the United States

IN CANADA

Badger—anonymous blogger believed to operate from Canada

Lloyd Axworthy—minister for foreign affairs, 1996–2000

IN LEBANON

Alastair Crooke—former British intelligence agent, European Union adviser in the Middle East, and founder of the Beirut-based Conflicts Forum

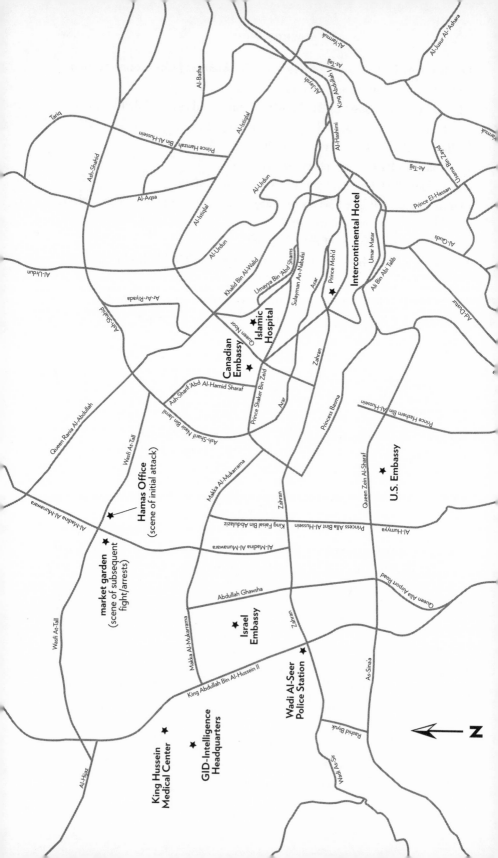

1

The Tourists

The Canadians arrived on different flights from different cities. Young, fit, and well dressed, they looked the part—Westerners with deep pockets dropping in to see Jordan's jewels . . . wondrous Nabatean ruins at Petra; stunning Roman relics at Jerash; and the desert wilds of Wadi Rum, where David Lean and Peter O'Toole created the cinema classic *Lawrence of Arabia*. If there was time, perhaps a beachside party at Aqaba on the Red Sea.

In September 1997, in the madness of the Middle East, Jordan was a pocket of relative peace. Usually a few tourists bobbed up among the suited foreign-business and white-robed-Arab traffic at Amman's Queen Alia Airport and the Canadians were quickly swallowed by the anonymous chaos of the arrivals hall. Immigration officials perfunctorily stamped their passports; half an hour later, all five were downtown, piling out of a couple of battered taxis in the paved forecourt of the Intercontinental Hotel. Checking in, they again presented Canadian papers and chatted easily with a desk clerk about which of the tourist attractions were within easy striking distance of Amman.

Only later, when all assembled in one of their rooms, did they abandon the pretense. These "Canadian tourists" were agents for Mossad, the fabled Israeli intelligence service. Their mission in this quiet, U.S.-friendly Arab city was state-sanctioned assassination—in the name of Israel.

With the door chained from the inside, they dropped the phony accents and spoke in their own language. Unpacking their gear, they sat for one last time, methodically rehearsing the deadly detail and schedule for the coming days. They ignored the minibar. But, instinctively cautious in a part of the world where selected guests were assigned rooms expensively rigged for others to eavesdrop, they turned up the volume on the TV.

A glass-topped coffee table became a workbench on which they spread the essentials of death. A street map of Amman, with hand-drawn circles on a west-side business district. Photographs of their intended victim, who was a forty-something Arab male—lean, round faced, and bearded. Few in Jordan, or Israel, would have recognized him. Oddly, there was a small camera too.

A practiced nonchalance masked caution and anxiety in all five of them. One of the men—blond and bearded—handled the camera with a care and respect that went way beyond any ordinary tourist's concern for holiday snapshots. The camera, in fact, was the killers' "gun."

One of his colleagues produced a pouch, from which he extracted a small and seemingly innocuous bottle that had been brought into the country separately and delivered to them at the hotel by a secret courier. It contained a small quantity of a clear liquid—Mossad's "bullet." This was a chemically modified version of fentanyl, a widely used painkiller. But in this potent, altered form it would kill within forty-eight hours, leaving no trace for discovery on the autopsy table. Their plan was murder—silent, unseen.

In the privacy of another room in the same hotel, a handsome brunette opened a small makeup bag to assure herself yet again that one bottle in particular had traveled well. She was the Mossad men's insurance policy.

Her inclusion in the plot was most unusual, but so lethal was the drug the agents would be using for the first time that Mossad's mission planners had demanded the presence of a doctor and an antidote in case one of the team accidentally exposed himself to the poison.

Their orders were to kill Khalid Mishal. The forty-one-year-old Palestinian activist had been overlooked by the legion of foreign intelligence agents operating in Amman. But at the Mossad bunker near Tel Aviv, Mishal was seen as the first of a dangerous new breed of fundamentalist leaders. He was hard-line, but he did not wear a scraggy beard or wrap himself in robes. Mishal wore a suit and, as the man accused by Israel of orchestrating a new rash of suicide bombs, he was, by regional standards, coherent in his television appearances. From the Israeli perspective Khalid Mishal was too credible as an emerging leader of Hamas, persuasive even. He had to be taken out.

They struck on Thursday, September 25, 1997. It was just after ten AM— and they botched everything. Had they been successful, Mishal would have gone home and died quietly; the agents would have been on their way home too, over the Allenby Bridge on the Jordan River and back in Jerusalem for a celebratory lunch. Instead, two of the Israelis were soon languishing in dank cells under an Amman security complex and the others were hunkering at the Israeli Embassy—which, incredibly for a supposedly friendly foreign mission, was locked down by a menacing cordon of Jordanian troops.

King Hussein of Jordan could rise to the occasion in a crisis. Filled with rage, he fired a shot across the Israeli prime minister's bow, warning Benjamin Netanyahu that his Mossad men would hang if Mishal died.

More deliberately, Hussein then picked up a phone and placed a call. It was answered across the world, where a woman with a sweet voice answered: "Good morning. Welcome to the White House."

2

Village of the Sheikhs

The young boy knew this truck. In the summer it delivered fleshy watermelons to stalls in the village market. Now Khalid Mishal and dozens of his stricken relatives were dumped on the back, where he was more accustomed to seeing fruit piled up like great green boulders. His mother, Fatima, was distracted, but he clung to her. Some of his aunts sat on the hard boards; cousins were squished between fat suitcases and bundles of bedding and other effects, which were held together in knotted blankets and bedsheets.

Heading east and away from their homes in the Jerusalem Mountains, they descended into an alien, inhospitable world. As the old truck lurched into the furnace of the Jordan Valley, the fertile familiarity of a village that had been the boy's entire world gave way to desolation—an arid, bone-dry moonscape.

As they made their way toward the Allenby Bridge, the crossing just north of where the indolent Jordan River fused with the glycerine depths of the Dead Sea, Khalid saw his first war dead—the bodies of fighters on the road. Taking it all in with a child's eyes, Khalid did not understand that, amidst this grief and sorrow, he and his family were being detached from their homeland. It was June 1967.

The traffic was chaotic. Trucks and taxis were bumper-to-bumper. Many other people were fleeing on foot. Hungry and thirsty in the heat of early summer, some wearily abandoned their baggage—suitcases and even a prosthetic leg were dumped along the way. Mothers with two-year-olds screaming for water could be seen. U.S. diplomats later estimated that tens of thousands had fled ancient Jericho alone.[1]

In the grim aftermath of the Six-Day War, Palestinians were repeating their own history. Just two weeks after Israel's snap conquest of the West Bank, Khalid was now another anonymous youngster in the second wave of Palestinians driven from their land. The first had been almost twenty years before, back in 1948, when so many were forced out to make way for the new state of Israel.

Fatima now ordered her teenage girls to keep a tight hold of five-year-old Maher, Khalid's younger brother. Yelling over the noise of the rattling truck on which they found themselves, she attempted to give the frightened children a simple explanation for this upheaval. "The Jews have taken our land," she said.

As they finally reached the river crossing, there was congestion and more panic when all were forced to abandon their vehicles. The old Allenby Bridge had been bombed and gaping holes in the timber planking made it impassable to cars. Now ropes were strung up as makeshift handrails, to assist the thousands of refugees as they carefully made their way across the splintered pathways that remained at the sturdier edges of the bridge's deck. Fatima and her children left their homeland on foot, inching across the river into Jordan.

Silwad was nestled in chalky high country in the heart of the West Bank. At the end of a track to nowhere, sixteen miles north of Jerusalem, about eight thousand people lived in a hillside pastoral that marked them as villagers—it was their relationship to the land, not their numbers that defined them.

The village straggled along a stoop-shouldered ridge running north–south. In front of its villagers lay a spectacular bird's-eye view of what, after the calamity of 1948, were the lost lands of Palestine—the coastal plains from Jaffa to Haifa. Behind them rose the lofty bulk of Al-Asour Mountain, which, at 3,370 feet, was the West Bank's second highest peak.

Silwad had been spared much of the bloodiness and brutality that shrunk the land of Palestine. But Khalid's father, Abd Al-Qadir, had left the village, as an eighteen-year-old, to find it. He had been riveted by the sermons of the firebrand preacher Izzadin Qassam, which he listened to at Al-Istiqlal Mosque in Haifa—the northern port city to which many young Silwadis went in search of work. In 1936 he had joined the ranks of the much-romanticized, but ill-fated, Arab Revolt against colonial British forces in the Arabs' attempt to preempt British support for the proposed state of Israel. In this uprising, which fueled Palestinian nationalism, Abd Al-Qadir sometimes fought with up to a hundred men; at other times, he roamed in a small guerrilla cell.

London had won control of Greater Palestine when the First World War's victors had carved up the Ottoman Empire. Thousands of Arabs died as their insurrection was brutally crushed by the British. When the revolt petered out in 1939, Abd Al-Qadir returned to Silwad with a new sense of the Palestinians' isolation and a deep disquiet about the failings of his people's fractured leadership. In the face of a persistent, British-backed push by the Jews for Palestinian lands, the Syrians had passed weapons and ammunition to the Palestinians, but the Arab leaders of the day had offered scant support and done little to help unite the bickering Palestinian leadership.

Amidst a rising sense of foreboding about Jewish ambitions, life in Silwad had continued for Abd Al-Qadir and his extended family of field workers and artisans. He had married Fatima, his first cousin and at that time a mere twelve-year-old, and together they had settled into a simple, if harsh, life.

Silwad was a bare-bones village with no electricity. There was just a single phone, which was locked away in the municipality office; water was drawn from the wells; and each family's only transport usually was a single donkey. Some here were wealthier than others, but the subsistence realities of life created a simple local egalitarianism—all cooked their bread on a hot steel dome, and all spread it with the same local tomatoes, homemade cheese, and olive oil for lunch. Such was the life of a Palestinian peasant.

Here, the children accepted as normal each family's deep engagement with recent Palestinian history, the sometimes coarse tribal ways, and the deeply conservative culture. In the same way, they took for granted the privations of a depressed rural economy that saw men go abroad for years at a time, working to supplement meager family funds. It was women who raised the families and crops. When Khalid was just fourteen months old, his father all but disappeared from his life—to distant Kuwait, sending back a few dinars each month. Sometimes the gap between his visits home was as long as two years.

For all that, there was a sense of security. Life was good. Their home was a single room, just twenty feet square, which had been walled off at the end of a building made of uncompromising gray stone. The rest of the structure was home to others in their extended family. Translated from the Islamic calendar to the Judeo-Christian, the dated keystone in the lintel read 1944.

More important than the house, however, were the salt-and-pepper fields of clay and broken limestone that came with it. Abd Al-Qadir was fortunate to have had a well-to-do grandfather who, on his death, bequeathed him forty *dunams*—about ten acres.[2] In these rough-terraced, boulder-strewn fields the family grew wheat, fruit, and nuts—olives, figs, apricots, grapes, and almonds. In her husband's absence, it was Fatima who marshaled her brood to work the fields between household chores and classes at a small local school, which was a walk of just more than a mile from their home in a spartan quarter of the village called Ras Ali.

Silwad was known as the "village of the sheikhs" because a long tradition of local men had undertaken spiritual studies at Al-Azhar, Cairo's fabled Islamic university. Most returned to the Jerusalem Mountains to preach and teach. They included the blind Sheikh Khalil Ayyad, who had a powerful hand in shaping Silwad's strict religious character at a time when Abd Al-Qadir and Fatima were finding their feet, somewhere about the middle of the local pecking order—socially and economically.

Abd Al-Qadir had a decent piece of land and, by local standards, a reasonable income. He was a restless man, often on the move, seeking the time of key political and religious figures. He had had only a brief, elementary school education, but he took to studying the Qur'an and in time his services were sought as a mediator, settling local disputes according to the tenets of Sharia or Islamic law. Fatima could neither read nor write, but she was philosophical, telling her husband, "We're not a wealthy family, but we have wealth in our brains."

After the 1930s revolt, violence had escalated—Arab on Jew, Jew on Arab. As Abd Al-Qadir saw it, the vacillating British were virtually giving Palestinian land to the Jews. "Piece by piece . . . in front of our eyes," he would say. Like the Palestinians, Jewish fighters had taken to attacking the British forces as Palestinians were shunted aside to make way for a new Jewish homeland. Against rising tension, it was the Jewish underground militias, the Irgun and the Stern Gang, that had created a specter that would haunt both peoples for decades—of deliberate and lethal attacks on civilian crowds. Arab fighters had gone on the attack with "the knife, the bludgeon and the fuel-doused rag," but the Jewish response had been the introduction to the conflict of the standard equipment of modern terrorism—"the camouflaged bomb in the marketplace and bus station, the car and truck bomb and the drive-by shooting with automatic weapons."[3]

In 1945, as the world reeled from the horror of the atrocities to which the Nazis and their supporters subjected the Jews of Europe, the Zionists went for broke in their campaign for a homeland of their own, demanding all of historic Palestine.[4] The emerging Cold War powers, Washington and Moscow, ignored Arab protests and, in November 1947, the United States and the Soviet Union backed a UN resolution calling for Palestine to be divided between the two peoples—with the exception of the holy city of Jerusalem, which U.N. Resolution 181 proposed be put under international control and accessible to Muslims, Jews, and Christians.

Inspired by an Islamist speaker who came to Silwad from Cairo in 1946, Abd Al-Qadir joined the Muslim Brotherhood—known in Arabic as "Ikhwan Al-Muslimun." The Brotherhood was a controversial group, established in Egypt in the 1920s to counter secular trends and to push for religiously oriented Muslim societies that would live by Sharia law. The Brotherhood was drawn to Palestine by the Arab Revolt.[5] Later it sent fighters to help the Arab resistance against the Jews and the British. It opened dozens of branches, and in Silwad most religious figures signed up—as much for political as religious reasons.

As Israel's War of Independence loomed, Abd Al-Qadir took up arms again. But he chose not to fight with the Brotherhood. Instead he went under the command of Abd Al-Qadir Al-Husseini, a legendary resistance leader who died as a Palestinian hero in heavy fighting at Qastal, west of Jerusalem, just weeks before the proclamation of the state of Israel in May 1948.

In the weeks before his death, Al-Husseini's paramilitaries so thwarted Jewish fighters in battles for control of steep hills on the strategic road between Tel Aviv and Jerusalem that the Haganah, the Zionist fighting force, devised what it called "Plan D." With the objective of clearing hostile and potentially troublesome Arabs out of Palestine, this was a military campaign that directly and decisively contributed to the birth of the Palestinian refugee problem.[6] The aim of the plan was the destruction of rural and urban areas of Palestine.[7] Water supplies were poisoned and massacres were counted in the dozens.[8] Yitzhak Rabin, a 1940s Israeli military officer who would serve twice as his country's prime minister, later wrote of his part in what the Israeli historian Ilan Pappe ranked with the biggest forced migrations in modern history. It was essential that fifty thousand civilians be driven out of Lod and Ramle, towns near Tel Aviv, Rabin wrote.[9]

"The population of Lod did not leave willingly. There was no way of avoiding the use of force and warning shots in order to make the inhabitants march the ten or fifteen miles to the point where they met up with the [Arab armies] . . . the inhabitants of Ramle watched and learnt the lesson: Their leaders agreed to be evacuated voluntarily."[10]

Palestinians counted more than five hundred villages destroyed. By the end of 1948, about seven hundred thousand people, more than 60 percent of the Arab population of what had been Palestine, were refugees in the West Bank and the Gaza Strip and in Jordan, Syria, and Lebanon.

The Declaration of Israeli Independence, read by the legendary David Ben-Gurion at a ceremony at the Tel Aviv Art Museum on May 14, 1948, deliberately omitted any reference to the national borders proposed in the UN's awkward attempt to evenly divide the disputed territory of the Holy Land because Ben-Gurion anticipated expanding beyond those boundaries. Within twenty-four hours of reading the proclamation he had his chance.

The next conflict, which began on May 15, would be perceived very differently by both sides. What Israel called its War of Independence, the Palestinians would call their *Al-Nakba*: "Catastrophe."

In the face of a collapse by the Palestinian resistance in fighting in the preceding months, the multinational Arab League threw its support behind them. Units of the Egyptian, Jordanian, Syrian, Lebanese, and Iraqi armies moved into Palestine the day after Ben-Gurion's declaration of independence. For decades Israeli historians would present the conflict as the Israeli David confronting the Arab Goliath. But in mid-May 1948, twenty-five thousand Arab troops in Palestine faced an Israeli force of thirty-five thousand. Both forces grew and by the end of the year Israel's hundred thousand men under arms outnumbered Arab forces by nearly two to one.[11] Israel began with inferior weapons, but arms shipments from Czechoslovakia, within weeks of the outbreak of war, tipped the balance in its favor.[12]

Israel was better manned and better armed, and it fought strategically.

By the end of the war, about six thousand Israelis and twice as many Arabs were dead. The Egyptians took and held Gaza and, with it, as many as three hundred thousand new Palestinian refugees who cowered along its mean coastal strip. Jordan's British-trained and funded Arab Legion moved in and held the West Bank along with the eastern quarter of Jerusalem—an outcome that was canvassed by Amman's wily King Abdullah I in a series of prewar meetings with Zionist leaders. Those secret encounters made the Jordanian monarch a weak link in the Arab coalition that Israel could exploit to its own strategic advantage.

The UN plan for Jerusalem to be an international zone was dumped. The city was divided along the cease-fire line, giving Amman control of the historic Old City and its revered shrines—for both Islam and Judaism. This was a cause of much bitterness for Israelis, who now were denied access to their holiest place of worship, the Western Wall. Palestine as a nation-in-the-making was erased from the map. As Israel, the world's newest nation, grabbed almost double the land mass allocated under UN Resolution 181, the burr of Palestinian dispossession was fixed firmly under the saddle of world leaders and armies of diplomats for generations to come.

In Silwad, shock at the outcome of the war and the failure of Arab leadership was acutely felt, as hundreds of Arab refugees from the new Jewish state found their way up the track into the Jerusalem Mountains. They came from Haifa and Jaffa, first borrowing outhouses and space in villagers' homes, but in time acquiring land, building houses, and marrying into village families.

Two years later, King Abdullah of Jordan formally annexed all of the West Bank—and, with it, the village of Silwad. Some locals yearned to be a part of an independent Palestine; others objected to being forced under the control of Amman. But Abd Al-Qadir lectured his family that, like it or not, Arabs would be better off under any Arab regime than under Israeli or British control, even if their new Arab monarch's clandestine dealing with Israel made him an outcast in the Arab world.

War, politics, and the hardships of village life aside, these were tragic years for Fatima. A rural Palestinian wife's first duty was to produce children—with the firstborn preferably being a son. Fatima's first five babies died within months of their birth—three sons and two daughters. Her first to survive were girls—Safiyah, born in 1950, and Miriam, in 1953. It was not until March 1956 that she fulfilled her marital duty by providing Abd Al-Qadir with a male heir. This was Khalid Abdul Rahman Ismail Abd Al-Qadir Mishal—whose name, in time, would be shortened to Khalid Mishal.

Any sense of joy was short-lived. Within months, her husband did as many other village men did—he took a second wife. Culturally, what seemed a cruel blow to Fatima was perfectly acceptable conduct. Abd Al-Qadir would draw quietly on his cigarette and profess himself well pleased with an arrangement that told the world he was a man of means, someone of stature. Fatima, then an attractive thirty-year-old, was furious. As her husband set up a second household and took to spending only half his time with Fatima and their children, she challenged him. "How can you do this to me?" she demanded to know. "I'm your cousin. I'm your wife. I've given you a son—why do you want another wife? Haven't I looked after you, the children, your mother, and the farm?"[13]

Her husband stonewalled her. Shrugging his shoulders, Abd Al-Qadir argued that polygamy was a right granted by Islam and Arab tradition. Such seemingly heartless behavior was a complex tale of Arab male indulgence. In Abd Al-Qadir's case, it became more difficult to understand when, a year later, this man who needed the world to believe he could afford to keep a second wife and home announced he was going abroad for work—to supplement the family funds.

The track abroad from Silwad was well worn. In the early days of the British mandate, young men hauled themselves to Nazareth to find work; through the 1930s and 1940s they went off to Haifa—to labor and to hear the fiery sermons of Qassam.[14] In the 1950s, a good number of Silwadi males packed their bags and headed for Kuwait, and now Abd Al-Qadir joined them. He went legally. Many others, including a cousin of his first wife and the first husband of his second wife, died traipsing the hot desert between Baghdad and Kuwait City as they attempted to smuggle themselves into the burgeoning emirate, oil rich and tiny, at the head of the Persian Gulf. His departure was doubly painful for Fatima, because Abd Al-Qadir had decided to take the newer of his wives to Kuwait. Fatima was abandoned in Silwad to run the farm and raise his first family.

Life was tough and lonely for women left behind. Fatima took solace from the farm and her children—especially Khalid, the all-important first son. At age four he demanded to be taught to read by his older sisters; soon, he was helping his illiterate mother to understand the labels on medicine bottles. She was proud of her son. His schoolteachers were pleased too. Khalid was at the top of his class regularly and became the school know-it-all. Village folklore recorded that whenever an exercise defeated his classmates, it was clever Khalid who provided the right answer. He amused Maher, his younger brother, by crafting cars and other toys for him from bent wire and tin cans.

Village play was a great leveler. Boys built kites, played marbles, and invented their own games of skill and chance. Much of their time was spent in the shadow of a giant, castle-like rock on the higher edge of Ras Ali, which the children had dubbed Ea'arak Al-Kharouf, or "Sheep Rock." When they fell over at play, they were immediately ordered to get up; as a child, Khalid split his head when he fell head-first from the living level of their home onto a rock floor in the basement below. The gaping wound was treated with a simple press of coffee grounds.

This was a parched corner of the world and, as the decade of the 1950s rolled into the 1960s, the infant Israeli state and its Arab neighbors were edging toward a new war footing—over water. Israel intended the Sea of Galilee as a great cistern for its new towns and farms. But only one of the three streams feeding it actually rose in Israel. The others—the Banias and the Dan—rose in Syria and in Lebanon. The Jordan River, flowing from the southern end of the Sea of Galilee, was a vital water source for Syria and Jordan.

Indignant Arab governments ordered their engineers to embark on a dramatic plan to divert the Banias and the Dan before the rivers entered Israel. But when they started digging, the Israelis bombed their bulldozers and dredges to a rude halt. There were frontier clashes between Israel and Syria, and an obscure but determined new Palestinian nationalist by the name of Yasser Arafat dispatched the first of his Fatah guerrillas on cross-border raids into Israel.

In Silwad, with her politically aware husband absent in Kuwait, Fatima was oblivious to the beat of the war drums. There was no television, and few newspapers reached the village; it was only the men, gathered around their battery-powered radios, who listened gravely to Radio Cairo and the BBC World Service. A fuse was burning but, apart from the fact that Fatima could neither read nor write, this was harvest time—she had just done cutting wheat and was drawing breath before bringing in figs and grapes.

Lasting just six days, the war was virtually over before a breathless nephew brought Fatima the news that it had begun. In a stunning series of strikes in the first week of June 1967, Israeli jets destroyed four hundred aircraft of the combined Arab air forces—most while they were still on the ground. The same morning, the Old City of Jerusalem was surrounded and, just hours later, Israeli ground forces penetrated deep into the West Bank. When they reached the outskirts of ancient Jericho, just before sunset on the first day, they received orders to snatch the entire West Bank for Israel.[15]

Fatima's nephew announced that nearby villages were being surrounded by Israeli forces—or, as he put it, in simple parlance, "the Jews." "We're losing our land!" he yelled. Next morning, refusing to panic, Fatima still sent eleven-year-old Khalid and his sisters to school while her father set off to work his fields. But the old man quickly returned. In great distress, he ordered Fatima to arm herself with a kitchen knife, telling her, "The Jews are coming. You can't die like an animal—defend yourself!"[16]

Like much of the Arab world, many in Silwad believed the propaganda that beamed in from Cairo. They believed the Egyptians' wildly exaggerated accounts of Arab victories in the making. In the streets of Amman, the Jordanian capital, crowds cheered fighter jets that roared overhead, going into Israeli airspace. These, they thought, were Egyptian fighter jets that would show no mercy to the Israelis.[17] In fact, they were the Israeli Air Force returning from the preemptive strikes, which had wiped out virtually the entire Egyptian air force. Abdul Fatah, Fatima's uncle who ran a grocer's store in Silwad, was captivated by Radio Cairo. He told his niece, "We are winning! We'll have lunch in Tel Aviv!"[18]

But a mere twenty-four hours later, Silwad fell without a struggle. There was no organized resistance—just a brief skirmish, in which one local was killed. Israeli troops moved through the streets, ordering locals to hang a white flag out front as a sign they would not resist. As the first nighttime curfew was imposed and their new Israeli overlords dug in across the West Bank, Fatima's mother submissively hung the universal sign of surrender on the doorjamb of her fearful daughter's home.

Fatima had no way to contact Abd Al-Qadir in Kuwait. Under the control of an occupying army of young Israeli men, she worried greatly for her daughters, seventeen-year-old Safiyah and fourteen-year-old Miriam. Her aunt Haleema wanted to flee to caves up in the mountains, but, as the head of her household, Fatima was defiant. "They can destroy my home if they want to—but I'm not leaving," she declared, words that rang in her children's ears.

Realizing just how badly the war had gone for the Arab armies, Abd Al-Qadir and Abdul, his older brother who also was in Kuwait, were gripped by fears that Israeli troops would repeat the killing and village demolitions of 1948. They rushed to Amman, where the older man asserted the authority of age. He argued that it was too dangerous for them both to enter the West Bank, now occupied by the Israelis, and ordered Abd Al-Qadir to remain in the Jordanian capital while he went to fetch their families from Silwad.

Arriving on Fatima's doorstep, Abdul told her to get the children ready for a quick departure. Instead of paying for the lunch in Tel Aviv that he had anticipated as a result of an Arab victory, Abdul Fatah, her grocer uncle, forked out his money for the owner of the watermelon truck to evacuate the family to the Jordan crossing.

As the truck pulled away from Silwad, Fatima looked back into the faces of her parents, who had elected to stay behind. She had packed lightly—just two suitcases for five of them—because the village men claimed they might be back within weeks, or maybe even days. This mess would be settled, they were sure; somehow the Israelis would leave and all the villagers would then return to complete the harvest. But something gnawed inside Fatima. Gazing into the fields, she burst into tears. She had nursed them as she had nursed her children. What troubled her most was the basics of rural life she left behind—

her stocks of homemade cheese, olive oil, dried figs, soap, and the grain she had just set aside as seed for next season.

In a swift and extraordinary mobilization, Israel had seized control of what then prime minister Levi Eshkol described as "a good dowry"—the West Bank snatched from Jordan; Gaza and the Sinai from Egypt; and the Golan Heights, strategically located above the Sea of Galilee, from Syria. Eshkol continued his wedding metaphor: "but it comes with a bride we don't like."[19]

Addressing the leaders of Israel's Labor Party, Eshkol was articulating the contradiction that would dog Israel's existential debate for decades. His anxiety was widely shared and very simple.

Israelis wanted the Palestinian land, but not its people. Amid suggestions that they be expelled—and even that the Dome of the Rock, the Islamic jewel on the Jerusalem skyline, be blown up—the fate of the Palestinians became "the question of the million."[20]

The Israeli lobby in Washington went into overdrive immediately, piling pressure on President Lyndon Johnson. American Jews feared that Israel might be forced to withdraw from its new turf without first negotiating a peace treaty with its vanquished foes.[21] But it was never clear that Israel really wanted one. Back in 1948, Ben-Gurion had concluded that time was on the side of the Israelis—that there was no need to rush to any formal peace talks, which might curtail future opportunities to create what his colleague Brigadier General Uzi Narkis described as "new facts."[22] When the fighting stopped in 1967, Defense Minister Moshe Dayan told the BBC that Israel was happy with its position—that he did not envisage negotiations. Cheekily, he added, "We're waiting for the Arabs to pick up the phone and call."[23]

There was fierce debate within the Israeli establishment about just what to do with the West Bank. Menachem Begin opposed returning it, and Dayan worked up plans for Israeli military outposts and new Jewish communities on high ground among the Arab villages and towns. The debate canvassed the Jordan River as a new international frontier—or having no border at all. Options for dealing with the Palestinian refugees were calculated clinically. To make them disappear from the new-look Israel, they might be resettled in Arab states—maybe in the Sinai, or across the river in King Hussein's shrunken kingdom of Jordan. But, even as this debate went on, groups of Israelis were given government grants and armed protection for the first of the controversial new Jewish settlements on Arab land.

There was a slight hiccup when Theodore Meron, a lawyer in the Israeli

Ministry of Foreign Affairs, produced a legal opinion that argued that the settlements contravened a Geneva Convention stipulation that an occupying country could not deport or transfer its own civilian population into occupied territory. Undaunted, the government countered with a claim that, because the final status of the West Bank had not been determined and its inclusion in King Hussein's Hashemite Kingdom in 1950 had not been executed legally, Israel could argue that the West Bank did not constitute occupied territory. To appease early American anger over the landgrab in the Golan, the first settlements were presented as "military" outposts and some settlers even were issued military uniforms. Just six months after the end of the war, there were already ten Jewish settlements in the Palestinian Occupied Territories.[24]

Vehicle-borne loudspeakers were dispatched to towns and villages, urging Palestinians to leave and threatening those who lingered. When they did leave, their homes were destroyed. Dayan was well pleased when refugee numbers crossing the Jordan River hit one hundred thousand. He said, "I hope they all go. If we could achieve the departure of three hundred thousand without pressure that would be a great blessing."[25]

The first of what would become decades of collective punishment by the Israelis was dealt to Arab villages and cities that resisted in any way—passively or aggressively. The Israelis imposed curfews; bus services were canceled and businesses were ordered closed. Homes were searched; individuals were arrested and tortured under interrogation. Some were deported, and more homes were demolished.

An effort to co-opt some Arab community leaders—as a precursor to an independent Palestine, whose sovereignty would be hugely compromised—was at times comic and very soon declared to be a failure. So too was a "transfer" program, which called on the skills of those Israeli operatives who had ferried Jews illegally into Palestine before 1948 to now turn their minds to making Palestinian refugees disappear from the Gaza Strip. Mordechai Gur, who was among the first Israelis to enter the Old City on the third day of the Six-Day War, was appointed military governor of Gaza; he cheerfully admitted he was doing his bit to pressure Arabs to leave by deliberately eroding their standard of living.[26]

And yet many Palestinians simply decided not to move. When an Israeli post office was opened at Hebron, the Arab mayor, Sheikh Muhammad Ali Jabari, treated the assembled dignitaries to a brief but pointed history lesson. He was just a boy, he told them, when the Turks opened Hebron's first post office in the days of the Ottoman Empire; later, during the years of the mandate, he had officiated at the opening of a British post office, and after that a

Jordanian one.[27] He was quite confident someone else would take the place of the Israelis.

When the Palestinian rush to the borders stopped, Uzi Narkis wrote: "We certainly hoped [the refugees] would flee, like in 1948. But this time they didn't. We made buses available. Whoever wanted to, could go to the Allenby Bridge. At first some left. Then fewer and fewer every day, until they stopped."[28] In the end, Israel estimated that the Six-Day War created up to 250,000 refugees.[29]

The creators of the Israeli state were digging in, making it impossible for their successors to agree to any concessions on what would continue to be the four burning issues at the heart of the Middle East crisis: a return to the 1967 borders, Arab access to Jerusalem, a right of return for Palestinian refugees, and the removal of Jewish settlements from Palestinian land.

In 1968, Moshe Dayan ended up in the hospital after he was trapped in a landslide on an archaeological dig. His many visitors included the Arab mayor of a town that had been assisted by Dayan in the postwar confusion. When Palestinian homes had been demolished, the Israeli warrior with the trademark eye patch had had some of them rebuilt. Later, Dayan spoke of the special bond he believed he had with the mayor, who had come to his bedside bearing oranges still on the branch: "The situation between us is like the complex relationship between a Bedouin man and the young girl he has taken against her wishes. But when their children are born, they'll see the man as their father and the woman as their mother. The initial act will mean nothing to them. You the Palestinians, as a nation, do not want us today, but we will change your attitude by imposing our presence upon you."[30]

The Six-Day War changed the Middle East—and the contest between Jews and Palestinians—forever. The two were locked in a crude vise that, in the abstraction of a child's mind, the boy Khalid could feel tightening. In Silwad, the children had been allowed to sit in the village circles, as old men drank their tea and told stories of Palestinian heroics amidst the overpowering losses of 1936 and 1948. In the weeks before the Six-Day War, the boy had had a sense of foreboding as the elders hunkered around the radio, and his instinct had sharpened as air-raid drills interrupted classes at school. The danger had become real and present when he raced to the top of Al-Asour, Silwad's mountain backdrop, to cock his ear for the thump of artillery as he and his schoolmates gawped in the direction of Jerusalem in June 1967.

Khalid Mishal would forget none of this.

3

The Tap Dancer from Amman

Randa Habib was just eighteen when she crossed into Jordan. The daughter of a well-traveled Lebanese career diplomat, she had attended primary school in Beirut. But, having spent much of her teens in the cities to which her father was posted, she knew Belgrade, Athens, Caracas, and Rio de Janeiro better than she knew her hometown—Beirut.

Over her father's objections, Habib was determined to be a journalist, and after finishing her education she took a job in 1972 at *Magazine*, a weekly journal published in Beirut. She showed promise, and within months of her signing on, the magazine's editor devised an ambitious project that was to involve nearly his entire staff—he wanted nitty-gritty portraits of the region's leaders. Having just resettled in Lebanon after a stretch in Brazil, the neophyte Habib was indifferent to her allotted subject—Hussein Bin Talal, the Hashemite king of Jordan.

Touching down in Amman to begin her assignment, Habib's eyes lit briefly on a group of American lawmakers, whose suits and skirts set them apart in an airport crowd of robes and veils. As the last of them wrestled their bags from a carousel, she observed a young government official attempting to herd them toward a fleet of VIP cars.

Habib took a cab to the city and checked into the Intercontinental Hotel, just across the road from the U.S. Embassy on Al-Kuliyya Street. In Amman, the "Intercon," as it was known, was the grease pit where officials, diplomats, and journalists fixed things—to such an extent that the government had been obliged to put a press office in the ground-floor lobby, so the regime could keep abreast of all the comings and goings.

When Habib settled in and informed the flaks ensconced in the lobby press office that she wished to interview the king, she saw their eyes glaze. Had she spoken to anyone? Did she have an appointment? Did she not think to call ahead? As she pondered what to do next, the answer walked through the door. The government official she had glimpsed at the airport introduced himself as Adnan Gharaybeh. When Habib explained her mission, Gharaybeh advised her to get herself the next morning to one of the government reception centers, where King Hussein would be revealing details of the latest version of his grand plan for a union of Jordan and the West Bank to an assembly of powerful tribal sheikhs. This would be her chance to see him in action—close up.

Grateful for the tip-off, Habib followed Gharaybeh's directions. Standing in line as the king made his entrance, she pushed forward with an outstretched hand. "Your Majesty, could I have an interview?" she asked bluntly. Hussein paused, took her hand, and smiled. "*Insha'Allah.*" That was all he said. It might have been another Jordanian brush-off—"God willing"—but Habib sensed that her forthright approach had amused Hussein. She returned to Beirut and was not at all surprised when her phone rang a week later. It was Adnan Gharaybeh, to announce that His Majesty would see her at three PM on the following Wednesday.

This time she drove. As her father's daughter, Habib traveled on a diplomatic passport. But when she pulled up at the Jordanian border the day before her appointment at the Amman palace, there was nothing diplomatic or even nice about the treatment she received. Such a delay and so many questions. "Why the Minolta camera? What's the tape recorder for?" she was asked.

"I'm going to interview the king," she said, with all of the excitement of a journalist on her first big assignment.

At the Amman Intercontinental the next morning, Habib could not help noticing that a rough-cut individual sitting nearby had quite deliberately placed a pistol on his breakfast table. He was watching her. Later, as she and her photographer colleague killed time by taking a drive around the city, they noticed they were being followed by a blue Volkswagen Beetle, the occupants of which seemed to be making a clumsy effort to keep them under surveillance.

Back at the hotel, the efficient Gharaybeh arrived to tell Habib that under no circumstances could her colleague accompany her to see the king—instead, a royal photographer would shoot pictures. On arriving at the palace she was subjected to an invasive search; her camera and tape recorder were confiscated without explanation and she was asked the same odd questions in a hundred different ways—Where was she from? What was her real name? Where was she in 1967? When had she last been to Jerusalem? The novice journalist complained; seasoned palace officials smiled obsequiously.

King Hussein himself was utterly charming. He had short legs that required him to perch on the edge of his chair, but he sat with his hands clasped in his lap and answered Habib's questions with warmth and enthusiasm. He was a fast talker and she was new to note taking. Sensing her panic as Habib fell behind his rapid delivery, Hussein gracefully slowed his pace.

The king seemed to enjoy himself immensely as he canvassed his plans for the West Bank. At the end of the interview, he urged Habib to stay on in Amman and take in the sights of Jordan. A sheepish Gharaybeh, who, she now noticed, had rather handsome black eyes and a fine nose, asked if she would join him for dinner that evening. He took her to the old Diplomat restaurant, where he explained the complex history and nuances of the king's words, while all the time the men she had observed earlier in the blue Beetle hovered near the door. Gharaybeh tried to put her at ease, explaining that they were following him, not her.

Habib's six-page article was the cover story of her magazine's two editions—in French and Arabic. But, just days before it hit the streets, it appeared that some of the detail might have been leaked. She received a blunt warning against giving prominence to Hussein's latest landgrab for the West Bank—in the form of a sham letter bomb that arrived on her desk. Days after publication, there was a more disturbing indication of what the Palestinian resistance made of Habib's first foray into the labyrinth of the Middle East crisis when the magazine's printing presses were bombed.

The next call from Adnan Gharaybeh was to register the king's satisfaction with her report. But then his calls kept coming. The young French-Lebanese Christian journalist was being courted by the Muslim official, who was a son of one of Jordan's more powerful northern tribes. Adnan made several visits to Beirut; Habib popped back to Amman. When the twenty-year-old told her Christian father she had found the man of her dreams, he was shocked to hear that his prospective son-in-law was a Muslim, and doubly shocked to be told that Adnan was not even from one of the Lebanese families over which her father might exert some influence. Attempting to head off the myriad ethnic and religious issues of such a mixed marriage, her desperate parents offered her an around-the-world trip, hoping an absence of some months might snap their headstrong daughter from her madness. Habib refused to go.

Three days after that holiday suggestion, Habib and Adnan eloped. Slipping themselves quietly onto a flight out of Beirut, they asked friends to deliver a letter to Habib's parents only when they were clean away. As a senior diplomat, Habib's father pulled out the government's big guns. Interpol came after the couple and the Lebanese ambassador to Amman tailed them to Adnan's family home in Irbid in the north of Jordan. Finally, after a visit to Amman by her father, a truce was called and the senior Habibs finally embraced their new son-in-law.

It was only after their June 1973 wedding that Adnan decided to tell Habib the real story behind the bizarre behavior of the Jordanians when she had first arrived in Amman twelve months earlier to interview the king.

The palace had received an anonymous warning that a Palestinian, masquerading as a reporter called Randa, would attempt to assassinate King Hussein by detonating a bomb that was to be concealed in her camera or tape recorder. The king had refused to cancel the appointment with Habib, on the grounds that he had given his word. The man with the gun at breakfast and the two spies in the Beetle were deliberate warnings by Jordanian security to let this would-be bomber understand that she was being watched.

The reason for the king's great good humor during the interview had been the arrival of a report from the Jordanian Embassy in Beirut, just minutes before they met, which revealed that Habib was the daughter of a Lebanese diplomat known to and much respected by His Majesty. The report had arrived too late for palace security officials to call off their protective gunmen, who, throughout the interview, had stood motionless behind the curtains in the king's office—in case Habib had made a false move.[1]

Dinner with Gharaybeh at the Diplomat had been the king's idea and it marked the beginning of Habib's new life in the Hashemite kingdom. Settling in Amman, she first worked at the Jordanian Information Ministry, but she quickly concluded that a bigger, bolder existence beckoned from beyond the Jordanian public service. She urged Adnan to quit and he did so, starting out in private business as the Jordanian agent for the Otis Elevator Company. She quit too, pursuing the independent career in journalism that she had wanted since being a teenager.

In time, Habib landed the plum post of Amman bureau chief for Agence France-Presse. This proved a remarkable vantage point in a region where Westerners perceived neat lines on maps as the borders between sovereign nations, but where today's crisis and yesterday's history were forever seeping across the flat desert frontiers, allowing all to demand a say in tomorrow's upheaval.

Geographically, the close proximity and scale of all of these countries was akin to a map of Toyland. On a clear night, King Hussein could see the lights of Jerusalem as he entertained guests on the terraces of his Hashimieh Palace, on the outskirts of metropolitan Amman. At the head of the Red Sea, just a few short miles of coast were shared by Egypt, Israel, Jordan, and Saudi Arabia. Cable and satellite TV would shrink distances even further and compress time.

The region was a veritable postage stamp, on which contemporary rivalries—territorial, religious, and political—predated the Great Powers' division of the Ottoman Empire at the end of World War I, a carve-up that was based entirely on Western interests. Later, what had been historic Palestine became Jordan, Israel, and the Palestinian Occupied Territories. Israel now controlled swathes of territory previously held by Jordan, Syria, and Egypt.

The spread of the refugees made the fate of the Palestinians a constant regional issue. There were sizable refugee communities in Jordan, Lebanon, Kuwait, Syria, Saudi Arabia, Egypt, and other pockets of the Gulf. These states sat almost on top of one another—Israel shared borders with Lebanon, Syria, Jordan, Egypt, and, virtually, Saudi Arabia. Religion complicated matters further—Jerusalem was revered and "owned" by and for all Muslims, all Christians, and all Jews. The upshot was that quite apart from U.S., Soviet, and European intervention, more than a dozen governments in the region claimed a right to stick in their oars.

What most saw in King Hussein was what they got. At the end of his posting in Amman, an American ambassador summed up the monarch this way: "King Hussein is not a reader. His life as a professional king doesn't revolve around briefing papers filled with bullet-pointed options and consequences. He is not especially devious or complicated—he is pretty straightforward, and that frustrates those around him who see the world in sophisticated and complex terms."[2]

As a sheikh of the desert, Hussein exuded a rare blend of tribal charm and Continental grace. His deep voice mesmerized even his most uncomfortable Western visitors. He assumed the role of father to his little nation. Sometimes he cajoled his mostly impoverished subjects; at others, he insisted he knew best. He had an appreciative eye for women and a passion for motorcycles and airplanes. But he was more bread-and-hummus than caviar king. Those who dropped by as he ate at his desk were bemused by his simple enthusiasm for melted cheese on flat Arab bread or a falafel sandwich. Senior officials took the precaution of lunching before they went to see him—lest he invite them to share his humble fare.

In Washington, Hussein had once emerged from what he deemed to have been a successful meeting at the White House, declaring to aides, "Let's celebrate—let's have hamburgers!" The burgers were so cold and congealed by the time they were delivered to the royal suite that only one member of the party wanted to eat one—an oblivious King Hussein.

He was a larger-than-life individual who seemed to cast a spell on people. His gestures and responses revealed not just a deep sense of tribal honor and duty, but also a sense of humanity that he indulged willingly—even in the face of threats to the throne.

When she was diagnosed with cancer, a granddaughter of the legendary Ethiopian emperor Haile Selassie wrote asking if Hussein would help to pay her doctor's bills. Her confidence was well placed, as the king fired off a check immediately. Perplexed, his advisers demanded an explanation. All of them Arabs, even they were astounded when Hussein cast back fourteen centuries to recount the story of King Najashi of Abyssinia, a distant forefather of Selassie's. Hussein told of a time when the armies of Muhammad were in trouble on the Arabian Peninsula, forcing the Prophet to send them to the land that became Ethiopia, where the Christian Najashi sheltered them. For Hussein, the plea from Selassie's granddaughter was a very simple matter: tribal honor required him to repay Muhammad's debt. Just as she was a direct descendant of King Najashi, he was a direct descendant of the Prophet.[3]

When one of Hussein's military tribunals jailed Layth Shubaylat, a vocal Islamist activist in Amman, the king had second thoughts and pardoned him. Contrarily, Shubaylat refused to leave prison unless others were freed along with him. Exasperated, King Hussein got into a car and drove himself to the prison, entered the cell block, and hauled out Shubaylat, whom he then drove to his home in the Amman suburbs.

Hussein forgave most who menaced him. At one stage in the 1970s, four of the chiefs of his six security services were individuals who, earlier in their careers, had been sent into exile amidst accusations that they were part of conspiracies against the monarchy. Unusually in the Arab world, all had been pardoned and given these positions of power.

But Hussein was no pushover, and the security of his throne was due in no small part to his ruthless capacity to keep the lid on tension. In the interests of keeping his subjects in their place and in deference to a regional flair for bending or breaking people, Hussein was prepared to inflict some pain on his people when it was deemed necessary. Chief among his security agencies was the General Intelligence Department (GID), which many Jordanians preferred to call the "Fingernail Factory."

Hussein's palace was in the Maqar, a historic hillside compound that included several royal palaces in the heart of downtown Amman. This was where the armies of the Great Arab Revolt camped when they liberated Amman in 1918 and where, after them, the governors of the British Mandate era were housed. It was where Hussein's grandfather Abdullah built his first palace as king of the Hashemite Kingdom of Jordan, a tumbleweed patch of desert between Iraq and what then was Palestine, which was granted to him by Winston Churchill during the post-Ottoman convulsions of the 1920s.

These days, the royal family lived in the Nadwa Palace, a grand building of stone and arches within the Maqar compound. Hussein's office and those of the royal court were in the Basman Palace, a separate building within the royal enclave. Portraits of his predecessors, whom he traced back to Muhammad the Prophet, adorned the walls. It might have been the workplace of any top executive, but in a region of royal opulence, it fell short of lavish. Apart from the rolling gardens and the tranquility of the compound amidst the madness of the city, an eye-catching nod to royalty was the pomp and color of the Circassian Guards. These were descendents of Muslim warriors who had fled the Russian advance into the Caucasus in the nineteenth century, and later served the Jordanian monarchy, much as the Swiss Guards did at the Vatican.

When he was fifteen, Hussein had witnessed the murder of his grandfather Abdullah, as the old warrior-king entered the Al-Aqsa Mosque in Jerusalem. Young Hussein had been saved from one of the assassin's bullets when it ricocheted off a medal on his military uniform. He had been crowned king as a schoolboy. Grappling with his unforgiving turf and the ease of death in the desert, he claimed he had taken to disguising himself as a taxi driver and cruising the streets of Amman so he could quiz his passengers on the performance of their new ruler.[4] Hussein was still in his teens when he fired his first prime minister.[5]

His cousin Feisal, whom the British installed as king of neighboring Iraq, was murdered in a 1958 military coup in Baghdad. Just months after this loss, Hussein put down an Egyptian-inspired military coup. Later, he called on all his skill as a pilot to survive an aerial dogfight. He was at the controls of his lumbering old twin-engine De Havilland Dove when two nimble Syrian MiG-17 fighter jets tried to force him to crash. Subsequently he was the target of serial assassination plots and uprisings as the Soviet-backed enforcers in Damascus and Cairo set out to break his independent spirit.

In the Six-Day War, Hussein was humiliated by the loss of his western flank to Israel and, with it, half of holy Jerusalem. At the same time, he was burdened by the displacement of almost half a million refugees from the Occupied Territories into his reduced kingdom.[6] This was an outcome that now put the king on a second collision course—with the Palestine Liberation Organization and its feisty leader, Yasser Arafat.

They were against each other immediately. Hussein came to see Arafat as an inveterate liar. A standing joke in the royal court was that Arafat had two signatures—one that his aides knew was to be acted on, and a second mark that told them to ignore whatever preceded it.

As a young fighter in 1968, Arafat—according to the king's reading of events—had stolen the credit for what Hussein believed was a Jordanian military victory over the Israelis at Karameh on the Jordan River.

The conflict over Karameh revolved around who did what to aid the victory. Arafat had undoubtedly beaten off the Israelis, but only after a senior Jordanian intelligence officer—acting on a CIA tip-off—had warned Arafat of an imminent Israeli assault. The Jordanian military had amplified that warning and, despite orders from Amman to stay out of the conflict, a sympathetic Jordanian army commander had provided artillery and tank support for Arafat at a critical moment in the battle. It was enough to force a humiliating retreat by the Israelis. Close to one hundred of Arafat's four-hundred-strong force were killed, but the cost to the Israelis was twenty-eight dead, sixty-nine injured, and thirty-four tanks hit. By the military metrics of the Middle East, that was enough for Arafat to proclaim Karameh "the first victory of the Arab nation after the 1967 war."[7]

Thereafter, Arafat touted himself as a seasoned guerrilla leader, whose ragtag militia had restored Arab pride by rising above the defeat of 1967 to repel a powerful Israeli incursion into Jordan.

He and the other factional leaders now saw Jordan's great strategic potential as a base for resistance against neighboring Israel, much as the Vietcong had used Hanoi as a base from which to retake South Vietnam. They infiltrated Hussein's military and security services. Their tens of thousands of unruly fighters, or fedayeen, became a state-within-a-state, owing allegiance to the fifty-plus Palestinian factions that had mushroomed in Jordan. Amidst talk of an overthrow and the seizure of Jordan as the basis for a new Palestinian state, King Hussein struggled to control his realm. The choice he faced was grim—he could allow the Hashemite throne to be undermined or he could act decisively.

Ignoring calls for brotherhood among Arabs, Hussein chose the latter course in September 1970. At a cost of thousands of lives, his loyal Bedouin military forces drove Arafat and the PLO out of Jordan—their refuge of first choice—to new bases in Syria and Lebanon. Palestinians called this episode in their history Black September.[8]

These events were to some extent precipitated by a dramatic episode that had sent a shiver down the spine of the international community. Leftist elements of the PLO had used Jordan as a stage on which to unveil a powerful new tactic in their guerrilla war when they hijacked four passenger jets and successfully ordered the pilots of three of them to put down at Dawson's Field, a former British airbase in the Jordanian desert. There they blew up two of the aircraft in front of a British TV camera while striking a deal to exchange three hundred passengers for seven Palestinians held as prisoners in Britain, Switzerland, and Germany.[9]

The manner in which the PLO had thus upped the ante was matched only by an extraordinary appeal by Hussein to London and Washington at the height of his showdown with Arafat. As an Arab leader, he asked Britain and the United States to relay a Jordanian plea to the Jewish state of Israel to buy time for his army by bombing Syrian forces that were set to enter the war on the side of Arafat.

Most of Hussein's subjects were Palestinian refugees, many of whom had squatted for years in miserable refugee camps run by the United Nations. In their squalor and poverty, they looked westward every day, clinging to the hope that they might somehow escape the pressure cooker of the camps to return to their villages and farms in Israel and the Occupied Territories. Their presence seriously complicated affairs in Jordan, a country about the size of Ireland but with scant resources. Their geographic proximity to the West Bank was a constant reminder of their loss. Their frustration could—and did—spark regular outbursts of anger and rebellion.

This was the environment in which the Muslim Brotherhood became a key presence. Its unregulated fund-raising drives, based on the religious obligation of all Muslims to donate to charity, made the Brotherhood one of the wealthiest welfare and political organizations in Jordan. In 1967, Hussein decided to do away with political parties, but he could not do away with the Muslim Brotherhood. In the 1950s and 1960s, the Islamists had sided with his regime against a wave of leftist challenges. Sometimes they did the regime's dirty work. To save Hussein the embarrassment of being seen to put a brake on what, elsewhere, might be read as a healthy political discourse, the Islamists sent crowds of baton-wielding thugs into the streets of Amman to smack down protests. By the letter of their charter, the Brotherhood's objective was a pure, Sharia-based Islamic society. But self-preservation was their first priority. Figuring any nationalist or leftist alternative to Hussein was a threat to their existence, they had a common cause with the king.

Hussein flattered them at the same time as he laid down "redlines," arguing that there was a difference between "enlightened" and "fanatical" Islam.[10] He was able to pull rank with his claim to be a forty-second-generation descendant of Muhammad, but he also made sure that those who were known as the East Bankers, the traditional Jordanians from the east side of the Jordan River, were in control of the Brotherhood. These elements were more tribal than those of the predominantly Islamist Palestinian Brothers.

In 1982, when Syrian president Hafez Al-Assad massacred up to thirty thousand people to put down an Islamist revolt and leveled the restive city of Hama to warn any other upstarts of the fate that awaited them, Hussein gave refuge to many of the Brothers who fled Syria. In 1971, he took in those who straggled out of Iraq after a Ba'athist purge.

The Jordanian regime sponsored the Brotherhood, which, in return, gave back something that Arafat and the PLO threatened—Hussein's legitimacy. The king clung to a belief that he among Arab leaders was the rightful representative of the Palestinian people. With the exception of the tissue-sized Gaza Strip, all of the putative Palestinian state had, for a time, been formerly Jordanian. As blow-ins from the Hejaz region of what became Saudi Arabia, the Hashemite family was without local roots—hence their reliance on Islam for legitimacy. They claimed a direct lineage back to the Prophet Muhammad and, as the emir of the Hejaz, Hussein's great-grandfather had been keeper of the holy cities of Mecca and Medina.

When he lost control of Jerusalem in the 1967 war, Hussein's legitimacy was put in doubt—notwithstanding a deal with the Israelis under which he continued to be custodian of the Islamic holy places in Jerusalem. Many Arab analysts had long suspected that the rationale for the British creation of Jordan, in that portion of the British Mandate that lay east of the Jordan River, was to build an alternative Palestinian homeland—thus to enable the Jews to have all the territory west of the river, so-called Eretz Israel.[11]

An Arab summit in the Moroccan capital, Rabat, in 1974 had dealt Hussein yet another blow, formally stripping him of the last vestiges of his role as a guardian of the Palestinians and vesting all legitimacy in Arafat's PLO. It was payback to Hussein for ousting the PLO from Jordan in 1970 and his refusal in the previous year—1973—to join the Egyptian-Syrian attack on Israel that brought on the Yom Kippur War.

The bitter lesson Hussein took from the murder of his grandfather on the steps of the Al-Aqsa Mosque in Jerusalem, and again as his Jewish and Arab neighbors squeezed him, was that, as a leader, he must act independently of all the noise in the region. He parlayed with some or all of his neighbors from time to time, but, as an Arab ruler, the king of Jordan was on his own.

From the throne on which he sat, this required talking to the West, especially Washington; and talking to Israel, which, in turn, meant the denunciation of Hussein in the Arab world. Cairo radio beamed into Jordan, urging Jordanians to assassinate the "Hashemite whore" and "the treacherous dwarf."

Hussein became Israel's most trusted Arab ally. In 1973, he warned Israeli prime minister Golda Meir of Egypt and Syria's plans for a surprise military strike as Israelis marked Yom Kippur. To her cost, she did not believe him. However, Hussein refused to give ground to the Israelis on the Palestinian question and, try as he often did to discredit the PLO, he knew that any deal he might broker with Israel or the world would not fly unless it had the endorsement of Arafat and the other Arab leaders.

Hussein, and his grandfather before him, had accepted the reality of the Israeli state decades before any other Arab leaders. Both had engaged in a long series of secret meetings in which they arm wrestled with Israel over the so-called Jordan Option, in which the West Bank and Gaza somehow might come under the aegis of Amman. Sometimes they met in London, at the clinic of Dr. Emmanuel Herbert, Hussein's Jewish physician, or in Paris, for a continuing covert dialogue. The Israelis estimated later that their leaders and key officials met face-to-face with Hussein for what amounted to five hundred hours.[12] In all this, Hussein saw himself as a realist. But to some in the PLO and among his Arab neighbors, he was naive and—worse—a collaborator.

His "loner" play meant that Hussein was never alone. He was the beneficiary of a cynical 1950s American plot to co-opt Arab leaders to protect Western oil supplies and block Soviet expansion in the first decade of the Cold War. Harrison Symmes, a 1960s U.S. ambassador to Amman, described Hussein and others in the region who were seduced with guns, money, and intelligence from the CIA thus: "These four mongrels were supposed to be our defense against communism and extremes of Arab nationalism."[13]

Hussein took the money, but there were times when his single-mindedness infuriated Washington. Better than most, the Jordanian leader knew the precarious threads by which his monarchy hung—and high on his list was the need for domestic popular support. "If your people and your tribe are not with you, you are nothing," he lectured his advisers.[14] The case studies he would quote were self-evident. In 1957 sufficient numbers of his army remained loyal to see off a menacing Leftist plot, and in 1970 they stood with him when Arafat's militias tried to overthrow the monarchy. Later, he would add 1990–91 to the list, when only his strong popular support among Jordanians kept Washington at bay at a time when it would have liked to punish Hussein for his refusal to support the American-led campaign against Saddam Hussein's invasion of Kuwait.

Western observers joked that the office of prime minister in Jordan was a good retirement post and to be a government minister was to be an ornament existing outside the circles of power. Conventionally, the Washington-Amman relationship should have involved the Jordanian Foreign Ministry and the U.S. State Department, but Hussein's line was direct to the White House and it was the CIA–GID (General Intelligence Department) axis that kept it oiled and functioning. During the Cold War, when tinpot dictators and corrupt generals could name their price for cooperating with Washington, Hussein's name was on the CIA's "financial support" list—alongside those of Zaire's infamous Mobutu Sese Seko and Panama's dictator in waiting, the unsavory Manuel Noriega. Quite apart from declared foreign aid programs, Hussein's "secret subsidy" was banked for twenty years.[15]

His more passionate Jordanian subjects liked to say God broke the mold after he made Hussein. Their king drew religious legitimacy from his claim to be a descendant of the Prophet, enjoying Islam as others enjoyed poetry. He knew the Qur'an intimately and loyalists wagered he could defeat the ayatollahs of Tehran and any other fundamentalists in a debate on the use—or abuse—of the holy book.

Hussein railed at the West's black-and-white simplification of the Arab world, its duplicity in the carve-up of the Ottoman Empire, and the shock treatment inflicted on the Arab world with the creation of the state of Israel. He wrung his hands at the scheming and failure of Arab leaders, and their destabilizing Cold War flirtations with Moscow. Yet, isolated and without refuge, Hussein turned to the West and the Israelis as partners in what became a tenacious and ultimately successful bid for Hashemite survival.

His much-touted Jordanian Option, which had featured in Randa Habib's first news report from Amman, remained on the table, sometimes buried under other proposals or simply deep in the hearts of the Jordanian leader and those around him. The art of being king of Jordan was in picking at the knots of tension. Did Hussein want to take the West Bank back under the wing of the monarchy, as had been the case for the two decades up to 1967? Was the Muslim Brotherhood, like the PLO before it, plotting to overthrow Hussein, to reshape his kingdom as a new Palestinian republic, or as a caliphate, perhaps?

Bitter experience made Hussein an exceptional tap dancer—but he fussed about his partners. He appreciated the difference between needing and loving his alliances with the Brotherhood and with Israel. He reserved his paranoia for Leftist nationalists and any who hitched their fortunes to the Syrian or Egyptian regimes. He was contemptuous of Arafat and the PLO.

King Hussein understood that being cozy with the Americans was a good thing—but that being too cozy was not. He often counseled friends with a parable of his power: "To be an enemy of the United States is dangerous; to be a friend of Washington can be fatal."[16]

4

The Education of a Terrorist

Kuwait University was still in its infancy. Richly endowed with the vast oil wealth of the ruling Al-Sabah family, it was poised to become one of the region's grander halls of learning. But there were humble beginnings.

There was great fanfare when it opened in 1966 with just four hundred students and a faculty of only thirty-one, teaching science, arts, and education. But as new colleges were incorporated, the campus was pulled into the slipstream of the turbocharged economy transforming the emirate from a barren back lot to an indulgent petrodollar emporium. Traditionally, Kuwaitis were more relaxed than some of their stitched-up neighbors, like the Saudis. It showed on campus, where classes were coeducational; women wore miniskirts and, on weekends, joined their male colleagues for desert picnics.[1]

The straitlaced Khalid Mishal's Islamist sensitivities may well have been offended by this progressive, liberal atmosphere. But, as a Palestinian, he had to count himself lucky just to be among his fellow students, miniskirts or not. Tuition was free, but only a few dozen places were reserved for Palestinians.[2]

In 1974, Professor Asad Abdul Rahman started lecturing at the university. Running a practiced eye over his first class as the students took their places for his eclectic course on Palestinian history, Abdul Rahman took in an intense, thin-framed student. Lingering momentarily on his ill-kempt, woolly beard—which Adbul Rahman well knew was a sure sign of fundamentalist tendencies—he inwardly dismissed Mishal as just another misguided youth. The professor concluded that the student was already aligned with the Muslim Brotherhood.[3]

There was no such thing as a neutral Palestinian. Their history was too new, too raw, and, of late, too humiliating. The professor saw the world through the prism of Fatah, the secular faction of Palestinian politics that had emerged from the refugee community in Kuwait to become the backbone of Yasser Arafat's PLO. A staunch believer in the supremacy of the PLO, he was more at home with his own kind, their leftist Arab sensibilities buttressed by a confident sense of their own ascendency. It was a simple equation: Fatah was in control; Islamists were fringe dwellers. Most of Abdul Rahman's students dreamt of armed revolution and perhaps a seat at a conference in Prague or Moscow, where they might see Arafat rub shoulders with Fidel Castro amid cries of "Come the revolution!"

Khalid Mishal might have looked out of place, but already he was a young man on a mission. In the absence of a homeland, Palestinian parents were obsessed with the notion of providing their children with a good education, in the hope that job skills might take them where they wanted—or needed—to go in the world. It was one of the reasons why Khalid Mishal's family had settled as grateful refugees in Kuwait.

After crossing the Jordan River with her children in June 1967, Fatima had eventually located her husband at the Amman home of a relative, where he had organized temporary lodging. In the 1960s, the Jordanian capital was a quiet little backwater, but compared to their former home in Silwad, it was enough to make a boy's head spin. But the greater shock for the family in coming so far down the track from the bucolic Jerusalem Mountains was in their sense of complete displacement. The parents, connecting with others in the same predicament, would talk for hours of what had befallen them.

Sponge-like, the boy Khalid soaked it all up—the dislocation, a grim realization that there might be no going back, and, worst of all, their deeply wounded Arab pride. It all had a profound impact, especially the onset of a painful psychological shift from living in a homeland to having the memory of a homeland live on in their minds. Fatima had wept as the truck left Silwad and, the family noted with dismay, she was inconsolable at some stage of every day for the next four years.

Two months after the river crossing, Abd Al-Qadir packed his family into an old Mercedes-Benz taxi for the long ride to Kuwait City, via Baghdad. The emirate had been generous to footloose Palestinians and it seemed the father's uncanny ability to land on his feet had not deserted him. He had survived two military wars with just a grazed chin; he had come through a marital war with his first and second wives waiting on him and his children. Now, in Kuwait, he found a well-placed benefactor.

In his early years in the emirate he had found work laboring on farms and in market gardens. But by continuing to memorize the Qur'an and acquiring a working knowledge of Sharia, he was soon tapped to be a mullah. First he served at a local mosque, where, as the muezzin, he went up the minaret five times a day to sing the call to prayers. He was invited to preach when the regular imam was absent. On the preacher's death, he was appointed to the post, and henceforth would be addressed as Mullah Abd Al-Qadir. Soon after, an aide to the Kuwaiti royals invited Abd Al-Qadir to take prayers at a private mosque where a senior member of the royal family prayed with his circle of palace aides and their families.[4]

Pumped up on its oil revenue, Kuwait was the most liberal—and sympathetic—of the Palestinian refuges in the region. The Kuwaiti royal family found ways to manage the anxiety of ordinary Kuwaitis about the growing number of refugees in their midst. Palestinians were not allowed to invest in property or other ventures without a Kuwaiti partner, and they were paid significantly less than Kuwaitis.[5] But apart from insisting on no interfactional feuding, the local authorities left it to Fatah to manage and police the Palestinians, whose numbers almost doubled in the months after the 1967 war. They now accounted for 20 percent of the whole population.

The Kuwaiti regime levied a 5 percent tax on all Palestinian workers to help fund the PLO. Most important, it created a crucible for Palestinian nationalism when it handed over its schools to the refugee communities for them to run their own de facto education system. Out of Kuwaiti school hours, impressionable Palestinian refugee pupils were immersed in their own history and an abiding sense of loss by Palestinian refugee teachers who were as distraught and angered as their pupils and their respective families. Each morning the children saluted the Palestinian flag, and the syllabus included paramilitary and political courses.[6]

In the eyes of his mother, Khalid was a perfect boy. He had always received good grades and in Silwad he had done his bit in the fields; as he raced through school in Kuwait, he took to spouting poetry and Islam and still was at the top of the class.

In Silwad, the family had lived in the shadow of a noisy minaret, but the young Khalid had rarely darkened the door of the mosque. Despite the village's deep conservatism and the strong influence of the Cairo-trained holy men, Islam was observed in Silwad more as a way of life than in regular communal prayer. Fatima had run a strict house, making the children curb their tongues and teaching them manners and respect—but her regime did not run to rounding them up to attend the nearby mosque.

In Kuwait, their father was back on the scene. He had kept his second wife, with whom he had several children. But as he reasserted authority over his first family, he asked his eldest son a simple enough question, which marked a turning point in the boy's life: why was it that he did not pray? "No one ever taught me," Khalid replied.

He began to accompany his father to the mosque and took to reading the Qur'an. In 1969 Khalid was selected to attend a Kuwaiti government center for high achievers—the Abdullah Al-Salim Al-Sabah School. It was another milestone. After having been steeped in Palestinian nationalism during his first years in Kuwait, this new school cast him on the Islamist tide that was enjoying a revival across the Muslim world. Almost overnight, the boy became deeply religious, and very soon he was announced the winner in a national competition that required students to memorize and recite two chapters of the holy book.

These were years in which Palestinian boys were forced to become men early. Primed emotionally by their parents' storytelling of the past and by a rising sense that they might have been duped into hastily fleeing their homeland, Khalid and his friends were galvanized by day-to-day shifts in the ongoing struggle. These "new" Palestinian refugees had a different view of their predicament from the "old" refugees—those who had fled Palestine in 1948. Suddenly, there was a demand for leadership, where previously there seemed to have been a vacuum. Arafat and the other factional leaders came to Kuwait to address thronging rallies. Rousing speeches by the likes of Salah Khalaf and George Habash were a poultice for the refugees' shriveled sense of national identity. Rediscovering themselves as Palestinians—and sharing the experience as a displaced community—had a powerful restorative effect.

Just as others of his generation, growing up in very different cultures, cheered for their favorite football teams, Khalid was jubilant after the 1968 Battle of Karameh, which left many of his contemporaries with a sense that they owed Yasser Arafat their allegiance and their blood. But he was devastated by the death of thousands in the brutal Arab-on-Arab fighting of Black September, which coincided with his first weeks at secondary school. Regular lessons were cast aside for an endless workshop on the clashes in Jordan, which, amidst great frustration and bitterness, were reported in the diaspora as an attempt by Jordan's King Hussein to undermine Arafat's Fatah, the PLO, and the newly emerging sense of Palestinian nationalism.

Sandwiched between Karameh and Black September was an atrocity that further enflamed passions among the refugees in Kuwait and across the Muslim world. Palestinians were still adjusting to the shock of Israel now controlling their holy places in Jerusalem when Michael Dennis Rohan, a seemingly deranged Australian Christian visiting Israel, torched the Al-Aqsa Mosque. Reputedly visited by Muhammad on his mystic steed, the mosque was one of Islam's holiest of holies. Its southeastern wing was gutted. A priceless one-thousand-year-old pulpit, known as a minbar, was destroyed.

Repairing the mosque ultimately cost about $9 million. Wild Arab conspiracy theories about Israeli complicity in the blaze flared after the authorities bundled Rohan off to a mental institution before deporting him. Anger served to harden the religious shell forming around Khalid Mishal's youthful nationalist sentiment, and very soon it was to trigger critical decisions that would shape his entire life.

Mishal took to rising daily for dawn prayers. He undertook the hajj, the pilgrimage to the holy city of Mecca in Saudi Arabia, which all Muslims aspire to at least once in their lifetimes. During his father's absences he became the man of the house, checking each day that all had prayed. When he started punishing those who had not, his younger brother Hashim took to lying to escape a beating.[7] As the family's senior male, Khalid Mishal demanded respect; he explained that in keeping order, he was merely "rectifying conduct—not imposing ideas."

In secondary school, young Mishal's reading was ecumenical and voracious. He ranged through Arabic translations of the classics—Charles Dickens and Fyodor Dostoevsky, Albert Camus and Victor Hugo. He took in the Arab and Islamic masters, both literary and spiritual. He spent much of his spare time in Kuwait's liberally stocked public libraries, engrossed in Arab history and world affairs. Fascinated, his younger brother Maher counted the volumes as they fell from Khalid's hands—by Maher's calculation, Khalid had read more than five hundred books by the time he was eighteen.[8]

When his father was home, the boy hung on every word of his stories of war and the Palestinian struggle. Maher, who, of all his siblings, was closest to Khalid, observed his older brother often reduced to tears by Palestinian anthems. In his quest for an "ideological and intellectual personality," Khalid joined his school's Islamic Society. Maher was perplexed again when Khalid resolved—at just fifteen—not to pursue adventure by joining Yasser Arafat's guerrilla fighters, who were then entrenched in Lebanon after the rout in Jordan. Instead, Khalid reached the lofty conclusion that, in years to come, he could better serve the Palestinian cause if he had a full education.

He signed up with the student branch of the Muslim Brotherhood, even though his father's brief membership in this fundamentalist organization had lapsed when he left Silwad, back in 1957. For a Palestinian teenager, joining the Brotherhood was as radical as it was contrary. The war cry of the day was guerrilla war, but because the Brotherhood eschewed armed resistance, Khalid effectively was opting to live to fight another day.

His classmates—filled with tales of Kuwait as the 1950s birthplace of Arafat's kaffiyeh-clad Fatah forces—were eager to go off and train for guerrilla missions in the Occupied Territories, or just to hang with the PLO in Beirut. But Khalid was hooked on what was called the "Islamist current." Undaunted by the arrogance of Fatah and the other leftist and secular factions, he told classmates of his realization that Islam was an essential element of their history and culture—and he felt duty bound to act on that.

Since its establishment in Cairo in 1928, the fortunes of the Muslim Brotherhood had waxed and waned with political developments in the Muslim world. When some of its foremost thinkers found their way to Kuwait during a brief easing of the crackdown on their activities by Egyptian authorities in 1970, Khalid Mishal was ripe for the taking. As he turned his back irrevocably on Fatah's secularism, he attempted to placate troubled friends who had taken the other path.

Insisting that his choice was not a rejection of Fatah and all it stood for, he articulated concepts way beyond his years. He explained that an individual cradling a weapon in the hill country of southern Lebanon was an insufficient expression of nationalism unless it was accompanied by a firm Islamic underpinning across the Palestinian people. Cocking an eye, as he always did to make a point, he argued that these were complementary, not contradictory, currents. "Islam has to be a part of the equation because it conforms to our Arab and Muslim heritage and culture," he told his friends.

As head of his school's Islamic Society, Khalid explained with remarkable self-awareness that he was quite deliberately building the various dimensions of his character—spiritually, personally, and intellectually. He confided to others a belief that his Islamist engagement was shaping his personality. In a way, Khalid was catching his generation's "new wave." Suppressed through the 1950s and 1960s, particularly in Egypt and its Arabic satellites, political Islamism was resurging across the Muslim world; with the arrival in Kuwait of the movement's scholars, Khalid Mishal drank in Brotherhood philosophy and spiritualism.

One whose oratory had him spellbound was the Sudanese sheikh Hassan Tannun, a man so moved by his own lectures that often he wept as he spoke. Like teenage groupies, Khalid and his friend Azzam Tamimi followed Tannun from mosque to mosque, using a newfangled cassette recorder to capture his sermons so they could be taken back to the classroom to be played for others.

In a school riven by a hardening Islamist versus secularist divide, Khalid parlayed his top-of-the-class authority into that of a self-appointed school preacher. "If I saw something wrong, I spoke out; if someone needed to be admonished, I admonished," he said of himself.[9] In the absence of an imam on school camping trips to the Kuwaiti desert, he continued his impromptu sermonizing and led the students in prayer.

The teenage Khalid stepped up his Islamic reading as well. In his excitement, he believed he was discovering tracts—such as the controversial Egyptian fundamentalist Sayyid Qutb's thirty-volume commentary on the Qur'an—for the first time.

This was a generation of young Palestinians who made their own choices. Failure by their parents' generation to defend and preserve their homeland had freed the children to go their own way. Azzam Tamimi observed his own father's lax Islamic devotion and concluded that he was an infidel. Khalid Mishal was moved by the war stories and religion of his father, but he was reluctant to admit that they may have guided his own path. When Fatah marked the twentieth anniversary of Al-Nakba with a new slogan—"The children of '48 are the fighters of '68"—Khalid and Azzam wondered where it left them. As the children of '67, they were roused more by contemporary Islamic heroics in Iran and Afghanistan than by Israeli sucker punches inflicted on Palestinians during two wars.

Khalid was a nerd before the term was invented. Arafat's overspun victory at Karameh made his schoolmates desperate to tote guns for Fatah, but Khalid kept his nose in his books and frowned on their indulgence in trivia. His friend Tamimi was thrown by Khalid's extreme certainty as he—Tamimi—wrestled with his love of Arab honky-tonk and tennis, both of which were considered un-Islamic. The increasingly rigid Khalid rebuked Tamimi, telling him he must choose one path in life. "You can't be in the Islamic Society and play music," he argued.[10] Driven more by his sense of being a young man in a hurry, Khalid told them matter-of-factly, "I don't want to waste time!"

When Tamimi signed up as a junior member of Fatah, Khalid tried to pull him back, hoping his friend would join the ranks of the Brotherhood. They played this tug-of-war right up until they finished school. Neither would give ground until Tamimi surrendered, in 1974, on hearing that Yasser Arafat was in New York to address the General Assembly of the United Nations. "It proves you're right; I'm wrong," Tamimi told him. "Arafat's sold out."[11]

Observing his friend at this stage, Tamimi felt that the Palestinian cause seemed to be of secondary importance for Mishal—and that the driving force in his life was a need to be a devout Muslim and a believer in the Brotherhood's Islamist platform.

But as an activist on the campus of the new Kuwait University, Mishal was finally able to strike a balance between these nationalist and spiritual elements, driven in part by Fatah's taunting of Mishal and his fellow sympathizers in the Muslim Brotherhood over their relegation of the nationalist cause. Tamimi would say, "There was a sense of guilt . . . but also, Fatah's failing was pushing the Islamists to provide an alternative."

The eighteen-year-old Mishal who arrived on campus in 1974 had come to study physics. But it was politics that he practiced and the Brotherhood brand of Islam that he preached.

By Western standards, 1970s Kuwait was just another highly regimented emirate. But by Arab standards it was liberal, even permissive. Cultural and intellectual life was robust and, despite the regime's ban on factional feuding among the Palestinians, the campus was a hothouse in which Mishal and his fellow believers had room to rally and organize.

Students were alive to the tumult of the time. Fatah was stepping up its guerrilla raids into Israel; the refugee community in Lebanon took sides in the Lebanese Civil War; and the Egyptian leader Anwar Sadat became an Arab outcast by breaking with the pack to go to Jerusalem to address the Israeli Knesset. Students went off to fight, but Khalid's response to the plight of his people was confined to the realm of verse. In the absence of any other overt response, his love of poetry provoked bitter sniping from his more gung ho compatriots—they wanted to run off to guerrilla training camps, while his response to reports of the gruesome treatment of a group of Palestinian commandos captured by Israeli settlers in 1975 was to write a poem when riding a bus home from lectures.

Arafat had long ago left Kuwait, where he and others had originally launched Fatah. But his secular movement was the dominant force in the PLO, and it claimed a mortgage on all aspects of life in the Palestinian diaspora—especially student groups, which were key recruiting centers. But Kuwait also was the beachhead for an emerging Islamist challenge to the Fatah-dominated status quo—and riding the crest of this wave was the bookish Khalid Mishal.

Some believed it would never amount to much. As the new Islamism spread on campus at the university, a senior academic, who also happened to be an Islamist, took it upon himself to outline the future to Asad Abdul Rahman, the history professor who on Day One had picked Mishal as an Islamist. Abdul Rahman thought his colleague had taken leave of his senses as he explained the methodical determination that underlay the Muslim Brotherhood's gradualist philosophy. Grand in its scope, it was a scheme to eventually cloak the university in Islamist mores.

Looking into the future, quite accurately as it turned out, the colleague predicted, "You see this liberal, progressive campus of yours, and all these young women in their revealing clothes? That's all going to change—the Brotherhood is working on the elementary schools now and, in fifteen years' time, we'll flood this university with student women in veils and men wearing beards and dishdashas."[12]

Persisting with his smorgasbord course, which Abdul Rahman described as "Palestinian history, the current situation, and the Zionist conspiracy," the professor was deeply impressed with Khalid Mishal—notwithstanding the political gulf between them. He found Mishal to be bright as he politely pushed his professor with questions that revealed both his extensive reading and a hunger for a more detailed understanding of his people's plight. Abdul Rahman remained a faithful Fatah disciple, even if he would later have a personal falling-out with Arafat. But politics aside, he rated Khalid as his brightest student ever. "There are lots of B-pluses and Bs in social science. He was my only A-student in nineteen years of teaching."[13]

Mullah Abd Al-Qadir became chief-in-exile to the several hundred members of his extended family who had found their way to Kuwait in the aftermath of the 1967 war. But such community standing could not insulate him from the rude shock in 1979 when his second wife abandoned him. Fatima, displaying remarkable good grace, welcomed him back into her family home along with his second family of three sons and two daughters, whom she blended with her own brood to make a single family of eleven.

Like so many Palestinian families in exile or under occupation, the boys were all hungry for education and travel. Mufid, the first son of the father's second family, went on to study in the United States and married an American. Maher did engineering in Britain and worked in Germany and South Africa before switching to human resources management in Jordan and the Gulf. Hashim became a sales manager in Dubai. Mithqal would end up running an auto-sales shop in Alabama, and Hisham was destined to become a senior accountant in a prestigious Abu Dhabi bank. Khalid himself would ultimately shed his religious pacifism and rise to become the leader of the violent Palestinian resistance movement Hamas, a man on the wanted lists of both Israel and the United States and a key player in his people's destiny. But that was in the future.

As he shed the awkwardness of youth, Khalid Mishal looked like both of his parents. He had his father's strong nose and deep-set eyes, but they were in a face more like that of his mother. As he wrapped up his university studies, his mother had good reason to worry that her firstborn son was moving into dark and dangerous terrain.

Fatima dared not question him, but she wondered about the quizzical looks from his visitors when she interrupted closed-door meetings in her house to serve them tea and coffee. The looks came when she urged them to attend to their studies, as it was clear that physics and commerce were not being discussed. Mishal became secretive, responding to her oblique queries about his activities only by urging her to pray to Allah to guide and protect him. He began preaching to student congregations in mosques in Kuwait, and occasionally he stood in for his father at the royal mosque. Suddenly he was traveling abroad frequently, often to the United States, where he became a popular fixture on the activist Palestinian lecture circuit.

At home, he confronted his mother finally with a request that revealed to her how far her son had traveled down the road of Islamist self-discipline. Decades later she could still quote word for word an exchange they had as they drove along one of Kuwait City's grand freeways:

"Mother, I need you to listen. I'm going to ask Allah for something and I want you to say 'amen.'"

"What is it that you want?" she asked.

"May he accept me as a martyr for Palestine," her son replied, placing himself on the furthest extremes of Islamist thinking.

"My son, I can't say 'amen' to that. It's too difficult," she countered.

The son persisted. Finally the mother compromised. But she would go no further than expressing a wish that he might live long and be martyred as an old man.[14]

Of all the boys, Mufid later would dance on the edge of the fire that seemed already to be burning in Khalid Mishal's mind. But only Khalid would grow up to achieve notoriety as an American-declared SDGT—a "Specially Designated Global Terrorist."

5

"Have You Guys Lost Your Minds?"

Israel was going backward in two wars—militarily in Lebanon and economically at home—when the technocratic Shimon Peres became prime minister in September 1984.

Israel's ill-judged invasion of its northern neighbor in 1982 had cost the lives of almost seven hundred Israeli troops and pushed the country's ailing economy to the brink.[1] To survive, Peres had to cut and run in Lebanon. At the same time, he needed to make pragmatic deals at home. He struck one such deal on the homefront with his defense minister—Yitzhak Rabin, his bitter Labor Party rival. If Peres was to convince his ministers and the public of the need for severe budget pruning, then the all-important defense allocation would have to take a haircut. Rabin agreed, but his acceptance was conditional—the prime minister must undertake in turn not to interfere in Rabin's running of defense.[2] These two men could not make room for each other and Rabin was determined to have his own way in his own portfolio.

Peres, with no options, agreed. He and his advisers had enough on their plate in attempting to salvage what was left of Israel's post-independence economic miracle. The 1984 budget deficit had shot through the $1 billion mark, hyperinflation had crashed through a thousand percent, and a $1.5 billion bailout by Washington would take the total American subsidy for the year to a politically sensitive $1,000 for every Israeli.[3]

In the summer of 1985, it was a cause of some irritation when there was a rude interruption to a meeting of Peres's advisers, a tight-knit group of academics who came with him into office as the "100-day team."

Few had the nerve to gate-crash the prime ministerial suite in Jerusalem in this fashion. But here, yelling at them as he barged through the door, was a pugnacious American. This was Dan Kurtzer, a thirty-something junior diplomat from the U.S. Embassy in Tel Aviv. They knew him well, but now the advisers stared blankly as Kurtzer launched, with no preamble, into a tirade: "Have you guys lost your minds? Do you ever learn from history? Do you know what you're doing in Gaza as we speak?"[4]

Kurtzer's previous posting was Cairo—he had been there when Islamists assassinated President Anwar Sadat in 1981. Now Hezbollah, also Islamist and tied to Iran, was running amok in Lebanon. And, as Kurtzer saw it, the Israelis were fooling themselves—or being fooled—if they believed the claim by fundamentalists in Gaza that their only interest was the spiritual well-being of the people. Aware that Israel was an island in an Islamist sea, and alive to the risks of an Islamist revival on the back of Ayatollah Ruhollah Khomeini's 1979 revolution in Iran, Kurtzer had been to and from Gaza for several months, doing his own investigation of what he regarded as an extraordinary development.[5]

Raising a hand to fend off the American's tirade, one of Peres's advisers pleaded, "Dan, what are you talking about?" Simmering down, Kurtzer proceeded to outline details of the presence and activities in Gaza of a man called Shmuel Goren, a former Mossad agent who was Defense Minister Rabin's operations coordinator in the Occupied Territories.

Gaza was a brutalized society even before Israel seized the Strip in the 1967 war. Previously under the control of deeply suspicious authorities in Cairo, its fundamentalists had suffered the same crackdown as their Muslim Brotherhood confreres in Egypt; this meant that the activists Israel had inherited were seasoned underground operators. Chief among them was an unlikely revolutionary—the crippled and wheelchair-bound Sheikh Ahmad Yassin.

In 1965, Yassin had been jailed as a Muslim Brotherhood sympathizer after yet another roundup by Egyptian intelligence. Now, as a refugee amidst the unrelenting squalor of Gaza, he regarded the Israeli presence in the Occupied Territories as no ordinary occupation. This, he believed, was a determined Israeli effort to completely obliterate the Palestinian sense of identity. Nevertheless, Yassin saw an opening he could exploit, enabling him to spread the Islamist creed. As long as he moved quietly, Israel would not block his activities.

As explained by Shalom Harari, a senior Arabist with the occupation authorities in Gaza, Israel's position was based on the historical thinking of Defense Minister Moshe Dayan. "The Islamists were okay as long as they were not shooting and bombing; as long as there were no disturbances. Dayan said we have to treat Islam as we treat Christianity."[6]

With a passport that gave his year of birth as 1929—making him the same age as Yasser Arafat—Yassin was a preacher who could bide his time. The way Yassin assessed the outcome of the 1967 war was that the Jews had adhered to their faith and triumphed. Meanwhile, the secular, nationalist ethos of the Arab armies and Arafat's PLO had brought defeat for the Arabs. It followed that the Islamic beliefs and values of Palestinians had to be restored before there could be any successful uprising.

Yassin's message found fertile minds as he worked the mosques of the refugee camps. "At school and university we all were obsessed with Nasser's belief in Arab nationalism," recalled an early disciple of Yassin's, who was struck by the simplicity and surprising humor of the crippled preacher's language. "He spoke of the shameful defeat of the Arabs by such a tiny state. In the camps, he spoke to crowds of one hundred, maybe two hundred. Some of us worked those crowds, seeking out the bright, intelligent ones, who we invited to smaller gatherings in private homes."[7] In these more intimate forums the likely recruits were offered the writings of the Muslim Brotherhood giants— Hasan Banna, the founder of the movement, and Sayyid Qutb, its intellectual firebrand. The new recruits were encouraged to spread the word in family and educational circles of the falsity of the secular ideologies.

Yassin stopped short of publicly trying to discredit the PLO. Arafat's guerrilla attacks on Israel from Jordan and Syria and the Battle of Karameh were already legendary. "We had no confidence that Arafat would liberate Palestine, but at least he was able to claim his men were still fighting the Israelis," the disciple continued.

In 1973, Israel allowed Yassin to set up an umbrella for all Brotherhood activities in Gaza—the Islamic Center, or Mujamma' Al-Islami. This was a one-stop Islamist shop—mosque, clinic, kindergarten, festival hall, training center for women and girls, and headquarters for the powerful *zakat* (alms) committee, which managed local and foreign donations. And it capitalized on a steady Islamic reawakening in the Occupied Territories. In the twenty years following the Six-Day War, the number of mosques in the West Bank doubled to 750; in Gaza they trebled to 600, nearly 40 percent of which would be controlled by Yassin's Islamic Center.

Islamist candidates were marshaled to challenge the PLO's traditional control of professional and trade organizations and community groups, dislodging Fatah and other secular office bearers as the Brotherhood garnered anywhere between 35 and 45 percent of the vote. Some of the 1980s campaigns for control of university faculty and student unions became so violent that the injured were counted in the hundreds. They included Mohammad Hassan Sawalha, a lecturer at Najah University in Nablus, who was thrown from a third-floor window.[8]

The Israelis blocked Fatah and PLO community initiatives. But Yassin's Islamists were granted official approval for what actually was the early infrastructure of a state-within-a-state—schools and clinics, mosques, charities, and community centers, all of which evolved into a vast Islamist network, through which political tracts and guidance were distributed.

The ideological gulf between the Muslim Brotherhood and the PLO was not over jihad itself, but over a question of timing. Arafat and the other PLO factional leaders had opted for shooting their way back into Palestine as early as the late 1950s. But Yassin held rigidly to a Brotherhood belief that liberation could be achieved only as a sequel to a long and serious program of ideological, spiritual, and psychological reeducation. In short, as he saw it, it was the banner of Islam that had driven the Crusaders from holy Jerusalem in the twelfth century; in the face of repeated secular Arab failure, the same spirit was needed in the late twentieth century. Even then, Yassin believed that Palestinians could only be a spearhead. To help them drive the Jews out of Palestine, they would need to wait for the Muslim Brotherhood to create an Islamic state in Egypt, Jordan, or Syria.

The Israelis utterly misread the situation. In the mistaken belief that Yassin's organization would undermine what had been near-monolithic support for the secular and nationalist credo of the PLO, they allowed the sheikh's operation to prosper.[9] Claims by the secular Palestinian factions that Israel was actually funding the Islamists were vehemently denied, but in the mid-1980s the Israeli military governor of Gaza, Brigadier General Yitzhak Segev, would describe a deliberate strategy to boost the Islamists at the expense of the PLO and the Palestinian Communists: "The Israeli government gives me a budget and the military government gives it to the mosques."[10]

In June 1982, Ariel Sharon, Israel's bullish defense chief, had sent a military blitzkrieg northward into Lebanon, setting the scene for a grueling eighty-eight-day siege of the PLO in Beirut. In the end, Washington brokered a safe-passage deal, under which Arafat's headquarters staff of about two thousand was evacuated to Tunis, more than twelve hundred miles away on the North African coast, and more than ten thousand of his fighters were dispersed to seven different Arab countries.[11]

Driving around Gaza alone after these events, the American diplomat Dan Kurtzer was struck by a stark contrast in the mood of the people. With Arafat's eviction from Beirut, his demoralized Fatah and nationalist supporters were being held on a tight leash by the Israelis. But there was a new Islamist dynamism—with women covering up, men growing beards, new mosques everywhere, and even an Islamic university. The Arafat loyalists moaned to Kurtzer about being squeezed out by the Israelis. But the Islamists had no need for dialogue with the American. They were satisfied with what the Israelis were allowing them to achieve on the ground.

Shimon Peres had been in office for less than a year, but he was totally engrossed by Lebanon and the challenge of rescuing the Israeli economy. His wunderkind advisers, miffed at finding themselves lectured to by an uppity diplomat from Washington, complained. Despite defense being an agreed "no-go" area, the prime minister sent them to see Rabin, who then gave them another lecture—this one on the brilliance of the former Mossad operative, Shmuel Goren, whose cunning plot to use the Islamists to defang the secular PLO was showing such success. "And then we were told to go mind our own business," one of them reported back to Peres.[12]

When Kurtzer first confronted senior Israeli military officials in Gaza, they denied the existence of the Goren scheme. But later they conceded that the American was right. Believing that they could create a counterweight to Arafat and the PLO, they were allowing an unchecked flow of funds to the Islamists from Saudi Arabia and the Gulf; Arafat's more secular followers were to get nothing.

It was a conscious policy. But Kurtzer did not expect to find a policy paper when he marched into the prime minister's office. He well knew the latitude enjoyed by the Israeli military and its reliance on what he described as "policy by schmooze" rather than by formal and documented decision making.[13] But, having interrupted Peres's men in 1985, he left them on a note of disbelief, saying of the Islamists, "You really think you can tame these guys?"[14]

What began as a policy of religious tolerance, which Israel hoped might win it some respect in the Islamic world after its crushing of the Arab armies in 1967, quickly became a strategy to exploit a widening gulf between Islamist and secular Palestinians, and to spur Arab-on-Arab violence. It was done as much by omission as by commission. For some years, the Israelis did not have sufficient manpower on the ground in Gaza—even if they had wanted to challenge the Islamists. They did not have enough language experts to translate sermons from the mosques under the control of the Islamists or even to adequately patrol the Strip, especially when the religious obligation of the Jewish security forces required them to absent themselves en masse.[15]

In occupying Gaza, Israel inherited a system by which the pre-1967 Egyptian administration had attempted to keep the Gaza fundamentalists reined in—appointing and paying the salaries for a small army of tame imams. However, there was a new twist: while the Israelis continued to maintain the funds flow, those imams not to the liking of the Muslim Brotherhood were simply elbowed out of the way or paid a second salary to step aside or to deliver sermons written by others.[16] If the Islamists could not seize control of an Israeli-funded mosque, they gave dramatic new meaning to the term "new facts on the ground" by building their own—often in just a day. Israelis who staffed the occupation's religious administration were recruited from nearby Jewish settlements; they too needed to observe the Sabbath, and that was the day the Islamist activists chose to marshal hundreds of workers to throw up the shell of a building to serve as a family or local mosque in less than twenty-four hours.[17] "On a Sunday morning, our people would round a corner and see a mosque where there was nothing on the Friday," the Israeli Arabist Harari later explained. Kurtzer, the American diplomat, was taken aback too, saying, "Suddenly there'd be a green and white building where there was nothing the previous week."

When the Israelis attempted to establish their own handpicked Palestinian leadership, it too was hijacked by Yassin and his Muslim Brotherhood followers. After what some perceived as the collapse of the PLO—when Arafat was ejected from Beirut by Israeli forces led by Ariel Sharon, the man Israelis called "the bulldozer"—a few secularists did emerge as potential leaders in the Occupied Territories.[18] But Tel Aviv spurned them, opting to fund and appoint its own local councils or Village Leagues, up to two hundred members of whom were given weapons training by the Israeli security forces.[19] The Israelis believed they were recruiting collaborators,[20] but, like the Israeli-appointed imams, some of these councils soon fell under Yassin's Islamist influence.[21]

Kurtzer was left scratching his head. With Arafat and his forces licking their wounds in distant Tunis, here was an opportunity for Israel to encourage a local leadership that was independent minded and secular. Instead, the Islamists were being given free rein.

Kurtzer was not alone in his anxiety about where this might lead. Philip Wilcox, who was on the U.S. consulate staff in Jerusalem, was aware of persistent rumors that Israel was covertly supporting the Muslim Brotherhood.[22] At the CIA, analyst Martha Kessler concluded that Tel Aviv was playing with fire. "I don't think they realized how dangerous it would become," she said later.[23] And an effort by officials in the Pentagon to have the Defense Intelligence Agency analyze the Palestinian Islamist phenomenon was quashed through the intervention of "friends of Israel in the Reagan administration."[24]

It was hardly surprising. At the time, the CIA, in cahoots with Pakistan and Saudi Arabia, had begun Washington's biggest-ever covert operation—a multibillion-dollar gambit, in which Islamic fundamentalists were armed and trained as a proxy force against the Soviet Union in Afghanistan. Breathtaking in ambition and wild in its execution, the operation forced the godless Soviets to retreat and, ultimately, ended the Cold War. But Afghanistan also was the conflict that brought the espionage term "blowback" into common use.

As Washington walked away from the Afghan mujahideen war of the 1980s, so too did a generation of triumphant Islamist warriors, hyped on jihad and seeking out new infidel enemies. Afghanistan degenerated into the Central Asian badlands that ultimately would host Osama Bin Laden and his Al-Qaeda terror network.

The United States was applying the same "my enemy's enemy is my friend" strategy that the Israelis were exploiting in the Occupied Territories. Ironically, Israel had its own part in Washington's Afghanistan play. As the Goren experiment unfolded in Gaza, Israel was doing America's bidding by quietly supplying arms to the Islamists in Afghanistan[25] and Iran.[26] Moving model armies around the Cold War planning board at the Pentagon, the Americans were fulfilling a 1957 call by President Dwight Eisenhower for an Islamic jihad against communism. The CIA needed to stress the notion of "holy war" against Moscow in its dealing with Arab regimes, Eisenhower had once told a White House strategy meeting.[27]

Since the turn of the decade, Israel had been surrounded by the kind of strife that might have made asbestos gloves a prerequisite for any dealing with Islamists. In Egypt, next door and to the south, the 1981 assassination of President Anwar Sadat, whose 1977 peace pilgrimage to Jerusalem had inflamed Islamists, seemed not to weigh in Goren's reckoning. In Syria, next door and to the north, President Hafez Al-Assad had just put down a Muslim Brotherhood revolt, massacring them by the thousand;[28] yet Goren and his team naively believed Israel could achieve the impossible, by harnessing the fundamentalists to Israel's own political and security ends.

By contrast, next door and to the east, the Israelis watched with rare admiration for an Arab leader as King Hussein developed a textbook example of how to deal with Jordan's Islamists. Hussein set himself apart from the other Arab regimes by engaging and co-opting the Islamists; he thus burnished his Islamic credentials, and yet at the same time contained them organizationally. That this was effectively a mutual coexistence pact helped as, from time to time, Hussein and the Islamists had enemies in common in Egypt, Syria, and Iraq. One of the king's closest advisers explained, "He knew there had to be a middle ground to accommodate the mainstream Islamists—but he was always able to deal harshly with the extremists."[29]

Hussein warned privately that the Saudi Arabian and Egyptian handling of the fundamentalists would backfire. The Saudis blindly financed and supported fundamentalists with no checks on their operations because they wanted to spread their hard-line Wahhabi strain of Islam. The Egyptians had made tactical mistakes that allowed numerous Islamist groups to emerge from the Muslim Brotherhood because of a vicious state crackdown on the parent organization after an attempt on the life of President Gamal Abdel Nasser back in 1954. "The response was brutal and this is where you have to start in terms of what went wrong," another of Hussein's advisers concluded.

In Gaza no one was inclined to listen to those who saw readily enough what the Islamists were doing. The PLO wised up to the risks long before the Israelis would. Nabil Shaath, a Gazan exile in the Arafat camp, observed his leader's rage over Israel's encouragement of the fundamentalists as an antidote to his PLO. "But that was the mistake of all who gambled on the Islamists; the fundamentalists would accommodate them, but they were always working for their own goals," Shaath would lament in much sorrow many years later.[30]

Observing events on the ground, the Israeli Arabist Shalom Harari did see in a new light Arafat's determination to have the PLO declared the sole representative of the Palestinian people—which he achieved at an Arab leaders' summit in Rabat, the Moroccan capital, in 1974. Arafat's desperation was always interpreted as an attempt to block the wily King Hussein's claim to speak for the Palestinians. But, from Harari's viewpoint, Arafat was driven as much by a need to block a march by the fundamentalists.[31]

Israel was not going to help him. Harari would recall a brief effort to mediate a truce when fratricidal violence flared. "But no one really complained, so we did nothing . . . [even] as the violence spread to campuses on the West Bank. I remember officers at the Erez checkpoint [on the northern edge of the Gaza Strip], calling us at HQ to say a busload of Gazan students wanted to pass to the West Bank to help the Islamists in a clash. I said, 'Let them go—they'll only be beating up each other.'"

As early as 1978, their own puppet Arab officials in Gaza had warned Israeli officialdom of the consequences of their actions,[32] but their government persisted with its claim that the unholy alliance was reasonable toleration of religious freedom.

In 1987, couriers dropped copies of a highly classified new report on the desks of more than one hundred senior figures in government, security, and the bureaucracy—Israel's top decision makers. It might have been described as a "yes, yes, but" document. Yes, religious fervor was up in the Occupied Territories; yes, the Islamists wanted an Iranian-style theocracy in all of historic Palestine; but its message was that the Islamists were not an immediate security threat.

General Shayke Erez, the military governor of Gaza, wrote in the report's foreword: "[They] want to focus on the process of winning hearts and minds . . . and only later [to] begin an active struggle against Israel."[33] Little did he know.

6

Arafat's Circus

When Khalid Mishal graduated from his physics course in 1978, job prospects in Kuwait were good for a non-Kuwaiti. But as the 1980s unfolded, it would prove to be an exceptional period for this Palestinian refugee's principal pursuit—preparation for jihad.

When the time for graduation approached in 1978, Mishal's friends feared that his neglect of his studies would be reflected in his final results. But even with all his religious and political distractions, his grades were sufficient for an appointment as a physics teacher in the Kuwaiti education system, which by then was a refugee redoubt—a quarter of all teachers in the emirate were Palestinian.[1]

In his third year in the classroom, Mishal decided he should marry. It was not a question of having met, or even seen, a woman he wanted as a mate; rather, it was an in-principle decision about another marker in what, culturally and socially, was becoming the very ordered existence of a determined young individual. By totally embracing the conservatism of the Muslim Brotherhood, Mishal found spiritual and philosophical reinforcement for the innate conservatism of the tribal and cultural traditions of the West Bank, which, after fourteen years in the Gulf emirate, were still the glue that held his family together. Azzam Tamimi would say, "I don't think Khalid experimented with anything."[2]

After he had expressed his desire to marry, Mishal was told about a certain man from the village of Bourin, near Nablus—"a good man"—who had daughters of a marriageable age. Knowing neither the girls nor the family, Mishal telephoned the father, Salih. "I told him I'd heard highly of him from a mutual friend, who said perhaps, if we got to know each other, I might be able to marry one of his daughters,"[3] Mishal explained later. They met outside a city mosque and agreed, as custom required, that his mother and one of his sisters would visit Salih's home. Afterward, the women of Mishal's family reported very favorably on meeting one of Salih's daughters, a young woman named Amal.

It seemed perfectly natural for this twenty-five-year-old teacher that the way to Amal Salih was through her father. Her family lived in Kuwait, but Mishal considered them West Bankers. He was invited to accompany both of his parents for tea with the Salih family—during which Amal was expected to enter the room, perhaps to serve biscuits and maybe to ask if Mishal would like sugar in his tea. The rule was that he could steal just a glance, but the young man shocked the four parents by engaging Amal in lengthy conversation. That evening they were required, separately, to recite the *istikhara* prayer, a request for guidance in making a big decision. "We both felt it was right," he said.

They married in 1981. But the calendar by which they then lived was more Palestinian than it was Gregorian or Hijri. In which month did they marry? "The anniversary of the Six-Day War," he would say. And when was the birth of Fatima, their first child? "Sharon's invasion of Lebanon" was the answer.

That was June 6, 1982, when the removal of the PLO from any country peripheral to Palestine seemed like a huge defeat for all Palestinians. The distance from their homeland would make resistance all that much more difficult. Certainly that was true as it applied to Arafat and the PLO. But, from Khalid Mishal's viewpoint, Arafat's banishment was one in a series of international circumstances that was falling into line with precision timing to make it possible to launch a new initiative that was gestating in the mind of this physics teacher in Kuwait.

These were global events that placed elements of the Islamist movement at key intersections of foreign policy calculations, from Riyadh to Washington. All geopolitical strategy was still informed by the Cold War, so when the CIA's new Counterterrorism Center opened in the mid-1980s, its targets were secular, leftist terrorist groups.[4] Washington's recruitment of Islamist volunteers for jihad against the Soviet Union meant that it was training new fighters at the same time that it was spawning interconnected fund-raising efforts in Muslim communities around the world. In the United States alone, there were dozens of recruitment and fund-raising centers for Afghanistan. Likewise, in the Palestinian Occupied Territories, the Israelis had concluded that of all the Palestinian bad guys, the Islamists were at least tolerable.

Washington was spending billions in Afghanistan. Saudi Arabia was matching it dollar for dollar, but Riyadh had been pumping money into the Islamist cause even before the start of the Afghan adventure. A senior figure in the Palestinian Muslim Brotherhood at the time explained, "Most Islamist parties in the Arab world had links to the Muslim Brotherhood. The Saudis were spending millions trying to buy the Brotherhood at the time of the Iranian Revolution [in 1979]. They needed a bulwark against Tehran."

Observing the region and the world, Mishal could afford to feel almost satisfied. Islamists had room to move in the Occupied Territories, and now, quite remarkably, the Israeli occupiers were allowing them to organize and to receive substantial funds from outside. The Islamic fighters in Afghanistan, the mujahideen, were getting good press, which legitimized Islamic fundraising in the Middle East, Europe, and the United States. In turn, this made it highly probable that funds could be raised for Palestine in the shadow of this greater Afghan alms effort, which was successfully targeting wealthy and middle-class Muslims who lived in First World economies, but still felt bound by the call of the Qur'an for *zakat* (charitable giving).

The only piece missing from Mishal's jigsaw was an ability for the Muslim Brotherhood to move freely in Kuwait, so that he and his cell of about ten Islamist colleagues might function more freely themselves. But in this regard too, the Kuwaiti regime was moving in the direction he wanted.

Kuwait depended on Palestinian refugees, who had an inordinate impact on the development of this tiny emirate, which, at one stage, was rated the fourth-richest country in the world.[5] An early Kuwaiti response to the spudding of the first oil wells in 1936 had been to call for teachers from Palestine.[6] With their traditional hunger for education and their desperate need of refuge in 1948, and again in 1967, the Palestinians were a ready-made labor force for Kuwait, which, in turn, made the emirate one of the most cohesive and active of the Palestinian diaspora communities.[7] When Palestinians bragged about their contribution to the emirate, Kuwaiti ruler Sheikh Jaber Al-Sabah would finish their boast: "Built on the shoulders of Palestinians," he would say.[8]

But, grateful as most Palestinians were for their material well-being in Kuwait, they remained aliens. Decades after their first arrival, the editor of the daily *Al-Watan*, Mussid Al-Saleh, observed bluntly, "We look at them as foreigners."[9] Kuwaiti anxiety rose as each new crisis erupted across the region, whether it was Black September in Jordan or the Lebanese Civil War, in which the headstrong Arafat took sides. Suspicion lingered that Palestinians might attempt an uprising in Kuwait.[10] Anxious about jeopardizing their jobs or residency rights, many of them kept up donations to the Palestinian cause but withdrew from overt participation[11]—and those who did take part were watched by the authorities.

In the 1960s the Muslim Brotherhood's presence in Kuwait was rated "insignificant" by diplomats and foreign intelligence agencies.[12] But in the aftermath of Arafat's lunge for power in Amman and its bloody denouement in 1970, the Kuwaiti royals opted for the same kind of insurance as King Hussein of Jordan. As a counter to an emerging leftist liberalism among Kuwaitis or any pushiness by secular Palestinians, the regime allowed the Muslim Brotherhood to put down roots. This was a breathtaking deal, which included establishing a $1 billion investment house that would become the epicenter of a web of Islamist business, social, and charitable organizations. In time, it would be accused of funding violent Islamist organizations in the region.[13]

Palestinians had to act with caution, and much of their activity was conducted underground. Both the secular and religious camps touted for membership numbers that would extend their support base, and for funds, which many donors were told were for welfare work in the Occupied Territories. Fatah had been actively recruiting students for two decades, and it protected its ascendency jealously.

Amid uproar over Egyptian president Anwar Sadat's "treacherous" peace pilgrimage to Jerusalem in 1977, Khalid Mishal had headed a slate of Islamist candidates who challenged Fatah's previously unquestioned lock on the council of the General Union of Palestinian Students (GUPS). As the angry young Muslim Brothers saw it, their attempt to break into this lowly level of the Palestinian power structure was blocked by a ploy straight from the Arafat playbook. Still in control of the union, the old man's disciples simply canceled the poll. Mishal was contemptuous: "The elections were not real because Arafat always decided who was in charge. They believed all institutions belonged to Fatah . . . [and] they worried we'd win."[14]

Wielding the knowledge that had so impressed Asad Abdul Rahman, Mishal had reveled in the fierce ideological competition between the factions, laying waste to Arafat's followers in campus debates that sometimes ended in violent clashes between rivals.[15] Undaunted as they went head-to-head, the Islamist bloc broke away to form their own student body—the Islamic Association of Palestinian Students, of which Mishal became president. That move sparked Islamist breakaways from the Arafat-controlled GUPS throughout the diaspora. Branches of Mishal's holy new union sprang up in the region and in sprawling émigré communities in the United States, West Germany, and the UK. In turn, these union branches became building blocks for more broadly based support groups, like the Islamic Association for Palestine, which opened for business in the United States in 1981.

Khalid Mishal became obsessed with what he described as "building and layering the foundations" of what he already saw as the "Islamist national project for Palestine."[16] Various intelligence agencies in the region would later conclude that his teaching job—particularly the hours—was a useful cover as he devoted his every waking hour to "the project."[17] But, a stickler for propriety, Mishal seemingly took great exception to any suggestion the job was just a cover for his underground activities, explaining: "My other role was not at the expense of my schoolwork . . . [and] I resigned from teaching the moment the project demanded more of my time."[18]

Mishal abandoned the classroom in 1984. By then he had already put in place the essential infrastructure for a fundamentalist flying wedge that would be unleashed just three years later on Israeli forces occupying Gaza and the West Bank. His project would become a multimillion-dollar global apparatus that delivered in arms and blood, dollars and diplomacy. Khalid Mishal would become its leader. Explaining the dynamic later, he pinpointed its origin: "It was done in parallel with the West Bank and Gaza. But the launch platform was student politics in Kuwait [where] rapid measures paved the way for this new project."

Steeled by the campus clashes and irked by taunts from the secular factions that the Muslim Brotherhood took an easy road, with its insistence that it must tend to the spiritual and moral needs of the Palestinians before it embarked on any armed struggle, Mishal reread the Muslim Brotherhood's history.

He would claim that it was the Brotherhood, not Fatah, that had given birth to Palestinian armed resistance. Brotherhood members from Egypt had carried arms against the British and the Zionists in the 1930s and 1940s, and it was from their ranks that the founders of Fatah had emerged to launch their organization in Kuwait in the 1950s. Mishal's argument was that Fatah actually was a splinter group, which had broken away in frustration at the gradualist philosophy of the Brotherhood. "We're the root; Fatah is a mere branch" was his triumphant boast.[19]

Claiming ownership of the historic roots of armed resistance, Mishal agitated for a radical shift in Muslim Brotherhood thinking. He wanted a resumption of war. Arguing that the historic Ikhwan project had merely been

overrun by Fatah, he now rationalized that there was no contradiction between fighting for Palestine and conducting a religious life.[20] He urged
fundamentalists to rejoin battle to restore Palestine as a part of the Islamic
homeland, the *umma*. To liberate Jerusalem and its holy places became essential elements in reclaiming the religious psyche of Islam. The young
physics teacher told his cell of fellow thinkers, "It's holy land; the first *qibla*
[the site toward which all Muslims turn for prayer] was in Jerusalem; it is
our country, the homeland of our fathers. We must have a role in liberating
Palestine."[21]

Fatah and PLO loyalists were outraged already by the Muslim Brotherhood's continued loyalty to the Jordanian monarchy in the wake of Black
September, and by its persistent description of the PLO as an instrument of
flawed Arab regimes. The Brotherhood saw the PLO's many failures and
setbacks as God's punishment for its secular ways. Retaliating, the PLO
mocked the Brotherhood for remaining aloof from the armed struggle; its
leaders continued to taunt the Brotherhood with demands to be told when
might be the right time for armed struggle.

Then the Muslim Brotherhood upped the ante. It accused the PLO's exiled leaders of squandering precious resources by getting caught up in other
non-Palestinian crises and conflicts in the region—by swanning around Arab
capitals where Islamists were being persecuted, and by allowing themselves to
be duchessed by heathen Eastern Bloc and Soviet leaders, while ordinary
Palestinians in the Occupied Territories endured the trench warfare symbol-
ized by the pistol on the swaggering Arafat's hip. In all of this, Mishal was
quite deliberately rebuking a figure seen by many in Fatah as an earthly god:
Yasser Arafat.

The old Egyptian Muslim Brotherhood, indeed, had been the crucible
from which they all had sprung. In Cairo back in the 1950s, Arafat was a cal-
low showman of just twenty-three when he first signed on for battle. As a
student activist, he had organized a petition written in blood, as a plea on
behalf of displaced Palestinians. At that time, Khalid Mishal was not even
born; yet now he was girding his loins for a new Palestinian war, making it
clear he believed that Arafat should be sidelined.

Mishal was not alone in advocating that the Muslim Brotherhood resume
the fight. As early as 1980, some Brotherhood members, frustrated with the
movement's passive policies, had broken away to form a small fighting group
called Palestinian Islamic Jihad. In mounting a daring campaign of violence
to achieve the Brotherhood goal of an Islamist state, they fired the imagina-

tion of young Islamists in Gaza and the West Bank with their success, prompting them to challenge the Brotherhood leadership to explain why theirs was the only Palestinian movement that believed it was necessary to abstain from the fray.[22]

In Kuwait a like-minded group of about ten was excited by Mishal's call for an organizational breakthrough that would transform the Palestinian struggle. There had been earlier efforts to link some of the Islamist groups in the diaspora. Now the Kuwait ten would workshop the teacher's idea for a first-ever conference of diaspora and territory delegates that was to upend the current Muslim Brotherhood's strategy on confronting Israel. It was Mishal who gave expression to their collective thinking in a paper that persuaded the formal Islamist leadership in Kuwait to embrace a new campaign of resistance.

In 1983 about thirty territory and diaspora delegates slipped into Amman, taking advantage of the Brotherhood's extensive local network of welfare, educational, and religious services to plan jihad under the nose of King Hussein's General Intelligence Department. They came from the United States, Europe, Saudi Arabia, and the Gulf. The proposal they heard from a strong Kuwaiti delegation was breathtaking—it was nothing less than a full-frontal assault on the supremacy of Yasser Arafat, the man indulged by much of the world as Mr. Palestine.

Miraculously, Arafat had always seemed to bounce back from defeat and travail. Arab leaders had blessed his PLO as the "sole legitimate representative" of the Palestinians and had opened their coffers to him. He rode out the PLO's eviction from Jordan in 1970, he weathered the petty jealousies and flagging interest of the Arab leaders, and he stared down protests from those Palestinians in the Occupied Territories who were angered by his meddling in regional affairs instead of focusing on their tragic plight.

But in the lead-up to the secret Amman conference, Mishal dismissed Arafat as a failed leader. He lambasted the Fatah strongman over his eviction from Lebanon in the previous year, which, he said, had put the Palestinian military campaign into retreat. "There was great anxiety in the minds of many for the future of the campaign and for the homeland," he would say years later. "It wasn't just what was happening in Lebanon. There was increasing talk of a negotiated settlement. Alternative activity had to be launched inside the Occupied Territories. As Islamists we had a responsibility to compensate— we had to offer a new model of resistance that would constitute an additional contribution to the battle with Israel."[23]

If ever there was a time to make a pitch to the neglected Islamic sensitivi-ties of Palestinians, this was it. With the PLO and Fatah effectively banished from the region, the dream to which so many Palestinians had clung for so long seemed to have evaporated. Islamist Palestinians across the diaspora tra-ditionally immersed themselves in the national branch of the Muslim Brother-hood in whichever country they found exile. Mishal proposed that the Palestinians within each national branch be brought together within a global Palestinian project that would exist within the folds of the Brotherhood's international movement.

The Amman conference adopted Mishal's sweeping plan, which also pro-posed that Islamist Palestinians around the globe be tapped as a legion of new fund-raisers and fixers for the cause. Either because they were religiously sympathetic or because they were jaded by the endless hoopla of the Arafat circus, Arab and Muslim governments, together with wealthy businessmen, were to be persuaded to provide all that was needed to sustain an alternative to Fatah and the PLO. The Muslim Brotherhood and Islamists around the world were to be mobilized behind a fundamentalist resistance campaign that would stand apart from the failing secular factions—in the eyes of man and God. This was truly audacious.

Mishal moved deeper into his new clandestine existence. On the strength of his early student activism, he had become a sought-after speaker in dias-pora communities, a role that gave easy cover for more secretive activities. He had entered the United States, Europe, and various countries in the region in the guise of a student lecturer, when his primary purpose was to raise funds and establish logistics for the jihad to come. Following the 1983 conference in Amman, all of the Brotherhood's varied Palestine-related activities were brought together under the auspices of the Kuwait-based Jihaz Filastin—the Palestine Apparatus—which gave Mishal effective control over funding for the activities in the Occupied Territories.

When Mishal had lived under his parents' roof, his mother had wondered about his endless meetings—yet she had thought it best not to inquire.[24] But when he married Amal, he felt a need for his wife's family to have a sense that she was also marrying the movement. The husband's role in laying the foun-dations for radical resistance was known only to the innermost circles of the Muslim Brotherhood, but swearing both his future father-in-law and bride to secrecy, Mishal thought it politic—and polite—to reveal some of what lay beneath the veneer of his being a conscientious teacher of physics. The bond with his father-in-law was almost immediate, and Salih came to see his new son-in-law filling an emptiness that had existed in his life since one of his own sons had died as a PLO fighter in Lebanon. Amal later told Mishal that she had often prayed for a husband who would serve both his religion and the Palestinian cause.[25]

In keeping her vow of silence, Amal soon found she was also cooking regular dinners for perhaps one of the most powerful Islamist preacher-philosophers of the century—the shaggy-bearded Sheikh Abdullah Azzam.[26] If Mishal had graduated from the push-and-shove of campus activism in Kuwait, he now had the opportunity for doctoral studies with a revered master of the complexities of global jihad. Azzam was fast becoming expert in all of it—spiritual justification, recruitment, fund-raising, and managing cash when it was delivered by the suitcase-full, politics, and diplomacy. But, most of all, Azzam could teach patience and planning to a young man in a hurry.

Azzam was playing a crucial organizational role in the Afghan conflict, but he was in Central Asia by default. He believed that Afghanistan took precedence over Palestine only for the tactical reason that the Afghan conflict could deliver a genuine Islamic state as a beachhead in what might be a new Islamic world order. At the same time, Azzam argued that the Palestinian cause had been hijacked by the secular "isms" of the day—communism and nationalism—along with what he derided as "modernist Muslims."[27]

As the rising star of the Muslim Brotherhood in Kuwait, Khalid Mishal was like a relay runner, poised and waiting for Azzam to pass the baton, to take Azzam's more sophisticated style of jihadi management on to Palestine. Making frequent fund-raising visits to Kuwait, Azzam became a regular visitor to Mishal's home. Responding to criticism by those Palestinians who claimed Azzam was fighting the wrong war and that he should have been directing his jihadi energies to the Occupied Territories, Mishal would apologize on Azzam's behalf, explaining that jihad in Afghanistan was an opportunity for action at a time when Islamists had no combat role in the Palestinian resistance. Azzam confirmed as much in his writing: "Afghanistan . . . does not mean we have forgotten. Palestine is our beating heart, it comes even before Afghanistan in our minds, our hearts, our feelings and our faith."[28]

Azzam's obsession was always Palestine. Born near the West Bank town of Jenin in 1941, he had fled after the Six-Day War—first to Jordan, before becoming something of a jihad gypsy in the region and the world. Fifteen years older than Mishal, he had a fighting spirit that surfaced much earlier than that of the eleven-year-old whose family also had fled the Israeli occupation of the West Bank. Azzam had the look of a firebrand—broad shouldered with dramatic daubs of white marking the extremities of his long, dark beard. His ability to differentiate on the finer points of the struggle might ultimately cost him his life, but outwardly Azzam was as uncompromising as his motto: "Jihad and the rifle alone—no negotiation, no conference, no dialogue."[29]

This man from Jenin fought before he thought. On arriving in Jordan as a refugee, Azzam was instrumental in the earliest post-1967 push for Islamists to fight alongside the PLO.[30] In a deal with Arafat, the Muslim Brotherhood took over a number of Fatah training camps in the Jordan Valley. Calling them the Bases of the Sheikhs—Qawaid Al-Shuyukh—Azzam trained his men with weapons before launching Islamist-only guerrilla raids into Israel.[31]

But this venture was short-lived. Some said the closure of the camps was forced by the rising pressure that other governments, such as Egypt, applied to the Brotherhood.[32] Others detected a finer tactical point: sensing the looming Black September clashes between the Jordanian regime and the PLO, the Brotherhood was obliged to quit to avoid becoming a victim of its conflicting loyalties.[33] As Islamists, they would have been expected to side with King Hussein against Arafat; as Palestinians, they would have been obliged to line up with the PLO against the Hashemite regime.

Azzam changed course. Opting to study Islamic jurisprudence at Al-Azhar, he launched himself on a trajectory that would make him one of the most influential Islamist scholars of modern times. He was the author of the fatwa that delivered plane-loads of young Muslims from the Middle East and the Maghreb countries to Afghanistan, on the grounds that fighting the Soviet occupation of a Muslim land was an Islamic duty. He moved to Pakistan in 1980 and became a role model and mentor for Osama Bin Laden before they fell out over a struggle for power and ideas. It was Azzam who set up the Peshawar-based recruitment center that Bin Laden commandeered as a forerunner to his Al-Qaeda network; and, when the CIA needed help holding the fractious Afghan factions together, it was to Abdullah Azzam that the American agency turned.[34]

For a time, the power of Azzam's ideas held sway over the millions of dollars being doled out by the charismatic Bin Laden. As the defeat of the Soviets loomed in Afghanistan, Azzam urged the Islamist forces there to turn to Palestine, but Bin Laden, together with an Egyptian clique that wanted to bring on the war of the worlds, managed to marginalize Azzam at that time. He fell from grace in the councils of Al-Qaeda because he refused to issue the fatwas that would sanction the attempted overthrow of Muslim regimes— such as those in Saudi Arabia, Egypt, and Jordan.

Azzam became a sensation on the international jihadi circuit for recruiting and fund-raising, particularly in the United States. His mystic portrayal of angels riding into war on horseback, and birds that sheltered mujahideen from Soviet bombs, raised the rafters at mosques in Brooklyn, St. Louis, Kansas City, Seattle, Sacramento, Los Angeles, and San Diego.[35]

But Azzam was also raising funds for Palestine. In 1988, he was guest speaker at a conference of the Islamic Association for Palestine in Oklahoma City.[36] An architect of the American Islamist network who became part of Mishal's global strategy identified Azzam as "essential" in building the Palestinian project, explaining: "The donations were huge. Azzam believed that Palestinians with Afghan mujahideen experience should return to Palestine for jihad . . . his plan after the defeat of the Soviets was to move into Jordan with handpicked fighters who he would dispatch to the Occupied Territories." Recalling the thrill of fund-raising functions in the United States, a well-traveled senior Hamas figure in Gaza revealed, "I was there when Azzam collected $250,000 in one night in New Jersey."[37]

Few Palestinians with Afghan experience were known by Israeli or other observers to have returned to the Occupied Territories, with one tantalizing exception. In 1986, Israeli authorities uncovered a small, unaffiliated Islamist cell that had recruited a nineteen-year-old woman as a suicide bomber. Under interrogation, their bomb maker, who was an engineer from the West Bank town of Tulkarm, revealed details of the camp at which he had trained in Afghanistan and of his trainers—who, he said, had included CIA agents.[38]

In the absence of the Palestinian phalanx that Azzam envisaged would come from Afghanistan, the process of establishing the Muslim Brotherhood's armed jihad in the Occupied Territories would have been a slow burn that might have ended in disaster. At the secret Amman conference in 1983, it was made clear that it would take time to get the project up and running. But, if only in their own minds, the organizers craved credibility in order to weave a narrative that might compete with the rich tapestry of Fatah and the other factions. In the Occupied Territories, this meant missions and martyrs.

The first whose names were engraved on the Brotherhood's honor board of martyrdom were Jawad Abu Sulmiyah and Saib Dhahab,[39] both of whom were Gazans enrolled at Bir Zeit University on the West Bank. Abu Sulmiyah and Dhahab were killed, and twenty others were injured, when Israeli forces put down a street protest in June 1986. It was one of the first such protests that the leaders of the Muslim Brotherhood authorized in the hope of easing pent-up anger and emotion in the ranks of their younger followers.

More curious and less clear-cut was the Islamists' first military mission.

Unbeknownst to most of the delegates, an inner circle decided in advance of the Amman conference to get cash to Sheikh Ahmad Yassin in Gaza to train and arm a small Brotherhood fighting corps. In his first foray into fundraising, Mishal produced the necessary $70,000 by tapping the circle of well-connected Kuwaitis he and his father had come to know from serving at the mosque of the Kuwaiti prince. At a time of need for the Muslim Brotherhood, their deep pockets opened obligingly when Mishal came calling.[40]

Yassin put the money to good use. Men were dispatched to Jordan for covert training, and orders were placed with illegal suppliers who could access Israeli weapons stores.[41] However, Yassin's buyers came up against two of the constants in the Palestinian conflict: people from their own side who collaborated with the occupiers, and agents of the occupiers who successfully passed themselves off as crooked arms dealers. The upshot was the arrest of Yassin, who, on being convicted of plotting to destroy the state of Israel, was jailed.

At the time, the sheikh was an oddity to his Israeli jailers. They were unaccustomed to having an Islamist among the thousands of secular Palestinians in their charge. Their bemusement dovetailed with accusations from Fatah, which presented the Muslim Brotherhood with a catch-22: lacking any record of their attacks on Israelis, how could they scotch persistent rumors that they were actually arming to fight Fatah, not Israel? In time, they would have their own sprawling record of terror and violence as the bona fides of jihad, but, more than twenty years on, the Israeli Arabist who served in Gaza at the time, Shalom Harari, remained convinced that Yassin's guns really were pointed at Fatah. "He'd had the weapons for a year, but he wasn't shooting at us—his targets were in the Arafat faction," Harari insisted.[42]

These were filthy Fatah rumors, the Brotherhood declared.[43] Either way, it all might have been a disaster. Mishal's new global machine for funding and logistics would become an essential element of the new jihad, but it would have had great difficulty functioning in the absence of Yassin's charismatic leadership and his canny management of the Islamist community networks in the Occupied Territories. Yassin was sent down for thirteen long years for plotting to destroy Israel. But, amazingly, in just over a year the preacher would be back in Gaza, negotiating its rutted alleys and lanes in his battered old wheelchair.

7

The Palestinian Project

Each day, when the children of Jabaliyah finished school, they could be found behind buildings breaking stones into easily hurled missiles. Then they took up positions at intersections throughout Gaza's most squalid and densely packed refugee camp. On this particular day, their first engagement was short and sharp. The target was a group of Israeli soldiers repairing the barbed-wire fencing around a military compound. Within seconds, two armored personnel carriers nosed out of the compound into the camp's boggy laneways. They moved this way and that, like irritated elephants, but the children's stones fell wide of the mark. Soldiers gave chase on foot, but halfheartedly.

The youngsters kept up the provocation. Sure enough, within thirty minutes a pitched battle was under way. More Israeli armored personnel carriers delivered reinforcements. Then the Israelis wheeled out one of their own special inventions: a stone cannon. In the land where stoning was a traditional punishment, the occupying force had created a machine capable of spitting rocks faster and more forcefully than any child might throw them.

The inventors of this brutal weapon gave it a strangely poetic name: the Chatsatsit. Snub-nosed, its wide-diameter barrel protruded from an armored housing on the rear of a vehicle on which the front wheels were conventional; those at the rear were tracked, like those of a tank. Inside, soldiers could be seen loading boxes of stones into a hopper attached to the firing mechanism. Its range was about one hundred yards.[1]

The Chatsatsit lumbered into full view, spraying dust and rock. Never mind that the street was choked with about one hundred primary school girls heading home for lunch. Rocks weighing as much as ten ounces each pelted down around them, off the road and crashing through the rooftops. Shrieking girls raced for shelter.

But the *shabab*, as the youths were known, stood their ground and so revealed the machine's futility. Displaying remarkable bravado, boys as young as ten and twelve ducked and weaved, around and under the rock bombardment, to press their own attack. The mesh grille on the windshield of one of the Israeli support vehicles finally gave way. Several stones later, the windscreen was smashed, and it and the Chatsatsit were forced to withdraw.

A great cheer went up, the girls and some passing mothers joining in. Now all entered the fray: mothers, sons, and daughters all hurling stones, prayers, and abuse at Israel's prime minister of the day. "Shamir, get to hell out of here! Dog!" they cried.

There were a few light injuries. Ultimately seven children and teenagers were arrested, and the rest went to do their homework. It was just another day in the third year of the War of the Stones.

Formally, this six-year-long uprising became the Intifada, the "shake-up." It erupted as an explosive campaign of grassroots resistance—with civil disobedience and strikes, boycotts and barricades. But it was the stone throwers who snapped the world out of its glazed-eye boredom with a crisis that found a need for catharsis in twenty-year cycles, hemorrhaging at least once in the life of each generation. In 1948, it was Israel's War of Independence; in 1967, the Six-Day War; and in 1987, this, the First Intifada. In the six years to the end of 1993, Israeli security forces killed eleven hundred Palestinians.[2] Hundreds more were killed by fellow Palestinians as a result of accusations that they had collaborated with the occupation forces.[3]

After decades of neglect and oppression by their Israeli overlords, and failure by their PLO envoys, Palestinians could no longer suppress a seething rage in the face of the relentless Israeli campaign of collective punishment for Palestinian resistance—of mass imprisonment and detention; land seizures and home demolitions; curfews and deportations; harsh taxes and economic privation. There had to be an escape valve.

The Intifada was a protest against both Israeli repression and the failure of Arafat, the PLO, and the Arab governments to deliver. The rhetoric of Arafat's dominant Fatah faction was rich, brutal, and exaggerated; yet, it had achieved little. As refugees and prisoners in their own homes, Palestinians had clung to and nurtured an enduring sense of place and identity. The world refused to recognize it, but the mere sense of being a nation sustained them under occupation.

The upshot was that the advice of the exiled and remote PLO leadership was losing credibility. More of the hated Israeli settlements were spreading like a virus on "their" land. At the same time, an ugly new political campaign was gathering steam in Israel. Called "transfer," it advocated that the Palestinians from the West Bank and Gaza be forcibly removed across the Jordan River, and into the lap of the hapless King Hussein—thus removing the problem.

The original spark for the Intifada had been a traffic accident in Gaza early in December 1987. The Strip was on tenterhooks. In the preceding days, spirits had been buoyed by the mass escape of six Palestinian fighters from a high-security Gaza prison, and the death of six Israeli soldiers at an Israel Defense Forces (IDF) camp in the north of the country after their Palestinian killer arrived in their midst on a hang glider. But also there was anger over the death of four Palestinians in a bloody shoot-out with Israeli troops. There was an expectation too of a heavy Israeli crackdown as it dawned on Gazans that the celebrated prison escapees may have been behind a new series of attacks on Israelis. These included the assassination of a senior Israeli military policeman, Captain Ron Tal, and, two days before the traffic accident, the stabbing death of an Israeli plastics merchant, Shlomo Sakal, in Gaza City's bedraggled Palestine Square.

On December 8, a truck driven by a twenty-five-year-old Israeli, Herzl Buchovzeh, careened into oncoming traffic near the tense Erez security post on the northern perimeter of the Gaza Strip. Four Palestinian workers died in the pile-up and seven more were injured. Three of the dead came from nearby Jabaliyah, the biggest and most overcrowded of eight miserable camps for Palestinian refugees in Gaza. Hard on the heels of news of the accident arriving in the camp came an unfounded rumor that the Israeli truck driver was a brother of Shlomo Sakal, and that far from being an accident, this deadly collision was a deliberate act of revenge.

Pent-up rage exploded first in Jabaliyah and then spread like wildfire up and down the Gaza Strip before leaping to the West Bank. Men took to the streets and, right behind them, women and children. As ammunition against an army with tanks and guns, they ripped up paving stones and hurled trash cans. Men who in the past had cowered in the face of Israeli authority now tore off their shirts and thrust out bare chests. The Israelis were dared to shoot[4] and, after they did, the endless keening from each funeral served as a kind of compounding siren call for more people to come into the streets, for more businesses to shut in defiance of Israeli orders to remain open, for more stones and bricks to be hurled at a foreign force that had imposed itself on every aspect of the Palestinians' lives.

All wanted to own the Intifada. But in truth, it was a genuinely spontaneous eruption of grassroots anger that took all by surprise—Islamists and secularists, Palestinians and Israelis alike.

In Tunis, Arafat paced. His usual anxieties kicked in: what were the implications for his own leadership? How could he control such combustible events from so far away? This was so totally unexpected, completely unplanned; none of the exiled leadership had ordered it or even anticipated it.[5]

And once it had begun, most misjudged its staying power. Mahmoud Abbas, the man who on Arafat's death would later become leader of Fatah, gave it "two or three months."[6] After just two weeks, Shmuel Goren, the official who had spearheaded Israel's strategy of engaging the Islamists as a ploy to undermine the PLO, reported that the people were exhausted—it was all "dying down."[7] Perplexed as he was, Arafat made a decision that was typical of what he often did in a dead end: he would run with the stone throwers, gambling on where they might take him. On the night of December 10, 1987, PLO Radio, then based in Baghdad, beamed his crusty voice across the region as he urged on the revolt.[8] Little did Arafat know that other hands also were set on seizing control of the protests.

The previous evening, seven men had met in a ramshackle house in Gaza's Jawrat Al-Shams district—the home of Sheikh Ahmad Yassin. Having been jailed in 1984, the preacher had barely settled into his Israeli prison cell before he was released in a celebrated prisoner exchange in which 1,150 Palestinians were handed over in return for three Israeli soldiers who had been captured by Ahmad Jibril's Popular Front for the Liberation of Palestine—General Command.[9] Yassin's guests included a doctor, a pharmacist, an academic, an engineer, and two teachers. All agreed this was the time to publicly launch the resistance movement envisaged at the secret Amman conference of the Muslim Brotherhood more than four years earlier.

The Islamists' first signed statement urging revolt was not released until December 14, four days after Arafat had hit the airwaves.[10] They chose the name Islamic Resistance Movement, or Harakat Al-Muqawamah Al-Islamiyah—the acronym for which was HAMAS, an Arabic word meaning "zeal" or "enthusiasm." Yassin and the older Brotherhood leaders were tentative, opting for a front organization lest they expose the Muslim Brotherhood or Yassin's carefully nurtured Islamic Center to a full-frontal clash with the Israelis. But looking on from afar in Kuwait, Khalid Mishal concluded that what was to become the Intifada was "the opportune moment to declare a project that was already born."[11]

Shalom Harari assessed the fatal traffic accident at Erez as a lit match igniting prestacked kindling. "The first Intifada was started by the Islamification of the streets," he proffered. "We could see them imposing their ideology and way of life. They took control of the streets—burning liquor shops and killing prostitutes—hundreds of them. Arafat was sending his terror cells to murder senior Islamists; and the Islamists were beating and stabbing Fatah activists."

Israeli neglect of the essentials Palestinians needed in their daily lives had left a vacuum that Yassin's charitable agencies exploited. Using funds marshaled by Khalid Mishal's external organization, the Islamists had stepped up the development of schools and kindergartens, and the provision of food and student loans. As communities were cleansed of drugs, prostitution, and gambling, the mosques controlled by Yassin became places of politics as much as prayer. With the exception of political and religious hoardings, advertising was effectively outlawed.

Harari had reported all of these dramatic changes and the risks he and his colleagues now saw in the Islamists, but the reports were received in silence. "Unless there was blood and crisis, there would not be a political, military or security response . . . and at that stage, the Muslim Brotherhood still wasn't shooting anyone," he said.[12]

Hamas was first mentioned in the foreign media early in 1988 when the Associated Press quoted its signed slogans appearing on the graffiti-daubed walls of Gaza City.[13] By then Arafat was a war-wearied revolutionary with three chaotic decades of struggle under his belt. Hamas published its "nosurrender" charter in August that year, just a few months ahead of what it saw as the Fatah leader's capitulation: his recognition of the state of Israel and his renouncement of violence.

Mishal read it as Arafat having played his last card. Equally, the Fatah leader's declaration of a Palestinian state in just the Occupied Territories, instead of all of historic Palestine, was futile. Quite apart from Arafat's inability to physically walk the soil he declared to be independent, few citizens of his new state could celebrate because they were locked down under an Israeli curfew.[14]

The first time anyone was quoted speaking on the record for Hamas was around the time of the charter, when Sheikh Mohammad Abu Teir, an intense young mullah in Jerusalem, hurled a warning at Israel through the columns of the *Chicago Tribune*, telling its reporter Stephen Franklin, "We won't leave them a single grain of sand."[15] The *Tribune* headline read: FUNDAMEN-TALISTS FIND PALESTINIAN NICHE.

And so it was. Hamas and the PLO made efforts to paper over squabbling that soon became murderous. For some of the time, the pretense worked for much of the English-speaking media. But they were at each others' throats in Arabic-language pamphlet wars in the Occupied Territories and in the columns of the Arabic press across the region. No one was above suspicion. A detailed internal Hamas report on a modern new hospital at Jenin, on the West Bank, took the trouble to analyze the Islamist allegiance of every staff member—either as signed-up members or as sympathizers—who were then ranked as "semi-brother," "good," or "inclined to us" before the report's author concluded that Islamist forces controlled the hospital and the local charity committee through which it was funded.[16]

Despite Arafat's endless efforts to co-opt Hamas, Yassin remained aloof as his followers went on the warpath—against Fatah as much as against the Israelis. An Islamist assessment of conditions in south Gaza in 1992 reported: "Arafat and his demons conspire against us . . . all agree that Fatah needs to be confronted, disciplined and its members tamed in their dens . . . we must be ready and prepared with . . . weapons."[17]

Hamas refused to take part in the joint Intifada leadership set up by all the PLO factions. Arafat always balked at the level of representation demanded by Hamas as the price for joining the PLO, alleging that the upstart Hamas was trying to pull off a reverse takeover of the most powerful body in all of Palestinian history. Coordination between the factions on the ground was limited[18] as Hamas insisted on calling its own Intifada strikes and running its own race.

Meanwhile Yassin's authority was expanding. As the limited civic institutions across the Occupied Territories collapsed, crowds would gather at Yassin's home on a daily basis, seeking his spiritual guidance and mediation in settling disputes. Arafat appealed to the Muslim Brotherhood leadership in Egypt to curb this dangerous new force, but to no avail. The Intifada was a powerful right of passage that made Hamas a dangerously militant challenger to the PLO's long-held claim that it alone embodied the dreams of the Palestinian people.

Various loose elements of the Islamist organization—political, communications, security, youth, and, more recently, the prisoners detained by Israel—were now pulled together under the Hamas banner.[19] Khalid Mishal managed the war chest from Kuwait.

The key means of communication was crude wall slogans: graffiti messages and instructions, painted on by masked youths to sidestep an Israeli restriction on printing. It was dubbed by locals "the Wall Street Journal."

The military wing of Hamas was formalized in 1991 as the Qassam Brigade, named after the Syrian-born resistance pioneer whose 1930s sermons in Haifa had so inspired Mishal's father. After a series of brutal stabbings, known as the War of the Knives, a massive Israeli roundup of almost seventeen hundred Palestinians suspected of links to Hamas drove many followers deep underground. It was from their ranks that the Qassam Brigade's first cells emerged.[20] These first recruits were believers who were seen to have nothing to lose.

Hamas's first weapons were bought or stolen from Israelis, or smuggled in. After several shooting attacks, one of Hamas's early bombing missions appeared to be the use of an explosive device, which killed Marnie Kimelman, a sixteen-year-old Canadian tourist, on a Tel Aviv beach in 1990. Israeli investigators concluded it had been assembled from sulphur, coal, and match tips, which were triggered by the timer from an old washing machine.

The new movement adopted the same tactic that the Irish Republican Army did, denying operational links between its political and military wings. And it was as ruthless as the IRA with anyone who aided its enemies. Yassin issued blunt instructions on the fate of those who collaborated with the Israeli occupiers: "Any Palestinian informer who confesses to cooperating with the Israeli authorities—kill him straightaway," he ordered.[21]

Israel cracked down immediately. The ease with which it detained hundreds of senior Hamas figures was again read by Fatah and other observers as proof of the extent of earlier coordination between the Islamists and the Israeli occupation forces. Four of the seven who had attended the launch meeting at Yassin's home were included in the first one-hundred-plus arrests early in 1988. An observer in Gaza at the time explained, "The key Islamist figures were effectively employees of the administration or its satellites. By organizing, they had identified themselves as a reservoir of people who opposed Fatah or were ready to undermine it. Now they could be rounded up in hundreds."[22]

Countering with stunning organizational and logistical depth, Hamas revealed the benefits of years of advanced planning as it defied every Israeli attempt to decapitate the movement. At times, it had up to four tiers of shadow leaders and, as one tier was scooped up, the next took its place—each as capable but more militant than its predecessor. "We expected they'd try to hurt us with waves of arrests, so we had to have these stand-bys. It was very important for us always to announce a new leader the day after anyone was killed or arrested,"[23] a senior figure from the time later recalled.

Israel provoked international condemnation by going a step further in 1992, rounding up hundreds of mostly Hamas leaders, whom they handcuffed and blindfolded, before dumping them in the winter snow at Marj Al-Zuhur on the Lebanese side of Israel's northern border. The laws of unintended consequences kicked in again. Locked out of Israel and the Occupied Territories by Israeli firepower, the deportees camped on a bare mountainside for the better part of a year, refusing to move from where they could at least see the land they laid claim to. Even America added its voice to a campaign, ultimately successful, in the United Nations and elsewhere, demanding that they be allowed to return to their homes.

Their predicament became a remarkable photo op for television crews introducing Hamas to the world. With members from sixteen to sixty-seven years of age, the group included seventeen university lecturers (many with doctorates), eleven medical doctors (some of whom were senior specialists), fourteen engineers, thirty-six businessmen, and five journalists. In addition, there were more than one hundred university students and two-hundred-plus bearded imams.[24]

Abdel-Salam Majali, a Jordanian official visiting Washington at the time, wondered if Israel was attempting to create its own monster. In a meeting at the White House, Majali challenged then president George H.W. Bush: "If Israel believes that Hamas is a terrorist group and that Lebanon is a haven for terrorism, why have they sent the Hamas men to Lebanon?"[25]

It was a good question. Hezbollah, the Shiite resistance movement, was by then well established in southern Lebanon and had considerable terrorist expertise. A senior Hamas figure in Gaza later confirmed the tuition the deportees received from their Hezbollah confreres—military techniques generally, but in particular, instruction on extracting explosives from old armaments and using readily available chemicals for homemade explosives. "Our guys were like sponges. The deportation was crucial—it gave us a shared experience with Hezbollah."[26] Fifteen years later, Isa Al-Najjar, one of the seven who had met at Yassin's house in Gaza, enthused wide-eyed about another unintended consequence for himself, saying, "It was the first time I saw snow!"[27]

Yassin's run of freedom came to an abrupt halt in 1989. When a new Hamas cell captured and executed two Israeli soldiers, Yassin was identified as the source of instructions and funds for the mission. After a prolonged interrogation, which Yassin alleged included the torture of both himself and his sixteen-year-old son, Abdullah,[28] the preacher was given a double prison sentence—a life term and an extra fifteen years. Given his poor health and his age, Yassin was destined to die behind bars.

President Bush figured that all was quiet when he retired for the evening on August 1, 1990. In the first briefings he had received from the CIA on Saddam Hussein's mobilization of his Republican Guard, the president had been assured that after a brutal, years-long war with Iran, Iraq's forces were too exhausted to venture into Kuwait.[29] Then, at the last minute, the agency flipped, warning that an attack was imminent. Wanting more advice, Bush did his own phone-around of the Middle East, calling the Egyptian president, the Saudi and Jordanian kings, and the emir of Kuwait. All of them told Bush that he could rest easy. They believed Saddam would not dare to invade his tiny southern neighbor.[30]

But he did. In Kuwait City, Mishal's father, Mullah Abd Al-Qadir, awoke to find that his country of exile had been stormed by Iraqi tanks and troops in the hours before dawn as they nailed down the whole emirate in just five hours. Twenty-four years after missing the invasion that had driven his family from the West Bank, Abd Al-Qadir now wandered streets filled with heavily armed Iraqi troops on a looting rampage of Kuwaiti homes, banks, and businesses. On foot, the old man was making his way to the People's Palace to inquire about the safety of his patron, the prince. Oddly, royal guards still manned the palace gates, but they ordered him to return to his residence.[31]

The mullah did as he was told, but back at home he went into deep shock. Sitting for days alone in a corner, he refused to eat, drink, or even speak.[32] But he should not have troubled himself about the well-being of the prince. In the first hours after the Iraqis gate-crashed the emirate, a fleet of limousines had ferried hundreds of Kuwaiti royals to the leafy tranquility of Taif, a luxurious mountain resort deep in Saudi Arabia's far western quarter.

Mullah Abd Al-Qadir had been living here half his life; Fatima and the older children for more than twenty years. Now all were to be thrown back on the road again. For more than three decades the emirate had been the setting for a wonderful marriage of convenience: Kuwait's fabulous oil reserves in an enduring union with the professional and management skills of Palestinians who had become the backbone of the economy. Among them had been the young Yasser Arafat. For decades the Palestinians had wired hundreds of millions of dollars a year back to their immediate families and other relatives still trapped in the Israeli occupation of the West Bank and the Gaza Strip.

But now, Arafat wrecked everything. In what had to rank as his most reckless stunt as the leader of a people fighting the invasion and occupation of their own territory, Arafat stuck his nose into this new crisis on the side of Saddam, an aggressor whose invasion of the emirate also caused fear and loathing in the other Arab capitals on which Arafat's PLO depended for much of its funds. The PLO leader would neither condemn the invasion nor make a clear call for an Iraqi withdrawal.

When the combat ended, and Kuwaiti sovereignty was restored, in February 1991, Arafat's posturing ensured there would no longer be a welcome for Palestinians in Kuwait. Less than 10 percent of the original Palestinian refugee population of four hundred thousand remained or were allowed to return. As a nationality, the Kuwaiti authorities now declared them to be a security risk. Those who remained in the emirate were the victims of vigilante gangs that were assumed to have the backing of the authorities. Dozens of revenge killings were reported; international observers cast doubt on a series of unconvincing show trials of Palestinian "collaborators."[33]

In the absence of Khalid—who happened to be on vacation in Amman, with Amal and their children—the Mishal family's decision making fell to his younger brother, the engineer Maher. Thanks to Arafat's loose lips, Palestinians at least had the cover of being seen by the invading Iraqis as allies. Biding his time as Iraqi occupation forces dug in, Maher quietly organized his brothers and a sister, ordering them to be ready for his signal that it was time to leave.

At dawn on August 16, they assembled a convoy of four cars, in which they packed their children and parents, and cautiously headed out of Kuwait City on the only route open to them—north into Iraq, before turning west at Baghdad for Amman. The roads were filled with convoys of buses, trucks, and cars, loaded with terrified Arab and Asian guest workers who were fleeing Kuwait, Iraq, and the neighboring countries as the threat of war loomed.

As his parents and extended family fled north, Khalid Mishal was traveling in the opposite direction, desperate to head off what could be a fatal blow to Hamas. Three years earlier the movement had been unveiled in the Occupied Territories, but its secret powerhouse had operated from Kuwait for almost eight years. Given Arafat's close relationship with Saddam, Mishal could not risk having the Iraqis discover Hamas's headquarters in the emirate, or the possibility that funds, donor lists, and other secret organizational files might be passed to Arafat as his reward for defending the indefensible in Saddam's invasion.

Leaving Amal and the children in Amman, Mishal first flew to Baghdad and then changed cars three times on the drive south to Kuwait. By further way of cover, he joined a handful of anxious Palestinian businessmen, some of whom he knew, who were returning to the emirate to see what, if anything, was left of their businesses after the early Iraqi looting. They arrived at the Safwan border crossing close to midnight. It was well into the Iraqi-imposed curfew, but they pressed on, hitching a lift and arriving in Kuwait City at 2:30 AM.[34]

Taking charge, Mishal offered the group accommodation for the night, thus ensuring they stayed with him, conveniently maintaining his cover. They decided any attempt to reach his neighborhood—Al-Salimiyah, which was deep in the downtown area—was too risky. Instead, they headed for the home of one of Mishal's aunts. She lived at Al-Farwaniyah, known to locals as the "West Bank" because of its concentration of Palestinians, which was closer to where the road from the north hit the city. The plan was to hunker at his aunt's till the curfew lifted.

They were on the last traffic roundabout—almost there—when their way was blocked by an Iraqi checkpoint. Ordered to pull over and held at gun-point, they were on the verge of being arrested before the edgy patrol accepted their claim to be Palestinians on Jordanian passports, returning to check the safety of their families and the security of their business premises. It was all true, with the exception of the bearded man from Hamas, who would have made a prized prisoner for the Iraqis, had they known who he was.

The next day, against a backdrop of chaos and fear, Mishal could still move with relative freedom during the non-curfew hours. Retrieving his own car from his family home near the seafront, he then met hurriedly with others in the underground leadership of Hamas. There was not a lot to debate—Saddam had just emerged from a brutal eight-year war against the Islamist regime in Iran, and Yasser Arafat was one of his few remaining friends in the world. The new reality, as Mishal described it, was that there was no future for Hamas in Iraqi-occupied Kuwait. Files were sorted quickly. What was not essential for continuing the operation elsewhere was destroyed; what was needed was packed into his car for the desert run back to Amman.

It was easy for Hamas to insinuate itself into the Jordanian capital, a prized location for the movement's forward base outside the Occupied Territories. A dozen or so came in the mass movement of Palestinians from Kuwait. The Hamas cell and returning Islamists may have been abstemious, but generally this wave of newcomers startled the sedate people of Amman with their demand for housing and jobs, at the same time as they imposed what locals described as their "Gulfie" ways—shopping-as-a-sport by day, eating out by night, and promenading.

The first some Ammanis noticed of the Hamas presence in their city was the vibrant tribal beat of music at the movement's anti-American rallies, which drew strong crowds to Amman's ancient Roman amphitheater as a U.S.-led coalition tightened the noose on Saddam Hussein ahead of the liberation of Kuwait in the first weeks of 1991. Ordinarily King Hussein might not have tolerated such behavior, but his people were so pro-Saddam and his economy was so Iraq dependent that this was one of those rare occasions when he concluded that the security of his throne was more important than American patronage.

The city quickly became a Hamas hub. It was already one of a string of capitals around the world that was a sometimes base of operations for the genial Dr. Mousa Abu Marzook, the head of the Hamas political bureau, whose deliberately high-profile role in the organization made him "Mr. Hamas" for many in the region. Now Amman would become a conduit for donations from Muslims in the United States, Europe, and the Gulf. It was the head of a funnel through which armaments were pushed into the Occupied Territories.

Jordan's Palestinian refugee community was the biggest in the world, providing depth and cover for a range of clandestine activities. Communications with the Occupied Territories were excellent, and there was great emotional and psychological comfort in the geographical proximity to Palestine. In time, Amman would become a relay station for orders to unleash devastating suicide bombers against targets in Israel.

Officially, there was a single Hamas office in Amman—Abu Marzook's political bureau. But as others—most of them Jordanian citizens—arrived from Kuwait, several other no-name establishments were opened. Khalid Mishal ran what appeared to be a nondescript commercial office on Garden Street, in the west of the city, and the movement's publishing and other ventures were sheltered under the wing of the Muslim Brotherhood and its various charitable satellites.

But, in a sense, Hamas was always in Jordan—because the Muslim Brotherhood was well established there. At this time, it seemed to make good sense to have Mishal nominally under the supervision of the general secretary of the Jordanian Brotherhood. Essentially, this was a cosmetic move that gave cover for his Hamas activities, as much as it acknowledged the Jordanian Brotherhood's enthusiastic embrace of Mishal's bold plan almost a decade earlier for a dedicated transnational Palestinian project inside the Brotherhood.

But with the sudden influx of these doctrinaire Islamists into the comfort zone of the Jordanian capital, the palace of King Hussein became wary and watchful. In time, it decided it needed to address some of the testiness developing in its relationship with the new arrivals. At one stage Abu Marzook, not a Jordanian, had been denied entry to the country. Nerves also were taut after a cache of weapons, thought to be worth as much as $1.5 million, was uncovered in several secret dump spots in Amman. The Hamas group scattered until the heat died down—Abu Marzook was in Washington at the time and several others joined him there; Mishal opted for London, which became his base for several months.[35]

There were a handful of arrests, all of them people who were from the East Bank, where the monarchy drew its staunchest support. These people were jailed and then pardoned quietly, but the escapade drove the Hussein regime to insist on a formal agreement to cover Hamas's operations in the kingdom. A venue for the meeting at which this would be thrashed out was a matter of some sensitivity, given the strains between Hamas and the PLO, and the tension this provoked in Jordan's Palestinian refugee communities. "We can't have them here [at the palace]. Everyone will know—it has to be discreet," one key palace official said early in a discussion on the rationale behind the proposed meeting with Hamas.

The various Palestinian groups were seen as gypsies in the region, hosted by leaders who would manipulate them to their own ends. Jordan had been badly burned in hosting Arafat and the PLO after the 1967 war with Israel, but, by accommodating Hamas, King Hussein now could deliver a calculated, if belated, insult to Arafat. At the same time, he would be able to use Hamas as a lever in the never-ending diplomacy of the Middle East crisis.

The senior official from the palace who was nominated to meet Hamas told his colleagues, "They need a secure base and for that they will have to pay a price—better here than a lot of other places." The official was a man who enjoyed his scotch, especially a ritual tilting of the glass as he rolled the liquor over the ice for some time before taking the first sip. But, when it came to setting the rules for Hamas, he knew well that his visitors were abstemious by nature and creed. He called on the household staff to brew coffee ahead of the secret meeting.

It was an unusual setting for the conduct of the king's business. The carved ivory and silver trinkets might have adorned the office of a high official, accustomed to foreign travel, and the wrought-iron window grills looking into a leafy garden might have passed for security at the palace. But when it came time to lay down the law to the men from Hamas, they were invited to a private home in a well-protected enclave in the inner city, where senior officials and their families enjoyed around-the-clock protection from a cordon of jeep-mounted machine guns.

A trusted middleman was sent by car to fetch Abu Marzook and Mohammad Nazzal, another of the Hamas team who had come in from Kuwait. Assessing them, the palace official would report later that Nazzal struck him as mediocre—a socially awkward man and seemingly not politically astute. He marked him down as "the messenger." Abu Marzook, by contrast, was a "more distinct political animal"—an Islamist, obviously, but with a sense of pragmatism and an awareness of the world.[36]

They all took their seats in the muted light of the heavily shaded floor lamps. As a flint-eyed young Bedouin woman looked on from the gilt-framed painting above his left shoulder, the official explained the terms on which Hamas's uncertain status in the country was to be legitimized: "It's very simple—you may have an information and PR office here, but you can do nothing to endanger Jordan's prospects with Israel . . . no forays into the West Bank, no claiming responsibility for bombings from Jordanian soil—do that from Syria or Qatar, if you have to. We can't afford it; we won't permit it. If you want to be our enemy, go right ahead!" He did not want an immediate answer; instead, he sent them away to consider his ultimatum. "We're with any voice that continues to underline Palestinian rights," he reminded them. "Go and think about it. Come back with a solid commitment."

It was Nazzal who made contact within days to accept the king's terms. Once Hussein was notified, Hamas signed a document that had been prepared by the General Intelligence Department. Hamas now was "in"— officially.

The aftermath of the Kuwait crisis was grim for both King Hussein and Yasser Arafat, his old nemesis. Each, for his own reasons, had stood with Saddam Hussein on the invasion of Kuwait, and each was being made to pay by his own suite of patrons. In the United States, President Bush accused Hussein of "betrayal,"[37] and aid checks from the Gulf and Saudi Arabia, on which the king relied, ceased to arrive as he grappled with the challenge of three hundred thousand Palestinians who had streamed in from the Gulf looking for homes and jobs.

Arafat was in the same boat. Many of his historic supporters cut the flow of funds, a move from which Hamas benefited greatly.[38] Still obliged to support the Palestinian cause, many wrote checks for Hamas in acknowledgment of two things. One, Hamas was not the PLO; two, it had been smart enough to adopt a nuanced approach to Saddam's incursion into Kuwait. Hamas opposed the U.S.-led armies massing in the Arab homelands but, unlike Arafat, it also opposed the invasion of Kuwait.

Hamas, however, had no time to gloat. Arafat was back on his feet just as soon as a tsunami of hope tore through the Middle East after hostilities were suspended in Kuwait. A decision by the White House to renew the search for a "durable" peace had the most peculiar result of seeming to succeed—initially, at least. Before the year was out, the parties were dragged to a conference table in Madrid, and then to extensive talks in Washington.

They deadlocked, but in the meantime Norwegian diplomats intervened quietly and opened a second, secret channel between Arafat and the Israelis. The outcome of what was to become known as the Oslo Accords was a deal under which Arafat could return to Gaza as the leader of his people. Initially he would control just the Strip; later, a tissue-sized piece of turf around the West Bank city of Jericho, and then other West Bank centers, which were to come under his control by means of a complex process of evolving autonomy.

It was a perverse response to an intractable problem. Arafat would be the "head," but there was no "state." Fundamentals—which ordinarily defined a people and their country—were to be dealt with later, and these included the area's capital and borders. Also postponed was how to deal with the continued existence of Israeli settlements, and the right of refugees or their descendants to live within the nonexistent borders of this new entity. Despite his mere toehold in the Occupied Territories, the deal also placed on Arafat's shoulders responsibility for a task that for decades had defeated the might of the Israeli security forces, even when they had full control of the Occupied Territories: halting terrorism.[39] But Arafat did emerge with a priceless trophy. Even the Israelis, who for much of the previous decade had flirted with the Islamists in the hope of destroying Arafat, now accepted the PLO as the "sole representative" of the Palestinian people.

As the ground shifted, Hamas and its international support network scrambled for a new footing. An early brainstorming session of Hamas activists took place in a most unexpected American setting: Meeting Room B at the Courtyard Marriott, an unprepossessing, clay-colored hotel just a stone's throw from the Philadelphia International Airport in Pennsylvania. Seated around what hotel staff call a "hollow-square" table were some of Hamas's leading fund-raisers. They included senior figures from two Hamas fronts in the United States: the Islamic Association for Palestine and the Holy Land Foundation, which was raising millions of dollars in the United States for the movement.

Planning this think tank, which took place in the first weekend of October 1993, Holy Land Foundation chief executive Shukri Abu Baker fretted about keeping the numbers down, lest they draw attention to themselves. "A large number, my brother, will be suspicious . . . will attract attention," he warned during a long conference call with two associates. They decided on no more than twenty-three delegates, who were to fly or drive from various cities in the United States and Canada. There was some urgency because early bookings could qualify for a 45 percent discount on the Marriott's room rate.[40]

Hamas was to be referred to only in code—the spelling was reversed, giving "Samah." Early in the first session, after a mention of Hamas, Abu Baker was sharp, issuing more specific instructions. "Please don't mention the name Samah in an explicit manner," he chided them. "We agree on saying it as 'Sister Samah.' " And lest any of them disclose they were meeting as Hamas, he added, "The session here is a joint workshop between Holy Land Foundation and the IAP. This is the official form . . . I mean, please, in case some [one] inquire[s]."[41] Minutes hardly elapsed before Abu Baker had to rebuke a loose-lipped colleague who uttered the H-word again, snapping at him: "Didn't we say not to mention that term?"[42]

Inside Meeting Room B, all eyes turned to Brother Abu Osama, who had just returned from a visit to the Occupied Territories, which coincided with blanket media coverage of the Oslo Accords and Yasser Arafat's imminent return to Gaza as head of the Palestinian Authority, the Palestinians' nominal new government. What followed became an hours-long analysis, as deliberate as it was revealing of the mind-set of the Hamas men sitting around the table in Philadelphia. It was Abdel Salem who voiced what was dawning on them: "This is a new thing for all of us."

A man addressed by the conference attendees as "Brother Gawad" framed the new Oslo Accords as a ploy by the Israelis and Arafat working together to wrong-foot Hamas and to strike at Islamist movements elsewhere in the region. Asking rhetorically about likely inordinate power in the hands of Arafat's security forces, he predicted with some accuracy the probable outcome: "We're at an historical crossroads . . . retaliation will be widespread against our individuals, our organizations, our supporters, our mosques, our presentations, our media, our boys, our girls, our women, [and] our relationships with our brothers in other Arab countries."[43]

Police power under Arafat was a recurring theme. Abdel Haleem Al-Ashqar predicted, also with some accuracy, that as many as fifty thousand Fatah loyalists would be enlisted in Arafat's new security force. In that, Brother Gawad saw dark times ahead: "When they have authority—a flag, an army, money, jobs, and IDs—what do you expect will happen? They'll be murderous criminals, my brother."[44]

Brother Gawad spoke at length, before arriving at a sobering thought for a ferocious new resistance movement. Warning that Washington and other capitals might now deem the Occupied Territories to be no longer "occupied," he said, "You'll no longer have the right to resist. [Resistance] will be classified as terrorism. . . . How are you going to perform jihad?"

He warned of inevitable confrontation between Hamas and Arafat's new forces within a year, but the debate then segued to a free-for-all on the notion of "derailing" Oslo. The deal had to be made to collapse. The new Palestinian Authority's failings would have to be exploited; its leaders should be accused of theft of the people's funds; it had to be "stripped of its confidence." Then, lighting on the movement's ability to play to several constituencies at the same time, one of the delegates articulated the propaganda challenge they faced. They had to make Palestinians doubt the honesty and integrity of the Palestinian Authority; they had to play on the anxieties of the wider Arab world about the sovereignty of the Islamic sites in Jerusalem and, in the United States, the accent would have to be on "human rights, justice and stuff."

They could have been forgiven for believing they had enough on their plates as, in the words of one delegate, Hamas "rearranged its papers." But no, there was some irritation about breakfast. Hasan, a quiet young man, had gone out to buy it and now was returning to the Marriott, where their rooms were clustered on the third and fourth floors. On a room-to-room call, Omar Ahmad Yehiya informed the Holy Land Foundation executive director, Haitham Maghawri, that Hasan was bringing doughnuts. Maghawri was unimpressed, complaining: "We were supposed to get hummus and stuff like that to eat for breakfast and lunch. Doughnuts don't fill you."[45]

It has to be assumed that such trifles could preoccupy them only because they were unaware of a far greater crisis. The FBI, in fact, had the place wired. Every word uttered, in conference sessions and in calls from one room to another, had been captured. FBI photographers were in the shrubbery, snapping the attendees as they came and went. And a few days later the FBI was back at the Marriott, photocopying the credit-card stubs and invoices for their $50 discount rooms. The FBI had everything, except the laundry lists.

8

The Bearded Engineer in a New York Cell

When the warning flashed that a suspected terrorist was attempting to enter the country, much would hang on what Nadia El-Ashi had hidden in her underwear as she arrived at John F. Kennedy International Airport. Her husband, Mousa Abu Marzook, possessed a passport that read like an international departures board. He had been in and out of New York so many times in the previous fifteen years, he figured he knew the drill. But for Nadia and their six young children, it was a relief to be arriving home in the United States after a dog-leg flight through London from the Middle East. She and the children had flown from Amman; her husband's journey had originated in Dubai. All in the party were ragged—he was self-medicating his acute diabetes; she needed aspirin. The kids were tired.

Nadia had snagged a green card in the U.S. Immigration and Naturalization Service's 1990 lottery, an official lucky dip by which a fortunate fifty thousand or so applicants were randomly selected each year from the queue waiting for permission to live and work in the country. As a result, Abu Marzook also became eligible for a card and all its benefits—it was pure gold for a stateless Palestinian exile. Presumably, card A41685264 was issued only after Abu Marzook's presence in the United States, as a student and businessman since 1982, had been vetted by the INS. Four of their children were U.S. citizens by birth, and now the parents were back after several years in the Middle East, planning to apply for U.S. citizenship and intending to set up home in Brooklyn.

It was eleven o'clock when British Airways Flight 117 touched down on a morning in July 1995. Terminal 7 was heaving as Abu Marzook led his family through to passport control. From outside the officer's booth, Abu Marzook could not see the computer screen as his Yemeni passport was processed. But the mood changed just as soon as the terror lookout system threw up a match for the Palestinian engineer's name and date of birth. No questions were asked, but the family's passports were snatched and hastily sent elsewhere; they were ordered to wait. Eventually, a customs officer escorted them to a carousel, where they were told to collect their four suitcases. It was then that two men whom they had not previously seen during the several hours of waiting introduced themselves—Special Agents Joseph Hummel and Michael T. Dougherty. The FBI was on the case.

The agents bundled Abu Marzook off to an interview room, where they probed his links to Hamas. At the start of the year, Washington had begun a crackdown on Hamas, declaring it a terrorist movement. President Bill Clinton had issued an executive order to freeze its assets and outlaw all business dealings with and donations to Hamas.[1] Abu Marzook gave away little. He admitted to being a "mid-level political activist" but denied fund-raising, training, or recruiting on the movement's behalf in the United States or abroad. He denied transferring funds to Hamas from the United States, however circuitously. But Abu Marzook did reveal he was on the move as a result of the termination of his residency status in Jordan two months earlier because of his Hamas ties.

This odd initial encounter between the engineer and U.S. authorities lasted almost eleven hours. It is fair to say that if Hummel believed he had a red-hot terrorist on his hands, Abu Marzook, perhaps carelessly, formed the view that he was dealing with a butthead. When it came time to file court documents, Abu Marzook and his New York attorney, the colorful and highly provocative Stanley L. Cohen, would make good use of a sharp tongue in their demolition of Hummel, who, though he did not use the word "expert" in his affidavit, implied as much in setting out his duties with the FBI's antiterrorism unit. But if attorney and client gained satisfaction from preparing to shoot holes in Hummel's account of that day's events, they were seemingly unaware that a juggernaut of chillingly serious terrorism charges, prepared by Israeli lawyers, was heading in their direction.[2]

Khalid Mishal might have believed he owned the Hamas project. But that was not how the peripatetic Mousa Abu Marzook saw it. As a dedicated servant of Sheikh Ahmad Yassin, his patron, Abu Marzook saw himself managing the political bureau in Amman on behalf of the preacher-prisoner. In Hamas's internal faction wars, Mishal was Kuwaiti and an outsider; Abu Marzook was Gazan and an insider—despite the obvious technicality of his living physically outside Gaza. Yassin had seen something special in the young Abu Marzook as he sat in the first group selected by the spotters the preacher had dispatched to trawl the mosque congregations of Gaza for talented youngsters in the aftermath of the 1967 war.

In time, Abu Marzook would become a heroic figure in Hamas. Since the early 1980s, the United States had been his home, but he was forever on the move to and from the Middle East, incongruously managing much of the affairs of Hamas from his various homes in the United States—in Springfield and Falls Church, which, in northern Virginia, were on Washington's doorstep and in the backyard of the CIA, headquartered at nearby Langley. It was only after the 1990–91 Gulf Crisis that the political bureau's operations stabilized in Amman.

Abu Marzook was expelled from Jordan in May 1995 because, notwithstanding the deal struck between King Hussein and the Islamist movement, the regime was under pressure from Israel and the United States to act against Hamas. At first, Hamas took Abu Marzook's expulsion from Jordan in stride. Several of the team were summoned to a meeting at the Foreign Ministry in Amman, during which their limited options were explained in blunt terms. If they made a fuss, they could jeopardize the deal under which the political bureau operated in Jordan.

But, if truth be told, Abu Marzook's colleagues were more accustomed to him working from the transit lounges of the region and the world than they were to seeing him at a desk in Amman. Phones, faxes, and e-mail all worked in the Jordanian capital. They expected Abu Marzook would continue as in the past, and there was no discussion of a need to appoint a replacement head of the political bureau. But, as Abu Marzook explored the possibility of resettling his family in the region—in countries like the United Arab Emirates, Egypt, or Sudan—the regimes were reluctant to take in an official of Hamas. As Abu Marzook's options narrowed, America beckoned.

Whenever he was asked, Samih Batikhi feigned shock at the suggestion that Jordan might have deported Abu Marzook. As King Hussein's intelligence chief from early 1996, Batikhi had a deft knack of making crude maneuvers sound almost ordinary. "Look, he was not one of us," he explained to one foreign diplomat almost apologetically. "But kicked out? Abu Marzook? No. No. No. No!" He paused reflectively as he lit up one of his favorite slim cigarillos, inhaling deeply before going on. "Because he was not a Jordanian citizen, we simply asked him not to return here . . . while he was abroad."

At the General Intelligence Department, or what locals called the

"Mukhabarat," Abu Marzook's expulsion fell into the category of "throwing a bone to barking dogs." During any of the regular meetings between Jordanian and Israeli officials, the Israelis complained bitterly about the Hamas presence in Amman. An Arab intelligence chief who had chanced to see Yasser Arafat would convey the PLO chief's bitter complaints about the Hamas presence in Amman. And when the Americans came to town, they conveyed their own bitter complaints and passed on the bitter complaints of the Israelis and of Arafat. When the "barking" reached a certain crescendo, the dogs had to be thrown a bone.[3]

It would have looked bad to deport some of their own citizens who were tied up with Hamas, so the non-Jordanian Abu Marzook had to go if Jordan was to be seen as a responsible ally. The king's pact with Hamas had been a delicate issue. Now a horrific campaign of suicide bombings orchestrated by Hamas in Israel had focused attention on the leadership group's presence in Amman, which put them on borrowed time. But news of Abu Marzook's expulsion had an inevitable side effect: it prompted discussions between American and Israeli agencies about Abu Marzook's name being added to the INS terror-suspect watch list at all points of entry to the United States.[4]

An intriguing character, with his silver mane and his natty wardrobe, Samih Batikhi was perhaps the second-most powerful element in the whole East-meets-West concoction that was the Jordan cocktail. Presiding over a wonderful deception—in a country that might be described as a desert meeting of Kafka and Orwell—King Hussein needed a local fixer to guard his interests while he was off on his frequent visits to the White House and the receptions in London and other capitals that he so enjoyed. That fixer was Batikhi. If a problem arose while the king was abroad, it was referred to the GID chief.

Batikhi delighted those he met socially, but the files and reports of human rights watchdogs contained disturbing reports on the fate of some who were processed at his headquarters on the western edge of the city. When Dave Manners, the CIA's Amman station chief, spoke of how his wife "adored" Batikhi, it was understood he was referring to the charmer she met at drinks and barbecues in the summer. When Manners described Batikhi as "the world's finest intelligence officer,"[5] his words had more weight, more edge. Clearly, Manners was not referring to the GID chief's resemblance to the actor Stewart Granger.

King Hussein was not in the same gory league as Saddam Hussein or others among the region's despots who ran classic police states. But democracy and human rights advocates invariably complained of a chill as they left Amman, taking away another haul of torture and abuse allegations. There was no meaningful freedom of the press, of assembly, or of association.[6]

Members of King Hussein's parliament were usually briefed on how to vote by the GID, not their party chiefs, and even poets like Sameer Qudah could be hauled in for a ten-day "analysis" of the meaning of their verse before being jailed for a year.[7] The GID's extraordinary brief included vetting applicants for posts in universities, the media, and the diplomatic corps.

The regime's justification for all this, in a country that was more tribal monarchy than constitutional democracy, was that it had to balance human rights with real security anxieties. Monitoring the likes of Hamas required invasive powers. All Jordanians remembered Arafat's tilt at the throne in 1970, and many understood the regime's belief that Jordan was the eye of a regional hurricane: a crazed Saddam Hussein to the east; the explosive violence of Israel and the Occupied Territories to the west; and to the north and south, regimes that ran hot and cold as the mood took them.

Hussein had no intention of allowing an Islamist takeover. But, within the strictures he had laid down, the Muslim Brotherhood was the only political opposition allowed in Jordan. In the early 1990s it controlled close to half of the MPs and even had a few ministers in the government. It adhered to its beliefs but pragmatically accepted King Hussein's framework of faux democracy over confrontation and his right to tweak the electoral and other laws as he saw fit to curb their power and influence. Hussein believed both Saudi Arabia and Egypt had failed in their dealings with the Islamists—Riyadh, because it gave them carte blanche to do as they pleased; Cairo, because of its hard-line club-and-cell tactics.

The Jordanian king insisted there had to be a middle ground. He would jail the troublemakers, but by regional standards his war against the rising Islamic tide would have a singular subtlety, setting it apart from the blindness of the Saudis and the heavy hand of the Egyptians. Hussein was not intimidated by the Muslim Brotherhood, but its leadership needed to function within his terms of reference.

Of course, there was another reason for hosting Hamas. In 1988, Hussein seemingly had abandoned his long-held hope of incorporating the West Bank back into his kingdom. But Jordan's national interests required that he continue to have a seat at the table in the so-called Middle East peace process. For that, he kept fighting and, like a seasoned guerrilla fighter, he won by not losing.

The neighbors were weary of how Hussein lectured both them and the

West on managing the Islamist current. They would remind his envoys that Jordan had harbored Abdullah Azzam, the author of the celebrated fatwa sanctioning the Afghanistan jihad. And languishing in Hussein's cells was another fearsome extremist scholar, Abu Mohammad Al-Maqdisi, who at this time was priming a fanatical disciple and fellow inmate who would not be unleashed on the region until after the U.S.-led invasion of Iraq in 2003: Abu Musab Al-Zarqawi.[8]

In suppressing local voices, the Jordanian regime gave weight to those from outside. One such voice was the Arabic service of Radio Monte Carlo, which, through its affiliation with the wire service Agence France-Presse (AFP), featured reports by the cigarette-smoking workaholic journalist Randa Habib, who had reached the top of her profession since the first fledgling interview in 1972 with the king of Jordan.

On first meeting, Habib came across as a quiet forty-something—almost shy. A graduate in political science and administration, she had an unruly auburn mane that she tried to tame by bunching it at the back of her head. The strength of much of her reporting hinged on a knack she had developed of reading King Hussein's mind by closely analyzing his seemingly innocuous comments and actions as he approached any key decision. When it came to the ease with which she extracted information from those around him, she would give a smile and a roguish explanation: "Ha! You know oriental men! You can always break their silence."

In a region where the new Arabic satellite channel Al-Jazeera was still finding its feet, many stopped in their tracks when they heard Habib's distinctive voice on RMC's medium-wave radio service. So much so that in 1991, when she dined at a restaurant at Mosul, in the far north of Saddam Hussein's Iraq, the waiters brought a young girl from the kitchen to do her party trick, a perfect imitation of Habib's rhythmic radio sign-off: "This is Randa Habib, for Radio Monte Carlo, in Amman."

The power of her radio reports had hit home in 1989, when price increases and corruption allegations sparked wild riots in the city of Ma'an, in Jordan's restive south. Amidst a news blackout and heavy-handed suppression of unrest while the king was abroad, Habib took to the air arguing that the people simply needed to hear from their king—not the truckloads of soldiers then shooting their way into town. Queen Noor offered King Hussein the same advice—privately[9]—but angry court officials accused Habib of inciting the uprising in which a dozen died and dozens more were arrested.

In a way she had. In the aftermath, which included a royal clean-out of the government and the country's first elections for more than two decades, some of the rioters went north to Amman to thank the AFP reporter, one of them telling her, "Your radio reports made us do it!"

Habib's reputation for courageous reporting and being on the spot was not confined to Jordan. Protesting at the jailing of a relative in the mid-1990s, an Iraqi general hijacked a military tank and proceeded to the infamous Abu Ghraib prison. Before attacking, he paused to make a satellite phone call to someone he believed would tell the world what was happening in Saddam's gulag: Randa Habib.

Later, when Saddam's security forces executed the dictator's two sons-in-law in the streets of Baghdad, a reporter in Amman received a dramatic eye-witness phone call as the bullets were flying. That too was Habib. And when Saddam concluded that he would have to sue a foreign reporter to shore up his credibility, it was Habib on whom he had the papers served.

All King Hussein's questioning, snooping, and eavesdropping required a staff of thousands, and nothing was left to chance. Randa Habib assumed it was the GID that regularly rifled through her files. She knew they listened in on phone calls, and she exposed their efforts to enlist members of her bureau staff to report on her latest movements and thinking.[10] Habib presumed that the peculiar disappearances of personal items—a picture from her bookcase, trinkets from her desktop—were deliberate messages to let her know she was being watched. She made it into a sport, leaving copies of sensitive documents where she knew they would be found—just to let the watchers know she knew they were watching.

Habib could afford to mess with them because she had protection. Once, when she went to the limit in a report, some in the intelligence service suggested hauling her before a military tribunal. The prime minister of the day stopped them in their tracks, exclaiming, "Are you crazy? Randa Habib is untouchable!"[11]

Others could not feel so safe. All the implicit menace of the GID machine was revealed to another female reporter whose line of questioning got under the skin of a senior GID man. "A woman is like a pencil," he told her, apropos of nothing. "When you break it, you can never fix it."[12]

Abu Marzook had new clothes—the bright orange overalls of a prisoner of the U.S. authorities. And by the time U.S. Attorney General Janet Reno announced that he had been snatched at JFK, he was in solitary confinement at the Metropolitan Correctional Center in lower Manhattan. The firestorm was immediate.

Threats of retribution by Hamas fed official anxiety in the United States, which sparked increased fears of terrorist attacks and a consequent tightening of security as airports around the country went to "Level 2" alert. Apart from Abu Marzook, the authorities had just arrested a Jordanian in connection with the 1993 bombing of the World Trade Center, and ten men charged with plotting to blow up New York landmarks would soon be sentenced if found guilty in a trial that was nearing its end.

Americans were still reeling from a horrifying act of homegrown terror that in fact had no connection with the Middle East: Timothy McVeigh's April bombing of the Alfred P. Murrah Federal Building in Oklahoma City, in which 168 had died and more than 800 were injured. Further complicating the security matrix, more than 150 world leaders were soon expected in New York for the opening of the UN General Assembly, and Pope John Paul II also was due to visit. Airline passengers were now being more closely quizzed about the contents of their baggage; patrols in terminals and parking lots were being stepped up.

On August 13, 1995, the threat of a car bomb all but froze New York's JFK Airport. Parking lots were barricaded, trash cans were removed from public areas, and unattended cars were towed away. Only passengers with tickets were allowed into the terminals.[13] The *Washington Post* reported the threat of a "suicide massacre" at JFK.[14]

Menacing fliers appeared on the windshields of vehicles used by United Nations aid workers in the Occupied Territories. "Every dirty American" was warned that they could be abducted and killed if Abu Marzook was not released.[15] A statement by Hamas in the Occupied Territories was confrontational: "The U.S. Administration is hereby held fully responsible for whatever harm that may befall Dr. Abu Marzook [if he is extradited to Israel]."[16] Clinton and other key figures received letters of warning. Orrin Hatch, chairman of the Senate Judiciary Committee, was faxed his own personal threat: "[His] continued detention or handing over to Israel will provoke a wave of outrage against the U.S. in various parts of the Arab and Muslim world. Serious repercussions could ensue as a result."[17]

An Israeli diplomat assured reporters the prisoner was a Hamas "head-honcho . . . a big fish."[18] The INS was preparing documents to apprise American courts of an alarming Israeli twist to Hamas's terror strategy. The movement had never acted violently outside Israel and the disputed Occupied Territories, but now the INS relied on briefings by Israeli officials to claim that Abu Marzook, who had the legal right to walk in and out of the country, was likely to engage in terrorist activity in the United States.[19]

Extradition talks were under way between officials in Washington and Jerusalem, but the Americans wanted firm undertakings that the case against Abu Marzook would withstand scrutiny in the U.S. courts. Unwittingly, Abu Marzook would be fighting in two arenas. In the media, he had to challenge the emerging Israeli case against him. But in the courts he wrestled on two more fronts: challenging Washington's right to hand him over to Israel; and at the same time, the decision of the INS to force him to return to Abu Dhabi. INS spokeswoman Carole Florman was quoted in the *Jerusalem Post*: "We believe he's engaged in terrorist activities . . . one of the key leaders of Hamas. We believe he has no right to be in this country."[20]

Despite all the official bravura in talking to reporters, in both countries there were some who were troubled that the case against Abu Marzook was not a slam dunk. In Washington, they doubted that a prosecution could be sustained on the basis of the Palestinian's past activities in the United States, even as a full-blown investigation was launched into the fourteen frenetic years he had spent as a student in Colorado and Louisiana, and as a businessman on Washington's doorstep. Israeli officials, including some of the government's top legal advisers, conceded privately that they might have insufficient evidence to tie Abu Marzook to specific terrorist acts.[21] On top of that, a second cause of anxiety in Jerusalem was the fear of backlash attacks by Hamas if the extradition was to succeed and the spectacle of the trial of Abu Marzook was to unfold in Israel.[22]

Since 1993, FBI eavesdroppers had followed the big hitters from the Hamas conference in Philadelphia. Forty-eight hours after Abu Marzook's arrest, the tapes were rolling in Dallas, Texas, as two of the Philadelphia alumni spoke by phone—Shukri Abu Baker and the Gaza-born chairman of the Holy Land Foundation, Ghassan El-Ashi, who also happened to be related to Abu Marzook by marriage. In this and two subsequent calls, El-Ashi was deeply distressed by the JFK arrest; both were caustic in their response to what they saw as the U.S. authorities succumbing to pressure from the Jewish lobby.

When El-Ashi told Abu Baker that he had managed to speak to Nadia by telephone, El-Ashi seemed to be suggesting that she was not even aware that Abu Marzook had a role in Hamas. He said, "She doesn't know what's going on even. She didn't hear anything. I hinted to her that they're saying they arrested someone with Hamas at the airport and stuff like that."[23] They proceeded to analyze Attorney General Janet Reno's statement on the capture of Abu Marzook, but Abu Baker then interrupted himself mid-sentence, thus revealing to the FBI agents who later read the transcript that he and El-Ashi had become aware of the bureau's eavesdropping: "We speak now and all this is being recorded!"

In the absence of immediate charges against Abu Marzook, they concluded that Reno's team was buying time. The two men ticked off the probability of Abu Marzook being deported, but another forty-eight hours would elapse before they addressed the possibility that he might be extradited to Israel. El-Ashi: "There is some disturbing news that the Israeli government is re-questing . . . not officially, but Rabin has issued a statement saying, 'We're preparing the papers, we want him.'" Abu Baker offered the agitated El-Ashi little comfort and seemed to allude to earlier debate within the movement on the wisdom of Abu Marzook daring to show up in the United States at all. "We told you this would happen," he complained.

U.S. law allowed Israel sixty days to consider its position. There was no need to rush, but, just three days after Abu Marzook's detention, Israel de-cided at the highest level to seek his formal extradition. Rabin, with his for-eign minister Shimon Peres and senior justice and security officials, had rolled the dice.[24]

Extradition cases could take years. The case of Joseph Doherty, an Irish Republican Army fighter, had dragged on for eight years before he was handed over to British authorities to be tried in Belfast for killing a British soldier.[25] In the case of Palestinians sought by Israel in the United States, results were mixed. There had been two cases in the 1980s, one of which had resulted in the defendant being successfully prosecuted and jailed; the other defendant had been freed after appealing the decision of a lower court.

On the eighth day of his detention, Abu Marzook attempted to cut his losses by offering simply to leave the United States and not return, but INS officials told a court hearing convened in his lower Manhattan prison that this offer was meaningless unless Abu Marzook admitted that he was en-gaged in terrorism.[26] Yet, at the same time, U.S. investigators were shifting away from Abu Marzook's role in front-line terrorism to the question of his transferring funds to Hamas because, as an unnamed official explained, "There's never been any indication that this is a hands-on guy on terrorist activity."[27]

It was not clear who derived more pleasure from their attorney-client relationship—Abu Marzook, the forty-five-year-old suspected Palestinian terrorist, or Stanley L. Cohen, his forty-one-year-old Jewish American lawyer who liked to walk on the wild side. Cohen had represented anarchists, communists, and suspected revolutionaries, including one charged with threatening the life of an American president.[28] But in the minds of some in the American press, Abu Marzook was Cohen's most controversial client to date, to which the bearded and ponytailed lawyer responded that his taking the brief merely reflected a Jewish tradition of "standing against the tide."[29] But for that trouble he was excoriated on Web sites supporting Israel and was the recipient of dozens of abusive or menacing calls, which ranged from accusations of Jewish self-hatred to the threat of a bullet in his head. Countering it all, Cohen explained, "I think my client is being made a scapegoat, a pawn in a huge international political game."[30]

On the first day at JFK, the FBI agents Hummel and Dougherty had worked on the premise that Abu Marzook's involvement in Hamas might be grounds to bar his reentry to the United States. Hummel accused Abu Marzook of concealing a leadership role in the political and financial affairs of Hamas and, more important in terms of creating immediate suspicion, of attempting to hide incriminating baggage that he had carried off Flight 117. When asked if the four suitcases on a carousel were "all of your bags," he had responded "yes," the agent swore.

Abu Marzook had in his possession a small pile of common identity cards, which he produced from a folder that he carried in the pocket of his jacket—they were credit, bank, and telephone cards. But, other than the passports now in the hands of the FBI agents, Hummel claimed Abu Marzook denied he carried any other travel papers, money or financial records, birth or marriage certificates. They did not believe him.

"Addresses? Phone numbers for where you say you lived in Amman, Cairo, or Dubai?" Agent Dougherty asked him. No.

"A phone or address book?" Hummel testified that he was told by Abu Marzook several times that he possessed none of these items.

"If you're trying to relocate to the US, you must have numbers to contact friends, business associates, or relatives in the event of an emergency?" No.

Hummel said Abu Marzook claimed he could access that kind of information from his hotel.

"Does your wife have an address book?" No.

Hummel also was dubious about the engineer's claim to earn no more than $35,000 to $40,000 a year, because an investigative report prepared by the U.S. Customs Service referred to millions of dollars passing through Abu Marzook's bank accounts in 1989 and 1990.

At this time Abu Marzook was returned to the waiting area—and it all might have ended there. But when Dougherty went out again to quiz Abu Marzook about $8,000 he had entered in his customs currency declaration, the agent noticed a small suitcase under Abu Marzook's chair—it was between his legs. Under the next chair was an attaché case. Dougherty wanted to know whose they were and, more important, if they had been searched. Abu Marzook told Dougherty they were his. He referred to the contents as "papers" and claimed the bags had already been searched, Hummel testified later. This, the agent said, was not true. The customs inspector who had searched the family's suitcases earlier had not been made aware of these smaller items.

The agents took the bags to an interview room, where they found the attaché case contained blank checks, birth certificates for Abu Marzook and the family, and what they described as "numerous expired travel documents." Also, the small suitcase held records for three bank accounts—one of which was in the United States and the other two offshore. As recently as four months previously, the balance in one of the accounts had stood at $490,000. Abu Marzook might have understood that now he was in a certain amount of trouble, but it would get worse.

Done with the attaché case and the small suitcase, the agents decided all family members would be strip-searched—even the three-year-old daughter. Two female immigration inspectors were summoned to take Abu Marzook's wife, Nadia, to a private room, where she was asked to undress. It was as she removed what Hummel described as her "undergarments" that the address book tumbled to the floor. When the women rushed it to Hummel and Dougherty, the agents were certain they had hit the jackpot—there were hundreds of handwritten entries in Arabic: names, addresses, and phone numbers; associates, friends and relatives; in the United States and abroad. In short, they had the story of Abu Marzook's life.

Nadia and the children were finally allowed to go. The address book was sent for translation and analysis by FBI experts on Hamas and other terrorist groups; meanwhile, Abu Marzook was dispatched to a jail cell.

In reporting the contents of the address book, Hummel focused on just a handful out of the hundreds of entries. These he described as "documented and suspected terrorists." They included Hasan Al-Turabi, the Sudanese extremist who had invited Osama Bin Laden to Sudan; Ahmad Mohammad Yousef, a former Sudanese diplomat who had been implicated in plots to assassinate Egyptian president Hosni Mubarak and to bomb the UN headquarters in New York; and George Habash, whose Popular Front for the

Liberation of Palestine was responsible for the series of 1970 hijackings that ended so horrifyingly in Jordan. Habash was not to be confused with Ahmad Jibril, leader of the Popular Front for the Liberation of Palestine—General Command, a PFLP splinter group that continued to mount its own separate guerrilla operations against Israel. Intriguingly, Hummel said that the FBI's "expert" analysis also had uncovered a "coded" reference to Yasser Arafat.

Now, under the glare of both an army of investigators and the news media, Abu Marzook was found to have left surprisingly few crumbs in his years as a renter on South Sixth Street in leafy Falls Church. This was part of greater Washington but in Virginia, just over the state line. Abu Marzook had not obtained a driver's licence; he paid no property tax; and neighbors had little to reveal, except occasional sightings of Abu Marzook mowing the grass.[31] He handed out a business card in the name of Mostan International, Inc., but it did not disclose the nature of the company's business. Mostan was not in the local phone directory, nor was it registered locally.

Abu Marzook had completed a master's degree in construction management and industrial development at Colorado State University in 1984. He then moved to Ruston, Louisiana, to embark on doctoral studies in industrial engineering at Columbia State University. There, what was remembered as a stop-go approach to his studies did not match the terrorism "head-honcho" image of his current predicament. One of his former lecturers told the *Washington Post*, "He didn't show [that kind of] leadership here . . . not a bright student."[32]

Now, having taken the Israeli intelligence offerings, federal investigators were proceeding on the basis that it was from the tranquility of Falls Church that Abu Marzook had masterminded Hamas's operations in the Occupied Territories. Through his lawyer, Abu Marzook finally acknowledged he had raised big amounts of money, but these had been for orphanages, schools, and other welfare programs in the Occupied Territories, he said—this despite Hummel's claim that Abu Marzook had earlier made a blanket denial of such activity. Together, lawyer and client now worked to produce a twenty-page, line-by-line rebuttal of Hummel's account of the events of July 25—the day the engineer and his family touched down at JFK.

Abu Marzook claimed that both he and Nadia El-Ashi had been in and out of their separate carry-on items many times under the eyes of various U.S. immigration and customs officials. He had produced their passports from one of these bags; at another stage, he had retrieved his medication from them. There had been no effort on his part to hide them.

The issue of the four suitcases being "all" of their baggage was an innocent misunderstanding, he argued. On being taken by an officer to a carousel and instructed to identify his bags, Abu Marzook now swore that he had answered truthfully when he said "yes" after being asked by the officer if the four suitcases were "all" his bags. He said he believed he had been asked whether those four bags were the only bags of his that were *on the carousel*.

Abu Marzook noted that Hummel contradicted himself on the currency issue. He had accused Abu Marzook of denying possession of hard currency, yet the agent's own affidavit confirmed that Abu Marzook had entered $8,000 on his customs declaration, an amount he was not required to declare and which he had voluntarily shown to a customs agent by opening one of the bags he was accused of attempting to conceal. Abu Marzook also suggested that the eye-catching entry in one of the three bank accounts—the 490,000 units of a particular currency, which had so excited Hummel—was for units of the less valuable UAE dirham, which would convert to a significantly lesser amount of $120,000.

The issue of the address book was a family mix-up compounded by Hummel's ignorance of Arab culture and custom, Abu Marzook swore. Ordinarily he traveled with a copy of his address book, while leaving the original at his home in Amman. In this case, he had inadvertently left the copy in Dubai when he flew to London. Unbeknownst to him, his wife had come upon the original in Amman and had popped it into one of her bags. During the transit stop in London, she had used the book to make a phone call to Amman, and then had tucked the book under her bra strap, he said, because the traditional garment she wore on that day, a *jelbab*, had no pockets. Contrary to Hummel's claim that the book had "fallen to the floor" as she was undressing, he insisted that Nadia El-Ashi had handed it to the women charged with searching her because "she had nowhere to put it."[33]

But there was no way around the record of some of the names and numbers of radicals or extremists in the book. Abu Marzook attempted to turn this fact to his advantage, arguing, "With the few 'provocative' entries, [Hummel] once again seeks to substitute fiction for fact; high drama for truth . . . to cast me in the worst light."[34] Hummel certainly was reluctant to cut any slack for Abu Marzook. The two-year veteran of the FBI's antiterrorism squad might have been expected to know that, as often as not, Yasser Arafat was alternately addressed, or referred to, as Abu Ammar—formally and informally, to his face and behind his back, in newspapers and on TV. To present the entry as a "coded reference" said more about Hummel's professional shortcomings, and those of the FBI terrorism experts who had analyzed the book, than it did about the company kept by Abu Marzook.

Notwithstanding Arafat's volatile history, to include the PLO leader on a "documented and suspected terrorist" list seemed to miss the point that, just weeks before Hummel had signed his affidavit, Arafat had been a welcome guest at the White House, where he and Israel's Yitzhak Rabin had signed what President Bill Clinton had described as "a courageous and historic peace accord." Arafat and Rabin had then participated in one of history's most-photographed handshakes.

It was a point that Abu Marzook and his lawyer attempted to leverage. Accusing Hummel of resorting to "sophomoric rhetoric ... to criminalize me," Abu Marzook argued that the FBI agent was attempting to mislead the court with a small, selective cull of titillating names from his address book. "[Hummel] conveniently fails to note that included among these [hundreds] of names and phone numbers are those of numerous heads of state and high-ranking government and law enforcement officials from throughout the Middle East." He listed some that had been ignored by Hummel: the head and various members of the Jordanian parliament; Jordan's ministers for higher education and information; the President of the Jordanian Reporters' Union; the speaker of the Palestinian parliament; the prime minister of Tunis; Syria's information minister; members of the Yemeni parliament; the heads of state security agencies in Kuwait, Jordan, and Egypt; and on and on and on.

On the question of the millions of dollars going through his bank accounts some years earlier, Abu Marzook insisted that these funds had come *into* the United States, as was known by the Internal Revenue Service and other U.S. agencies that oversaw the activities of the American-based Mecca Investments, for which Abu Marzook solicited funds from the Middle East.

Abu Marzook and Cohen continued the fight by attempting to ridicule Hummel's expertise, denouncing the FBI agent as "the expert on Palestinian affairs, [who] again proves himself hopelessly lost with no true understanding of the problems, politics, and dynamics of the Middle East."[35] But in his more introspective moments, as he sat alone in his Manhattan cell with a tearful Japanese prisoner next door,[36] Abu Marzook can only have wondered at the wisdom of his risky gamble in coming to the United States at this time. After his eviction from Jordan, it was very likely that even if the Americans did not think to put his name on their terrorist watch list, then the Israelis were sure to press them to do so.

Two weeks after his arrest, Abu Marzook was hauled before an extradition hearing in the Federal Court in Manhattan, during which prosecutors accused him of raising hundreds of thousands of dollars for Hamas and of authorizing the purchase of weapons for "holy war." Acting on evidence provided by Israeli authorities, they also charged that Abu Marzook had overseen the recruiting and training of would-be terrorists in the United States. Days later, Israel formally requested that any move by the United States to simply return Abu Marzook to the country from which he had commenced his journey, the UAE, be put on hold pending the arrival in New York of its detailed request for extradition, which would allege that Mousa Abu Marzook was complicit in murders, grievous bodily harm, and injury with malicious intent.[37]

The formal Israeli document, signed by Irit Kohn, of the Justice Ministry's International Affairs Department, constituted a chilling litany of violent upheaval in more than 200 civilian lives—46 had ended in death; more than 140 others had been torn apart by injury. Abu Marzook must face trial in Israel, Kohn said, for "murder, attempted murder, manslaughter, harm with aggravating intent, harm and wounding under aggravating circumstances and conspiracy to commit a felony in connection with his criminal responsibility," arising from ten Hamas attacks over four years.[38] Set out in detail, the attacks escalated in force and sophistication from the beach bomb that killed the sixteen-year-old Canadian tourist at Tel Aviv in 1990 to the death of twenty-two people in a suicide-bomb attack on a commuter bus in Tel Aviv four years later.

More than one thousand pages of accompanying affidavits by Israeli investigators, together with records of the interrogation of Hamas operatives captured by Israeli forces, presented a macabre account of the inner workings of Hamas's increasingly violent campaign against the Israeli occupation of Gaza and the West Bank. Kohn's twenty-two-page opening statement demanded that, as a Hamas leader, Abu Marzook be held criminally liable because he had "aided and abetted, counselled, solicited and procured others—members of Hamas—to commit these criminal offences."[39]

Abu Marzook remained legally feisty, but by mid-November he was in poor health. He complained of dizzy spells and at times his hands shook uncontrollably. The American prison diet did not agree with him and his weight loss worried his doctor,[40] who complained that Abu Marzook was allowed only a "brief" daily predawn exercise session on the roof of a forbidding prison building[41] sandwiched between the headquarters of the NYPD, the federal judicial complex, and the towering Municipal Building in lower Manhattan.

Despite all the dire threats by Hamas, the judges of the U.S. District Court held their nerve. On May 7, 1996, Judge Kevin Duffy approved the Israeli application to extradite Abu Marzook. In his thirty-three-page decision, Duffy wrote that "probable cause exists that Abu Marzook knew of Hamas's plan to carry out violent, murderous attacks, that he selected the leadership and supplied the money to enable the attacks to take place."[42] Along the way the judge challenged Stanley J. Cohen's expectation that the case still had years to run, putting a flea in the attorney's ear: "Mr. Cohen expects to delay the proceedings by his refusal to comply with any schedule set by this court. The delays end now."[43]

On appeal several months later, Judge Kimba M. Wood backed the soundness of Duffy's decision, without reservation. Abu Marzook, it seemed, had nowhere to go—except to the dock of an Israeli court.

9

Violence Is the Only Weapon

As a Palestinian and longtime resident of Bridgeview, on the South Side of Chicago, Mohammad Salah traveled frequently to his homeland, using his American passport.

But in 1993, Salah was picked up by Israeli authorities as he wandered the West Bank with almost $100,000 in cash in a bag. A trophy captive, he was delivered immediately to interrogators at Israel's domestic intelligence agency, the Shin Bet. In the "interviews" that followed, it emerged that Salah had completed a successful bagman run from the United States to the Occupied Territories in August 1992, during which he had distributed more than $100,000. Five months later, the used-car salesman born in Jerusalem was back, planning to dole out more than $600,000 for Hamas in Ramallah, Nablus, and Hebron—at least half of which appeared to be earmarked for military operations. He was drawing funds from an amount of $300,000 that had been deposited in his account at the LaSalle Talman Bank in Chicago, Illinois, and he was anticipating a further deposit of about $350,000. But his arrest abruptly stopped everything, after just three disbursements that totaled $140,000.[1]

Salah later claimed that everything in almost five hundred pages of the transcript of his interrogation was untrue, because it had been extracted under physical and mental torture.[2] In keeping with a human rights watchdog's description of the Shin Bet system of torture, ill-treatment, and humiliation of its detainees,[3] Mohammad Salah swore he was kept naked for long periods and threatened with being photographed in that state unless he cooperated. He was made to sit on, and then was tied to a child's chair—eight inches high—for long periods. His captors struck him repeatedly and subjected him to music played at "deafening" levels. At times, he claimed, they pulled a sack over his head and deprived him of sleep for up to forty-eight hours at a time. He was warned that Israeli and FBI agents would inflict violence on his family back in the United States if he did not incriminate Hamas's clandestine hierarchy.

Salah's account under interrogation would subsequently be used by Israel in an effort to persuade an American court that Mousa Abu Marzook should be extradited to Israel to face terror-related charges. In eventually approving the extradition in 1996, Judge Kevin Thomas Duffy of the New York District Court was unmoved by Salah's torture claim. Much of Salah's interrogation had been translated from an interview conducted in Arabic to a written record in Hebrew, and then translated again into English. But Judge Duffy argued that a long and crucial part of Salah's confession to the Israelis, which happened to be in his own hand and in the Arabic language, had "certain hallmarks of reliability which cannot be ignored."[4]

The handwritten document had been extracted from Salah in a complex investigative double cross, by which Salah was tricked into believing that fellow captives in his cell block were also arrested Hamas operatives. In fact, they were prisoners already collaborating with Israel. "Nadav"—a pseudonym for the head of the Shin Bet investigations unit at Ramallah, whose identity was suppressed for security reasons when Israeli authorities included his account of Salah's activities among the pile of documents in its case against Abu Marzook—admitted to setting up the sting. Salah was made to believe that he was confiding in other Hamas members incarcerated in the same jail. "To do this, we directed other prisoners who were cooperating with [us] to pose as Hamas activists," Nadav began. "They persuaded [Salah] to confide in them regarding the true scope of his activities. At their request, he provided a lengthy, narrative description."

In admitting later that he had been fooled, Salah recounted how he had been placed in a cell with Palestinian prisoners who presented themselves as genuine Hamas prisoners, in whom he could trust. Salah said they threatened him on the grounds that *he* was suspected of collaboration. Outlining the sting, he explained, "[They] said unless I proved to them that I was not a collaborator, I and my family would suffer violence." The test they set for Salah to prove his bona fides was that he had to reveal what he knew of the Hamas leadership and membership: "They intimidated me, and produced paper and pen for me to use, all the while screaming their threats,"[5] Salah wrote in a subsequent affidavit, which Abu Marzook produced at his U.S. court hearings in a failed bid to undermine the Israeli case against him.

Quite apart from lifting a veil on the tactics used by Israel's investigators, Mohammad Salah's revelations sparked a chain reaction of Israeli arrests and interrogations, all of which merged to offer a rare insight into Hamas operations in the Occupied Territories.

The Israelis could now go after the local men to whom Salah had handed money, and then the next leadership layer down—men like Musa Dudin, a student at Hebron University who used $45,000 of Salah's funds to buy a small cache of weapons: two Uzis, a carbine, a Kalashnikov, and a short-barreled M16, which he hid in a water culvert before distributing them.

When the Israelis captured Musa Dudin, he in turn coughed up the names of a group of his associates, who had been tooling around the West Bank in a Volkswagen sedan, their weapons hidden under the seats. And then he gave the names of another group, with whom he had attacked an Israeli patrol before he lost his nerve and was ordered to pass the weapons to a masked man driving a Peugeot 305. This was the kind of needlepoint detail that the obsessively secretive Hamas was loath to see revealed, and it was the sort of raw information that Israeli authorities were loath to disclose they had obtained.

Salah's confession on its own would always have been legally questionable, given what a senior Clinton administration official later described as his "Star Chamber" treatment at the hands of his interrogators.[6] However, the Israelis—having taken possession of Salah's address book, containing the names and numbers of his local and U.S. contacts—quickly cracked the code that Salah believed protected his database from exposure. Much of the detail, in what became sixty-three pages of a typewritten account of Salah's adventure in the Occupied Territories, dovetailed with accounts of Hamas's funding and logistics that the Israelis subsequently extracted from other Hamas figures whose covers were blown by Salah. The FBI also obtained bank documents in the United States that matched Salah's version of how the funds were moved into his bank account and their subsequent transfer to Israel. In turn, the Israelis produced bank documents that revealed how the money was processed on the ground in the Middle East.[7] The jigsaw was all but complete.

In his confession, Salah placed Abu Marzook at the center of Hamas operations in the United States and in the Occupied Territories, organizing the money and directing military operations. It was Abu Marzook who had recruited him, early in the Intifada, to what he described as a paramilitary organization. Abu Marzook also had attempted to make Salah a full-time military commander in the Occupied Territories—an offer he had declined, Salah insisted, because he was in the middle of building a house in Chicago and Hamas did not pay well enough to cover his commitments.

But, as a freelancer, his first task had been a stalled effort to recruit trainees from the ranks of the diaspora community in the United States to fight in the Occupied Territories. He started with twenty-seven candidates, who were tested in their claimed fields of expertise, such as remote-control aviation, agricultural pesticides, and the use of basic chemicals to prepare bombs and explosives. "The result was very little success," Salah complained. "The required know-how . . . was not shown."

Salah was aided in this endeavor by "Brother Yousef" from Jordan and two others with combat experience, who had come to the United States from Lebanon. But, with the exception of three of the trainees, the program was abandoned because of surveillance of the Muslim community by U.S. authorities in the aftermath of the Iraqi invasion of Kuwait. These three new recruits continued to be trained in the use of detonators by a Palestinian who had fought as a mujahid in Afghanistan, but this program was terminated when Salah was arrested by the Israelis.

Oblivious to the prison double cross his Israeli interrogators had set up, Salah took his cellmates through a plot to murder the prominent Palestinian intellectual Sari Nusseibeh because of his role in U.S.-backed peace talks between Israel and the PLO. He said Abu Marzook had been initially in favor, but then the assassination plan was abandoned. Salah walked his fellow prisoners through his efforts to reinforce the layers of local Hamas leadership after another wave of Israeli arrests. And then there were what Hamas operatives might have described as the "usual frustrations": how to respond to provocation by Fatah; how to get local branches and cells to report their activities; and how to rein in local leaders who decided, on their own, to direct funds earmarked for military purposes to other projects.

One of the Hamas operatives named by Salah was Abu Saab, who headed the Hamas militia in Gaza. Salah said Abu Saab had pleaded with him for additional funds to meet a steep rise in the black-market price for firearms.

In Ramallah, an operative identified as Abu Khalid had sought Salah's advice on the wisdom of his plot to execute three Israeli road engineers. He was anxious about the impact the killings might have on Israel's willingness to allow the 1992 deportees to return from southern Lebanon. But, not mincing his words, Salah told the Ramallah man, "Kill them and take their weapons." He also was attempting to investigate the "fantastic" expenses of the Nablus branch—which had run up debts of $290,000—and how best to manage Gaza's explosive debts, which exceeded $1 million.

It was difficult to see how he—and the whole movement for that matter—could function under such relentless pressure. For example, covert shelter and weapons were needed by Hamas for fighters in Gaza, and a military trainer had to be spirited in from Lebanon. A local supplier of medical equipment might have had a Swiss bank account, but he demanded a 2 percent commission to launder funds through the account for Hamas.

Now stuck in prison, Salah's humiliation was complete when he was forced to list the errors of his mission. These included that he had returned to the West Bank at the wrong time; it had been a mistake for him to carry an address book; he had "forgotten" that Hamas was outlawed in Israel and it was an offense to contact members; if he had had to carry information, it should have been concealed in a capsule; and he had organized too many meetings with locals at a time when Palestinian Americans visiting Israel and the Occupied Territories were kept under close surveillance by the Israelis.

In the first weeks of his ordeal, Salah took comfort in holding tight to a nugget of information he had committed to memory before arriving in Palestine. It was the detail of a sketch map acquired by Mousa Abu Marzook during one of his visits to the Hamas deportees in southern Lebanon. It purportedly marked a secret grave in which Hamas killers had placed the body of Ilan Sa'adon, an Israeli sergeant they had kidnapped back in 1989. Before being arrested, Salah had failed in his own efforts to locate the grave, which was supposed to be near Yavneh, on the old coast road to Gaza.

Now he offered the Israelis a deal—in return for his help in retrieving Sa'adon's body, he wanted the release of three hundred Hamas prisoners, including those whose capture he had provoked, and the return of Hamas's $100,000, which had been confiscated from him. Salah committed what he could recall of the map to paper, including its key features: a big tree and a well in the area of Yavneh. He accompanied Israeli search parties on a futile twelve-day search, which included digging to a depth of more than six feet near several wells, but they could not find the body.

An eternal optimist, Salah then placed his faith in an expectation that his U.S. passport literally was a "get out of jail" card. He fully anticipated the arrival of an American diplomat to rescue him. Instead, the gates of an Israeli prison closed on him after he was sentenced to five years in jail by an Israeli military tribunal.

Back home in Chicago, significantly more than the $350,000 anticipated by Salah had been deposited in the LaSalle Talman bank account that he held jointly with his wife, Azita. Individuals described by the FBI as close associates of Mousa Abu Marzook had already lodged almost $1 million in the account. In the last week of December 1992, $300,000 had been wired from a Virginia bank account held jointly by Marzook and an associate. The rest of this rush of funds came from sources in Geneva and Dubai. But a single deposit of $99,985 puzzled federal agents. It had been wired in the name of Gazi Abu Samah. As a name, Samah was common enough, but it also was Hamas spelled backward—the coded reference by which some within Hamas referred to the movement.

Just four days after Salah's arrest in Israel there was an unseemly rush to get at the funds in his account.

A person described by the FBI as an unidentified individual attempted to cash a $299,950 check, which supposedly had been signed by the imprisoned Salah. It was payable to Nasser Al-Khatib, who worked in the United States as a private secretary to Mousa Abu Marzook. The bank refused to clear the check and later the FBI concluded that the handwriting was not Salah's.

Three days after that attempted check fraud, it was Salah's wife, Azita, who lunged.

She withdrew an amount just shy of $750,000, depositing it in a new account at the Standard Bank and Trust. Two months later, she drew $97,067.93 to pay down the mortgage on their home, which was in Salah's name, even though she well knew that the funds had been deposited for distribution to foreign charities. "Azita Salah stated she decided to keep the money herself after her husband was arrested in Israel," Special Agent Robert Wright swore in an affidavit. "[She said she] transferred the money into a new account because she feared the U.S. government might attempt to take it."[8]

In the Occupied Territories, others on a list of forty names culled from Salah's address book were being dragged in by the Israelis. One was Bassam Musa, a spiritual teacher and low-ranking Hamas activist from Khan Yunis, in the south of the Gaza Strip. His interrogation produced an astonishing account of Hamas's on-the-ground efforts to survive a determined Israeli campaign against the organization.

In 1991, Bassam Musa had agreed to become a stand-by leader, in case there was another mass roundup of the senior Hamas figures by Israel. His time came as hundreds of Islamists were jailed in early 1992. The man who had recruited Musa into Hamas fled to Sudan ahead of the roundup, but not before introducing the teacher to one of the senior leaders of Hamas in Gaza, Ghanem Hashash. Musa was told that if Hashash disappeared, he would be required to step into the leader's shoes. When he did, his first task was to establish contact with other leaders who had survived the roundup or the other shadows, who, like himself, were novices taking the place of the prisoners. These links were fixed through what were called "dead-letter boxes," or DLBs, up and down the Strip, in which handwritten notes were secreted, to be collected by trusted couriers for delivery to the right operative. It was primitive, but it worked.

Musa adopted the Intifada best practices, in which he had been instructed. When he set up face-to-face meetings between mid-level leaders, they were required to verify one another's identity through coded exchanges, sometimes as they took their place at the Sheikh Shaaban Mosque or by being seen to read a particular *sura*, or chapter of the Qur'an at other designated mosques in Gaza. Cells were kept small and unaware of one another, and individual code names were adopted. Bassam Musa's was Abu Mujahed.

When news or instructional leaflets were faxed in from abroad, he would have them photocopied, five or six at a time, and distributed to people who in turn would make another five or six copies, and so on "until every man in the street receives one," Bassam Musa explained to his interrogators. He retained the services of a personal courier, "who can keep his mouth shut," and he regularly switched the all-important DLBs, through which he passed money or instructions to his comrades. At one stage, while he was using an empty Coca-Cola can, at a point about three-quarters of a mile south of the gas station on the road between Rafah and Khan Yunis, someone else was using a 7Up can on a different stretch of road. At another time, Musa used a hole in the partition between the third and fourth stalls in the men's restroom at the Al-Rahma Mosque.

The various departments of Hamas communicated internally and with one another through DLBs, with the exception of the military wing, the Qassam Brigade, which ran its own show. Bassam Musa dealt with the militia chief Abu Saab through a DLB in the cistern in the third cubicle in the public bathrooms of the Islamic University Mosque.

Some of the money from abroad came in $50,000 parcels from bank accounts in Switzerland and Egypt, which Bassam Musa distributed for military, *dawa* or preaching, and community and welfare operations.

Musa also revealed another conduit for funds from the outside: a local academic, Dr. Fares Muammar, who from time to time would send a fax to say that money had arrived in Gaza. Over about a year, almost half a million dollars came via the doctor, which was over and above a separate amount of $370,000 for community projects and an additional $400,000 for the Qassam Brigade.

Asked by his Israeli interrogators about his repeated references to "Hamas abroad," Musa explained he was referring to "the head of Hamas," Abu Marzook, who, he said, generally operated from Jordan. "I receive many faxes . . . from him," he said.

After his arrest, which took place just days after the detention in Ramallah of Mohammad Salah, Musa tried, but failed, to relay a coded message through his lawyer for his cousin Fathi Subhi to "burn the things."[9] Musa told his interrogator, "He would understand that I was referring to the archive, but I don't understand why he didn't burn it."

Shubi's failure to act was seized on by the Israelis in the struggle to suppress Hamas. "Abu Hamed," another Shin Bet intelligence officer who operated under a pseudonym for security reasons, filed a report on the detention of two Hamas fighters near Khan Yunis, just days after the detention of the teacher Bassam Musa. Abu Hamed explained that one of the fighters "advised" that a trove of Hamas documents was hidden in a barrel buried at a nearby house. "I observed that after exposing the barrel, [the fighter] opened it and extracted a number of plastic bags which he identified as the Hamas archives."[10]

Among the hundreds of documents was a letter that undercut any of the bravura displayed by Hamas captives to their Israeli interrogators, such as that by Salah Arouri, another who had been rounded up as a result of Salah's bungles. Arouri told his interrogator how he spirited two men wanted by the Israelis from the West Bank to Gaza, by piling three thousand dollars' worth of toilet tissue around them as they crouched on the tray of a truck going to Gaza.[11] But the letter recovered from the Hamas archives was a desperate plea for help from an organization reeling amidst disruptive waves of Israeli arrest. Its author was Bassam Musa.

Written in October 1992, his seven-page letter was addressed to Abu Marzook. In it, Musa complained that no funds had been received for Hamas's vast program, and just $100,000 had come through for the military, which he referred to in code as "the positive apparatus." Things were so bad that Hamas members were selling their wives' gold in order to continue operations, he said. Some local branches were so angered that they were threatening to go their own way. There was great embarrassment in the Qassam Brigade because a dealer was offering thousands of weapons, and without funds they could not stand in the market. Musa told Abu Marzook, "We are in dire need of every cent we are supposed to get in order to support our [militia] and our *dawa*."

Despite the intense Israeli pressure, Hamas was also fighting hard on another front at this time. Both the Islamists and Arafat's Fatah organization were locked in near-mortal combat for control of a range of vital groups and organizations whose elected councils provided powerful community and political bases. The contest had reached fever pitch in 1992.[12] Backed by other secular-minded PLO factions, Fatah won control of the engineers', doctors', and lawyers' associations in Gaza, but Hamas swept the chamber of commerce. On the West Bank, the Islamists seized control of the business and student bodies at Hebron, but not the Red Crescent Association. Palestinians were stunned when the fight moved to Ramallah and it was Hamas that stole power in the chamber of commerce, long assumed to be a citadel of secular or Christian nationalism.

Both sides slugged it out in each lecture room, on every campus, right down to the last pieces of business in every chamber of commerce. Hamas packed such a punch in these power struggles that a secular PLO delegation, engaged in peace talks with the Israelis in 1992, had requested that an Israeli proposal for municipal elections in the Occupied Territories be deferred.[13] The Islamist brew was becoming more potent. At a time of violent clashes between the two organizations over Arafat's commitment to a negotiated peace settlement,[14] there was a growing sense that Palestinians needed to become more self-reliant. Hamas's Islamist credentials were a powerful elixir that fused patriotism and nationalism, together with religiously pure hearts and minds, into what, for many, was the seductive essence of jihad.

The diplomatic breakthrough in Oslo had rekindled long-dormant international interest in, and hopes for, a negotiated settlement to the Middle East crisis. A by-product was that more diplomats and intelligence experts came through the region, and they all stopped in Jordan. But any who attempted to intercede on Arafat's behalf when they got to see Samih Batikhi at the General Intelligence Department in Amman got short shrift. "Arafat's paranoid" became his two-word distillation of Jordan's deep and decades-old distrust of the PLO leader.[15]

But paranoid or not, Arafat now had a Nobel Peace Prize on his mantelpiece—premature as it might have been. For the seeming triumph of Oslo he had shared the award with two others. First, with Yitzhak Rabin, who, as Israeli Defense Minister in the early 1980s, had encouraged the

Islamists as a foil for Fatah, but now had become the Israeli prime minister who would recognize Arafat and the PLO. The third recipient was Shimon Peres, his foreign minister, who, as prime minister in the mid-1980s, had agreed to Rabin's demand that he stay out of defense matters as Rabin egged on the Islamists. Convincing a Norwegian judging panel was one thing; the challenge Arafat now faced was to convince his own people that Oslo was such an award-winning effort.

Hamas, his arch-opponents, had come to stand for all that Arafat had abandoned as he came in from the diplomatic cold. Principally, Hamas reserved the right to use violence and terror as legitimate weapons of struggle, and it laid claim to *all* of historic Palestine as a homeland for their people. It viewed renouncing violence and compromising on territorial claims as, in a sense, the "last cards," which could be played only when the Palestinians knew precisely what they would get in return. Key figures in Hamas proved adept at tap-dancing, accusing Arafat of treachery at the same time as they made oblique offers of long-term truces and the like. But they always ensured that they could not be seen to make Arafat-like policy retreats, and the Israelis would buy none of it.

At a time when Arafat was adrift on perilous seas, Oslo was a life raft. He needed the deal to secure the huge international development funds that might help stop a rising Islamist tide that was corroding his power base across the Occupied Territories. One of the PLO's last cash injections before the Kuwait debacle had been $50 million from Saddam Hussein. Arafat knew he was gambling when he authorized the talks in the Norwegian woods, but he also knew he was broke. PLO staff were being let go by the thousand, and Arafat's guerrillas, who had been scattered since their eviction from Beirut in 1982, had not been paid for seven months. Welfare payments to refugee camps across the region had stalled, and PLO departments, including the all-important information unit, were shuttered.[16]

There was edginess but an unmistakable air of triumph when Arafat and his entourage settled in Gaza to establish the Palestinian Authority in mid-1994, as agreed with the Israelis in the Oslo negotiations. But instead of all the economic excitement of a Dubai-on-the-Mediterranean, or the democracy showcase they were promised, Gazans had quickly discovered that things would change little. Giving life to the fears expressed at the Hamas workshop at the Courtyard Marriott in Philadelphia the previous year, the new Palestinian security forces were stacked with thousands of Fatah loyalists from abroad. Arafat cronies returning from exile won the lion's share of jobs and contracts, allowing them to fritter vast quantities of foreign aid on their own lavish villas and on foreign education for their children. They involved themselves in dubious business deals with various Israeli businessmen who had made an art form of milking the occupation.

Arafat had come home a stranger. But he was determined to impose himself and his ways on a fractured and unstable society that had known only occupation—Israeli, Jordanian, and Egyptian—since 1948. This was a hostile and angry place, in which the radical Hamas was already establishing itself as the only cohesive political force.[17]

Arafat was unable to shed the skin of the gnarled revolutionary; nor could he break with the Arab propensity for the one-man state and its inevitable companion: corruption. He relied on almost a dozen thuggish and competing security services to enforce his writ.[18] These were backed by a justice system that relied on unannounced midnight trials, which sometimes lasted just minutes. The response to media criticism was to charge editors with sedition and to sentence them to long jail terms.[19] When the highly respected Raji Sourani, head of the Gaza Center for Rights and Law, critiqued the new Palestinian legal framework, the police came on a midnight run, snatching him from his bed. Arafat had re-created a version of the darkest days of the fiefdom he ran in Beirut.[20] But in the face of local defiance, Arafat resorted to what some perceived as one of his double plays—the rough-handed roundups continued, but some who were convicted by his kangaroo courts were released soon after being sentenced.

Far from any rebuke, the PLO leader won international praise and support, particularly from Washington.[21] One of the indignities inflicted on Mousa Abu Marzook as he bided his time in a New York cell pending finalization of Israel's extradition request was his incarceration in the city while Arafat was the toast of five days of diplomatic partying, as New York and the world celebrated the fiftieth anniversary of the United Nations.

Observing the post-Oslo landscape from his new lair in Amman, Khalid Mishal felt he could detect another anxiety—apart from budget woes—that had hastened Arafat along the road to Madrid and Washington, before his dramatic detour to Oslo. Few would have taken Mishal seriously at the time, but he sensed that the PLO leader had belatedly realized that Hamas had the leadership, internal discipline, and popular support to confront Arafat and his Fatah organization in the Occupied Territories.

Initially, King Hussein was shocked by Oslo. Quite apart from any highbrow geopolitical implications, he was furious on personal grounds. On the one hand, he had been frozen out of the Oslo loop, notwithstanding his essential role in getting the Madrid and Washington legs of the peace talks off the ground; on the other, Arafat had been allowed to rob him of his cherished role as the Arab poster boy for peace.

Publicly, it would have been churlish not to fall in with all the congratulatory backslapping, but privately the king saw Oslo as a bad deal. On first hearing the news from Oslo, the king told his aides, "We have to seek peace—not a piecemeal settlement."[22]

But then Hussein performed his own spectacular backflip. If Arafat had concluded what amounted to a Palestinian treaty with Israel, then the way was open for Jordan to do likewise, he reasoned. This had been a long-term objective of the king's, and so, just two weeks after Oslo, he authorized a start to treaty negotiations during a secret meeting with Prime Minister Yitzhak Rabin at the Red Sea port of Aqaba.

Khalid Mishal barely had time to draw breath. Hamas had drawn strength from Arafat's decision, as the Islamists saw it, to go to bed in Oslo with the "devil" Israelis. Suddenly, Hamas also needed to come to terms with the fact that Jordan, the host country for its campaign in the Occupied Territories, was prepared to jump into the same bed by signing its own treaty, formally ending almost three decades of hostility with Israel and bringing into the open what, until then, had been Hussein's long, covert relationship with his western neighbors.

There was a calculated stepping-up of Hamas violence after Israel and the PLO signed a deal granting Palestinians interim self-rule for Gaza and Jericho at a White House ceremony in September 1993. There was no coincidence in the timing and nature of the Hamas response. To discredit Arafat and his Oslo life support, Hamas needed to destabilize the proposed new PLO regime. Thus, on the first morning of the supposed peace, nineteen-year-old Bahaa Al-Din Al-Najjar tried to blow up the central police station in Gaza, one of four such attacks in the space of thirty hours.[23] But Hamas also needed to draw the ire of the Israelis, and in order to do that, the movement would introduce a terrible new weapon to the conflict.

After the arrest of Abu Marzook at JFK Airport, the FBI Agent Joseph Hummel claimed that Abu Marzook had admitted knowing a twenty-nine-year-old Palestinian called Yehiya Ayyash. Hummel would go further, claiming that Abu Marzook described Ayyash as a "hero, a great man."[24] There would be hairsplitting on this point—was this the opinion of Abu Marzook, or did he say this was the view of a good many Palestinians? Either way, they were talking about the man who had single-handedly engineered an appalling new madness sweeping Israel and the Occupied Territories. They called Ayyash "the Engineer."

In a conflict in which blood was the first unit of measure, a suicide bomb that exploded outside the Israeli Army headquarters at Beit El, on the West Bank, on October 4, 1993, drew media attention, despite past efforts by Israeli security forces to play down such attacks.[25] The driver of an explosives-laden car, twenty-year-old Kamal Bani Odeh, was the only one to die, but thirty passengers on an Israeli commuter bus were injured. Most of the wounds were slight; none was life threatening.[26] But just the fact that thirty injured might have been thirty dead was sufficient to make a wary public realize that the Beit El device was the fifth in a series. The others had also been deemed failures but only because the drivers of these car-borne bombs had died.

Like all who were members of militia cells in Hamas's Qassam Brigade, Ayyash was lying low in the face of another wave of arrests. Religiously devout and an electrical engineer by training, he went back to his books after the first failures, broadening his understanding of homemade explosives and refining his knowledge of how best to direct the explosive force of his crude devices for maximum deadly impact. In the meantime, the cyclical nature of violence in the region intervened to give Ayyash's Hamas masters the last element necessary for a terrifying bombing campaign, to gnaw at the Israelis' national psyche and their preoccupation with their own existential fate. As events stood, these early, ineffectual bombs were targeting the peace process and Arafat as much as Rabin. Hamas needed the knife to go deeper.

As Hamas was on the cusp of intensifying its attacks, a devastating attack from the other side set the scene for the gruesome death counts to come. In the early hours of a Ramadan morning, late in February 1994, the Brooklyn-born and reared physician Baruch Goldstein rose from his bed at Kiryat Arba, an Israeli settlement overlooking the West Bank city of Hebron. Dressed in reservist fatigues, he drove to the ancient Ibrahimi Mosque at the Cave of the Patriarchs. Armed with an automatic Galil rifle, the Israeli version of an AK-47, Goldstein slipped through an Israeli security checkpoint and entered the crowded mosque—and then he opened fire. By the time he had been clubbed to death by members of the enraged congregation, the extremist settler-doctor had massacred thirty Palestinians. During the protests that followed, Israeli troops would kill another dozen.[27]

Ayyash was bent on what he regarded as the noble cause of Arab revenge. In the first week of April, after a suicide bomber killed nine Israelis and wounded forty-five at Afula, in the north of Israel, Hamas announced that it was the first of five payback attacks for the murders at the mosque in Hebron.[28] "[Each one will make] the Zionists cry blood on their dead," the statement said.[29]

A week later, six died and twenty-five were wounded when a bomber detonated his charge on a bus at Hadera. In October, another bus was bombed in Tel Aviv—with twenty-two dead and forty-eight injured. A month later, a bomber rode a bicycle into the Jewish settlement of Netzarim in Gaza, killing three Israeli soldiers and wounding eleven. In July 1995, on the day before Abu Marzook's arrest, six Israeli civilians were killed in a suicide attack on a bus at Ramat Gan, near Tel Aviv.

All this was a radical policy shift for Hamas, requiring a brutal mind-set and nerves of steel. Ayyash's leadership of the Qassam Brigade was acknowledged later by a senior official of Hamas who would attempt to explain the macabre logic of Ayyash's bloody campaign in stark but simple terms: "Violence is the only weapon that makes the Israelis bleed as we bleed and we always have people who are ready to do it."[30]

Arafat and Rabin refused to allow the peace process to be derailed, but their retaliatory crackdowns were ferocious. Both the Israelis and the new Palestinian security forces controlled by Arafat rounded up hundreds more Hamas suspects. There was widespread speculation that the Qassam Brigade at this time numbered no more than a total of one hundred fighters who, working in small independent cells, fought to the death, giving their enemies little opportunity to capture them.

Arafat banned street protests and Israel introduced even harsher interrogation tactics. In November Arafat's forces provoked outrage among Palestinians when they opened fire, killing fourteen protesters at a rally in Gaza, earning Arafat the ignominy of being held responsible for one of the highest daily Palestinian tolls since the start of the Intifada seven years before. The more Arafat responded to Israeli and American pressure to round up the Islamists, the more the Islamists' campaign to chip away at the credibility of the Palestinian Authority seemed to work.

Arafat's associates described his policy on managing Hamas as "carrot and stick." But, stripped of superficial nicety and pragmatic acts of goodwill, the relationship between the key Palestinian factions—Fatah and Hamas—was governed by much stick, and virtually no carrot. Mutual suspicion and zero-sum games would dictate the terms from now on.

In the process, it all became deeply personal. Street crowds denounced

Arafat as a collaborator after angry protests over the death of an Islamist figure by what was presumed to be a car bomb, planted by Israeli agents. There were reports that jostling crowds knocked Arafat's trademark kaffiyeh from his head[31]—a grave insult for any Arab male. It was never clear if this was the particular incident that seared itself in the minds of Arafat's security men, but years later his old guards still complained about the indignity Hamas supporters had visited on Arafat by forcing him to flee a Gaza mosque. More than a decade on, one of his senior enforcers at the time remained incensed. Complaining that Arafat had been attacked while praying, he thundered, "They tried to capture him; he escaped in a taxi, but there was no time for him to get his shoes or his kaffiyeh."[32]

In just a few accelerated years since the start of the Intifada, Hamas had achieved what it had taken the PLO more than twenty years to do. Just as the young Khalid Mishal had plotted in Kuwait in the early 1980s, this was a "new model of resistance." Hamas had become a force that could not be ignored.

10

A Little Obscurity Is Good

She was a vision in pink. As Ranya Kadri stepped out for the day, her pink linen pants moved in the Amman breeze; her paler pink vest was adorned in gold threads and stones of iridescent blue. Even the Gucci handbag slung on her bare shoulder was pink. Gem-encrusted YSL sunglasses were fixed to her nose until some arbitrary moment in the day, when they were swapped capriciously for a more spacey pair by Chanel.

In her early thirties, Kadri moved too often for a casual observer to count the dozens of diamonds in her gold necklace. Once, on a famous occasion when a member of her household staff had produced baseball caps for the young guests attending a poolside birthday party for one of her children, she had pounced on the pile of hats, extracting one in a fit of genuine panic. It seemed that one of her cherished brand names had inadvertently found its way among the party hats. "Not the Prada," she had yelled.

As Kadri left home each morning, her driver, Khalil, headed for the blue Land Rover just beyond a front gate decorated in gilded vine leaves. As taut as a razor strap, Khalil carried her priceless contact book, her three or four mobile phones . . . and "Madam's" giant coffee flask. "I like it only the way I make it," she explained matter-of-factly, breezing into the homes and offices of state officials as calmly as she did those of terror suspects, corrupt regime cronies, or tribal sheikhs.

Kadri had studied law before setting out to make herself a journalist's journalist in a crossroads city of the Arab world. Such was the procession of foreign correspondents beating a path to her door as each crisis loomed that cabdrivers on the ranks at the Four Seasons or Intercontinental hotels only had to be told: "Ranya's house." For all her outward gloss, Kadri was a wise and skeptical observer of Arab societies and an incisive analyst of their interwoven flaws and foibles, their rich cultures and traditions. A regular visitor to the Palestinian camps, where she spent hours discussing politics while sitting on the floor in refugee homes, she was deeply offended by rising corruption and greed in Jordan. Kadri spurned the veil, but to many she represented the best of Jordanian tradition.

Whether it was the *New York Times* or the *Washington Post*, CNN or CBC Canada, the well-sourced and informed analysis of journalists was often shaped over muddy Turkish coffee and hash brownies at Kadri's chaotic table, where all were received, from senior political players to tribal sheikhs to the many who had heard she might be able to help them get out of a fix. Kadri's contact book was the envy of all. "Even Barbies have brains," she teased newcomers who stared askance at her wild ensembles. Visitors marveled at her instinctive reading of the lay of the land, sometimes displayed in her judgment call on when it was appropriate for her to arrive at Mukhabarat headquarters bearing a plate of cookies . . . or to stare down the local G-men with demands that they arrest her or stand back as she went about her business.

Kadri was a frequent visitor to the main Hamas office, in a small complex behind the Amra Hotel, on the fringe of the diplomatic quarter. She had found Mousa Abu Marzook to be moderate, more sophisticated and smarter than the recently arrived Khalid Mishal. "He was the least interesting of them," she would say of Mishal. "Abu Marzook always had to introduce him, because people never seemed to remember him." When Abu Marzook was arrested, Mishal became acting head of the political bureau. But, as Kadri understood it, this was a stopgap arrangement and Abu Marzook remained the boss. She decided that Mishal was "just an assignment guy, chosen for his mediocrity, so Abu Marzook can resume the leadership later." Still, her antennae told her to keep a watch on the low-key Mishal.

Mishal had slipped into Amman so quietly in 1990 that few noticed him at first. It was a deliberate ploy. Abu Marzook and several others were the frontmen who dealt with government, chatted with diplomats, and briefed reporters. Mishal, on the other hand, continued to operate invisibly, as he had done in Kuwait.

Abu Marzook had a certain style. Like most senior Hamas figures, he did not smoke. He stayed trim, offering visitors the traditional, heavily sugared Turkish coffee while he stuck to a Diet Pepsi or Nescafé, which he sweetened from a pocket pack of Canderel. One foreigner described the bearded fundamentalist's appearance as "dapper." If a woman visitor put a hand on her heart, a common no-contact greeting in the Arab world, Abu Marzook usually would lean in and offer his hand for a conventional Western handshake.

Abu Marzook's office was adorned with the usual Qur'anic readings and framed posters of the jailed Sheikh Ahmad Yassin. But its loud fittings and furniture were what conservative Ammanis looked down on as "a bit too Gulfie," with heavy black fixtures trimmed in red. Marzook kept a gun in a filing cabinet and there was always a buzz around his office as a stream of government officials and others came through. "When we spoke to him, we understood we were talking to the leader of Hamas," Kadri said.

Power in Hamas was deliberately blurred and scattered. It suited much of the organization's far-flung and clandestine leadership to have international media focus on the jailed Sheikh Yassin in the Occupied Territories, his spiritual and welfare organizations and the bomb throwers and marksmen of the Qassam Brigade.

There were personal centers of power. They included Yassin, as founder of the grassroots operation in Gaza, and Mishal, as author of the strategic plan agreed to at the Amman conference and as the driving force behind the Kuwait project. Yassin had installed Abu Marzook as the first head of the political bureau, hoping that he would give Hamas a visible presence beyond reach of the Israelis and that he, and those around him, would balance the internal pull of the Kuwaitis.

The political bureau, in turn, was scattered, with its members doubling as Hamas representatives in Amman, Tehran, Damascus, and Beirut. Some of the senior fund-raisers in the diaspora communities—in the United States in particular—also were influential. A political bureau member visiting the Agence France-Presse office in Amman once asked if he could make a phone call, before he and the reporter Randa Habib could resolve a row over Hamas's bullying of her AFP colleagues in the Occupied Territories. When the man left, Habib hit the auto redial to discover that the Hamas authority figure in this case was in the British Home Counties.

To external eyes, an even more opaque layer of authority in Hamas was the Majlis Shura, an appointed advisory council of sixty-plus whose identities were a tightly guarded secret. Sitting above the layers of local, military, and political bureau leadership in the early 1990s, most were religious figures, and about half were drawn from other national branches of the Muslim Brotherhood across the region.[1] The Majlis Shura set broad policy, such as contesting elections; it assessed internal performances; and it elected a high-level committee, from which members of the political bureau were appointed. Explaining the heavy outside membership, a senior Hamas figure in Gaza explained, "That's why we say Palestine *is* 100 percent a Muslim issue, and *is not* a 100-percent Palestinian matter."[2]

Hamas decision making was based on the principle of the *shura*, which insisted on exhaustive internal consultation before arriving at a decision, after which all were obliged to stand by it. The intent was to protect the organization against the ambition or willfulness of single individuals, but when Mishal and his team arrived from Kuwait in 1990, some in Hamas wondered if the Jordanian capital was big enough for both Khalid Mishal and Mousa Abu Marzook.

Unlike Abu Marzook, Mishal remained invisible to the general public. The minutiae of policy debates and a good deal of Hamas's internal politicking were covered in the Arabic-language news media and in the records of the movement's internal discourse, a quantity of which were seized by the Israelis. But curiously absent from debate and all leadership consideration was the name of Mishal, even after his arrival in Amman. Pressed later on his early anonymity, Mishal would only say, "A little obscurity is good. My comrades and God know what I have been doing."[3]

But many in Amman did not understand the role of the blow-in from Kuwait. "We were told he did international liaison," a senior Jordanian Islamist explained. "He dealt with other Islamic organizations and some of the PLO factions. He was trying to open relations with different regimes, but no one really knew who he was or what he did."[4]

Sometimes engaged, at other times aloof, Mishal spoke well. But, for some, there was no sense that they were listening to their future leader. He was observed to harness the *shura* process to his sense of the movement's needs, privately canvassing all options ahead of any meeting, during which he would then urge all to speak before a decision was made. He was even tempered, they said, and had an understated elegance that matched his preference for a suit and a collared shirt. A close colleague from the period observed, "At first, there was no charisma, no spark. But, as I got to know him, I saw potential—he struck me as a hard worker, a man of the movement who seemed not to have a personal agenda."[5]

Whenever Mishal moved, his intelligence file followed him. Shortly after his arrival in Amman, the Mukhabarat desk tasked with monitoring both the Muslim Brotherhood and Hamas in Jordan was briefed by Kuwaiti intelligence. The Jordanian agents were absorbed by what they were told were three key aspects of Mishal's activities—funds, weapons, and military infrastructure.[6] In 1994, he was in Kuala Lumpur and Islamabad, lobbying for support and seeking a venue for a grand conference of Islamic scholars on the fate of Jerusalem. Back at the Mukhabarat office in Amman, it was noted that when Mishal went to southern Lebanon to visit the Hamas deportees, he shunned public highways and instead drove on roads reserved for the exclusive use of Syria's military forces.

An Israeli report on Hamas in the mid-1990s, described as an "expert opinion" from within IDF intelligence, gave Mishal just a single bracketed mention as it listed the membership of the political bureau, and there was no reference to his membership of, or role in, the Kuwaiti-based Jihaz Filastin.[7] Insiders later described Mishal's duties at the time as "communications and finance." But a senior Arab intelligence agent added a third element by referring to what his Jordanian colleagues called the "secret line." This, he said, was an internal intersection of power in Hamas that vested significant power in Mishal. Still holding the purse strings for what had become the relocated Kuwait project, he also was part of a three-man "outside" military committee that oversaw the operations of the Qassam Brigade. This, they concluded, amounted to a veto that made Mishal the single most powerful individual in the leadership of Hamas.[8]

Hamas insiders agreed. "The number one guy is the one who controls the money, because that gives him control of the weapons. In Hamas that guy was Mishal," a member who was close to Mishal in the mid-1990s explained. "He told the military wing which operations were required." Some in the Israeli security services would describe him as "the prime minister of Hamas."[9]

It was 1995 before Mishal began to make official appearances as one of Hamas's leaders. Among his first public duties was to wait on the Jordanian Foreign Ministry and be informed that Abu Marzook was to be deported.[10] As Abu Marzook packed up to leave Amman—a journey that ultimately would see him fall into the hands of U.S. authorities—there was no sense that Mishal was hankering for his job.[11] As some saw it, Abu Marzook was being pushed by the Jordanian regime at the same time as the Mishal machine, which had arrived from Kuwait, was crowding in. Mindful that Kuwait had been the biggest Hamas operation outside the Occupied Territories up until the Iraqi invasion of the emirate, a senior figure in the Jordanian Brotherhood observed, "All the outside people came from Kuwait, except Abu Marzook."[12]

There was, however, an intriguing sign of the invisible man's rising ambition. Mishal had changed his name.[13] Until this point in his forty-odd years, Mishal's formal, seven-part name had been abbreviated to Khalid Abd Al-Qadir, in keeping with the Arab naming custom that identified him simply as his father's son. Now a cocktail of vanity, psychology, and resistance tradition seemed to kick in. Adopting a nom de guerre was common enough among Arab fighters. Often they were grandiose—as in the Iraqi Shiite warlord Abu Deraa, meaning Father of the Shield. Others simply honored a fighter's place of birth—as in Abu Musab Al-Zarqawi, who was born in the Jordanian city of Zarqa. But, in the absence of any combat heroics in his career, Mishal followed the resistance practice without dwelling on glorification. By his new appellation, he was Khalid and he was of the extended Mishal family of the Palestinian West Bank. The message here was that Mishal was ready to lead from the front. And in becoming the acting leader of the Hamas political bureau in Amman in the absence of Abu Marzook, he emerged from underground.

Mishal and Abu Marzook were a study in contrasts. As Palestinians, their families had suffered greatly from Israel's occupation of their homeland. Yet, compared to the relative comfort of Mishal's flight from the West Bank and his upbringing in Kuwait, life for Abu Marzook had begun in classic refugee circumstances. He was born on the floor of a tent in a fetid refugee camp at Rafah, at the south end of what was Egyptian-controlled Gaza, in 1951. After being ordered at gunpoint by Jewish forces to abandon their home, his market-gardener father, mother, and five siblings trekked through the south of what was to become Israel for four months before landing in the overcrowded, under-resourced UN camp at Rafah.[14]

By age sixteen, Abu Marzook was a committed Islamist activist, and a year later he was dispatched to Cairo by his mentor, Sheikh Ahmad Yassin. After studying engineering at the Helwan College of Engineering and Technology, he graduated in 1976. His first jobs were in the United Arab Emirates, but Abu Marzook continued to be driven by the urgency of Gaza's needs. In 1978, he returned to become a founder of Yassin's Islamic University and to marry Nadia El-Ashi, whom Yassin had chosen from the ranks of the Muslim Brotherhood as a suitable wife for Abu Marzook.

In the early 1980s, Abu Marzook plunged into a frenetic new life in the United States. Living first on their own savings and scholarships from the UAE, Saudi, and Kuwaiti governments, both husband and wife studied at Colorado State University's Fort Collins campus. At the same time, they were raising a family and managing a lucrative series of property purchase-and-renovation projects. A prolific fund-raiser and organizer for Hamas, Abu Marzook helped establish the Islamic Association for Palestine, a critical support group in the United States, which was set up on the direction of Khalid Mishal.[15] He contributed $210,000 in seed capital to Hamas's main American fund-raiser, the Texas-based Holy Land Foundation.[16] From his home in Virginia, almost within the shadow cast by the Washington Monument, Abu Marzook had run much of Hamas's logistical and support operations in the late 1980s and early 1990s.

If none of that amounted to anything heroic, Abu Marzook had excelled himself in 1989, when he was credited with single-handedly saving Hamas from extinction. It was the second year of the Intifada and his mentor Yassin was in jail again. Israel was attempting to decapitate the movement with another mass roundup of activists when Abu Marzook dropped his doctoral studies in Louisiana and went home to Gaza.

When the Hamas activist Said Abu Msamah was arrested early in 1991, he gave Israeli interrogators an eyewitness account of how his old acquaintance Abu Marzook managed to fireproof the grassroots organization and its structures sufficiently to keep it on its feet until international pressure forced Israel to allow old hands among the deportees in southern Lebanon to return.[17] Installing Abu Msamah as a member of the new leadership team, Abu Marzook had carved Gaza into five districts and appointed a leader in each. Together these five became a new central administrative committee. As Abu Msamah recalled, "In his region, [each leader was to] recruit three committees— security, activities, and propaganda. They will do [as they are] told and they will report to the person in charge." Abu Marzook forbade face-to-face recruiting. It was all to be done through DLB so that, as Abu Msamah put it, "if somebody is arrested he won't be able to tell who recruited him."

For money, Abu Marzook first handed out blank checkbooks from Bank of America, in which he had signed all the forms. "I just had to write in the sum," Abu Msamah said, before explaining that he disliked this form of exchange and instead had asked for cash. In due course an anonymous courier began delivering banknotes by the brick. "He would tell me that [Abu Marzook] sent him . . . in this way I received a total of $100,000," he revealed. Later, the Israelis admitted that they did not discover the extent of Abu Marzook's rescue effort until the 1991 roundup that bagged Abu Marzook's star recruit, Abu Msamah.[18]

Abu Marzook was uniquely qualified to be dropped into Gaza at a time of crisis. As a Gazan and a disciple of Yassin, he was the only leadership figure capable of getting in and around the deep suspicion of outsiders. But because he was an "insider," the effect of Abu Marzook's new structures was to deliver effective control of Hamas to the "outsiders," whose role so far had been to support an "inside" operation that had been making its own decisions. To protect Hamas from being undermined by the Israelis and by the PLO, the outsiders would become the decision makers.[19]

As the political bureau established itself in Amman in 1990, Mishal and Abu Marzook were revealed as two sides of the Hamas coin: one a visionary strategist; the other a go-to guy with the energy required to shuffle funds in Virginia one week and, in the next, to be parachuted into Gaza on a daring mission, so as to pull the operation back from the brink. But trouble loomed as a policy gulf began opening between them.

Hamas had fortified itself sufficiently to endure. However, in some quarters of the movement debate had begun on its ability to survive, particularly since Yasser Arafat's return to parts of the Occupied Territories in mid-1994 and the unleashing of his security forces on Hamas, which was still under intense pressure from the Israelis.

In Israel, the security and intelligence establishments were entitled to feel quite smug. Since 1989 they had kept the extraordinarily influential spiritual leader, Yassin, behind bars, and the Americans had been nifty in grabbing Abu Marzook at JFK Airport in 1995. With the Israeli campaign of on-the-ground assassinations, Hamas was being whittled away. Think-tank analysts wondered how much longer the movement could withstand such pummelling without suffering grave organizational injury.

At the U.S. Embassy in Tel Aviv, Ambassador Martin Indyk thought it was not a question of Hamas merely having been contained. As he saw it, the movement was in serious trouble and the rawness of his language seemed somehow appropriate to the security landscape. "They're getting screwed by the PA forces on the orders of Arafat," he told colleagues. "Operationally, they might just be finished off."

Diplomatically, there was something quite perverse about the Middle East triangle—Israel, Jordan, and the United States. All three were close allies, but while Washington and the Israelis ranted about Hamas, their ally King Hussein still hosted the movement, which was as bad as Arafat's PLO in its enfant terrible days. The king had swatted away Israeli and American complaints by expelling Abu Marzook, but now he was getting briefings on a harder, more rigid Hamas line being taken by Mishal in the absence of Abu Marzook.

The U.S. ambassador to Jordan, Wesley Egan, was a practical career diplomat who found it rewarding to serve as a senior U.S. diplomat in countries
snubbed by Washington's pointy-elbowed, A-list appointees. In his past, he
had had a stint as ambassador to Bissau, the capital of handkerchief-sized
Guinea Bissau in West Africa. He had been on the embassy teams in Cairo,
Johannesburg, and Lisbon. Egan was engaged yet cautious and he had a firm
personal rule to never keep a diary, or make notes that could be seized by investigators or subpoenaed by inquiries.[20] The ambassador kept his secrets in
his head.

More than three years into his Amman posting, Egan found that he enjoyed both king and country. Activity in Amman came in bursts, but Egan
and his wife Virginia found time, whenever calm seemed to prevail, to in-
dulge their shared passion for archaeology. Egan talked of slipping away to
dig among the Nabataean ruins at Petra, famously described by the poet John
William Burgon as "a rose-red city half as old as time."

The only problem was distance. Petra was a good three-hour drive south
from the capital. Egan was off digging in 1995 when Hussein Kamel, Saddam Hussein's son-in-law and the man in charge of Iraq's weapons programs,
surfaced in Amman, claiming he wanted to reveal all. Egan's absence as the
defection drama broke prompted a running royal gag. King Hussein would
joke that if Egan was at Petra, then a spike of drama would surely rear up in
Amman.

If Egan sought pleasure digging at Petra, his principal work duty was to
persistently hammer away in the capital. He was under permanent instruction from Washington to give King Hussein a hard time, all the time, about
Hamas. He had been "banging away" at Hussein for a solid three years.

In the royal office or over a meal, Egan would lecture the king on the inconsistency, as Washington saw it, of his sheltering Hamas and what the
ambassador described as Hussein's "otherwise fundamentally positive role in
trying to negotiate a Middle East peace." The king would parry that the
Hamas operatives in Amman were Jordanians. "They've done nothing bad in
Jordan; or in Israel that can be traced to Jordan. I can't just bundle up my
people and dispatch them."[21]

While Egan attempted to negotiate with the king in Amman, in New York
the fortunes of one of Hamas's most senior officials took a dramatic new turn
early in 1997. Mousa Abu Marzook had been languishing in jail since his
arrest in 1995, fighting Israeli efforts to have him extradited. After the decision by Judge Duffy in 1996 to grant the Israeli request, Abu Marzook's

lawyers had launched a battery of appeals to stay the extradition. But now, after spending more than eighteen months in his six-by-eight-foot prison cell in Manhattan, the Hamas leader dramatically changed tactics in an attempt to bluff the Israelis, who he did not believe had a substantive case against him.

Abu Marzook, who was Israel's most high-profile catch since Sheikh Ahmad Yassin almost a decade earlier, announced that he was dropping all appeals. He was prepared to be flown to Israel to stand trial as a terrorist before an Israeli court—providing the Israelis had the evidence. In a statement to the U.S. Court of Appeals, where his latest appeal bid had languished, he mocked American justice, telling the court he had concluded that maybe he stood a better chance before the judges of Jerusalem than before their New York brothers. Embellishing his stance with the proclamation that he was ready to go to Israel and suffer martyrdom, he lectured the bench and the Clinton administration on the detail. "The law of the U.S. requires that I be extradited to Israel within sixty days from the withdrawal of my appeal," he pointed out.[22]

As a ploy to garner attention, this was a huge success. The prospect of Abu Marzook actually being handed over to the Israelis caused renewed Hamas threats to rain down on the United States, yet stunned Washington officials were obliged to await a response from Israel. Amid speculation that Abu Marzook was attempting to manipulate Israeli and American fears of a Hamas backlash to hasten his freedom, the *New York Times* declared the Palestinian to be "a diplomatic time bomb."[23]

Washington immediately began the process of transferring the prisoner to Israeli custody. American diplomats in Tel Aviv were instructed to extract Israeli assurances on how Abu Marzook would be treated. "WE HAVE CLEAR ASSURANCES FROM THE GOI [government of Israel] THAT IT WILL AFFORD ABU MARZOOK HUMANE TREATMENT AND FULL LEGAL RIGHTS," Washington was told in a "secret" diplomatic cable dated January 29, in which the U.S. Embassy reported the outcome of talks between Ambassador Indyk and Israeli justice minister Tzachi Hanegbi.[24]

But after all Israel's strident demands that Abu Marzook be handed over, there was a hint of hesitancy in a personal plea by Hanegbi that Washington stall on the transfer until as late as possible in the two months set by statute for deportation.

In Israel, the political mood and the government had changed in significant ways since Abu Marzook's arrest. Bringing him to trial in Israel now

seemed a fraught business. As a precaution, Indyk warned Washington that
things were not as clear-cut as they seemed. "THE NETANYAHU GOVERNMENT
HAS JUST BEGUN TO GRAPPLE WITH THIS NEW DEVELOPMENT IN THE MAR-
ZOOK CASE WHICH IT INHERITED FROM THE PERES AND RABIN GOVERN-
MENTS," the cable said.

The hard-line Benjamin Netanyahu had been elected months earlier and,
though his new government might try to wash its hands of this difficult case
and its concomitant risk of a terror backlash—on the grounds that it had been
initiated by his predecessor—Netanyahu needed to work through the domestic politics. The Abu Marzook case had been big for Israel. Its government
had told the world that here was one of its worst terrorists, and considerable
legal, security, and diplomatic capital had been invested in getting this far.
Allowing Abu Marzook to walk away at such a late stage would require careful handling. As speculation on Abu Marzook's fate mounted, the Jewish
Telegraphic Agency quoted authoritative Israeli sources making the point
that Israel still had the revered Sheikh Yassin locked up. As one of them said,
why should they let Abu Marzook go? "Impossible," a former head of the
Shin Bet, Carmi Gillon, told the agency. "It's not a matter of political interests. It's a matter of law."[25]

Netanyahu was the politician who had urged that terrorists never be released, and it was his get-tough-on-terror platform that had won him the
election.[26] But his advisers were said to have a better understanding of the
powerful dynamics of cyclical violence in the aftermath of the assassination,
presumably by Israeli agents, of two prominent Palestinian militants. One of
these had been the Hamas suicide bomb maestro, "The Engineer," Yehiya
Ayyash. In retaliation for this assassination there had been four suicide bombings, which not only killed nearly seventy Israelis but also provided the
springboard of public anger that propelled Israeli voters to entrust their government to Netanyahu in May 1996.[27]

In mid-February, there were news leaks in Jerusalem to the effect that
Washington and the Israelis were quietly looking for ways to make the Abu
Marzook problem go away. In Washington, reporters were backgrounded on
the Americans' fury over the embarrassment caused for them by Israel's
change of heart. Then, in Amman, a late-night meeting between Ambassador Egan and King Hussein produced the circuit breaker, when the monarch
declared, "I'll take him." Relieved, an Israeli diplomat in Washington told a
reporter, "It's not a bad solution. They know us, they cooperate with us
and King Hussein knows how to deal with these people."[28] Suddenly Abu
Marzook was free, and Israel had wriggled its way out of a menacing crisis.

But all was not entirely as it seemed. Certainly the three capitals had engaged in an exercise of mutual back-scratching as they tossed the Abu Marzook problem between them. But far from clear was just who had manipulated whom, and to what end. In all three countries, the public comments of government officials were accepted at face value, and they were allowed to close the account on the arrest by the Americans, and then the remarkable release of Abu Marzook.

Benjamin Netanyahu came to power in Israel in a vacuum of grief and uncertainty after the assassination of Prime Minister Yitzhak Rabin. Rabin had died on a November evening in 1995 after being shot at close quarters by a right-wing Jewish fanatic bent on destroying the Oslo peace process. Rabin's death, as a Hussein loyalist in Amman said, made an orphan of the faltering peace process. Gone was a unique trust and mutual respect between two leaders in a region that seemed to have become inured to its own brutal history. On the day of Rabin's funeral, King Hussein spoke to the AFP's Randa Habib in his suite at Jerusalem's King David Hotel. Overcome by emotion, he told her through his tears, "I have the impression that today I have also, in some way, buried the peace."[29]

Believing that the only way to stop the Oslo process going down the drain altogether was to strengthen the forces of moderation, King Hussein decided that Hamas would have to be moderated and then be brought into the negotiations that it had spurned since the Norwegian-engineered breakthrough in 1993. But if he was to point Hamas in a different and more amenable direction, it would have to be under a different leadership, he concluded with characteristic confidence. This was the daring strategic framework in which the king of Jordan realized that it had been a mistake to bow to American and Israeli pressure by deporting Abu Marzook in the first place.

The Jordanian intelligence reports coming in on Khalid Mishal's leadership of the Hamas political bureau were damning. After more than a year's scrutiny, the assessments of Mishal by Samih Batikhi's Islamist Desk rated Mishal to be shallow, brittle, and unbending. He lacked credibility, they said, and failed to grasp the mutual-interest element of the relationship between the Jordanian monarchy and the movement. "The word 'Israel' does not exist in his ideological dictionary," Batikhi barked at one of his senior colleagues.[30] There was a claim too that Mishal was moving beyond Hamas and its focus on the Occupied Territories, in a bid to establish a local power base within the Jordanian branch of the Muslim Brotherhood.

Hussein's plan to reform the leadership of Hamas was as dangerous as it was grandiose. One false move could provoke the combined ire of Hamas and the Muslim Brotherhood's powerful Jordanian wing. At the same time, it could stir the simmering anger of his own huge Palestinian refugee community. However, the king saw his gambit as vital, both to creating a new negotiating reality and to his own role as a regional peacemaker and a defender of his own national interests. He reasoned that Abu Marzook was conciliatory by nature, a man whose Gazan roots and enduring relationship with Yassin and those around the sheikh made him a valuable conduit to Hamas's more amenable local leadership in the Occupied Territories. Abu Marzook had traveled the world and understood its ways. He had a green card; some of his children were American citizens. The Americans had got to know him during his incarceration.

But if all the jailed engineer's fine attributes were to come into play, the king's plan required cooperation by others on three crucial fronts. First, he had to get Abu Marzook back to Jordan. Second, once there, he had to be shoe-horned back into the leadership. Finally, once reinstated, he needed to understand that he owed a debt at the palace for having rescued him from the Israelis and the Americans.

The extent to which this Jordanian plot was part of the decision-making mix in the other two capitals was moot. Ambassador Egan later said it was not raised with him, but he assumed it would have been dealt with in discussions between Washington and Israel.[31] One of Netanyahu's advisers was disarmingly frank. "Batikhi briefed us on the plan to weaken Hamas," he said. "King Hussein was gambling on Abu Marzook, whose mind had been opened by his time in the US. Mishal was much more extreme. . . ."[32]

Egan was shocked. Perhaps naively for a career diplomat, he attempted to explain what he described as "this slight inconsistency" to his masters at the State Department. "You're demanding that King Hussein shut down Hamas at the same time as you say to him 'Please take Abu Marzook, Hamas leader, off our hands?' This is crazy." But in the dry manner of a practiced career diplomat, Egan would explain later that his protest had no impact. "I was advised Abu Marzook would be arriving in due course," he said.

Still wearing the prisoners' standard issue, the familiar orange jumpsuit, Abu Marzook was triumphant as he alighted from an American military jet in Amman on May 6. His armed escorts kept him handcuffed and in leg irons for the eleven-hour flight from New York. But ahead of leaving his Manhattan cell, his words would have cheered King Hussein. Interviewed at length in the weeks before his release, Abu Marzook laughingly assured reporter Roger Gaess that he still was the leader of Hamas's political bureau.[33] Forty-eight hours after arriving in Amman he proclaimed, "I'll still be in the same role, performing the same activities."[34]

Abu Marzook wanted his job back. Quite apart from his extraordinary past, he saw himself as the conquering Hamas hero, who had bearded the Israeli and American lions in their den and walked away, head high, while the superpower and its Middle East pawn squirmed in embarrassment before the world. That, he believed, was leadership material. He saw in himself an amalgam of dizzying profiles and he wanted others to believe his publicity lines.[35] His lawyers had told the New York courts that he was Hamas's de facto ambassador to the world; he himself had taken to telling reporters he was the Gerry Adams of the Middle East.

But there was a problem, and his name was Khalid Mishal. When Abu Marzook was arrested in 1995, Mishal had been nominated in an acting capacity to keep the chair warm. But in 1996, when there was no way of knowing what Abu Marzook's fate would be, Mishal had been formally elected to lead the political bureau. Abu Marzook was doubly shocked—not only did Mishal refuse to step aside upon his return, but quite a case had been built up against him in his absence.

First, there was the question of his lapsed judgment in thinking it would be safe to go to the United States at all. He had done this in defiance of political bureau colleagues who had advised him in the strongest terms that Washington's anti-Hamas rhetoric had been rising.[36] It seemed the height of recklessness for Abu Marzook to have arrived at JFK Airport just twenty-four hours after a suicide bombing that killed six Israelis and wounded thirty-one near Tel Aviv; it was only six months after Washington had begun the formal processes that, in time, would see Hamas and its leadership declared to be SDGTs.

There was another internal political problem too. Until his arrest, Abu Marzook was the only political bureau chief his comrades had known. In his absence, however, they had experienced a more collegiate, less domineering leadership tone that seemed more suited to Hamas's *shura*-style institutions.[37] Observing that it was too late for Abu Marzook to pull back the reins of power, one of his colleagues explained, "By then there was a strong current for Mishal. Abu Marzook marginalized himself by marginalizing too many others."

Some of this was raw politics. The group around Mishal was known internally as the Kuwaitis. All were Palestinian, but they had been exiled in Kuwait. A second group, mostly Gazans, coalesced around Abu Marzook.

Analysts had no real sense of the "Kuwaitis" until they started rubbing up against Abu Marzook's "Gazans" in Amman in 1990.[38] A Gazan supporter of Abu Marzook explained: "Yassin was vital for Abu Marzook. The old man had never met Mishal, but Abu Marzook was 'a son of Gaza.'"[39] Asked why Mishal had been selected in Abu Marzook's absence, he replied tartly, "I don't know. There were older people; better people. Mishal just got lucky."

A Mishal loyalist countered, "Khalid Mishal did not spring from a vacuum. Abu Marzook had strong links with the inside organization. But the outside Hamas was driven from Kuwait and Saudi Arabia and in that way, Mishal was a much bigger wheel than Abu Marzook. And as a West Banker, Mishal was able to build strong alliances with the Hamas leadership on the West Bank."[40]

Inevitably there were policy issues as well. In the lead-up to the first Palestinian elections in 1996, Middle East observers were on the edges of their seats, waiting for Hamas to decide if it would effectively endorse the Oslo process by participating in the historic poll. It was a harrowing, divisive debate and, in urging participation, Abu Marzook found himself on the losing side. Subsequently, and despite the decision by the movement to abstain, he had given prison interviews in New York in which he argued against the majority decision to boycott.[41]

Some of the endorsements he received when he was arrested might have appealed to King Hussein, but they left some of Abu Marzook's comrades with a sense that perhaps he was in the wrong movement. Khalil Shikaki, the director of the Palestinian Center for Policy and Survey Research in the West Bank city of Nablus, was quoted as saying, "He is the leader of the most pragmatic wing of Hamas. Without him, it would be difficult for Hamas to make the fundamental move into a political force. Without him, there are a lot of radicals who would take over."[42] In perhaps the cruelest gibe, some in the movement gave Abu Marzook a new nickname: Mr. CIA.

The king's aides believed their plan to co-opt Abu Marzook was working, even if it did lack the monarch's customary subtlety. They reported up the line that Abu Marzook had intimated that he understood the debt he owed and that he believed he could deliver in the name of Hamas. Inside Hamas, however, Abu Marzook's colleagues were deeply suspicious of the amount of time he was spending at the Mukhabarat and in the offices of senior government officials. Believing that it could count on a relationship that was older than Hamas itself, the regime had made clear that it would deal only with Abu Marzook. "Mishal was the leader of the political burea, but he did not have the authority to step between Yassin and Abu Marzook," Ranya Kadri recalled later. "As far as King Hussein was concerned, a channel to Abu Marzook was a channel to Sheikh Yassin. The regime figured, why bother with Mishal when you can get to Yassin through Abu Marzook."[43]

Despite Mishal's injured pride, the organization stood back as the king and his intelligence chief curried favour with Abu Marzook—having the Hamas deputy and his family up to the palace and giving him the king's direct phone line. In reality, Hamas had little choice. When he was challenged, Abu Marzook described his encounters with the regime as "social," but he conceded that face-to-face or by telephone, the conversation with his powerful hosts often was bent to questions of how Hamas might respond to varying sets of circumstances. He did not disclose the details.

An uneasy sense that 1997 was to be a watershed year emerged as early as the month of March. By then the new Israeli prime minister, Benjamin Netanyahu, had become an embarrassment for King Hussein. All too quickly, Netanyahu seemed to have forgotten the support he had received at a critical time from the Jordanian leader. In the lead-up to the Israeli elections in May 1996, Hussein had invited Netanyahu to Amman, knowing well that he was giving the hard-line leader of the Likud Party the opportunity to offer himself to Israeli voters as a more acceptable partner to their closest Arab ally than was Shimon Peres, who had struggled to finish the late Rabin's term as leader of the country. Believing Netanyahu to be a man he could deal with,[44] Hussein had pleaded with other Arab leaders to give the new prime minister a chance.

The sense of betrayal came early for Hussein. A landgrab by Netanyahu for a controversial new Jewish settlement on the outskirts of Jerusalem fueled King Hussein's anger at the same time as it became one of a series of reasons for the collapse of peace talks between Arafat and Netanyahu. Hussein churned, sensing that in the eighteen months since the assassination of his friend Rabin, the peace treaty he had so courageously signed with Israel was being cheapened by neglect. In March 1997, it seemed to be up for grabs when Hussein wrote to Netanyahu, warning of the dangers of his persistent humiliation of the Palestinian people. "I sense [you want] to destroy all I have worked to build between our peoples," he admonished.[45]

Four days after Hussein's letter to Netanyahu, one of the king's soldiers snapped, murdering seven Israeli schoolgirls and wounding six others on a school outing to an island on the Jordan River. A devastated Hussein angered many in the Arab world by going across the river and into the Israeli homes of all seven victims. In each, he dropped to his knees to apologize. He commanded that every one of these family visits be broadcast on Jordanian television and, quietly, he sent a US$1 million check as compensation.[46]

Come the summer, the smell of trouble hung in the air like spent cordite. Netanyahu seemed oblivious. Displaying more of the arrogance that now frightened Hussein, the prime minister took to the airwaves in the last week of July, declaring that an absence of major terror strikes was proof that he could deliver on his election promise of peace *and* security.[47]

Just forty-eight hours later, on July 30, the drumbeat's tempo increased markedly. Twin suicide bombs detonated in Jerusalem's popular Mahane Yehuda produce market, killing 16 Israelis and wounding 178. A keen-eyed American reporter who went to the bloodied scene noticed one of the prime minister's wall stickers, still in place from the previous year's election campaign: "Netanyahu, making a secure peace."[48]

In the aftermath of the twin bombs, Arafat refused to be pushed by Netanyahu's accusations that the Palestinian Authority was failing to deliver on its security undertakings. Defying the prime minister's repeated demands that he crack down on Hamas, Arafat set about stabilizing his own position, which had become increasingly parlous in the eyes of Palestinians. He attended a conference with delegates from the hard-line factions, at which he welcomed the likes of Hamas's Abdel Azziz Al-Rantisi with traditional kisses. In a speech, Arafat kindled memories of the Intifada and warned that Palestinians were prepared to resume their violent revolt against Israel. This filled Netanyahu with horror, but that was exactly what Arafat needed within his domestic constituency.

Just weeks after the twin bombs, the violence ramped up dramatically. In the first week of September, a triple suicide attack on boutiques and cafes along the stone-paved Ben-Yehuda mall in Jerusalem killed 5 and wounded 181 more. Both bombings were the work of Hamas. The statement claiming responsibility for these latest strikes demanded the release from prison of the movement's spiritual leader, Sheikh Ahmad Yassin. "We cannot continue this way," Netanyahu said after visiting survivors in Jerusalem's Shaarei Tzedek Hospital. "When [Arafat] embraces and kisses Hamas, instead of fighting it, the message is that Hamas can strike at Israel with impunity."[49]

A day later, Israelis already fearful of the renewed onslaught were told that twelve elite Israeli commandos had been killed in an ambush deep inside Lebanon, while they were engaged on a mystery nighttime assignment authorized by Netanyahu. As a nation, they had a huge military and technology advantage, and great diplomatic heft in the world. But seemingly these were no shield against lethal bombings at home and a declared need for foreign incursions that could go so disastrously wrong.

In Jerusalem, Netanyahu shuttled almost frenetically between appointments. Emerging from meetings with his military and security chiefs, he did back-to-back media interviews, warning of tough new measures against the Palestinians. But the prime minister also immersed himself in long sessions with advisers, finessing his bid to abandon the step-by-step path to Palestinian statehood drawn up in Oslo in 1993, in favor of a take-it-or-leave-it offer of his own, which he must have known was as unacceptable as it was provocative.

Netanyahu wanted Palestinians to accept just half of the disputed West Bank, along with the continued existence of most of the controversial Israeli settlements. He now believed that the Palestinian Authority should be no more than a quasi-state, like Puerto Rico or Andorra; that it should have neither arms nor an army; and that Israel should retain control of its borders, airspace, and precious water resources. Finally, on the volatile issue of Arab control of Jerusalem, Netanyahu believed Palestinians should be grateful if he permitted a new entity whereby they might be allowed to look after the Muslim holy places in the disputed city.[50]

Palestinians reeled under Netanyahu's punishing response to the Jerusalem bombings. Tens of thousands of laborers were denied access to their jobs in Israel proper; huge tax-revenue transfers to the Palestinian Authority were frozen; and Yasser Arafat seemed to wilt under the impossible burdens of the Oslo process. Back in 1993 he had accepted a deal that effectively made him the guarantor of Israel's security. Now, with the backing of Washington, Netanyahu was demanding that he deliver. At the same time, demands by Arafat's own people for their Oslo dividend drove a destabilizing anticorruption campaign against Arafat and his cronies.

Having gone to the brink after the July bombing, rhetorically at least, Arafat returned to the dictates of the Oslo script after the September attack, arresting dozens of Hamas activists and shuttering sixteen of the movement's relief and educational institutions in Gaza. In Amman, the ailing Ibrahim Ghosheh, Hamas's media spokesman, was thrown into jail for overstepping the regime's redlines after the September 4 attack in Jerusalem. The other members of the political bureau braced for something more to come.

Just as Hamas had never struck outside the borders of historic Palestine, the Israelis had not pursued them beyond Israel and the Occupied Territories. But anxiety about imminent Israeli retaliation surfaced at a gathering of political bureau members on the evening of September 24. Meeting at the Amman home of the jowly Mohammad Nazzal, it was a gut reaction rather than any lucky intelligence break that prompted Sami Khater to raise the subject of Khalid Mishal's personal safety. "You are a target of Mossad, Brother Khalid. Something is about to happen," he ventured. "You must be careful."

Mishal was disturbed by the sense of foreboding in the room and he thought carefully before responding. "Nah," he said finally. "Who in their right mind in Jerusalem would allow Mossad to jeopardize the Jordan Treaty for the sake of taking any of us out?" He closed the debate, assuring them that nothing like that could happen in Amman.

In the days after the triple suicide attack, U.S. secretary of state Madeleine Albright came to the region, and then left empty-handed. Despite the air of impossible gloom, King Hussein again wrote to Netanyahu. Quite out of the blue, the Jordanian leader struck a surprising note of optimism. And he had top-secret information to impart. Hussein informed the Israeli leader that Hamas was prepared to discuss a thirty-year truce, or *hudna*. As this extraordinary letter was prepared for hand delivery to David Silberg at the clandestine Mossad station at the Israeli Embassy in Amman, one of Samih Batikhi's close colleagues noted the chief revealing a rare flash of genuine excitement. Alluding to Mishal and all the others, whom he bundled together as the Hamas hotheads, Batikhi said to those around him, "These guys will be sixty years old by the time this expires—maybe they'll fade away."[51]

There had been *hudna* talk in the past, usually for lesser terms. But never had such a formal offer been delivered, and never with the imprimatur of the king of Jordan. Hussein figured four days—perhaps more—would pass before he would hear back from Netanyahu.

11

"They Used a Bizarre Instrument"

As she dressed for work on a Thursday late in September 1997, Randa Habib's mind was elsewhere. The father of a friend had died and today there would be traditional Arabic condolences—women in the morning and men in the afternoon. As a mark of respect she chose a white blouse and a simple black suit. Habib lived in Rabiyeh, just off Amman's Sixth Circle, and she drove herself to work each day, down into the old quarter, a ten- or fifteen-minute trip depending on the traffic.

Habib was conscious of the time as she arrived at the AFP office, a graceful old building that once had served as a private home on a tight corner on Ibrahim Al-Mouelhi Street, just off the Second Circle. Habib planned to leave for the home of her colleague's grieving family no later than 10:45 AM.

All was quiet. She had passed the reception desk and was pulling the door closed behind her when she heard a phone ring; seconds later, her longtime assistant Rebecca called after her, "Mohammad Nazzal. He says it's urgent."

Habib knew Nazzal well, and she groaned. As a press aide for Hamas he was always calling, taking hours of her time to workshop the resistance group's latest position. The last thing Habib needed right now was to have her ear numbed by Nazzal. But the sixth sense of a reporter kicked in and she took the call at the reception desk.

Nazzal was agitated. Dispensing with the customary long-winded Arabic greeting ritual, he proceeded rapidly, issuing a formal statement on the phone: "I want to inform you that Khalid Mishal was the victim of an assassination attempt."

Habib was stunned. Mishal was the emerging light in the Hamas firmament and an attempt to kill him on Jordanian soil was as good as a declaration of war. Recovering her wits, she quickly asked if Mishal had survived.

"Yes," Nazzal said. "He's here, beside me. They attacked as he entered the building."

"Did someone try to shoot him?" Habib asked, finding it hard to believe even as her mind raced to the story she would write.

"No," said Nazzal.

"Was it an explosion?" demanded Habib, starting to wonder about Nazzal's reticence. What was going on?

"No—they used a bizarre instrument," Nazzal told her. In Arabic, this was a strange choice of words.

Minutes later, when Habib got to accent it in French for the five-line report she dashed off to AFP in Paris, it would sound even more dramatic. But, right now, the reporter demanded of Nazzal, "Put Mishal on the line."

Like the rest of the press pack in Amman, Habib knew Mishal only in passing. On the phone she judged him to be coherent and composed. But at the same time he seemed shaken as he swore two things—his attackers were foreign, he said, and they worked for the Israeli intelligence agency, Mossad.

Habib was still skeptical but she asked Mishal the basic reporter's question: what happened? Mishal tried to explain: "I felt something in my ear, a whispering." He made a hissing sound. "They tried to inject me with this bizarre instrument, but I moved, so it didn't work."

As Habib hung up, she wondered what the story here was and how to write it. If there was a story, what might it say? Khalid Mishal seemed unharmed. His claim that his attackers were from Mossad counted for little because Hamas blamed the Israelis for everything. Neither Mishal nor Nazzal could adequately explain this claim of a "bizarre instrument." And where were the eyewitnesses to this so-called assassination attempt?—apart from Mishal, who seemed to be okay.

Yet she was swayed by their desperation to get the story out to the public and, even more so, by their readiness to agree that if she reported the attack they would drop their usual insistence that Hamas officials not be quoted by name. For now, this strange tale would have to come from their mouths, not Habib's. But if they were right, she had a sensational story.

Habib stood in the AFP reception area pondering the details but instinctively believing the story. She conceded to herself that, as it stood, the story was weak. But ultimately this was what convinced her to run with it: had

Mishal and Nazzal invented it, they would have come up with something less vague and more dramatic. They would have produced a more plausible tale than this mysterious hissing noise in Mishal's ear.

In that snap decision, Habib returned to her desk and hit the keyboard. She filed a first, brief report just after eleven AM local time. Relying again on her instincts, she took the precaution of calling Paris to warn the news desk that a weird story was about to lob. "But go with it," she urged.

AFP subscribers around the world got the flash at 11:14 AM, Amman time, and minutes later Radio Monte Carlo was beaming it across the region. "September 25/Amman: The chief of the political bureau of Hamas, Khalid Mishal, was not hurt in an assassination attempt today, Hamas representative Mohammad Nazzal told AFP in Amman. But Mishal's bodyguard was injured in the attack."

Thirty minutes later, Habib fleshed out some remarkable details in a longer account of the attack: "Nazzal said that two assailants and three accomplices were arrested by Jordanian police. Mishal was attacked at about 10:15 AM as he alighted from a car to enter his office. Nazzal said that two unknown men with foreign features—one bearded, the other wearing glasses—got close to Mishal brandishing what seemed to be an explosive device, which prompted Mishal's bodyguards to intervene. The attackers ran away, but were pursued by the bodyguards while three accomplices waited nearby. Jordanian police intervened and arrested all five. This is the first incident of this kind against a leader of Hamas in Jordan."

In fact, Habib's report marked just the beginning of a spectacular episode in a covert war. Eventually it would involve the governments and intelligence agencies of Israel, the United States, and Canada. Its ripple effects would stretch from the spy programs of Mossad and the deep underworld of illicit killer drugs all the way to the White House of President Bill Clinton.

Thursday started lazily in Amman, because it was the first day of the weekend. It had been ten AM before Mishal set out for his office on Wasfi At-Tall, a busy commercial strip, in the Tlaa Al-Ali district. Abu Maher, his driver, was behind the wheel; Mishal's three small boys—Omar, Walid, and Bilal—were along for the ride. Tailing them, in a second car, was Mohammad Abu Sayf, Mishal's regular bodyguard. Abu Maher was to drop Mishal outside the office and then take the boys on to a local barber to have their hair cut.

Early in the drive, Mishal's wife, Amal, had called his cell phone to warn that, as he left home, she had observed non-Arab strangers in the vicinity of their apartment. As Mishal ended the call, his driver was worried himself about whether a green Hyundai he had picked up in the side mirror was following them. But then it switched lanes, overtook them, and disappeared from view.

Nearing the colonnaded facade of the five-story building in the western suburbs where Mishal had a fourth-floor office suite, the Hamas leader sensed something was up. The green Hyundai had put him on edge. He alighted from the car but instinctively took the longer way, going around the tail end of the vehicle as he made for the broad, covered pavement.

A young man, blond, bearded, and wearing sunglasses, stood about five meters back from the curbside, braced as though ready to pounce. He was dressed in jeans and an open-necked shirt. His right hand was wrapped in what looked like surgical gauze. When Abu Maher stepped out of the car, he wondered if the young man had been injured. As Mishal's foot touched the curb, the blond dropped toward the pavement. One hand was touching the ground for half a second, but the other was poised for action, and he reared up as though to strike the left side of Mishal's head. But his clenched and bandaged fist stopped just short of Mishal's ear.

Several eyewitnesses claimed later that this was when they heard a small explosion. Abu Maher immediately jumped to Mishal's aid, smashing the weight of his body into the blond assailant and dropping him to the pavement.

It happened fast. As Abu Sayf stopped his car at the curb, the attacker and a darker, more solidly built accomplice, who had been lurking behind a column, attempted to flee, but not before Abu Sayf had raced from his car and knocked the darker of the two men to the ground. Oddly, as he got back on his feet, this man hurled a soda can at Abu Sayf before bolting from the scene.[1]

The bodyguard gave chase on foot. Gaining on the two men, he realized the attackers were making for a getaway car. It was about two hundred yards east of the scene of the attack on Mishal, parked outside the Sarawat Restaurant, which was on the edge of a warren of doglegged side streets, through which an escape route could be easily found for a quick break to Medina Munawara Street and the anonymity of its four lanes of heavy traffic. The driver was already gunning the engine.

Abu Sayf had the presence of mind to slow down for as long as it took to scrawl the car's registration-plate number on his hand—5473. He memorized the make and color of the vehicle. But the behavior of his quarry confused him—why did they not look back? Despite the pavement struggle, it seemed they believed they had accomplished their mission and already were clean away. But as the unarmed Abu Sayf catapulted himself down the street after them, he was buoyed by his own deep conviction: "Allah is with me!"

Hearing a car behind him, Abu Sayf turned. His arms flailing dramatically, he stood in the middle of the street, forcing the driver to slam on the brakes. Wrenching open the front passenger-side door, Abu Sayf piled in, yelling at the driver: "There's a problem—the green car! Chase the green car!" Remarkably, the young motorist obliged. He hit the gas, chasing the Hyundai as it careened at speed through the backstreets, zigzagging past the local mosque and on toward Medina Munawara Street.

Suddenly the Hyundai stopped and Mishal's assailants jumped out. The car roared off again as they lunged into the traffic on foot, pausing briefly on the raised median strip before reaching the pavement on the far side. Abu Sayf feared he would lose them as they broke into a steady canter, heading south with the traffic, as though expecting or hoping for a second getaway car to come alongside to whisk them to safety.

Tugging at the door handle, Abu Sayf yelled for his unknown but compliant driver to stop. As he hit the brakes, Abu Sayf leapt from the car. Like a man possessed, he struck out at a diagonal to the road, hurtling over rough, open ground, and then through the traffic, as he sprinted after his quarry. They had a thirty-odd-yard break on him, but over about 220 yards Abu Sayf whittled down their lead, hurling abuse as he ran. "Cowards! Dogs!" he shouted.

Abu Sayf finally closed in on them as all three passed an urban market garden, which fell away steeply on the western side of Medina Munawara Street. Panicking, the assailants veered into the garden. "Like wounded dogs, they didn't have a clue," Abu Sayf exclaimed later. He collared the darker, thickset man as he set off across a footbridge over a small irrigation channel.

Abu Sayf figured both men were unarmed. He noticed that during the brief time they had been in the green Hyundai, the blond man had stripped the bandages from his hand and forearm. As Abu Sayf tried to get a firm grip on his captive's clothing, the blond came at him, smashing his head with a sharp-edged instrument.

The bodyguard reeled. A gaping wound opened in his head and blood streamed into his eyes, blurring his vision. But he clung to his prey, and with a heavy punch to the man's face, Abu Sayf dropped him to the ground screaming.

Now the blond lunged at him again. They rolled down the embankment, coming to rest in about ten inches of muddy water. Scrabbling in the mud,

Abu Sayf clenched a rock in his fist and slammed it into the other man's head. Now both had blood pouring from their wounds.

As all three men staggered to their feet, Abu Sayf registered for the first time that a crowd had gathered. But no one came forward to help. He still had the blond man by the scruff of the neck and, as the accomplice made repeated efforts to land a blow, the bodyguard used the blond man as a shield.

Because it was the day before Friday, Islam's holy day, Abu Sayf was fasting, and this, combined with the loss of blood, soon made him feel groggy. All three stumbled again, and as they hit the dirt, one of the attackers fell across Abu Sayf, pinning him to the ground. The second broke free and was staggering back toward the other prone figures with his arms wrapped around a very big boulder[2] when finally Saad Na'im Khatib, a passerby, intervened.

Khatib, thirty-six years old and an officer in Yasser Arafat's Jordan-based Palestinian Liberation Army, had been in a taxi on the way to visit his father. They had just come through the Waha Circle, the eastern exit of which would have taken him past Mishal's office, and were driving past the Omar Mukhtar School when he noticed the small crowd transfixed by three grown men locked in a filthy brawl in a market garden.

Khatib jumped out even before the taxi had come to a halt. Running toward the wrestlers, he heard Abu Sayf shouting, "They killed Khalid Mishal— they're Mossad!" First, Khatib jumped on the rock bearer, laying him out with a powerful jab from his knee into the man's stomach. Then, with Abu Sayf seeming to have lost consciousness, Khatib grabbed at the clothing of the other man, who had Abu Sayf pinned to the dirt. He pulled the man to his feet and was twisting his forearm high behind his back when he noticed his captive's accomplice crawling away on his hands and knees.

Now his own PLA training in killing and ambush techniques kicked in. Khatib thought he knew enough about Mossad teams—they did not act alone, and there was a good chance that Israeli observers or backup men were in the crowd. Hearing a foreign voice calling, "Wait for the police," he feared someone was trying to buy time for the attackers by having the rest of the crowd stay back. Thoughtfully, the cabdriver had waited, keeping the meter running.

Now Khatib bundled all three men into the vehicle—Abu Sayf, drowsy and bleeding in the passenger seat; the two foreigners squeezed in with him on the backseat. Khatib asked the driver to head for the nearest police station, which was at Shmeisani, near where Mishal lived.

But once they cleared the area, he started to worry that if other Mossad agents were in the crowd as it pressed around the departing taxi, his instruction to the driver might have been overheard. So he set them on a new course, heading southwest and away from the city center toward Wadi Al-Seer, where a big police compound huddled beneath a concrete freeway overpass on the Ninth Circle.

It was an uncomfortable ride. Abu Sayf sat up front, hurling abuse over his shoulder at the would-be killers. "Bastards! Dogs!" the bodyguard angrily growled, over and over. Finally, in a fury, the two captives resorted to their own name-calling, and then pleaded with Khatib in heavily accented English to silence Abu Sayf. Khatib pretended he did not understand English, but all the while he was eavesdropping on an argument between the two men in the backseat about whether or not to announce that they were innocent Canadian tourists who had been set upon by the bully in the front seat.

At Wadi Al-Seer, Saad Khatib called for an ambulance to take Abu Sayf to the hospital and suggested that armed guards accompany him. But his hackles rose when two foreigners suddenly materialized, one with a video camera, and demanded access to the police station on the grounds that they were journalists.

Had they been followed? "They've got to be Mossad," he warned the guards on the gate to the compound. "How could any journalists know yet that these guys are here?"

With Abu Sayf dispatched to the hospital, Khatib's role in the drama was now elevated to the extent that, instead of merely being allowed to watch, he was able to participate as a PLA officer in the subsequent processing and body search of the two foreigners. When a police lieutenant arrived on the scene, Khatib became his right-hand man. Khatib took a blocking position in front of the captive who had a small bag strapped firmly around his waist, and when the man asked if he could go to the bathroom, Khatib shouted, "Don't let him! He wants to get rid of something."

In an extraordinary breach of accepted police protocols, the police lieutenant raised no objection when Khatib proceeded to search the two prisoners himself. One of the local police officers, responding sympathetically to the assailants' claim to be Canadian tourists who had been set upon, tried to insist that Khatib and the other police stop handling the captives so roughly. But Khatib, guessing that Samih Batikhi's men would soon arrive, admonished the police upstart, "It's not your call—the Mukhabarat will be here soon." When he discovered a Canadian passport in each man's pocket, Khatib extracted these and decided to slip them into his own.

Apart from the fact that the two assailants had used a boulder to smash the head of a local claiming to be the bodyguard of Khalid Mishal, two other aspects of the situation were more than passing strange. Both captives had their elbow and knee joints firmly bandaged, as a prize fighter might as he entered the ring. And the bag that one of them wore around his waist contained a strange camera-like item.

This seemed to be the object seen in the blond's bandaged hand as he had jumped at Khalid Mishal earlier in the morning. Dark metallic gray in color, it was about the size of a cigarette packet. At first glance, it had the look of a camera. But later, a policeman who had been present at the search pointed out that it had neither a viewfinder nor any of the other features typically found on a camera. Instead of a lens, there was an odd-shaped protrusion from the middle of one of its flat surfaces. It was seized by the police lieutenant, presumably as evidence, while the pair themselves were hauled off to holding cells.

Back at the scene of the attack on Garden Street, Abu Maher had called a friend to take Mishal's distressed children to their mother before he took the Hamas chief into hiding. The first that his Hamas colleague Mohammad Nazzal heard of the attack was when a runner rushed into his office, announcing that there had been an assassination attempt. "Brother Khalid is waiting near your house—he wants you there now," the messenger told him breathlessly. The lugubrious Nazzal was as deliberate in his movement as in his speech, but hurrying as best he could, he made his way home. Here he found Mishal hiding nearby in a parked car. "Brother Khalid came to my place because he was afraid a Mossad backup team would go to his own house," he later explained.

But Nazzal was skeptical about Mishal's claim that his attackers were Israeli. As the seemingly healthy Mishal burbled out his story, Nazzal raised questions. "Maybe someone just wants to frighten you? They'd use a pistol if they were going to kill you. . . . How can you be sure it was Mossad?"

At this early stage the only evidence of Mossad's involvement was Mishal's gut feeling. He insisted his attackers were foreign and "looked Jewish." Nazzal pushed him: "Well, if you're sure, then we have to get this story out—tell the media!"

But Mishal hesitated. Hoping other members of the Hamas political bureau would arrive, he wanted to canvass tactics more widely before embarking on Nazzal's strategy. There was no certainty about how the Jordanian regime would respond to a full-frontal accusation by Hamas against Israel.

"You don't have time," Nazzal pushed him. "Delay now and we'll lose this battle."

"What do you want to do?" Mishal asked.

Nazzal responded, "I'll call Randa Habib."

Habib's experience with the authorities in Amman shaped the way she dealt with news reports. She preferred to report sequentially. It was a practice that suited the around-the-clock demands of a wire service like AFP for the piece-meal telling of a developing story. But more important, Habib used it as a device to deny the local authorities an opportunity to discredit or dismiss her reports before they went out. She would make sure her words were on the air and on the wires in Arabic, French, and English before contacting Jordanian officials.

On the Mishal story, she thought to herself, "I don't need confirmation from Jordan for a first report that a man says someone tried to kill him." But she definitely needed a response because, in effect, Mishal was accusing Israel of shredding the letter and spirit of the historic peace treaty it had signed with Jordan in 1994. She needed an official explanation, and she needed a whole lot more information on who was trying to kill whom in the streets of quiet little Amman.

She worked the phones. Officials at the Information Ministry knew nothing. And the reaction when she called Samih Batikhi, the powerful, all-knowing chief of the GID, convinced her that he too knew nothing, apart from per-haps having heard her report on Radio Monte Carlo. Batikhi was at his desk and, she thought, eager to take her call. Pouring out the little she knew, Habib decided he was genuinely surprised. He seemed anxious to get her off the line. "I'll call you back," he said. Among the many calls that Batikhi made next was one to Mousa Abu Marzook, ordering him to rein in Mohammad Nazzal, who, he claimed, was spouting lies and nonsense to Randa Habib.

Batikhi paused to take an incoming call from General Nasouh Muheiddin, the director of public security in Amman. Muheiddin thought Batikhi needed to hear about reports of strange goings-on in the Tlaa Al-Ali district of the capital. But none of what the general said made sense to Batikhi: "Khalid Mishal was taking his kids somewhere . . . two foreigners approached; he felt something on his neck . . . yelling and screaming in the street and then a fight . . . claims of Mossad being involved. Hamas guards gave chase. One of the attackers seemed to be heading for the Israeli Embassy."

Batikhi locked on to three elements of what Muheiddin had told him: the presence of foreign tourists, the hand of Mossad, and a man bolting for the Israeli Embassy. Heaving a sigh, he added a fourth: Hamas.

"A misunderstanding," he decided. But he instructed the director of public security to isolate the prisoners: "We'll need to get to the bottom of it," he said. "If they're tourists, then there'll be consular procedures."

Try as he might, Batikhi could not ignore the Israeli dimension to the problem now before him. He hated Hamas, and any involvement by the resistance movement had to be treated with caution. But however he looked at it, this still was surely just a street brawl. Given any chance, Hamas would blow it out of all proportion. The starting point for the Islamists, always, was that the CIA or Mossad was the guilty party. Batikhi needed facts.

In a short time, facts started to dribble in. Muheiddin was back on the line. "They're Canadian," he reported.

This was not exactly what Batikhi had expected, but his off-the-cuff analysis still pulled away from, rather than toward, a crisis. "But we don't have a record of Canadians being bad guys," he replied.

Five minutes later, Batikhi was at his dismissive best when he got back to Habib. "Randa, come on! You know Hamas . . . there was no assassination attempt. It was just a simple row between two Canadians and a Jordanian companion." As if to prove the story had no legs, he told her, "Mishal wasn't even at the scene of the fight."

But inadvertently, Batikhi was confirming Nazzal's claim that this story did have two locations. And by revealing the foreigners as Canadian, Batikhi had opened a new line of inquiry for the reporter, who promptly pounced. Surely the embassy would be informed? After being stonewalled all morning, now she had the excitement of a fresh lead to pursue.

As the GID machine kicked into life, Batikhi ordinarily might have sent the tourists' names to the liaison officer at the Canadian Embassy, but he decided not to do so. Batikhi's agency was doing what it was supposed to do and attempting to do so in its customary below-the-radar fashion, but Hamas was not making it easy. Mishal was well known to Batikhi, and now he and his sidekick, Mohammad Nazzal, were making so much media noise that the one person Samih Batikhi did not call, quite deliberately, was Khalid Mishal.

The whole story, Batikhi thought, was exaggerated nonsense. No weapons had been found; there was not even a hint of someone wielding a gun. When the next report to reach his desk included a wild claim about some kind of chemical spray, his eyes rolled in disbelief. Since the signing of the 1994 peace treaty between Jordan and Israel, and even long before that, the GID had a good working relationship with Mossad. Batikhi thought of Mossad director

Danny Yatom as a genuine partner in the fight against terrorism. Channels already existed for Yatom to roll into the GID's hilltop complex in Amman to make his case if he saw a need for Mishal's leash to be tightened. The Jordanians would, in all probability, have gone along with that. Mossad was well briefed on King Hussein's firm belief that it made sense to have the outside leadership of Hamas pinned down in Amman, where Batikhi and his men could watch them.

The election in the previous year of the hard-liner Benjamin Netanyahu as prime minister of Israel had cast a pall over Arab observers and the participants in the Middle East peace process, but Hussein was still appealing to all sides to give the voluble Netanyahu a chance—and the Israelis knew that too. Netanyahu had been badly received in the region. He had taken to abusing Hussein's trust, but the king and the GID had been reluctant to rush to judgment so far. The Amman regime was against anything that was anti-Israeli, and that included the lunatic fringe in Hamas. Still weighing fantasy and reality, Batikhi told one of his officers, "I don't believe that Mossad would be so stupid, so irrational to try something like this. . . . And why would they try it in Jordan?"

But if Batikhi thought he could keep a lid on things, Randa Habib, at AFP on the other side of town, was steadily prising the story open. At 1:23 PM, Habib filed an update. She was reluctant to make it a denial, but she gave prominence to Batikhi's withering comments. In the meantime she had been back to Nazzal, who was at his home with Mishal. They were standing by their story. Venturing into treacherous territory by daring to contradict the head of intelligence, Nazzal now told her, "Indeed there was an assassination attempt. This was no tourists' row."

When she tried to call other government officials, Habib quickly realized the regime was now in crisis mode. No one was available, and a staffer at the office of one senior official told her in an unguarded moment, "He's at an urgent meeting with the king." All Habib's alarm bells started to ring at once.

Batikhi had received another report. In a preliminary interrogation, the Canadian detainees claimed they were staying at the Intercontinental Hotel. They had been sightseeing, they said, when they were set upon by an aggressive local. But Muheiddin added that, for a couple of "innocents," they seemed quite terrified about the circumstances in which they found themselves.

Batikhi's mind went back to the geography at the scene of the fracas. The fight had taken place perhaps a mile from the Israeli Embassy, and several of the updates in the last half hour confirmed the earlier claim by Nazzal that one or two likely accomplices had headed in that direction. Was it a coincidence?

Then more firm detail filtered in from eyewitnesses. Two other men had definitely run away from the fight. They were seen jumping into a taxi that continued toward the embassy. As a professional, Batikhi still had difficulty coming to terms with it all, but the idea of two men bolting for the Israeli mission started to outweigh Hamas's lack of credibility. Then Batikhi did two things: he decided not to rule Mossad out of this game, and he put a call through to King Hussein.

"*Sayyidna,*" he began, using the Arabic term by which those in the inner circle addressed the king of Jordan. It translated as "Our lord." Batikhi gave the king a brief account of the facts, stressing that the investigation had been under way for less than an hour and that many questions remained unanswered. The two key elements for the king's ears were that Hamas was involved, and Mossad might be involved too. "We can't say Mossad because we don't know, but we're checking," Batikhi told Hussein. The king listened quietly before ending the call, saying, "I'll need to hear back from you."

About an hour after realizing the regime was in lockdown, Randa Habib reported a new development over the AFP wire: "Nazzal said that Mishal's wounded bodyguard was being treated at King Hussein Medical City."

Then she had reason to pause. Under siege from reporters racing to catch up with her first spectacular news flash, the government news agency, Petra, had issued a statement in the name of the information minister, Samir Mutawi. He lashed out at Habib. "The AFP story is totally false," he charged. "The Canadians were shopping when they were provoked by Mishal's driver. This degenerated into a row—both sides were throwing stones at each other. A police search found no weapon in the Canadians' car—just a wallet."

Stone throwing? Foreign tourists shopping in humdrum Tlaa Al-Ali? None of it made sense. Soon enough the minister was on the phone to Habib, calling personally to trash her and her professionalism. "How can you do this?" he admonished her. "Why do you believe Hamas when Mishal's driver was harassing these tourists?"

The damning subtext to the minister's rant was not lost on Habib. His first jab was that the driver of Mishal's car was a mere Palestinian West Banker, not a solid East Bank Jordanian. His counterpunch was to use an unsavory, colloquial term reserved by Arab women to describe an unwelcome male advance—*tharkash*—to characterize the driver's harassment of the "unfortunate Canadians." The minister's unambiguous inference was that the driver had made an unseemly approach to a couple of reluctant, innocent foreigners who were good enough to spend their foreign currency in Amman.

Just as Habib was inclined to believe the men from Hamas because their story lacked imagination, she concluded that the minister's denial was overly imaginative. But her editors in Paris had a brief bout of the wobbles. When one called to test how solid she was, Habib stood her ground, telling the Frenchman, "Don't dismiss what Khalid Mishal said."

Jordanian police checked car rental agencies. But when none reported renting a car to Canadians, what was seen as a Hamas fantasy took a small step toward reality. All foreign embassies had official diplomatic plates. The recently arrived Israeli ambassador, Oded Eran, had his own special bulletproof vehicle, but Batikhi knew there was one group of foreigners in Amman who were permitted to use green-plated rental cars as a security cover—the secret Mossad unit at the Israeli Embassy.

When King Hussein next called, Batikhi could hear the worry in his voice. He informed Batikhi that a phone call had just come directly to the palace from the prime minister of Israel, Benjamin "Bibi" Netanyahu. "He's sending Danny Yatom to see us on an urgent matter," the king said.

When Hussein had asked Netanyahu the reason for this hasty, even mysterious visit by the director of Mossad, the prime minister had revealed scant detail, saying only that it could have bearing on the peace process.[3] The king momentarily wondered if this was a first, informal response to his letter three days before, advising Netanyahu that there was a secret proposal on the table from Hamas for a *hudna*.[4] But Batikhi needed no time to leap to the seemingly obvious conclusion: "So they did it!"

Hussein agreed to receive the Mossad chief at Bab Al-Salam, his less-formal family home on the northern outskirts of the city. He wanted Batikhi to be present. The Jordanians sensed this would be a difficult encounter. While an aide canceled all his appointments indefinitely, Batikhi called General Muheiddin and barked orders down the line. "The 'Canadians' are Israeli agents—isolate them," he said. "Don't even tell your assistant where you've put them! And seize the embassy!"

An order to seize the Israeli Embassy was unprecedented. Ordinarily, a small number of Jordanian guards were posted on the perimeter of what was the most sensitive foreign mission in the Jordanian capital, whose bland exterior had the appearance of a European-style suburban villa topped by a tower with the look of a pigeon loft. Ordinarily, the crews in two Jordanian armored personnel carriers were required to keep a constant wary eye out for external threats to this vulnerable diplomatic mission. Now all that was reversed. In a flash, those high-caliber machine guns were pointing at the embassy. Guests of the Jordanian regime, Israel's entire diplomatic staff in Amman had suddenly become a security threat.

Majali Whbee, a senior Israeli civil servant who chanced to be in Amman on government business, needed to get to the embassy. But he came away much affronted by the Jordanian military rollout. He had just left a meeting with King Hussein in which there had been no hint of a new chill in relations that might warrant such an insult. "The guards said I was crazy trying to go in," he said later, recalling a cordon of dozens of soldiers around the Israeli building.[5] Military backup units and Mukhabarat teams descended. Their orders were that no one was to enter or leave.

For the first time since the Israeli mission opened in 1994, Jordanian eyes and weapons were directed into, not away from, the compound. As part of the Oslo process, several of the smaller Arab states had agreed to limited Israeli representation, but the diplomatic mission in Amman was one of just two fully fledged Israeli embassies in the Arab world (the other in Cairo), and it was a hugely significant geopolitical dart on any map of the region. Suddenly, it was locked down. Even worse, it was the normally mild-mannered King Hussein who was giving the orders and saying of those pinned down inside: "They're not going anywhere."[6]

An adrenaline surge enveloped Batikhi's spacious, dimly lit office. A wall of obfuscation was quickly thrown up to push back the army of reporters now laying siege by telephone—including the leader of the pack, Randa Habib. The curbside punch-up was developing into an international crisis. How it was handled could very well decide the fate of the Jordanian monarchy.

Batikhi had only the most basic grasp of what had happened and he was not yet ready—certainly not publicly—to point a finger at Mossad, because he still did not know how all sides would emerge from this, and on what terms. By inclination, agencies like the GID—and the CIA or the KGB, for that matter—lived by a siege mentality. It was the nature of the beast. Veteran intelligence officials might puff up their chests, claiming they awoke each morning ready for a crisis like this, but in his gut Batikhi knew Jordan had never faced anything quite like the story now engulfing Amman.

Racing down from his second-floor office, Batikhi jumped into a car for the dash to Bab Al-Salam, which was set in a royal enclave on a shoulder of the Jordan Valley, just north of the capital. The airy new palace looked out toward the old cities of Salt and Jerash. Queen Noor had designed it around a huge mosaic-adorned fireplace and hanging space for portraits of the Hashemite dynasty, right back to the days when Hussein's forefathers ruled ancient Mecca. A sunken rock garden, fragrant with orange blossoms and jasmine, served as a private open-air extension to the king's study and his magnificent library. The Syrian-American Noor also gave herself a treat in the gardens, with lots of palms and bougainvillea to remind her of childhood days in Santa Monica, California. Ironically, the name Bab Al-Salam was taken from one of the grand entrances to the Great Mosque in Mecca. It means "Gate of Peace," but that did nothing to quell the volcanic anger rising in Batikhi as his chauffeured car hurtled through the squat and square suburbs of the capital.

At this very moment, the thermal activity over the Jordan Valley was bumping a light aircraft that had just cleared Israeli airspace as it flew eastward toward Amman. Its sole passenger was the hapless head of Mossad, Danny Yatom.

On the ground below him, there was always a sharp contrast between the Israeli security paranoia on the west side of the lazy Jordan River, and a more workaday attitude on the Jordanian side. But, in the immediate aftermath of the attack on Mishal, the Jordanian border guards had become much more rigorous. It was ironic that the mastermind of the bungled assassination attempt would get the red-carpet treatment when his aircraft put down on a secured military airstrip in Amman, because he came as an official guest of King Hussein. Meanwhile, his fellow Israelis going in either direction through the border post were subjected to the most intense scrutiny in years, lest they were somehow involved in the Israeli plot.

Yatom could not relax. He could be in no doubt about the kind of reception that awaited him at Bab Al-Salam. Just a week earlier, he had been in Jordan for a holiday with his family at Aqaba on the Red Sea. King Hussein had entertained him at his summer palace by the beach, and he had taken time during the last days of his break to drop in on his GID colleagues up in Amman. He had been hospitably received for chummy chats on the routine matters then cluttering their joint intelligence radar. But Yatom had revealed to them none of what he was planning for Amman.

12

Mishal Must Not Die

Khalid Mishal's mother, Fatima, was pottering at her hillside home on the western outskirts of Amman when a friend called to tell her about Randa Habib's latest AFP report. The mother quickly called her daughter-in-law, Amal, who assured her that Mishal was fine. She suggested that her in-laws, now in their seventies, come to their home and await his return from Mohammad Nazzal's house.

But by the time a taxi was organized to deliver the older couple to the apartment block in Shmeisani, Khalid Mishal's health would take a turn for the worse.

At Nazzal's house, the Hamas gang had been debating how best to manage a crisis that they assessed as a win-win for their side. Despite all of the panic of the morning, Mishal seemed in good health and the Jordanian authorities had two prisoners whom they confidently expected would be revealed as Israelis. Over lunch, Mishal enthralled them all as he attempted to explain the impact of what he now described as an electrical device: "There was a ringing in my left ear and something like an electric shock or a shivering sensation went through my body." Then he recounted his sense of a surreal, momentary connection with the blond attacker. "We looked into each other. I could sense panic, maybe because the plan needed him to get in close to me," he told his riveted listeners.

But then, quite suddenly, Mishal felt overcome by tiredness. Distractedly, he asked Nazzal if he could use the bathroom. He could feel a severe headache developing and he had an urge to vomit. For someone who had been so quick to phone Randa Habib earlier in the day, Nazzal now was slow to realize what was happening. At first he suspected Mishal was suffering from something they had eaten. He thought briefly about the curative effect of a glass of lemonade. Only then did he make his second, very sensible call of the day. "Brother Khalid, you're going to hospital," Nazzal declared.

Brother Sami Khater, relatively unknown as a member of the political bureau, was quickly delegated to drive Mishal to the Islamic Hospital. It was a logical choice. The hospital was a sophisticated medical facility situated in central Abdali. But for men who lived under their own siege mentality, it represented a special safe haven—the Islamic Hospital was owned, operated, and staffed by the Muslim Brotherhood.

Still, as seeming fantasy morphed to reality before their eyes, they all moved at a slow pace in these first moments. It was agreed that Abu Marzook would remain on standby at his own office near the Amra Hotel, to deal with the regime and any questions that might arise from the morning's events, and that Nazzal would return to his office, where the media army, previously camped at the Information Ministry, was now clamouring for his ear.

As Sami Khater bundled him out of his car and into the Islamic Hospital's admissions section, Mishal was still conscious. But soon he started fading in and out, suffering from what he giddily suspected was the influence of a powerful tranquilizer. Though his brain scrabbled for detail, he assumed the vomiting was somehow caused by a surreptitious injection that had been administered to him during the weird encounter outside his office. Mishal was gathered into the arms of the doctors as he began losing consciousness entirely.

Protocol required that all who were to see King Hussein should assemble before he entered the meeting. Samih Batikhi was at Bab Al-Salam first. When the heavily perspiring Danny Yatom arrived from Israel, he was escorted into Batikhi's presence by the director of the king's private office, the bluff General Ali Shukri. They gathered in the grand sitting room, and as Yatom took his place next to Batikhi on one of three couches, the Mukhabarat boss studied the troubled features of his Mossad counterpart. The color had drained from his face; he seemed discomfited.

With Yatom cornered on the same sofa, Batikhi pounced from close quarters: "I hope you are not here because of what happened in Amman this morning?"

The Israeli said nothing. Batikhi took his pained grimace as confirmation. This was going to be explosive.

King Hussein entered and had barely lowered himself into an armchair before Yatom's mouth opened. "We did it. He'll die in twenty-four hours. We sprayed him with a chemical. There's nothing you can do about it," he blurted out.

The king had a reputation as a master of diplomacy. He would often remain silent to mask anger; he would smile to conceal hurt; by saying little, he could convey a lot. Batikhi and Shukri watched him now, trying to contain their own shock as the king resorted to a customary clenching of his jaw—but with a ferocity neither of these senior officials had witnessed previously in their years of service at the palace.

Hussein's eyes slowly scanned the room, taking in each man in turn as he asked himself a thousand questions. But just one was etched on his face: "What have they done?"

Hussein had a way of directing a gathering with imperceptible nods and gestures that his staff well understood, but which were lost on outsiders. General Shukri was the silent note taker, and it was to the highly emotional and volatile Batikhi that his highness signaled to open the verbal assault.

Batikhi started shouting at the head of Mossad. "Tomorrow? He'll die tomorrow morning? His funeral will be Friday prayers? All of Jordan will be at that funeral! I'm telling you, if he dies, you can say good-bye to the peace treaty! Danny, he can't die. . . . You are jeopardizing everything!"

Everything! Quite literally. The regime had gone out on a limb to sign the treaty with Israel—a vital element in a tortured search for peace in the region. The pact bound the two countries to bilateral security based on mutual confidence, promotion of common interests, and cooperation. Both undertook to abstain from any threat or the use of force. Each undertook never to resort to terrorism.

Hamas had been designated a terrorist organization by the White House because of the movement's disruption of the peace process. Yet just three days before, King Hussein had personally conveyed a message to Prime Minister Netanyahu saying that Hamas was prepared to discuss a halt to attacks on Israel in the context of a thirty-year truce. Now Israel, the American ally that had urged Washington to lock Hamas out in the cold because of its reliance on terror as a weapon, was admitting it had engaged in its own state-sanctioned terrorism against Hamas—but on the home turf of another loyal U.S. ally, Jordan. It was inconceivable.

Most Jordanians were highly suspicious of their king's closeness to the authorities in Jerusalem, *his* holy city from which they had been barred since the

Arab debacle of 1967. King Hussein was a fervent believer in a negotiated Palestinian-Israeli peace, but now, in one reckless stunt, Jerusalem had given every Jordanian good reason to trust neither the Israelis nor those—such as their own king—who promoted them as capable partners in peace. Worse, with Jordan's parliamentary elections just six weeks away, the death of Mishal would be an electoral bonanza for Islamist candidates. These bunglers from Mossad really had built a fire.

Batikhi could imagine how it all would unfold. Huge prayer crowds on Friday would be enlisted as Mishal's mourners. Their anger would spark a blaze. Religious fervor and raw nationalism were an incendiary mix; no one would believe that the king and the Mukhabarat did not have a hand in Mishal's assassination.

The masses would see the regime in cahoots with the Israelis against Hamas, the unbowed new voice of Palestinian rights that had emerged after decades of failure by others to advance the Palestinian cause. That failure was blamed on a regional cast that included no less a figure than King Hussein himself. And then there were the other Arab leaders, corrupt and fickle, who used and abused the Palestinians' plight for their own intrigues, to say nothing of the erratic PLO and its mythic Yasser Arafat, who had promised so much and delivered so little.

The conspiracy theorists would insist that Israel would not have dared act like this in Amman without at least a nod from the regime and some tacit cooperation from its agencies. How else could a Mossad team get into the place so easily? How did they bring in the poison?

All Batikhi could see was a nightmare. Hussein now had to save the life of Khalid Mishal to save his own neck. The king would never be able to clear himself in the eyes of his own people if the resistance leader did not survive. Right now, Hamas heavies like Abu Marzook and Mohammad Nazzal would be at the Islamic Hospital, plotting at the dying Mishal's bedside. Muslim Brotherhood activists would be working a growing crowd of confused and angry supporters in the hospital corridors, rounding them up to bring oil and kindling for Mossad's Bonfire of the Hashemites.

Yatom was cold-bloodedly emphatic about the irreversible nature of Mishal's fate. He told the small gathering, "He's been poisoned and all his bodily functions will deteriorate. There'll be no apparent cause of death. It's done. He was hit and he'll die in the morning. We'd better deal with the consequences."

Batikhi was certainly thinking of the consequences himself, particularly

Hamas's already published claim that Mishal's attackers were from Mossad. "All of Jordan will know that you killed him!" he expostulated.

Yatom volunteered no remedy. Death was inevitable, he said. They might as well chalk it up as another success in Israel's systematic campaign of targeted assassinations against key Palestinian leaders.

Batikhi would have none of this: "Danny, he's not allowed to die! There must be an antidote—you have to give it to us."

Hussein at first said little, but then he too spelled out the dire risk to the treaty and, therefore, to Israel and Netanyahu. He could see that Yatom well understood that by bungling their mission and being captured, the Israelis had given Jordan the upper hand. Now the message Yatom needed to take back across the river was that Netanyahu was about to take a beating. King Hussein succinctly warned the man from Mossad, "I'll have to act."

Once Yatom had revealed the imminence of Mishal's death, the king and his security chief were desperate to save the Hamas leader. They hammered the Israeli for a treatment—any treatment—for the dying man. Finally Yatom seemed to relent. But he would have to consult Netanyahu first, he said. Could he use a secure phone, please? One of them escorted him to another room, where he would have privacy.

He rejoined them within minutes. "One of our team at the Intercontinental Hotel has the antidote," he announced. They were thrown when he added the extraordinary postscript: "She's a doctor."

Further discussion was pointless. The Jordanians dismissed Yatom when he asked for the king's permission to collect the four agents corralled at the Israeli Embassy so they could be taken home with him. "Nobody leaves," Batikhi yelled.[1]

King Hussein's own political survival depended on keeping Mishal alive, and that was the end to which he directed his men. The king's confidante Shukri was assigned to liaise with the shattered Yatom and the Israeli Embassy to fetch the cure from the hotel and deliver it to the doctors now treating Mishal.

From the palace, Shukri and Yatom left in pursuit of the antidote as the king and his intelligence chief set about working up a strategy to handle the crisis. Conscious of the chaos engulfing them and certain of even greater tumult ahead, the only way they saw to safely negotiate their way out of the maelstrom was first to bring down a shroud of silence.

Apart from Hussein, Batikhi, and Shukri, only one other Jordanian would be brought into the loop. That was to be the scholarly Crown Prince Hassan, the king's brother and long-serving counselor. Ministers might be wheeled out from time to time, such as the information minister who had attacked Randa Habib's first news report. But for now not even the prime minister was to be told what this uproar was about.

Now Batikhi had to bring the doctors up to speed. But which doctors? There was a major security problem in Mishal being admitted to the Islamic Hospital, where all the doctors and nurses were dues-paying members of the Muslim Brotherhood. There was no way they would be persuaded to use an antidote or anything else supplied by the Israelis, to treat one of their own whom the Israelis had tried to kill that very morning. They could also be relied on to be contemptuous of the regime's demands for secrecy.

Batikhi concluded that, if they were to snatch Mishal back from death's door, they first had to get him out of the clutches of the Islamists and into the care of more trustworthy doctors at the regime's principal military hospital— a complex called King Hussein Medical City. Here there were military professionals who knew not to ask questions. They knew not to talk when the regime called for silence, and they would obey orders.

Batikhi understood it would take artful negotiations to get Hamas to agree to move Mishal. A sneaky early effort by the GID chief to force the issue failed. A paramedical team he dispatched with orders to effect what might have appeared to be a "routine" transfer was confronted by an Islamist flying wedge, which denied the team access to Mishal's room. One of the Hamas activists made a frantic call to Abu Marzook. "They're trying to steal Brother Khalid from the hospital!" he warned.[2]

Batikhi had other urgent calls to make. He found the director of the CIA, George Tenet, lazing on a Delaware beach. Tenet's family outing was interrupted by a member of his security detail whom he saw racing toward him, across the sand, brandishing a phone. There was an urgent call from Jordan.[3]

The CIA chief recognized the voice. It was Batikhi, telling him that America's friends, the Israelis, were the bad guys in a grave new crisis. The Jordanian told Tenet the call was still precautionary. He could not predict how events would unfold, but he had a hunch that Amman would need Washington's help before this crisis blew over. Tenet needed to be on standby.

At the Canadian Embassy in Amman, there was complete confusion. Staff were on the case as soon as a local employee drew attention to radio reports that two Canadians were cooling their heels at Amman's central lockup. The radio was reporting two separate incidents, and the detention of their nationals had not been linked publicly to the attack on Mishal. But nobody in Amman would talk to them—not the Interior Ministry, not the Foreign Ministry. Even the Americans were playing dumb.

Ottawa had its embassy staff under ferocious pressure to provide information. The media back home were going berserk with a wild story of two Canadians acting as Israeli hitmen. The opposition hammered the government, demanding to know if the passports were real—and had Canada provided them to Mossad? Arab embassies in Ottawa needed to be reassured that Canada was not in the business of trying to whack Palestinian leaders on behalf of Israel.

A woman consular staffer in Amman was rapidly dispatched to investigate. At the Wadi Al-Seer cellblock she found that the detainees, one of whom was barechested, were bashed and bruised. Her cursory examination of their passports compounded Ottawa's problem, because she concluded they were genuine and, therefore, that these men indeed were Canadian. But, oddly, they rejected her offer of consular assistance and pleaded that their names not be published.

When a Jordanian guard explained to her that one of prisoners was in a state of half-undress because his shirt had been ripped from him in the street fight, the diplomat sympathetically dashed to her home to fetch one of her husband's shirts for him.

The two men had been through the mill with Abu Sayf, Mishal's bodyguard, and later they would complain that they had been knocked about in detention, but the prisoners still refused to answer questions. Now, reportedly with video cameras rolling, they were being put through the mill again by Jordanian interrogators, whose response to their silence now included a threat to publish their photographs, ending whatever might be left of their covert careers. Despite Danny Yatom's frank admission of guilt, King Hussein wanted full confessions from the agents on the ground.

After squaring away George Tenet in the United States, Batikhi headed back to his office to see Abu Marzook, hoping to persuade him to agree to Mishal being transferred to another hospital. As the route took Batikhi near the lockup, he decided to take a look at the two prisoners himself. When they gave him their half-baked cover story, Batikhi took some satisfaction in revealing that he knew exactly who they were—and even more so, that he had just come from a meeting with their boss, the director of Mossad.

The GID chief was so pumped up that he had not even noticed the presence of the Canadian woman diplomat, who by now had returned with a shirt for one of the prisoners. The reaction to her return was dramatic. "Your interview is over," she was told abruptly before being escorted off the premises.

Batikhi's office was on the second floor of the GID building. Wood paneled and with the window curtains always drawn, it had a sofa and a large armchair set in a corner. This was where he confronted Abu Marzook.[4]

Despite the tension in the GID-Hamas relationship, Batikhi had put much store by the usefulness of Mousa Abu Marzook. Unlike the dying Khalid Mishal, he trusted the Hamas deputy and believed he could be made to deliver. "The only way to save his life is to get him to the military hospital. If you want to save him, you'll have to cooperate," Batikhi said.

But Abu Marzook hedged. Deferring to the collective Hamas leadership, he told Batikhi it was not his decision to make. "The others are back at the hospital. They'll have to be convinced," he said. Batikhi was grateful that at least Abu Marzook seemed receptive.

Abu Marzook left, but within minutes he phoned back. "No," he said. It was not hard to translate his one-word response: the Islamists did not trust the king's military hospital.

Batikhi yelled, trying to convey the seriousness of the situation, but Abu Marzook was unmoved.

Then Shukri called in by phone. He had been on the phone with Dr. Yousef Qussos, the director of the Royal Medical Service, and there was a new sense of urgency as he briefed Batikhi. Specialists at the KHMC's Queen Alia Heart Institute had warned Shukri that every minute lost before administering an antidote lessened Mishal's chance of survival.

When they arrived at their son's address in Shmeisani, Khalid Mishal's parents were shocked to find his apartment crawling with men from the Mukhabarat. The whole building was surrounded by police. They were doubly shocked because, while they well understood that their son was deeply committed to the Palestinian struggle, they did not know that he worked for the hard-line Hamas or that his activities could warrant such an incredible operation by Mossad.

At about four PM, one of their nephews arrived, telling them he had instructions to ferry them to the Islamic Hospital.

In a report filed at 4:09 PM, Randa Habib quoted a formal statement issued by Mohammad Nazzal, in which he firmed up Hamas's claim that the attackers were from Mossad. "Hamas accuses Israeli agents. . . . We reaffirm without hesitation that there has been an attempted assassination—it failed."

Developments at the Islamic Hospital an hour later cast doubt on the certainty of this last assertion. As Mohammad Nazzal picked up the phone to take another call from Habib, the reporter immediately detected the fear in his voice. Again Nazzal refused to be quoted by name, but he provided the information for another news flash that clinched Habib's story. "Khalid Mishal is in hospital, suffering dizziness and nausea after being attacked by two Canadians with a bizarre instrument," Habib's report began.

It was close to five PM when General Batikhi decided he had to get to Abu Marzook alone. He demanded another meeting in his office.

Abu Marzook was surprisingly calm. His discussions with the GID boss went around and around in endlessly unproductive circles, until it finally dawned on Batikhi that the man across his desk saw him only as the heavy-handed spook whose job was to keep Hamas in check. Batikhi and the king had believed they had Abu Marzook in their pocket, but now the Mukhabarat chief could see the other man's dilemma. As a fallen senior figure who believed he could still recover his standing in Hamas, Abu Marzook could not afford to be seen by his colleagues to be a tool of the GID. But there was no way Batikhi could divulge all that he knew in this matter.

It occurred to Batikhi that Abu Marzook might respond to another, more sympathetic voice. He picked up the phone: "The king, please. . . . *Sayyidna*, I have Abu Marzook here, but he is having difficulty convincing his people to move Khalid Mishal to the Medical City."

The intervention of the king was finally sufficient for Abu Marzook. This proof that his royal benefactor was so intimately involved in the bid to save Mishal softened him. But it was just then that Batikhi gave him a calculated slap—a stick to balance the king's carrot. "If you guys don't cooperate in the transfer, whatever happens is on your heads—not ours," he warned with some menace.

Abu Marzook left the GID. Back at the Islamic Hospital he was able to talk convincingly to his colleagues about a plea coming from the king, rather than from the dreaded Mukhabarat. Abu Marzook called back to Batikhi, laying down three conditions. First, an Islamist delegation would have to be by Mishal's bedside at all times; second, Hamas would have the right to invite its own doctors to examine the patient at all times; and finally, Islamist visitors would not be denied access to the KHMC.

Batikhi agreed to it all. Abu Marzook put him on hold while he had a final discussion with the Islamists and doctors at the Islamic Hospital. When he came back on the line, he told Batikhi: "All right, move him."

Sinking deeper into a dangerous, unknown void, Mishal was only half-aware of the disembodied voices around his bed, arguing about whether or not he could or should be moved. Finally all had agreed, except for one key holdout: his mother. Fatima wanted him to be kept at the Islamic Hospital in the city center, which was more accessible. Even as Mishal was loaded on to a stretcher, she continued to make a fuss. In the end it was the fast-fading patient who half rose on an elbow to hush her protests. "Mother, stop causing trouble," he pleaded.

Within the KHMC, the Queen Alia Heart Institute normally was reserved for members of the royal family and for VIPs from across the region. As its director, Dr. Bassam Akasheh, prepared to manage the Mishal case himself, he wondered about fate and why the life of an unidentified patient could be so important to his king. The bespectacled surgeon had just emerged from a long session of open-heart surgery when General Shukri had called half an hour earlier, revealing little as he told him, "King Hussein wants to transfer an attempted homicide case to the institute."

Switching his focus to the condition of the mystery patient, Akasheh asked a single question: "Is it safe to move him?"

Shukri replied in a voice that told the fifty-one-year-old Akasheh that the urgency was dictated by other, nonmedical considerations: "He's at the Islamic Hospital. He's very weak. He can hardly breathe—but we *must* transfer him to you."

This was no ordinary patient transfer. The ambulance carving its way through the evening rush hour—first through the hilly warrens of the old downtown before hitting flat, concrete highways—was from the king's personal health unit. As it entered the sprawling grounds of KHMC, it was escorted by wailing police and military vehicles fore and aft. Strapped in the back of the vehicle, Mishal could hear the noise as he drifted in and out of consciousness.

As the convoy slammed to a halt outside the ground-floor admission center, two of the country's leading specialists were waiting in an office near the second-floor cardiac-care unit. Akasheh had earlier called his chief anesthesiologist, Dr. Sami Rababa, at home to discuss antidotes, but, minutes later, he was back on the line demanding Rababa's urgent presence at the elite hospital. Akasheh had already issued instructions for the patient to be brought up to the cardiac-care unit immediately. Now, as the doors to one of the elevators opened, the gurney carrying Mishal was whisked into a treatment room. And, as the doors to another elevator parted, armed guards tumbled into position in the corridors and at all entry points to the heart unit.

In the controlled chaos, it was never clear who spoke as observations were made, monitors frantically checked, and instructions sharply issued. "He can't breathe—intubation!" someone called.

As a medical and nursing team crowded in around them, the two specialists went to work, inserting a new tube in the near-comatose Mishal's throat, hoping to assist his dangerously weak breathing. They hooked the patient to a mechanical ventilator, as Shukri explained the details as they were known. "He was injected by an Israeli agent with some kind of poison. We don't know what it is."

Khalid Mishal was a strong, healthy specimen. But Akasheh was struck by how weak and limp he seemed. Rababa was curious about finally putting a face to a name he had read in the news. Now, as Mishal's respiratory system began to shut down, the patient was barely breathing. Rababa tried to keep him talking—ordering him to breathe, desperately trying to pull him back from the brink of a deep and deadly sleep. Before they put a tube down his throat, Mishal was lucid enough to give Rababa a somewhat garbled account of the attack—of a strange noise and a weird instrument.

Akasheh issued orders for Mishal to be stripped naked. Then they began a meticulous examination of his lean body—chest and abdomen, neck and head, arms and legs. He had no abrasions. He didn't seem to have been man-handled. What Akasheh most needed to find was a fine puncture where Mishal's skin might have been pierced by a syringe, but there was none. The patient was fading fast. "If the breathing stops, he's dead in three minutes!" Akasheh muttered.

It was the unenviable lot of the wire-service reporter to file bit by bit as a story broke and then, at a break in the traffic, to cobble the bite-size pieces of the day into a coherent whole. Some in the trade called it a "wrap." As dusk began to settle over the dusty Jordanian capital, Habib sat down to do the day's wrap. At 6:26 she filed the story, adding a single new element: "A spokesman for the Israeli Embassy in Amman, Roy Gillad, denied that Israel was implicated in any attack on Khalid Mishal. He said: 'The Hamas accusation doesn't surprise me and doesn't deserve a response.'"

This was an evening when there would be no going home for the Amman press pack. The first Ranya Kadri had heard of the crisis was in a phone call from Joe Contreras, the Middle East Bureau Chief for *Newsweek*. Calling from elsewhere in the region, he told her that AFP was reporting that Mossad may have killed Khalid Mishal. "No," Kadri insisted, her political insight kicking in, "there's something wrong there—Mousa Abu Marzook would have been the target."

Randa Habib had been in full flight at AFP for several hours; Kadri soon raced to catch up. Habib's early reports on the AFP wire about Canadian tourists being caught up in a fracas in Amman had lit a fire under editorial executives at CBC Canada. A reporter had been sent to Amman, but they needed more, and for that they rang Kadri. In the way of television, what CBC desperately wanted was footage—any footage. Kadri pulled in a free-lance cameraman and set off to start reporting the story herself.

At the Canadian Embassy, behind the smoked-glass facade of the Pearl of Shmeisani building on Abdalhameed Shoman Street, a receptionist politely told Kadri to go away. Next stop was the police compound at Wadi Al-Seer, where the Canadian tourists were in custody. A novice in the field of news gathering, the cameraman approached the building brandishing his camera. He was detained on the spot. When Kadri ran to his rescue, she too was detained.

Randa Habib's first, unvarnished understanding of the extent to which Mishal's health was in freefall came at about the same time that Ranya Kadri was detained by the police—just before seven PM. Having moved from the Islamic Hospital to KHMC with the patient, a panicking Sami Khater had been on the phone to Mohammad Nazzal: "We need you here—it's bad! He's dangerous!" Then Nazzal had gotten back to Habib, who in turn broke the news to Paris: "Hamas representative Mohammad Nazzal said Khalid Mishal's condition was so grave he had been transferred from Amman's Islamic Hospital to the better-equipped KHMC. He has difficulty breathing and suffers from a lack of oxygen to his blood."

Minutes later, the AFP reporter finally got through to the Canadian Embassy. Habib had a sense that Steve Bennett, the first secretary, was treading his way through a minefield—he had little to say, but he said it with such hesitancy that she knew she had to keep him on the line. On the record, he provided the kind of information she expected from any foreign diplomat whose nationals were in a tight fix. She later quoted Bennett in an eight PM update to her story: "A member of the embassy staff met two Canadians in custody. One was slightly wounded . . . they have been implicated in a street brawl, but there is no detail."

But not long after, she was back on the phone to the embassy. This time Bennett produced a nugget of information, which he imparted only as background. His diplomatic colleagues had returned from the lockup in great confusion, he said, because the Canadian prisoners had refused to talk. He did not mean that they had said, "No, thanks, we don't need consular help." He meant precisely what he had said—they sat in a cell, staring blankly and refusing to open their mouths.

While she still had Bennett on the line, Habib wondered out loud, "Why would a foreigner incarcerated in the Arab world refuse to speak to an envoy from his embassy? It's odd, isn't it?"

"Yes. We're still trying to understand it," Bennett replied.

By nine PM, the Jordanian Muslim Brotherhood had backed in behind Hamas. Their PR machine went into overdrive, demanding that Jordanian authorities immediately reveal the identity of Mishal's attackers. Mohammad Nazzal was in full rhetorical flight. In a new statement on behalf of Hamas, he declared, "The government of the Zionist entity headed by the terrorist Netanyahu is totally responsible. This cowardly aggression only reinforces our determination to pursue the fight."

Unable to get past the hospital switchboard to ask her own questions, Habib now co-opted Nazzal as a go-between. She persuaded him to enforce the terms of Abu Marzook's agreement with Batikhi, when Mishal was transferred, and to demand that the doctors brief him—Nazzal—on Mishal's condition.

The doctors, Nazzal reported back to her, seemed rattled. They made no mention of any poison; they told him that, for reasons they did not fully understand, Mishal's respiratory system was failing rapidly. Nazzal was not far off the mark when he reduced one of the doctor's long technical explanations of the Hamas leader's health to a perfect sound bite: "Khalid Mishal is dying."

Habib pounced. All the weight of the day's official denials and ministerial rubbishing of her reporting lifted from her shoulders. "The story's right," Habib called to colleagues as she hastily belted out another line in the intrigue: "Jordanian authorities have seized the instrument used by the assailants, but they are being very discreet about its nature."

Earlier she had dispatched her photographer colleague Jamal to the Islamic Hospital. Luckily, he had arrived just as Mishal, strapped to a stretcher, was being placed in an ambulance. Habib was shocked by the images Jamal brought back. "I know a dead man when I see one," she exclaimed when she saw the pictures on Jamal's computer screen. The patient in the images was motionless. Mishal's thick black beard was the only relief against a swathe of pale blue hospital sheets. A blue plastic fitting held the end of a green hose in his mouth. Another plastic device had been inserted to prevent his choking on his tongue. Mishal's left arm lay heavily across his chest. As he was pushed into the back of the ambulance, a nurse had thrown a blanket over him.

At the military hospital, the medical staff had Mishal hooked to a heart monitor. Other machines analyzed his blood, testing for liver and kidney poisoning and to ensure that the right quantities of oxygen and carbon dioxide were getting to his brain. Mishal's parents had arrived with a group of anxious relatives, all of whom immediately were enlisted in an effort to keep Mishal talking, to keep him awake, and to keep him breathing.

But at no stage did Mishal realize that he was dying. As an Islamic believer does when he is unwell, he recited verses from the Qur'an in his mind. He recalled later that he did not broach the incantations reserved for imminent death.

With an eye on a bank of monitors, Dr. Rababa and the bullet-headed Dr. Akasheh concluded that, with the exception of his almost nonexistent breathing, all Mishal's other vital signs were strong—his blood pressure, his heart rate, and his pulse.

Akasheh came from one of Jordan's most trusted medical families. His father had delivered all the royal babies and the son had trained first at Guys Hospital, London, and later in Houston, Texas, where he did most of his postgraduate cardiac studies. Rababa was London trained too. Now, they were required to make a call on saving the life of the patient they already thought of as the Palestinian VIP.

Mishal's mother, Fatima, told them that Allah would save her son. But, being more earthbound, the doctors concentrated on the task at hand with a cool professional confidence. "He's not breathing, so they must have given him a respiratory depressant. It wasn't an injection, but whatever's in his system has to be a muscle relaxant," Akasheh concluded. "That's why he's not breathing."

They were flying blind. So far there was no sign of the antidote promised by Danny Yatom. In any case, the doctors were determined to make their own clinical assessment, rather than to blindly accept a diagnosis from an Israeli spy. In this at least, they were in accord with their professional colleagues at the Islamic Hospital. By a process of elimination, it seemed that the poison had to be either a benzodiazepine—that is, something from the family of drugs that includes Valium and Librium—or a narcotic.

They gave Mishal an intravenous cocktail—Narcan, a widely use postoperative drug that reverses the effects of anesthesia; and Anexate, which would reverse the impact of a benzodiazepine. Mishal had been with them for a good thirty minutes and they were starting to understand the clinical picture.

They also grasped the national consequences of failure. They did not need to know how or with what Mishal had been drugged to appreciate that they had to keep him breathing in order to keep him alive. Whatever he had been given, the sedation effect was profound. Both Narcan and Anexate were effective for just a few minutes, so they would have to keep the mix pumping through him.

Finally they told Mishal to let go—he could go to sleep while a machine did his breathing. They posted a vigil by his bed, hoping that this state of total life support would keep him going until they had a better idea of what was killing him. Then the treatment could be more specific than the one-size-fits-all Narcan-Anexate brew that they hoped would prevent the Israeli's unknown poison from achieving its aim—for now.

Armed with the advice and assistance of Danny Yatom, the Jordanians did not find it too difficult to get their hands on a sample of the antidote. Yatom had directed them to Mossad's Amman station chief, a figure well known to Batikhi's men, whose appointed task that day was to swim laps of the pool at the Intercontinental Hotel, so as to suggest that Mossad was having a quiet day. He now informed Shukri that the woman doctor had fled to one of a number of backup rooms, which had been reserved at the Meridian Hotel in case any of the Mossad team needed to bolt from the Intercon.

The doctor had in fact switched hotels and, by the time Shukri and several members of the Royal Guard came to arrest her, she was biding her time in a nearby coffee shop. She was quickly detained and, as the guards went through her bags, they found two liquid-filled syringes, similar to the short-needled hypodermics used by diabetics for the administration of insulin.

Immediately, however, the amalgam of reasonable suspicion and deep paranoia so prevalent in the Middle East kicked in. It was one thing to confiscate the syringes, which the woman said contained the antidote for whatever had been administered to Mishal, but it was entirely another thing to believe her—or Yatom for that matter.

"Think about it," Batikhi warned Shukri. "How can we use a doctor who was part of the plot?"

"Yep," General Shukri replied. "We need to know what this shit they've injected into him is."

When the Israeli doctor was brought to the hospital by Shukri and four members of the Royal Guard, she confirmed she was the Mossad agent who, as Danny Yatom had explained to King Hussein, had been on standby at the Intercon. A pretty brunette, she looked sullen and worried as one of the guards shoved her into the corner of Akasheh's visitors' sofa.

Akasheh demanded that she reveal what had been injected into his patient.

"I don't know," she said, insisting she had been told nothing of the nature of either the poison or the antidote—only that one would counteract the impact of the other.[5]

"He seems to be doing well," Akasheh told her. Skating over the reality of a ventilator doing Mishal's breathing for him, Akasheh wondered what sort of response might be elicited from her by news that Mossad's intended victim was still alive. But she stared back blankly, saying nothing.

Canvassing their options, Batikhi and Shukri—and eventually the team of doctors around Mishal—became hostages to their own imagining. They convinced themselves it was plausible that, in producing this "antidote," the Israeli doctor was capable of handing over an additional poison that would complete the assassination task, in the event that Mishal was not yet dead.

Their anxiety was further heightened by a garbled report that came through to Batikhi's office, suggesting that an Israeli doctor had in fact contacted the KHMC medical team, offering the outlandish suggestion that Mishal be disconnected from the mechanical ventilator keeping him alive. That too would have completed Mossad's dirty work. This was so bizarre that it kindled even greater suspicion of anything and everything the Israelis might do.

Akasheh, who at this stage was taking no chances, sent the two liquid-filled syringes off for immediate analysis at the government forensic laboratories. "We'll not use it before we've had it tested," he told the Israeli agent. "It could be a medication to finish him off completely."

Through Thursday evening, there was another stroke of luck in the accidental presence in Amman at this time of a fifty-five-year-old American, Dr. Walter Wilson, who was head of the world-renowned infectious diseases division at the Mayo Clinic in Rochester, Minnesota. King Hussein had recently suffered a mystery fever and other odd symptoms; Wilson had been brought to Amman to work with the royal medical team.

Now the king press-ganged Wilson into service on the case of Mishal, who the local team was satisfied had finally been stabilized in his drug-induced, deeply comatose state. The taciturn Wilson was allowed to examine Mishal only after Hamas's nonmedical expert Nazzal had vetted his credentials. Wilson reiterated to Nazzal: "To treat him, we have to know what kind of poison they used."[6]

How, they wondered, could reliable information be extracted from the Israelis? What they needed was a description of the precise chemical that had been used in the attack.

King Hussein was in another of his flights of rage by the time Batikhi called to present this latest obstacle in the race to save Mishal. "We'll make them hand it over," the king snapped. "We need that formula."

Throughout the night the king and his aides besieged the doctors. Shukri stayed at the hospital, shadowing Akasheh and Rababa as they hovered over Mishal and continued to debate the risks of using the antidote taken from Mossad's doctor-agent. Both Hussein and Batikhi were on the phone every half hour, making sure their Palestinian VIP was still alive.

As the day's drama unfolded, Netanyahu had twice tried to call Hussein. The king had refused both calls, opting instead for an underling to convey a message. "If Mishal dies, we're all in deep trouble," it said. "You had better make sure he doesn't die."[7]

13

"Who the Hell Is Khalid Mishal?"

The Canadian diplomat Steve Bennett was determined to get something on these suspected Canadian hitmen. A cocktail party at the British Embassy to commemorate the Battle of Britain was an opportunity to press others on the diplomatic circuit. But the British were not in the picture. He next browbeat his way into a meeting with Interior Minister Nathir Rashid, which, he later reported back to Ottawa, was "tense, unpleasant and entirely unproductive."[1] His plea for photographs of the men and copies of their fingerprints drew only blank stares. Bennett then set his sights on the Swiss, who had invited much of dress-circle Amman to a reception at the embassy to mark Swiss national day.

Bennett had the taut figure of a rugby player who also had a black belt in martial arts. He was admired at the Canadian mission as a colleague who could crash through when all else failed. The pressure from Ottawa had become unrelenting. Prime Minister Jean Chrétien was helpless in fending off opposition and news media attacks claiming that his government was complicit in the Israeli plot to kill Khalid Mishal.

Seized by the urgency of the matter, Bennett resorted to tactics that were quite undiplomatic at the Swiss function. Taking a drink, he scanned the gathering for high-ranking Jordanian figures. He then insinuated himself among the guests nearest to his prey, whereupon he complained loudly about Ottawa being unfairly kept out of the loop at a time of acute embarrassment for his government. When he espied Prince Raad Bin Zeid, the head of the exiled royal house of Iraq, whom he knew to be a confidant of King Hussein, Bennett moved in more closely and grew louder. "Why is

Amman treating its Canadian friends in this manner?" he demanded to know. "There's great difficulty at home. Ottawa insists on answers. The embassy has none."

Bennett's calculated rudeness had the desired effect. By the next morning, an anonymous phone caller invited him to the first of several cloak-and-dagger drives that would deliver him to a series of meetings, first with General Ali Shukri and later with King Hussein himself. Initially, Bennett was instructed to have an embassy driver drop him in one of the capital's back streets—next to a silver Mercedes-Benz. The Jordanian driver of the Mercedes then took him to an office where Shukri allowed him to inspect the two passports. Like his female colleague earlier, Bennett concluded, after his own unscientific examination, that the documents indeed were genuine. This was not what Ottawa wanted to hear.

But then Bennett was taken to the holding cells at the Amman headquarters of the Public Security Directorate, where the two culprits had been moved from the Wadi Al-Seer police complex. Bennett was allowed to interview them one at a time. Both refused to disclose their identities, which the registration book at the Intercon had recorded as Shawn Kendall, twenty-eight, the blond assailant of Mishal, and Barry Beads, thirty-six, his darker accomplice. Their details were among those of three other Canadian passport holders who had checked in to the hotel at the same time. The two spoke with strong Israeli accents but, after listening for a time, Bennett concluded that one had learned his English in Australia.

Watched by bemused Jordanian guards, Bennett then subjected each man in turn to his unique test of Canadian-ness. Could he name a street in Canada where he had lived as a child, or a town in which he went to school? No? Perhaps he could name one of his teachers? No, they each replied.

On the basics of Canadian geography, they knew nothing. The men also had an equally disappointing knowledge of Canadian sport. Four years earlier the Toronto Blue Jays had caused a heartstopping sensation by defeating all comers in the United States to win back-to-back World Series titles. At the time, it was said, even the dead in the cemeteries of Canada sat up to celebrate. Now these supposed Canadian true-bloods stared blankly at Bennett, asking "The Blue whats?"

Perhaps his last question was cruel, but the diplomat was determined to nail this down. He asked them to sing a few bars of "O Canada," the national anthem. Bennett helpfully hummed the opening line: "O Canada! Our home and native land. . . ." After their failure to join in, he was satisfied that both men were impostors.

.   .   .

Any embarrassment for Ottawa was the least of Benjamin Netanyahu's worries. The twenty-four hours just past had been among the worst in his turbulent career, and he knew that by the time this crisis was over, his prime ministership too might be finished.

Yesterday was meant to have been a day of triumph. In a week's time his country would shut down for three days to celebrate Jewish New Year. By tradition, the prime minister visited Mossad in the days before the holiday break to toast the agency's contribution to national security.

Staff were already assembled in one of the dining halls when the prime minister's armed motorcade had pulled into the Mossad compound near Herzliya, on the coast north of Tel Aviv, at close to noon on Thursday. If all had gone as planned in Jordan, he would have arrived shortly after a coded "Mission Accomplished" signal had been relayed from the Mossad station hidden in the Israeli Embassy in Amman. Instead, a distracted and crestfallen Danny Yatom had greeted him. And, instead of escorting the prime minister to the festivities, the director had taken him aside to report the shattering news from Amman.[2] "We've got a problem," he began.

Violent retaliation against the leadership of Hamas—wherever they were in the world—had first been sanctioned by an emergency meeting of the Israeli cabinet after the twin suicide bombings almost two months earlier, on July 30, in which sixteen people had been killed at the Jerusalem produce markets. Netanyahu had emerged from that meeting declaring, "I'll get those bastards, if it's the last thing I do."[3]

As Yatom revealed the extent of the covert mission's failure in Amman, Netanyahu listened in silence, his rising anxiety betrayed by beads of sweat forming on his brow. Two of Mossad's agents were behind bars in Jordan. As many as six others had been captured or were on the run from the local authorities, either heading for the border or hunkering at a Mossad safe house or, perhaps by now, at the Israeli Embassy in Amman. Two other agents, including one whose cover was that of a thirty-year-old Canadian named Guy Eris, were thought to have fled Amman and were probably finding their own way home.

The pre-mission briefings by Yatom and his hands-on director of operations, known only as H, were a distant memory. The team had begun to assemble in Amman weeks earlier. Flying in from different cities around the world, at least five of them had masqueraded as Canadian tourists. The woman doctor, a practicing cardiologist from Israel's southern Negev region, and one of her male colleagues had checked in as husband and wife.

The inclusion of the specialist doctor had underscored the detail in the planning—she was to be on hand with the antidote, to save any of her colleagues who might accidentally come into contact with the killer drug. Backup rooms had been booked at the Meridian Hotel, on Queen Noor Street, just in case any of the team needed to beat a hasty retreat from the scene.

The team had used unsuspecting passersby on the sidewalks of Tel Aviv to play the part of Khalid Mishal in rehearsals for the mission. While one agent distracted the target by "accidentally" popping open a shaken can of Coca-Cola as he and the target approached each other on the pavement, another agent was to glide past on the other side of the target. Using a sophisticated nebulizer, concealed in the body of a tourist's camera, his job was to spray a killer dose of the poison into the target's ear.

In these test runs, water was substituted for the poison. A third operative would be present as a field commander. All three had been trained to communicate by facial expressions. They had clear instructions on the circumstances under which the operation was to be aborted, one of which was the presence of any of Mishal's usual entourage.

It could not go wrong, Yatom had assured Netanyahu. There had been much planning and great attention to detail. The team had been hand-picked from the ranks of Caesarea, one of Mossad's three specialist killing teams. The mission required them to be in the street literally for just a few seconds.

Some time later, according to the plan, Mishal would be presumed to have had a heart attack. But, just to provide Mossad with more cover, a cleverly conceived subterfuge had been set up, underlining the planning sophistication that the prime minister, and frankly the world, had come to expect of Israel's security organization. In the knowledge that Samih Batikhi's GID had supervised the installation of the surveillance video cameras at the Intercon and had full access to both the tapes and a team of paid informers planted among the hotel staff, Mossad's Amman station chief—who was not privy to the planned hit—had been instructed to take himself off to do his usual laps of the pool at the hotel. The plan was that the inevitable discovery of images of him, apparently so relaxed at the time of the hit on Mishal, would remove Mossad from the frame in the event of an investigation into the cause of the mysterious death of Khalid Mishal.

But now, instead of Mossad's customary espionage showmanship, what had actually happened in Amman seemed like the work of amateurs. The clever plan for the three agents to communicate with each other had fallen apart, because Mishal and his driver had broken their lines of sight.

During the pursuit and arrest of "Kendall" and "Beads," four others who were in the squad had managed to sneak away to the relative sanctuary of a Mossad safe house in Amman. But Yatom had then ordered them to move to the embassy.[4]

When the Jordanians threw a military cordon around the embassy, they had been acting simply on a hunch. Several witnesses had claimed they saw members of the team driving or running in the direction of the Israeli mission. The agents in fact had veered off to the safe house, but, acting on subsequent orders from Yatom, after the capture of "Kendall" and "Beads," the agents backtracked to the embassy before the cordon was in place. They had made themselves prisoners of the Jordanian military.

Still, they believed at first that the poison had been administered successfully and Mishal would die, thus fulfilling the mission's objective. The agents had even reported their "success" to a member of the getaway team before realizing that Mishal's bodyguard was on their tail.[5]

Washington in the fall is beautiful, and the last week of September 1997 was no different. The U.S. capital was relatively quiet. The perennial congressional brawl on political fund-raising had flared again and, after thirty-two years of Medicaid, a better health care deal for millions of children had just been agreed upon. Big tobacco had balked at a tough new liability deal. Young Chelsea Clinton was off to college—to Stanford—but President Clinton's political landscape was now permanently blotted by the tawdry Paula Jones sex scandal. The accompanying scandal over his relationship with a White House intern, Monica Lewinsky, had yet to be revealed publicly.

On the day before the hit on Mishal—Wednesday—President and Mrs. Hillary Clinton had headed for home turf. They planned for a hectic four days, during which they would operate from Little Rock, their hometown. To that extent, the West Wing team had drawn breath.

Given the time difference, Bill Clinton slept through the first hours of the crisis in Amman. By the time Mishal was being rushed between hospitals—late afternoon in Amman and mid-morning in Little Rock—Clinton was leading a moving commemoration of the fortieth anniversary of the Little Rock Nine. Arkansas was revisiting the desegregation turmoil of the 1950s when President Eisenhower had laid on a one-thousand-strong military escort for nine black students to get to their desks at Little Rock Central High.[6]

It was unheard of for a foreign leader to cold-call the White House. Kings, presidents, prime ministers, and generals often came on the line—but only after days of negotiations between their ambassador in Washington and a White House staffer who, as the Clinton aide Bruce Riedel put it, would "grease the skids."[7]

When King Hussein phoned, no one quite knew what to do with his call. Clinton was on a platform in Arkansas with all nine of the Little Rock Nine; his national security advisor, Sandy Berger, was tied up elsewhere. King Hussein was patched through to Riedel, a twenty-year CIA veteran who was now serving as a presidential adviser on Near Eastern affairs. But, apart from his declaration that there was "a crisis in the Middle East," the Jordanian leader refused to elaborate. All Riedel could do was undertake to have the president return the king's call when he could. "All he'd say was he needed to talk to the president," a somewhat startled Riedel told Sandy Berger when he finally ran him to ground.

Intelligence agents worry if phones do not ring, if people are not talking. They listen and they process, but if there is a lull, they might throw on their sweats and head for the gym. That was what Dave Manners was doing on Friday morning. As the forty-something CIA station chief in Amman, he had taken a call the previous day from a local contact who, in going through a laundry list of issues, had made a brief mention of a strange attack on an Amman-based official of the Hamas movement. Reports later in the day had been garbled and contradictory.

Threading his way through light morning traffic, Manners decided the Hamas business was too half-baked to get his blood going, on what was the first day of the Jordanian weekend. "A Palestinian being attacked by who knows who," he asked himself. "Not really a story, is it?"[8]

He was heading for the embassy gym, but he had yet to reach the high-walled American diplomatic compound when his mobile phone lit up. A breathless Mohammad Dahabi, executive assistant to Samih Batikhi, was on the line: "Immediately! Come now—the boss needs you to go with him to see His Majesty!"

Manners enjoyed irritating people with his casual dress. He religiously wore denim jeans and a flapping polo shirt. But right now he was in a T-shirt and sweatpants, which, he thought, did not quite meet royal dress standards. He dashed home and changed—into the inevitable jeans and polo shirt—and then drove to Batikhi's bunker on the outskirts of the city.

Something obviously was up. Instead of the usual tight stop-and-check security, the gates had been thrown open, the boom was up, and Manners was waved straight through. Before he cut the motor, Batikhi's man Dahabi was already tumbling down the steps: "*Pasha*"—an Arab term of respect for a senior man like Batikhi—"couldn't wait. You must drive after him . . . go, go!"

"What's going on?" Manners demanded. "Why's everyone so hyped up?"

"I don't know," Dahabi told the CIA man. "But it's important—go fast!"

King Hussein was at the Hashimieh Palace. Arriving there, Manners found that what awaited him was even more mysterious than the panic back at the GID compound. He was escorted to a reception room and into the presence of Ali Shukri and King Hussein's eldest son, Prince Abdullah.

Two things struck him immediately—Batikhi was not there and, on what Manners understood was a laid-back Friday morning, the prince was in full military uniform. "What's going on?" he demanded.

It was Prince Abdullah who replied hesitantly, saying, "I'm not really sure."

Manners turned to Shukri. "Okay—what's up?" he repeated.

"We'll tell you in a few minutes," General Shukri said. "We're waiting for Wes."

Wes? As far as Manners knew, right then Wesley Egan, the American ambassador, and his wife, Virginia, were on another of their regular archaeological digs at Petra. If the king was hauling him back to town, this had to be serious. He chuckled at the timing as he recalled the king's gag about there always being a crisis in the capital when Egan was in Petra. But when Shukri revealed that Hussein had dispatched a helicopter, instead of requesting the ambassador return by car, Manners understood that something very serious was afoot.

Ambassador Egan had been digging since sunrise. A couple of hours into the day's work, at about eight, he was engrossed in a pillar of undisturbed dirt—what practiced archaeologists call a "baulk"—when a member of his Jordanian security detail leaned over the edge of the pit in which he was working, informing him that the king needed him back in Amman—"now."

As the guard spoke, the *wap-wap-wap* of an approaching helicopter could be heard, and seconds later, one of the palace fleet of Pumas cleared the nearest ridgeline. Caught up in the drama of the royal command, Egan was all for jumping aboard immediately. But Virginia was a woman of standards—his wife insisted he return to their hotel to shower and change into attire that was more appropriate when responding to a summons to the palace.

Manners attempted some small talk, but no one would play. He toyed with his ornate gold knuckle-duster ring, which featured a fat, milky sapphire and the figure 76, the year in which Manners had graduated from the U.S. Naval Academy in Annapolis, Maryland. All sat in this awkward void for about thirty minutes before the silence was broken by the rattling roar of a helicopter landing outside. Flustered, but looking smart in his clean slacks and sports coat, Egan gave Manners a quizzical look as he entered. But there was no time to exchange even a few words—Hussein and Batikhi were right on the ambassador's heels.

The king strode in with his usual purposeful manner. But Manners was taken aback by his friend Batikhi's demeanor. "He was aggrieved, devastated," Manners said later. "Really, really pissed."

Turning his gaze back to the monarch, the CIA man detected something quite apart from the deliberate calm he had come to expect from Hussein— Manners made a mental note of what he later would describe as the king's "cat-eats-a-canary look." As Hussein and Batikhi poured out the essentials of the last twenty-four hours, it became apparent that the two most powerful men in Jordan were reacting very differently. It was evident that Hussein— furious as he was—could not quite believe his good fortune: after more than a year of Netanyahu's treachery and deceit and after decades of condescension by some in the Israeli establishment toward his desperate but dignified little kingdom, he was going to settle for nothing less than the complete humiliation of Benjamin Netanyahu.

"The president will have to weigh in on this one," Hussein explained to Egan. Not pausing to draw breath, the king then set out how and why Clinton had to be made to force Netanyahu to reveal the original formula for the poison the Mossad team had used on Mishal—and urgently.

Maintaining a salvo of rising anger and bitterness, the king declared that the death of Mishal on his turf would be so destabilizing that Netanyahu must have been in deliberate pursuit of two outrageous objectives. Quite apart from making it impossible to rescue the now comatose Oslo process, the Israeli leader also must have been attempting to destabilize the Hashemite dynasty, probably as a prelude to clearing Jordan to make way for some sort of greenfield site on which to create a new Palestinian state.

"Is Netanyahu seriously committed to this treaty of ours, or is this his attempt to wreck it?" Hussein demanded of his audience. "If Jordan is Israel's only true friend in the Arab world, why this knife in the back?"

The king found it even harder to accept that Mossad was the instrument of his discomfort. Just days earlier he had hosted a visit by senior officials of Mossad and Israel's Defense Ministry to discuss their joint efforts in counterterrorism. Now Hussein was convinced that these recent guests at his table had to have been aware of the plot against him.

Several times, Hussein clasped his hand dramatically to his forehead, complaining about Netanyahu: "I simply don't understand that man."

Manners was quick to agree. "This whole thing is so idiotic," he said. "You got to wonder if it wasn't a deliberate message, as you suspect, Your Majesty."

Like a chess master, Hussein proceeded to arrange the board to his advantage. Egan had to understand that he still needed to talk to the president of the United States. Then Hussein upped the ante. Calculating that, as the authors of the crisis, the Israelis would not be received at the White House, Hussein demanded that Clinton receive a high-level Jordanian delegation as soon as it could be arranged. The royal jet was ready, but, he pointed out, Egan would have to move fast to ensure that Clinton would be available both to take a phone call from Hussein in Amman and to receive the planned delegation to Washington, to be led by his brother, Crown Prince Hassan.

Hussein was sharply issuing orders. Batikhi should accompany the crown prince, and so should Manners. "The president needs to hear directly how seriously we view this incident," he thundered.

Egan nodded, and Manners said to himself, "Looks like I'm off to Washington."

As the Americans prepared to leave, Hussein returned to his key point—Netanyahu must be forced to deliver the complete details of both the antidote and the poison. The king had spoken hardly a single sentence without mentioning the Hamas leader—it was Khalid Mishal this, Khalid Mishal that. When they finally broke up and headed for the palace portico, Ambassador Egan piled in with Manners for the ride back to the embassy.

As he pulled the car door closed, Egan looked blankly at the CIA man and asked, "Who the hell is Khalid Mishal?"

It did not help that President Clinton was on the road. With back-to-back public engagements, the Washington-based officials found him where they could—inevitably between appointments and usually in a limousine bottled up in a noisy motorcade.

As well as being commander in chief, Clinton was the Democrats' fundraiser-in-chief, and his handling of the Mishal affair was to be bookended by big party functions. On the Friday he made a seventy-minute dash by air to Houston, Texas, for a lavish dinner at the gated mansion of Tilman

Fertitta, a forty-year-old millionaire restaurateur. In less than two hours, Clinton got stuck into a three-course seafood extravaganza and then, as he posed for individual photographs with guests, gathered more than $600,000 from the pocketbooks of about seventy of Houston's wealthier Democrat supporters.[9]

Air Force One put the Clintons back on the deck at Little Rock just after ten PM local time on Friday. It was now a day after the attack on Mishal.

Both Hussein and Netanyahu were racing to get Clinton's ear. Just as the king had abandoned protocol to make his own first call to the White House, so too did the prime minister—as Dennis Ross was to discover way too early on Saturday morning. As Clinton's special envoy to the Middle East, Ross endured constant travel, which meant too many nights sleeping on aircraft and in hotels or embassy compounds. So an opportunity to sleep in, in his own bed, in his own Maryland home, was to be savored—at least until Netanyahu telephoned.

It was about seven AM when the White House called Ross to advise him that the Israeli prime minister needed to come through on a secure line. That was all it took—Ross needed no more information to understand that he had a crisis on his hands. Familiar with Netanyahu's personal habits, Ross was aware that the Israeli leader habitually slept into the afternoon on a Saturday. "This is Saturday. It's two PM in Jerusalem and Netanyahu's out of bed," he mumbled to himself. "I've got a problem."

A breathless and, at times, seemingly incoherent Netanyahu was patched through for what would be a very difficult exchange, not least because the prime minister presumed Ross had already been briefed on the detail. Ross knew nothing. Dispensing with any greeting, Netanyahu blurted out his key point: "The king—he's threatening to cut relations."

"What are you talking about?"

"We tried to kill Khalid Mishal—he's in hospital."

"Tell me what you did—"

As Ross listened, Netanyahu stumbled through the essentials of the botched Mossad mission, coming to a halt roughly where he had started when Ross had first picked up the phone: "If we don't give him the formula and the antidote, he'll break relations."

Ross was direct—there were no options. "You don't have a choice, do you? Give him what he wants."

But Netanyahu pushed back. He wanted another solution. He was loath even to consider Ross's suggestion that Israel make doctors available as advisers to the Jordanian medical team trying to keep Mishal alive.

Still in his bed, Ross nearly fell out of it when Netanyahu countered by suggesting that, if King Hussein wanted to save Mishal, he should send him over the river for treatment in a good Israeli hospital. Having dispatched the would-be killers, Netanyahu seemed to believe he might now be trusted with an offer to save the victim's life.

Then the prime minister swung wildly, helplessly in the opposite direction: "But . . . if we were ready to cooperate, I'm not sure that he would accept our help. . . ."

"What's most important to you?" Ross asked.

"The president [Clinton] must talk to him," said Netanyahu, his rising panic clear to the American diplomat.

"I can try to make that happen," said Ross. "But tell me this—what were you thinking?"

"We went after him because of the Hamas attacks."

"What you're saying is you went after him in Amman. Did it occur to you that it might go wrong?"

After a long silence, Netanyahu replied: "No. . . ."

"How could you be so irresponsible? Don't you understand how essential the Jordan relationship is for you?" Ross demanded. "If you put Hussein in a corner, he's got no choice but to respond like this. . . ."

At this stage, Netanyahu simply stopped talking. The American had to call down the phone line a couple of times to confirm that the prime minister was still there.

"If you had a problem with Mishal, why didn't you go talk to the Jordanians? At a minimum, they'd certainly have arrested him; they might even have deported him—he would not have been able to operate from Jordan any more."

There was no response from the Jerusalem end. Just silence.

But there was sufficient ambient noise for Ross to conclude that the phone line remained open. They were at cross-purposes. As an attuned diplomat, Ross was attempting to get Netanyahu to explain why the Israelis believed they *had* to go after Mishal in Amman. But all that was coming back to him was Netanyahu's slightly unhinged plea for Washington to extricate him from a mess of his own making.

Seemingly unaware that he was repeating himself, the prime minister resorted to mantra-like repetitions: "Break in relations . . . Clinton must call the king. . . . Break in relations . . . Clinton must call the king."

"I understand what's at stake. But you made this mess," Ross told him. "If you don't want the king to make good on his threat, you'll just have to cooperate."

"He's holding two of my men."

"I can't rescue this unless you do as Hussein asks," said Ross implacably.

Ross got off the line and immediately called Sandy Berger. When he was done with Berger, he called Martin Indyk, Washington's ambassador in Tel Aviv. As Ross recounted his exchange with Netanyahu, Indyk's first response was one of shock: "Stupid! If that treaty goes, it's a three-alarm blaze!"

Not long after these exchanges, the first of a daylong series of extraordinary phone calls was put through to the president of the United States. Before nine AM that Saturday, the Clintons were in the air on a thirty-five-minute helicopter ride from Little Rock southwest to Hot Springs, the president's boyhood hometown, for a $25-a-head fund-raiser to restore his old school. By mid-afternoon they were scheduled to be back in Little Rock, at the Ray Winder Baseball Field for another Democratic fund-raiser with a guest list that ran to about six hundred. But whenever Clinton was in his car that day—at least eight times, his diaries would later reveal—he engaged in business that was deemed too sensitive to be included in extracts from the official record, which would be released a decade later.[10]

It was all done by phone. Egan pitched in from Amman, insisting to Berger at the White House and to David Welch at the State Department that the king's demands must be met. Netanyahu must be made to hand over a detailed account of the composition and properties of the poison, plus a verifiable antidote, before Mishal could be safely moved on to a more specific course of treatment.

"Right now, they're just holding him—you've got to get that antidote!" Egan urged. But Berger told the ambassador that it was not quite as simple as that. Clinton had a day filled with public appearances, and getting him to a secure line was not as easy as it sounded.

"Figure it out," Egan told Berger. "These guys need to talk."

Through Saturday, the pitch of the negotiations became so heated that the ever-frenetic Berger moved his team to the Situation Room—the intelligence nerve center beneath the West Wing that, since the Cuban missile crisis, was the U.S. president's eyes and ears to the world in times of upheaval. All calls were on secure lines—except for some to and from Dennis Ross. Because this new crisis clashed with his nine-year-old daughter's soccer match, Ross was seen several times scurrying away from the sidelines of a playing field in the suburbs of metropolitan Washington, to take yet another call on a very ordinary cell phone.[11]

With Ambassador Egan and General Shukri as pointmen in Amman,

King Hussein finally was connected to President Clinton. The king's smelter-like anger had not dissipated. Riedel, and others listening in, could sense the rage—the ink had hardly dried on the peace treaty that Hussein had so courageously stepped outside the Arab tent to sign with Israel, and now a bumbling Mossad team had attempted an assassination in broad daylight in the streets of the king's own capital. "Not actually conducive to peace, is it?" Hussein snapped at the Israel-friendly Clinton, who was seen as the godfather of the 1994 treaty.[12]

Hussein knew just how to twist Clinton's arm. He made it clear he was on the verge of abandoning the peace treaty, a cornerstone in the interminable process. On the American end, Riedel advised that Hussein was not bluffing; the treaty that Clinton had signed was in jeopardy. "He can't be left looking like a stooge for the Israelis, and the Israeli Embassy in Amman can't become a den for assassins," Riedel warned.

The U.S. mission in Amman reported through its secure channels that Hussein was threatening to hang his Israeli prisoners and that senior officials at the royal court were urging Hussein to allow his eldest son to lead a commando mission to storm the Israeli Embassy in Amman—with the foreign press invited to watch. Palace aides were busily making arrangements with Jordanian TV networks for Hussein to address the nation—to reveal the sordid details of the Mossad intrigue and how Netanyahu had overplayed his hand.

The early months of the Clinton presidency had been marked by the dramatic Oslo breakthrough in the search for peace in the Middle East. But intransigence all around and the latest Hamas bombings had put the whole process on life support. Now Hussein's threat to respond to Netanyahu's provocation by publicly dumping the treaty could be a fatal throw of the switch. "You know these people didn't dare behave like this when we didn't have the treaty," a livid Hussein barked down the line. "How can we ever cooperate with them again?"

Clinton could see well enough that the king had been put in an impossible position. Unless Mishal survived, Washington's loyal and lonely Arab ally would be exposed and vulnerable to his many enemies. With so much hanging in the balance, and a good friend demanding help, Clinton agreed to assist in getting Israel to deliver both the formula for the poison and the antidote. He also undertook to keep the pressure on Netanyahu to stick to the terms of whatever was agreed between the two countries and to commit to reviving the peace process.

"But, I've got to say—this guy really is incredible," Clinton told Hussein as the king poured out the details of what Netanyahu had attempted in his capital. Having allowed the king to vent as much anger as he needed to, Clinton in turn extracted a commitment from the Jordanian monarch that he too would stick to the terms of whatever the deal would be and that he would then put his shoulder to the bogged wagon of the Middle East peace process.

Agreeing, the king left the president with a thunderclap warning: "[You need to know that] the life of the peace process hangs on the life of this Jordanian. If this man dies, the peace dies with him."[13]

Ordinarily the king would not speak so bluntly, but as he heard this exchange, Dennis Ross understood what was at stake for the monarch. "Hussein was yelling at Clinton," he would recall later. "He felt utterly exposed. How was he ever to trust the Israelis again? He was angry, bitter, and embarrassed." The two leaders would talk several times more as the king milked his moment of power, with the president trying—and, most of the time, failing—to talk the king down from the peaks of his anger.

The phone traffic did not let up—Hussein to the White House; the White House to Clinton in Arkansas (with Berger, Ross, or Riedel on the line, either individually or with some or all of them in teleconference); Clinton to Hussein; Netanyahu to Ross; Berger to Netanyahu; the U.S. Embassy in Amman to the State Department, to the CIA, to Dennis Ross at a playing field in Maryland. But in all this flow of calls, Bill Clinton did not talk to Netanyahu. That task was assigned to the unfortunate Sandy Berger, causing Bruce Riedel to quip at one stage, "Bibi is Berger's baby!"

Berger came from the tsunami school of crisis management. Everything was classified "urgent," and when the issue of the day actually did have its own urgency—as the Mishal affair did—the force multiplier was a sight to behold. "It made life miserable for the people around him—but it meant nothing fell through the cracks," one of his overwrought staff said.

At the big desk in the Situation Room, Berger handled the phones. If the logic of his argument was failing to make an impression, he resorted to the power of his voice. "Sandy's going to make it happen—he's screaming down the phone," an aide observed as he left the Situation Room.

Remarkably, this was an episode in which no one at the White House was prepared to go to bat for Netanyahu. All apparently understood just how badly the Israelis had bungled. "Sandy is being quite firm in his position that

Bibi must satisfy the king's demands—that's a huge price for Israel to pay," a staffer who had spent time in the Situation Room was heard to say late in the day.

Stunned by the enormity of the unfolding drama, a recent arrival on Sandy Berger's White House staff likened it all to a James Bond movie. "It's like a thriller—one country needs an antidote held by another to treat an illness it doesn't understand. And the clock is ticking."

King Hussein set midnight Saturday as the deadline for the storming of the Israeli Embassy and the arrest of the four Israeli agents who were hiding inside the building. By then, just over sixty hours would have elapsed since the attack on Mishal. At the same time, he warned, all relations between Israel and Jordan would be severed.

Oded Eran, Israel's ambassador to Amman, was so new in the job that he had yet to present his credentials to the king. But credentialed or not, the ambassador was unlikely to forget the reaction when he attempted to explain to Shukri that Netanyahu was still refusing to reveal the formula for the drug used on Mishal, on the grounds that it was a "state secret."

"It's impossible," Eran told the director of the king's office. "We can't do it."

Stunned, Shukri asked him, "Could you repeat that?"

When the ambassador obliged him, Shukri exploded. "Why is it that in Israel you call it a top state secret, and in Iraq you call it a weapon of mass destruction? We're trying to save someone here, not kill them."[14]

The negotiations had become a global triangle, with Amman and Washington putting the squeeze on Jerusalem. Having received his riding instructions from the White House, Netanyahu well knew that, even if he complied with King Hussein's demand to hand over the secret formula, he was still unlikely to emerge from the crisis unscathed. But having plunged to the depths on the back of his own and Danny Yatom's wild call, the prime minister now needed to bring others into the decision making, to attach as many names as he might to the precarious process of reversing out of the quicksand in which he had sunk the axles of state.

Precise instructions were issued to a select group of senior Israeli officials early on Saturday evening. Staggering their arrivals, they were to attend a nine PM meeting in the Cabinet Room, off the prime ministerial suite in Jerusalem. Some were to use a side door to access the building; none of the military types were to wear uniform. Despite the late hour on a weekend night, there was a risk the news media might be tipped off to this emergency session. If the story leaked, it could be fatal.[15]

Up to now, they had managed to maintain an effective media blackout within Israel. But Randa Habib's reports were piling up on every editor's desk and, despite a strict censorship regime, questions were inevitable. Already a few reports, submitted as pull-togethers of what the foreign press was reporting from Amman, had been smacked down by the Israeli censor.

Netanyahu had summoned the inner circle of his government. Those taking their seats in the Cabinet Room included Defense Minister Yitzhak Mordechai, Infrastructure Minister Ariel Sharon, Attorney General Elyakim Rubinstein, the chiefs of the three Israeli intelligence services—foreign, domestic, and military—and a clutch of advisers and officials. They had been called together to decide if Israel should comply with what amounted to an ultimatum from Washington to hand over details of the drug.

It barely needed saying that, if it complied, Israel would be admitting that it was dabbling, in a very boutique way, in the sort of chemical warfare research that appealed to the likes of Saddam Hussein and other unsavory leaders. Some who were present sensed that Netanyahu was getting on top of the panic that had been apparent in his behavior earlier in the day. When they inquired what had happened to Mishal, they were told rather bluntly, "In hospital—a few minutes into death."

An official who attended the meeting later tried to sum it up: "We had decided to kill the guy, and we almost did it," he said. "Now we were being told that, to save our relationship with Hussein, we'd have to save the guy we'd nearly killed. Not an easy decision . . . everyone was aware of the political and practical consequences of saving Mishal."

And there was some scorn for the pressure that came from Washington in an endless stream of phone calls. "We well understood the mess we were in—we didn't need much encouragement from the White House," another attendee added.

Whichever way they cut it, they saw in the end that they had no choice. Within minutes of their unanimous decision to cooperate by handing over the antidote and the classified details of the poison, the news was flashed to Washington through the usual channels.

If Clinton was going to break the news personally to King Hussein, the West Wing team had to achieve split-second timing. In the Situation Room, Sandy Berger would have two opportunities to get the president's ear before his next public appointment, the Democratic fund-raiser at the baseball field back in Little Rock. Clinton would have ten minutes in the car between the school and boarding Marine One at the Hot Springs end of his journey, and another ten motorcade minutes as he was driven from Little Rock's Adams Field airstrip to the fund-raiser at the Ray Winder Baseball Field.

The first ten-minute window was used to update a somewhat relieved president on the decision taken in Jerusalem. And in the second, he was patched through to the palace in Amman, where a more gracious King Hussein shared his sense of relief at the same time that he indicated he would be remaining on guard.

"Thank you, Mr. President," the king said several times. "Thank you very much."

14

Pulling a Rabbit from the King's Threadbare Hat

In the panicked hours after the attack on Khalid Mishal, Benjamin Netanyahu had instinctively believed that somehow he would extract himself and his government from catastrophe. He knew that Israeli voters might punish him for trashing the Jordan treaty, but he knew too they would punish him twice over if he failed to rescue the Israeli agents now jailed in Amman, or their colleagues who might be snatched at any time from the embassy by Jordanian commandos. That was his priority.

When Danny Yatom returned empty-handed from Amman on Thursday afternoon, soon followed by the cabinet secretary, Danny Naveh, Netanyahu experienced a rare sensation for an Israeli leader dealing with the Palestinians on his doorstep and his Arab neighbors. It was when his attorney general, Elyakim Rubinstein, who was held in particularly high regard in the Jordanian capital, also could not get the ear of the king that the prime minister finally understood that this time he did not have the upper hand. The balance of power had been reversed.

Netanyahu understood his predicament well enough. But it was his military liaison officer, Shimon Shapira, who identified perhaps his only likely savior—a man versed in the arts of diplomacy, but also a cutthroat warrior with a steel-trap mind. Now Shapira urged Netanyahu to recall Efraim Halevy from Brussels, where he served as Israel's envoy to the European Union.

For all his diplomatic polish, Halevy had another side. For almost three decades before going to Brussels, he had been a fixture at Mossad, where the last five years of his service were spent as deputy director. Over time, and particularly when the Jordanian treaty was being negotiated, Shapira had observed Halevy's deep personal bond with King Hussein. Having witnessed the respect that he and Hussein had for each other, Shapira fully appreciated why Halevy was known with some affection as the "Father of the Treaty." It also helped that Halevy knew Mossad like the back of his hand.

Netanyahu agreed immediately. This was of the utmost urgency—not another precious hour could be lost. When the first phone call went out, late on Thursday afternoon in Europe, Halevy was on a shopping expedition with his wife. They were on a train to Antwerp, to buy furniture for the home they expected to move into in Israel when their posting ended in a few months. Shapira gave no explanation, no detail; he simply instructed the ambassador to return home immediately.

A forceful and independent character, Halevy refused. He would not return until his own boss, Foreign Minister David Levy, approved this sudden, mysterious assignment. "Can't be done," Shapira replied. "Levy is in New York."

It was clear the recall was an emergency. But the gruff and grumpy Halevy held his ground. He had traveled once before at the sudden request of the prime minister, who had not first cleared the matter with the foreign minister; the outcome had been a public shellacking for Halevy.[1] Finally, a Mossad agent was dispatched from Washington to the United Nations headquarters in New York to brief Levy on the crisis and to get his official approval for Halevy to be brought in to help save Netanyahu's political neck. Jerusalem needed a troubleshooter with rare skills and, as much as it grieved some in the conference room back at Mossad's headquarters to have someone else come in to clean up their mess, Efraim Halevy was perhaps the only Israeli up to the task. And at least he was one of them.

There were no immediate connections from Brussels to Israel's Ben-Gurion International Airport. Such was the sense of urgency in Jerusalem—or perhaps it was desperation—that an attempt was made to divert an El Al 747 freighter to pluck the ambassador from Brussels. But by the time it would get to him, Zaventem Airport would be closed for the night. Halevy investigated charter aircraft—but he balked at the $80,000 price tag to travel in the speed and comfort of his own jet.

That suited the ambassador in any case. The next available commercial connection would be Friday morning. Through his own channels, he had established an understanding of the Mossad madness in Amman. Now Efraim Halevy wanted some time to think.[2]

What might Halevy deliver that would satisfy King Hussein? If the king was to emerge from this crisis with his reputation intact and his throne secure, the Jordanian leader would have to appease four angry constituencies, by getting either something for all of them or something so remarkable for some of them that it would be transparently churlish for the others not to cheer him on.

By the king's own analysis, Jordanians generally were angry. He knew they saw little for themselves in the treaty he had signed with Israel. The Islamists—in the guise of Hamas and the Muslim Brotherhood—saw themselves as victims of the Israelis. Now they wanted blood and sport. Yasser Arafat's protests would raise the rafters if Hussein extracted Israeli concessions that gave Hamas a boost. And the regimes in the region that, along with the so-called Arab Street, had trashed Hussein's belief in peace with Israel would ramp their ridicule unless the king pulled an exceptional rabbit from his threadbare hat.

As Halevy wrestled with the challenges, King Hussein put himself at the center of the crisis in Amman. He talked to Hassan, his brother; he held meetings with General Batikhi; he bounced ideas off General Shukri.

Batikhi controlled the key official channel to Jerusalem, but there were other personal back channels, some of which were based on years of secret assignations before the signing of the treaty in 1994. Others were built on personal relationships that had evolved during the more formal diplomatic, political, and commercial engagements after the historic signing. With Mishal suspended between life and death, fevered phone calls went in both directions across the valley, as would-be peacemakers searched for the slimmest idea that might be massaged into a solution.

It all seemed like Mission Impossible. But, as he peered into the abyss, King Hussein finally discerned a ghostly, blank-eyed visage. It was a card held by the Israelis, but it was his trump card to play—it bore the face of Sheikh Ahmad Yassin. Freedom for the jailed founder and spiritual leader of Hamas needed to be the centerpiece in a deal that would have to be even more elaborately embroidered if King Hussein was ever to hose down his baying constituencies. But it all would have to start with the preacher.

As the living symbol of Islamic resistance, the crippled Yassin was the most prominent and most venerated of the thousands of Palestinians held in Israel's jails. His release would be a cruel concession to extract from Netanyahu, but this was the price he would have to pay for gaining the freedom of the Israelis under Jordanian arrest and those hiding out in the Israeli Embassy in Amman. Freedom for Yassin would be seen as a triumph not just by the Palestinians of the Occupied Territories, but also by the Palestinians who accounted for more than half of the population of Jordan.

Admittedly, freedom for Yassin would greatly destabilize Arafat. But how could the PLO leader complain, especially if the Israelis were so desperate that they too believed this was a good idea?

A cautious man, Halevy used words sparingly, and he was capable of the odd deferential compliment to make others feel they had his respect. Whether he arrived independently at the same ideal solution as Hussein—or whether it was broached in the incessant phone traffic to and from Amman, and perhaps even to Brussels, before he finally arrived in Jordan to see the king on Sunday morning—was unclear.

On landing back in Israel on Friday afternoon, just over twenty-four hours after the attack on Mishal, Halevy had been taken directly to Mossad's headquarters, where he made his presence felt immediately.[3] His former colleagues were startled when he insisted that he did not want to be briefed on what had happened in Amman. Instead, he wanted to know what ideas they had come up with to get all their agents back alive.

It was clear to Halevy that the Israeli intelligence establishment had been unable to grasp the enormity of what was at stake. They viewed this as just another crisis to be glossed over. They seemed unable to understand either the extent of the Jordanian king's sense of betrayal, or the risk and consequences of his being branded a traitor in his own country, should he accept any simple trade-off for Mossad's mess.

It was lean pickings. They had thought of offering a supply of infrared night sights for Jordan's military tanks, or perhaps upgrading some of the Jordanian air force's aging fleet.[4] Halevy quickly concluded they were in completely the wrong headspace—they were looking at how to solve their own problem, rather than how to solve King Hussein's problem. When he asked for something better, he was met with sullen silence and ill-concealed resentment.

Halevy devoted his first twenty-four hours back in Israel to getting the nation's most senior political and security figures to appreciate just what was at stake. He was accused of being overly dramatic, of failing to understand that the king would probably step back from his threats if Israel tossed him a supplement for his meager defense budget, or some such palliative. But Halevy was very much of the view that the pact he had helped to negotiate with Jordan was a cornerstone in Israel's long-term diplomatic strategy. A major concession was required.

When he threw Yassin's name into the mix, Halevy was met with shocked silence before being howled down by both his colleagues and his superiors. They pelted him with all the reasons that releasing the blind and crippled Palestinian hero was as impossible as it was inappropriate.

This kind of gesture had been raised recently by Washington during ongoing dialogue with Israel, but Netanyahu had told the Americans that freedom for Ahmad Yassin would greatly undermine Israel's security.[5] The Israeli public, still oblivious to this crisis, would never accept Yassin being allowed to walk from the cell in which they expected him to end his days.

Apart from the moral objection, Halevy's audience was politically opposed as well. Yassin's release would inflict harm on Yasser Arafat and the PLO, who, nominally at least, were Israel's formal partners in the peace process. If Yassin was to be released, they argued, he should be handed over to Arafat, not to King Hussein.

Halevy warned that without a gesture as weighty as Yassin's release, King Hussein would be written off as a collaborator with Israel. In that case they could expect all the vital defense and security cooperation between the countries to cease. This, he argued, was a potential development that would put both governments—Israeli and Jordanian—in jeopardy.

After arguing themselves into an angry stalemate, the Mossad team decided that the Yassin idea should be put to Netanyahu. He rejected it out of hand.

But by the next day, Saturday, the crisis was taking a heavy toll on Netanyahu. He was now confronted by three countries demanding a resolution: the aggrieved Jordanians, whose sovereignty had been traduced; the Canadians, who were furious about the passports; and the superpower Americans, who were fighting a losing battle in their efforts to hold the Middle East peace process together and were angry about the stupidity of the failed assassination plot.

Netanyahu was forced to change his position. Under extreme pressure from Washington to deliver the antidote and the formula to Jordan immediately, he would also have to hand over perhaps the most revered of the Palestinians' spiritual leaders, in order to save a peace process he might have preferred to sink. The release of Yassin would be a step so repugnant to Netanyahu that it would sting forever, but he was in a vise of his own making and there was only one way out.

The Israeli leader was concerned primarily about his captured agents and the domestic impact this would have on his political life. But all who were advising him could see that much, much more was at stake. Whatever Israel was going to offer in redress had to be significant and it had to be substantial. On Saturday morning, the prime minister finally relented and telephoned Halevy to give him explicit authority to offer the release of Sheikh Yassin. Being a cautious man, Halevy insisted that Netanyahu actually utter the word "Yassin" on the phone, so that later there could be no going back.[6]

Late on Saturday, just around midnight, a light aircraft flew west to east, over the Jordan Valley, before landing on the same military airstrip used by Danny Yatom when he had arrived in Amman forty-eight hours earlier.

A lone figure waited on the tarmac with an outstretched hand as the Israeli doctor stepped from the aircraft and walked toward him.[7] The two-page document and small bottles handed over possessed a value impossible to calculate. Mossad's top secret formula and more of the precious antidote were now in Jordanian hands. For King Hussein, however, this was merely an opening shot.

By Sunday morning in Amman, there was restrained jubilation and a tentative sense of relief at the King Hussein Medical City. The man from the Mayo Clinic had been back to check on the Palestinian VIP, and Akasheh's team were increasingly optimistic about the patient, even if they were disconcerted by the dozens of Mukhabarat, Hamas, and Muslim Brotherhood personnel in the corridors and the armed guards who hovered commando-like around his room.

Mishal had been treated so far only with the clinical cocktail devised by his Jordanian doctors, Bassam Akasheh and Sami Rababa, but now the doctors had a breakthrough, confirming their careful case management.

Shukri had earlier delivered the antidote syringes seized from Mossad's woman doctor. The first batch of the antidote they analyzed proved to be Narcan, one of the drugs already being fed into Mishal's body. When the new batch of the antidote, flown in from Israel at Washington's behest, was analyzed, it too proved to be Narcan. Akasheh was extremely pleased when the test results came back—they had been on the right track all along.

The medical team finally decided it was time to begin the process of bringing Mishal back from his enforced slumber. Gingerly at first, Rababa started to ease back on the ventilator around dawn on Sunday.

The doctors could only guess at how much of the killer drug was in Mishal's system, but, whether it was because the Israelis had bungled the dosage or its administration, Rababa the anesthesiologist concluded it was just short of the right amount. "If he was older or lighter, he would have been in more trouble.

His age and his weight—about a hundred kilograms—helped his body to cope sufficiently till we got him on the ventilator," he said.[8]

Up to now, the closest Mishal had ever come to death had been his involvement in a traffic accident in Kuwait some years earlier. But, by Akasheh's reckoning, the attempted assassination had taken him to "the dark tunnel with the light shining from the other end. It was that close."

Another intriguing piece of the pharmaceutical jigsaw fell into place when the royal palace faxed Akasheh the two-page document that the Israeli courier had handed over with the antidote on Saturday night. This was the chemical formula that the pincer movement of President Clinton and King Hussein had extracted from Netanyahu's reluctant clutches.

Finally, the poison had a name—levofentanyl—and it raised more questions than it answered about Mossad's acquisition of the drug, and the Israeli intelligence agency's involvement in the sinister world of industrial espionage and illicit drug research.

Shortly after receiving this fax, Akasheh took a strange phone call, which a hospital switchboard operator told him was being patched through from the royal palace in Amman. The caller did not identify himself by name, but he said he was a university professor attached to a reputable Israeli hospital, and he claimed to be the author of the document then in Akasheh's hand. The caller proceeded to give the Jordanian surgeon the same extraordinary account that was being fed to the CIA, of how Mossad had acquired the drug.[9]

Levofentanyl, he explained, was the product of failed research by the Belgian firm Janssen Pharmaceutica, which, in turn, was owned by the New Jersey–based American pharmaceutical giant Johnson & Johnson. Janssen had been looking for a spin-off from its hugely successful product fentanyl, then widely used to treat postoperative chronic pain.

It was common business practice in the drug industry to tinker with the chemical composition of a successful product in the hope of finding another marketable drug that might have similar or different applications. Levofentanyl, Akasheh was told, was such a hybrid, but it had proved to be far too potent and so had been deemed a failure.

The original fentanyl was a synthetic, morphine-like drug. But it was as much as one hundred times more potent than morphine. Traditionally, fentanyl was administered by a conventional needle injection into deep tissue. Functioning as both an analgesic and an anesthetic, it was an effective pain-killer, but it also affected a patient's consciousness and respiratory system.

When the drug was administered sparingly, the patient's blood became a very fast "taxi" that took just seconds to deliver micromanaged quantities of fentanyl to its "destination": the brain. There it connected to receptors where it could mimic the body's natural endorphins to control the pain neurocircuitry and the neurons that instruct the body to breathe. It was this latter aspect, away from the lifesaving environment of a hospital, that turned fentanyl and its even more powerful derivatives into killer drugs. "When the victim stops breathing, it's a death sentence," Akasheh concluded.

Akasheh was then at the peak of his profession and consulting widely, but he had never heard of levofentanyl. The databases he checked were utterly silent. Akasheh wondered how, if it had never gone on the market, this mysterious professor, who said he was calling from Israel, knew so much about levofentanyl. The Jordanian surgeon later told puzzled colleagues, "He was aware of its most minute detail, so he had to have been involved in testing it."

Akasheh concluded from this conversation that Mossad had somehow illicitly acquired the formula for the drug from within the Janssen organization and brought it back to an Israeli laboratory where it was manufactured. In Mossad's line of business, levofentanyl had added appeal because the death it induced was utterly unremarkable, making its cause impossible to trace.

Mossad's use of the drug might have been dismissed as a one-off dabble in boutique chemical weaponry had it not been for Netanyahu's bluster about protecting a "national secret," and for the insights of a small group of opiate experts in the United States. These clues suggested a more sinister possibility.

Others had tinkered with fentanyl before. In the 1970s, illicit drug laboratories on the American West Coast had unlocked the magic formula, manipulating it to produce the lethal "China white" analogues. These had the hallucinogenic strength of an elephant kick, but they left no traces that could be discovered in toxicological analysis of more than one hundred drug addicts whose deaths in Southern California were attributed to these so-called designer drugs.[10]

In other covert laboratories in the United States and abroad, the formula was manipulated in the search for a drug that military and civil authorities might use to control crowds—a sort of mega mace spray, which security experts referred to euphemistically as a "less than lethal" or "calmative" weapon.

Many fentanyl derivatives were spun off in legitimate commercial establishments. The Janssen laboratories in Belgium produced alfentanyl and sufentanyl, for use on humans; carfentanyl was marketed to tranquilize huge animals. But such was the extraordinary potency of most of the derivatives that even a tiny dose was an overdose. Most were locked away—deemed by their creators as way too risky for any commercial pharmaceutical application.

Internationally, this was a very specialized field of expertise. Perhaps no more than a dozen scientists were involved in any one of the advanced economies, and much of the technical information was proprietorial or held secretly by governments. But, fiercely competitive, all watched one another like hawks—and some on the fringes resorted to an old research trick to stay abreast of developments without doing their own laboratory legwork. Often using the letterhead of unknown institutions, they formally requested "reprint" rights for the best research, a process by which they were handed detailed accounts of the work of their competitors, in the expectation that they would be published for the benefit of a wider readership. However, many of the research papers never saw the light of day again.

One of America's opiate experts was fascinated by what he described as a "huge" stream of such requests from Israel and the former Soviet Union, which first came to his notice in the 1970s. "And from my interaction with people in U.S. agencies, I believe the Israelis . . . were up-to-date on novel ways to deliver these drugs," he added.[11]

The Soviet link was intriguing. Later it would be alleged that Mossad had recruited scientists from among the wave of Soviet Jews then resettling in Israel, to create a bank of toxins and nerve agents that were outlawed by international treaties.[12] In 2002, the world had a tragic insight into where the covert Soviet research might have led, when Russian authorities pumped quantities of a mysterious knockout gas into a Moscow theater in a bid to end a hostage drama in which Chechen guerrillas held a thousand hostages. The Russians used the same nebulized delivery mechanism that the Israelis had used against Khalid Mishal, albeit on a grander scale. The shocking outcome was the death of 129 of the unfortunate hostages.

At first, Russian authorities denied that the gas was the cause of death. But after four days of intense speculation driven by the families of the victims, Russian health minister Yuri Shevchenko admitted that "a substance based on a derivative of fentanyl" had been used with the intention of "neutralizing" the terrorists.[13] When urine samples from the Moscow victims were subjected to the most sensitive and sophisticated analysis available, none of the suspected fentanyl derivatives were found.[14] In the absence of the known, commercially produced derivatives such as sufentanyl and carfentanyl, experts concluded that the Moscow authorities had created their own fentanyl derivative, which was not capable of being detected in the West.

Dr. Akasheh could see the technical attraction of this drug for Mossad: there would be little chance of detecting the hand of a killer because an autopsy was highly unlikely to reveal the real cause of death. "If you are not looking for levofentanyl, you don't find it. You might conclude that there was some kind of narcotic—but how would you know what to look for?" he asked. "You start a street fight and the guy goes home feeling there's nothing wrong with him. In a while he starts to feel drowsy and says he'll just have a nap. But he never wakes up—the drug takes effect while he's asleep. It's a homicide, but nobody knows."

There was no known research on the clinical efficacy of administering fentanyl through the ear, and as Akasheh saw it, it made no sense medically. The human eardrum was a membrane that effectively sealed the ear, making it a slow point of absorption for any drug. Far better, he thought, to have sprayed it in Mishal's mouth, where absorption through the fleshy surface of the tongue would happen within seconds, or through the skin, which also would facilitate its rapid delivery to the bloodstream. But, for Akasheh to understand where Mossad was coming from, he needed to invert his analysis. Trained in the business of saving lives, he failed to consider the potential of levofentanyl in the hands of an assassin.

Mossad's decision to deliver the drug into Mishal's ear was quite brilliant. They needed Mishal dead, but they wanted him to die in his own time. They wanted the drug to act slowly. Ideally, Mishal was to expire at least a few hours after the "innocent" street encounter and at a location removed from the scene. In those circumstances his family and colleagues would hardly be likely to connect his death to a stranger having "accidentally" brushed against him in the street that morning. But the plan had a fatal flaw. Because the drug was administered through his ear, the hours before Mishal was expected to die also became the hours during which he might be saved.

Randa Habib was running ragged. Ordinarily there was logic to the division of her time between the office and home. But she had been living at the office for four straight days now, chained around the clock to her glass-topped desk. Her hair was bunched in a topknot that signaled "crisis" to all around her, and she was smoking more heavily than usual to calm her nerves. But even in the middle of this crisis, she found time to distractedly play mindless hands of solitaire on her desktop computer as she waited for those she called to pick up the phone.

It was a spacious, welcoming office, the cream walls set off by furniture and fittings in black and the finest red trim. Usually pristine, the office was now becoming a pit as files and notebooks were strewn on every flat surface. As with any journalist on a big breaking story, for Habib it was the story—and only the story—that mattered.

Habib had reported on virtually every development in the case so far. There had been her early conversation with Mishal, which had first implicated Mossad in this whole business, then his wife informing her that Mishal was on a respirator. Subsequently, there had been her sensational confirmation that Jordanian experts were examining a mysterious appliance, which sources close to the inquiry had told her was intended to kill Mishal. This appliance, she was led to understand, would have killed the Hamas leader without his death being linked to Thursday morning's scuffle in Garden Street and so without any adverse effect on relations between Jordan and Israel.

Late on Sunday morning, Habib reported that the Hamas leader was starting to emerge from the controlled coma in which he had been blanked out for more than two days. It would be another four days before Mishal could breathe unaided, but Habib—first again with the story—quoted Mishal's wife, Amal, as saying that early on Sunday, Mishal had stunned the bedside vigil by getting up and walking a few steps, before collapsing back into the bed.

Jordanian border guards had already been alerted, but the sight of a Jew in a baggy suit striding across the metal-framed Allenby Bridge on a Sunday morning still took their breath away. It was a neat affectation by the patrician-looking Efraim Halevy. He came alone and he came on foot. To outsiders it might have seemed reckless for a former top Israeli agent and current senior ambassador to stroll across any of Israeli's borders. But Halevy well knew he was under double layers of electronic surveillance, both Israeli and Jordanian—as was anyone who might wish to do him harm. He enjoyed the walk, but his idiosyncratic arrival was also about sending a considered message to his Jordanian hosts. "We know each other; we trust each other," he was saying.

A car dispatched by the palace collected Halevy and delivered him to the Little House in the royal compound in downtown Amman, where he was received by Crown Prince Hassan and the GID chief, General Samih Batikhi. As the Israeli was ushered into a reception room, he took comfort from his long friendship with the crown prince and his brother, the king, but Batikhi, the security head, was an unknown quantity. Oddly enough, the timing of Batikhi's appointment as director of the GID and Halevy's departure from the top echelon of Mossad for Brussels meant they had never met. But Halevy could feel the oxyacetylene anger radiating from the man with the silver hair.

Halevy and his wife were regular houseguests at Hussein's palaces. All this was taken on board at the GID, but as the Jordanian intelligence chief took in Halevy, he decided to treat him for what he was. In Batikhi's estimation, the Israeli was a "smart Zionist"—just as capable as Danny Yatom of ordering Khalid Mishal's assassination, and then going home to have dinner with his family and a good night's sleep.

The Jordanians got straight down to business, revealing to Halevy for the first time much of the minute detail of the previous Thursday's attack on Mishal. Quite apart from their understandable outrage, what Halevy heard in the telling was a deep sense of hurt that Mossad's senior people considered their Jordanian counterparts so stupid that they could get past them with such slipshod planning. They were equally offended by the conclusion that Mossad now seemed to believe it could act with impunity in Jordan. The crown prince complained he was still suffering waves of nausea from just thinking about what the Israelis had perpetrated.

Halevy bided his time, allowing them to let off all the steam they wanted. When he finally thought it might be acceptable, he requested permission for himself or one of his Amman embassy colleagues to visit the Mossad prisoners. Batikhi refused point-blank. Halevy then asked for the release of the four Mossad agents still hunkering in the embassy. In the face of more stonewalling by Batikhi, Halevy recast his plea as a simple request to go to the Israeli Embassy. "Yes," Batikhi finally consented, Halevy could do that.

A car was made available to drive him to the Israeli mission, where, in a brief meeting, the former Mossad boss assured the four anxious agents he was doing all he could to extract them quickly. "Be ready to move fast," he instructed.

When Halevy returned to the palace, the group was joined by King Hussein. Halevy was struck by what he detected as a deep sadness, rather than any sense of anger, in his friend. "It showed in his eyes," the Israeli explained later. "It was genuine hurt. He spoke in the same soft way that he did after we did the Oslo agreement with the PLO without his knowledge."

For either side to have raised the fate of the jailed Sheikh Yassin at this point in an already explosive political situation might have been expected to be the equivalent of removing the pin from a grenade. Yet, as it transpired, groundwork by both sides in advance of this meeting had created circumstances in which the issue could be slipped effortlessly into the dialogue, as though steered by its own inevitability. But the Jordanians would want more. They made it abundantly clear that they needed what might best be described as a "Yassin-plus" outcome. Halevy would recall later, "[King Hussein] intimated he would be accepting the offer of the release of Sheikh Yassin together with others, yet to be specified."[15]

Changing gears diplomatically, Halevy suggested that the crisis could not be allowed to fester. Acknowledging that Israel well understood it would have to pay dearly to resolve it all, he proposed a meeting at the highest level—which he urged should be organized for that very night. Hussein agreed and Halevy excused himself. Dashing back to the embassy, where he had access to a secure line, he succeeded in arm-twisting Netanyahu into agreeing to what promised to be a high-risk encounter.

Halevy then returned to the palace, and they all stood in an awkward circle. Hussein, Hassan, Batikhi—and their Israeli friend. This was the moment Halevy chose for a considered gamble. He complained to the monarch that Batikhi was being unreasonably harsh in his treatment of the six agents.

Privately, the Israeli concluded that there was no chance of winning immediate freedom for the two held in jail. But he threw himself on the mercy of the king, pleading for permission to take out the four still hiding at the embassy. After all, the woman doctor had been permitted to leave the country after handing over the syringes.

Hussein was a gambler too. He knew it was unlikely that the Jordanian authorities could lay their hands on these four without shooting their way into the embassy compound. The king was aware that Israel was a country capable of going to war for the lives of a handful of its soldiers. But such was the stupidity of this Mossad operation that the two Israelis languishing in his prison might as well have walked into their cells and thrown away the keys themselves. His majesty could afford to be gracious.

Too gracious, Batikhi thought. His own preferred strategy was to keep tightening all the screws on the Israelis. Halevy now made his third dash back to the embassy and organized an Israeli air force helicopter to come immediately to lift himself and the four agents out of Amman. He was determined to be off the ground before there could be any change of heart. The helicopter took off from the embassy within thirty minutes of Halevy having left the royal palace late on Sunday afternoon.

Dropping the agents off at Mossad's headquarters, Halevy flew to Jerusalem, where he barely had time to draw breath again before he was rounding up the most senior members of the Israeli government to brief them on his Amman outing. At the conclusion of Halevy's lengthy account, they adjourned, again under cover of darkness, to the helipad at the Knesset, the Israeli parliamentary complex in Jerusalem. The helicopter crew awaiting them was ready for takeoff.

The Israeli cabinet team entered Jordanian airspace after midnight, in the early hours of Monday, September 29, creeping across the Jordan Valley and up toward Amman. With all lights blacked out to prevent identification, they were running late.[16] Nerves frayed as the big helicopter rose and fell in the darkness, with all on board peering out for any sign of welcome from the Amman authorities. They thought they were being snubbed.

Waiting on the ground, the Jordanians concluded that their clandestine visitors must be lost. The Israeli helicopter pilot had been given coordinates for the royal guard helipad at Hashimieh, on the western outskirts of metropolitan Amman. But Jordanian air-traffic control was reporting the chopper to be way off target—hovering over Al-Mafraq, about thirty miles northeast of the designated drop point.

In the interior gloom of the helicopter, Efraim Halevy became more agitated as each tense minute ticked longer into the next. As a veteran of too many national security crises, his eyes darted around the crowded cabin, taking in his prime minister, ministers Ariel Sharon, Yitzhak Mordechai, and Elyakim Rubinstein, plus enough senior military brass and government bigwigs to fill him with dread. As an espionage agent turned diplomat, Halevy could see a national tragedy in the making.

It was against all security guidelines to have the prime minister and even just one of his ministers travel on the same helicopter. Yet, here they were—almost half the cabinet at the mercy of a single rotor blade, risking crashing into another aircraft or colliding with low-slung power lines as they groped in the dark for somewhere to land. The possibilities were too frightening—Halevy wanted to hightail it back to Jerusalem.

Unable to make himself heard above the engine noise, he scratched a message on a piece of paper for the prime minister: "Let's go back," it said. But Benjamin Netanyahu had come this far. His response was to slash his hand through the air a couple of times—"No way! No way!"

Ultimately, a Jordanian chopper flew abreast of the Israeli machine to guide them back toward the Hashimieh helipad. Just a few minutes away from there by car, the place chosen for this extraordinary meeting was a small farm owned by the king's office director, Ali Shukri. Given the late hour, its remote setting, and the presence of a royal guards compound nearby, King Hussein thought it was sufficiently secure for such a team of VIP visitors. But, even though the prime minister of Israel had flown into the night to see him, such was Hussein's still incendiary anger that he chose to have no part in this visit, quite calculatedly snubbing Netanyahu. Instead, he sent Crown Prince Hassan, Batikhi, and Shukri.

When the Israelis straggled into the farm, they were not invited indoors. They were offered nothing to eat, not a bowl of nuts, not even a drink. It was probably the only time a foreign delegation arriving as guests of King Hussein was so pointedly denied traditional Arab hospitality. As they were ushered to a small table beneath a shade cloth that swayed in a cool September breeze, no civility was extended at all.

Netanyahu was defensive, but he also attempted an apology. He took full personal responsibility for what had happened and, he said, he did not want it to reflect on the peace process. But Batikhi, in particular, did not hear the prime minister's words as a "sorry." What he heard was Netanyahu attempting to downplay the whole affair, at the same time as he tried to justify it on the grounds of Hamas's attacks within Israel. As the crown prince tried to pull the meeting back within the bounds of diplomatic decorum, Netanyahu made an ill-judged attempt to hose down Batikhi's unbridled anger. "General, I see you are taking this very personally," he told the GID man. "Please don't—these things happen."

That was a mistake because Batikhi was indeed taking it very personally. The intelligence channel he managed was probably the most important conduit between their two governments, even on political issues, and here were the Israelis trying to play his men for half-wits. General Batikhi had often been described as the first chief of Jordan's GID whose operational paradigm was not hatred for Israel; like the king, he believed in the treaty. He had worked hard to put into effect Hussein's vision of peace and cooperation between difficult neighbors, despite the carping of just about every man and woman in Jordan. Now Mossad had besmirched all that, creating circumstances in which Hussein would be made to look a fool, if not a collaborator, before his people and the region.

The general knew he was firing bullets for his king. In Hussein's absence, he resorted to a calculatedly coarse Arab response to Netanyahu's "these things happen" jibe: "I'll tell you why I'm angry," he snorted. "This business is like meeting someone, trusting him, and building a new friendship. You invite him home and, the minute you turn your back, he's fucking your wife."

Batikhi had taken the precaution of apologizing in advance to Crown Prince Hassan for the crude language he planned to use, but he still felt a sharp knock to his knee under the table at this juncture. "Done," Prince Hassan was saying. "You've made your point."

Batikhi's point was about the Arab male sense of honor, of trust, and of dignity between friends, and, as it turned out, he was not quite done. Batikhi now put a name on the scalp that he and King Hussein wanted as a personal partial payment for Israel's messing with Amman: "Danny Yatom is finished. Intelligence cooperation is over. I'll never work with him again, even if King Hussein fires me!" Batikhi declared.

Even before the attempt on the life of Khalid Mishal, Netanyahu might have anticipated payback from King Hussein if he were to drop his guard and give the Jordanians half a chance. The king's heartfelt letter five months earlier, complaining about the Israeli prime minister's contempt for the peace process, should have been warning enough. What deeply offended Hussein and his aides was that Netanyahu's most outrageous acts were timed so closely to visits by senior Israeli officials to Amman that the Hashemites could easily be painted as collaborators, acquiescing in Israel's most provocative deeds—deliberately so, they suspected.

One of those deeds had been Netanyahu's go-ahead, twelve months earlier, for a controversial tunnel under the Muslims' Al-Aqsa Mosque in Jerusalem, sparking violence in which almost seventy people had died—just twenty-four hours after Hussein had received a high-level envoy from Jerusalem. Another, which colleagues said burned in Batikhi's brain, was the Israeli leader's personal assurance to Hussein six months earlier that he had abandoned plans for thousands of new Jewish homes on the expropriated Palestinian land known in Arabic as Jebal Abu Ghneim and in Hebrew as Har Homa. This would be the last in a chain of Jewish settlements encircling Jerusalem, a prospect that drove the Palestinians to despair. Almost immediately after giving Hussein that assurance, Netanyahu gave the green light for the bulldozers. Now he had to face the consequences.

Amidst all the anger at Shukri's farm, a galled Crown Prince Hassan formally registered Jordan's complaint that the attack on Mishal in the streets of Amman constituted a violation of the treaty between their two countries. "We're always reminded that Israel is the only democratic state in the region . . . and yet you find the only democratic state in the region being associated with an act of terror," he said.[17]

As those at the meeting agreed in the broadest terms that it would require a substantial deal to get them all out of the mess, Hassan and Batikhi shuffled the pack. The occasions on which the Jordanians were dealt all the aces were too rare, but this was one of them. Hamas had already initiated a legal process against the two Mossad agents in custody, petitioning for a public trial that would play very badly for Netanyahu in Israel. Furthermore, King Hussein had agreed with President Clinton's plea the day before, that he should attempt to negotiate a deal that would win so many kudos for Amman that he would not need to cave in to the rising chorus of demands in Jordan that he must abandon the treaty. Batikhi's eyes bored into the squirming delegation from Jerusalem: "Jordan's leadership has to be preserved. We are the victims in this, and you guys are going to pay."

But agreement on what exactly those terms might ultimately be would have to wait. All accepted the need to ensure that Khalid Mishal's health was fully restored before there could be any further detailed talks. It was well after three AM on Monday when the Israelis retreated into the night.

In her AFP story on the Sunday night reporting Mishal's return from death's door, Randa Habib revealed that the suspect "Canadians" had been moved to secret custody, not a common prison. And, she added, "Jordanian authorities have put a total news blackout on their [investigation of the Mishal affair]."

Later, and despite the blackout, Habib reported that the official investigation demanded by Hamas was moving at breakneck speed. Already, the file had been referred to the Higher Criminal Court. The message here for Netanyahu was blunt—his men might still be put in the dock in Amman at what, for the Arab world, would be a sensational public examination of a botched Mossad mission.

But also in her report was the first hint that the Jordanian investigation might conveniently run out of steam. "Jordanian authorities have cautioned the Hebrew state and summoned the Israelis to identify the chemical," Habib reported. "If Israel agrees, Jordan would make as little noise as possible and resolve the matter discreetly."

Across the river in Israel, the media was still in its censorship straitjacket. But Smadar Perry, a senior journalist on the Tel Aviv–based daily *Yedioth Ahronoth*, was attempting to wriggle free. Believing Randa Habib to be the best-connected journalist in Jordan, Perry had been electrified by Habib's AFP reports, which she was hearing on Radio Monte Carlo. Off duty on the day when the reports first hit the wires, she thought them odd—except for the fact that they were Habib's.

The *Jerusalem Post* had reported the attack on Mishal as a page-two item the day after it occurred. The newspaper covered Hamas's allegation that this had been an assassination attempt, with Jordanian authorities hosing it down and the Israeli government refusing to comment. But thereafter, coverage in the Israeli media virtually dried up. In Cold War terms, it was the equivalent of a CIA team being arrested by the British, after bungling the lunchtime assassination of a prominent Soviet figure in London's Trafalgar Square—and the *New York Times* making no mention of it.

Calling her Tel Aviv office, Perry urged a senior editor to pick up the AFP accounts of the strange behavior of Israel's intelligence service in Amman. "Are you crazy?" he thundered down the line.

Perry continued to monitor Habib's reports. The detail was too exquisite to have been concocted, she concluded. Convinced that Israel's controversial Netanyahu was attempting to ride out a national crisis under cover of censorship, Perry went back to the same editor. "Look," she said, "Randa Habib does not invent this stuff!"[18] But he would not budge.

Resorting to an old fallback for Israeli journalists, Perry suggested they outfox the censors by legitimately reporting what the foreign media, such as AFP, were reporting from Amman. "No. Habib is hallucinating," the editor told Perry. "Who'd believe it?"

15

The Price Bibi Paid

Mousa Abu Marzook was back on top. As Khalid Mishal's life hung in the balance, the engineer had eased back into the leader's chair, crisis managing the Hamas political bureau in Amman. He lashed out at the Israelis, warning that if the attack on Mishal was the start of an Israeli campaign to strike at Hamas targets beyond historic Palestine, then Hamas too would strike at Israeli targets in the wider world.

For good measure, Abu Marzook took a swipe at Yasser Arafat and the PLO as well, warning that they would be targeted in new clandestine operations by Hamas's military wing unless Arafat backed off. In the aftermath of the latest suicide bombings, Arafat's security forces had been involved in an ongoing crackdown across the Occupied Territories, detaining dozens of Hamas activists and shutting down a dozen or more of the movement's community institutions, including medical clinics, a soup kitchen for the needy, a girls' dormitory, a school supplies agency, and a pirate television station.

Abu Marzook was pleased to have the cameras and microphones back in his life, and to see reporters lining up at his door. He had fun, especially with Jewish American reporters, some of whom would garble their surnames lest their antecedents be an issue when meeting top Hamas officials. Abu Marzook enjoyed toying with them, asking them to articulate each syllable as he made a studious examination of a business card. Only then would he put them at ease. "Ah," he would begin mischievously. "My lawyer was a Cohen. Did you know that the Cohens are the rabbis of the Jews?"

But the fun stopped when the call came from Samih Batikhi early on Sunday. The chief of the Mukhabarat needed to see Abu Marzook.

The GID boss took his time. In formulating a strategy for this discussion with Abu Marzook, Batikhi had decided that he would not immediately raise the prospect of freedom for Sheikh Ahmad Yassin. Instead, what he needed to know was under what circumstances Hamas might agree to drop its legal action against the captured Israeli agents?

King Hussein was now contemplating acting above the law to free the Mossad men. Hamas, however, was demanding that the regime stay within the law and prosecute the Israeli prisoners, who it saw as terrorists. As a non-Jordanian who lived in the kingdom by Hussein's grace and who by now was quite familiar with Batikhi's style, Abu Marzook had the sweaty-palmed feeling of someone who knew he was about to be asked again to return the king's favor.

Finally, they broke off for consultations with others. When they resumed their negotiations by phone—holding four or five conversations during the day—Abu Marzook detected a more strident tone in the GID man as the stakes went ever higher. Batikhi needed Abu Marzook to engage in a classic barter, but that required the man from Hamas to talk. Instead, he chose to listen. Abu Marzook needed to protect his own position, preferring that Batikhi put firm proposals on the table, which Hamas might take or leave.

The GID director was aware that Hamas vehemently opposed the king's treaty with Israel and the whole foundering peace process. The risk was that Abu Marzook might be tempted to gamble. By choosing not to cooperate with the regime, and instead using the attack on Mishal as a platform from which to ignite anti-regime anger, Hamas conceivably could force the king of Jordan to kill two birds for the movement with a single stone. If Hamas and the Muslim Brotherhood were to whip up sufficient popular protest, an anxious Hussein might be obliged to abandon the treaty with Israel, which, in turn, would be a grave setback for the Clinton-sponsored Middle East peace process. This was power to be exploited to the hilt by Abu Marzook, unless, of course, the regime was to make an offer that Hamas could not refuse.

Having failed to elicit an opening bid from Abu Marzook, Batikhi was obliged to play the Yassin card. Sheikh Ahmad Yassin, whom Abu Marzook, in particular, revered more than any other human being, had been languishing in an Israeli prison for eight years.

What if Netanyahu was forced to release Yassin? Batikhi asked in a deadpan voice. Wide-eyed, Abu Marzook batted it straight back. "The Jews would never agree," he said, well aware that the only response to the demand for Yassin's release that had followed each Hamas bombing had been a hardening of the Israeli resolve against their leader.

At this stage, it might have helped if Batikhi had trusted Abu Marzook

sufficiently to brief him on the whole story of the Israeli antidote. To have
done that might have engaged Abu Marzook in the wider complexities of the
crisis, but as Batikhi saw it, that was too much of a gamble. If his attempt to
lock in Abu Marzook were to sour, just the hint of any such dealings by Jordan with Israel and the United States could be used by Hamas to embarrass
the regime.

Instead, Batikhi pressed on with the prisoner release issue, trying to ice the
cake: "And some of the other prisoners—the release of Yassin and more
Hamas prisoners?"

Abu Marzook wondered if Batikhi had taken leave of his senses. But the
GID chief, who knew that any such deal needed the blessing of Hamas before Yassin could be released, assured him he was deadly serious.

Always a pragmatist, Abu Marzook took the proposal back to his colleagues and, among them, they decided to test Batikhi's patience by demanding more. Some began to imagine the Israelis being made to release thousands
of Hamas prisoners.

In a celebrated prisoner swap in the past, hundreds of Palestinian inmates
had been freed in return for a few Israelis held by Palestinian forces. The
Hamas men now decided to press King Hussein to push ahead with the criminal trial of the two Mossad agents unless Israel was ready to release hundreds
of Palestinian prisoners.

Abu Marzook had gone too far. Batikhi quickly pushed back, with a reminder that, in attempting to preserve his own honor and his throne, King
Hussein was far more concerned with his own fate than with any advantage Hamas might gain in the crisis. Batikhi now spelled out some harsh
realities—dozens, not hundreds, would be released; also, the Hamas legal
team could fold their tent—there would be no show trial for the Mossad hit
men in Amman.

Abu Marzook finally agreed, fully appreciating that the release of Yassin
would be a fabulous and unimagined prize. He was not to know, but the
acceptance by Hamas of the king's terms locked in the deal with the Israelis, just as Hussein had envisaged. Jordanian and regional public opinion
might be relied upon not to turn against the monarch if the Islamists could
be satisfied.

Now, as Hussein and Batikhi finalized the list of demands they would formally present to the Israelis, the king decided he would also need a couple of
dozen Fatah prisoners to keep Arafat quiet too. And, while he was at it, he
should insist on the release of all Jordanians in Israeli custody. There would
be something for everyone in this.

.   .   .

In the aftermath of the meeting at Shukri's farm, Netanyahu was as desperate to win the release of his two Mossad agents as he was to get Washington, Ottawa, and Amman off his back. Yet, curiously enough, when the Israelis returned to Amman yet again, late on Monday night for another meeting, they presented an almost entirely new lineup. Efraim Halevy had now returned to Brussels and, with the exception of one, all of the ministers who had made the Sunday midnight dash to Amman ceased to be involved in the Jordanian end of the drama.

That exception was Ariel Sharon, perhaps the member of the Israeli establishment most hated by the Palestinians. As Israel's defense minister, Sharon had mounted the 1982 invasion of Lebanon for the express purpose of destroying the PLO. His audacious plan at the time was to see the Palestinians of Lebanon and the West Bank herded into Jordan in sufficient numbers to topple the Hashemite regime. That would allow the creation of a new Palestinian state, which, the bullish Sharon thought, would solve all of Israel's problems. He was even ready to help the Palestinians to depose King Hussein, and he had advocated Israeli military action "against the terrorist headquarters in Amman."

Sharon had been no friend to Amman but had apparently seen the light after King Hussein and Prime Minister Yitzhak Rabin signed the peace treaty. When the pact was presented for approval in the Knesset, Sharon refused to vote for it, but later, observing its popularity among Israelis, he repackaged himself as Amman's new best friend in the region.[1]

Now Netanyahu, embarrassed and facing off against Sharon in an internal power play, agreed to send the Likud strongman to Jordan to engage in a talkfest with the palace. If Sharon was successful, well and good—all would benefit. If he failed, Sharon could wear the blame. It was a classic political double play by the cornered Netanyahu. Sharon, for his part, did not hesitate to grab an opportunity for the limelight.

Accompanying Sharon on his journey to Jordan on Monday evening, now five days after the attack on Khalid Mishal, was his intriguing aide, Majali Whbee. An Arab-Israeli, he was a member of the Druze sect of northern Israel, and one of the back-channel men between Amman and Jerusalem. Whbee had been denied access to the Israeli Embassy by the cordon of Jordanian military sealing the building off on the day of the hit on Khalid Mishal, when he returned there after a meeting with the king himself. When Netanyahu later demanded to be put through to Hussein at two o'clock in the morning, it was Whbee who had had enough presence of mind to dial the wrong number, rather than disturb the king.

For the meeting with Sharon on the Monday night, King Hussein chose a venue that was more appropriate than Shukri's farm—a small palace in the royal compound in the heart of Amman, which was reserved for guests of the crown prince. Hassan and General Batikhi were waiting to greet Sharon and Whbee when they arrived. Again it was almost midnight before the meeting began.

Once King Hussein had made his entrance, the Israeli and Jordanian delegations sat in a lounge setting, attempting small talk for a good thirty minutes. Batikhi was pumped up; Sharon too had come ready for a brawl. Finally Sharon let fly—the only mistake on the part of the Israelis, he declaimed, had been the Mossad agents' failure, not their choice of target, and not the location. "If they did it properly, Mishal would be dead and wouldn't that be just great for everyone," he declared, needling Batikhi.

Batikhi refused to take the bait. Rolling his eyes, he demanded to know if Sharon, in the presence of the king of Jordan, intended to continue as rudely as he had begun.

Taking his cue, Whbee steered his Hebrew-speaking boss toward more conciliatory language—words like "sorry," "apology," and "error."[2] But the king of Jordan took these verbal offerings and, wrapping them in salt, threw them straight back. "How do you apologize after such a huge mistake? This appalling error threatens the whole peace process," he rebuked the rogue bull of the Israeli establishment.

On this occasion there was some semblance of Arab hospitality, and food was offered to the guests from Israel. While they were eating, Whbee tried to steer the meeting in a different direction. Sharon refused Whbee's whispered suggestion that he take the initiative, so Whbee did it for him—regaling the Jordanians with an amusing account of how Sharon's wife had recently phoned in from the farm and insisted on being put through to a formal session of the Israeli cabinet to report to her husband on the successful birth of a calf.

Whbee's ploy seemed to work. Sharon got the king's attention with his theory of piping chilled drinking water to his sheep in a bid to improve their milk. In turn, Sharon was goggle-eyed as Hussein explained some of the more complex aspects of raising horses. But it was going to take more than a bit of farm talk to hoodwink King Hussein. When Sharon thought he had segued seamlessly to the fate of the two agents, Hussein merely gave Batikhi one of his meaningful looks.

Sharon was noticeably impatient as Batikhi long-windedly set out the need for Jordan to survive the crisis with no scar tissue. When Batikhi bullet-pointed Amman's specific demands, Sharon hit the ceiling. First his face went red, then, at the mention of Yassin's name, it went white. Despite the preliminary discussion with the Israelis the previous day about the need to free Yassin, Sharon appeared utterly taken aback. He gave the impression that he had no idea that this question had already been canvassed with his own leader. "Impossible! General, you are asking for the impossible," he exploded. "Not even the prime minister of Israel can do this."

Batikhi, as his master's voice, pressed on, making clear that Jordan was not proposing that Yassin be released to exile in Jordan. "He goes back to Gaza," he said, flourishing his own trump card. "And the other prisoners will have the right to go back to their homes and villages in Gaza and the West Bank."

Flustered, Sharon said he had come to Amman only to listen. He claimed he could see no possible connection between the Mossad attack on Mishal and the release of Sheikh Ahmad Yassin. But in any event, he was not authorized to make concessions. He would have to report back to Netanyahu.

It was about four AM when Sharon left with Whbee, advising Batikhi to be more realistic. "Netanyahu will not accept," he told him. "So you're going to have to reconsider."

Batikhi shoved a list of the Jordanian demands at Whbee, and went home to grab some sleep. At about six AM he was roused by the bedside phone. On the line was an operator on the GID switchboard, requesting permission to patch through a call from Jerusalem. The heavy voice of Ariel Sharon came down the line: "General, you've got yourself a deal."

Batikhi left nothing to chance. Abu Marzook was squared away and the Israeli government was basically prepared to accept the king's demands. Batikhi was finally clear to embark on the next stage in the king's strategy to hold Netanyahu to the fire—a dash to Washington with Crown Prince Hassan to see President Bill Clinton, to make sure that the United States was absolutely clear on all the facts of this crisis.

During his absence, Batikhi's men combed the city in a relentless investigation of every aspect of the activities of the "Canadians" in Amman. Their eyes were everywhere. Ranya Kadri found herself in the spotlight again when she took the *Washington Post*'s Barton Gellman to Garden Street, to attempt to reconstruct events at the scene of the crime. The search for eyewitnesses took them into a nearby fabric shop. Minutes later they were back in the street, planning their next move, when Kadri observed two men entering the shop. "Mukhabarat!" she exclaimed before racing back into the shop to find the two men, with notebooks open, copying down the details of the business cards she and the American reporter had left with the merchant.

Over at the AFP offices, Randa Habib stayed up all night on Tuesday. The king's every public word now was crafted as a bullet or a shield. Habib's antennae told her a dramatic development was imminent when Hussein seemed to go out of his way in a speech at Zarqa to address the issue of prisoners held by Israel. This was how it worked in this part of the world—public hints by the king laid down a marker for news of what officials were hammering out behind closed doors.

There was haggling over which prisoners could be released. The Jordanians were derisive when the Israelis challenged some names they had submitted. When Whbee objected, arguing that some had "blood on their hands," he was mocked by Saed Khair, one of Batikhi's senior men. Khair suggested that, if this was so, perhaps Israel might nominate the "respectable, good people in Israeli jails" who should be released.

Finally, up to seventy names were agreed. Many of the Jordanians had been serving sentences of twenty or more years. Israeli officials tried to "spin" the list, arguing that some had been arrested *before* executing their violent crime against Israel and thus it was of no great concern or embarrassment for Israel to see them walk free. But the Jordanians let it be known that most were "senior Hamas leaders."

King Hussein now became increasingly confident of his own survival. In public, he continued to flail at Benjamin Netanyahu; yet, at the same time he allowed a little give-and-take. For now, he insisted that the timing of the release of the two Mossad agents be left up in the air. His Majesty also refused outright a plea from Israel that Ottawa should be denied access to the incriminating Canadian passports, which had been seized from the agents.

With his own deal in place, King Hussein started setting the ground for the collapse of the Hamas case against the Israeli agents, which was a complication he didn't need. "We don't have a weapon that was used against Khalid Mishal, and from the depositions of Mishal's companions, the aggressors failed to touch him directly," the king announced, much to the astonishment of Randa Habib, whose inquiries through her own sources suggested quite the opposite.

In a single sentence King Hussein had revealed the pragmatism that underlay the difficult but, for him, necessary relationship with his Israeli neighbors. Exposure of the weapon—and all that it would reveal about a thriller-like departure from Israel's usual practice of eliminating its enemies with conventional bombs and bullets—was a headache Benjamin Netanyahu didn't need. On this issue, Hussein would oblige him.

As they left Amman late on Tuesday, there was a slight hiccough with regard to the important issue of royal dress standards among King Hussein's hand-picked delegation to Washington. The departure abroad of any of the senior royals required that they be formally bidden farewell to on the tarmac by family members and officials. The problem arose with the arrival of the CIA station chief, Dave Manners, who, at the express wish of King Hussein, was to accompany Crown Prince Hassan and General Batikhi on their visit to the United States. As the American mingled with the assembled suits in his trademark denim jeans and polo shirt, one or two of the Jordanian retainers had conniptions at such a breach of protocol. Fast on his feet, Ali Shukri quickly hustled Manners up the rear stairs of the aircraft, with instructions to remain out of sight until they were airborne.

The Jordanians were fixated on getting the ear of President Bill Clinton. King Hussein knew he had Israel's prime minister against a wall for as long as he held his trophy prisoners, the Mossad duo. But any lingering trust he had in Netanyahu was so shattered that Hussein would leave nothing to chance. He wanted Clinton to be intimately versed on the details so that, in the event of any last-minute breakdown in Amman's negotiations with the Israelis, the American president could make informed decisions. Hussein's willingness, at this critical stage of the crisis, not to have his closest advisers—his brother Hassan and Batikhi—at his side indicated how great was his need to have the full backing of Washington. Hussein understood too the diplomatic punch of a personal meeting with the president.

The Americans understood as well. Such was the anxiety in Washington that as the sleek Gulfstream IV eased to a halt on the tarmac at Andrews Air Force Base, just outside the Beltway, late on Wednesday morning, no less a figure than CIA director George Tenet was there to receive them. Batikhi and Manners found their own way to CIA headquarters at Langley while Tenet drove the crown prince to the fashionable Madison Hotel, just off Massachusetts Avenue, near Du Pont Circle.

Batikhi later held a hurried session with Tenet at the CIA and managed to squeeze in a half-hour session with his Canadian counterpart, who had flown down from Ottawa, hoping to extract more information from the tight-lipped Batikhi about Israel's misuse of Canadian passports. But the real reason for this trip was thirty vital minutes in the Oval Office that Clinton's staff had managed to slot into the presidential diary for early on Wednesday evening, October 1.

Prince Hassan and General Batikhi were received at the White House by the president and National Security Advisor Sandy Berger, Secretary of State Madeline Albright, and the man who had taken King Hussein's first telephone call to the White House, Bruce Riedel, Clinton's special adviser on Near Eastern affairs. The contents of a polished briefcase that remained in the firm clasp of the crown prince throughout this visit were a closely guarded secret. By several accounts, it was stuffed with "evidence" against the Israelis, including damaging statements by the two Mossad agents during their interrogation in Amman. There were oblique references to a show-and-tell video recording of the Israelis' confessions. But all subsequent questions about the contents of the case and in whose hands it was left were met with a stony silence.

The Americans listened in amazement as first Hassan and then Batikhi walked them through the results of the GID's investigation to date. The president promised his backing to King Hussein and offered to hold Netanyahu to the terms of whatever exit deal might finally be agreed. Clinton also undertook to continue pressing Netanyahu to moderate his behavior, in the hope that there might be a resumption of the stalled peace talks between the Arafat-led Palestinian Authority and the government of Israel, the outcome of which was vital to Jordan. All spoke in saintly tones of the absent King Hussein.

Hassan, the king's younger brother, was not the stereotypical Arab prince. He arrived at the White House in his customary conservative business suit with a neatly knotted tie, not in flowing robes. He had a reputation as a man of words, but one who had the ability to lose his audience between the start and finish of a single sentence. He was a graduate of Christ Church, Oxford, and he involved himself in education and the sciences. In religion, he was ecumenical. Hassan could speak to Arabs and Jews, to the English, French, and Germans, and to the Turks in their native tongues. But the most powerful language in this Oval Office encounter was symbolic.

Though he was not present, the meeting was an extraordinary moment in the life of Khalid Mishal. Here in the Oval Office, the unquestioned epicenter of global power since the end of the Cold War, the president of the United States was receiving one of the more refined princes of the Arab world to ensure, not that the man accused by Israel of dispatching suicide bombers was dead, but rather that he was alive and, hopefully, getting better. The prince had swept in from halfway around the world for a meeting with the president that was a turning point for Mishal as much as it was for Hamas. Until this point, they had been locked out of the Middle East club, as its members engaged in the push-me, pull-you Oslo process. But now Mishal and his movement had been acknowledged as key players.

For Benjamin Netanyahu, also absent, the meeting was more problematic. Riedel, for one, came away from it quite baffled by what he later described as the "foolishness" of the Israeli prime minister. "He was so willing to endanger Israel's and America's best friend in the region," he told colleagues. "On top of everything else he's done, this is dangerous, out-of-control stuff. . . . All talk, little thought."

In the air, going to and from Washington, Samih Batikhi went through great emotional swings. At one moment, he was on a high, wanting to celebrate the Clinton response as much as Hussein's fine management of the crisis. In the next he was down, warning that Mossad director Danny Yatom would still pay personally for Netanyahu's "criminal" conduct. He declared that all security cooperation between the two countries was frozen and relished recounting how he had ordered the closure of the Mossad station in Amman. "I can't deal with a cheat," he said with finality. "Do you know the stuff I've done for that man? And he does this to me? It's treachery—I just can't deal with it! If they wanted to kill Mishal, they should have told us."

It explained perhaps the reason why such a hardened professional as Batikhi had taken the matter so personally. Dave Manners, flying high over the Atlantic, was left wondering if perhaps his Jordanian colleague had had some sort of tip-off on the Mossad plot against Khalid Mishal. Perhaps he had, but then had presumed—or maybe had been led to believe—that the Israelis would not attempt the assassination in Jordan. Batikhi had complained previously about the Israelis' whining about the Hamas leader. Now he snapped, "I tell you, if I could prove that Khalid Mishal was operational, he'd be in jail immediately."

Manners fully understood the depth and detail of the GID-Mossad relationship, and he commiserated with Batikhi over his personal sense of violation. "And now they pull this shit in your front yard," he said by way of comfort for his aggrieved friend.

"What does it tell you about them—and their regard for us?" Batikhi went on. Clearly the GID chief would need time to recover, but there could be no wallowing in self-pity at this stage.

They were away from Jordan for just thirty hours, most of it up in the clouds in the king's Gulfstream. After swooping into Shannon, in Ireland, to refuel and then proceeding straight on to Washington, their feet barely touched the ground before they were wheels-up again and jetting back home.

While Hassan and Batikhi were in the United States, events on the ground in Jordan were unfolding rapidly.

Mousa Abu Marzook had been to the hospital on Tuesday afternoon to brief the now conscious Khalid Mishal on his meetings the previous day with Samih Batikhi about the possible release of Sheikh Yassin. On Tuesday night the king had set the scene with his reference to the release of prisoners during his speech at Zarqa. That news had both the reporter Randa Habib and the patient Khalid Mishal riveted.

Habib decided to stay at her desk working the phones through the night, and so she was able to report to AFP at about midnight on the drama that was to unfold in the coming hours. Mishal's own sense that something was already afoot was heightened when hospital staff advised him to prepare for an important visitor, who would arrive well after midnight.

Just minutes before four AM on Wednesday, not many would have noticed Israel's military media machine spluttering into life, for just the few seconds it took to issue a brief statement in the dead of night: On the grounds of his poor health, Sheikh Ahmad Yassin was to be released. At about the same time, lying in his hospital bed in Amman, Khalid Mishal realized that the king of Jordan was standing at his bedside.

The king did not stay long. He inquired after Mishal's health and care, but it seemed he was visiting the hospital at this ungodly hour on other business. Within minutes of the king leaving his room, Mishal detected the slow thump of an approaching helicopter. It became so loud that it had to be dropping into the hospital grounds. He hauled himself to a window.

In the eerie early half-light, no less a figure than the king himself stood patiently at the edge of the hospital helipad as the ungainly aircraft clattered in from the west, its Jordanian pilot crab walking it into position so that its cabin door would open to face the king. Paramedics rushed to extract a stretcher. A brown-checked blanket obscured the patient's wraith-like form. But any Palestinian observer, from the squalor of the West Bank to the queue in a Chicago Dunkin' Donuts, would have known, from the instant they saw the banged-up wheelchair being offloaded from the aircraft, that Sheikh Ahmad Yassin had been freed.

This was the massive price Israel was forced to pay for the rush of blood to the head that had made Benjamin Netanyahu think he could pull off an assassination in the streets of Amman on a Thursday morning in September.

In Washington there was helpless hand-wringing as the release of Yassin was locked in. A glum Dennis Ross declared it to be "an idea that didn't really thrill us." But he endorsed Bruce Riedel's analysis. Describing Yassin as the "guy who orchestrated the bombings that elected Netanyahu," Riedel accurately assessed Yassin's impending release as "political dynamite" on both sides of the Jordan River. However, he warned that, had Netanyahu refused to go ahead, the survival of the Israel-Jordan treaty would have been at stake. "Certainly a disaster; possibly fatal," he judged.

They had never met face-to-face. Yet here they were now—Yassin the spiritual leader and Mishal the strategic brain behind the Hamas movement and the whole Islamification of the Palestinian cause—in the same hospital, not too many bed lengths away from each other. For decades they had worked together and in parallel—one "inside" and the other "outside," to use the argot by which Palestinians separated the Occupied Territories from the rest of the world.

Mishal demanded that he be taken immediately to Yassin. Nurses said no, arguing that Mishal was not well enough. Doctors were summoned and they backed the nurses, but Mishal wore them all down. After about an hour, he was lifted into a wheelchair and pushed along a connecting corridor to the next building, where Yassin was settling in.

Despite the nature of this encounter, and all that it meant for the rebirth of Hamas, Mishal was oddly stiff. He later described to outsiders this meeting, which might have been expected to be intense, even emotional: "It was an auspicious occasion, especially when you think of a person who, despite his disability, had withstood all the pressure and imprisonment to lead the movement in difficult times," he said. "The overwhelming sensation was pride and gratitude to God that the attempt on my life was cause for his release. Success for Hamas out of failure for the Israelis confirmed our Islamic belief in the limitless power of God."[3]

As word of Yassin's arrival in Amman spread, there was pandemonium as the hospital and its sprawling grounds took on the air of a Hamas revival meeting. Mousa Abu Marzook—almost in tears at being reunited with Yassin—and Mohammad Nazzal ran the whole operation by mobile phone from the shade of a tree in the hospital garden.

But there was confusion over Yassin's precise fate—in Gaza, his family issued a statement denouncing the old man's removal from the Occupied Territories. "He should be allowed to die in Gaza," it said. At this stage, Israeli officials sought to stir the pot, spreading word that Yassin would not be allowed to return to Gaza.

The Israelis had a hidden agenda here, driven by their anxiety that the Jordanians had departed from the deal as they understood it. As originally agreed, the first of the two captured Mossad agents was to have been freed when Yassin arrived in Amman in the early hours of Wednesday; the second was to be returned to Israel once Yassin was back in Gaza, which was scheduled for the coming Sunday. It was true the Jordanians had shifted ground, deciding that, because they could no longer trust the Israelis, they would keep *both* Mossad agents until Amman was fully satisfied with the completion of Yassin's relocation.

By casting public doubt on the sheikh's return to Gaza at this stage, the Israelis were more interested in telegraphing to Hussein that they still had a card to play: their military forces on the ground in Gaza and their control of the airspace over the Occupied Territories gave them the power to block Yassin's return until their men were freed.

To see King Hussein now being branded the architect of Yassin's deportation beyond historic Palestine, rather than enjoying his freedom in Gaza, was a tricky moment that Abu Marzook had anticipated, not so much on the king's behalf as on Yassin's. The preacher's right to return to Gaza had been such a fundamental issue for Hamas that Abu Marzook had insisted on an audience with the king, so that he could spell this out to Hussein after he and Batikhi had crunched the prisoner numbers.

When Batikhi had finally allowed Abu Marzook to speak to King Hussein, the man from Hamas had just one imperative plea. The Hamas brothers' greatest fear was that, irrespective of any stalling by the Jordanians, the Israelis might pull a counter-stunt such as that which now seemed a distinct possibility. As Hamas saw it, a spiritual figurehead like Yassin had currency for the movement whether he was in Gaza or in an Israeli jail, but to be exiled in Amman would render him just another exile. He might as well be in Paris. "Sheikh Yassin must be allowed to return to his home in Gaza!" Abu Marzook had pleaded to the king in his slightly falsetto voice.[4]

It was to ensure that this happened that King Hussein had extracted a written undertaking from the Israelis guaranteeing that, even though Yassin was to be flown beyond Israel's international borders on the day he was released from prison, he would also be free to return to Gaza, which was under the control of Israel. Each element of this deal had been checked and rechecked in extraordinary detail.

The first that Yassin had known of his pending freedom was in the very early hours of Wednesday, when Israeli guards entered his cell, handing him a typed letter. Over the signature of General Yom Tov Samia, commander of Israel's southern military headquarters, its halting Arabic explained that Sheikh Ahmad Yassin was being pardoned, not deported. It went on to say that, as a result of an accord between His Majesty King Hussein of Jordan and Prime Minister Benjamin Netanyahu of Israel, Yassin was to be liberated to Jordan; that the Israeli leader was acceding to a Jordanian request based on Yassin's poor health; and that King Hussein would be sending his personal physician and a trusted envoy in a Jordanian helicopter to accompany Yassin to Amman.

It concluded, "The king agrees with the prime minister that Yassin be given a pardon document and identity papers—this is not a deportation and the state of Israel is committed to this."

Having digested its contents, Yassin was secured in his wheelchair and then wrapped in the brown blanket. In the middle of the night, he was wheeled out of the prison to be loaded into a Jordanian air force helicopter and flown to freedom.

At the King Hussein Medical City, doctors fought their way through a throng of visitors to examine the old cleric. It seemed he had a problem with one of his ears, but for a paraplegic who had spent eight years in a harsh prison environment, Yassin was in surprisingly good shape, so much so that within hours he demanded to speak to the people of Gaza. Mousa Abu Marzook cradled a hospital telephone next to his pallid cheek, and at the other end the handset was held to a microphone at the premises of the Union of Arab Journalists, from where loudspeakers relayed Yassin's reedy words through the rutted streets of Gaza City.

He came out fighting: "Young men and women, those who fight and those who stay in our country, we will continue in our way, which is the way of Muhammad. I salute those who sacrifice themselves so that we might see light at the end of the tunnel. Hamas will not cease the fight till we have liberated all of Palestine—from the river to the sea."

Hours later, Randa Habib interviewed Yassin by telephone, and his defiance was the same. Instead of savoring his freedom, the sheikh railed against the Israeli authorities and against Arafat for the latest round of closures of Hamas institutions. With bravado out of all proportion to his physical frailty, Yassin lamented Arafat's weakness in caving in to Israeli pressure. "The Israelis never dared to close these associations when I was running them" was his withering dismissal of the PLO leader.

King Hussein now was in a position to take some mischievous pleasure from a crisis that had been thrust upon him, so he called Yasser Arafat himself. The tension was exquisite—Hussein well knew the PLO leader would be enraged that it was he, Hussein, who had achieved Yassin's release, just as he knew that Arafat would have to smile for the cameras and hail this victory for all Palestinians. Arafat had already been on the phone to Washington, complaining to Dennis Ross. "Why should I pay a price for this," Arafat whined to Clinton's special envoy to the Middle East. "It's going to create problems. . . . It undermines me."

Having informed Arafat that his nightmare was about to resume, that Sheikh Yassin would be returning to Gaza, where, once again, he would continue in his inevitable way as a thorn in Arafat's side, King Hussein made a gesture. Some would see it as magnanimous, others Machiavellian, but the king dispatched yet another helicopter to the Occupied Territories, this time to fetch Arafat, so that he too could appear in Amman, where he might bask in the shadow of the victorious Hussein as he congratulated Yassin.

Hussein and his PLO guest, both short in stature, were lost in a media throng that descended on Yassin's room.

At Queen Alia airport, another welcoming party was preparing to rush to Yassin's side as the Gulfstream touched down on its return from Washington shortly after 2:30 PM on Thursday. Wanting to miss none of it, Crown Prince Hassan ordered Batikhi and Manners into the passenger seats of his car as he jumped behind the wheel himself for a mad dash to the hospital to join the official greeting circle for Sheikh Yassin.

Arafat emerged after the hospital visit declaring Yassin to be his ally in the peace process. But he was subjected to ridicule, with reporters pressing him on how he had showered kisses on the freed leader of Hamas at the same time as his security forces were cutting a swathe through the ranks of Hamas and its institutions in the Occupied Territories. Arafat blustered and instead thanked Yassin for supporting the peace process—an interpretation that could not be placed on the cleric's words, which at best were ambiguous.

On October 6, a huge crowd assembled at the hospital for Yassin's departure. Their eyes were fixed on the inert form of a Jordanian helicopter that sat, rotor blades drooping, on the KHMC helipad. Yassin's departure had originally been planned for twenty-four hours earlier. Now it was announced that takeoff would be at one PM. But as reporters killed time in the gardens, one o'clock came and went; they were informed that there was to be a further delay.

Standing in the sun, Randa Habib stabbed at her mobile phone, deciding to take her irritation out on any Jordanian officials who might answer her calls. As she attempted to get to the bottom of the delay, she wandered away from her colleagues and, quite by chance, she ended up doing what no other reporter had done.

The hospital was on one of Amman's prominent hilltops and, instead of looking into the gardens and the waiting helicopter, Habib turned her gaze out over Amman. It was then that she saw them—two more helicopters. They were hovering over the Mukhabarat bunker on the next hilltop, about half a mile away. She could not be certain they were Israeli, but she concluded they were foreign because, in appearance, they were nothing like the machine that sat in the garden, which she knew to be Jordanian.

The first official to whom she spoke revealed that there had been a last-minute wrinkle in the negotiations and that this had required the return to Amman of Ariel Sharon and his sidekick Whbee. She made more calls about the mysterious choppers, and at about 2:30 PM, she phoned an URGENT to Paris.

With just a few stunning exclusive lines, yet again, she was the first journalist to reveal to the world that the Mossad team was to be released and would return to Israel by helicopter within the hour. Quoting unnamed officials, she had the full gist of the deal that had been negotiated in the ten days of mostly secret talks since the attack on Mishal. She now revealed that Hussein would allow the Israeli agents to walk, but that the penalty on Israel was not only the repatriation of Yassin but the release of an additional seventy prisoners—both Palestinians and Jordanians.

Had she had the time to delve deeper, Habib might have discovered that the Israeli machines had been sitting, waiting, in the GID compound since seven o'clock that morning. Her counterparts in the Israeli media would already have discovered that the deal was under way at about mid-morning, when the first twenty prisoners to be released had been shepherded to a military helicopter base in central Israel in preparation for their return to Jordan. There were eleven Palestinians and nine Jordanians.[5]

There was a further revelation embedded in what Habib's sources had told her—the four Mossad agents who had been pinned down in the embassy had already been released, about a week earlier. But she had no time to dwell on that because at 2:47 PM there was thunderous applause from the gardens as a smiling Sheikh Ahmad Yassin was wheeled into the afternoon sunlight.

With the tails of a dazzling white kaffiyeh draped over his slight shoulders, Yassin emerged at his hectoring best. "The fight must continue," he cried. At this point his words were drowned by calls of "Allahu akbar! Allahu akbar!"

As they always do at Arab media conferences, the cameramen lunged forward as waves of emotion erupted from the crowd. Yassin's every statement was met with a "God is great" chorus from Hamas and Muslim Brotherhood activists and supporters on the ground and from the hospital balconies, which were thick with patients and uniformed staff. They clapped and cheered for Hamas and King Hussein. It was impossible for the media scrum to hear the feeble Yassin above the din, and it fell to Mohammad Nazzal to repeat his every word.

Was it true that that Yassin had endorsed a cease-fire? "We want peace," the preacher began, in what was to be another of his lessons in ambiguity. "But if it's not possible to restore our rights by peaceful means, we'll not accept the occupation of our land," Yassin said through Nazzal.

What about the friction between himself and Arafat? At this stage even the acerbic Yassin tried to gloss over the gulf between Hamas and the PLO. "We'll not allow the blood of Palestinians to be spilled for the benefit of our enemies," Nazzal repeated.

It was Randa Habib who then stepped in, with a question that punctured the triumphal mood. "How does Sheikh Yassin feel about the price of his freedom being freedom for the Mossad agents who tried to kill Khalid Mishal?"

There was stunned silence. Yassin looked at Habib and then turned to Nazzal. The holy man said something that could not be heard, but Nazzal then eyed Habib. "Are you sure?" he asked her. "Has this happened?"

When she nodded in the affirmative and pointed to two helicopters heading into the haze of the Jordan Valley, Nazzal and Yassin went into a brief huddle. Nazzal then announced that there would be no further comment. The press conference was over.

Yassin was lifted from the wheelchair onto a stretcher, which the paramedics then strapped into the chopper as the pilot revved his engines for takeoff. Two doctors and a paramedic clambered in to watch over Yassin during the forty-minute flight to the Gaza Strip.

Habib had watched the Israeli helicopters, with the freed Mossad agents as passengers, lift out of the Mukhabarat compound at 2:50 PM and then swing westward toward Jerusalem. At 3:05 the Jordanian machine, with Yassin on board, took off, tracking on a more southerly bearing in the direction of Gaza. She filed each departure as a separate news bite and, between them, the last details of the Israeli-Jordanian haggling over the botched attempt on the life of Khalid Mishal.

Habib's last question had sent Yassin off in a mood of uncertainty. Despite Abu Marzook's talk with Batikhi about a trade for the release of Yassin, Hamas had not reckoned on King Hussein being quite so accommodating to the needs of Mossad and the Israeli leadership. On his release from the hospital a couple of days earlier, a pale-looking Khalid Mishal had spoken to reporters: "Hamas insists that the authors of the attempt on my life must be judged and punished," he told them.

But the atmosphere on the Israeli helicopter that ferried the freed agents was just as strained, even more uncertain. Apart from their Canadian aliases, the agents were never identified publicly, other than as "A" and "D." On being freed from the cells beneath Samih Batikhi's office, they had stumbled into daylight, and the noise and hot air of a helicopter preparing for takeoff. They were uncomfortable, confused, and uncertain about what would come next.

They had been informed they were going home, and indeed the helicopter looked like an Israeli machine. But their only escort appeared to be an Arab. This was Majali Whbee, whom the agents had neither seen nor heard of before. For the duration of the flight, the noise of the machine enveloped the awkward personal silence that embraced all three. Whbee sensed the agents were ashamed of themselves and, despite his assurances, they refused to believe they had been freed until the helicopter put down in the Mossad compound.[6]

With Yassin back in Gaza and the Mossad agents returned to Israel, the next stage in the deal had been accomplished. Just before five PM, an Israeli helicopter delivered the nine Jordanian prisoners to Amman, and the eleven Palestinians were simultaneously released in Ramallah. Fifty more prisoners were to be freed in the coming weeks.[7]

As the Jordanian helicopter landed in Gaza, a crowd of more than fifteen thousand well-wishers engulfed the sixty-one-year-old Yassin. Most of the Israeli media covered Gaza by phone from Jerusalem or Tel Aviv, but a few brave reporters made it their business to understand the life and mood of the Occupied Territories and, for them, an event as tumultuous as Yassin's return was not to be missed.

Mingling among the crowd, they were confronted by a group of armed Palestinian security men. Nahum Barnea, a journalist on the Tel Aviv–based daily *Yedioth Ahronoth*, was surprised when one of the Palestinians asked him in perfect Hebrew, "Who are you?"

"Who are you?" the reporter countered.

They claimed to be members of Yasser Arafat's Preventive Security Service, but it seemed improbable that they would be fluent in Hebrew. Acknowledging the reporter's quizzical look, the Palestinian explained that he had learned Hebrew while doing time in an Israeli prison.

Having broken the ice, the security man then offered some advice. "You can walk around," he said. "But please do not mention that you are Israelis—and no talking Hebrew."

"Sure," Barnea told him. "We'll say we are Canadians."[8]

16

The Legendary Image of Mossad

Khalid Mishal would disappear for a while. On his release from the hospital eight days after the attack, he was still pale and drawn, but he had survived heroically. Hamas operatives prepared a safe house, enlisting the Muslim Brotherhood in Amman to provide a more secure office in one of its lesser-known establishments where Mishal might lie low. But before he dropped from sight, Mohammad Nazzal summoned reporters for Mishal's victory interviews.

Accusing Israel of state terrorism, the chief of the Hamas political bureau gave ritual thanks to God for his survival before resorting to saber rattling at the Israelis and the PLO. "It's evident Israel wanted to get rid of me," he told the reporters as members of his new, five-man security detail looked on. "[But this attack] will not deter us from continuing our struggle." Declaring himself to be more strong willed than ever, he reserved his most cutting words for Prime Minister Benjamin Netanyahu and his intelligence chief, Danny Yatom. "[They've] destroyed the legendary image of Mossad," Mishal declared dismissively before he was hustled into hiding by colleagues who fretted that the Israelis would come after him again.

The fiasco in Amman was a savage, self-inflicted wound for the Israeli intelligence community. There was great moral indignation in Israel, but it was less about the propriety or efficacy of the state sending killers abroad than it was about their failure to complete the task. The mythology of such a young state, planted in a hostile corner of the world, required the exploits of Mossad and its sister organizations as nerve-tingling embroidery in a national narrative in which there could be no room for failure. Mossad had had its share of embarrassment in the past, but if the legend was to persist as a fearsome deterrent in its own right, Israel needed to be seen to be eliminating its enemies relentlessly and efficiently.

As the political keeper of this holy trust, Benjamin Netanyahu had intimate personal knowledge of the standard required of him. In 1976, Israel had stunned the world with a daring transnational operation. An Air France flight from Tel Aviv to Paris, carrying one hundred passengers, had been hijacked to Entebbe Airport in Uganda. The rescue mission was code-named Thunderbolt.

A fleet of Israeli Air Force Hercules air transports dropped men and vehicles on the ground at Entebbe. To take care of the hostages, they landed a Boeing 707 flying hospital. And, to coordinate this operation of daunting complexity, another 707 hovered overhead in the night as a command-and-control center.[1] All was put in place without being detected by the hostage takers. During the rescue, three hostages died in the crossfire, along with just a single Israeli commando. That commando's name was Yonatan Netanyahu. He was an older brother to the prime minister, who, for his effort on the streets of Amman, now featured on the cover of the *Economist* under the headline "SERIAL BUNGLER."

All Israelis were steeped in tales of Mossad's daring. Danny Yatom was a fifteen-year-old schoolboy when the success of an audacious mission by his predecessors became a foundation strand in the Mossad mystique that was to be entrusted to Yatom decades later. Sixteen years before Entebbe, this was a mission that cut to the core of the atrocities in Nazi Germany during World War II. Thousands of miles from home, in the streets of Buenos Aires, Mossad snatched a factory hand who gave his name as Ricardo Klement. But the prisoner's true identity was Adolf Eichmann—the Nazi war criminal who had overseen the deportation and extermination of millions of Jews as he executed Adolf Hitler's Final Solution.

The Mossad operatives slipped into Argentina as members of an Israeli delegation invited to attend the one-hundred-fiftieth-anniversary celebrations of Argentinean independence. Operating in a country that sheltered war criminals, they grabbed Eichmann on a suburban footpath. They dressed him in an El Al flight suit and filled him with whisky before dousing themselves in alcohol. Playing the part of drunken foreigners unable to cope with the strong local liquor, they then drove their prisoner through all checkpoints and got to the Israeli aircraft that was due to fly the official Israeli delegation home, just before it took off from a military base in the Argentinean capital. Eichmann was tried and, ultimately, executed.[2]

Compared to Entebbe and Buenos Aires, the task that Netanyahu and Yatom had set for themselves in Amman was the espionage equivalent of going to the corner store for a loaf of bread. One of the more devastating critiques of their attempt to assassinate Khalid Mishal came from Zvi Malchin, the Mossad agent who physically collared Eichmann in the Argentinean capital back in 1960. Age sixty-seven, he was hauled from retirement to give his verdict. "Doomed to failure from the outset," he began. Using words like "childish," "amateurish," "impractical," and even "clumsy," Malchin concluded that the plan was enough to make "a junior recruit blush with shame."[3]

The combination of media censorship and a four-day national shutdown, as the celebration of the Jewish New Year ran into the Sabbath break, gave Netanyahu and Yatom respite—an unbelievably lucky news blackout, during which they tried to limit some of the damage.

Newspapers like Smadar Perry's *Yedioth Ahronoth* did not publish on the Friday or Saturday immediately after the attack, which had taken place on Thursday, September 25. But under the reporter's relentless pressure, her editors wilted, finally allowing Perry to cobble together a report based on foreign media reports and some of what she had learned from her own Israeli contacts. She deliberately padded the story with information that invited the censor to wield his pencil, in the hope that sufficient meaningful material might survive. She and her boss were both stunned and nervous when the report came back from the censor. "It was clean—untouched!" Perry recalled later.[4]

In the perverse relationship that existed between the government and the Israeli media, the state censor had an intriguing role. The nervousness of Perry and her editors sprang from a practice by which the censor sometimes conveyed a helpful warning to editors that there was something wrong with a report that might have more to do with, say, accuracy than a perceived need for state suppression. He was letting an editor know he should not touch a story, by not touching it himself.

"I don't want to touch it," the editor exclaimed. And that was where the influential *Yedioth Ahronoth* coverage might have ended, at least for the time being, had the prime minister not overplayed his hand. It was a phone call from Netanyahu to the paper's chief editor, pleading that there be no publicity, that convinced them that Perry's story was correct. It appeared on Sunday, under the slightly tortured heading KING HUSSEIN TOOK PERSONAL CARE OF THE HAMAS OFFICIAL ATTACKED IN JORDAN.

Perry was then dispatched to Amman. But the Israeli media continued to treat the story in a desultory fashion until the tenth day, when the government was finally engulfed by a political storm.

A FAR-REACHING FAILURE was the headline in *Haaretz*. Amidst calls for Netanyahu's head, *Ma'ariv*'s banner read, SORDID BUSINESS IN JORDAN.[5] Former prime minister Shimon Peres and Labor Party leader Ehud Barak demanded Netanyahu's resignation. A fatal combination of arrogance, inexperience, and obtuseness that characterized Netanyahu's actions had come to a head in this operation, opposition MK Dalia Itzik declared.[6]

In the face of the eruption, Netanyahu went on the attack. "Hundreds of Israeli citizens were wounded," he retorted, trying to turn the debate back to suicide bombings in Jerusalem, rather than his own reckless response. "Twenty-one Israelis were murdered . . . these disgusting acts angered the entire Israeli population. These are criminal acts that no one is prepared to accept. As prime minister, I'm obligated to fight this terror in any way."[7]

Seeming to have forgotten the humiliating compromise into which he had just been forced, Netanyahu likened his government to an insurance company that had to guarantee the success of its 24/7 security cover for Israelis. He vowed there would be no compromise in Israel's hunt for terrorist leaders.[8]

When a reporter had the temerity to ask if he might resign, Netanyahu twice ignored the question before snapping back that he had no intention of quitting.[9] In a striking denunciation, a former Israeli ambassador to Jordan, Professor Shimon Shamir, accused the Israeli prime minister of a "complete misunderstanding of the essence of peace."[10]

All the events that had unfolded during the eight weeks between the angry cabinet decision to go after the Hamas leaders and the stomach-churning morning when the Amman assassination mission fell apart would soon be picked over by a special Israeli investigative commission and by two parliamentary committees.

But many influential Israelis did not wait for the formal findings. The criticism came in great waves, and it came from all sides. The media, politicians, expert commentators, and foreign diplomats had a field day.

Fault was found in virtually every aspect of the mission—its location and timing; the damage to Jordan; Mishal's value as a target and the ease with which he could be replaced in the Hamas leadership; the release of Yassin. Mossad had not bothered to survey the scene of the attack. Escape routes had not been planned.

The prime minister had personally approved the target. There were allegations that number one on Yatom's list of likely candidates had been Hamas's more notorious Mousa Abu Marzook, recently allowed to walk free from U.S. custody because Israel suddenly lost its nerve when the time came to put him on trial in Israel. Abu Marzook's frequent travel might have allowed them to eliminate him on a different continent. But Netanyahu had personally overruled his intelligence chief. Instead, he had painted the bull's-eye on the lesser-known Khalid Mishal, who rarely traveled beyond Jordan.

The prime minister also had endorsed Yatom's decision to steer Mossad, for the first time, into the realm of the exotic in his choice of how Mishal would die. For Cold War aficionados, this was a leap back in time—to the 1978 execution of the Bulgarian dissident Georgi Markov near London's Waterloo Bridge, by a mystery assassin who used an umbrella to fire a dart filled with poisonous ricin.[11] Yatom had been absolutely confident that his 1997 sequel to that London attack would be just as successful and had even gone to the trouble of having a film made, to show Netanyahu how the operation was to unfold and how the poison would impact Mishal's body.

There was a long history of consultation among the top tiers of the Israeli government before any controversial missions such as this were ever authorized, including with the high-level body that operated under the intriguing title of Committee X. But Netanyahu had not consulted as widely as he might have among his senior ministers or his other intelligence chiefs. In the aftermath, he was accused of having sought a quiet but quick hit to exploit as a New Year's "present" to lift flagging national spirits at a time of renewed crisis for Israelis. Shimon Peres, Netanyahu's predecessor as prime minister, described the operation as "nonsense."[12]

At a personal level, Yatom was denounced as an incompetent amateur. One of his most senior colleagues was inflammatory in his critique. "People credited Danny with too much intelligence," the colleague complained. "Military intelligence and the Shin Bet didn't have a useful target ready, so Yatom said, 'If they can't do it, I will.' He just had to prove that he could do what a lot of others thought was not such a really good idea."[13]

Danny Yatom was no one's fool. His habit of donning his favorite black leather bomber jacket might have suggested a personal affectation, but he had graduated at the Hebrew University of Jerusalem in a weighty mix of mathematics, physics, and computer science. Over three decades, he had had a distinguished military and antiterrorism career before his appointment in the early 1990s as military adviser to Prime Minister Yitzhak Rabin. It was the assassinated Rabin's successor, Shimon Peres, who parachuted Yatom into the top job at Mossad, just three months before the 1996 general election.

But there were immediate complaints within the agency that, as a military man, Yatom would never be accepted in Mossad. There was resentment that he had not served his apprenticeship, had not spent nights in a cold car in a strange city to meet an informant or to intercept a target who might or might not show up.[14] All he knew of Mossad was observing its dangerous missions from the comfort of his desk as a prime ministerial adviser, they scoffed. In fairness, Yatom had worked in antiterrorism for nine years, helping to release hijack hostages and sneaking into Beirut to blow things up. But in the one-upmanship of the Israeli intelligence milieu, his record did not rate because, at the end of the day, he was a political appointee.[15]

At age fifty-one, Yatom was trapped in a complex relationship with Netanyahu. Once a week they would spend an evening together, over beers and olives.[16] One was a relatively inexperienced politician, hungry for results; the other was a military man more used to obeying orders to produce those results than he was to questioning the manner by which they might be achieved.

Senior intelligence figures argued that that as the chief of Mossad, Yatom should have had a dozen persuasive devices at his disposal to head off his wayward prime minister: the wrong place or the wrong time; a target inaccessible; a target gone to ground. A good intelligence chief had a drawer full of such excuses to peddle to a headstrong politician who needed to be saved from himself.

People who knew Yatom argued that his can-do attitude made up for a lack of imagination. "He's a military man" was the assessment of a close acquaintance. "Order Danny to take the hill—and he'll take the hill!"[17] Others swore by his attention to detail—throughout his career he had been obsessive about taking copious notes of meetings. "Yatom is a *yekke*," explained his longtime colleague Ephraim Lapid, using the Hebrew for "a man of detail."[18]

With Yatom relatively new to the intelligence business, Netanyahu also was relatively new to the office of prime minister. Netanyahu's bid for hands-on involvement in this operation had disturbed some in Mossad, who were accustomed to the agency's practice of keeping operational detail at arm's length from their political masters. It was a sound tradition that offered protection to both sides.[19] But Netanyahu had taken to calling Yatom at all hours of the day and night, each time demanding a more detailed progress report.[20]

Publicly, Netanyahu and his advisers spoke protectively, even warmly, of Yatom in the aftermath of Amman. But in background briefings to reporters, the Mossad director was crucified. "It was Yatom who failed to deliver," one of the prime minister's advisers concluded darkly. "He promised a very quiet, discreet operation—that was the boss's condition for the go-ahead. It was not to be noticed by anyone. No one else was to get hurt—there was to be no shooting in the street."

It was made known that Netanyahu would not demand Yatom's resignation but that if submitted, the prime minister would accept it. Nahum Barnea, the reporter who had joked about being a Canadian in Gaza, now told his readers how this preferred outcome was to be achieved. When the prime minister spoke on the record, he would bury Yatom in compliments, Barnea reported. But the real objective was to bury Yatom—period. "[Do it] slowly and wisely," he wrote as he articulated the strategic logic he understood to be at work in the prime minister's office. "Let the [investigative] committee take care of it. Let the media take care of it, with our guidance."[21]

More than a week after Israel's bid to kill Khalid Mishal, Canadian prime minister Jean Chrétien was still fending off strident charges at home that his government had been complicit in the bungled Mossad mission. And the stakes were higher than they might ordinarily have been because this was yet another episode in an embarrassing history of Israeli killers abroad taking cover as Canadian citizens.

In 1973, a woman member of a Mossad team that was systematically shooting its way through a list of Palestinians held responsible for the massacre of Israeli athletes at the Munich Olympic Games carried a Canadian passport. She was arrested in Lillehammer, Norway, and jailed along with five others, after the hit team killed an innocent Moroccan waiter in the mistaken belief that he was Ali Hassan Salameh, a key figure in the previous year's attack in Munich. Before Lillehammer interrupted their progress, Mossad had clinically deleted eleven targets whom it claimed were associates.

The arrested woman was Sylvia Raphael. South African born and age thirty-five, she was the Christian daughter of a Jewish father, who migrated to Israel in her late twenties after reading Leon Uris's *Exodus*. Posing as a Canadian photojournalist, she was credited with being one of the first Mossad agents to penetrate Yasser Arafat's bases in Jordan and Lebanon in the 1960s.[22] For the Lillehammer killing, she had assumed the identity of Patricia Roxborough, whose passport had disappeared some months earlier from her desk at a Montreal law firm, where she had worked as a legal secretary.[23]

In 1974, about fifty blank Canadian passports disappeared from a vault at the Canadian Embassy in Vienna. In Nicosia a year later, Cypriot authorities seized the kit of a Mossad team after a hotel bombing in which a Palestinian guerrilla leader was killed. The passport used by one of the Israeli hit men bore a number that revealed it to be from among the fifty stolen in Vienna.[24]

In the aftermath of its transgressions in Lillehammer and Nicosia, Israel had given Ottawa an undertaking that it would stop using Canadian cover. Now the Mishal affair brought forth a raft of new allegations against the Israeli security agencies, and sinister claims of Canadian complicity in Israel's program of state-sanctioned killings.

Shawn Kendall and Barry Beads, whose identities had been assumed by the Mossad agents arrested in Amman, were Canadian Jews living in Israel who had been asked if their passport details might be "borrowed" by one of the Israeli security services.[25] These were not isolated cases. A former Canadian kibbutznik emerged to reveal that Israeli agents had gathered up passports on a kibbutz where he had worked in the late 1970s and early 1980s.[26] A Canadian diplomat in the region would explain later that the Israeli authorities had proved adept at extracting current or expired passports by pressuring Canadian passport holders living in Israel to view their willingness to lend their identities to the authorities as a test of their loyalty to Israel.[27] When an enterprising Canadian TV journalist managed to track down Shawn Kendall at his home in Jerusalem, the computer programmer refused to open the door. "I'm an innocent victim in some screwed-up situation . . . and I'd like it to go away" was all he said from behind the door.[28]

Others were more voluble, piling on pressure that Ottawa was unable to push back before it could extract the passports used in the Amman attack from the Jordanian authorities. The diplomat Steve Bennett's testing of the arrested agents satisfied Ottawa that the men were not Canadians, but all the doubts about the authenticity and origin of the passports on which they had traveled left the Canadian government vulnerable.

Most damaging were explosive allegations by Norman Spector, a Canadian Jew who was publisher of the *Jerusalem Post*. Spector brought a unique insight to the Israeli-Canadian relationship because he had served as Ottawa's ambassador to Tel Aviv between 1992 and 1995. He now accused the Chrétien government of knowing and attempting to cover up Israel's use of the fake Canadian passports; he described as ongoing the "very close cooperation" between Mossad and Canada's CSIS. Making his point, he claimed that there had been a meeting between officers of the CSIS and Mossad just days before the attempted assassination. The implications of this further embarrassed Ottawa.[29]

The former envoy explained that the Canadian intelligence agency's complicity in Israeli spy ventures was the only price it was able to pay for useful intelligence provided by the Israelis.[30] "Canadian authorities knew, in general, that passports were being used by Mossad," he said, claiming to speak on the basis of his own personal experience. "It was known to people at the embassy and they essentially turned a blind eye to it."

Spector's allegations gave resonance and a whole new legitimacy to old claims by Victor Ostrovsky, a Canadian-born former Mossad agent. In a book published in 1990, Ostrovsky claimed to have seen "more than a thousand" blank Canadian passports in a Mossad forgery factory in Israel. Most of the companies used by Mossad as fronts for its operatives around the world were Canadian, he wrote.[31] Indignant and exposed, Canadian foreign minister Lloyd Axworthy rounded on Ottawa's critics, accusing them of creating new risks for Canadian travelers by heightening suspicion of their passports in the Middle East. A Canadian diplomat in the region warned that violence could follow Canadians home. "If the biographical data borrowed by the Israelis ends up in the hands of Hamas, then some night an innocent man of the same name in Winnipeg could open his door to get blown away by a revenge killer."[32]

After recalling David Berger, Canada's ambassador to Tel Aviv, for consultation—a symbolic diplomatic rebuke—Axworthy went to the United Nations headquarters in New York, where he corralled ambassadors from Arab and Muslim countries in a bid to dissociate his government from the Israeli madness in Amman.

It was not until the morning of October 4, a day after Mishal's release from the hospital, that the Canadian ambassador to Amman, Mike Molloy, and his first secretary, Steve Bennett, received new instructions by telephone from the Jordanian regime. They were to stand in the same Amman backstreet where a driver from the royal palace had rendezvoused with Bennett in the first days of the crisis. The same silver Mercedes-Benz was there, and this time they were driven northwest from the city to a California-style home built on a ridge with views over the biblical beauty of the Jordan Valley. They had been brought to the heart of the inner sanctum—Bab Al-Salam.

They were ushered into the presence of the director of the king's office, Ali Shukri, who spoke for ninety minutes, but still failed to produce the passports. Increasingly stressed, Molloy wondered if the documents that Ottawa needed so desperately might be in an aluminum briefcase, which the ambassador thought was chained to General Shukri's leg. It was around noon and

Shukri was still talking when they were joined by a short man who wore a black turtleneck and a salt-and-pepper sports jacket. It was King Hussein, with a pertinent question: "Have you boys eaten yet?" he inquired. "Do you eat Arabic food?"

Thus began one of the simple adventures for foreign diplomats in Amman—an intimate lunch with the king. Hussein led them to a sheltered terrace off his study, where a table was spread with mezza dishes, a kebab platter, and lots of flatbread. There was no alcohol. As they ate, Hussein threw morsels to the household cats and, despite having sat through Shukri's account of the whole affair, the Canadian diplomats then had to listen while Hussein rehashed it all.

After a time, he paused. On the king's signal, Shukri opened the aluminum briefcase and produced two small, blue-black books; these he handed past Molloy to the king. "You know, the Israelis had the nerve to ask for these passports to be returned to them," he said indignantly. "They wanted to give us something quite different to give to you gentlemen. Can you believe that?"[33]

Molloy and Bennett broke from lunch as quickly as they could without appearing rude. Back at the embassy, the passports were removed from Molloy's suit pocket by a colleague with gloved hands. After a brief examination, they were sealed in an envelope, which would be hand couriered to Ottawa by a member of the embassy's security team. One of Molloy's staff booked the courier's travel via Amsterdam. But then a message was received from Ottawa, insisting that the courier travel via Paris "because we don't have sufficient assets on the ground in Amsterdam." In a word, they had more agents in France than in the Dutch capital.

Canvassing options on how best to get their man and his package to Amman's Queen Alia International Airport, about twenty miles south of the city, they decided nothing should be left to chance. Molloy's bulletproof limousine—with the maple leaf on the hood—was hauled from the garage. As they finalized their plans, Ottawa's warning that the passports needed the full security treatment hung in the air. Some present wondered if they had gone over the top when one of the embassy security men looked to Molloy and said: "Ambassador—if anyone stops us, we'll fight!"

Other special arrangements were made. Molloy and Bennett were allowed onto the tarmac at the airport to escort their man to his aircraft. As the courier disembarked in Paris, he was intercepted by Canadian intelligence agents who guarded him through the entire transfer to make sure he and the two passports caught the transatlantic connection to Ottawa.

When the passports arrived in the Canadian capital, they were subjected to a thorough scientific examination. A relieved Lloyd Axworthy declared them to be "total, complete forgeries. . . . They weren't even using Canadian stock."

Given the history of Israel's abuse of Canadian passports, Ottawa's retaliation was surprisingly light—the brief recall of Ambassador David Berger. There was no threat—or even a hint—of trade sanctions, nor of tougher visa conditions for Israelis wishing to enter Canada. And certainly there was no suggestion that there might be an application to extradite the Mossad hit men—"A" and "D"—to face charges in Canada. Ottawa, it seemed, just wanted the whole thing to go away.

King Hussein was bitterly disappointed by the role played by Yatom, for whom he had considerable affection.[34] They had first met when Yatom served as a military liaison officer to Yitzhak Rabin. They had worked together on the peace treaty and they had cried together over the assassination of Rabin. Yatom and his family had been entertained at the royal palaces, where they had sometimes stayed overnight. But on leaving the Hashimieh Palace on September 25 after confessing to what Mossad had done, Yatom was informed by a senior Jordanian official that, so long as he headed the Israeli intelligence agency, he was deemed to be persona non grata in Jordan.[35]

President Clinton's Middle East envoy, Dennis Ross, hurried back to the region within days of the attack, but the stalemate in the peace talks dragged on. Israel did not believe that Arafat's historic renunciation of violence was genuine. For their part, the Palestinians concluded that nothing was going to divert Netanyahu from his plans for more and bigger settlements on their land.

With no other options, Arafat and the Palestinian Authority were going through the motions of the Washington-backed peace process. But the real negotiation had become a dialogue of violence between two parties that were opposed to the Oslo formula—Hamas and Netanyahu.[36] And the one message for Hamas and others to take from Amman was that force was the only language that Benjamin Netanyahu understood.

Amidst the gridlock, King Hussein's truce offer to Netanyahu went up in smoke. Efraim Halevy, returning to Brussels to see out the last weeks of his ambassadorship, was concerned that his political masters had missed a rare opportunity to engage Hamas more constructively than they had done in the September street war. In Amman, palace officials claimed they had been reliably informed by their Mossad associates that King Hussein's written proposal for himself to mediate in talks with Israel on an offer by Hamas for a truce of up to thirty years' duration had been delivered to Jerusalem *before* the attack on Khalid Mishal. Claims to the contrary by Netanyahu and his advisers, however often made, were simply not believed in the Jordanian capital. King Hussein read the attack on Khalid Mishal as Netanyahu's crude, informal response to his very important letter.

Halevy was not naive. He too had reservations about where the king's proposal might have led. Nonetheless, he believed there was an onus on the Israeli leadership to test it seriously. Halevy did not share the widely held view in Israel that force was the only language understood by Hamas. As he read it, King Hussein's message might have contributed to a new Israeli understanding of Hamas as a serious and potent element of the Palestinian community. "We'll never know," he later commented, "[because] there was never a discussion of their offer of a truce at the time [when] it could have been operative."[37]

One of the more revealing demonstrations of the fierce competitiveness in the relationship between the Israeli and Jordanian intelligence services was a struggle that started immediately, and would continue for years. It was about who could claim the credit for the breakthrough proposal that a gesture as momentous as the release of Sheikh Ahmad Yassin was required. Both sides claimed ownership.

Halevy said it was his idea.[38] He well understood that Netanyahu would have to make a dramatic move to send the right signal to King Hussein. But was it conceivable that the Israeli's opening bid would be so audacious? And if senior Israelis had already discussed the idea among themselves and with their Jordanian counterparts, why had Sharon been left in the dark? Majali Whbee said that when Batikhi raised Yassin's name in the critical Monday night meeting in Amman, Sharon was so shocked as to be nearly speechless. "I don't know if Yassin had been discussed through other channels," Whbee said. "But it definitely was the first time that Sharon heard it mentioned."[39] Batikhi swore later to colleagues that the Yassin proposal had first come up in a meeting between himself and King Hussein.

As this contest played out between the agencies, both had only to turn to a heartbreaking letter, published in the *Jerusalem Post* the day after Yassin's return to Gaza, to be reminded that Yassin's name had always been in the frame. All that was required to put him in play was a previously undetermined measure of Israeli desperation.

The letter writer was Esther Wachsman, who was the mother of Nachshon

Wachsman, a soldier abducted three years earlier by Hamas. She questioned the recent revision of her compatriots' values. At the time he was seized, all of Israel had watched as the soldier Nachshon had pleaded, in a Hamas video aired on national television, for Sheikh Yassin and two hundred other Hamas prisoners to be freed so that his own life might be spared. The prime minister of the day, Rabin, had refused to trade, and Wachsman had died in the cross-fire as Israeli commandos attempted his rescue. In her letter now, the mother addressed Benjamin Netanyahu: "The principle of not yielding to blackmail died three years after Nachshon's death." Laying out the twin failures of the Mishal assassination and the attempted rescue of her son, Esther Wachsman wrote, "Perhaps Yassin had to be released to save two Jewish lives, but it is three years too late to save one precious life—my son's."[40]

The Mossad men had returned to Israel escaping trial, but Hamas and the Muslim Brotherhood still had great cause to celebrate. On the evening of October 20—a Monday that fell just twenty-five days after the attack on Khalid Mishal—they came in the hundreds to Jabri's Banquet Hall on Garden Street, just a few blocks from the scene of the attack.

There were only a few women at this gathering, and one of them was Randa Habib. The phone call by Mishal and Nazzal to Habib on the day of the attack was the call that had saved his life. Ordinarily they might have been expected to call a trusted Hamas or Muslim Brotherhood insider, who, in such circumstances, might have achieved little. Instead they had played a wildcard—calling a journalist they didn't really know, who had flashed a report around the world before the local authorities had an opportunity to smother it.

Hamas wanted Habib at the celebration because her stories had laid the groundwork for Mishal's recovery. And what journalist would forgo the chance to observe the inside story of Hamas letting its hair down—albeit in a Hamas kind of way?

Habib was struck by how physically well the reborn Mishal seemed to be as he and Nazzal headed the official receiving line.

The Hamas night was about militancy, nationalism, and a victory over the Israelis that, despite the best efforts of the Jordanian regime, had played on a world stage. Chants, slogans, and the heavy beat of rousing Islamist anthems filled the hall, the walls of which were draped with readings from the Qur'an and the protest banners of Hamas. The menu was the classic celebration fare of the region: mezza and mounds of meat and rice were followed by the sweets for which Jabri was famous—including his chocolates and *knafeh*, a rich reddish pastry filled with Nabulsi cheese and soaked in syrup and rose-water. There was no alcohol, but there was as much Pepsi and 7Up as people could drink.

Habib was obliged to sit at "the women's table" with Amal, Mishal's wife, and the partners of the other senior Hamas and Muslim Brotherhood figures. She found them cheerful, happy, and veiled. Habib was the only female whose head was uncovered.

Cautiously—and wisely, as it turned out—Canadian foreign minister Lloyd Axworthy said he could take only at face value Israel's renewal of its past "ironclad" assurances to have Mossad abstain in the future from issuing its agents with Canadian cover.

Just weeks after the debacle in Amman, Leslie Lewis, a Canadian Jew living in Israel, contacted Canadian authorities to report that he had just been approached by what was believed to be a Mossad front.[41] In his fifties and an accountant by training, Lewis admitted he had cooperated with the Israelis in 1996, giving them his expired Canadian passport and other forms of identification, including his Canadian driver's license. But in the aftermath of the Mishal hit, he had rejected their latest request to borrow his new Canadian passport. They had also tried to persuade his daughter, Devora, to fly to Canada to apply for a passport, and then to fly back to Israel, where she would hand the new travel document to the Israelis.[42]

It was Netanyahu who would script the aftermath of the Mishal affair for his own people. Someone would have to pay the price, and by the reckoning of most, if Netanyahu was to get off lightly, then Danny Yatom would have to fall.

Yatom was soon hit by damaging leaks that cast further doubt on his performance. In November it was revealed that Israel had been on the brink of war with Syria because one of Yatom's top spymasters had fabricated reports to exaggerate threats from Damascus. The spy had pocketed the money he was presumed to be paying informants for more than five years. But even with this new blow Yatom refused to acknowledge that his days as head of Mossad were numbered.

The Israeli investigative commission into the Mishal affair finally produced a report of 110 pages. Few of its findings were published formally, but just enough seeped out for Israelis to grasp that Netanyahu and Yatom had run the attack on Mishal pretty much on their own. There was no surprise when the few pages of the report publicly released on February 14 condemned Yatom's handling of the matter. But there were howls of derision from the political opposition and media analysts when Netanyahu was exonerated.

Yatom had become a *yatom*—in Hebrew, the word meant orphan. The Mossad director was abandoned politically. Other senior Mossad figures with a hand in Amman had already resigned or stood aside. But Yatom stood his ground, even when faced with a staff revolt over his refusal to resign. It would take another bungled mission to dislodge him.

Four weeks later, two elements of a plan to put listening devices on the phone lines used by operatives of Hezbollah—the Lebanese Shiite militia—in seven European cities went disastrously wrong. In London, three of the Israeli agents attracted attention before they could plant the device and had to flee the country.[43]

Days later, Mossad agents in the Swiss capital of Bern made more mistakes. Their target was Abdullah Zein, believed to be an operative for Hezbollah. A team of five Mossad agents was sprung in the process of fixing a listening device to a phone junction box in the basement of the apartment building where Zein lived, in the Liebefeld quarter. An alert housewife spotted two of the agents, who were posing as a couple while on lookout. Four got away, but the man holding the listening device and a bag of tools was arrested.[44]

Finally Yatom gave up the fight. But in a caustic resignation letter, he rejected the investigative commission's finding that he was at fault in the attack on Mishal. Yatom reluctantly conceded only that he bore "overall" responsibility for Mossad's activity.

Once again, Efraim Halevy was called in to pick up the pieces. His time as Israeli ambassador to the European Union had come to an end. After unpacking the new furniture he and his wife had purchased in Belgium, he was named to replace the disgraced Danny Yatom as Mossad director.

As the dust settled on Yatom's espionage career, two other players found themselves in better shape than before. King Hussein of Jordan had fended off a dire threat to his throne, and the Palestinian resistance movement, Hamas, had been reborn and was ready to rejoin the battle for Palestine.

Benjamin Netanyahu became the first prime minister of Israel obliged to publicly acknowledge flaws in the Mossad glass. Having ridden out the toughest crisis of his career, Netanyahu pointed the finger internally. "I cannot deny that Mossad's image has been affected by certain failed missions," he acknowledged with a certain amount of understatement.[45]

17

Brother Against Brother

The homecoming was chaotic. Between fervor and delirium, tens of thousands of Gazans poured into dusty streets and playgrounds, into the broke-back Yarmuk sports stadium and the campus of the Islamic University, to see Sheikh Ahmad Yassin, a frail old man who seemed an unlikely enemy of peace.

As a child, Yassin had been raised by his widowed mother at the Shati, or Beach, refugee camp, within earshot of the murmuring Mediterranean. He had been paralyzed from the neck down since a sports accident when he was twelve years old. Despite his incapacity, he had fathered eleven children and worked as a teacher; at the same time he had built the spiritual and welfare network that became the backbone of Hamas. Through all this, Yassin offered Gazans a spirit of redemption more appealing than the corrupt and venal ways of the PLO and Yasser Arafat's Palestinian Authority.

In the excitement of his release from jail, some got carried away, likening Yassin to Iran's Ayatollah Khomeini. The comprehensive moral authority that he had exercised over the Occupied Territories from his prison cell might more appropriately have been compared with the leadership-in-exile from jail of South Africa's Nelson Mandela. But it was a wall slogan that appeared near his home that depicted him accurately enough. It hailed Yassin as the "sheik of the Intifada."

Now sixty-one, he arrived back in Gaza in early October 1997 with further complications—a problem eye, hearing difficulties, and a respiratory disorder. He was emaciated, and sometimes lolled off to the side of his wheelchair, his failing eyes fixed on a distant nothing. All pale skin and eggshell bones, it seemed he was held into the wheelchair only by the weight of the blanket in which dutiful family members wrapped him. For many Israelis, Yassin was the devil incarnate. But for a good many Palestinians, the words of the wispy-bearded preacher, his life, and what they saw as his selfless sense of service to them were the embodiment of their struggle.

As he toured the Gaza Strip, tribal drums and chants, both holy and nationalist, filled the air. Schoolgirls in pretty white dresses danced. Young men paraded with banners featuring images of Yassin and other Hamas heroes. Ecstatic crowds gave thanks for what was Yassin's second remarkable escape from being a prisoner of the Israelis. In 1984, he had been sentenced to fifteen years in jail after the discovery of his weapons cache, only to be released in a prisoner exchange just a year later. Now here he was again, prematurely winning freedom in a remarkable deal. The enormity of what had transpired would take some time to sink in—for Palestinians and Israelis alike.

To appreciate just what Jordan's King Hussein and President Bill Clinton had orchestrated, it was necessary to go back to the first weeks of 1997, to view the Occupied Territories as they might have looked from the desk of Danny Yatom. After about a year in the chair at Mossad, Yatom was entitled to a sense of smugness when he reviewed the Hamas file.

Yassin, the founder and spiritual light of the movement, was then in the eighth year of his sentence in Israel's Kfar Yona Prison. Mousa Abu Marzook, who had been Yassin's trusted pointman in the Amman-based political bureau, had been snatched by the Americans and was locked up in a Manhattan penitentiary, ready to be extradited to Israel, where they would surely jail him and throw away the keys.

And then there was Khalid Mishal, the mysterious operative from Kuwait, who had stepped into the outside leadership post on the jailing of Abu Marzook. Danny Yatom was going to kill Mishal—the plan had been drawn up the previous year, and then had been placed on hold. It was just a matter of time, Yatom judged, before Mishal would be liquidated.

Quite apart from this Israeli decapitation of the Hamas leadership, a surge of popular faith in the Oslo process had helped to marginalize Hamas, effectively neutralizing the movement.[1] As well, Arafat's security forces had spent the last two years hounding Hamas on the ground in the Occupied Territories, rounding up activists and sympathizers by the thousand. Official seals, in the form of globs of red wax, marked the doors of dozens of Hamas institutions that had been shut down by Arafat. Here was proof of the PLO leader's readiness to crush the Islamists if they persisted in challenging his writ in the Occupied Territories. Sheikh Yassin complained publicly about the effectiveness of Arafat's campaign, bemoaning the fact that the PLO leader's security agencies had foiled more than 170 military strikes by Hamas against Israel in the previous two years.[2]

Even Washington had concluded that Arafat's Preventive Security Service was working well—in cahoots with Israel's domestic security agency, Shin Bet—to "screw" Hamas.[3] Despite the two Jerusalem bombings that so infuriated Netanyahu, American diplomats in Israel judged that the combined efforts of Arafat and the Israelis were driving Hamas to the brink of organizational and military paralysis. "It wasn't just that we had Abu Marzook in jail and the Israelis had Yassin locked up," a senior U.S. official explained. "Hamas was having its worst year. But then Mossad's balls-up in Amman turned their fortunes."[4]

By their failure to assassinate Mishal, Israel's Netanyahu and Yatom had pulled Hamas back from the grave. Abu Marzook was succinct in assessing how circumstances then changed for the movement. "If [our] enemy fails," he said, "it means [we] are stronger than at any time before."[5] Abu Marzook may have been supplanted at the top of Hamas's outside leadership during his own incarceration, but now he was free; Mishal, his replacement, had come back from the dead; and in the aftermath of the extraordinary bungled assassination attempt, Sheikh Yassin too was back among the living.

Furthermore, Netanyahu's strategy of forcing Arafat to crack down on Hamas before the Palestinians could enjoy Israeli concessions was in tatters, because the combined impact of the Mishal affair and the near collapse of the Oslo peace process was to make Hamas more popular in the Occupied Territories—and Arafat less so. In the absence of a peace dividend for Palestinians, it had become too great a risk for Arafat to continue doing what, in the eyes of many of his own people, was the Israelis' dirty work of suppressing Hamas.

Yassin had been absent from Gaza for much of the Intifada and all of the Oslo process, a tumultuous period that had been as politically character forming as it was frustrating for Palestinians. On his return, he found his community and his movement barely recognizable.

Importantly, Arafat too was back in Gaza, and the shared history of these two men boded ill. In the early days of Hamas, Arafat had dismissed Yassin's followers as ants he might crush underfoot.[6] Later, because Yassin in the

1936–1939: The Arab Revolt. Mishal's father, Abd Al-Qadir, pointed to the scarfed figure in the middle of the front row of this group of Palestinian fighters, saying, "That's me." ABD AL-QADIR'S FAMILY ALBUM

August 2007: Fatima and Mullah Abd Al-Qadir, the parents of Khalid Mishal, at their home in Amman while being interviewed by the author. PAUL MCGEOUGH

1971: As a fifteen-year-old at Abdullah Al-Salim Al-Sabah School in Kuwait, Khalid Mishal opted to be an Islamist. HAMAS ARCHIVES

October 1977: Khalid Mishal as a final-year physics student at Kuwait University. HAMAS ARCHIVES

June 1974: Mishal's graduation class at Abdullah Al-Salim Al-Sabah School in Kuwait—Mishal is standing behind the teachers who are seated fifth and sixth from the left. HAMAS ARCHIVES

November 2007: Ras Ali, at the northern end of Silwad, where Mishal lived as a child. PAUL MCGEOUGH

November 2007: Khalid Mishal's shuttered family home at Silwad, on the West Bank. PAUL MCGEOUGH

August 1993: Randa Habib, the Agence France-Presse bureau chief in Amman, interviews King Hussein of Jordan. RANDA HABIB ALBUM

March 1997: Khalid Mishal at his office in Amman. HAMAS ARCHIVES

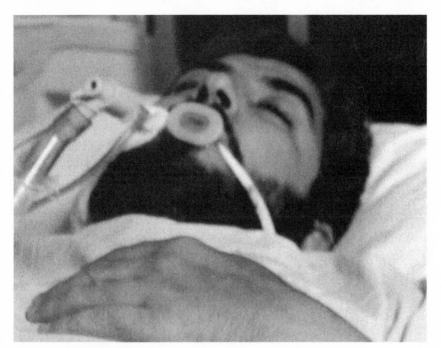

September 25, 1997: Mishal on a gurney as he is transferred between hospitals in Amman in the hours after the failed Mossad attempt to poison him.
AGENCE FRANCE-PRESSE

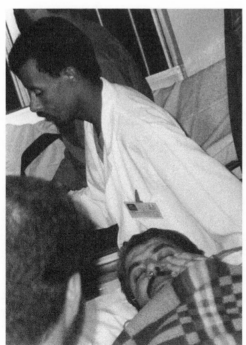

September 25, 1997: A doctor at Amman's Islamic Hospital supervises Mishal's transfer to King Hussein Medical City.
AGENCE FRANCE-PRESSE

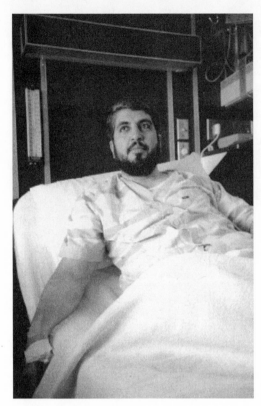

October 1997: In the days after the Mossad attack, Mishal is still confined to his bed at King Hussein Medical City. HAMAS ARCHIVES

October 1997: Mishal with his eldest son, Walid, one of his three children who witnessed the Mossad attack. HAMAS ARCHIVES

November 29, 2000: Two months into the second Intifada, Mishal rallied Palestinian refugees at the Yarmuk camp in Damascus. "Negotiations are absurd and useless," he declared. "The only choice is maintaining the Intifada and escalating the resistance." HAMAS ARCHIVES

March 27, 2004: A quiet exchange between Mishal and Hezbollah leader Hassan Nasrallah during a conference of officials from both their organizations in the days after the Israeli assassination of Sheikh Ahmad Yassin. HAMAS ARCHIVES

June 11, 2003: Emergency and forensic crews examine the bus destroyed by a suicide bombing that killed sixteen Israelis and

February 3, 2005: Four security men form a cordon around Mishal as he preaches during Friday prayers at a mosque in Tehran—one guard on the left, two on the right, and another below and in front of Mishal, looking out into the congregation. HAMAS ARCHIVES

November 11, 2005: Mohammad Abu Sayf, the bodyguard who captured two of the Mossad agents who attacked Khalid Mishal in September 1997, stands at his leader's shoulder during a Hamas rally in Damascus. HAMAS ARCHIVES

February 3, 2006: Mishal is greeted in Damascus by Syrian vice president Farouk Shara. HAMAS ARCHIVES

February 16, 2006: In Ankara, Mishal speaks to reporters after meeting Foreign Minister Abdullah Gul. The *Turkish Daily News* reported that Prime Minister Recep Tayyip Erdogan canceled a planned meeting with Mishal after pressure from Israel and other governments. HAMAS ARCHIVES

February 21, 2006: Mishal is received by Iranian supreme leader Ayatollah Ali Khamenei just weeks after Hamas's election win. HAMAS ARCHIVES

February 21, 2006:
In Tehran, Iranian
president Mahmoud
Ahmadinejad
welcomes Mishal.
HAMAS ARCHIVES

February 27, 2006:
Mishal in talks with
Syrian foreign minister
Walid Al-Mu'allim in
Damascus. HAMAS
ARCHIVES

March 3, 2006: Khalid Mishal puts the Hamas case to Russian foreign minister Sergey Lavrov (back to camera) at a meeting in Moscow—the first major crack in the international blockade of Hamas. HAMAS ARCHIVES

March 3, 2006: Mishal and the Hamas delegation hold a press conference after a round of official meetings in Moscow. Seated, left to right: Mohammad Nazzal, Mousa Abu Marzook, Khalid Mishal, Said Siam, and Sami Khater. Standing behind them is the Hamas security detail—including Mohammed Abu Sayf (with black beard), Mishal's personal bodyguard. HAMAS ARCHIVES

March 2006: Russian president Vladimir Putin's invitation for Mishal to travel to Moscow in the aftermath of the Hamas election win was the highest acknowledgment of the Islamist movement outside the Middle East. Here, Mishal is briefed on Russia's past wars during a visit to a military museum in the Russian capital. HAMAS ARCHIVES

March 5, 2006: In a meeting with the head of the Russian Orthodox Church, Patriarch Aleksiy II, Mishal heard support for a Palestinian homeland—but it came with a stern reminder that a homeland could be achieved only through dialogue. HAMAS ARCHIVES

March 5, 2006: Mishal and Hamas were frozen out by most capitals, but they were welcomed in Moscow, after President Vladimir Putin warned against isolating Hamas. "I am profoundly convinced that burning bridges in politics is the easiest thing to do, but it has no perspective, no future," he told reporters. HAMAS ARCHIVES

August 27, 2006: After meeting Khalid Mishal in Damascus, the Reverend Jesse L. Jackson told reporters that Mishal had assured him that Gilad Shalit, the Israeli soldier captured by Palestinian militiamen two months earlier, was still alive. HAMAS ARCHIVES

September 2007: Khalid Mishal during an interview in Damascus. Behind him is a portrait of Sheikh Ahmad Yassin, Hamas's spiritual leader who was assassinated by Israel on March 22, 2004. PAUL MCGEOUGH

December 15, 2007: Hamas supporters rally in Gaza to celebrate the twentieth anniversary of the founding of its movement. REUTERS/MOHAMMED SALEM

September 2007: Almost ten years later, the journalist Ranya Kadri returns to the scene of the crime—the pavement where Mossad agents attacked Khalid Mishal on September 25, 1997. PAUL MCGEOUGH

1980s had been encouraged by Israel as a foil to Arafat's dominant Fatah movement, he had been branded a collaborator by the PLO.

During Yassin's absence in jail, Arafat had opted strategically for a different deck of cards, undertaking to Israel and the Americans that he would control Hamas, along with the lesser rejectionist factions whose fighters were not affiliated with his PLO and whose orders came from beyond the Occupied Territories. Since Arafat had gained control of Gaza and small portions of the West Bank in 1994, he had taken to handling Hamas much as the Israelis had treated the Palestinians in the past. In 1995 and again in 1996, he had rounded up more than one thousand Hamas activists and sympathizers.

Hamas members and other detainees were held incommunicado, often for months without facing trial. Torture was widespread, resulting in fourteen deaths in custody since Arafat's return. Ordinarily Palestinians were vocal, but in a new reign of fear many had become reluctant to criticize the regime.

Arafat had seized control of Yassin's mosques and attempted to shut down many of Hamas's welfare agencies. Describing the mosques as "castles which have been the fortress of rebellion against occupation," a Hamas leaflet, published before Yassin's release, warned Arafat, "Maintaining the free and independent status of mosques is a redline our people will observe strictly." From his cell, Yassin had lashed out, warning that any assault on Hamas institutions "should be resisted violently."

Yet now, here was Yasser Arafat taking the newly freed Yassin's hand and telling him reassuringly, "God willing, we'll pray together in Al-Aqsa Mosque [in Jerusalem]."

Yassin was not taken in by this seemingly placatory gesture. With hundreds of his senior Hamas associates locked away in Arafat's prisons, he belittled the PLO leader, provocatively claiming that Hamas was all that Arafat had left to push back the Israelis. "What else does he have?"[7] Yassin demanded. "He has tried to restore our rights, but if he can't he should step aside and allow others to try."[8]

Even as it ratcheted up its rhetoric, Hamas seemed to appreciate that it needed to pull its punches; all-out war with Fatah was a schism that would play to Israel's advantage. When it seemed the stage was being set for civil war, Mohammad Dahlan, Arafat's security chief in Gaza, warned of the consequences of so much as a squeak of opposition from the Islamists. "I don't care if it's armed or unarmed," he thundered, warning that any Hamas activity would be viewed as an obstacle to the peace process.

Yassin's return to Gaza effectively required Arafat to share power. Inevitably the PLO leader, who earlier in his career had been dubbed Mr. Palestine, was diminished—put simply, both he and Yassin were vying for space on the same Palestinian plinth.

Yassin discovered as well that in his enforced absence, Hamas had changed. The ragtag militia run by the movement at the time of his jailing had morphed into the sophisticated, disciplined, and brutally efficient Qassam Brigade, whose attacks could kill dozens of Israelis and injure a hundred more.

Other changes were profound. Many of Yassin's generation of gradualist Muslim Brotherhood leaders—men whose authority came from their piety and religion—had been displaced by a new generation of Islamist revolutionaries.[9] The Yassin old guard, who had placed survival above outright confrontation with the Israelis, had been elbowed aside by a harder new axis of power—men more intent on nationalism and politics than on religion. In the 1980s and early 1990s, the most senior men had been almost entirely religious leaders; in 1997 about 95 percent of the new lineup greeting Yassin were devout but had a broader outlook. These were the university-educated professionals whom Khalid Mishal referred to as Hamas's intellectuals.[10]

If the old Hamas had been defined by the inside-outside roles of Sheikh Yassin and his disciple Abu Marzook, their imprisonment on opposite sides of the globe in the 1990s created a vacuum filled on the outside by Khalid Mishal and on the inside by Abdul Azziz Al-Rantisi, a Gaza firebrand and pediatrician who, despite regular stints in Israeli jails, refused to dilute any of Hamas's core claims or to soften the rhetoric in which they were articulated. The new leadership had been seared in the cauldrons of deportation to southern Lebanon and by the struggle for survival against Arafat's Palestinian Authority and Israeli forces. More technocratic than they were overtly religious, these were men whose vision of the movement was more nationalist and their perception more hierarchical than was Yassin's. If the sheikh was a reformist, they were more revolutionary.

Yassin had always been a man of patience. From a reference in the Qur'an he had divined that local history went in forty-year cycles. The Palestinians first had been denied their land in 1948, and the Intifada had erupted in 1987. So, he concluded, the fight to regain their lost homeland could last until about the year 2027.[11] Up to the end of the 1980s, Yassin had eschewed violence, insisting instead that his duty was to prepare Palestinians, spiritually and morally, for the long haul. But then he threw himself into the Intifada. Now, after an absence of eight years, every word he uttered was analyzed to the last syllable in a search for clues on how he might direct Hamas.

All sides were taken aback when Yassin urged that Israeli civilians be spared in Hamas attacks. And then, while talking to foreign reporters at his home two weeks after his return, he announced that Hamas had put all attacks on Israel on hold. "We have stopped [again]. Many times we have stopped for months, but the Israelis still continue their attacks. Why don't they stop?" he asked. Stressing that he was talking more of a cooling-off than a cease-fire, he went on: "The occupation compels our youth to fight. If [the Israelis] stop, we'll stop."[12]

The deal Yassin seemed to be putting on the table was a dramatic departure from the Hamas charter call for Palestine to be liberated from "the river to the sea"—in other words, all of historic Palestine, from the Jordan River in the east to the Mediterranean Sea in the west. Now Yassin appeared to be proposing peaceful coexistence, with Israelis on one side of the Green Line—the 1949 armistice line between Israel and the Occupied Territories—and Palestinians on the other. But he added that it was too soon after their dispossession for the current generation of Palestinians to forgo their claim to all of historic Palestine. That was a decision to be made by a future generation. "What we are accepting," he explained, "is what this generation will accept."

Some now detected other significant shifts in Hamas's rhetoric. Crude anti-Semitic references were less prevalent, and the discourse in which Yassin sought to engage Benjamin Netanyahu amounted to a new, de facto recognition of Israel.[13] They detected a move by Yassin away from jihad as a bloody and holy commandment to stating "political" goals that could be read by Israel, if it chose, as a willingness to engage in political, nonviolent dialogue.

David Bar-Illan, a spokesman for Netanyahu, deemed the sheikh's commentary to be a "positive development." Relieved Palestinian Authority officials judged that this was a new, more moderate tone, which, they hoped, might signal a shift of the Hamas center of gravity back to Gaza and away from the more radical outside leadership.[14]

But, in a matter of days, Yassin had gone full circle. The moment of compromise had been a chimera. As the Islamic University campus pulsated during his third week back in Gaza, Yassin told a crowd of about five thousand students, "Our people must choose the path of holy war because, if we do not fight, our people will die. This world only understands the language of force."[15] When Yasser Arafat demanded that Hamas cease its military operations, it was Yassin the militant who responded with the impatience of someone tired of repeating himself. "I have said many times that we are defending ourselves against occupation. The occupation continues, so there will be struggle." Deferring to his interpretation of Islam, he hectored, "If the enemy kills [our] civilians, it is our right to kill their civilians."[16]

An explanation for these wild swings by Yassin was that he was sticking to the ambiguity he had used as a shield for decades, allowing himself plausible denial if the import of his intended message offended the Israeli authorities. But it was clear enough too that on his return, an internal struggle was being waged and that Yassin was being brought into line with the harder outlook of the younger leadership that had taken control in his absence. These were professional men who had been revolutionized by the Intifada.

Now Yassin framed his core message as a warning that it was up to Israel to decide how the crisis might unfold. Suicide attacks? "The Jews are those who will determine that," he said. "If they stop their attacks on civilians, land confiscation, house demolitions; and if they release prisoners and detainees, then we'll definitely ease up—God willing!"[17] And what if his terms were rejected by Israel? "It is inconceivable that a person should stand idly by while his soil is occupied and his people and his homeland are degraded." He told the students at the Islamic University, "We have one enemy and we will wage war and fight him until we return to our land. No to a cease-fire! A nation without jihad cannot exist!"[18]

On the surface, these were euphoric days for Hamas. But behind the excitement, the question of *hudna* was just one in a series that made the period after Yassin's release a time of great reckoning for the movement.

The concept of a truce did not sneak up on Hamas. Writing from prison in 1994, Yassin had raised the prospect of a *hudna* lasting anywhere from fifteen to thirty years.[19] In the same year, Abu Marzook had written about the concept in a Jordanian journal, and both, along with others in the movement, had pushed the idea as a circuit breaker to the crisis.

Within its Islamic context, a *hudna* was a sacred undertaking—it made peace a religious duty, but it did not concede the issue fueling the conflict. In other words, a *hudna* would allow Israelis and Palestinians to live side by side in their respective parcels of what was historic Palestine, but the Palestinians would not relinquish their claim to what had become the state of Israel. This was not what Oslo was about, and whenever the prospect was raised, it was dismissed by Israel.

When news reports of a *hudna* offer surfaced, and King Hussein publicly confirmed that he had indeed written to the Israeli prime minister, offering on behalf of Hamas to "put an end to terror and violence in return for discussion on all issues," Hamas attempted to bury the story in denials. The movement ran its own internal investigation into who might have led the king to believe he could make such a bold gesture on behalf of Hamas and, inevitably, the finger of blame was pointed at Mousa Abu Marzook.

But, when challenged by a senior figure in the movement about what he might have communicated to the royal palace, the engineer denied having put anything in writing, either to Samih Batikhi or to King Hussein. "Abu Marzook thinks maybe Batikhi drew some conclusions from their little chats and gave them to the king," the senior figure explained.

Quite apart from the business of the *hudna* proposal, the Israeli bid to kill Khalid Mishal now prompted questions on the long-term viability of the movement's vital Amman bureau and who should head it. Inevitably, Yassin's freedom rekindled the leadership yearning of his protégé, Mousa Abu Marzook. It would be only a matter of time before Abu Marzook sought a showdown with Mishal over which of them would be Hamas's link to the region and the world—its banker and its bagman. Which of them, as the outside leader of Hamas, would be held responsible for the next bomb?

Given that King Hussein had in fact worked hard for Abu Marzook's return to Amman, so he might displace Mishal from the leadership of the political bureau, the movement was not being overly conspiratorial in attempting to understand just who at this time had been pulling the strings and to what end. They were not alone. Questions about the existence of what some in Amman described as "another truth" were posed inside and outside the movement as observers explored events that seemed to have unfolded between the sliding doors of unreality.

Abu Marzook became jumpy when asked if he was privy to any plot by the king to interfere with the hierarchy in Hamas. "I couldn't accept criticism of Brother Khalid; he was appointed to the job [in the political bureau]," Abu Marzook said, showing noticeable disquiet, even years later. "If I had accepted what King Hussein was thinking, it'd be a big problem for me and for the organization." But then Abu Marzook changed pace: "Maybe the king did prefer me as head of Hamas. . . . It's a Palestinian organization and King Hussein did not like to see Jordanians in charge of it." Then, taking another tack, he said, "I've never heard it suggested that I should be put back into the top job!"[20]

The stakes were high and so too were emotions. One of the most powerful drugs yet discovered had been used in a bid to eliminate a leadership figure who in Abu Marzook's absence had become better known in the movement and now commanded considerable respect and admiration. "They wanted Mishal out of the leadership, and the only way to achieve that was by a quiet assassination," insisted a source close to the leadership.

Real or imagined, all this fed into the movement's internal reckoning. Feigning disbelief, one observer who convinced himself that the Israeli assassination bid had to be a deliberate element in the Jordanian regime-change plot, framed his suspicions in these words: "They released Brother Mousa and four months later they try to kill Brother Khalid?"

Stunned by Mishal's refusal to relinquish the leadership after he was freed from custody in the United States, Abu Marzook bided his time. But when Hamas held internal elections early in 1998, he challenged Mishal again, pitting his claim to have outsmarted the combined might of the United States and Israel by beating the rap in New York, against Mishal's battle scars after evading Danny Yatom's silent bullet.

It was a defining standoff in Hamas history, in which the candidates' competing celebrity claims were part of a far more significant strategic struggle. The movement was an international pariah, but Mishal remained convinced that its strength came from military resistance. The world ultimately would respect it, he reasoned, and would therefore seek an accommodation on terms more advantageous to Hamas. Abu Marzook disagreed—he argued that a greater openness, combined with more liberal thinking and policies, would win the respect craved by Hamas. He was supported by key figures in the Occupied Territories who, being preoccupied with daily events and hardships on the ground, were more receptive to Hamas participating in the uncertain political process driven by the Oslo Accords.

Mishal countered with an argument that Hamas could not go the same way as the Palestine Liberation Organisation and Fatah. They had watched Arafat rewrite the PLO charter, renouncing violence as a weapon and dramatically shrinking his territorial claims. "Where did it get him? Where's his independent state?" Mishal asked.[21] "He talked with [Israel]—did the occupation end?" What Mishal's faction now laid down was a more nuanced strategy, geared to a rough coexistence with Arafat. Hamas could not afford to alienate its grassroots support, so attacks on Israel had to be presented as retaliation for excessive force by Israel; but at the same time it would travel a different road. And, lest doubt was taking hold among the cadres, Mishal added, "Operations against the occupation are honorable and legitimate."[22]

It was the Gazans who most vehemently clamored to reinstate Abu Marzook as leader of the political bureau. "Brother Mousa was the closest we had to a Western mentality," a Hamas insider said, with genuine admiration for the engineer. "Prison makes you either more—or less—radical. Abu Marzook became less radical during his jail time in Manhattan." Another of his supporters spoke of Abu Marzook as one of Yassin's handpicked future leaders who, in the 1980s, had been sent to the United States for study and exposure to a world that might open their minds. "Some of them came back to the Occupied Territories, bringing new ideas with them," he explained. "They were more pragmatic in their vision and their politics. They understood that things we previously thought could be achieved only by resistance also could be delivered by negotiation."

The forces that lined up now—behind Mishal on one side and Abu Marzook on the other—had squared off once before, in 1996, in a bitterly contested internal debate on whether or not Hamas should have fielded candidates in the elections for the first Palestinian parliament. At that time Sheikh Yassin and Abu Marzook had backed participation, while Mishal had rejected it. In a letter smuggled from Israel's Kfar Yona Prison, Yassin had revealed his momentous conclusion that it was time for Hamas to join the political process. "Is it permissible," he asked, "that a Muslim may serve as an errand boy in a Cabinet minister's office or in parliament, but he may not be a deputy in parliament, in which capacity he is better able to serve his faith, his calling and his *ummah*?"[23]

Was it permissible? After a torrid discourse in the movement, the answer at that time was no. Participating in the poll, Mishal had argued, would amount to Hamas condescending to play by rules devised by Arafat, Netanyahu, and Clinton. In acknowledging the "humiliating and shameful" Oslo agreement, he had said, contesting the election would amount to endorsement of Israeli domination. Also, it would blur Hamas's crucial point of difference with Arafat and Fatah. If Hamas were to fold its resistance banner, walk away from jihad, and then function as just another political party, it too would become a hostage to Oslo. A balance needed to be struck, but on Hamas's terms—not those of Arafat, the Israelis, or the Americans.

Mishal had carried the day in 1996, and he did so again in 1998. Hamas was not in the business of disclosing voting figures, but Khalid Mishal ultimately won the 1998 political bureau election. Mousa Abu Marzook was the leader the Israelis had freed, but Mishal was the leader they had tried, and failed, to kill.

Mishal's heroic survival now guaranteed him the leadership of the political bureau, but it did not diminish Abu Marzook's belief that somehow he had been cheated and therefore should be reinstated. "It's his psychology," a colleague explained. "In his self-estimation, he still believes he's the leader. The trouble is the assassination attempt made Brother Khalid stronger and even more famous, and he wins the elections. Marzook might have brains; but Mishal has charisma. . . . He's our Malcolm X; he's like Louis Farrakhan!"

Khalid Mishal emerged as a changed man from his brush with death. He saw himself in a very different light, and so did the movement's members. Overnight, he had become a household name—for Palestinians, Israelis, and the whole Arab world. In a Mossad flash, Mishal had been hauled into the pantheon of Palestinian heroes. It had a profound impact on him.

During an interview soon after he had checked out of King Hussein Medical City, the Amman journalist Yasser Abu Hilalah was taken aback when an emotional Mishal burst into tears as he revealed a deeply held sense that he had been reborn by divine intervention.[24] "I've been given a new life for a new role," he told the journalist several times.

Jordanian intelligence agents also were struck by a sense that they were dealing with a new man. "Every time you met him then, you found a different person—his ambition was unbounded," one of them later explained. Previously, Abu Hilalah had thought of Mishal as an average-quality chief executive in the way he ran the political bureau. But after his near-death experience, the West Banker concluded that he had been blessed with a new historic role. His first task, he told Abu Hilalah, would be to break the Gazans' traditional lock on the leadership of Hamas.

With Hamas now decisively choosing one of its leaders over the other, the movement confronted two new realities. Sheikh Ahmad Yassin's supreme authority had been significantly diluted, and such was the bad odor around Abu Marzook, because of his dealings with Batikhi and the Jordanian regime, that his ambition had been permanently thwarted. For the time, Abu Marzook had sufficient support, mostly Gaza based, to assure him of a position in the leadership team, but he would henceforth always have a lesser role to that played by Mishal.

The gross miscalculation by Netanyahu and Yatom had thus effectively anointed Mishal the leader of the future. And, quite apart from resolving the personal rivalry between the candidates, this hard-fought contest for the political-bureau leadership had answered a vital question posed by observers when Yassin was released: for the time being, at least, Hamas was opting for the bullet over the ballot.

As Yassin settled back in at home, Hamas and Fatah tried to maintain a dialogue. These efforts were rough and rude, but they did address some of the essentials of coexistence under occupation. Liaison committees were established to deal with areas of mutual interest, like the welfare of Palestinians in Israeli jails. But when the issue of Hamas joining the PLO was broached, the negotiations deadlocked. Arafat preferred to make his own appointments to the PLO's ruling council, while Hamas argued that there should be elections. Hamas claimed sufficient popular support to warrant the allocation of 40 percent of council seats; Arafat countered self-defensively, offering less than a quarter.

For one brief moment there seemed to be the possibility of a thaw locally in Gaza when, contrary to what an observer described as Yassin's "sixth sense that embodied the organizational consensus in Hamas," the sheikh chose to ignore advice from Mishal by announcing he would accept an invitation from Yasser Arafat to attend a meeting of the PLO council. But Mishal was disturbed that Yassin's attendance would amount to acceptance by Hamas of the PLO's claim to be the "sole" representative of the Palestinians.

Ultimately the spiritual leader was forced into an embarrassing backdown, leaving the meeting after the Hamas political bureau in Amman issued a statement saying that Yassin's decision to attend was personal and not to be seen as representative of Hamas—effectively disowning the sheikh.

In the overall scheme of things, this was small potatoes. But, in Hamas lore, it was recorded with significance as the point at which the Gazans finally got it—that the Amman-based political bureau was the senior decision-making body of Hamas.

In the face of Netanyahu's stubbornness through 1998, Arafat pulled back from the Oslo process, angering Israeli officials by positioning himself closer to Hamas—to the point, at one stage, of publicly greeting the Gaza hardliner Abdul Azziz Al-Rantisi with a traditional man-to-man Arab kiss. Twelve months after the misadventure in Amman, the full dimension of Israel's strategic error was clear. After almost a decade of attempting to lock Hamas out of the structure of formal relations within the Middle East crisis, Israel had confirmed Hamas as an essential, if uninvited, partner. By halting talks with Arafat as a response to Hamas atrocities, Prime Minister Netanyahu had handed the rejectionists a new card to play—effectively a veto over any progress.[25]

Sheikh Yassin appeared to be in fine health after receiving treatment for his various ailments during a four-month trip abroad in 1998—much to the amusement of Israeli commentators, who enjoyed reminding Netanyahu of his claim, at the height of the Mishal affair, that Yassin had to be released because his health was poor.

Elsewhere, however, the outlook was grim—the peace process remained on life support and King Hussein of Jordan was seriously ill. In the aftermath of the attack on Mishal, Jordan's Queen Noor had begun to refer jokingly to her husband's worrying symptoms—which now warranted visits to Amman by more Mayo specialists—as the "Bibi virus."[26] In fact, this was the early onset of the cancer that would consume him.

A five-month program of chemotherapy for King Hussein at the Mayo Clinic in Minnesota overlapped with a marathon bid by President Bill Clinton in October 1998 to break the stalemate in the Middle East peace process. It culminated in nine days of extraordinary talks in a bucolic setting at Wye on Chesapeake Bay, about seventy miles east of Washington, D.C. Netanyahu led the Israeli delegation; Arafat headed the Palestinians. Clinton finally browbeat them into an agreed form of words, but none present was prepared to call it an agreement. Instead, the document they signed was called the Wye Memorandum.

The memorandum was to extend the area of the West Bank under full Palestinian control to slightly more than 17 percent and that under partial control to a further 22 percent. In return, the Palestinian Authority had to honour a series of security obligations that applied only to the Palestinian side.[27] This deal perpetuated the flaw in the original Oslo agreement that to date had defied implementation—Arafat was accepting a security task in return for Israeli concessions, in an environment in which all parties knew that Netanyahu had vested Hamas with the power to thwart the implementation of its terms through his loud proclamations that he would not comply unless Arafat brought Hamas to heel.

As they inked the document, in a ceremony in the East Room at the White House, Netanyahu was hailed as the "moderate" who had finally accepted the concept of trading land for peace. Arafat was cheered for declaring war on Hamas.[28] Only time would tell whether this deal could change the course of a crisis that gave every sign of holding to Sheikh Yassin's prophecy that it would take another twenty-odd years to be resolved.

In reaching an understanding, the delegates only got as far as they did at Wye because they were shamed and cajoled into it by a dying man. Finding himself cornered by the intransigence of the two sides, and desperate for advice, Clinton had phoned Hussein while the king was waiting for a bone-marrow transplant at the Mayo Clinic. Despite his condition, Hussein volunteered to pitch in and the presidential helicopter was sent to fetch him to the Wye conference center.

Hussein's appearance on arrival shocked all who were familiar with the

Jordanian leader's customary fine bearing and charming good looks. The man who stood before them was gaunt, gray, and balding. The risk of infection for Hussein was so severe that all were ordered to wash their hands in a special antibacterial soap before greeting him. "It's time to finish," Hussein told them.

That was not quite the case. After another stormy session, during which Clinton was heard to refer to the Israeli leader as "that SOB [who] doesn't want a deal," Hussein was brought back to Wye one more time to push them to the line.[29]

Within hours of the ceremonial signing of the Wye Memorandum on October 23, Arafat again moved against Hamas. More than one hundred activists were rounded up and Sheikh Yassin was placed under house arrest. Amid warnings from Hamas that it would turn its guns on Arafat's security forces if they went ahead with his renewed undertaking to break up militia groups and confiscate illegal weapons, the telephone lines to the homes of Yassin and others in the Hamas leadership were cut. Yassin's house was sealed off by guards who disarmed his security detail while masked security men rifled through his files and cupboards.[30]

The restriction on Yassin was lifted by Arafat on December 24, as a goodwill gesture for the Muslim holy month of Ramadan, which, in 1998, overlapped with the Christian celebration of Christmas. Yassin wasted no time. The next day he traveled in his Land Rover—a gift from the Saudi government that had been customized to take the wheelchair—to Shati, the refugee camp by the sea where he had been raised. The occasion was the eleventh anniversary of the founding of Hamas and, as he was wheeled before a crowd of more than ten thousand cheering followers, the aging spiritual leader began: "We must continue on our path to holy war...."[31]

From the news clips at the signing of the Wye Memorandum, the world knew that King Hussein was gravely ill. But, as he returned to his kingdom after almost half a year in the Mayo's Minnesota medical complex, only one person was aware of the firestorm he had planned—Randa Habib, Agence France-Presse's redoubtable Amman bureau chief.

Despite his illness, the avid aviator Hussein was at the controls of his Gulfstream IV for the entire flight on his final homecoming leg from London to Amman. He acknowledged a farewell salute from pilots of each air force whose territory he overflew: first, a fighter escort from the Sixth Squadron of the RAF as they left British airspace; then, in quick succession, aircraft from the French, Italian, Israeli, and Jordanian air forces handed him on one to the next, in what Queen Noor described as a motorcade in the sky.[32]

Having reigned for almost fifty years, Hussein was the only ruler most Jordanians had known. But now he was required to name a successor—undoubtedly one of the most important moments in all of Jordan's brief history.

It was Randa Habib who stopped all in their tracks, and shattered the dreams of the presumed successor and his faction of royal hangers-on, with her revelation on the AFP wires that King Hussein's brother, the dutiful Crown Prince Hassan, was to be passed over. On his deathbed, Hussein had anointed Prince Abdullah, a thirty-seven-year-old son by his second marriage to the English princess Muna. The ever-composed Noor, the fuming Prince Hassan, and all the royal plotters and schemers were ambushed by Hussein's decision to make the succession a fait accompli by leaking it to Randa Habib before he took any of them into his confidence.

At the end of five months of what, ultimately, turned out to be futile cancer treatments at the Mayo Clinic, Hussein had made a series of phone calls to Habib. Breaking his homebound journey in London in mid-January 1999, the king acknowledged the forensic manner in which the journalist approached a story. "And keep following your gut feeling," he advised her. But it was his last words to Habib that underscored their shared knowledge that Habib's best-placed "senior palace source" had little time left. "Randa, will you be able to take the heat on this one?" the king asked gently.[33]

The succession was a dynastic intrigue of rare proportions. It culminated in a fourteen-page deathbed missive that Hussein seemed to have written in a fit of blind rage. Shakespeare would have been proud of him.

Back in 1965, Hassan's appointment as crown prince had been a device to protect the family and the vulnerable Hashemite throne. At the time Hussein's logical heir, his firstborn son, Prince Abdullah, was a mere three-year-old. An adult had to be in the wings in the event of Hussein's untimely demise; thereafter, one of the constants in Jordanian affairs had been an assumption that Hassan would succeed Hussein, who was his older brother by twelve years. But in his fourteen-page letter, the sixty-three-year-old dying king now excoriated the younger brother who had patiently stood behind him for thirty-four years; he dismissed Hassan as a parasite and an opportunist at the same time as he charged him with a litany of wrongdoings.[34]

Royal watchers in Amman discerned two motives and a single objective for the brutality with which Hassan was cut adrift. Hussein had been deeply offended by his brother's failure to deny an Israeli press report that had predicted—quite accurately as events transpired—that the king would be dead within three months. Hussein was troubled too that, in the event of Hassan being appointed ruler, they could not agree on the necessary guarantees for the royal succession to return to Hussein's line on the death of Hassan. For these reasons Hussein needed to destroy Hassan in the eyes of the military and the bureaucracy, lest he attempt to derail the reign of the new greenhorn king, Abdullah.

Amman woke to sultry skies on Sunday, February 7, and by lunchtime the heavens opened, sloshing the city in torrential rain. Queen Noor noted that, when King Hussein expired during noon prayers, one of modern history's most extraordinary spans of leadership had reached its conclusion.[35]

The king's funeral would be as much a logistical challenge as it was a security nightmare. Most of Hussein's friends from around the world, and some of his enemies, needed to find their way to Amman on less than twenty-four hours' notice, because Islamic rites required that the king be buried as soon as possible. Kings and queens, prime ministers and presidents got there on time. The leaders of the Arab and the Islamic world came to pay their respects. President Bill Clinton headed an American delegation of no less than four presidents: Gerald Ford, Jimmy Carter, and George H.W. Bush flew in with Clinton aboard Air Force One.

It was an illustrious turnout that far exceeded the relative insignificance of Jordan the country, but was a mark of respect for its accomplished king. Apart from the Japanese, Spanish, Dutch, and Belgian royals, the mourners included Britain's Prince Charles and Tony Blair, Russia's Boris Yeltsin, Germany's Gerhard Schroeder, France's Jacques Chirac, and Czech president Vaclav Havel.

Protocol demanded that some mourners be brought together—Clinton had a brief, private meeting with the newly crowned Abdullah. Security insisted others be kept apart—like the Israeli prime minister, Benjamin Netanyahu, and the man he had tried to execute fifteen months earlier, Hamas's Khalid Mishal. Here in the flesh at the funeral of the inveterate peace seeker Hussein, these two represented the extremes in an intractable crisis. Floundering in a no-man's land between them was Yasser Arafat, wearing his aged soldier's battle dress and the black-and-white kaffiyeh, the folds of which he liked to drape from his shoulders in the shape of a map of Palestine.

Traveling to Amman for Hussein's burial, Netanyahu was confronted by three points of Israeli failure. If they had settled with King Hussein in the aftermath of the Six-Day War in 1967, they might have avoided dealing with Arafat and the PLO. If they had settled with Arafat and the Palestinian Authority, they could have headed off the subsequent confrontation with Mishal and Hamas. Hanging in the somber Amman air was this question: who might Israel have to deal with if it persisted in refusing to deal with Hamas?

In their own way, each was a guerrilla fighter—Hussein and Netanyahu, Arafat and Mishal. None of them had made significant advances, but in this grueling epic, not losing was as good as winning. From time to time each had had his tactical victories, but the Israelis could not rid themselves of the Palestinians, nor could the Palestinians rid themselves of the Israelis.

More than three decades after capturing what became the Occupied Territories, the Israelis had "imposed their presence" on the Palestinians, but not quite as the eye-patched defense minister Moshe Dayan had predicted in 1967. After thirty-two years, they were stuck in a divorce court, but the Israelis had failed to prise the good land "dowry" from the unloved Palestinian "bride," as foretold in the memorable wedding metaphor of Israeli prime minister Levi Eshkol in the wake of the Six-Day War.

18

Handcuffed and Deported

Samih Batikhi launched his dragnet in the last week of August 1999. Upon his orders for a full assault on Hamas, Batikhi's security forces swooped on addresses across Amman and trucked away files and computers. The movement's five separate offices were isolated and a handwritten notice fixed to the door of each. CLOSED BY ORDER OF THE GENERAL PROSECUTOR FOR STATE SECURITY, it said with officious finality.[1]

More than a dozen staff were arrested, including Mohammad Abu Sayf, the bodyguard whose fast wits in 1997 had provided King Hussein with the trophy Mossad prisoners he needed to humiliate Israel after the attempt on Mishal's life. But two key Hamas operatives escaped Batikhi's roundup—Mishal himself and Mousa Abu Marzook, now his deputy. In fact, the raids seemed to have been timed to allow them to evade capture. The GID was in the business of knowing the whereabouts of these two, and forty-eight hours earlier they had flown out of Jordan to Tehran.

The garrulous Mohammad Nazzal, who was Hamas's formal linkman with the Amman regime, remained at large too. Having chanced to leave his office to go home for a late lunch, Nazzal was interrupted there by a phone call that alerted him to the crackdown. He managed to go underground before the GID could bag him, but Batikhi kept his home under surveillance for weeks. Nazzal's wife was tailed whenever she went out, and members of their extended family were hauled in for questioning.

In the wake of the Israeli attempt to execute him, Mishal's office had been moved to his new family home, which was fortified against further attack and under constant surveillance by the GID. Now it was his former protectors who stormed in, startling his wife, Amal, as she went about her chores. "They searched all his papers," she said, complaining that she had been given no explanation. "They shut down the office and arrested four of his staff."

Amal had met the challenge of being a Hamas wife. She was seared by the assassination attempt in 1997, but even so, her resilience surprised her more worldly brothers-in-law, two of whom lived in the United States. One of them was thirty-nine-year-old Mufid, an engineer with a double degree from Oklahoma State University, employed by the Dallas City Council in Texas. In the days after the raids in Amman, Mufid phoned his younger brother Mithqal, who ran an auto-sales shop in Alabama. Referring to his sister-in-law as Um Walid (which means mother of Mishal's eldest son, Walid), Mufid seemed quite awed. "By God, between you and me I was very impressed," he swore. "She's formidable, man. She *is* formidable. Her morale is high, believe me."[2]

The brothers, with the FBI listening in, held a cautious, broad-ranging, and family-oriented conversation. Inter alia, they discussed their aged father's health, the need to get funds to Mishal's family while he was on the run from Jordan, and the difficulty Mishal's daughters had in concentrating on their studies amidst this crisis. But, clearly concerned that the U.S. authorities might be eavesdropping, the younger Mithqal became agitated when Mufid revealed that he had put a call through to Mishal in Tehran. "You called Khalid? You called direct, huh?"

"Ah-ha. Direct. They answered me right away."

"There's no fear?"

"I did not speak with them about anything."

"Huh?"

"I [just] talked about an ordeal and patience. I mean, we didn't talk. We didn't say anything about where Abu Walid was. . . . Only chatting, I mean."

Mithqal was anxious that the FBI most certainly would have been interested in the call. His prodding irritated the voluble Mufid.

"Huh?" Mufid asked, his temper rising.

"The call itself is—" But that was all Mithqal could get out before Mufid blew up. "May God damn them!" he began in an apparent reference to the FBI. "May God damn them dogs! I mean, I can't even speak with my brother! [To] hell with them. What . . . what can they get? I mean, my phone number? [To] hell with them! I mean, what can I do for them? I need to speak to my family, or are we going to abandon them? . . . I'll [keep] calling."

Mithqal calmed Mufid down, but he soon blew up again, abusing the Jordanian authorities. "These bastards, man," he exploded. "The bastards . . . are servants to the [Israelis]. Lower than servants. Lower. . . . The [Israelis] use them as prostitutes. . . ." Mufid then steadied himself, inquiring after Mithqal's children and how Mithqal himself had fared in some recent exams. "What happened with your CPA?" Mufid wanted to know,[3] as the brothers shifted with familiar ease from struggle in the Middle East to the travails of living the American dream.

In Amman, King Abdullah II was taking a very different exam. As a significant departure from his father's policy settings, his clampdown on Hamas won praise as the "boldest move so far"[4] by a young man thrust on the throne at short notice. Already Abdullah had revealed a surprising deference to Yasser Arafat. This clearly posed a challenge for Hamas and, by issuing it, the son seemed to have set himself up to jettison his father's historic baggage. "Every good soldier knows it's best to fight his battles at the time and place of his choosing," a pumped-up Abdullah explained. "I was going to have to take these guys on sooner or later."[5] Jordanian officials confirmed that the raids on Hamas had resulted from security cooperation with Israel and Arafat's Palestinian Authority.[6] "We're helping the Palestinians in their peace talks with Israel,"[7] an official explained.

The new Jordanian regime was watched attentively by the Americans, on whom it depended for essential foreign aid. Secretary of State Madeline Albright was due in the region within days, to renew efforts to breathe life into the Wye Memorandum. She intended to visit Amman, where it was becoming increasingly evident that King Abdullah had succumbed to the constant badgering from Washington that his father had long resisted.

Jordan issued warrants for the arrest of Mishal, Abu Marzook, Nazzal, and Ibrahim Ghosheh, their old and sickly media-relations man who had departed Jordan with Mishal, Abu Marzook, and four of their staff. Two lesser-known members of the political bureau, Sami Kather and Izzat Al-Rishiq, also became wanted men.

With the exception of Abu Marzook, the others were Jordanian citizens. Batikhi's strategy to erase Hamas from the local landscape appeared to hinge on his belief that the threat of long jail sentences on their return to Jordan would prevent them from returning.[8] But, taking a leaf from Abu Marzook's Manhattan strategy, in which the engineer had dared the Israelis to extradite him to face trial, Mishal sent a message from Tehran. "We've done nothing illegal," he said. "We're coming home—we're not strangers . . . not beggars."

Interviewed by Al-Jazeera, Mishal upped the ante, lecturing the new king on the subtlety of his late father's ways. "The Hamas movement that was known to your father Hussein, God bless his soul, is the same Hamas that

lives today in Jordan." Reminding the young leader of the rescue of Abu Marzook from U.S. detention, and then of King Hussein's deft handling of Mossad's attempt to kill him, Mishal noted the differences between father and
son. "[King Hussein] took a manly stand full of determination, wisdom, and
gallantry. . . . Unfortunately the attitude toward Hamas has changed."[9]

The crackdown was in truth a nightmare for the movement. Amidst rising
uncertainty in the Occupied Territories, Jordan was by far the most convenient of the states neighboring Israel through which Hamas could move arms
and money. Its huge Palestinian refugee population provided excellent cover
for Hamas operatives, and communications and access to the Occupied Territories were good.

But the crackdown was not a complete surprise. Hamas had picked up
veiled warnings weeks earlier that if its operatives left the country, the local
authorities might make it difficult for them to return. Around the same time,
Mishal had been subjected to a humiliating personal search at Amman's
Queen Alia Airport, which he assumed was a message from Samih Batikhi.
Airport security staff would not have dared touch him without express orders
from the top.

Bizarrely, the offices from which Hamas had operated for almost a decade,
under intense GID scrutiny, now were deemed to have been functioning illegally in Amman. It became impossible to separate fact from fiction as unnamed officials leveled a spray of allegations that, if only half true, might have
led to the unlikely conclusion that Batikhi's intelligence agency had previously been asleep on the job.

The claims included that thousands of pages of "serious and sensitive" information on Jordan and on key individuals in the kingdom had been confiscated from the Hamas offices; Hamas was training operatives in remote areas;
arms and explosives caches had been uncovered in various parts of the country; Jordanian passports were being forged; and Mishal had been recruiting
Islamists from local refugee camps and campuses as fund-raisers and couriers
to move messages into the Occupied Territories.

A week later, the screws were tightened when the same unnamed officials
sent tremors of fear through Jordan with claims that evidence had been uncovered of Hamas militant cells operating in Jordan. These allegedly threatened a repeat of the 1970 bloodshed and mayhem when Yasser Arafat's forces
had challenged King Hussein.[10] "We found ourselves in a situation similar to
Black September," an official told AFP's Randa Habib.

For all that, the only formal indictments against any of those arrested were for membership of an illegal organization and possession of an illegal weapon—a pistol. Behind the regime's bravura, it emerged that it was Batikhi who recommended that Hamas be stamped out. The GID chief's long-standing ill will toward Khalid Mishal was no secret. Batikhi had always had the resources to close down the Hamas political bureau, but in the past he had been blocked by the late King Hussein.

Now Batikhi took advantage of a new king's insecurity. There was little substance to the orchestrated leaks against Hamas in the weeks after the raids, but the GID did perceive Mishal as an Arafat-type figure—not necessarily as the possible instigator of another Black September in Jordan, but as a significant leader in his own right. The GID believed his appeal to the big Palestinian community in Jordan could undermine the standing of a raw king who was himself, a close observer noted, "obsessed with screwing Khalid Mishal."[11]

A version of the allegations against Hamas might have been cobbled together at any time in the previous decade. But in the uncertain early days of King Abdullah, Hamas's strength was greatly magnified in the GID's national security assessments. "Batikhi's rationale was that the kingdom comes first," a regime insider explained.[12] "Abdullah is weak; Mishal is strong—ergo, he has to go." Batikhi raised anxiety levels among senior officials as he posed the longer-term problems. "The day will come when Mishal will be a symbol for the Palestinian people," he warned.[13]

From time to time, the fugitive Nazzal would pop out of hiding. To the great irritation of his GID pursuers, he offered newspaper commentaries—one of which was given page-one treatment in the Hamas-friendly daily *Al-Arab Al-Yawm*. He worked the phones, lobbying his Islamist contacts and journalists on the right of the political bureau to return to Jordan and promoting his belief that the crackdown was driven by Batikhi's fevered hatred of Mishal.

In the ten years that Hamas had been based in Amman—for five of which Mishal was head of the political bureau—these two men had had just a single, icy meeting—after the attempted assassination of Mishal, and only then through the intercession of an Islamist member of the Jordanian parliament.

After the crackdown, Mishal and the others hunkered in Tehran for several weeks deliberating how to respond. Another member of the political bureau, Imad Al-Alami, who was based in Damascus, flew to Tehran for discussions. Mishal traveled to the Syrian capital, where he consulted with members of Hamas's Majlis Shura, the movement's clandestine, supreme decision-making body, and met emissaries from the Jordanian Muslim Brotherhood, who, Mishal and others concluded, were being manipulated by Batikhi. The advice they now received from their Brotherhood associates was an echo of the GID's message: it was best not to come back to Jordan.

On Mishal's return to Tehran from Damascus, he decided to stare down Batikhi, calculating that he would not dare to arrest the top ranks of the movement. He booked return flights to Amman, via Dubai, for the Hamas seven who by then had been stuck in the Iranian capital for almost a month. But Mishal had miscalculated. When the Emirates flight touched down at nine AM on September 22, Queen Alia Airport was ordered into total lockdown.

Abu Marzook, the non-Jordanian, managed to disembark. But in the arrivals lounge he was grabbed and forced to reboard the aircraft on which they had arrived, for the return flight to Dubai.

The others, also seized in the arrivals hall, were forced to hand over their passports to a Jordanian security agent. They were handcuffed and bundled into vehicles for a circuitous drive across the city as their captors attempted to shake off a press posse.

Finally they were hauled before a military tribunal at the Marka military complex. In the tribunal, there was a lot of noise, but little process. Hamas engaged a prominent Amman lawyer, Salih Al-Armuti, and a team of others volunteered their services. Amidst angry denials of any wrongdoing, Ghosheh in particular was incensed at being pinned with a weapons-possession charge. When the military prosecutor shouted at Ghosheh, Hamas's lead lawyer, Al-Armuti, gave him a tongue-lashing: "Lower your voice," he told him. "The person you are speaking to is a *mujahid* [struggler] who is respected by the entire people of Jordan."[14]

In the absence of any progress, they were taken to the cells for the night. After another unproductive court appearance the following morning, the tribunal ordered that all six be detained indefinitely at Juwaydah Prison, on Amman's southern perimeter.

While elements of the local Muslim Brotherhood attempted to broker a truce, the prisoners refused demands by the regime that they renounce Hamas or voluntarily leave the country of which they were citizens. They insisted on being charged in a public court.

Instead, they were kept before the tribunal. The regime pressed a battery of new charges that carried the death penalty: possession of three unlicensed Kalashnikovs, a hand grenade, and a forged Egyptian government seal; applying for mobile phones under false names; raising funds for an illegal organization.

Isolated from other prisoners, the Hamas detainees ran their cellblock as a fundamentalist cell. They observed all their religious obligations, ran a strict exercise regimen, and conducted daily quiz games to improve their minds. After two weeks they went on a hunger strike. It was called off after just five days, but Mishal continued to refuse to negotiate with the authorities while they had him locked up. Fixed in his belief that their arrest and the shutting down of Hamas in Jordan were wildcat acts by Batikhi, Mishal clung to his hope that King Abdullah might be persuaded to respect his late father's long-standing view that it was better to have Hamas inside his tent than outside.

Despite the brinksmanship in Amman, Mishal's half brother Mufid, who monitored developments from his home in Dallas, was confident the king would buckle. "It's just to prove their words," he said in a putdown of the regime during a phone conversation with Shukri Abu Baker, the influential head of the Holy Land Foundation. "Yes, it's just a media gathering and that's it," Abu Baker agreed, "until Albright is done with her tour."[15]

But King Abdullah was serious—he wanted Hamas out of his kingdom. Mishal dug in; Abdullah and Batikhi would have to kick him out of the country of which he was a citizen. As a last resort and only after Mishal and his group had been in jail for two months, regime negotiators returned to the idea that they could remain in the country if they publicly renounced Hamas. "We do not relinquish our principles and we'll never relinquish our movement," Mishal snapped back.[16]

What came next was a variation on the offer—they must leave the country, but, by negotiation, they would be allowed to return every few months. As an added sweetener, if they were to agree, they would be spared the humiliation of wearing handcuffs as they were deported. "No" was Mishal's response.

Mishal's lobbying effort from Tehran had included calls to key figures in Doha, the capital of the emirate of Qatar, where Mishal conducted a significant part of his fund-raising operation. In the end, following a behind-the-scenes intervention by ministers of the Qatari government, a deal was put together whereby charges were dropped and, as Mishal put it, they were all "compulsorily deported."

On November 22, Mishal and Ghosheh were cuffed, blindfolded, and placed in a prison truck without being informed of a destination. After about an hour on the road, Ghosheh suggested, after sniffing the air, that they were among the popular coffee-roasting shops of the Marka quarter.[17] Minutes later, he was proved correct as the truck stopped and they were unloaded. When the blindfolds were removed they found themselves on the tarmac at a military complex near the market—a private jet was waiting.

"We were forced onto that plane," Mishal recalled later.[18] The Qatari foreign minister, Ahmad Abdullah Al-Mahmoud, was on board the aircraft too, but he curtly informed Mishal and Ghosheh that he was not at liberty to discuss their travel plans.

The presence of the Qatari foreign minister demanded by protocol the attendance of his Jordanian counterpart, Abd Al-Ilah Al-Khatib, who moved quickly to shut down loud protests by Mishal. "But you did call the Qatari foreign minister, didn't you?" the Jordanian minister said sarcastically as they waited for the aircraft to takeoff.

Mishal protested that they had never asked to go to Qatar. But he was cut off by the Jordanian minister, who handed them their passports. They were being deported.

Flying out in executive-jet style to the unexpected comfort of a suite at the Sheraton Hotel in Doha, Mishal left the new king of Jordan stranded between two textbook examples of how to deal with the diplomatic cut and thrust in the region. Abdullah's royal father had nurtured alliances with the United States and Israel, but he had also hosted Hamas; now the Qataris were taking in the Jordanian deportees, at the same time that Doha was home to the controversial Al-Jazeera satellite TV network and to thousands of U.S. troops, while maintaining its friendship with Israel.

By denying himself the ability to play the Hamas card any more—either by acting against the movement or, conversely, by refusing to do so at the request of the Israelis or the Americans—Abdullah was perceived to have weakened his own hand in the region's endless diplomatic jousting. Without the presence of Hamas in Jordan—as a foil to the relentless pressure from Israel or the United States—he would be less able to protect his kingdom's vital interests, particularly when it came to the Washington-mediated peace process.[19] Abdullah had cut himself out of the action.

Mishal, Abu Marzook, and the rest of the political bureau had pulled a narrow escape. Nothing might have pleased the Oslo club more than to have seen them all permanently behind bars—but King Abdullah II did not dare to take this final step. Once again, Hamas had lived to fight another day.

For Mishal, there was something deeply offensive in the young king's last offer. In assuming that Mishal would prefer to be spared the humiliation of being frog-marched out of the country, Abdullah appeared to have forgotten the tumult when he was nine years old, when Yasser Arafat had slunk across the border out of Jordan and into Syria in the dead of night, rather than stand with his men to face the late King Hussein's army in the Black September clashes. "I was blindfolded; my hands were tied," Mishal would respond when the circumstances of his deportation from Jordan were compared with those of the PLO leader. "I was kicked out. Arafat ran away."[20]

Israel had paid a huge price for the Mishal debacle in September 1997, but the eviction of Hamas from Jordan two years later was also Mossad's belated revenge. It had taken time to accomplish, but with the death of King Hussein, it had become possible to drive a wedge between the Jordanian regime and the movement. Batikhi was able to make clever use of the Black September scare to fracture support for Hamas in the ranks of the local Muslim Brotherhood. He believed he was saying good-bye to Hamas.

Batikhi's own position in Jordan's circles of power would not last long after seeing off his old Islamist foes. Within a year, the security chief would be fighting for his survival. In December 2000 he was abruptly replaced as head of the GID, and within a year he would be mired in scandal as stories of a $485 million embezzlement gripped the salons of the capital.

Abdullah's decision to ban media reporting on the investigation was taken in some quarters as proof that the move against Batikhi was more an exercise in ritual character assassination than a lesson in business ethics. Local editors were banned from publishing statements by the defendant. The weekly *Al-Majd*, under the feisty editorship of Fahd Al-Rimawi, was ordered to remove reports from its pages before being allowed to publish. *Al-Hadath*, another periodical, was hit with the same order, and found itself in deeper trouble when its editor decided to leave blank the page on which the report was scheduled to appear. Batikhi's humiliation seemed complete when it was decided that pending his release on bail, he was to be held in the GID cellblock of which he once had been the master. Batikhi denied any wrongdoing, but he was sentenced to eight years in jail—which his successor immediately cut to four.

Batikhi had won praise at home and abroad for the smooth implementation of a difficult succession. But in a royal court that ran on cryptic pronouncements, intrigue, and gossip, Batikhi was in an invidious position—he would always be seen as the eyes and ears of the dead king. Some of the Americans who had worked closely with Batikhi did not buy the story of corruption. "Too powerful; too much influence" was the assessment of former Clinton adviser Bruce Riedel. "He looked like he was running the show. He went down because he became too powerful for his own good."

The tail end of the twentieth century was an uncertain time. By the standards of the Middle East, it was a period of peculiar if relative quiet, almost as though ineffectual characters in the Israeli-Palestinian tragedy were being cleared out ahead of the explosive eruption that would soon come to be known as the second, or the Al-Aqsa, Intifada.

In May 1999 Israeli voters saw off Benjamin Netanyahu, bidding farewell to him as a "destroyer of dreams,"[21] a politician who "would walk over his mother to further his ambition"[22] in his relentless sabotage of the peace process.[23] Netanyahu gave way to Ehud Barak, another single-term prime minister, who was Israel's most highly decorated soldier.

As the country's fourth prime minister in just seven years, the fifty-eight-year-old Barak had a plan—he wanted to put the hard-won Wye Memorandum on hold. Instead, he wanted to sue for a separate peace with Syria, in keeping with what was known in diplomatic circles as Israel's Syria First strategy.

Syria was a genuine strategic threat. A treaty with Damascus might curb several of Israel's enemies who were also allies of Damascus, including not just Tehran, but also the so-called Palestinian rejectionist factions, among them Hamas.

Israel had concluded peace treaties with Cairo in 1979 and with Amman in 1994. Barak reasoned that Yasser Arafat's ability to maneuver in future negotiations might be usefully constrained if a treaty between Israel and Damascus was in place.

Barak convinced the Clinton White House to back a series of high-level meetings. Syria's President Assad had long made clear that he would be no pushover, famously conveying a message to Bill Clinton that he was not like Egypt's Anwar Sadat, who was assassinated by his own people after agreeing to peace with Israel, nor like King Hussein, who had traded one bit of land for another, nor like Arafat, who had concluded the hollow Oslo deal.

Syria very precisely wanted the return of all the land it had lost in the 1967 war.[24] Clinton put considerable political capital into bringing the parties together, but by the time Barak arrived in Washington in December 1999, he had been cowed by opposition at home to any surrender of the Golan Heights or to giving Damascus access to the Sea of Galilee. "I can't do it," Barak told Martin Indyk, who by then was assistant U.S. secretary of state.[25]

As the negotiations progressed haltingly, the Americans concluded that Barak was the obstacle, allowing his negotiators no leeway and ultimately scuttling the talks. The Syrian foreign minister Farouk Shara told Barak, at a tense dinner hosted by Clinton, "You simply got cold feet."[26]

The same charge could not be leveled at Barak several months later when he began withdrawing Israeli troops who had been stationed in Lebanon for almost twenty years—thus fulfilling one of his election promises.

The pullout was scheduled for July, but in late May crowds of Hezbollah activists and Lebanese civilians began to march on Israeli positions.[27] Barak hastily decided to collapse the weeks-long withdrawal schedule into just twenty-four hours,[28] and the ensuing chaos was a public relations triumph for the Shiite Hezbollah militia led by Hassan Nasrallah. His fighters commandeered abandoned Israeli tanks—in one case the motor was still running and rice was cooking on a small stove—while Lebanon celebrated and Israeli commentators likened the humiliation to the American withdrawal from Saigon twenty-five years earlier.

Within weeks, Barak was ready to execute another plan, this time on the Palestinian front. Instead of allowing further parcels of the Occupied Territories to pass to Arafat as required in the Wye deal, the prime minister wanted to use the prospect of Israel's relinquishment of land as a lever in negotiations with Arafat on the substantive issues: borders and settlements, Jerusalem, and the refugees' right of return.

The play-off on these so-called final-status issues ended in deadlock and what would become years of recrimination over who had been the spoiler at an extraordinary fifteen-day summit in the summer of 2000, hosted by Bill Clinton at the Camp David presidential retreat.

As a sound bite for the evening news, the proposals Barak appeared to put on the table ought to have sealed the deal for Arafat.

Palestinians would have won back all but 9 percent of the West Bank and a parcel of Israeli land adjacent to Gaza to compensate for the 9 percent retained by Israel; they would have "permanent custodianship" of Al-Haram Al-Sharif, which was surpassed only by Mecca and Medina in its sacredness to Muslims; they would enjoy sovereign control of the Muslim and Christian quarters of the Old City and much of the Arab neighborhoods of East Jerusalem; an international presence on the border between Israel and Palestine would be established; and a "satisfactory solution" would be discussed on the refugee questions.

There were as many versions of precisely what happened in those fraught days at Camp David as there were participants.

Clinton's Middle East envoy, Dennis Ross, was convinced that a historic agreement could have been concluded had Arafat not crumbled at the end. "Unfortunately for the Palestinians they were led by Yasser Arafat, a revolutionary leader who could not transform himself and become a statesman,"

Ross observed later. "Conflict had defined him ... he could not end the conflict."[29]

Clinton's adviser on Arab-Israeli affairs, Robert Malley, held both Arafat and Barak to account for the failure. He argued that Arafat had been singled out as a convenient culprit in what he described as a torrent of shallow analysis of a summit that became "a tragedy of errors."[30]

As Malley acknowledged, the Israeli prime minister had broken every taboo, particularly on the issue of Palestinian control of any part of Jerusalem and on the notion of a land swap. No Israeli leader before him had promised so much.

But Malley also judged that in reality there was never a true Israeli offer at Camp David. Barak's team had always stopped short of actually making a formal proposal; nothing had been in writing; Barak had avoided any substantive meeting with Arafat during the fifteen days. There was talk of a land swap—but the actual land to be swapped was not identified; there was no detail on what the "satisfactory solution" of the refugee question might entail.

The Palestinians, as they viewed their circumstances, already had conceded 78 percent of historic Palestine under the Oslo Accords, which had proved to be more about terms of surrender than about terms of peace. Arafat was afraid to be caught again. Far from being a final deal, whatever was to be agreed to at Camp David was to be the basis for further negotiations. It would also have required a shift away from the Palestinians' greatest diplomatic insurance— the protection they had in crucial United Nations resolutions on borders and the return of refugees. They wondered why they would trust Barak when he had refused to honor previous commitments.

The reasons for failure at Camp David appeared to be more personal and tactical than they were substantive. In a nutshell, neither side trusted the other and even Clinton's legendary persuasive skills could not shake Arafat's fears that a deal might imperil his position at home, even as it might burnish his reputation abroad.

"Mutual ... suspicion meant that Barak would conceal his final proposals, the 'endgame,' until Arafat had moved ... and Arafat would not move until he could see the endgame," Malley observed. For Barak every step had been a test of wills; for Arafat, a potential trap. Arafat had fought for years to have a relationship with Washington, but when it came to the crunch he did not understand how to use it to his advantage.

Malley teased out the ephemeral nature of the Israeli-Palestinian encounter at Camp David and just what was on the table. "Ask Barak, and he might volunteer that there was no Israeli offer and, besides, Arafat rejected it. Ask Arafat, and the response you might hear is that there was no offer; besides, it was unacceptable; that said, it had better remain on the table."[31]

On their respective homecomings from Camp David, Arafat and Barak received very different welcomes. The Palestinian leader was hailed as a hero who had stared down the United States and Israel. But, in the eyes of many Israelis, Barak had failed; worse, based on leaks from the talks, he was deemed to have been far too generous, while Arafat had simply thumbed his nose.

Washington was left with nowhere to turn. Clinton was just months away from leaving the White House after two terms as president. He had expended much energy on years of talks seeking a truce between Israel and the Palestinians—looking for the victory of stability in the region and, of course, his own foreign policy legacy.

A furious Clinton vented his anger at Arafat. Alluding to an already agreed redeployment of Israeli troops and a handover of three villages on which Barak had stalled, Clinton sided with the Israeli leader. "You were ready to cut your legs off for this guy. . . . If I were you I wouldn't have done the re-deployment [either]."[32]

As the delegates packed up to leave the president's Maryland retreat, they could not have fully appreciated the desperate milestone that this failed summit would represent in the history of the conflict. With the exception of a last spluttering effort by Clinton in his final days in office in December 2000 to make something of the shards left on the table at Camp David, these would be the last formal negotiations between the Palestinian and Israeli leadership for years to come.

The spark that lit the second Intifada was a calculatedly provocative visit by the Israeli opposition figure and leader of the right-wing Likud Party, Ariel Sharon, to the Old City in Jerusalem just weeks after Camp David. It was September 28, 2000. Flanked by hundreds of security men and with a media circus in attendance, Sharon insisted on his right as a Jew to go to what Muslims called Al-Haram Al-Sharif, the compound enclosing Al-Aqsa Mosque. This was Islam's third holiest site, but the Jews knew it as Temple Mount, because it sat atop the ancient ruins of their own most sacred site, the Second Temple. Since Israel's seizure of East Jerusalem in 1967, the Haram had been left in the semi-autonomous control of Jerusalem's Muslim religious authorities.[33]

Sharon was hated by Palestinians. In the 1980s, he was dubbed the "Butcher of Beirut" after his attempt to wipe out Yasser Arafat and the PLO in Lebanon. He had been held responsible by an Israeli commission of inquiry for the massacre by Lebanese militias aligned with Israel of up to three thousand Palestinians in the Sabra and Shatila refugee camps on the outskirts of the Lebanese capital. And as the godfather of the Israeli settler movement, Sharon had declared memorably in 1998, "Everybody has to move, run and grab as many hilltops as they can to enlarge the settlements because everything we take now will stay ours."[34] Seared in the minds of most Palestinians was Sharon's answer to the "question of the million" that senior Israelis had posed in the days after the 1967 annexation of the West Bank. Implied in the question was how Israel might dispose of the inhabitants of the West Bank, while at the same time keeping the land for itself. "Jordan is Palestine," Sharon had often declared, implying that the Palestinians of the West Bank should be driven into Jordan.

Sharon's abrasiveness and his visit to Al-Haram Al-Sharif certainly were the spark. But some reasoned that the cause of what quickly became an incendiary explosion of Palestinian anger in response to his provocation must have been something much more profound.

In searching for an explanation, the director of the Ramallah-based Palestinian American Research Center, Mouin Rabbani, drew attention to the little-noticed seventh anniversary of the signing of the Oslo Declaration of Principles, which had occurred two weeks before Sharon's foray up the mountain.

Rabbani compared the Oslo Accords with all that came after it—Oslo II in September 1995; the Hebron Protocol in January 1997; the Wye Memorandum in October 1998; and the Sharm Al-Sheikh Agreement of September 1999. Overlaying these five documents, he distilled a consistent theme, which he concluded was the root cause for the bitter disappointment of Palestinians. "[There's] a clear pattern," he said. "Israel first refuses to implement its own commitments; seeks and obtains their dilution in a new agreement; subsequently engages in systematic prevarication; and finally, demands additional negotiations, leading to yet a further diluted agreement."[35]

By Rabbani's reckoning, seven years on from Oslo, Israel still had effective control of 60–70 percent of the West Bank and more than 20 percent of postage-stamp Gaza. In the areas under nominal Palestinian control, the Israeli military and settlers still did as they pleased. In recognizing the state of Israel in the first Oslo document, Palestinians had signed away 78 percent of historic Palestine, but Israel still wanted to "compromise the compromise," he said.

The never-ending talks between Israelis and Palestinians, including the debacle at Camp David, were understood to be a "peace process," but, since they had begun in 1993, there had been an explosion of Jewish "settler colonization" in the Occupied Territories, land that supposedly was to be relinquished by Israel. Roads connecting the settlements bypassed Palestinian communities, and military control over Palestinian movement had reduced the territories to noncontiguous enclaves. The provocative Jewish settler population had increased by 77 percent.

Despite Barak's claims that he ran a "peace cabinet," the approval rate for Israeli settler housing on Palestinian land in his first year in office had been 65 percent higher that in the first year of the hard-line Netanyahu. If there was any doubt, Barak's celebrated Camp David proposals were conclusive proof that the "apartheid-Bantustan" scenario of separation, which was envisaged by the critics of Oslo, had arrived. "By September 28, 2000, life [for Palestinians] under Oslo had become an intolerable proposition," Rabbani concluded.[36]

On that day, the fuse began to smolder as Sharon concluded his controversial walk on Al-Haram Al-Sharif. In the first twenty-four hours, the reaction was limited to wild protests in the vicinity of the mosque and the wounding of a small number of protesters and police. It was on the second day that the powder keg exploded. Stones were thrown from the forecourt of the Al-Aqsa Mosque at Jews worshipping below, at the Western Wall. Shots were fired, killing seven Palestinians, creating the first martyrs of the new Intifada. Protests spread like wildfire across the Occupied Territories.

Ariel Sharon had ascended Temple Mount as an opposition leader who wanted to stand above Prime Minister Ehud Barak and who needed to set himself apart from the indefatigable Benjamin Netanyahu, who, at the time, was mounting a strong challenge to Sharon's leadership of the Likud Party. Sharon descended from Al-Haram Al-Sharif ordained as prime minister designate. He was destined to lead the Israelis in a long and brutal new chapter in the war of attrition with their Palestinian neighbors.

More than thirty Palestinians were killed in the first three days of the new Intifada; an estimated five hundred were wounded. In just over a month, more than one hundred and sixty Palestinians were dead—a third of them under the age of seventeen. In the same period twelve Israelis died.[37]

The Palestinians had thrown stones and insults during the first Intifada, but now they were shooting back. Israel retaliated with its full arsenal—jet fighters, attack helicopters, and tanks—against an enemy that was lightly armed or unarmed. The Palestinians hit back with waves of horrific but crudely effective suicide bombs. Israel upped the ante with a campaign of targeted assassinations of Palestinian leaders.

Arafat's leadership fell apart. Caught between demands by the international community to retrieve a peace process in which his people had lost all faith, and a merciless, disproportionate military response by the Israelis, the PLO leader was reduced to equivocation and prevarication. Cornered, he would condemn the violence, but few listened to him. When the hardcore Al-Aqsa Martyrs Brigade emerged as a new fighting force from among the younger ranks of Arafat's own Fatah movement, he inevitably was accused of speaking with a forked tongue.

In the period before he lost office, Ehud Barak certainly had given Palestinians food for thought on the avenues that might best move the crisis in their favor. Ironically, though, it was what he did in Lebanon in the weeks preceding Camp David that prompted many Palestinians to rethink their strategy in terms of war or peace.

In ending Israel's eighteen-year occupation of southern Lebanon, Barak had handed to Hezbollah—the Hamas equivalent in Lebanon—a victory that was celebrated across the Islamic world. Seven years of talks with Israel had won back for Palestinians a sliver of their land, but little control of it and nothing approximating a peace dividend. Hezbollah, on the other hand, had bombed the IDF out of Lebanon. In revealing himself as a leader who could be moved by Arab force, Prime Minister Barak's underlying message would resonate in the privations of the Gaza Strip and the West Bank. Mohammad Dahlan, the head of Arafat's Preventive Security Service, offered a succinct interpretation for Palestinians: "violence wins."[38]

From the day Sharon was confirmed as prime minister in February 2001, he turned the conflict into a highly personal bid to settle old scores with Arafat, who had survived Sharon's onslaught in Lebanon in 1982. It quickly emerged that Sharon's grand design was to obliterate Arafat's Palestinian Authority, its leadership, its operating systems, and its symbols. Declaring Oslo to have been "the biggest catastrophe that ever happened to Israel,"[39] Sharon set out to bury all manifestations of the accords beneath the rubble of unremitting war.

At the same time, the tension between the biggest Palestinian factions continued to damage their supposedly common cause. Relations between Fatah and Hamas faltered from crisis to crisis. Each was capable of helping the other at various times, but the mainstays of the relationship were antagonism, distrust, and a good measure of contempt. Like a bickering couple who could not divorce, Hamas and Fatah would accept cohabitation only if one could dominate the other. The gulf between them—on policy, tactics, and religion—was wide and complex. The few bridges that existed were personal, not organizational. Both Palestinian camps—Islamist and secular—had emerged from the first Intifada with bloodied knuckles and long memories.

Ten days after Sharon's encroachment on Al-Haram Al-Sharif in old Jerusalem, Yasser Arafat presided over a rare display of Palestinian factional unanimity. Present at this meeting, at Arafat's presidential compound in Gaza City, was Ismail Abu Shanab, a senior figure in Hamas. This was the first time that the movement had been represented at such a session of Palestinian leaders.

Clearly, the three-hour gathering suggested a rapprochement between Arafat and Hamas. In Israel it was interpreted as the PLO leader turning a blind eye to the Islamists' hardcore violence against Israel. As the meeting broke up, Abu Shanab emerged and stressed the importance of unity. "All factions were there," he told reporters.[40] Then he explained that he had discussed "stepping up the uprising" with Arafat. "We discussed ways of developing this Intifada and ways to confront the challenges being thrown down by the Israelis."[41]

Abu Shanab also provided an insight into how the Intifada might unfold. As he explained, Hamas wished to emulate the tactics of Hezbollah. "Those who are negotiating will continue to do so, and those who use the armed struggle will continue to do so, because the two are complementary," he said.[42]

That too was Arafat's strategic thinking as Israelis and Palestinians dug in during the first weeks of the second Intifada. It was not as though the PLO leader had options. Having donned the Oslo straitjacket, he could not utter an outright "no" to the Israelis or to Washington; at the same time, he could not keep saying "no" to all or any of the Palestinian factions, including the Islamists.

Seven years had passed since Arafat had signed on for Oslo. And since Sheikh Ahmad Yassin's 1997 return to Gaza, there had been three years of muttered insults and mutual suspicion between the Hamas spiritual leader and Arafat. Israeli analysts were in a bind as they attempted to read the complexities of the Palestinian leadership double act—were Arafat and Yassin irreconcilable adversaries or was this a clever good-cop/bad-cop routine? Some in the Israeli intelligence services concluded it was a devilish mixture of the two.[43]

One of the clearest signals was the dramatic release of Hamas operatives and other fighters from Palestinian prisons in the early days of the renewed

violence of the Al-Aqsa Intifada. First a dozen here, then a dozen there; finally, hundreds were back on the streets, prompting anxiety in Israel of a repeat of the mid-1990s wave of suicide bombings. Some of the explanations
for the mass releases were plausible enough—some prisoners had simply broken free when their Palestinian guards had fled in the face of Israeli attacks
on the Palestinian Authority security compounds; others had been set free
because Arafat's men did not believe they could protect the prisoners from
harm by Israelis.

There was another explanation, however.

The go-between was Khalid Mishal's old university professor, Asad Abdul
Rahman, who by 2000 was a senior figure in the PLO. Through a series of
phone calls with Abdul Rahman, Mishal put his pitch to Arafat for the release of 240 of Hamas's best fighters from Arafat's grimy prisons.

Speaking to the PLO leader through Abdul Rahman, Mishal said,
"We [Hamas] are champions of resistance—if we are to be brothers, fighting under the same banner as Fatah, these men must be freed to join the
fight."[44]

Mishal suggested that Arafat would be seen as a traitor to the Palestinian
cause if he refused. He did not refuse, but the old man could not resist this
opportunity to show Mishal who was the boss. The prisoners were dribbled
from detention—a few here and a few there—until just one remained behind
bars. Mishal was back on the phone to Abdul Rahman: "Can you try to get
him out?

"Arafat says he has to keep him—to protect him from the Israelis," Abdul
Rahman responded.

"Is that Arafat's way of saying 'no'?" Mishal inquired.

"It's an Arafat 'yes' and 'no,'" Abdul Rahman told him. The PLO leader
was showing Mishal just who was Mr. Palestine. Arafat believed he could
arrive at an accommodation with Hamas, but personally and psychologically,
full cooperation was beyond him. He might release prisoners but he would
never share weapons, funds, or intelligence. Most of all, he would never share
the leadership limelight.

Still smarting at his eviction from Amman, Mishal was trying to make Doha
work as a base. The Qatari regime allowed him to come and go as he pleased,
which kept him in close contact with Abu Marzook and Imad Al-Alami,
who had moved to Damascus. The Syrian capital, in turn, was easily accessible to other key members of the movement and the contact points for Hamas's
covert conduits to Yassin and others in the "inside" leadership.

But the onset of the second Intifada made it imperative that Mishal relocate closer to the action in the Occupied Territories. Qatar, far away in the Gulf States, would always be a temporary bolt-hole. Hamas needed to operate from one of what sometimes were called the "frontline states"—Egypt, Jordan, Syria, or Lebanon. But the options were limited; King Abdullah had made it clear there would be no going back to Amman; Cairo's suppression of the Muslim Brotherhood ruled out Egypt; and Beirut was deemed not to be an option because Lebanon was too accessible to the Israelis.

Logic dictated that Damascus, with its Palestinian refugee population of about half a million, was Mishal's best choice. Already it was home to almost a dozen Palestinian factions, spanning the whole spectrum of Palestinian politics—from Muslim fundamentalism to Marxism. Collectively, they were known as the "rejectionists" because of their opposition to the Oslo peace process, and they included the Palestinian Islamic Jihad, the Popular Front for the Liberation of Palestine, and the Democratic Front for the Liberation of Palestine. Washington was convinced that Damascus hosted training bases for all of these groups in the Syrian-controlled Beka'a Valley in neighboring Lebanon.

Yet Mishal still had cause to hesitate. There were several reasons why he had not automatically headed to Damascus when Hamas was evicted from Jordan toward the end of 1999. If Israeli prime minister Ehud Barak had succeeded in his efforts to negotiate the treaty he sought at that time with Damascus, the Syrians would have come under immediate pressure to give up some or all of the hard-line Palestinian factions operating inside Syria's borders.

And Mishal was alive to the implication of reports that Damascus had buckled less than a year before to threats of military action from neighboring Turkey when Syria had provided sanctuary to the Kurdish guerrilla leader Abdullah Ocalan. Forced to flee, Ocalan had been arrested in Kenya three months later.

Also, Hamas needed to overcome a historical anxiety before it could move north of Amman. The movement could never forget, and would find very hard to forgive the Syrian authorities for, the massacre of more than ten thousand Muslim Brotherhood sympathizers and activists when their uprising in the Syrian city of Hama was brutally suppressed in 1982.

Ultimately, though, Hamas had nowhere else to turn, especially after a bizarre postscript to their deportation by King Abdullah sparked fresh tensions and considerable diplomatic discomfort for Qatar in June 2001.

On June 14, an old man arrived unexpectedly at Amman's Queen Alia Airport on a flight from Doha. Ibrahim Ghosheh had served for years as the

Hamas media spokesman in Jordan, but he was now sixty-seven years old and had been stuck in Doha for two years. He wanted to go home.

Ghosheh was arrested as soon as he got off the plane. He might have been old, but he was still a stubborn Hamas operative and he refused the Jordanian demand that he "resign" from Hamas before being allowed into the country.

Jordan seized the Qatar Airways Airbus-320 Ghosheh had arrived on, refusing to allow its crew to leave unless they took him away with them. The crew had strict orders from Doha not to do so. All flights between the two countries were then canceled.

During the fraught negotiations that followed, the region was treated to an extraordinary standoff. Ghosheh was detained at the airport terminal for two weeks—with a mobile phone hidden under his blankets and a doctor on standby to monitor his diabetes and high blood pressure.

The governments of Yemen and Libya offered to help, but to no avail. Insisting that Ghosheh must first leave Amman before he could be granted formal approval to return, Jordanian agents finally ordered him to board a scheduled Royal Jordanian flight surrounded by a GID security posse that included the deputy director of the GID. Ghosheh thought he was going to Yemen. But, once on board, the pilot announced they were bound for Thailand.

Within minutes of landing at Bangkok's Don Mueang International Airport, Ghosheh and his guards checked into a transit hotel to haggle over the wording of a statement. But events took a turn for the worse when Thai authorities discovered that the Jordanians had brought a "known terrorist," Ghosheh, into their midst. They were forced to flee on the next available flight—this time, to Kuala Lumpur.

Ghosheh finally agreed to "freeze" his activities for the movement. It was a semantic point, but he would not be labeled a quitter. The party returned to Jordan the following day, where Ghosheh resettled himself in Amman and quickly disappeared from public view.

Khalid Mishal was on the move too. He finally packed up his bags in Qatar and headed to Damascus, where the Hamas political bureau was reassembled in a city where the ground rules were even tighter than they had been in Jordan. In the Syrian capital they were banned from all public activities, and it would be five years before the local authorities gave permission for an event as harmless as Khalid Mishal's first press conference in Damascus.[45]

19

Dead Men Walking

In Damascus, it was late afternoon when Khalid Mishal clicked on the television in the discreet suburban property that was provided by the Syrian regime as an office and home for its newest official guest. It was a short pause in a busy day to catch up on the news.

"I was watching Al-Jazeera. Suddenly there was news of an aircraft hitting one of the towers," he later recalled. "And then there was another one."[1]

It was September 11, 2001, and Mishal was speechless.

The Doha-based Arab satellite news channel had just flashed its first reports of Al-Qaeda's attack on America, where hijacked aircraft filled with passengers were flown at full throttle into the iconic towers of the World Trade Center in New York and into the Pentagon defense complex in Washington. Mishal struggled to take it in. "It was like watching a movie. It was unbelievable," he said later. "It wasn't just one strike—it was a succession of them."

Mishal always objected to his own activities being categorized as terrorism, and as the carnage in Manhattan and Washington unfolded, he had difficulty grappling with the enormity of the project of the master terrorist Osama Bin Laden. "It was incomprehensible that this was happening to the most powerful nation in the world," he said. "At first I was overwhelmed by it all. I just followed the news."

Fairly quickly, however, the likely dire consequences for Hamas began to register. September 11 would overshadow the world's view of the second Intifada, much as Saddam Hussein's invasion of Kuwait in 1990 had dramatically altered perceptions of the first Intifada. If the end of the Cold War had dulled the attraction of freedom fighting in various corners of the globe, 9/11 would reduce adherents like Mishal and his movement to an endangered species.

More important, their opponents—in Mishal's case, Israeli prime minister Ariel Sharon—would move quickly to adapt Washington's reaction to Al-Qaeda to their own purpose. America's new antiterrorism rhetoric would be co-opted to justify increasing Israel's military force in a very different conflict. Quite suddenly, Mishal's struggle against the occupation of Palestine was to become a focus for George W. Bush's so-called war on terror.

On the ground in the Middle East, the mood was angry. As the Intifada entered its second year, neither side could beat the other. More than eight hundred Palestinians had died since the end of September 2000.[2] In the same period, more than one hundred and seventy Israelis had been killed. Thousands had been injured on both sides. The Palestinian economy had shrunk dramatically, with three hundred thousand Palestinian jobs evaporating, and Israel's tourism industry was shot.

In the weeks after the attacks on New York and Washington, all Palestinian factions lay low, in what appeared to be a collective decision to avoid being lumped in with Bin Laden's global operation. The tension was unbearable. It snapped toward the end of November, when Israeli security chiefs authorized an airborne missile strike to assassinate Mahmoud Abu Hanoud, an elusive Hamas military figure on the West Bank.

The movement promised vengeance. Ignoring one of Yasser Arafat's many cease-fire calls, it delivered in the first weekend of December. Two suicide attacks—one in Jerusalem, the other in the northern port city of Haifa— killed twenty-six Israelis and wounded more than two hundred others. The Jerusalem attack was particularly brutal—first, the simultaneous detonation of two powerful suicide bombs. Then, after a twenty-minute pause, during which paramedics and security teams arrived at the scene, a third device—an unmanned car-bomb—exploded.

Khalid Mishal was not in the habit of recklessly poking his head above the parapet. So the interview he gave to the Moroccan newspaper *Attajdid* on the day of the Haifa bombing had to be seen as calculated and incendiary. Bragging and baiting at the same time, Mishal put both Sharon and Arafat on notice as he proudly chalked up most of the Israeli dead in the Intifada as victims of Hamas. "More than three-quarters of Zionists killed have [died] by the hand of Hamas," he declared. Insisting that well over half of the activists and protesters who kept the uprising roiling were from his movement, Mishal seemed intent on elbowing all other factions away from the front line.[3]

Though Hamas had loudly identified itself as the author of the latest bombings, Sharon's forces went after Arafat, blowing up the PLO leader's helipad and two of his helicopters. "We want to ground him and humiliate him" was how a senior Israeli official explained the choice of targets.[4]

It was George W. Bush who struck at Hamas. Lifting his gaze from Al-Qaeda for the first time since September 11, the U.S. president met hurriedly with Ariel Sharon in Washington on the day of the Haifa bombing. Sharon came with a special request. He wanted Bush to shut down a vital Hamas cash cow, the Holy Land Foundation (HLF). In the previous year, the HLF had raised $13 million in the name of Islamic charity.[5]

Bush wasted no time. The White House press corps was summoned to the Rose Garden just before eleven AM the next day. "Those who do business with terror will do no business in the United States," Bush declared, as he reduced the Hamas welfare network, on which thousands of Palestinian families depended, to a menacing sound bite.

"Money raised by the Holy Land Foundation is used by Hamas to support schools and [to] indoctrinate children to grow up to be suicide bombers," he said.[6]

And the fund-raising was happening on American soil. The HLF was entrenched in the Muslim communities on which the federal authorities mounted their raids—in unlikely settings like the suburbs of Dallas; in Bridgeview on the south side of Chicago; in Patterson, New Jersey; and in San Diego. Despite denials and protests by executives of the multimillion-dollar fund-raiser, HLF's records and documents were seized as federal agents raided its offices in the four states. Holy Land Foundation assets were frozen, along with those of a bank and an investment company that the Bush administration claimed were financial arms of Hamas.

Months earlier the HLF had retained a private countersurveillance company to sweep its Dallas headquarters and had been advised that the premises had been "under technical surveillance by unknown entities for an undetermined period of time."[7] These federal raids were a dramatic revelation of just who the "unknown entities" listening in were. Included in the trove of information hauled out of the HLF offices were such intelligence gems as a secret account of a Hamas council of war that had taken place at an undisclosed venue in the Middle East in January 2001, three months into the Intifada and eight months before September 11.

The report provided a rare glimpse inside the supreme decision-making authority in Hamas, the clandestine Majlis Shura. About eighty of the movement's most senior and mostly unknown figures, including an unnamed handful from the Occupied Territories, were present. There was just a single agenda item: survival. The discussion ranged over strategies to be devised to keep the Intifada burning, and also to inoculate Hamas against the rising Israeli onslaught and Yasser Arafat's erratic attempts to break the movement. Hamas was digging in for a long conflict.

Orders were prepared in painstaking detail for all Hamas branches in the Occupied Territories to set up local planning committees to resist any move to shut down the Intifada. This report,[8] dated January 2001, revealed instructions for the preparation of rapid responses that would insulate the movement against the arrest of its leaders or the closure of its mosques and institutions. Alluding to military operations, the meeting ominously judged the Intifada to be "a very suitable atmosphere, God willing, for us to rebuild our work, selecting those who are suitable for it and preparing them in the proper manner in light of these hot, daily confrontations with the enemy."

The report warned branches that the political bureau could not be linked publicly to Hamas's military activity. But at the same time, it ordered the appointment of military contacts who were to be provided with "proper direction and logistical support" from the outside. Promising a better-organized delivery of funds from abroad, the report made a cryptic reference to a system of Hamas couriers operating between the Occupied Territories and the outside, for use by branch activists who were unable to maintain contact by facsimile or e-mail. In the event of emergencies, they were given a coded introduction and a phone number to call—in Switzerland.[9]

For Mishal and for Hamas, the HLF bust was a catastrophe, cutting it off from generous community support networks and from lifeblood funding, the vast bulk of which was spent on community welfare in the economically shattered Occupied Territories. The "dire consequences" that Mishal had envisaged after September 11 had arrived.

Confronted with attacks such as this abroad, Hamas became obsessive about putting defensive structures in place in the Occupied Territories.

The tasks of the Hamas outside leadership were fund-raising, diplomacy, and military planning. It was essential that all three be stepped up if the movement's vast inside operation was to be sustained. Driving it all was Mishal—his reelection as chief of the political bureau was confirmed by the secret account of the January council of war.

. . .

On his return home to Israel from his successful trip to Washington, Ariel Sharon declared his own "war on terror" as he turned his attention back to an old foe. "This will not be an easy war," he said, paraphrasing the Bush declaration in the aftermath of September 11. "This war will not be a short war. But we shall win."

During this televised address, the Israeli prime minister revealed the extent to which his personal rivalry with Yasser Arafat infused his sense of the conflict. "Arafat will not succeed in deceiving the government I head," he declared.[10] Twenty years earlier Arafat had stood across the street from a block of apartments in Beirut, which he had vacated minutes earlier, watching as Israeli fighter pilots pulverized the building in a bid to take him out.[11] The pilots were acting on orders from Sharon, who at the time was Israel's defense minister. Now it was 2001 and it seemed Sharon believed he had unfinished business to attend to.

Some of Sharon's ministers and security chiefs were already making noisy demands for Arafat to be deported, even eliminated. There was a rising chorus of support for an old idea of attempting to make the West Bank disappear behind a huge wall, similar to the barricade that divided the city of Berlin into east and west in the early 1960s.

Arafat was in a hopeless position. In the forty-eight hours after the Hamas bombings in Jerusalem and Haifa in December 2001, he rounded up more than two hundred Islamists. His security services detained a prominent activist, and they shoved Yassin back under house arrest as Arafat wrestled with Washington's demands that he destroy the Islamist militias.

There had been a time when, in the tradition of the strongest Arab autocrats, Arafat might have imposed his will. Even though he had worked so hard for the funding and status that Oslo was intended to deliver to him, his position as *the* leader of the Palestinians had become so precarious that now he had to frame his cease-fire proposals according to the dictates of the other factions. The vast majority of his people still were behind the Intifada, staunchly supporting attacks on settlers and the Israeli military in the Occupied Territories. They flatly rejected his claim that suicide missions were terrorism.[12]

If the conflict was viewed as a balance of power, the Palestinians were hopelessly outgunned by Israel's sophisticated, high-tech arsenal. Hamas, however, conjured up a more even playing field when they portrayed the contest as a balance of fear.

Ismail Abu Shanab, fifty-three years old and the father of eleven children, was a founding member of Hamas. An engineering graduate from Colorado, he explained this other prism as the measure of success for Hamas. "Look," he said. "They are afraid when we destroy an Israeli tank. That's evidence of success. When we kill an Israeli soldier, it's a major success. When we cross Israeli defenses and borders, it's a major success. And when we can hurt them inside Israel, then that is indeed a great success."[13] Abu Shanab conceded that suicide was a primitive weapon. "But," he insisted, "it's all we have and it's less harmful than F-16s loaded with tons of explosives."

Arafat was trapped in a void between two seemingly contradictory expressions of popular sentiment. A poll at the end of 2001 found that a strong majority of Palestinians supported a cease-fire and a return to negotiations. But the same poll found that nine in ten Palestinians were of the view that no cease-fire would hold and, in that eventuality, they would support armed attacks on Israeli soldiers and settlers in the Occupied Territories.[14]

As a leader who was out of step with Palestinian public opinion, Arafat was required to do the splits—between a world pleading that he keep faith with the fractured Oslo Accords and his own people's overwhelming loss of faith in that process, which, by the measure of their existences, was bankrupt. The weaker Arafat was made to look in the eyes of his people and of the world, the more Hamas pulled ahead.

The crisis had become a poisonous stalemate. As Israel's peace partner, Arafat would get nothing until he had destroyed Hamas. But Arafat could not destroy Hamas without destroying himself, because by now the Islamist movements represented a significant body of Palestinian opinion no longer believing in the deal that nominally, at least, made Arafat and Israel peace partners in the first place.

Now attempts at foreign intervention were either badly timed or badly thought out. When Washington—under outgoing president Bill Clinton—had dispatched CIA chief George Tenet as the Intifada first gathered steam late in 2000, oxygen was sucked from his visit by ghoulish images from Ramallah, where an Italian television crew chanced upon a Palestinian mob lynching two Israeli soldiers who had lost their way. When former U.S. senator George Mitchell had called for an end to violence and a freeze on Israeli settlements in a report prepared in May 2001, he was howled down by Sharon, who had declared all settlement activity to be a "vital national enterprise."[15]

September 11 froze all attempts at peacemaking. Clinton, who had made the Middle East peace effort one of his signature foreign policy ventures, was gone. In his place was the insular George W. Bush, who made it clear that clamping down on terror was his mission—not bolstering the Middle East mission of his predecessor.

In the aftershock of the Jerusalem and Haifa bombings in 2001, Arafat did insist on a "complete halt to all operations, especially suicidal operations."[16] In response, Hamas and the other factions held their fire; the Israelis chose not to do so.

Arafat's shaky cease-fire had entered its third week when one of the Israeli intelligence services received information on the whereabouts of Raed Karmi, a Fatah activist they believed had killed twelve Israelis. Hearing that Karmi regularly passed through the cemetery at Tulkarm, in the West Bank, Israeli agents planted a bomb at head height in a wall by a path that the suspect used. It was detonated when Karmi next passed by; he died in an instant, and so did the cease-fire.[17]

Within weeks, Amnesty International enraged Sharon with the release of a report charging Israel with multiple breaches of the United Nations Convention against Torture. The human rights group accused Israeli forces of consistent cruel, inhuman, or degrading treatment, and sometimes torture, of thousands of Palestinians.[18]

In the first few months of 2002, more than five hundred buildings, in which more than two thousand families lived, were "wantonly" destroyed without any absolute military necessity, according to the Amnesty report. Whole villages and towns were closed, denying freedom of movement to entire communities—even those who needed medical attention. On top of these closures, curfews forced thousands to remain in their homes for weeks at a time.[19]

The violence was merciless. March was dubbed "Black March." Almost 240 Palestinians died as the IDF mounted back-to-back incursions into Palestinian communities; more than 130 Israelis were killed in a rapid-fire sequence of seventeen suicide missions, which, by the end of the month, rocked Israel at a rate of almost one a day. By the end of March the total Palestinian death toll had overtaken that of the first Intifada: 1,442 dead in just a quarter of the time—and the Israeli toll had reached 400 dead.

Dressed to look female and foreign, Death wore sunglasses and carried a handbag when it arrived, almost by accident, at Netanya's Park Hotel. On the afternoon of March 27, 2002, Mohammad Odeh strapped on a belt that contained twenty pounds of explosives, which he then covered up with his female disguise. Accompanied by Fathi Khatib, a driver attached to Hamas,

Odeh then set out on a random search for a target, anywhere up and down Israel's coastal strip.[20]

Meticulous planning had gone into the operation. The bomb had been prepared; passes were acquired to get past Israeli checkpoints; the disguise had to be subtle enough not to draw attention. Yet, as the two men drove away from Tulkarm, where Odeh lived at the northern end of the West Bank, all the attention to detail was left behind. After so much effort, the selection of a target had been left purely to chance.

Ideally, they hoped to find a gathering of Israeli military personnel. First, they drove south to Herzliya; then further south along the Mediterranean to Tel Aviv. Frustrated, they turned around, heading north again. Odeh was already on the Israelis' wanted list, but, despite an intense security clampdown, Khatib and Odeh were able to nose around vulnerable communities for more than four hours before Khatib finally dropped the twenty-three-year-old bomber outside the Park Hotel on Netanya's beachfront.

As the first day of Passover—the commemoration of the exodus of the ancient Israelites from Egypt—this was one of the most solemn dates on the Jewish calendar. As dusk fell, about 250 Jews took their seats in the hotel dining room for the ritual Seder feast.

Odeh evaded the hotel's security guards. At about seven PM some guests finally registered that there was something not quite right about the "woman" who had wandered hesitantly into the hotel foyer, but by then it was too late. The force of the blast peeled fittings from the walls and ceilings; bodies, body parts, and broken furniture were hurled through shattered windows to distances of fifty yards.

The toll rose through the evening. The first reports said nineteen had died. At the Netanya hospital, chief medical officer Avinoam Skolnik said sixty-eight people had been admitted, twenty-two of them critically injured. In the end, thirty were dead and another hundred and forty were injured, all of them civilians. Shockingly, most were in their seventies or older. It was the sixtieth suicide bombing in one and a half years of renewed conflict.

The ease with which Odeh and Khatib had arrived at the Park Hotel underscored the fear that gnawed at the Israeli national psyche—no one felt safe. The toll from the suicide attacks was horrific, for the living as much as for the dead.

There had been many more shooting and stabbing attacks on Israelis, but it was what the Palestinians called martyrdom missions that draped the land in a leaden blanket of fear. As Israel used targeted assassinations and a regime of stifling curfews and lethal incursions in a bid to break Palestinian spirits, the combined Palestinian factions retaliated with wave after wave of suicide strikes.

Anywhere Israelis assembled was a target. Already, the list of Palestinian hits had included bus and train stations; pedestrian malls and busy intersections; gas stations and shopping centers; pizzerias, cafés, and discos; checkpoints and kibbutzim; and anything to do with the Israeli military.

The Passover Massacre, as the Netanya bombing would be remembered, took on special significance. It was the most destructive suicide attack to date, but its timing also was crucial. Quite apart from the sanctity for Jews of the day of the attack, it collided with fevered diplomatic efforts in the Western and Arab worlds to avert a looming cataclysm.

Arab leaders were meeting in Beirut, attempting to finesse a Saudi Arabian peace proposal. President George W. Bush, long disdainful of the Palestinians and their plight, had been forced to dispatch his envoy General Anthony Zinni to the region in a bid for a cease-fire. Both the Saudi plan and the Zinni cease-fire were stillborn—the Israelis were not interested in what the Saudis had to say; the Palestinians would not listen to Zinni.

Formally declaring the Palestinian Authority to be a "terror-supporting entity," Sharon abandoned the usual rhetorical depiction of Arafat as Hitler and the PLO as the Third Reich,[21] opting now for more contemporary comparisons with Osama Bin Laden and Al-Qaeda. Sharon's Ground Zero was the mangled remains of the Park Hotel.

The prime minister addressed the nation again. "The state of Israel is at war," he said as his generals put the final touches to a military campaign they called Defensive Shield. "We must . . . uproot these savages," Sharon declared, leaving little to the Palestinian imagination as to what they might expect.

Five days later, as Israeli emergency crews pulled the bodies of fifteen victims from the rubble of the Matza restaurant near Haifa's Grand Canyon shopping mall—the scene of another suicide mission—celebratory calls rang out from the mosque loudspeakers in the refugee camp at Jenin, on the West Bank and about thirty miles southeast of Haifa. They announced that the perpetrator of the Matza bombing was Shadi Tubasi, an eighteen-year-old local.

Hundreds poured in to Tubasi's family home for condolences and coffee. Senior members of the Tubasi clan formed a greeting line, handing each arrival a postcard celebrating the "hero" of the Haifa explosion. In a corner, an unsmiling Walid Fayed, thirty-one, clutched an M16 rifle as he explained the unusual absence of sugar in the cardamom-flavored coffee served in tiny china cups. "Today we drink it bitter, so that we can share the Tubasi family's bitterness for the Israelis," he explained.

Fayed waved away any suggestion of revulsion at his young neighbor's reduction of a roadside restaurant to a cavern of death. He dwelt instead on his expectations for Israel's Operation Defensive Shield. "It'll be a massacre," he said. All in the Jenin camp awaited their fate: "We'll go out with bomber's belts, because that is better than sitting at home waiting for them to kill us. But before they kill me, I must explode myself with some Israelis."[22]

In Gaza, the same air of defiance was tinged with recklessness. Sheikh Yassin reiterated the Hamas philosophy—"We might as well die fighting"—before declaring martyrdom to be an "exceptional weapon."

His lieutenants beat the jihad drum. "They wanted to kill us without paying a price," Abdel Azziz Al-Rantisi scoffed at the Israelis. The fifty-five-year-old pediatrician was the second-most important figure in the Hamas leadership in Gaza after Yassin. He had been among the Hamas prisoners released by Arafat in the first weeks of the Intifada. "Now they're finding that there is a price after all," Al-Rantisi said. Mahmoud Al-Zahar, a practicing surgeon and member of the Gaza-based leadership, focused on the need for the Palestinians to wound Israelis psychologically. "Since we can't touch Israeli dignity without martyrdom operations, everyone encourages more attacks. What else can we do?"[23]

These men understood that they were targets for assassination by Israel. Al-Rantisi had abandoned the use of cell phones after the Israelis began loading them with explosives and coercing Palestinian collaborators to swap them for the intended target's phone. Al-Zahar had been switching cars almost daily since the previous year, when Israel began missile strikes on vehicles in which its intended victims traveled.

All the Palestinian security services' buildings in Gaza had been demolished by Israeli jets or helicopters in the previous weeks. The security chief, General Saeb Al-Ajez, was operating from a makeshift office built of sandbags, next to the rubble mountain that had once been his security headquarters. Three mobile phones and a pistol were spread on a plastic table. If he seemed to be in reduced circumstances, his bravado was undiminished. "If Sharon enters this city, he'll be in big trouble," the general insisted as coffee was served at the curbside.[24]

When it came, Defensive Shield was a raw, grinding display of Israeli power and force. Starting in the first days of April, Israeli tanks and armored personnel carriers churned the West Bank into a bleak humanitarian disaster as thousands of troops reoccupied much of the territory that had been ceded to Palestinian control under the Oslo Accords. More than one million people were locked down under blanket curfews. Thousands were detained amid complaints of widespread human rights abuses.[25]

Ariel Sharon revealed himself to be the equal of Ahmad Yassin and Khalid Mishal in his judgment of the military or strategic value of human suffering. "The Palestinians must he hit, and it must be very painful," he told reporters during an impromptu briefing in a Jerusalem cafeteria. "We must cause them losses—victims—so that they feel a heavy price."[26]

With the relentless Israeli aggression and the resultant Palestinian misery being conveyed on television screens around the world, Sharon soon came under intense pressure to withdraw—from President Bush, the United Nations, the leaders of Russia, Europe, and the Arab world, even the pope. Sharon stared them down, announcing he would do so "when the mission is accomplished." Mindful that the Intifada was undermining White House efforts to win Arab support for the looming invasion of Saddam Hussein's Iraq, a Bush spokesman insisted that, when the president had said "without delay," he had actually meant "now." The Israeli leader was unflustered. He undertook merely to "expedite" his campaign. Bush did nothing.

The impact of Defensive Shield was felt across the entire Occupied Territories, and it significantly altered the power and direction of the second Intifada. But when the dust finally settled, two of its most dramatic components would be seared in the international consciousness: the Israeli assault on Jenin and the effective removal of Yasser Arafat from his role as Palestinian leader.

The Israelis described Jenin as "Suicide Central" because as many as thirty suicide bombers had emerged from its fetid alleys in just eighteen months. This included the young Shadi Tubasi, the Hamas suicide bomber who had detonated himself in the Matza Restaurant in Haifa.

Starting on April 3, the Israeli attempt to take the camp met fierce resistance from an estimated two hundred Palestinian fighters. In one incident, the IDF lost thirteen men after they stumbled into a building that had been booby-trapped by the camp defenders. The Israelis called in tanks and missiles. Their ground troops then took to moving in clumps, crouching behind huge armored bulldozers that flattened all in their path.

By the time this Israeli attack on Jenin paused on April 11, its demolition was reminiscent of the destruction of Dresden. Its alleys were silent—bent and broken. In one, two human feet protruded from a low mound of rubble. In another, an aid worker interrupted an interview to point to a human foot that lay on the ground between the reporter's feet.[27] The shredded leftovers of a woman's orange skirt blew in a lump of fractured masonry, which dangled like a macabre mobile held by a thread of reinforcing steel. A green shirt was caught on the edge of a jagged hole that once held a window. A stack of mattresses were splayed like a hand of playing cards, in what was left of a bedroom. And on a cardboard box, half-buried in the fresh rubble, there was a printed label: SAVE THE CHILDREN.

When the shooting stopped, fifty-two Palestinians and twenty-three Israelis were dead. About 150 buildings had been demolished, and an estimated four thousand people were homeless. The scene, flashed around the world, that was most damaging for Israel was what Palestinians named their own "Ground Zero." The center—perhaps 10 percent of the whole camp—had been razed. There was nothing. Just rubble, the smell of rotting flesh, and complaints from humanitarian agencies that the Israeli authorities needlessly restricted their access to three thousand Palestinian civilians still huddled elsewhere in the camp.

Because of who he was, one of the first foreigners to enter the wreckage of Jenin compounded the public relations problem for the Israelis. Terje Roed-Larsen was a Norwegian diplomat whose credibility in the region was out of all proportion to the size of his small nation because he had been one of the key instigators of the whole Oslo peace process. What Roed-Larsen saw in Jenin made him furious. "Horrific beyond belief" was how he described the devastation to foreign reporters. "Israel has lost all moral ground in this conflict."

Arafat was pinned down in his sprawling compound, known in Arabic as the *muqata*, by an armored column that included forty tanks. "They want me to become a prisoner or fugitive, or dead," Arafat told Al-Jazeera in a live interview. "But I tell them no, [I'll be] a martyr, a martyr, a martyr. May God grant me martyrdom."

The Israeli bulldozers ate their way through perimeter walls that locals had thought to be impregnable. The tanks followed, crunching over vehicles in Arafat's parking lot before commencing to demolish buildings around the one in which Arafat was making his last stand. As electricity and water supplies were cut, Israeli commentators joked that Yasser Arafat now needed permission from Ariel Sharon to go to the bathroom.

Behind the heavy-handedness with which Sharon's forces pursued Arafat through the month of April, the first surreptitious steps were taken to execute an ingenious Israeli plan to ditch Arafat as the elected leader of the Palestinian people.

This new strategy was the brainchild of the then head of Mossad, Efraim Halevy, who, back in 1997, had been recalled from Brussels to rescue Prime Minister Netanyahu from the nightmare outcome of his attempted assassination of Khalid Mishal. At that time, Jordan's King Hussein had been attempting to find a resolution to the Middle East crisis by engineering regime change within the leadership of Hamas. Now, as head of Mossad in 2002, Halevy was setting out to impose regime change on Hamas's strongest competitor in the Occupied Territories—the Arafat-controlled Palestinian Authority.

As Operation Defensive Shield unfolded, the Mossad chief did not share the sense of triumph that gripped sections of the Israeli establishment. He had a brain that functioned like an over-the-horizon radar, and in analyzing the likely outcomes of Defensive Shield, two strategic problems alarmed him. The first of these was that an international outcry was sure to rob Israel's generals of the time they needed to achieve their objectives. The second was how to address that operational failure.

The generals said they needed months, but that was a luxury they would be denied. Within weeks the White House was despairing over the implications for its planned Iraq adventure of the Israeli campaign in the Occupied Territories. Washington insisted that Sharon had gone far enough in the siege of Arafat. Under threat of being denied an opportunity to visit the White House during an upcoming visit to Washington, the Israeli prime minister finally backed off.

This, then, was the context in which Halevy devised his scheme. Israel could not remove Arafat, but Halevy believed Israel could manipulate others to rearrange the infrastructure of Palestinian power in a way that would allow much of it to be vested elsewhere.

Putting to one side the fact that Israel was engaged in bloody war with the Palestinians, what Halevy was proposing was nothing less than a bloodless coup. Acknowledging Arafat's immense popularity among Palestinians, the spy chief explained, "The idea was to leave him with his title of president, but to devolve his power in such a way that he would become a titular head of state, comparable . . . to the Queen of England."[28]

According to the Halevy blueprint, Palestinians would get a newly empowered prime minister who would exercise most of the power held by Arafat. Their dozen-plus security agencies had to be reformed. Funds control should be in the hands of a minister who reported to the new prime minister—not to Arafat.

Ignoring any quibbles about the geopolitical morality of the plan, Halevy concluded that he had to deliver a new Palestinian leader who would be a "credible partner" to work with Israel. It was in fact a classic maneuver from the playbook of American foreign policy interventions from Vietnam to Central America—the quest for a cooperative or puppet leader.

Once Sharon had blessed this strategy, Halevy and Moshe Kaplinsky, the prime minister's military secretary, took a highly clandestine roadshow touting the advantages of Palestinian regime change to Amman, Cairo, London, and Washington. They apparently went to other capitals as well, which Halevy was reluctant to identify, but wherever they went their plan was well received. "The world was prepared not only to listen, but also to adopt the ideas as if they were their own," he explained.[29]

On June 24, 2002, President George W. Bush strode into the Rose Garden at the White House. As he broached the lectern he was flanked by Secretary of State Colin Powell, National Security Advisor Condoleezza Rice, and Defense Secretary Donald Rumsfeld. Waiting in Jerusalem, Halevy was anxious to see how much of his blueprint had become the Bush blueprint.

It was all there. The president did not name Arafat, but it was clear that the PLO leader was being sidelined by Washington. He would have to go before American support and funding for a new Palestinian state would be forthcoming. The Palestinians needed "new institutions, new security arrangements . . . a new constitution," Bush said.[30]

Halevy was mightily pleased. "I could not recall another instance when the intelligence community had made such a strong showing in charting strategic trends in the region," he wrote later. "I felt that we were making history."

President Bush's Rose Garden speech was the start of the tortured gestation of yet another Middle East plan: the road map. Israel reportedly had nearly one hundred initial reservations about this particular plan—one for each twenty words in the document, which would not be released officially until April 2003. Ultimately, these objections and qualifications were ground down to fourteen, some of which amounted to dealbreakers.[31]

Along the way, however, significant changes took place in the Palestinian Authority. They were sufficient to give Israel and the United States a new working partner, and Efraim Halevy a sense of satisfaction. Surprisingly, Mr. Palestine had capitulated to Bush's demands for Palestinian reform—at face value, at least. Arafat would allow the appointment of a prime minister—but then he resorted to using all his guerrilla talents to make life miserable for the unfortunate appointee.

The first difficulty in creating this new Palestinian order was to find a candidate other than Arafat who had a half-decent public profile. One of the old man's golden rules in his decades in public life had been to ensure that none around him acquired the experience or exposure that might lead to a challenge to his own authority. The eventual nominee was Mahmoud Abbas, also widely known as Abu Mazen. Abbas was finally appointed in March 2003, just twenty-four hours ahead of the U.S.-led invasion of Iraq.

A nondescript backroom operator since the early days of Fatah, the slightly stooped Abbas had been a key player in the Oslo process. He was a party functionary, always present and well-connected. But he was a gray figure and not often noticed—even by Palestinians. When he took office, most polls scored his popularity in single digits.

Effusive praise for his appointment by the Americans, and by Israeli officials who spoke to journalists on background, hinted to some Palestinians that their new prime minister might well suit Efraim Halevy's refrain of a "credible partner." Age sixty-seven, Abbas was vehement in his opposition to what he called the "militarization" of the Intifada, which he firmly believed had been hijacked by Hamas for the purpose of eliminating the Palestinian Authority.

Khalid Mishal was tart in welcoming Abbas's appointment. He argued that resistance was legitimate and that the Bush vision, under which the new prime minister had come to power, was a sellout. Throwing down the gauntlet, he drew a dividing line between these two fierce factions of Palestinian resistance. "No Palestinian will accept [you] . . . confiscating weapons," Mishal lectured the hapless Abbas.[32] "Real leadership must remain true to the resistance . . . it does not induce the people to retreat, to change their minds, to wave the white flag."[33] There would be no love lost between Abbas and Hamas.

The road map revealed both Bush and Abbas as putty in the hands of the wily Ariel Sharon. At a ceremony at the Jordanian port of Aqaba to mark the unveiling of the new document, fast footwork by the Israeli leader and slow thinking by Abbas left many Palestinians thinking their new prime minister was indeed either a puppet or, at best, incapable of standing up to his heavyweight cosignatories. Abbas allowed himself to be bullied into giving a speech, which was written by the Americans and televised back to the Occupied Territories, in which he all but prostrated himself before the Israeli and American leaders.[34]

Abbas had been led to believe that Sharon would speak in a similar vein, but the Israeli was having none of that. Sticking firmly to his own script, he went to the lectern breathing fire, vowing that terrorism had to be defeated before there could be a Palestinian state.

In Damascus, Mishal was scathing in his critique of Abbas's performance at Aqaba. "Imagine a Palestinian speech that speaks of the resistance as terror and about putting an end to the armed resistance," he said. "And the speech says nothing of the rights of Palestinians. The eight thousand of us who are prisoners are not mentioned." Abbas returned to the Occupied Territories with Mishal's condemnation ringing in his ears.

Still, Abbas pressed on. With grim determination, he pleaded with Hamas to cooperate in a cease-fire. While talks went on, Israel embarked on a new round of the targeted assassinations that had already eliminated more than one hundred Palestinian militia figures.[35] Hamas warned likely targets in its ranks to shave their beards and dress as women, to escape both detection by the collaborators who informed the Israelis on their movements and the helicopter gunships sent after them.

The Israelis assassinated another four militant leaders before a failed attack on June 10 on Abdel Azziz Al-Rantisi, the most high-profile target to date in their programmed elimination of the Islamist leadership. Al-Rantisi escaped with multiple wounds after six Israeli missiles turned his Jeep SUV into a colander. Back on his feet, Al-Rantisi, who spoke fluent English, thundered: "The expression 'cease-fire' does not exist in our dictionary."[36]

Despite the attack on Al-Rantisi, Yassin led a strong internal campaign to push Hamas to agree, in the last week of June, to join the other factions in a cease-fire—initially for three months. This was the leadership breakthrough that Abbas needed, and, amazingly enough, the cease-fire held for about six weeks. Then Israeli forces took out a militia leader attached to the Palestinian Islamic Jihad at Hebron in the West Bank and the gloves were off—again.

On August 19, a Hamas suicide bomber killed twenty-three Israelis in Jerusalem. On August 21, a successful Israeli helicopter strike in Gaza on Ismail Abu Shanab, judged by many to be a Hamas moderate, was the first of a dozen such killings of Hamas figures in as many days. On September 9, two Hamas suicide bombers were dispatched: one killed nine Israeli soldiers near the Tzrifin military complex; the other killed seven civilians at a café in Jerusalem.

Any lingering hope that the cease-fire might be salvaged was blown away on September 6 as ground crews at an undisclosed Israeli air force base armed an F-16 with a half-ton bomb. With a flightplan logged for airspace over Gaza, it became clear that Israel's political, defense, and intelligence chiefs had resolved a debate that had dogged them for months. "It was unheard of, but the first question was 'Could we assassinate a mufti?'" one of the participants in the debate explained later.[37] "In the old days we wouldn't touch a mosque or a holy man. But now they were in up to their ears in the violence. The other question was 'How do you hit a cripple?'"

They were going after Sheikh Yassin.

He was old and sick. Confined to his wheelchair, Yassin had long been a defining symbol of Hamas's struggle. Dropping a bomb on a building he was in or firing missiles at a target not physically capable of escaping was an exceptional act of extra-judicial killing by the state. But the Israeli generals concluded that this was a hit that they could justify by holding Yassin personally responsible for the tally of Hamas violence throughout the Intifada—74 suicide bombs, 251 Israelis dead, and more than 1,500 wounded. And with the United States now engaged in its own "hot" wars in Iraq and Afghanistan, the international climate had changed. Israel framed its campaign in the Occupied Territories in the same colors as the Bush war on terror.

They decided to strike against Yassin when an informer in Gaza reported that the Hamas spiritual leader and several other senior Hamas figures were scheduled to meet in the apartment of Dr. Marwan Abu Ras, an Islamist academic. "We had information a summit was being convened," said Gideon Meir, a senior official of the Israeli Foreign Ministry.[38]

The size of the ordnance chosen for the attack was a measure of Israeli caution. In July of the previous year, Israel had been censured internationally for dropping a one-ton bomb on a house in Gaza that killed Salah Shehadeh, one of the Hamas founding seven who had met at Yassin's home on the eve of the first Intifada back in 1987. But also killed were sixteen civilians, including nine children, who lived in the building. Since then Israel had limited itself to targeted assassinations employing missiles and rockets.

Yassin's September 6 meeting was deemed to be a golden opportunity, but it would take more than rockets and missiles to penetrate the building. They calculated that a smaller bomb than the controversial one-ton device used in the previous year would be sufficient because they had been told the Hamas meeting was to take place on the top floor of the building.

Apart from Yassin, others at the meeting included Ismail Haniyah, a leading political figure in Hamas, and Mohammad Deif, a senior member of its military wing, the Qassam Brigade. Deif had survived an earlier Israeli attempt on his life. As they were about to sit for lunch, those present were alerted by the sound of the approaching aircraft. All fled, escaping with minor injuries, although a piece of flying shrapnel wounded Yassin's right shoulder. He was treated at Gaza's Shifa Hospital and by nightfall was preaching in a local mosque. "They've lost their minds," he told worshippers. "The Israeli people will pay a dear price for this crime." Al-Rantisi, who did not attend the meeting, told Al-Jazeera, "The gates of hell have opened."

By the third anniversary of the Intifada, in September 2003, both sides remained undefeated, but at a terrible cost. More than 2,100 Palestinians had been killed by Israeli forces—380 of them children—and about 750 Israelis had died, most of them civilians. Tens of thousands had been injured on both sides, many of them maimed for life. More than three thousand Palestinian homes had been destroyed; hundreds of workshops, factories, and public buildings had been demolished in the West Bank and the Gaza Strip. Vast acreages of cultivated land had been bulldozed; olive groves and orchards had been uprooted, field crops and greenhouses flattened.[39]

Ariel Sharon had abandoned the prospect of a negotiated settlement with the Palestinian leadership. Despite international protests, he had commenced building the long-mooted wall around the West Bank. This "barrier," as Israel preferred to call it—lest parallels be drawn with the likes of the Berlin Wall— was billed as the bigest-ever public works project in Israeli history. It was deemed vital for Israeli security, but in a scathing assessment, the New York–based Human Rights Watch declared it to be another illegal landgrab under a "regime of belligerent occupation" that would cause disproportionate harm to the lives of tens of thousands of Palestinian civilians.[40] Except for a handful of permit holders, more than one hundred thousand Palestinians would be confined to enclaves carved by the route of the combined wall and fence. Scores of homes were hit with demolition orders,[41] and olive and other fruit trees were uprooted as great tracts of agricultural land were destroyed, in some cases with just twenty-four hours' notice, Human Rights Watch said.[42]

Suddenly, Sharon stunned Israelis and Palestinians alike when he embarked on yet another gambit, announcing that Israel would unilaterally "disengage" from Gaza and parts of the West Bank. Sharon sold this move, and Washington bought it, as an essential element of the road map. Others saw it as the making of Gaza as the first Bantustan, one of the Palestinian pockets Sharon would tolerate within his long-held vision of Greater Israel.[43]

Publicly, the prime minister had abandoned his hope that Israel could incorporate all the Occupied Territories into Israel proper. But the proposed route for the wall—well inside the Green Line, the old 1949 armistice line that originally defined Israel—amounted to yet another Israeli landgrab, permanently consolidating its hold on another parcel of the long-disputed territory.

In July, Mahmoud Abbas had been feted as the first Palestinian leader to be received by President George W. Bush at the White House. Publicly, administration officials had framed the visit as important to bolster Abbas's popularity and standing at a time when he was still locked in a power struggle with Yasser Arafat, who was refusing to relinquish power. In Washington, Abbas displayed a map of the West Bank to support his argument that Sharon's wall would shrink the area by 55 percent, making a Palestinian state a "factual impossibility."

"It's a problem," Bush said in a rare concession to Palestinian sensitivities.[44] But he then proceeded to cut the ground from under the Palestinian prime minister. Echoing Sharon as he lectured Abbas, Bush told him that terrorism was the main obstacle to peace, and he played down Abbas's pleas for the release of prisoners held by Israel. Sending Abbas home, Bush told him, "I will continue to discuss this issue [the wall] with [Sharon]." Meeting Bush just days later, Sharon refused to back down. When he argued that the wall had to go up for security reasons, Bush declined to press him.

In September 2003 Abbas quit in disgust, complaining that he had been hobbled by Israeli and American intransigence and by Arafat's persistent undermining of his office. He had had little joy from Hamas either.

After Abbas resigned, Hamas backed away from suicide missions for three months. The movement was determined to position itself for maximum political advantage in the event that Sharon did proceed with his mooted "disengagement."

Quite suddenly, Khalid Mishal began agitating for greater acknowledgement in the Palestinian political process of the growing popular support for Hamas.

In mid-2000, Arafat's Fatah had been almost four times as popular as Hamas in Gaza, but by the end of 2003 Hamas had pulled ahead. "The brothers in the PA and Fatah must recognize the reality of the changes and what's incumbent on them," Mishal asserted. "They must accept genuine participation of the resistance factions and forces, and go beyond the mentality of marginalizing them."[45]

Sheikh Yassin backed Mishal with more explicit language. "If the Israeli withdrawal [from Gaza] is absolute and total, Hamas in essence will become a political party . . . and begin participating in government," he told a Hamas Web site.

Mohammad Dahlan—the PA security chief who had won the admiration of George W. Bush for what he presented as a 'can-do' approach to knocking Gazans into line behind the Oslo Accords—was not impressed by Hamas seeming to jump the rails in this blatant fashion. "Unfortunately, the authority has lost some of its standing," he said. "[But] Hamas is exploiting this and trying to impose an alternative authority."[46]

In the early hours of March 22, 2004, the Israelis finally succeeded in their attempts to assassinate Sheikh Ahmad Yassin with a spectacular dawn strike on his wheelchair by Israeli helicopters.

He was an easy target. In his late sixties, Yassin rarely left home, except to be pushed and pulled in his wheelchair by family minders and bodyguards as they took him to pray five times a day at the nearby Islamic Association Mosque, which had been the first activist hub in Hamas's early days in Gaza.

On this Monday morning, the AH-64 Apache gunships swung in from the north, shredding Yassin's body when he took a direct hit from one of three missiles fired as he left the mosque after dawn prayers. Spitting short slivers of metal, which local children later rushed to gather for souvenirs, the missiles punctured sharp holes in the footpath, about the size of an American quarter. Lethal enough to cut through a steel door on a nearby building, they killed seven others who were close by.

Trash bins were set ablaze in protest. Tire fires at street corners pushed fingers of acrid, black smoke into the clear, blue Mediterranean sky. The city was draped in flags of all the factions, a sea of black, yellow, green, and red bunting swelling behind the recycled-timber coffin as it was carried shoulder high at the head of a two-hundred-thousand-strong procession through the rutted streets of Gaza City. Along the way, masked gunmen let off endless rounds of automatic fire and detonated hand grenades. After a tumultuous funeral procession, Yassin was buried at Gaza's Martyrs Cemetery. Two cinderblocks marked his simple grave in the sandy earth.

A few days later, a surging, flag-waving crowd of about twenty thousand stirred the dust in Gaza City's Yarmuk Stadium. Black-hooded marshals fought to control them, to clear a space on the sports field for a daring display by the Qassam Brigade, Hamas's outlawed military wing. Hundreds of armed fighters jog-marched into the arena, pledging their readiness to die for Palestine in chants that were echoed by the crowd.[47]

It was more a call to arms than a funeral. Men and boys, some of whom hung from the rafters, raised high their right index fingers, as cheerleaders led them in devotion to the cause: "Who is our God? Allah! Which is our party? Hamas! What is our goal? To die for God!" The stadium reverberated to wild gunshots, powerful explosions, and the pounding bass drums of rousing Arab anthems. Then the fighters melted away into the night as quickly as they had come.

Amidst all the burning anger, there was ecstasy at what Khalid Mishal described as Yassin's excellent good fortune. "It's a blessing from God!" he exclaimed. "A miracle!" The jihadi logic here was that Yassin was too old, too ill, and too incapacitated to have had any real hope of martyrdom, but now the Israelis had obliged him. "Our people pray to be martyrs," Mishal explained. "[But] because he was so handicapped, Yassin could not have wished for such a death." Even Arafat, Yassin's old foe, opened a condolences tent in Ramallah, where the PLO leader saluted the slain sheikh. "To heaven, you martyr," he declared in a generous send-off.

Israelis were in high spirits. Despite a wave of condemnation from Arab and other capitals, the chief of the General Staff, Moshe Ya'alon, warned that Israel would be stepping up its assassinations program. Arafat could be next, he threatened. Sharon, who had risen in the night to monitor preparations for the attack on Yassin, declared his victim to have been the "mastermind of Palestinian terror." Defense Minister Shaul Mofaz likened Yassin to Osama Bin Laden, declaiming "his hands were soaked with the blood of Israeli children." Others stopped short of assigning operational control of the Hamas suicide bombings to Yassin, arguing that his role was more that of a very influential cheerleader.

There were hasty predictions that, in the absence of Yassin's steadying hand, a weakened Hamas would probably splinter, becoming politically less capable at a time when the Palestinian factions needed to negotiate how to run Gaza if the Israelis did disengage.

Warnings that this assassination could actually strengthen a movement that was driven more by popular rage against the occupation than by the charisma and character of individual leaders were ignored. Arguments that within the Hamas spectrum Yassin had actually been a force for moderation were dismissed.

Hamas was not blind to Sharon's objective. It galled Israelis that the Shiite militia, Hezbollah, still claimed it had forced Israel to retreat from Lebanon in 2000. Hamas would not be allowed to gloat over an Israeli retreat from Gaza. The assassination frenzy under way was intended to weaken the Islamists, in a bid to clear the way for the other, more secular factions to gain ascendancy.[48] Palestinians needed to understand that, as Israel saw things, a takeover by Hamas was not an option.

That was how Mishal read it from Damascus. "Sharon thinks he broke the resistance," he said. "[He wants to] clean Gaza of the resistance and all the elements of power in it, whether political leaders, military commanders, resistance weapons, or resistance cadres . . . to organise it for the parties Sharon and the Americans are wagering on. He's deluded."[49]

The death of Yassin was a crushing blow to Hamas. The officer in charge of the Israeli military in the West Bank, Brigadier General Gadi Eisencott, produced statistical proof that Hamas surely was being ground down. In the first two years of the Intifada, he reported, its suicide attacks had jumped dramatically—from 28 missions in 2001, which had claimed 94 lives, to 62 missions in 2002, accounting for 234 dead. But in the 12 months up to the end of 2003, the number of attacks had fallen away to just 18, in which 137 Israelis died. And those 18 successful attacks had to be measured against more than 400 that had been thwarted—a 96 percent success rate for the combined Israeli security agencies.

Mishal cautioned Israel's commentariat, advising them to examine the movement's track record. "Hamas has always presented to its nation convoys of leaders, mujahideen, and martyrdom-seekers." Claiming to be more than a cult of personality, the movement proved Mishal's point within forty-eight hours of Yassin's death when it named Abdel Azziz Al-Rantisi as the new leader of Hamas in Gaza.

But Hamas certainly had entered a new era. No one in the movement had Yassin's unique stature. For all his frailty, he was one of the most influential personalities in the Middle East. Mishal quickly ruled out another such appointment.[50] The sheikh was to be immortalized as a spiritual symbol for the movement, and Khalid Mishal would become its sole leader on earth.

Taking pains to explain that Al-Rantisi's role as a local leader in Gaza was not to be confused with the expansive powers enjoyed by Yassin as a founder of the movement, a formal Hamas statement confirmed the Al-Rantisi position but went on to say that Mishal had "become the movement's leader everywhere."[51]

Fifty-four years old and trained as a children's doctor, Al-Rantisi was a combative hard-liner. Always reluctant to compromise, he had opposed the short-lived cease-fire of the previous summer and he was a reluctant participant in interfactional talks on Palestinian power sharing. He had been both deported and jailed by the Israelis. Arafat too had locked him up without trial for two years in the late 1990s, as punishment for his relentless criticism of the Palestinian Authority.

There was jubilation when Al-Rantisi's appointment was revealed on the second day of condolences for Yassin at the stadium. Amidst wild cheering and more gunfire, the most senior figures in the movement queued to congratulate their bespectacled new leader. Al-Rantisi called on Palestinians to unite in resistance. And, nailing his colors to the Hamas doctrine of violence, he urged Hamas's military wing to new heights, telling them, "The door is open for you to strike all places, all the time and using all means."

Al-Rantisi then sat quietly in the front row of seats cordoned off for VIPs, seemingly lost in thought. He went through the motions of accepting condolences—a handshake and a kiss to each cheek for every mourner. An ill-fitting suit hung from his heavy frame and his black shoes were scuffed from a day in the dust. He seemed to emerge from his reverie only when a small, curly-haired child tugged at his hands, which were clasped tightly in his lap.[52]

During a lull in proceedings it became apparent that, after three days of incessant speeches and interviews, Al-Rantisi's voice was failing him. After croaking a brief apology, he deferred to his deputy, the surgeon Mahmoud Al-Zahar, who was still in fine voice.

Defending calls that came from all quarters for Yassin's death to be avenged, Al-Zahar set out a Palestinian plea that seemed to have lost sight of any restraint. "Everyone expects us to retaliate," he said. "It's the only way to stop the Israelis killing more of our people. Armed struggle is the only option we have, so Israelis will pay the price. They have killed many, many of us in the past. They have arrested us and deported us. They have driven us into hiding but they can't suppress us. All that happens is our popular support escalates." But then, stopping to draw breath, Al-Zahar flicked the switch from war to diplomacy. "We are also willing to talk and to reach agreement that we will keep," he concluded.

In the aftermath of Yassin's death, the leadership dynamic was affirmed amidst some confusion. A system of internal elections had for a long time replaced the process of simple appointment to high office that had come as a right to Yassin in the early days of Hamas, because he had been the founder of the movement. But tension was evident as the new post-Yassin order was delineated.

Mishal's announcement of Al-Rantisi's appointment had made it clear that the pediatrician was in charge "in the Gaza Strip."[53] Al-Rantisi had first told reporters that he had been elected "overall head of Hamas and the political bureau," but he quickly conceded the overarching role of Mishal during an interview with Al-Jazeera. He pledged to "obey" the Mishal-led political bureau.

Subsequently, Israeli negotiators succeeded in extracting two remarkable commitments from Bush as a "reward" to Sharon for his planned disengagement from Gaza. The core Palestinian issues in the crisis always had been the return of all of the land occupied in 1967; a right of return for refugees to their homes on either side of the Green Line; the evacuation of all Israeli settlements; and for Jerusalem to become the capital of a Palestinian state.

At the heart of the Oslo Accords was a provision for these hoary old chestnuts to be confronted by negotiation when an initial peaceful coexistence had been achieved between Palestinians and Israelis. But, without consulting the Palestinians, Bush caved in to Sharon's insistence that Palestinian refugees could not be allowed to return to Israel proper and that the border between the two states needed to be further east than the disputed Green Line to allow Israel to retain strategically located tracts of Palestinian land on which it had already settled tens of thousands of people.[54] Sharon demanded written guarantees; the president of the United States gave them.

At the stroke of an American pen, the Middle East crisis had just become even more intractable. For Palestinians who had looked to the United States as their last hope, it was devastating.

Three weeks after the attack that killed Yassin and three days after Sharon's White House triumph, Israel stamped hard on Hamas—again. On April 17, an Israeli AH-64 Apache helicopter hovering above Gaza's Sheikh Radwan neighborhood let off two missiles as Abdul Azziz Al-Rantisi's white Subaru neared his home, just before eight o'clock on a Saturday night. The car was mangled; two bodyguards and one of Rantisi's sons were dead; and Rantisi was all but dead.

He was rushed to Gaza's Shifa Hospital, where he died as cameramen from the Arab satellite channels fed live footage to the region of the desperate fight by doctors to save one of Hamas's shortest-serving leaders.

Like Yassin, it seemed that Al-Rantisi too had been granted his wish. While chatting with foreign reporters in the days after the death of the old sheikh, Al-Rantisi had speculated lightheartedly on how he himself might die. "It'll come by killing or by cancer; by Apache or by heart attack. I'll take the Apache."

The funeral began at Gaza City's ancient Omari Mosque, where Ismail Haniyah told angry mourners, "They say they killed Al-Rantisi to weaken Hamas. They're dreaming." A raucous procession then carried Al-Rantisi's open coffin to the cemetery, where he was buried next to Yassin.

Mishal now was the uncontested leader of the movement. He had already consolidated his grip on the leadership outside the Occupied Territories, and there was no challenger to be found among the shell-shocked ranks of the movement inside the Occupied Territories.

Reports in the Arabic-language media suggested that the appointment of a three-man council to run Hamas was imminent. This appeared to be an attempt to put a brake on Khalid Mishal's power and authority. He was named as the likely head of this council, but his two co-members were to be the Hamas leaders from Gaza and the West Bank—in other words, two grassroots "insiders," who would be positioned to constrain a headstrong "outsider." But the council was not formed and Mishal now wielded power from his Damascus lair as first among equals in the most senior councils of the movement.

After the deaths of Yassin and Al-Rantisi, more high-profile assassinations seemed likely, and Mishal, who had survived the extraordinary assassination attempt in 1997, seemed certain to be in the bull's-eye. An Israeli commentator declared Hamas's collective leadership to be "dead men walking" and the Israeli minister without portfolio, Gideon Ezra, went out of his way to put Mishal on notice. "The fate of Khalid Mishal is the fate of Al-Rantisi. The minute we have the operational opportunity, we'll do it," he threatened. There were new Israeli warnings that no one in the movement was beyond their reach.

"Yes, I'm being threatened, like many others, and we'll take precautionary measures," Mishal threw back. "But these threats don't shorten our lives, because God alone decides our fate."

As small crowds of Palestinian refugees gathered outside the Damascus bunker to greet their leader on the night of Al-Rantisi's death, there was a touch of melancholy among observers who paused to contemplate the stepping stones by which Khalid Mishal and Hamas had come this far.

Yassin had instilled the movement with rare single-mindedness and determination. Mishal had been visionary in his 1983 plan for the "new jihad" and
how to fund it. The movement had been on its knees in the mid-1990s, but
Benjamin Netanyahu had given it a leg up, helping to restore the leadership
and its mystique with his botched attempt on the life of Mishal. Intriguingly,
Efraim Halevy was there for Sheikh Yassin's remarkable release from prison
in 1997 and he was a behind-the-scenes player in 2002, helping to remove
the single biggest obstacle to Hamas's eventual arrival in the Palestinian political arena: Yasser Arafat.

With Yassin and Al-Rantisi in their graves, some were mindful of U.S.
secretary of state Colin Powell's words of caution as Ariel Sharon left the
White House in the aftermath of September 11, believing he had carte
blanche from the Bush administration to conduct his own war on terror and
hell-bent on getting rid of Arafat.

"We always say to both sides . . . you better think about the consequences
of what happens the next day or the day after," Powell counseled. "Will your
actions make things better? Will your actions make things worse?"[55]

Six months after President Bush had caved in to Ariel Sharon's demands
for a "reward" for his plan to disengage from Gaza, the real intent of his strategy was revealed when the prime minister's confidant and chief of staff, Dov
Weisglass, agreed to a frank interview with the Israeli daily *Haaretz*.

Truly a revelation, the report was spectacular not just for its content, but
also for its hubris as Weisglass explained a Machiavellian policy that had been
sold in many quarters as the U-turn Sharon had had to make. The message
had been that Gaza was being given back to the Palestinians and so too, in
time, would some of the West Bank, as Sharon abandoned the settlements he
had fashioned as foundation stones for Greater Israel.

Claiming to be on first-name terms with Condoleezza Rice, then the U.S.
national security advisor, Weisglass was Sharon's conduit to the White House.
The son of a Polish fur merchant, he revealed disengagement to be a classic
policy feint, choosing to describe it as the "bottle of formaldehyde" in which
Bush's road map was to be preserved.

"It supplied the amount of formaldehyde necessary [to ensure] there will
not be a political process with the Palestinians," he revealed with much self-
congratulation. "We have in our hands a first-ever American statement that
[the West Bank] will be part of Israel," he said of the Bush letters, preferring
to use the Jewish names Judea and Samaria when he referred to the West
Bank. "Out of 240,000 settlers, 190,000 will not be moved from their
place."[56]

Weisglass wanted to be clearly understood. "The political process is the evacuation of settlements; it's the return of refugees; it's the partition of Jerusalem. And all that has now been frozen," he said, claiming that a nightmare for Israel had been postponed. "[And it came with a U.S.] presidential blessing and the ratification of both houses of Congress."

The Palestinians would turn to Finns before their demands were met, Weisglass gloated.[57]

20

Follow the Money

Bernard C. Welch Jr. had always kept odd hours, staying in during the day, but stepping out most afternoons, at around five PM, before returning several hours later. He kept up this strange nocturnal schedule during all the years that he and his partner, Linda Hamilton, lived in Great Falls, a well-heeled quarter of Fairfax County, Virginia, in the late 1970s.

When she was asked what her husband did for a living, Linda Hamilton would explain that Welch invested in coins, jewelry stores, and real estate. He spent much of the day managing his investments. She did the paperwork. Their home was estimated to be worth $1 million. They had a housekeeper and "his" and "hers" Mercedes-Benzes in the driveway.

Oddly enough, they had once rented a house in nearby Falls Church, Virginia, where a few years later a Palestinian engineer by the name of Mousa Abu Marzook would set up the family home from which he ran whole sections of Hamas's operations in the Occupied Territories. But it was not the address in common that would give Hamilton and Welch their cameo role in the American fight against terror in the 1990s.

Welch had five aliases. He was an escaped convict, a thief, and a killer. When he went out in the evening, he was breaking into people's homes, stealing anything precious. In the basement at Great Falls, Welch's inventory was stored neatly in as many as fifty big boxes. There were thousands of items of stolen jewelry, furs, antiques, and other valuables that he would slip into the market at an appropriate time. Welch had two small smelters in the garage—one for gold, the other for silver. A cautious man, he reduced jewelry to ingots before selling it.[1] In total, the loot was worth about $4 million, and life was good.

But everything fell apart on the night of December 5, 1980. When Dr. Michael Halberstam, a noted cardiologist and author, and his wife, Elliott Jones, returned to their home in northwest Washington, they were taken aback to discover a thief going through their possessions. Welch was at work.

With the advantage of surprise, the thief ordered the couple to drop to the floor, which they did. But, outraged by this violation of his home, the forty-eight-year-old doctor then leapt up at Welch.

Two shots were fired from a .38-calibre revolver. Halberstam took both in the chest, at close range. Welch fled. Badly wounded, Halberstam struggled to his car, intending to drive himself to the nearby Sibley Memorial Hospital with his wife in the passenger seat.

As he was driving away, Halberstam saw a man on foot whom he believed to be the thief. Jerking the steering wheel, he mounted the curb and ran him down.

He then tried to drive on to the hospital but lost control of the car and crashed into a tree. Within hours, he died in a hospital operating room.

When police arrived on the scene, the man Halberstam had knocked down was still unconscious. It was Welch, wearing gloves and still in possession of the gun and a burglar's toolbox.[2]

In the American way, Welch became a dark celebrity. *Life* magazine bought his story. Elsewhere, he was written up as the "super thief" and the "society burglar." But on his conviction there was nothing to celebrate. The District of Columbia Superior Court locked Bernard C. Welch Jr. away for nine consecutive life terms.[3]

That left the widowed Elliott Jones to confront her losses. She sued for damages, naming the imprisoned Welch as a defendant, but also roping in Linda Hamilton on the novel legal grounds that Hamilton had knowingly lived on the earnings of Welch's crimes.

The courts agreed. "[Hamilton] was compliant, but neither dumb nor duped," and that made her a joint venturer and a co-conspirator, one of the judges, Judge Aubrey E. Robinson Jr., declared. Much to the surprise of legal observers, Hamilton was ordered to pay the bereaved Elliott Jones $5.7 million.

Fifteen years later, it was the judges' portrayal of Hamilton as a "passive and compliant" partner in crime that became a backdoor through which Nathan Lewin would put the fate of Linda S. Hamilton at the center of the U.S. campaign to destroy Hamas.

Nathan Lewin was at the forefront of a new warrior force that now began to throw itself into battle. Their theater of war would be the chrome-and-glass towers of Washington and New York, Chicago and Dallas. Most wore smart pinstripes and carried bulging briefcases. Their weapons were computers, dictaphones, and photocopiers. Their smart bomb was the law and their trenches would be the courtrooms of the United States.

For years American criminal investigators had flopped around on the heels of the usual Hamas suspects, but they seemed to make little progress. In the early 1990s, Israel had handed over a mountain of leads from the dramatic interrogation of Chicago's Hamas bagman, Mohammad Salah. The interrogation of other captured Hamas activists also had pointed to the activities of Mousa Abu Marzook and to the Dallas-based Holy Land Foundation as the centerpiece of an extensive Islamist organizational and fund-raising framework in the United States. It was this intelligence that had directed the FBI to the Hamas conference on which the agency had eavesdropped so intently in Philadelphia back in 1993.

Already, there had been several civil actions against Hamas itself. Two U.S. courts had ordered the movement to pay damages totalling $330 million to the families of American citizens who had died in Hamas attacks in Israel. But getting the organization to pay up on these default judgments was impossible.

In other civil actions, American courts had issued judgments against states sponsoring terrorism. A grieving New Jersey family won a $247.5 million verdict against the Iranian government after the death of their daughter in a Gaza bus bombing in 1995. But collecting from foreign governments was a fraught business, and lawyers for families of the hundreds who died when Pan Am Flight 103 blew up over Lockerbie, Scotland, in 1988, were locked for years in a grueling struggle with the government of Muammar Gadhafi of Libya.

But the Hamas fund-raisers—plus the big banks that held and moved the money they raised, and even the influential financial advisers who audited their books or advised them on funds management—were literally in George W. Bush's backyard. They were vital cogs in the Hamas machine. If a legal action could be mounted against any of them in the United States, they would be obliged to defend their assets, cash, and reputations. The objective would be to shut some of them down and for the others to be forced to walk away from the business links that made life easier for Hamas.

The Israeli authorities wanted their American counterparts to launch major criminal investigations in the United States. However, when they first attempted to convince Washington that Hamas had built an extensive and successful front operation in America, they were met with deep skepticism.[4]

But no such foot-dragging was possible when private or civil litigation was launched. The seventy-one-year-old Nathan Lewin made it sound like hand-to-hand combat as he spoke of tackling "defendants who are real entities, real lawyers . . . a real fight . . . not ephemeral targets like in other cases."[5] His daughter Alyza, who worked in law with him, was passionate. "We went into this knowing there might be no compensation," she explained. "But there had to be a moment of justice . . . of understanding that the people responsible for the senseless killing and wounding should have their day in court."

Lewin & Lewin ran a small law office nine floors above L Street, on the Foggy Bottom side of Dupont Circle in Washington, D.C. Behind the locked doors of this shoebox suite, there was something quite deceptive in the appearance of these two.

Together, they were a formidable legal tag team. But the father had the look of some of the more rumpled characters on the sidewalks of Manhattan's diamond district—a shaggy white beard, a slight paunch, and a wardrobe that looked more Wal-Mart than Brooks Brothers. When Lewin sat at their cramped office conference table, he seemed to list to the right, as though he might fall from his chair. His daughter was a string-of-pearls mom, doting on her dad and the law in equal measure. Like an old married couple, they would finish each other's sentences until they reached some point in the discussion when he would inevitably cut her off with: "As I was saying sometime back . . ."

What the daughter called "Nathan Lewin's Novel Legal Theory" sprang from her father's distress after a chance meeting in Israel with Joyce and Stanley Boim, whose seventeen-year-old, Brooklyn-born son David had died in a hail of Hamas fire as he waited at a crowded bus stop north of Jerusalem in 1996. Lewin decided he would take the case as a civil matter after he had been told of the Boim parents' inability to get U.S. authorities to launch a criminal case against their son's killers, who had been arrested by Palestinian police.

Back in the United States, the Polish-born Lewin stared at a blank legal pad. In 1941, he had landed in America as the five-year-old grandson of the rabbi of Rzeszow, east of the city of Krakow. The family was part of the Jewish flight from the German horrors in Europe. Opting for a career in law, he had worked in government, for both the Kennedy and Johnson administrations. He had taught law at Columbia, the University of Chicago, and Harvard. He had clerked in the U.S. Supreme Court and had later gone back to argue dozens of cases before the highest court in the land. Along the way, he had bagged his share of celebrity clients—Richard Nixon, Jodie Foster, and

John Lennon. But much of Nathan Lewin's more recent caseload had to do with what he described as "Jewish public interest work."

Frustrated by the reluctance of U.S. authorities to pursue Boim's killers, Lewin ventured legally where others had not dared, cherry-picking statute and precedent law to build a case of far greater consequence than nailing a couple of lowly Hamas killers on the West Bank. If the justice department refused to go after mere foot soldiers, he and his girl would go for the leadership of Hamas and their American bagmen. "I'll look at the books," he told his daughter before adjourning to his library.

The law that began to exercise Lewin's mind was a 1992 statute passed in response to the brutal killing of a sixty-nine-year-old American Jew—the wheelchair-bound Leon Klinghoffer. A passenger on the Italian ocean liner *Achille Lauro*, Klinghoffer had been shot and thrown overboard by the merciless Palestinian gunmen who commandeered the ship as it cruised the Mediterranean in the mid-1980s. The 1992 statute sanctioned action by American citizens for injury abroad, and, as Klinghoffer's revenge, it contained a special clause that authorized a presiding judge to multiply whatever damages a jury awarded by a factor of three.

But this provision had not been used domestically, possibly because, even though it allowed a legal action to be taken, it was oddly silent on just who the defendants might be.

Lewin decided that it didn't make sense to think just of the men directly involved in Boim's shooting. The individual Hamas operatives in the Boim circumstances were hardly relevant anymore. The gunman who had fired the shots that killed David Boim had gone on to greater notoriety as one of the suicide bombers whose attacks in Jerusalem early in September 1997 had provoked the botched Mossad attempt on Khalid Mishal's life. The gunman's driver had confessed to Palestinian authorities and had been jailed for ten years. But he was released early and reportedly had died in a subsequent clash with Israeli forces.

Lewin concluded that the 1992 law had to be interpreted as an authorization for action against *any* individuals or groups in the United States who might have aided those who had killed an American abroad. But what kind of aid would he be required to prove? Did he have to show that the defendants had actually provided a weapon, or had sat in on detailed planning for the attack? Lewin found he was repeating himself—"That doesn't make sense . . ."

Much to the alarm of former legal partners and others he consulted,

Lewin began to formulate a belief that Congress had intended a much wider meaning in the Klinghoffer law. With that in mind, he settled into finding support where it mattered most: American case law. His eureka moment came as he fused the legal outcome from two very different sets of real-life circumstances.

The first was the case of Linda S. Hamilton, who, despite being nowhere near the scene of the murder of Dr. Michael L. Halberstam, nonetheless was ordered to pay damages because she was a partner in Bernard C. Welch Jr.'s criminal enterprise.

Then Lewin turned to the stellar advocacy of Morris Dees, a civil rights lawyer in the South, who, in the aftermath of racist lynchings and church torchings, had resorted to a strategy of taking civil action against white supremacist groups. The effect of these actions by Dees was to bankrupt these organizations by holding them accountable for the consequences of their incitement of the perpetrators of race crimes. Dees's most recent success had been a $37.8 million verdict against the Christian Knights of the Ku Klux Klan after a church was burned down in South Carolina in 1995.[6]

The case law, as Lewin read it, was saying that, if Hamilton knew what her partner Welch was up to and not only did nothing about it but also lived on the proceeds, she could be held responsible. Equally, if the KKK preached hatred and its redneck followers acted accordingly, then the KKK too was liable. Lewin asked, "If Hamilton and the KKK are as vulnerable as that, why not supporters of Hamas?" Amidst barely suppressed guffaws from his circle of old partners, Lewin extrapolated, "*Anyone* in the U.S. who contributes to Hamas, knowing that the movement is involved in acts of terror in the Middle East, can be held liable."

David Boim died in 1996 and the Klinghoffer law under which Lewin opted to proceed had a statutory limit of four years. Lewin & Lewin filed the Boim papers in a Chicago court just a day before the limit expired in the spring of 2000. When Lewin revealed his slate of defendants, there was another intake of breath in the profession, and further questions about the old man's sanity by the very colleagues he had hoped would help in running what he knew would be a huge case.

David Boim's two killers were on the list of defendants, and so too was Mousa Abu Marzook, the Hamas leader best known to Americans, who by then was in Damascus and safely beyond the reach of American justice.

Mohammad Salah, who had enjoyed notoriety as a Hamas bagman and "military commander," would be a defendant. As a resident of Chicago, he reportedly had been working various jobs—car salesman, van driver, college teacher, and storekeeper. Like Linda S. Hamilton, he had not been charged with any crime in the United States, but in the Boim case he would become the human face of terrorism for the nightly TV news.

But Lewin's real targets were several Arab organizations in America. The most prominent of these was the Holy Land Foundation, a highly respected and very successful Muslim charity. The other defendants would be the Chicago-based Quranic Literacy Institute and the Islamic Association for Palestine. Lewin was alleging that they all comprised a network of front organizations that laundered the funds that financed Hamas's terrorism. In terms of the HLF's public standing in particular, the Christian equivalent might have been for Lewin to accuse the St. Vincent de Paul Society of terrorism.

"They all thought I was batty," he said.

The daily scorecard in the Intifada was tallied in death and injury, Palestinian houses demolished, and humiliating hours spent queuing at Israeli roadblocks. But in the back rooms of the respective war machines, it was money from all corners of the globe that greased the wheels in this conflict.

Israel had been the biggest single recipient of U.S. foreign aid since 1976, collecting about $3 billion a year in military and economic assistance.[7] The Arafat-controlled Palestinian Authority, according to the World Bank, collected about $1 billion a year from a range of regimes in the region, plus the United States and some European governments. All the Palestinian factions drew covert funds and assistance from Arab governments and Iran, and interwoven into that money matrix were big donations from diaspora charities that were aligned with individual factions, as the Holy Land Foundation was with Hamas.

Hamas did not reveal the size or source of funds in its annual budget. But there was no shortage of guesstimates; most of these ranged from $20 million to $70 million, more than 90 percent of which was dedicated to its social services network.[8] The U.S. Treasury estimated that Hamas raised "tens of millions of dollars a year." Washington acknowledged that a goodly portion of the money was spent on "legitimate charitable work," but, it then argued, "this work is a primary recruiting tool for the organization's militant cause."[9] In the second year of the Intifada, Sheikh Ahmad Yassin estimated that payments to families that had been victims of Israeli violence cost Hamas from $2 million to $3 million a month.[10]

The economic crisis in the Occupied Territories had reached the point where Hamas, together with an estimated one hundred affiliated NGOs working in the Occupied Territories,[11] were bailing out the Arafat-controlled Palestinian Authority. A significant challenge for critics of the movement, particularly those who believed Hamas's community work needed to be stamped out in order to reduce its popular appeal, was the sheer efficiency of their grassroots community operations. Often, when international aid agencies needed to check the accuracy of their own beneficiary lists, it was to the Hamas-linked *zakat* committees that they turned for cross-checking, because of the local charities' reputation for professional accuracy.

By January 2003 it was estimated that three-quarters of Palestinians existed on less than $2 a day, and the United Nations estimated that 150,000 Palestinian households were being propped up by the four biggest Islamist charities in the Occupied Territories. Afflicted by its own corruption, organizational inefficiency, and a paucity of donor funds, the Palestinian Authority was incapable of responding to the hardship blanketing the Occupied Territories.

Israel did little to alleviate the suffering of those whose land it occupied, and few others did either. The key UN agency in the Occupied Territories—the UN Relief and Works Agency, which regularly fed 11,000 Palestinians before the new Intifada and more than 700,000 in the second year of the conflict—pleaded for an emergency cash injection of $94 million. The Swiss put up $1.5 million, and the rest of the world put up nothing.[12]

For many Palestinians, their only respite was the grants that came from Arab regimes and Muslim charities. Most generous in the eyes of Palestinians—and consequently the most controversial for Israel—was Saddam Hussein, who paid $10,000 to the families of the dead. Saudi Arabia was next with a grant of $5,300 for families of the dead. The Palestinian Authority paid bereaved families $2,000; and Qatar and the United Arab Emirates pitched in with $500 each for the families of the dead.

The Holy Land Foundation had a full-time staff of thirty-five. At this stage in the Intifada, they were pacing themselves in what was expected to be an open-ended, ongoing conflict in the Occupied Territories. But, despite the foundation's essential role in Hamas's global fund-raising, there were days when the recording jacks, which the FBI had attached to the HLF lines at their local phone exchange, revealed the enterprise to be as humdrum as the headquarters of any other American business.

Behind the austere, gray-brick facade on International Parkway, in north suburban Dallas, staff could be heard grousing about overbearing superiors.

They recycled office jokes about how they might be made more amenable or dared to raise the forgotten promise of new work contracts and, hopefully, a much-needed pay raise.

May 14, 2001, was such a day. When Kamal Tamimi picked up a phone in the HLF office in Hebron, a volatile city in the West Bank, it triggered a fifty-four-page FBI transcript.[13] Eight foundation staffers on opposite sides of the globe came on the line at various times, addressing issues in their own lives, or in the lives of Palestinians then living through the seventh month of the Intifada. On the day of Tamimi's call, seven Palestinians would die in the Occupied Territories, taking their toll for the first half of the month to twenty-three.

In Dallas, the business day had just started. It was 9:30 AM. But the West Bank was eight hours ahead of Texas, and Hebron was winding down for the day at 5:30 PM. In each city colleagues passed the call around as they dealt with the minutiae of running a charity that, even before the outbreak of the new Intifada, was channeling funds to Hebron at a rate in excess of $1 million a year.[14] Finally, the outer limits of the HLF's endeavor were revealed with chilling clarity, in an exchange between Sister Mirvat in Hebron and the surly Akram Mishal in Dallas—a cousin of Khalid Mishal.

Mirvat had raised the need for HLF to respond to emergency welfare cases not linked to the Intifada. "If you mean illnesses that befall people, such as needing surgery or being sick with cancer ...," Akram began uneasily, before changing tack. "In the Intifada, we give priority to ... to the injured and those who are wounded. . . . As for disease ... I mean ... we don't support them, based on the fact that we do not have the budget for them ... most of our budget is ... earmarked for the injured of the Intifada or those who were shot during the Intifada. These actually have the priority."

Public gatherings in the Occupied Territories usually were a male affair. But given that their men were dead or in jail, widows, mothers, and sisters were among the crowd that climbed three flights of stairs for a meeting—the first of its kind—at the Chamber of Commerce at Tulkarm, about sixty miles north of Jerusalem.[15]

Previously, Saddam Hussein's representatives went door-to-door to convey the Iraqi president's condolences to the families of Palestinians killed in the conflict, to ease their circumstances with a check for $10,000. He paid lesser amounts where a member of the household had been wounded or jailed, or where the house had been demolished. But the numbers were getting out of hand. Instead of a separate visit to each home, the men of the Baghdad-aligned Arab Liberation Front decided to streamline the process by inviting the families to meetings such as the gathering in Tulkarm.

As the aroma of shwarma lamb and rotisserie chicken wafted in from cafés on the Abdul Nasser traffic roundabout, members of forty-eight families who had suffered a death, detention, or demolition sat patiently through the inevitable speeches. Four of the families were to receive martyrs' checks—two men had died as suicide bombers; the others were a nine-year-old boy who had been shot by Israeli forces and an ambulance driver who had died in the crossfire. The atmosphere was subdued, but there was an audible intake of breath by the two hundred or so people present when it was announced that, on top of the usual $10,000 for those who had been killed, two of the checks included a new $15,000 bonus, which Saddam would pay to the families of suicide bombers, to encourage others to volunteer for martyrdom missions.

By the end of the meeting, checks for about $500,000 had been distributed. The silver-haired Rakad Salam, secretary-general of the Arab Liberation Front, did the mental arithmetic before confirming that Saddam had contributed in excess of $10 million since the Intifada began. For Palestinians, this meeting in March 2002 was filled with pathos; for the Israelis it was the worst provocation.

When a bystander asked Salam how the money in his handy little briefcase actually got from Baghdad to Tulkarm, he looked at the man asking the question as though he was an idiot. "It's transferred by the banks, from the Iraqi banks to the banks in Palestine," he explained, as though it was the most normal thing in the world.

And it was. On one level the meetings were a calculated exercise in public relations—Saddam was looking for support from the Arab Street as the rising tempo of Washington's war drums confirmed the likelihood of an American-led invasion of Iraq. But this very public presentation of benefit payments to bereaved Palestinians was exceptional. Tens of millions of dollars from charities in Saudi Arabia and elsewhere in the region, and from the HLF and its counterparts in Europe, had for a long time now been transmitted seamlessly through the global banking system, as direct transfers to the bank accounts of the recipient families in Palestine. The Amman-based Arab Bank had been using its sophisticated monetary software to deposit about $90 million from such charities into individual accounts in the West Bank and Gaza.

Israeli and American authorities saw the payments as incentives that encouraged Palestinian violence. But it was not just families involved in the

Palestinian resistance who were offered financial assistance. At the extremities of this makeshift welfare system, the families of suicide bombers were looked after, but so too were the families of those who had been executed by the Palestinian factions for collaborating with Israel.

When Operation Defensive Shield was unleashed across the West Bank in 2002, special orders were issued for Israeli troops to raid the paper and electronic archives of the Palestinian Authority's security services and departments, of local charities and of any of the Palestinians' factional offices. Typical of the files they brought back was that of thirty-four-year-old Mahmoud Abu Hanoud, a Hamas militia leader whose family was being assisted by the Hamas-controlled Al-Tadhamun Society in Nablus. Israel had assassinated Abu Hanoud, and Hamas had cited this as the provocation for a resumption of suicide attacks in the weeks after the September 11 attacks on the United States.

Born in the first weeks of the Israeli occupation of the West Bank in 1967, Abu Hanoud was one of a family group of seven surviving on just 1,500 shekels (about $400) earned each month by one of his brothers, who was a teacher. The number of his family's account at the Arab Bank in Nablus was recorded in the file, as was the observation of a social worker who had visited their home. "The family is materially well off, resilient, and patient," he reported.

Noting that Abu Hanoud had been unemployed because he was on the Israelis' wanted list, the file went on to explain in heroic terms the manner of his death: "Bombardment by Israeli Apache helicopter killed the martyr. There were two previous attempts on his life some months ago—the first, when the Israeli Army destroyed the house he was hiding in. [Abu Hanoud] then killed three members of the [IDF] Special Forces, wounded nine others [before he] managed to escape.

"He was later arrested by the Palestinian Authority and sentenced to 15 years in prison. On May 18, 2001, an F-16 bombed the prison in which the heroic commander was being kept and killed 13 policemen, but Abu Hanoud escaped again. He then renewed his jihad activity until he rose to heaven on November 23, 2001. May Allah have mercy on the heroic commander and situate him in the broad expanses of paradise."[16]

Abu Hanoud's file spoke volumes for the *Rashomon*-like complexity of the Middle East crisis. In death, he was a terrorist to the Israelis and a warrior-hero to Hamas. Earlier, to the Palestinian Authority, he had been in the wrong place at the wrong time and so had to be jailed when Yasser Arafat needed to prove to Washington that he could lock up his own people.

All sides were watching one another as intently as they watched their own pounds and pennies. In his crumbling compound at Ramallah, Yasser Arafat kept a hawklike eye on the funds flow.

A key task the PLO leader set for his security services was to monitor Hamas and its affiliated charities and community groups, and to report back to him on the source of their funds and what they did with them. Little went unnoticed. The reports that landed in Arafat's in-box dealt with a wide range of issues.

Early in 2001 there had been trouble over a sizable cash donation from a charity in Saudi Arabia for Palestinian prisoners. Arafat's staff at Bethlehem accused Hamas of hoarding the money and not sharing it with inmates from the other factions. One of Arafat's security agents reported to his superiors how he had stumbled on the funds because of the circumstances of two brothers who were doing time at Israel's Megiddo Prison. Ziad Zaud Ahmed Radaidah was a fighter with Islamic Jihad and his brother Hisham fought for Hamas. Hisham had made the mistake of informing his brother that Hamas was distributing the funds among its own prisoner network.

"The money was given to the brothers in the Hamas movement, which concealed it," the agent noted in his report to Arafat. Explaining that the prisoners' cross-factional leadership in the jail had taken control of the funds, the agent concluded, "The [Palestinian] prisoner club became involved and about one week ago the money was paid to all of the organizations in the prisons. Each prisoner received 10,000 shekels [$2,922]."[17]

On another occasion, there were ructions when it was discovered that a Muslim charity in Bosnia-Herzegovina had dispatched $50,000 to a Hamas-controlled welfare group in Nablus. Arafat's lieutenants issued orders in an effort to intercept the payment, and an emissary was dispatched to Gaza to heavy the Hamas leadership.

If one of the Hamas charities received a donation of meat to distribute to the poor at the end of Ramadan, a report went up the line on the fairness of the distribution. When word went around that a Ramallah-based Hamas activist and businessman, Ahmad Mohammad Abdullah Al-Sharuf, had come into $2 million with which he had opened a new furniture store, a report was duly passed along.

It was one thing for junior officials to handle the prisoners' squabbles over the Saudi donation or to investigate the factional affiliation of whoever ended up with the sheep's hindquarter, but when $33 million apparently went missing, it was Yasser Arafat himself who leapt into action.

Early in the second Intifada, Arab leaders had agreed to set up a $1 billion aid fund, the dividends from which would go to the Palestinians. As a precaution, in December 2000 Arafat had directed his ambassador to Riyadh to arrange for a delegation from the Palestinian Authority to be received in the Saudi capital, to ensure that the earnings "will reach those who deserve it." Translated, Arafat wanted the money sent to him—not Hamas.

Four weeks later, a second appeal to Riyadh on Arafat's behalf was more plaintive. Signed by the future Palestinian prime minister Mahmoud Abbas, it was delivered to the head of a wealthy Saudi charity. Abbas complained that Saudi funds were being channelled directly to groups affiliated with Hamas. "This has a bad effect on the domestic situation," he said. "[It] also strengthens these [Hamas] brothers [because the Saudi] committee does not send money or aid to the Fatah members."[18] Abbas proposed sending computerized data to ensure that the Saudi funds reached the "real beneficiaries, thus ensuring the rule of the PA over its people . . . so that there will not be a disaster in which the PA loses its honor and leadership."

A week later, Arafat hit the roof when a summary sheet of the day's television news for January 7 landed on his desk. It included a line in a report carried by the Saudi-owned news channel MBC: "The Saudi Interior Minister [says] a sum of 123,750,000 riyals [$33 million] was paid as assistance to the families of the Intifada martyrs, its prisoners, wounded and handicapped."[19] Addressed to Abbas, Arafat's curt reaction was scrawled in his own hand in the margin of the news summary: "Please inform me where did this money go and who received it," he snapped, "since the martyrs and the wounded received nothing."

Presumably Arafat meant Fatah's martyrs and wounded. In the file of letters snatched from the Palestinian Authority by Israeli forces during Operation Defensive Shield, the fate of the missing $33 million was left hanging.

At the time, regular items in the Arabic-language media in the Middle East faithfully reported the dispatch of each installment of Saudi funds to the PLO. But about a year after Arafat's outburst over the missing millions, Khalid Mishal and some of his Hamas colleagues held a long meeting in Riyadh with Saudi Arabia's Crown Prince Abdullah, who, due to the prolonged illness of King Fahd, was de facto ruler of the oil-rich kingdom.

According to a written report to the Gaza leadership by one of the Hamas delegates in Riyadh, Mishal thanked the prince for continuing "to send aid through the civilian and popular channels, despite all the pressure America exerts on them."

"This is indeed a brave posture deserving appreciation," Mishal told the prince, leaving little doubt that whatever official transactions took place between the Saudi royals and the PLO, Hamas was the beneficiary of a back-channel from Riyadh that delivered an estimated $5 million a year.[20]

In America, civil litigators like the father-and-daughter team Lewin & Lewin clearly were well ahead of the Clinton administration's criminal investigators' efforts to attack the Hamas support network that moved funds through and from the United States.

However, in Chicago, Agent Robert Wright of the FBI's Counterterrorism Task Force was put to work on material provided by Israel concerning the activities of Mousa Abu Marzook and Chicago bagman Mohammad Salah. In 1996, this investigation was expanded under the code name Vulgar Betrayal. The task force uncovered a remarkable web of cross-directorships and family ties among commercial and charitable entities, in which all the threads seemed linked to Hamas.

Three senior figures from the Holy Land Foundation had been present at the 1993 Philadelphia conference. One of the organization's more colorful and energetic fund-raisers was discovered to be Khalid Mishal's brother, Mufid; a senior executive based in Dallas was Mishal's cousin, Akram. Two of the key figures in the HLF were found to be cousins of Mousa Abu Marzook's wife.

Despite his pleading of meager earnings while he had been in U.S. custody from 1995 to 1997, it seemed that Abu Marzook had sprayed serious money around in the United States in the early 1990s. Quite apart from being linked to the near $1 million that was deposited into Mohammad Salah's bank accounts in Chicago in 1992, Abu Marzook had deposited checks worth more than $200,000 in the accounts of the HLF and a further $125,000 in the accounts of the Islamic Association for Palestine,[21] which he was believed to have established on instructions from Khalid Mishal.

Abu Marzook had also invested $200,000 in InfoCom Corp., a computer sales and Web-hosting company that operated from premises across the road from the HLF in Dallas. The FBI concluded that InfoCom was a Hamas money laundry. In the same period Abu Marzook invested close to $1 million in an oddly funded Maryland property development. His co-investors had included members of the wider Bin Laden family and a Saudi businessman who would be accused by U.S. officials of links to Osama Bin Laden. Just ten miles from the White House, those who bought into this smart residential development called it Barnaby Knolls. In time, federal investigators would dub it Hamas Heights.[22]

In 1998, federal authorities in Chicago instituted proceedings to confiscate the money that had been in the Salah family's bank accounts as well as his assets. Included among the latter was the house, which had been paid off by Salah's wife with money snatched from Hamas funds.

But suddenly, in 2000, Vulgar Betrayal mysteriously folded. Amidst allegations of institutional turf wars, bureaucratic bungling, sexual harassment within the ranks of the FBI teams, and Washington's reluctance to offend Riyadh because of the involvement of a Saudi Arabian bank, the criminal investigation of Islamist activities in the United States was put on ice.

"It was a huge investigation, but it went bad because it overreached," an official close to Vulgar Betrayal explained.[23] "It failed, partly because the people driving it thought they could bring down Islamic terror in its entirety . . . instead of pursuing individual targets."

Elements of the investigation continued, but the scope had been greatly narrowed. In the first week of September 2001, a multi-agency federal task force raided the Dallas offices of InfoCom after its bank records and garbage had been sifted.[24]

Sitting back in Damascus, Mousa Abu Marzook could afford simply to ignore the civil action in which the Lewins had named him as one of the parties responsible for the death of young David Boim. But the U.S.-based defendants opted for a high-risk strategy. Because Lewin's theory was so novel, the HLF and the others named in the action took the unusual course of marching off to the Court of Appeals in Chicago, seeking to test its legal validity, even before any of the facts of the case had been argued.

Then the world changed. Two weeks before the defendants' appeal was to have been heard, almost three thousand people died in the September 11 attacks on New York and Washington. Suddenly, what many in the profession regarded as Lewin's legal whimsy ceased to be just about the Boims and the friends of Hamas in the United States. In as long as it took for four hijacked airplanes to crash into the Twin Towers in Manhattan, the Pentagon in Washington, and a field in Pennsylvania, the import of the Boim case shifted from a single shooting at a bus stop in Jerusalem to the rights of the families of the thousands who had died in the 9/11 attacks.

In these dramatically altered circumstanced, the Chicago appeal bench decided it needed to hear the views of the Bush administration on what otherwise was likely to have remained an obscure case. Given the anguished mood of America in the aftermath of September 11, the Department of Justice backed in behind Lewin and his novel theory. It argued that, far from being confined to action against Boim's actual killers, the Klinghoffer law indeed was intended to go after *anyone* in the causal chain of an act of terrorism.

When Lewin's phone rang in December 2001, the caller was a friend who urged him to switch on CNN immediately. George W. Bush was in the Rose Garden, announcing overnight raids on the Holy Land Foundation in four states. At midnight, all HLF offices had been sealed; its multimillion-dollar funds and assets frozen; its bank accounts blocked; its phone lines cut. "The net is closing," Bush intoned. "Today it just got tighter."[25] Lewin felt vindicated. A stream of calls from well-wishers wrenched him away from the television as he declared with satisfaction, "The world is beginning to understand what we've been saying all along."[26]

In this new, post-9/11 environment all bets were off. Hamas had nothing to do with Osama Bin Laden, his Al-Qaeda terrorist network, or the attacks on New York and Washington. But just the idea of the Islamist movement raising funds in the American Muslim community was repugnant to an administration that had set the task for itself of "smoking out" terrorists at home and abroad.

Suddenly, the Vulgar Betrayal task force was reactivated in Chicago. In quick time the five Elashi brothers, who ran InfoCom and who also were involved with the HLF, were declared by Attorney General John Ashcroft to be "terrorist moneymen." In December 2002, all five were charged with money laundering and with exporting computer components to Libya and Syria without the required U.S. licenses.

In August 2003, the U.S. Treasury declared Khalid Mishal to be an SDGT. He was formally accused of skimming charitable donations to fund military operations, including assassinations, bombings, and the killing of Israeli settlers. In July 2004, a slew of criminal charges were levelled against the HLF and five of its executives. "Today, a U.S.-based charity that claims to do good works is charged with funding works of evil," Attorney General John Ashcroft told reporters.[27]

And just weeks later, it emerged that the Vulgar Betrayal evidence had been knocked into shape with charges against the bagman Mohammad Salah. Indicted along with Salah was Abdelhaleem Ashqar, formerly a professor of business studies at Howard University in Washington, D.C., who also had attended the Philadelphia conference more than a decade earlier. Despite being granted immunity, Ashqar was twice detained for refusing to cooperate with grand jury investigations into Hamas. He opted instead to go on hunger strikes. Eventually he was force-fed on the order of the court, but he declared, "I'd rather die than betray my beliefs and commitment to freedom and democracy for Palestine."[28]

Ashqar was accused of using his bank accounts in Oxford, Mississippi, as a clearinghouse for Hamas funds being moved within the United States and abroad, and of running a covert Hamas phone exchange. Instead of two Hamas operatives drawing the attention of authorities by calling each other directly, an ingenious scheme had been devised by which they were linked through Ashqar's Mississippi phone.

Back in 1991, when Mousa Abu Marzook was on the ground in the Occupied Territories resurrecting the Hamas leadership structure after it was crushed by Israel, a Hamas operative captured by Israel had named Ashqar as the go-to man for money when they ran out of the blank checks distributed by Abu Marzook. "There was another way to get money," the captive Said Abu Msamah told his interrogators, according to an Israeli-provided translation of his questioning.[29] "It was through a fellow in the U.S. and his name was Abdelhaleem Ashqar. He called me [at] my house and told me he was the mediator between me and [Abu Marzook]." The captive Abu Msamah then explained the response after he had called Ashqar to request that $300,000 be deposited in an Egyptian bank account. "[Ashqar] called me twice and told me the first time [that] he [had] deposited $200,000 and the second time that he [had] deposited $100,000."

The FBI claimed that its agents, when they trawled Ashqar's home in 1993, had found a trove of incriminating material: minutes of secret Hamas meetings, detailed reports on Hamas attacks on Israeli soldiers, and a fax from the everywhere-man Abu Marzook, instructing Ashqar to shift $40,000 to the account of another activist. Abu Marzook was also named as a defendant in the Chicago case, but given that he was in Damascus, he now was deemed to be a fugitive from U.S. law.

The grand jury that sifted the evidence accumulated by the Vulgar Betrayal task force threw the book at Salah and Ashqar. Alleging a racketeering operation over fifteen years, the indictment accused the two men of soliciting; conspiring and executing murder in the first degree; killing, kidnapping, maiming, or injuring people abroad; laundering money; obstructing justice; aiding foreign terrorists; hostage taking; forgery; and traveling to aid their racketeering enterprise.

Branding Hamas a criminal enterprise under racketeering law, the Chicago prosecutors hoped they might hold the defendants accountable for activities by Hamas before U.S. authorities had declared the movement to be a terrorist organization in 1995, a date that would prove crucial in subsequent litigation.

If the Holy Land Foundation lawyers had erred tactically in their pre-9/11 rush to challenge Nathan Lewin's theory in the Court of Appeals, their mistake was compounded when they opted to go back to court to challenge the federal decision to freeze the HLF's assets and funds.

As was the case for the appeal against Lewin's theory, this separate action to challenge the freeze also was rejected, with a three-judge panel in the D.C. Circuit Court of Appeals ruling that there was "ample record evidence" that the HLF continued beyond 1995 to maintain its ties with Hamas and continued to give money to entities controlled by and associated with Hamas.[30]

By failing in both these legal challenges, the HLF and the other defendants had driven themselves into a legal dead end. By denying in the latter appeal that the HLF had any knowledge of Hamas's activities, they had sprung a legal trap for themselves. American law does not allow defendants to run an argument in one court that has already been rejected in another; this prohibition now robbed them of any opportunity to run the same we-know-nothing defense when the facts of the Boim case were argued.

The jury in the Boim case came back in December 2004 with a $52 million verdict against the HLF and the others. But because of the congressional response to the death of Leon Klinghoffer, which authorized a presiding judge to multiply the jury's damages award by three, the final amount awarded to the Boims was $156 million. Of course this was subject to appeal, but Nathan Lewin liked the idea that in dollar terms, the verdict qualified as one of the top ten of 2004.

21

Government from the Trenches

Leaden skies cloaked Paris as General Christian Estripeau ventured into the chilly Thursday dawn. As official spokesman for Percy Military Hospital, he was about to deliver the biggest media statement in his career. Throughout the night, a media pack had huddled at the entrance to the hospital, located in Clamart on the southern outskirts of the French capital. As the balding general approached the reporters, his dress uniform was immaculate. His notes were brief.

It was 5:15 AM when Estripeau announced to the world that Yasser Arafat was dead. It was November 11, 2004. An old man had died and the earth had moved.

Reduced to a sad caricature of the guerrilla fighter who had become a Nobel Peace laureate but lost his way, Arafat had been airlifted two weeks earlier from the bombed-out remnants of his Ramallah compound, where he had been pinned down by Israeli forces for much of the past two years. Age seventy-five, the PLO leader had been unable to shake off what initially were described as flu-like symptoms. In Paris he developed nausea and stomach pain. A week later, he suffered a stroke, which had dropped him into a deep, deep coma.[1]

There was the brief distraction of a soap-opera struggle between the dying Arafat's wife, Suha, and his PLO lieutenants over information on the patient. There were unfounded rumors that Arafat in fact had been dead for days, and then wild allegations that maybe the Israelis had poisoned him.

But when dignity was needed the French provided it. A military band struck a poignant note during a ceremony at the presidential air facility at

Villacoublay, not far from Versailles. An honor guard of French soldiers carried the flag-draped coffin on board a French aircraft. As the PLO leader's remains were ferried back to the territory he had always called Palestine, French President Jacques Chirac, bid farewell to Arafat as "a man of courage and conviction."

The void left by Arafat was enormous. Despite, or perhaps because of, all Arafat's paranoia and autocracy, he and his people had endured. "We have made the Palestinian cause the biggest problem in the world," he said just weeks before his death. "One hundred and seven years after the [founding of the global Zionist movement at the] Basel Conference . . . Israel has failed to wipe us out. We are here, in Palestine, facing them. We are not Red Indians,"[2] he responded when the veteran Middle East correspondent Graham Usher asked him to assess his legacy.

The resistance careers of the two most powerful Palestinian leaders had overlapped for more than twenty years, but Arafat and Khalid Mishal had met face-to-face just three times. They spoke, however, by phone, especially in Arafat's last years. "The Israelis and the Americans ganged up on him . . . and even some of his own people," Mishal recalled later.[3] "We [were] Hamas, not Fatah. But when we saw what was going on, it was natural and moral for us to stand by Arafat."

Standing by Arafat, however, was not the same as standing by his corrupt and broken Fatah organization. The two factions tried dialogue, but they could never bridge a yawning gulf that was about power as much as policies.

There now was a job opening in Fatah for a leader with exceptional skills, but the man who finally stepped into the outsize shoes of the dead Palestinian Authority president was the hapless Mahmoud Abbas, the man who had been appointed prime minister in March 2003 on the urging of Washington and the Israelis—but had resigned six months later after finding that his hands were tied. Abbas was one of a dwindling band of survivors from the heady days of five decades earlier, when Arafat had founded Fatah. Abbas was elected as president and Arafat's successor in January 2005, sixteen months after he had quit as prime minister.

In keeping with its opposition to all that emanated from the Oslo Accords, Hamas boycotted the election. Nonetheless, the movement had proved itself deft in grassroots politics and had steadily insinuated itself into many areas through the electoral process. Since the late 1980s Hamas had fought politically to control the elected committees of a range of student, professional, and community organizations across the Occupied Territories. Toward the end of

2004, little notice had been taken of the fact that Hamas was standing candidates in the first Palestinian municipal elections allowed in almost thirty years.

More than a hundred of these contests would be staggered over several months, but included among the first batch to vote—in the last week of December 2004—was Silwad, the remote mountain village of Khalid Mishal's childhood.

Much had changed in Silwad in the years since the Hamas leader's family had fled in 1967. The isolated hamlets of the 1960s had merged to become an untidy urban sprawl clinging to a chalky ridgeline at the northern end of the Jerusalem Mountains. Intrusive Israeli watchtowers had been foisted among the stumpy limestone pinnacles and slender minarets of the high country. Like communities across the West Bank and the Gaza Strip, Silwadis compiled their own heartfelt catalogue of local land seizures, water supplies commandeered, and olive and other fruit trees uprooted as Jewish settlers, backed by the overwhelming power of the IDF, worked tirelessly to create their version of Greater Israel on Palestinian land.

Just to get up into the mountains from the coastal plain had become a logistical lottery. In the gridlock of Israeli checkpoints, cars from Jerusalem, Ramallah, or Nablus experienced endless delays or were forced onto circuitous backroads. Sometimes they were unable to reach the villages.

A Jewish settlement, Ofra, had been planted hard up against Silwad. In the evenings, its harsh security lighting glowed eerily in the soft mountain air. Ironically, the first furtive steps to impose Ofra among the Palestinian villagers—making it an Israeli fact-on-the-ground without formal government approval[4]—had been taken at about the time that Khalid Mishal had last trodden the Silwad soil. It was in 1975 when, as a second-year university student, Mishal had been permitted to return to the West Bank for the summer vacation. Al-Asour, the mountain he had climbed as an eleven-year-old to listen to the bombing of Jerusalem during the Six-Day War, was out-of-bounds to Palestinian locals now. It had been crowned by a high-fenced Israeli military base.

In Ras Ali, at the northern end of the ridge, the flat-roofed stone building that the Hamas leader's family had shared with another branch of the clan was shuttered and somewhat run-down.

Over sweet black tea spiked with wild sage, which their children fetched from nearby Wadi Zaitun, villagers liked to boast that for its size Silwad had given more than most communities to the Palestinian struggle. A calendar published in the lead-up to the municipal election celebrated the memory of sixteen locals who had died in clashes with Israeli forces. A pamphlet adorned with red roses and bent prison bars commemorated another seventy-odd who had been jailed.

But in the local pantheon of resistance heroes there was a fine balance between the two dominant and rival organizations. Hamas and Fatah had two local heroes each. Astonishingly, all four came from different lines of the same extended family: Khalid Mishal's own Hamed clan.

Apart from Mishal, who operated from exile in Damascus, there was also Ibrahim Hamed, who at the time of the 2004 elections had been on the run from the Israelis for almost six years. Hamed was celebrated as the leader of Hamas's military wing in the West Bank. Israel had accused him of masterminding a series of car bombs and suicide missions that had claimed more than sixty Israelis' lives and wounded hundreds. Age thirty-nine, Hamed had been a toddler when Mishal, who lived just a stone's throw away at the Ras Ali end of the ridge, left Silwad.

On the Fatah side, the feisty Qadura Fares was emerging as an influential member of a frustrated younger Fatah generation positioning itself to wrest control of the faction from the Arafat old guard.

The other Fatah hero was known simply as "the Sniper."

Most in the village had wondered about his identity since the day in the spring of 2002 when a mystery marksman had secreted himself behind an olive tree on a hillside terrace, high in a nearby gorge known as the Valley of Thieves. The importance of Nablus Road, running through the narrow gorge, demanded the presence of Israeli security forces, which often ran a checkpoint at an old British police post that could be seen from near Mishal's house.

A first shot rang out at about 6:30 AM on March 3. With a hunter's expert eye, the shooter first picked off soldiers on the checkpoint; then reinforcements as they arrived; and next, stunned Jewish settlers as they slowed their vehicles on approaching the checkpoint. Incredibly, the marksman's twenty-five single shots, fired over twenty-five minutes, killed seven Israeli reservists and three settlers.[5] Four others also suffered direct hits, but they survived.

He shot so precisely and got away so cleanly that settlers and investigators alike wondered if the killer was from the Irish Republican Army or perhaps had been trained as a marksman by the IRA.[6] Later there were unconfirmed reports that he had died while making a bomb. But when IDF and Shin Bet units finally moved into Silwad to arrest the Sniper in the weeks preceding the local election at the end of 2004,[7] the man who was thought to have been an IRA mercenary was revealed as Thaer Hamed, just another twenty-something Palestinian desperate to avenge the death of a much-loved uncle who had died in a clash with Israeli forces during the first Intifada.

Mayoral candidate Taleb Hamed, who described himself as a "former" Hamas activist, was another from the clan of the same name. He ran on a modest platform of needing to complete a half-built hospital, to improve local schools, and to lure a bank to Silwad.[8] But these contests across the Occupied Territories were about more than filling local potholes or whether Silwad might get an ATM.

Historically Silwad had been a Fatah fortress where, especially in the 1960s and 1970s, young men grew up in the thrall of Yasser Arafat. More recently, however, Hamas held sway. The Islamist movement had swallowed the local branch of the Muslim Brotherhood, which Khalid Mishal's father had joined briefly in the 1940s. Hamas also had won control of many of Silwad's institutions and associations. When votes were counted in the local poll, Silwad's Fatah loyalists were slack-jawed as Hamas edged ahead, capturing seven of the thirteen council seats to take control of the municipality.

These town and village polls were the curtain-raiser to a more defining test of popular support for the two factions claiming to be the true guardians of the Palestinian dream. With an election for members of the Palestinian Authority scheduled for mid-2005, under the leadership of new president Mahmoud Abbas, Fatah saw the local ballots as an important first step in hauling its legitimacy back from the Arafat grave.

In the circumstances, Hamas—and particularly Khalid Mishal—had decided the time had come for a comprehensive review of the movement's odd policy on PA elections: it had consistently refused to stand candidates, but it did not interfere with the conduct of the elections. Hamas tossed and turned for months. As the intense debate unfolded, the movement made promising gains in the first two rounds of local voting. The final decision to participate in the Palestinian Authority elections was taken in the easy knowledge that Hamas had already made a strong preliminary showing—taking control of sixteen local councils against Fatah's twenty.

The decision to stand candidates was announced in March 2005. Finally, Hamas would put its money where its mouth was. The movement had driven the Fatah cadres demented with its oft-stated claims that it represented anywhere up to a half of the popular vote. Now, all its barking would be put to the test.

Mishal was cagey when he explained later how he had vaulted from his doctrinaire opposition to standing candidates in the 1996 PA polls to whole-hearted endorsement a decade later. He had previously been sensitive to the perception that the PA was a creature of the Oslo Accords and that Islamist participation would be seen as acceptance by Hamas of that shaky edifice. "1996 was not the right time," he elaborated.[9]

Insisting that the death of "Mr. Palestine" at the end of 2004 had had nothing to do with his ideological U-turn, Mishal argued that by early 2005 it was well understood locally and internationally that Oslo had failed. The second Intifada had introduced a new, post-Oslo dynamic to the conflict. And Palestinian voters deserved an alternative after suffering more than a decade of Fatah's abuse of the hard-won funds and resources of the Palestinian Authority. Eventually, Hamas would go all the way, following its participation in the local elections in 2004 and 2005 with full participation in the 2006 elections for a government for all of the Occupied Territories.

"We had to run if we were to be in a position to fight corruption and to reform the PA," Mishal claimed. But, rather than ending armed resistance, the Hamas leader saw the decision as broad protection for the violent option. "It would make the people more steadfast as they opposed Israeli aggression," he argued. Mishal insisted that electoral participation was a decision by the movement—not an imposition by Khalid Mishal. "A majority of the cadres wanted to take part," he said, acknowledging that there had been some opposition. "So did I. It was the leadership that decided no in 1996; and it was the leadership that decided yes in 2006."

Mishal saw participation as a calculated two-way bet—Hamas seemingly entering the system in order to stand apart from it. The formal peace process might well have been in a state of collapse but, away from the battlefield, it was the only forum in which the parties to the crisis interacted. All needed to understand—and to have it demonstrated to them—that Hamas was too big a player to be left on the sidelines. "To some, that might seem like de facto recognition of Oslo," he later acknowledged. "But [if we could win], Hamas would play a much bigger role in Palestinian politics—without being dragged into the peace process."

There was an awkward bump on the road after Hamas revealed its intentions. In a third round of municipal voting in May 2005, Fatah managed to pull itself together sufficiently to win in fifty communities, taking control of almost two councils for each of the twenty-eight contests in which Hamas had prevailed.

As it maneuvered to gain the upper hand over Fatah, Hamas tempered its rhetoric and continued to honor a cease-fire on attacks against Israel agreed during a conference of the Palestinian factions in Cairo, in March 2005. The cease-fire was a helpful break for the colorless new President Abbas. But in return, Hamas had extracted an unambiguous endorsement by Abbas and Fatah of two bedrock objectives: the Palestinian right to resist the Israeli occupation and the right of refugees to return to their homes.

As the local elections played out in the Occupied Territories, there were renewed violent clashes between Fatah and Hamas loyalists in Gaza. It was against this background that Hamas had moved to come in from the cold. Curiously, though, Hamas seemed to believe either that it *could* not or *should* not win outright control of the PA.

Instead of making a pushy claim for Hamas to rule in its own right, Mishal urged at the start of the elections that the factions should jointly appoint a collective leadership for the post-Arafat era.[10] In Hebron, a senior figure in the movement argued that Hamas wanted to be in a position merely to "influence" the Palestinian leadership, rather than to assume leadership itself.[11] In Gaza, Ismail Haniyah, who had been a senior aide to Sheikh Yassin, also seemed to suggest a preferred role for Hamas as the political opposition when he envisaged that the movement would be better placed to confront corruption from inside the parliament.

There were ominous warnings from Israel that Hamas, as a designated terrorist organization, should not be allowed to participate in the elections—at least not without laying down its arms. Israel argued that there was a "fundamental contradiction" in violent resistance and Hamas's pursuit of parliamentary representation, and ordinarily Washington might have been expected to sympathize. But there were two problems here: President Bush was now in full cry in his grand push for democracy in the Middle East, and Abbas simply did not have the personal authority to enforce disarmament ahead of the election. However, Abbas did figure that having won the election, he would be better placed to co-opt Hamas. Washington wanted the election, so it backed Abbas—just as it had in 2003 when it sought to reorganize the Palestinian Authority around Yasser Arafat. But in agreeing to the Islamist resistance movement's participation, Abbas was steering all parties into uncharted waters. Armed resistance movements did not usually contest fully democratic elections.

Like angry bulls pawing the earth before locking horns, Hamas and Fatah stomped around the electorate, campaigning in all parts of the Occupied

Territories. The Intifada was running out of steam as a result of the Cairo cease-fire and the death toll had fallen dramatically on both sides. Almost 260 Palestinians died in the twelve months after the calling of the cease-fire, which was less than a third of the toll in the preceding year. At 53, the Israeli toll was about half that of the previous period.

Abbas needed this relative calm if he was to have any chance of making progress in negotiations with Israel. But amid widespread anxiety in the ranks of Fatah that his faction was so ill prepared it dared not risk a campaign showdown with Hamas, the president announced in August 2005 that he intended to defer the election for six months.

In the meantime, Israeli prime minister Ariel Sharon pressed ahead with his own plans for a unilateral separation of Israelis and Palestinians. He commandeered another substantial slice of the West Bank by pushing the route for the wall and fence he was building well into the Palestinian side of the 1967 Green Line. In September 2005, he ordered the leveling of many of the Israeli settlements in Gaza before completing his so-called disengagement plan.

The plan did away with the need for Israeli security forces to be deployed inside Gaza and, by claiming they no longer occupied the Strip, some Israelis argued that they had increased the proportional Jewish head count in their Jewish state by effectively uncoupling 1.4 million Arabs from the demographic mix. But the evacuation of the settlers, amidst angry protests by the Greater Israel lobby, and the withdrawal of Israeli military forces to the perimeter of the Strip did little to alter the reality that Gaza was still the world's biggest, meanest prison.

Despite all the disengagement talk, the Jewish free-for-all had continued on the West Bank. As urged by Sharon in the past, settlers had seized the hilltops and now enjoyed water allocations that greatly exceeded the trickle allowed to Palestinians. Arguing that they needed greater security, they had uprooted Palestinian olive groves and orchards, and they had carved out a network of roads through Palestinian land for their own exclusive use. They went armed in public.

Cowering defiantly behind high walls and sharp fences on an exquisite biblical landscape, the settlements were slices of America and Europe, dormitory suburbs that looked utterly out of place in the sunbaked Middle East. The sight of the huge hydraulic arms of concrete pumps, or of the lumbering crosses of construction cranes demonstrated Israel's contempt for Palestinian pleas for a halt to settlement expansion on what was their land—all of it in defiance of both UN resolutions and the occasional censure from foreign capitals, on which there was little or no follow-through.

In mid-December 2005, Ariel Sharon was suddenly admitted to Jerusalem's Hadassah Hospital after a minor stroke. Israelis heaved a collective sigh of relief when Sharon was discharged within days. But three weeks later, at the start of the new year, the heavily built prime minister suffered what his doctors described as a massive brain hemorrage while at his Sycamor Ranch, in the southern Negev region.[12] He was rushed back to the hospital, where, amid grim prognostications by doctors, he fell into a long-term coma.

Sharon's illness was another of history's thunderclaps. First Arafat, and now, just fourteen months later, his archrival had exited the regional stage. Gnarled old men, they had been authors of the script for much of the crisis that had locked their respective peoples in an ugly, decades-long embrace. Just as the irascible Yasser Arafat had been unable to escape the clutches of the headstrong Ariel Sharon, the Israeli prime minister could not be rid of the seventy-five-year-old PLO leader until he was firmly in his grave.

By comparison, the men who replaced them could not have been more lackluster or more uncertain as they grasped the levers of power. Palestinian Authority president Mahmoud Abbas and Ehud Olmert—Sharon's deputy, who became prime minister of Israel—were relative novices who would need to stretch every leadership fiber in their beings if they were to meet the expectations of their respective peoples.

As the Palestinian election loomed in the West Bank and in Gaza, the endless politicking sorely tested one of the constants of Palestinian life—a tradition of family unity that was based on respect for the parents as much as it was for older siblings, especially brothers.

The family of Ahmad Yousef, a senior Hamas figure whose family was based in Khan Younis, on the southern edge of the Gaza Strip, was split down the middle. "Three in Hamas and three in Fatah," he would explain.[13] But Yousef's colleague, the German-trained surgeon Bassam Naim, could easily up the ante, outlining the dinner-table dilemma that confronted one of his aunts. "She has seven sons," he recounted later. "Two are in Hamas," he would begin, pausing for an imaginary bugle blow to mark the absurdity of what was to come, "two in Fatah, and two are in Islamic Jihad. The last is agnostic."[14]

But the election drama that truly laid bare the explosive intersections of modern Palestinian life—Hamas vs. Fatah, religious vs. secular, glitzy foreign vs. hokey local, brother vs. brother—was the story of the Rajoub family.

This was played out in Hebron, a West Bank city with its own built-in volatility due to the insistent presence of 500 Jewish settlers who were protected by a heavily armed, 2,000-strong IDF force. A measure of the resentment and bitterness of the 150,000-strong Palestinian community was provided by the off-field performance of the local soccer team, who were sponsored by a Hebron mosque and called themselves the "Jihads." Eight members of the team had died in successive suicide bombings, in which they had killed more than 20 Israelis and injured dozens more.[15]

Despite the traditional notion of respect due an eldest son, in the Rajoub family fifty-three-year-old Jibril had to mask his embarrassment in the face of stiff early competition from Nayef, his younger brother by eight years.

The elder brother was considered to be one of the toughest characters to walk the West Bank. He was celebrated in song as "the lion of the south." And while some referred to him as "the King," others who claimed to have worked closely with him acknowledged Jibril's reputation as a thug.

But he was Fatah's thug and, up to the time of Arafat's death, he had been the PLO leader's thug. As a mainstay of the first Intifada, Jibril had been jailed several times by Israel before he was deported in 1988. On returning to Gaza with Arafat in the mid-1990s, Jibril had been appointed security chief for the Occupied Territories. In that role he had even jailed the younger brother who now had the cheek to stand against him in the general election—as a candidate for Hamas.

Jibril wore a scowl and a mustache—tightly clipped, like a smudge of steel wool on his upper lip. Nayef had that look of serenity that came with spiritual certainty, and he wore a beard—the full, fundamentalist fuzz, from one ear to the other. A beekeeper in his spare time, Nayef also was a professor of Islamic theology at Hebron's Al-Quds University.

Jibril campaigned from behind the tinted windows of an armored Chevy Suburban, invariably accompanied by gun-toting Fatah bodyguards. He preferred to wear a Western suit as he handed out glossy brochures and spoke through a proper amplifier. His style was to summon local businessmen and other power brokers to a meeting room in one of Hebron's finer hotels, where he would introduce himself as "an obedient servant of Fatah."[16]

Jibril had honed a pitch that, in the circumstances, failed to match the potency of his younger brother's spiel. "We've nothing to learn from Hamas," he would explain in a voice that sounded like a spade in gravel. "Hamas believes armed struggle is the only way to confront Israel. . . . [But] they should learn from us—we've led the revolution, we've led the Palestinian people for forty-one years."[17]

Campaigning against the corrupt ways of Fatah, the younger Rajoub brother dodged Israeli checkpoints as he tooled around the district in a banged-up Hyundai sedan. Green Hamas bunting flew from the radio antenna, and there was always a gaggle of Hamas helpers, who wore baseball caps in Hamas green and scarves embroidered with snippets from the Qur'an. Nayef's most sophisticated campaign technique was to chat with groups on the mosque steps, declaring Hamas to be "the ears, eyes, and heart of the people."[18]

Opinion polls in the early days of campaigning indicated that support for Hamas in Hebron was running as high as 40 percent. With nine regional seats up for grabs, there was a good chance that the Rajoub family's honor would be redeemed with both brothers being elected to the 132-member Palestinian Legislative Council.

As the Islamists rolled out a highly professional and disciplined campaign, voters were given a more nuanced sense of what Hamas stood for. The movement's candidates went heavy on rights for women; they played down the whole religious side of their platform and succeeded in making corruption and law and order the focus of the campaign debate. Opinion polls revealed that issues that Fatah might have bent to its advantage—the economy and the peace process—were of little interest to voters.

Ironically it was not Hamas's but Fatah's campaign literature that put greater emphasis on struggle and violence. While it was a badge of honor for Fatah candidates to brag about their time spent in Israeli prisons, it became mandatory for Hamas candidates to boast about the time they had spent in Israeli *and* Palestinian prisons.

Hamas packaged its campaign in the romanticized notion of "resistance," rather than the brutal reality of suicide bombs—but the subtext was understood. And while it was understated, there were hints of a pragmatism that Israel and the West might have picked up on. In the previous year, Hamas had not mounted a single suicide mission inside Israel. In the last days of campaigning, Mahmoud Al-Zahar, a leader in Gaza, made clear that Hamas was prepared to talk to Israel through intermediaries, be they from the region or from Europe. On one level the door was opening, not closing.

But there was little change in how Hamas was perceived in Israel, Washington, and other capitals: this was a terrorist organization, and should its members be elected, both they and the voters—the Palestinian community—would be punished. The Israelis and Abbas loudly demanded that Hamas renounce violence and recognize the state of Israel. Washington warned that a promised $350 million aid package would be reviewed if any Hamas MPs were appointed to the PA ministry.[19] Senior Fatah figures swore they would not join Hamas in a government of national unity.

Khalid Mishal campaigned as "the invisible man," speaking to rallies up and down the Occupied Territories through a mobile phone held to the microphone of a loudspeaker system. He did not dare to contemplate outright victory, but in Damascus he received a flood of reports from colleagues in Gaza and the West Bank that became increasingly more confident. The most likely result anticipated by Mishal was a neck-and-neck finish between Hamas and Fatah.[20] Given that other secular parties and independents could be relied upon to prop up Fatah, his expectation was that Hamas would wind up in the relative safety of the opposition benches.

Even this would be an extraordinary development for an organization that had cut its teeth on jihad and had remained in the extreme reaches of violent resistance for two decades. But a handful of foreign correspondents began to sense a tectonic shift in Palestinian affairs and in their last reports for the campaign indicated that change was afoot. While late opinion polls found that as much as 30 percent of the electorate was undecided, the consensus was that Hamas would poll respectably but would capture significantly less than half the seats in the legislative council.

The final result was slow in revealing itself. More than one million voters had been to the ballot box and Hamas was doing well. But exit polls predicted that Fatah would win, and early counting suggested that they were well on track. As Palestinians went to sleep on the night of January 25, the election results seemed much as they had anticipated.

In Ramallah, presumed to be a Fatah heartland, groups of rowdy young Fatah supporters took to the streets. Impatient for a result, they allowed themselves to be convinced by the exit polls and so spent the night partying, noisily cruising the city by car and letting off volleys of celebratory gunfire. In the morning they woke to find that their world had changed.

In Hebron, nothing could save Fatah and the eldest son of the house of Rajoub. The tough-talking Jibril was swamped as Hamas romped home, taking all nine seats in the district. Seven seats went to activists, including Jibril's beekeeper younger brother Nayef, who had been among the mass deportations to southern Lebanon when Israel had attempted to crush the Islamists in the pre-Oslo years. Nayef topped the ballot.

Somewhat to its embarrassment, Hamas had won convincingly in its own right—with 74 seats in a parliament of 132 members. "We didn't expect to be in government," said the astonished new Hamas MP Riyad Mustafa. "We thought we'd be a strong opposition. We're stunned!"[21]

Nine of Hamas's winning candidates would not be attending parliament, as they were locked up already in Israeli prisons. One who would be there was Miriam Farhat, otherwise known as the Mother of Martyrs. She had seen off three of her sons as suicide bombers and had produced a campaign video of herself helping her seventeen-year-old boy into his bomb vest before he went off to kill five Israelis.

Fatah, the party with so much history, won just a paltry forty-three seats. Worse, Abbas's secular faction might have saved itself from this humiliation had the leadership contained the brawling between the returned exiles of the Arafat old guard and the angry young Turks who believed, reasonably enough, that their time had come. The refusal of the two camps in Fatah to agree on who should stand had resulted in Fatah-aligned candidates standing against each other for some seats. By splitting the non-Hamas vote, they had helped pave the way for the Islamists to capture 56 percent of the seats with just 44 percent of the popular vote.

Recriminations inside Fatah were immediate. "The people punished us because of mismanagement and the corruption by the mafia that came from Tunis," Ramallah activist Nasser Abdel Hakim said, complaining of the excesses of the Arafat old guard.[22] Days would pass before Hakim and others became aware that Abbas himself had ordered the suppression, until after the vote, of a report that identified $700 million of corrupt deals inside the PA and suggested that possibly billions in public funds had been lost in the same fashion.[23]

There were angry calls for Abbas's head—from within Fatah. In fear for his life, the president canceled a planned meeting that required him to travel to Gaza. His supporters went on a rampage—torching cars, shooting up public buildings, and threatening the lives of some of Fatah's failed candidates. Hundreds of Fatah loyalists gathered in the presidential compound at Ramallah, seeking forgiveness at the grave of Yasser Arafat.[24]

Instead of coming to terms with its new opposition role, many senior figures in Fatah immediately began plotting the overthrow of the newly elected government. They spoke in terms of being at war with Hamas, and they urged the United States and other foreign donors not to bail it out.[25] Privately, even Abbas supported the tough quarantining of a government that had just been elected by his own people.[26]

The vote had upended the peace process: Hamas, the outsider, had been legitimized; Fatah and the PLO had been cast out. Any lingering doubt that Hamas held a veto over Palestinian decision making evaporated. The movement that had always claimed to have the support of about 40 percent of Palestinians had captured 44 percent of the vote.

Less than five years after September 11 and the launch of the war on terror, Israel and Washington found themselves reluctant midwives at the birth of an Islamist government. More dramatically, an armed resistance movement that was as disciplined as it could be brutal and that had been declared a terrorist organization in America and in Europe had won. And it had prevailed under a repressive occupation, while running on a platform to oppose the occupation by all means—including what it called military operations, which others classified as terrorism.

This was a geopolitical earthquake. In a stunning turnaround for a movement that had flagged its desire to be a parliamentary watchdog, Hamas now held the whip hand in the Occupied Territories. Both the Americans and the Israelis were wrong-footed by a vote that had been given a clean bill of democratic health by an army of international observers. Compared with other elections in the region—by Saddam Hussein in Iraq, by the mullahs in Iran, and by Washington's friends and aid recipients, Hosni Mubarak in Egypt and King Abdullah in Jordan—the Palestinian election had been a model of democratic fairness, despite being held under occupation and siege.

Abbas complained bitterly that he had been abandoned by both Israel and Washington. He had urged peace negotiations, but Israel had left him looking impotent as a negotiator. It had refused to make the kinds of concessions on settlement expansion, checkpoints, and economic development that Abbas needed if he was to be seen as a strongman by his people. Rightly or wrongly, Hamas had been lionized by voters for driving Israel out of Gaza. Palestinians had been entitled to conclude that the gun and the bomb had worked, and that talk had failed.

Four days after the vote, U.S. secretary of state Condoleezza Rice was still trying to get her head around the outcome as she spoke to reporters who accompanied her on a flight to Europe. "I've asked why nobody saw it coming," she said in a frank revelation of Washington's failure to even consider the possibility of Hamas winning. "I don't know anyone who wasn't caught off-guard. It does say something about us not having a good enough pulse."[27]

When Rice visited the Middle East just weeks later, her calls for democracy had lost much of their previous urgency and enthusiasm. Abbas's Fatah regime was the first Arab government ever to lose office through the democratic expression of the will of its people. It would not be a good look for the United States to openly seek the overthrow of the newly elected government. But if Hamas was allowed to succeed, it would transform not only the Palestinian internal dynamic but also the conflict with Israel. At the same time, it would embolden Islamists chaffing under Arab regimes that, even though they were allied with America, had little interest in Washington's gift of democracy.[28]

In the region, the American stand on Hamas drew scorn. There were accusations of hypocrisy and barbs from media interviewers demanding to know why Washington now refused to accept the outcome of the very same election it had insisted be held in the Occupied Territories. "Is this some kind of designer's democracy then, Dr. Rice?" she was asked pointedly on Egyptian television.[29]

Back in 2003, Washington had insisted that key powers be stripped from the office of the Palestinian Authority president in a bid to break Yasser Arafat's grip on Palestinian affairs. As prime minister at the time, Mahmoud Abbas had been the beneficiary. He had needed to weaken the presidency of Arafat so that he might be a strong prime minister. Now Abbas moved with indecent haste to strip power from the same prime-ministerial office he had once held.

Showing neither embarrassment nor shame, Abbas set out to emasculate the incoming prime minister by robbing his office of control over key sectors of government. Those powers were to be re-vested in the presidency, to bolster Abbas and to allow Fatah to protect a system of patronage that for years had put the interests and the financial security of the faction's members before those of ordinary Palestinians.

The security forces, which were quickly quarantined from Hamas, were a Fatah enclave. Just months earlier they had been described by a U.S. general attempting to advise on reform as a "social-welfare net." Almost 60,000 men were on the payroll of these paramilitary services, but only 22,000 even bothered to show up for work.[30]

The Palestinian Monetary Authority and the broadcasting service were roped into the president's orbit. Fatah loyalists were put in charge of the government's anticorruption watchdog. They were installed in the agency that managed the salaries and pensions of government employees. All these were posts in which they were expected to look out for Fatah's interests. This orgy of vested interest climaxed on the last sitting day of the outgoing Fatah-dominated parliament, when it set up a new court with the power to cancel any decision by the incoming Hamas-controlled parliament—and it gave Abbas the power to appoint all of its nine judges. This was a recipe for chaos.

Hamas did, however, offer the vanquished an olive branch. In a speech relayed to a victory rally in Khan Younis, Khalid Mishal appealed to Fatah to share power with the Islamists. "We are one people," his disembodied voice boomed across a flag-draped crowd that, by some estimates, was fifty thousand strong. "We lived together in the resistance trenches, so let us stay together in the trenches of politics."[31]

Hamas leaders on the ground in the Occupied Territories made the same offer, over and over. It was rejected. Days after the Khan Younis rally, Mishal seemed to have accepted that Hamas would be on its own in this new Palestinian era. "We talked to the brothers in Fatah, [but] they tied themselves to a premature and hasty stand of an unwillingness to join Hamas in the new government," he said.[32]

Fatah was utterly humiliated. Faced with the collapse of political power, Mohammad Dahlan, the former Arafat lieutenant and a hardman in Gaza, took to taunting Hamas on the daunting challenges it faced. "You are about to enter the [Palestinian] Authority—we warmly greet you," said the man who would play a critical role in crises to come. "It's time for you to become acquainted with the suffering of being in government," he said, almost leering through the television screen during a broadcast panel discussion.[33]

The level of anger in Fatah prompted fears of renewed street violence and, while Mishal played them down, he felt a need to appeal to Hamas supporters during a news conference beamed into the Occupied Territories from Damascus. Pleading for his supporters to be "modest at this time of glory," he urged them not to provoke others.

Votes were still being counted when the first of a barrage of demands landed at Hamas's door. Israel, the United States, and the European Union quickly put the new government in the deep freeze, refusing to fund it or even to talk to its members until three critical demands were met. Hamas was ordered to renounce violence, to formally recognize Israel, and to abide by all agreements previously signed in the name of the Palestinian people. Predictably enough, Hamas refused. When it did, Washington and Brussels promptly blocked the flow of aid, leaving observers with a feeling that their real objective had been to bring about the swift collapse of the Hamas government[34] and that the conditions had been deliberately framed to provoke Hamas to respond as it did.[35]

Israel blocked the transfer of tens of millions of dollars in tax revenue it had collected on behalf of the Palestinian Authority. The first monthly transfer put on hold was for $50 million of revenue that rightfully was Palestinian, but which had been collected by Israel as an occupation exigency. Hamas responded with its own regional roadshow—an appeal for funds led by Khalid Mishal. Provocatively, Mishal's itinerary included Tehran, where the Iranian leadership undertook to help the new government financially.[36]

Benjamin Netanyahu, who, as Israeli prime minister in 1997, had hoped to cripple Hamas by assassinating Mishal, lunged at what he deemed to be the failed policies of the Israeli government. These he said had contributed to the frightening election outcome. "Before our eyes, 'Hamastan' has been established," he said in his role as leader of the opposition Likud Party. "It is the stepchild of Iran and the Taliban."[37]

Within the Israeli establishment, the finger of blame was quickly pointed at the IDF's intelligence wing for its "total failure" to detect what critics claimed, with the benefit of hindsight, had been blindingly obvious.[38]

Hamas had survived against the most incredible odds. Since the early days of the first Intifada in 1987, the movement had withstood a relentless American-backed onslaught by the combined forces of Israel and Arafat's Palestinian Authority. It had withstood deportations and mass arrests. Leader after leader had been the victim of Israel's systematic campaign of assassination; Mishal himself had almost been killed. Hamas's institutions had been shut down; its fund-raising operations across America and Europe had been intercepted by the FBI and its sister agencies and dragged into the courts; its publications had been banned. And yet, as Islamists, its leaders had won the trust of an electorate that was devout but that had previously not embraced Hamas's religious-nationalist recipe for dealing with the occupation. In the political pressure cooker of Palestine, Fatah had become the faction that ate itself through greed and corruption and its own internecine wars.

With the governments of the world, the region, and Israel breathing down their necks, the Palestinian factions were like coiled springs. Conflict between them was inevitable. Hamas rightly claimed it had a mandate even if Fatah asserted that its platform had been legitimately endorsed by the electorate when Abbas was elected president just a year earlier. "The two programs were put to the Palestinian people, who in turn chose Hamas," Mishal argued, rejecting a reporter's suggestion that the two platforms be "harmonized."[39]

Sensing confrontation, Abbas made it known that he still commanded the loyalty of the sixty-thousand-strong Palestinian security forces, which, in the aftermath of the election, were eager for revenge against Hamas. As Hamas began to establish its own security forces, both factions were moving closer to the confrontation they professed to abhor.

Fatah had failed politically, but, as it wrestled internally with its own demons, its leadership became convinced that Hamas could not survive in government. Built around a near-delusional belief in power for power's sake, this was the Fatah reckoning: if Hamas refused to compromise with Israel and Washington, it would be punished by the world; if it did compromise, Palestinians would condemn the Islamists as hypocrites. For Fatah, that was a win-win ticket back to the power and control over Palestinian society, which it saw as its birthright.

The initial Israeli reaction to the election result was predictable. There were dire warnings that the Hamas government on Israel's doorstep would serve as a terrorist Trojan horse. There were warnings that all seventy-four Hamas MPs could be thrown into jail, and threats by trigger-happy Israeli officials that if there was a single terrorist strike, the names of all the MPs would be added to the hitlist for targeted assassination.

But a few Israelis wanted to see where the Bush democracy experiment might lead. Shalom Harari, who had been on the ground in Gaza as a member of the Israeli administration team in the days when the late Sheikh Yassin was establishing his grassroots Islamist network in the 1980s, argued that Israel had nothing to lose. "Israel must take a chance with Hamas inside the system," he ventured. "We're already faced with a failing peace process that has them on the outside. They're already here. Let's try to tame them."[40]

Refusing to bow to unconditional demands, Hamas gave mixed signals on how easy Harari's taming process might be. "The Europeans and Americans are telling Hamas to choose between having weapons and being in government," said an indignant Ismail Haniyah, the man who would be appointed the first Hamas prime minister. "But we say we'll go for arms—and parliament."[41] At the same time he revealed a touch of pragmatism. "Israel exists and is a state recognized by many—and I have to deal with this," he offered in what might have appeared to be a statement of the obvious.[42]

In a media blitz, Khalid Mishal adopted strikingly different tones as he lectured Palestinians and Israelis on the new realities in their separate and collective lives. "We are partners with our brothers in Fatah and the other factions," he said, before turning to his point—which was that he saw no contradiction between democracy and resistance. "Israel, like any occupier, only respects the logic of force," he argued. "[But] history confirms that if a party opts for the political solution and has no [force] to back it, it'll make no progress, it will regain nothing."[43] For the time, Mishal said, Hamas would not demean itself by repeating past offers to Israel. "We say that Israel must recognize our rights first," he insisted. "The killer must first admit that there is a victim."[44]

In a commentary in the Palestinian newspaper *Al-Hayat Al-Jadidah*, Mishal told Israelis that Hamas would not be recognizing their state. "However, if you're ready to accept a long-term truce, we're ready to negotiate with you on the conditions for it," he added, in what read almost like a throwaway line from the lips of a man who rarely wasted a word.[45]

It seemed that Hamas did understand its electorate. In an opinion poll taken shortly after the vote, just 1 percent of those polled wanted Hamas to make a priority of introducing Islamic law. By contrast, more than 70 percent supported a two-state peace deal with Israel.

With this in mind, the Islamists sent a range of signals that might have been interpreted as nods to the kind of moderation around which dialogue might have begun. Thieves would not have their hands chopped off, as required under Sharia law. The Hamas charter, with its crude anti-Semitism that so offended Jews, was to be rewritten. There was acknowledgment that "just the crazies"—who, by implication, were seen by the movement as a fringe minority—would demand that Hamas hold out for the liberation of Palestinian land beyond the West Bank and Gaza.[46] The cease-fire could be extended. If Abbas negotiated a deal with Israel that was approved by the Palestinian people, Hamas would accept it too. And when Al-Qaeda Number Two, Ayman Al-Zawahiri, urged Hamas to stay with violent jihad, he was promptly pushed back into his cave. "Hamas believes that Islam is completely different [from] the ideology of Mr. Al-Zawahiri," a statement by the Islamist movement said.[47]

These tentative offerings by Hamas were ignored or rejected. Two days before the poll, Israel's acting prime minister, Ehud Olmert, had spoken of resolving differences by negotiation "between the two countries" and had urged his country to hand back more of the territory it currently controlled. But later he did a backflip. "Israel will conduct no negotiations with a Palestinian Government of which even a part is a terrorist organization that calls for Israel's destruction," he hectored.[48]

Given that in the last five years there had been no substantive talks, Palestinians hardly received these Israeli warnings as the fearsome threat intended by Olmert. "Israel already refused to deal with the governments of Mahmoud Abbas and Yasser Arafat" was Khalid Mishal's "so-what" riposte.[49]

When Ismail Haniyah was challenged on Hamas's refusal to recognize Israel, he retaliated with an easy demand for reciprocity by Israel. "Has Israel respected agreements?" he began. "Which Israel should we recognize—the Israel of 1917; the Israel of 1936; the Israel of 1948; the Israel of 1956; or the Israel of 1967?"[50]

Haniyah had a point. As Sharon's successor, Ehud Olmert had lunged for the same "bottle of formaldehyde," committing to the closure of just a handful of West Bank settlements. But he also was insisting on Israel's right to retain substantial existing settlement blocs, and control of the Jordan Valley and all of the disputed capital, Jerusalem. Even Bush's sacrosanct road map had been effectively rejected by Israel. When it was published, Sharon had insisted on fourteen significant conditions, and up to the time of his collapse, he had rarely referred to the document without adding a significant rider: "as accepted by Israel's government."[51]

"Given that no one [else] is abiding by the provisions of the road map, the Palestinians do not see fit to abide by it either," Mishal told the Russian newspaper *Nezavisimaya Gazeta* ahead of a high-profile visit to Moscow in the weeks after the election. Elaborating during the Tehran stopover for his fund-raising roadshow, Mishal was more strident in playing to his audience: "Israel has obstructed, disregarded and torn up the agreements that it has signed . . . [so] it is inconceivable for the Palestinian people to remain committed to agreements that have been . . . disregarded by the other side."[52]

Under pressure from Washington and other capitals, the world's banks refused to process the electronic movement of funds to Gaza. By the middle of the year, Hamas complained that various Arab banks had frozen more than $300 million that had been donated by Iran and several Arab regimes.[53]

Hamas ministers and officials had to become inventive. Whenever they returned from abroad, they hauled back suitcases filled with cash. The last hurdle in getting the money into the Occupied Territories was at the Rafah border crossing between Egypt and Gaza, which was under the control of the Israelis and Palestinian security forces loyal to Abbas. In mid-May, Hamas spokesman Sami Abu Zuhri was discovered to have stuffed the equivalent of more than $800,000 in euros inside his clothing as he returned to Gaza from Qatar, where, over the years, Hamas had tapped a plentiful stream of donations.

Weeks later, Foreign Minister Mahmoud al-Zahar was luckier. After a trek through Iran, China, Indonesia, and Pakistan, Al-Zahar managed to lug four suitcases containing an estimated $20 million through the Rafah crossing.[54] But all this was petty cash, given the new government's accumulated debt. Already, unpaid government salaries had reached $300 million. Individual workers were handed two or three $100 bills from Al-Zahar's kitty. But at an average of $10 million a month, Hamas's currency smuggling could never catch up with its galloping wages bill, on which one-third of the population depended.[55]

Fatah had lost the government, but it still was refusing to relinquish power.

Within the PA public service there were more than five thousand directors general who, for the most part, were Fatah loyalists. Hamas accused them of obstructionism. In some ministries absenteeism rocketed beyond 50 percent. In the absence of funding, there was little to do for those who did attend their workplaces. When small caches of funds became available, it was not possible to devise a payroll distribution that all agreed was fair—and some demanded their due at the end of a gun. The funds flow to the PA was more tightly crimped when Abbas argued that, if there was to be any emergency foreign aid, it had to be channeled through his presidential office.

The election had introduced a fraught new dynamic to the Middle East conflict. And yet events on the ground seemed to prove the adage that the more things change, the more they stay the same.

There was a promise that February's government salaries would be paid in mid-March, but March came and went without relief. And as tens of thousands of Palestinians came to terms with the reality of no paycheck in April either, Khalid Mishal exploded. It was three months after the election, it was in public, and he had a microphone in his hand.

The venue was a rally in a camp for Palestinian refugees in Damascus, to mark the anniversary of the Israeli assassinations of Sheikh Ahmad Yassin and of Abdel Azziz Al-Rantisi. Mishal's vitriolic speech marked a dangerous new low in relations between Hamas and Fatah.

Mishal taunted Israel and the United States as would have been expected by his audience. "We prefer starvation to going down on our knees," he jeered, reiterating Hamas's refusal to abide by the three conditions for acceptance set by Israel and Washington. He mocked the Israelis. "[They are losing confidence] and need Hamas's recognition!"

But if all that might have been dismissed as crisis-time rhetoric, Mishal's jibes at Fatah and Abbas seemed calculated to provoke and offend. It was one thing for the Hamas leader to insult long-standing enemies like the Americans and the Israelis. It was quite another to publicly take potshots at a fellow Palestinian, a fellow Arab. "Why do some of our own people conspire against us and draw up a thought-out plan to render [the Hamas government] unsuccessful?" he demanded.[56] "Today, it is high time to unmask . . . these traitors."

Mishal coyly stopped short of naming the "traitors," but there was no doubt about whom he spoke. "They sacrifice the interests of the homeland . . . in order to serve the interests of the enemy," he railed. "They contribute to the starvation of their people and the state of lawlessness." Drawing a line between the activities of a loyal opposition and what he suggested was Fatah's support for a U.S.-Israeli-backed coup, Mishal declared, "The Palestinian people will thwart the conspiracy!"

A few days before the Damascus rally at which Mishal spoke, the successful candidates in Israel's March 28 national election had been sworn in as members of the Knesset, Israel's parliament. But just hours after this ceremonial swearing in, a suicide bomber detonated twenty-one pounds of explosives at the entrance to a restaurant in Tel Aviv, killing eleven people and wounding seventy others. This was the first such attack since Hamas's election victory and was claimed by Islamic Jihad, the Islamist faction that had shunned the political process. Abbas roundly condemned the bombing, but spokesmen for Hamas justified it as a logical response to Israeli oppression. Coincidentally, the swearing in of the new Knesset had occurred on the same day that Palestinians customarily commemorated Prisoners' Day—their annual protest against Israel holding thousands of Palestinians in its jails.

Targeting the Palestinian Authority president and his Fatah colleagues in his Damascus speech, Mishal drove home his attack. "[The new Hamas] ministers told me that they have entered their ministries to find that their [Fatah predecessors] have stolen the couches, desks, tea, coffee, and notebooks," he charged. "Can shame be on the one who blew himself up in Tel Aviv? Is disgrace for the one who blows himself up in Tel Aviv, or the one who dines and drinks in Tel Aviv?"

The speech was ignored by virtually the entire English-language media, but it electrified the Arab world. Apart from reiterating the standard Hamas charge of corruption against Fatah, Mishal was now accusing the secularists of theft and treachery, collaboration and fraternizing with the enemy.

In Ramallah, gunshots were fired in anger. In Gaza, stone throwing and fistfights broke out among hundreds of students from the rival Islamic and Al-Azhar universities. Fatah's central committee denounced the Damascus speech as "sick" and "idiotic."

Apologies were demanded. Mishal was accused of fomenting civil war, of sedition, and of suffering his own personal crisis. Mohammad Dahlan, now Abbas's security chief and long a thorn in the side of Hamas in Gaza, lectured Mishal on a need for pragmatism. Abbas's spokesman Ahmad Abd El-Rahman spoke directly at Mishal in an interview for Al-Jazeera: "We want you to let us solve our problems . . . without your interference and without your speeches!" But it was Jibril Rajoub who nailed the point of this particular wrangle. "That speech lasted more than fifty-five minutes," Rajoub grumbled.

"It included insults to Fatah, its history, leaders, and symbols. It was not a slip of the tongue."[57]

Hamas had more or less abided by the cease-fire agreed in Cairo in March 2005. The movement's suicide attacks had been put on hold. But since the Israeli military pullback and the settlers' evacuation from Gaza in September 2005, about three hundred crude, homemade missiles had been launched on wild, erratic trajectories from just inside Gaza. Fueled by a mixture of sugar and common fertilizer, the missiles were fired by the other Palestinian militia groups, but Israel claimed that these attacks were orchestrated by Hamas.[58]

As a psychological weapon they packed a punch. But as artillery pieces, they bordered on the ineffectual. Israel estimated that almost 200,000 of its population lived within range of the Gaza rockets. Disparaged by some Israeli analysts as "flying stovepipes," the rockets had killed an average of three Israelis a year since the first such death in June 2004.[59] In the eight months since the so-called disengagement, injuries to Israelis caused by the rockets numbered in the dozens and just a single Israeli death had been recorded.[60]

Israel's powerful return fire, which on one count included as many as five thousand artillery shells between January and May 2006,[61] exacted a far heavier toll. More than seventy Gazans were killed, almost forty of whom were identified as combatants, twenty-six as civilians, and sixteen as victims of Israel's ongoing assassination program.[62]

With firepower of that intensity, it would be only a matter of time before the pressure became unbearable. That happened early in June 2006.

Hamas formally abandoned its cease-fire amidst outpourings of Palestinian rage, after the death on June 9 of seven members of a single Palestinian family picnicking on one of Gaza's northern beaches. Two years earlier, four members of the same family had died when an Israeli shell hit their farm at the northern end of the Gaza Strip. On both occasions Israel offered the same explanation—it was attempting to stop Palestinian rocket fire into Israel.[63]

Heartrending pictures flashed around the world of a distraught Huda Ghalia, a ten-year-old member of the family who had survived, as she fell weeping beside the body of her dead father on the beach. Nearby lay the mangled remains of the girl's stepmother and five of the girl's brothers and sisters.

The Israeli army admitted that its tanks were in action at the time and at first it apologized, expressing sorrow for the beach killings. But after its own internal investigation, it then denied firing the killer shell. Backtracking, the

IDF absolved itself with a claim that the beachside carnage more likely was caused by a device planted by Palestinian militants.[64]

The night before the beach deaths, Israeli aircraft had attacked a resistance training camp in southern Gaza. Among the four Palestinians killed was the high-profile Jamal Abu Samhadana, the leader of a cross-factional militia group known as the Popular Resistance Committees. Israel claimed that Abu Samhadana was not the intended target, but the Hamas government had just appointed Abu Samhadana to head its Executive Force, the paramilitary force it was setting up in opposition to President Abbas's security forces.

For Israeli officials, it was a provocative appointment because they held Abu Samhadana responsible for much of the rocket fire into Israel. Hamas marked the end of its sixteen-month-long cease-fire with a barrage of fifteen of its signature Qassam rockets.

Brutal as it was, all this might have been seen to be within the highly elastic bounds of action and anger, reaction and resentment, in a never-ending crisis. But on June 24, Israeli forces mounted a cross-border raid, enraging Hamas. Penetrating about eight hundred yards into southern Gaza, the Israelis' objective was Umm Al-Nasser Village, where they captured the brothers Mustafa and Osama Abu Muammar, who they claimed were Hamas operatives in the throes of planning an attack.

The snatch-and-grab was the first raid of its kind since the Israeli retreat from the Gaza Strip. Now Hamas snapped.

22

"No Gold Bars Left"

Kerem Shalom had the air of an improvised holiday camp. Date palms and other greenery cast gentle shadows for a community of just thirty adults and twenty-five children. Tucked deep into a corner of Israel, where its borders met those of Egypt and Gaza, the kibbutz potato fields sprawled toward the fence separating Palestinians from Israelis.

Despite the fence and the leaden symbolism of the local lookout towers, members of the kibbutz hoped one day to run a fruit-and-vegetable export venture with their Palestinian neighbors. Negotiations had been under way, but by late June 2006 it all seemed like a pipe dream. The border crossing, through which they had hoped to bring Palestinian produce into Israel and then to the kitchens of Europe, had been closed several times in recent weeks, after intelligence alerts of likely militia attacks in the grassy flatlands of the south.

Israeli surveillance over Gaza was so sophisticated that the IDF could almost do a house-by-house catalogue of who was in and who was out for dinner on any given night. But the famed electronic eyes had failed to detect what had to have been weeks, perhaps even months, of unusual activity around a nondescript building close to the crossing.

The source of the warning of an attack was Israel's domestic intelligence service, Shin Bet. Alerted by its network of Palestinian collaborators that "something" was going on, Shin Bet passed the information on. It even mentioned a tunnel, but inexplicably the message had lost its urgency by the time it was transmitted to some of Israel's frontline army units.[1]

Since well before the killing of Jamal Abu Samhadana and the mass deaths of the Ghalia family on the beach in Gaza, Hamas had been digging a tunnel—a very serious tunnel. In a joint venture with Abu Samhadana's Popular Resistance Committees and another smaller militia group, Hamas had brought in a team of specialist tunnelers who ordinarily opened passages for military and commercial contraband coming into Gaza from Egypt.

This time their task had been to dig and burrow deep under Israeli territory. At depths of up to twenty-five feet below the surface, they had to dig for 400 yards just to reach the border fence. Then they kept going, for another 300 yards, all the way to the edge of Kibbutz Kerem Shalom.

The tunnel had to be wide enough for men and weapons.

Apart from Israel's failure to detect the movement of diggers going to and from the building that Hamas had rented, there was also a small mountain of earth that had to be spirited away from the site. All of this Israel's renowned surveillance apparatus had missed.

The day after the Palestinian Abu Muammar brothers were abducted by Israeli commandos in Gaza, Hamas activated its own audacious raid. This time, the Islamists were in the driver's seat.

In the predawn darkness of June 25, eight Palestinian militants slithered through the tunnel. Wearing what passed for Israeli uniforms, they dragged a cache of weapons with them. By punching out the last clods of earth at about 5:30 AM, they were able to surface inside Israel under cover of darkness. They were right beside an IDF forward post.

Four Israeli soldiers were in a tank. Several others manned a seventy-five-foot-high observation tower. An unmanned armored personnel carrier had been deliberately parked off to one side as a decoy in the event of such an attack.

Emerging from the tunnel to the rear of the Israeli tank, the Palestinians silently split into three teams. Then, guns blazing, two of them tried to storm the observation tower. Two others attacked the decoy armored personnel carrier, and the last four went for the tank with hand grenades, while militia units operating from the Gaza side of the border fence opened up with anti-tank fire and hand weapons.[2]

Two Israeli soldiers were killed and a third was wounded when the hand grenades exploded inside the tank. A fourth member of the crew, nineteen-year-old Corporal Gilad Shalit, was captured.[3] Two of the Palestinians were killed by Israeli fire. But the rest quickly started manuevering Shalit toward the border fence. During the assault on the tank, the corporal had been wounded in the left shoulder and hand, but he was able to walk to where the

Palestinians used explosives to blow a hole in the fence. They then melted back into Gaza.[4] They had been in Israel for precisely six minutes.

By the cruel calculus of conflict, Shalit was doubly burdened. Quite apart from his wounds and the shock of the attack and his capture, he had just become the Palestinians' first prisoner of war in more than a decade. Israel, at the time, held more than nine thousand Palestinians in its jails. Shalit was a prize bargaining chip and Hamas was ready to trade.[5]

Israelis were horrified, even outraged. Senior officials warned there would be no forgiveness unless Shalit was safely returned. By the time Israel was done with it, the new Hamas government would cease to exist, they threatened.[6]

From the Palestinian perspective, this Israeli response was quite hysterical. If Israelis were to believe that a military and diplomatic onslaught was a justifiable response to the capture of a single Israeli soldier, what kind of Palestinian response was warranted by Israel's imprisonment of thousands of Palestinians?

Israeli anger was stoked even more by the grim satisfaction the Palestinians—and Hamas in particular—took from the abduction of Shalit.

While Hamas had been holding its fire through the last sixteen months, Israeli analysts had accused it of taking advantage of the cease-fire to stockpile more and better-quality rockets. That may have been so. But when Hamas had sprung back into action, it was with a daring display of all the military finesse that most presumed to be the exclusive preserve of the "invincible"[7] Israeli security forces. Palestinians knew they could not redress the imbalance of military power. But Hamas celebrated this stunning foray into Israel as a substantial tweaking of the balance of fear.

Khalid Mishal went underground in the immediate aftermath of Shalit's capture. Senior Israeli officials repeatedly named him as the mastermind behind the operation, prompting claims within Hamas that Israel was attempting to create the pretext for another attempt on Mishal's life. "Indeed, we have received threats to liquidate Brother Khalid, and we take that very seriously," declared the movement's representative in Beirut, Osama Hamdan.[8] Mishal later pronounced himself proud to be "a bone in the enemy's throat."[9]

Hamas officials, in Gaza, Damascus, and Beirut, worked hard to convince the world that only the clandestine leadership of the movement's military wing, the Qassam Brigade, had prior knowledge of the mission. That defied belief. The brains capable of attending to the meticulous planning and execution of Shalit's abduction could not have ignored the diplomatic and political sensitivities of the time. The elected Hamas government was fighting for survival against a U.S.-led campaign to deprive it of oxygen. At the same time it was engaged in a faltering dialogue with Abbas's Fatah, which might have led to a respite for all the Palestinian factions with the establishment of a government of national unity.

In the fog of these wars, it was difficult to be certain about who was lying. Was it the Islamist spokesmen, who insisted that members of the elected Hamas government had no prior knowledge of the mission, because those officials needed to be distanced from it? Or was it the Israeli officials briefing reporters on Mishal's central planning role, simply because any excuse to go after Mishal was a good excuse? "Khalid Mishal, as someone who is oversee-ing, actually commanding the terror acts, is definitely a target [for assassina-tion]," Israeli justice minister Haim Ramon warned.[10]

The thrust of the Israeli argument, which was amplified by Fatah, was that Mishal had hijacked the Gaza-based government to his own demonic ends. But the artistry of leadership in Hamas was more complex than that. Mishal certainly was the movement's supreme leader, but its deep-rooted system of *shura*, or consensus consultation, made it difficult for him to unilaterally hi-jack the Palestinian government.

Far more likely, as the man who knew what all elements of the movement were doing at any given time, Mishal was sending multiple messages. One was about buying time, and it was directed to Fatah. In reigniting the conflict with Israel so spectacularly, Hamas was pushing for the interfactional brawl to be put on a back burner. At the same time, Mishal was articulating for local and foreign consumption articles of faith that were well understood and ac-cepted within Hamas—this was a movement that could "do" government and "do" resistance. More important, it could do both better than Fatah could, and it could do both *without* Fatah.

At first, Hamas demanded the release of five hundred Palestinian women and minors from Israeli detention in exchange for Corporal Shalit. But then the movement insisted on the release of one thousand Palestinian prisoners as the price of freedom for the Israeli soldier who, they had confirmed to the world, was still alive.

After four days, during which Hamas refused to buckle to threats and de-mands, Israel retaliated with a vengeance. In an operation code-named Sum-mer Rain, it raided Palestinian communities in the West Bank, snatching sixty-four Hamas officials—including eight cabinet ministers and twenty members of the newly elected parliament. As Israeli tanks and ground troops powered into Gaza, airstrikes knocked out the main Gaza power station, several bridges, and a series of government buildings, including Hamas prime minister Ismail Haniyah's office and the Palestinian Ministry of Foreign Affairs.

In a stab at Syria for harboring Khalid Mishal, four Israeli fighter aircraft penetrated Syrian airspace, drawing ground fire as they buzzed President Bashar Assad's summer palace, on the Mediterranean coast, near the ancient port city of Latakia.[11]

A full two weeks elapsed after the capture of Shalit before Mishal re-emerged. The setting was a press conference in Damascus, where his aides so ratcheted up their customarily intense security procedures that they felt obliged to apologize to those attending. Mishal capitalized on the opportunity provided by the Shalit drama to launch a propaganda campaign boasting of Hamas's success.

"The world has panicked and has been flabbergasted because an Israeli soldier was 'abducted,' as they say," a defiant Mishal told reporters.[12] "We say he was captured in a clean military operation. They speak about [one] soldier and we have 10,000 who are prisoners with them. They claim that 200,000 Israelis around the Gaza Strip are threatened by the simple and primitive missiles of the Palestinian heroes. We have almost four million Palestinians who are captives, besieged and threatened, in one big jail in the Gaza Strip and the West Bank."

Mishal argued that the "heroic operation" had been intended to dispel the new Israeli prime minister Ehud Olmert's illusion that Palestinians would capitulate. "Our people in Gaza say that in order to protect our dignity, and for the sake of our sons and daughters and the 10,000 in enemy jails, we'll not hand over the soldier except in exchange for Palestinian prisoners," he said, making clear there would be no stepping back. "They say that [a prisoner] exchange is a must."

Almost daring the Israeli leadership, Mishal warned that Israel's campaign "to break our will" would not succeed. "I say that you are liars," he charged, dismissing Israeli claims that Israel would work with a "moderate" Palestinian leadership. "Take a shortcut," Mishal urged—the whole crisis could be ended if Israel recognized the rights of Palestinians.

And so the summer continued, with the kind of Middle East madness that passed for normal in the region. As if the inexperienced new Israeli government did not have enough on its plate, Israel opted to invade Lebanon on July 12, 2006, after Hezbollah, an ally of Hamas, had mounted its own daring cross-border incursion on Israel's northern flank.

Hezbollah's capture of two Israeli soldiers drove the Israeli leadership to levels of anger that seemed to cloud their decision making. They unleashed the full force of Israel's military machine in merciless attacks on southern Lebanon and major infrastructure across Lebanon. But when the shooting stopped, Corporal Shalit remained a prisoner, as did the two Israelis taken by Hezbollah. And rockets still flew out of Gaza.

Under near-constant Israeli gunfire, it was virtually impossible for the Palestinian leadership to deal with the immediate internal political challenge: the shape of a unity government. Hamas and Fatah had finally been edging toward common ground, but the interfactional diplomacy evaporated in the face of Israel's ongoing attacks on Gaza, which coincided with the disastrous, month-long war in Lebanon, in turn leaving Israeli prime minister Olmert fighting for his own political survival.

Palestinian Authority president Mahmoud Abbas was also proving ineffectual in his stop-start efforts to establish himself as a genuine leader of his people, as opposed to merely being a factional leader driven by an overweening sense of entitlement. In a bid to pressure Hamas to play by his rules, he threatened to hold a referendum on a peace plan drafted by a group of cross-factional leaders among Palestinian prisoners held in Israeli jails—and then he balked. He warned that he would call new elections, but this came to nothing. And his orders for the Hamas government to disband the Executive Force provoked a defiant Hamas announcement that, actually, it was planning to increase the size of the new force. It was already being deployed in the streets of Gaza.

Constantly at war with Abbas and Fatah, Hamas in government initially tended to perform as the opposition it had expected to be. Besieged by the world and inexperienced in managing the day-to-day burden of a bankrupt government, it was also hostage to its own interminable processes of internal consultation, which dictated that any policy shift would be more gradual than what crisis management demanded. For all its strength and rhetoric, Hamas was struggling to capitalize on Fatah's weakness.

Under American pressure, Fatah closed ranks against any power-sharing deal with Hamas. At various meetings of envoys to the Middle East Quartet—a body that comprised representatives of the United States, the European Union, Russia, and the United Nations, and was intended to coordinate diplomatic efforts to resolve the crisis—Washington's message was that Hamas must be kept isolated. "We were told that the U.S. was against any 'blurring' of the lines dividing Hamas from those Palestinian political forces committed to the two-state solution," Alvaro de Soto, the UN envoy to the Quartet, re-called later.[13]

In Gaza the Americans' isolation tactic was wholly embraced by the Fatah strongman Mohammad Dahlan, who warned that he would rough up and humiliate any Fatah members tempted to help Hamas by joining a unity government. Unaware that he was speaking within earshot of an open micro-phone during a visit to a Gaza radio station in June, Dahlan suggested that it was he who was masterminding a campaign of incitement and disruption in Gaza. "The march will go on and if our brothers [in Fatah] seek to stop it, they'll be roughed up," he threatened.[14] Boasting that he had learned from Yasser Arafat that "the rod" was the most effective means of political persua-sion, he made quite clear what he thought of Hamas: "I told [Hamas] that they would eat shit if they recognized Israel and would eat shit if they didn't recognize Israel. They would eat shit if they recognized the Arab [govern-ments' Beirut peace] initiative and they would eat shit if they did not."[15]

Dahlan vowed to hunt Hamas through to the end of its four-year term in government as he alluded to his own role in creating the lawlessness on the streets. "I just deploy two Jeeps and people would say Gaza is on fire," he bragged.

There was no real need to signpost the way to Gaza. Israeli citizens were not allowed to go there; Gazans for the most part were not allowed to leave; and the Israeli military used high-resolution maps to find their own way around in the dark. But for the keen-eyed, a distance marker near the Israeli port city of Ashkelon—or Al-Majdal, as Palestinians knew it—indicated that Gaza was another fifteen miles to the south.

Sanctions had forced a halt to diplomatic traffic to Gaza and, in the face of rising violence and fears of abduction, foreign journalists and aid workers were increasingly reluctant to make the trek. For those who did, the taxi ride from central Jerusalem ended in a windswept wasteland, where they were let out in the forecourt of the otherworldly $35 million Erez Terminal.

On the Israeli side, Erez had the look of a modern airport complex: soar-ing glass and polished aluminum finishes. Young Israeli passport-control officers—sometimes an ebony-skinned Ethiopian or maybe a straw-blond Russian émigré—manned discreetly fortified booths that maintained the sense of this being a conventional transit facility.

But these officers were a last point of human contact on the Israeli side. At the press of a button, a security officer activated a door that opened into a world of soulless science fiction. Here were narrow interconnected voids of steel mesh and blank concrete. Monitored by a network of unseen cameras and guided by instructions from a disembodied and distorted voice blaring from tinny loudspeakers, travelers were directed through cages and turnstiles, sliding blast doors and metal detectors. It had the ambience of a state-of-the-art abattoir.

When the last steel door slid open, travelers were almost in Gaza. Here they might chance upon the odd northbound traveler, waiting to enter Israel through an adjacent, parallel channel that was even more sophisticated.

On exiting the steel door, travelers found themselves at the mouth of a caged tunnel, perhaps three hundred yards long, that doglegged over dunes and drains, finally opening onto a bleak landscape where many buildings had been demolished and trees uprooted. Occasionally there was a Palestinian official waiting to check travelers' documents. Taxi drivers who hoped to bag a fare risked being pushed back by warning gunfire from the Israeli side if they dared to drive too close to the tunnel's exit.

If it was tough traveling from Israel to Gaza, the journey in the other direction was far more difficult. Anyone attempting to enter Israel would first be processed through an electronic body scanner, which generated a holographic image said to be so sensitive that even a tissue in a traveler's pocket could be checked. And yet some still were ordered to strip to the waist for another examination by unseen eyes. One journalist carefully counted almost two dozen gates, scanners, doors, and turnstiles as he left Gaza.[16]

The new Erez terminal was another monument to the failed peace process. It was built around the time of disengagement, in the expectation that it would process thousands of travelers a day. Instead, only dozens, or maybe hundreds, were allowed through. Often the crossing was shut for security reasons. The area to the immediate south was prime Palestinian rocket-launching territory, and often enough the terminal came under direct attack. Israel had logged nine major attacks over the years, including a female suicide bomber who had killed four Israeli soldiers in 2004.

Fifteen minutes south of the crossing, the main road tumbled into the dusty maze of Gaza City, where the Mediterranean beaches were a rare but limited escape from siege and war.

At the end of August 2006, late on a hot, humid day, there were colorful umbrellas, flags in the breeze, and a lifeguard's shrill whistle beckoning from the city's main beach. School holidays were almost done, and small boys squealed in delight as they darted away from family picnics and into the surf.

Aloof from the games on the sand, two young men stood out. One, bronzed and bare chested, reined in a prancing horse. The other sipped a minted lemonade and pulled deeply on a narghile, or water pipe, which enveloped him in clouds of apple-scented tobacco smoke. In the fading light, fishing boats and paddleboards hugged the curved breakwater as they darkened to silhouettes against the sun. A group tried to coax a reluctant donkey into the water as children raced to meet incoming fishermen.

It looked like a postcard, but this was Gaza City seven months after its people had, in the eyes of the world, elected the wrong government. It was six months into their collective punishment for refusing to turn on Hamas, as Israel, Fatah, and the U.S.-led Quartet had anticipated. It was also a little over two months since the explosion that killed so many members of the Ghalia family at another beach farther north and closer to the Israeli shelling from the border. Small crowds could usually be found the length of Gaza's beaches. But the fate of the Ghalia family had forced most beachgoers back to the city beach, where they felt safer somehow, as though they were beyond the reach of weapons.

But there was no escape. Heads on the beach turned as an Israeli navy destroyer heaved into view, the thump of its turbines pulsing through the water as it carved a southerly course. A series of heavy thuds signalled incoming artillery exploding in the north. And overhead there were twin sounds—the lawnmower squawk of an unmanned surveillance drone and, much higher, a growling jet fighter.[17]

Even fishermen were not spared the hardship of life in Gaza. Casting in barren shallows, they were forced to stay well inside an Israeli navy blockade. Boats venturing into the deep risked being shot at. When half a dozen fishermen tied up in the afternoon, their catch was so miserably small that one of them was able to haul his own catch and that of two others to market on the back of his bicycle. After five hours netting in the shallows, another man had less than a bucketful of sardines, which he sold on the dockside for thirty shekels (about $8). It was the same story right across Gaza, with economic privation spread deeply and evenly.

Gazans of a certain age could remember a time in the 1950s and 1960s when women wore bikinis on the city beachfront. Now, as the impact of the Islamic regime was felt, there was not even a one-piece swimsuit to be seen.

Some women moved their plastic chairs to the water's edge—revealing naked toes. On a day of 104°F heat, there was great hilarity when a few dared to plunge in, dressed head to foot in swaths of black cloth that ballooned on all sides as foam washed over them. Some also revealed their hands and the pale, skinny reminders on their bare fingers of wedding bands that they had sold during furtive visits to the gold market, either to feed their families or to buy clothes and books for children about to start the new school year.

Plying their trade against the stone walls of the seventh-century Great Omari Mosque, Gaza's gold traders had grown idle. Five months earlier, when families first began to feel the pinch of financial cutbacks, some of the twenty or so dealers were buying as much as twenty-four pounds of gold in a single day.

Traditionally, Arab women held as much solid gold as they could afford, keeping it in reserve to sell down in bad times. Summer was a time for weddings, and there was much excitement when young brides bought their first gold. But when women came to the market to sell their wedding rings, traders knew that another family had reached the end. "I can tell from the numbness in their faces that there was a battle at home about when to sell the gold, about how much they would lose and how the money I pay them will be spent immediately," the dealer Hamdi Basal explained. "There are no gold bars left in Gaza . . . just a few more wedding rings."[18]

For some in Gaza, commercial suffocation came in a flash. At Beit Hanoun, a few miles north of the city, sixty-five-year-old Mohammad Hussein sat amidst a dusty pile of rubble. He had spent almost thirty years as a resistance agnostic, he said. But now he was committed to Hamas.

The new fire in his belly was the result of an Israeli airstrike that had pulverized a four-story building in which his children and their families lived, and from which he had run one of the bigger supermarkets in the neighborhood.

"I worked for twenty-two years in Saudi Arabia for the money to build it. The Israelis called at one o'clock in the morning on my son Hussein's mobile, saying everyone must be out of the building in fifteen minutes. 'You must leave immediately,' they told him." The son had asked for proof that the call was genuine. "The voice told him to go outside, to look up and he would see the F-16 circling," the old man said. Although two missiles hit the house minutes later, much of it still remained standing. Neighbors rushed in to help the family move their belongings from the building. "But the Israelis called again," Hussein said. "They said to get people away, because there will be another strike. Six minutes later, two more missiles knocked the rest of the building down."[19]

On a rise overlooking the flat blue of the Mediterranean, north of Gaza City, a more palatial residence was still standing.

This was the home of Dr. Nabil Shaath, foreign minister in the former

Fatah-led government. Here the swimming pool, the manicured gardens, and the Asian household staff were seen by ordinary Palestinians as proof of the rampant corruption that had caused voters to turn against Fatah.

A pistol-packing bodyguard hovered as Shaath canvassed some of his party's options as it struggled to regain its political footing. "We've made many mistakes," he began, in what might have been a declaration of contrition. Shaath acknowledged that the loss of face at the January election had initially enraged many in Fatah. "So we refused to be a part of a Hamas government," he said. "But they need partners. Maybe we can help them now."

As a former minister, Shaath acknowledged but denied allegations that Fatah was a driving force behind U.S.-Israeli pressure to bring down Hamas. "Not true," he insisted, seemingly of two minds about which was the better side to be on.

"Hamas doesn't suffer one bit—it gets funds from Iran and the Arab world, and they make sure that their own people don't suffer," he observed. Complaining that international sanctions and Israel's arrest of Hamas leaders gave the Islamists a plausible excuse for their failure in government, he added, "The U.S. dictated that we had to have elections, but it can't dictate the outcome. That's not how democracy works."

By now, most shops were remaining closed all day. Smoldering garbage was piling up in the streets. Traffic steadily thinned as fewer Palestinians could afford to fill their cars with gas. Some ran their vehicles on cooking oil. By late 2006, men and women wept as they stood in ATM queues, waiting to withdraw the last funds from their bank accounts. Most of the government's 160,000 employees had received just two paychecks since the election at the start of the year. The Gazan economy was being crushed.

Since the West had cut funding, as many as 170,000 families were without an income, and there was little else to prime the local economy. About 90 percent of Gazans lived below the poverty line; as many as 85 percent were said to be jobless, and more than one million individuals had come to depend on United Nations agencies for their household supplies of oil, flour, beans, rice, sugar, and milk. It was a measure of the intractable nature of the conflict that the United Nations Relief and Works Agency was in its fifty-sixth year of caring for Palestinians who first became refugees when the state of Israel was established in 1948.

Government workers who had gone for months without pay took to staging wildcat protests, shutting down whole sections of Gaza City with stone throwing and gunfire. The Israeli airstrikes on Gaza's main power station had reduced it to a few erratic hours of power each day. Housewives complained they could no longer save by cooking in bulk because they could not rely on refrigeration. No power also meant no domestic pumps, which meant no water either. But so long as the Hamas government existed and Gilad Shalit remained a prisoner, Israel was not going to wind back the pressure.

As the summer of 2006 trailed into autumn, the increasingly bitter contest between Islamists and political secularists was developing a dynamic that mirrored all the intractable shortcomings of the Palestinian-Israeli struggle. In the first Intifada, which had erupted almost twenty years earlier, Hamas and Fatah could agree to quarantine schools from the struggle. Now their gunmen fought running battles in the corridors of Gaza's hospitals. After decades of nurturing the flame of Palestinian national unity under the weight of a foreign occupation, Palestinians now had their own sectarian civil war.

Gunmen from both sides, usually in the garb of the respective security services, clashed at street corners or mounted tit-for-tat attacks on buildings and institutions associated with "the enemy." The enemy had become Fatah or Hamas more often than it was the Israelis. Two people died when Hamas launched a rocket attack on the Rafah headquarters of Abbas's Preventive Security Service (PSS). Fatah loyalists retaliated in Ramallah, setting fire to a PA cabinet building seen as a Hamas base, and then tried to block the firemen racing to the blaze. Dr. Shaath lost his shiny green BMW to carjackers who struck in broad daylight. And in his efforts to travel to the parliament in Gaza City, Hamas's prime minister Ismail Haniyah was thwarted by protesters who mobbed his convoy.

As the violence escalated, the numbers killed or wounded and the seniority of those targeted on both sides ratcheted up. A senior PSS man in Jabaliyah was dragged from his home and executed. Another died when a hand grenade was dropped into the elevator taking him up to his office at the military intelligence headquarters. Gunmen opened fire on Wasfi Kabha, Hamas's minister for prisoners' affairs, as he drove through Ramallah. A security officer in Gaza was abducted; three children of one of his Fatah-aligned colleagues were murdered.

By the end of the year, the two factions were on a semiconstant war footing. Dozens were wounded in daily clashes as the black-market price for weapons went through the ceiling. An M16 that cost $5,400 in 2005 sold for more than $13,000 in 2006. Bullets sold at a dollar apiece.[20]

There were ructions at the Rafah crossing on the Gazan-Egyptian border when Israeli and Fatah-aligned security services joined forces to block Prime

Minister Haniyah's return from overseas, with more than $35 million stashed in his luggage. As Hamas gunmen rushed to Rafah to defend Haniyah, a hole was blown in the border wall and eighteen people were wounded in a shoot-out that paralyzed the crossing terminal. The injured included one of Haniyah's sons and a prime ministerial adviser.

As the first year of Hamas's term in office neared its close, it seemed that Khalid Mishal no longer felt it necessary to maintain even a veneer of civility for President Abbas. "Have you not yet grasped the fact that he counts for nothing?" Mishal snapped at an Italian reporter who had mentioned that Rome supported Abbas. "Nothing when he was Arafat's second-in-command and nothing when he was prime minister in 2003."[21]

With that sort of fallout at leadership level and in the streets, Gazans had taken to cowering in their homes, ordering their children to sit in their baths or to play in concrete stairwells, in the hope that they could dodge the bullets.

23

Everything Is Not as It Seems

When the battle-scarred British secret service agent Alastair Crooke arrived in Beirut in late 2004, the Lebanese capital was on an upswing. Striking modern architecture sat cheek by jowl with jewels from its Ottoman and French-mandate past, many of which were still bruised and broken from the civil war that raged until 1990. But now designer stores fought with international hotel chains for space downtown. The Corniche again was the place to be seen in the late afternoon, and the cafés and bars of Achrafiya pumped into the night. Beirut's reputation as a crossroads for intellectuals in the Arab world had been restored, even against the background of rising Islamist sentiment and the emerging dominance of Hezbollah in Lebanese affairs.

It seemed like a good fit for the fifty-eight-year-old Crooke. Beirut nursed old war wounds but looked ahead, and Crooke needed somewhere to start the rest of his life. The abrupt halt to Crooke's career in British intelligence and European diplomacy had left him feeling the future had vanished.[1]

He had spent thirty years with Britain's Secret Intelligence Service, more commonly known as MI6. He had years of experience in Northern Ireland, South Africa, Namibia, Afghanistan, Cambodia, and Colombia. He had been a hostage negotiator; he had pursued cease-fires; and his last, fateful posting had been as a special adviser to the European Union in the Middle East. Northern Ireland had shaped Crooke's opinions on the link between security and politics. Afghanistan had given him an insider's appreciation of the significant differences between Islamist groups.

On arriving in Jerusalem in 1997, he had viewed Hamas less as a terrorist organization and more as what he called a "political insurgency." In Gaza and the West Bank, Crooke often went by local taxi, alone and unarmed, to meet-ings with Sheikh Yassin and senior figures in Hamas and the other Palestin-ian militias. He attempted to engage them in the art of politics as a tactic that one day might supplant raw resistance. He wanted to get past simplistic de-bates about good and evil, to go beyond isolation and demonization, to en-gage Islam on behalf of Europe. He was fired when a Palestinian cease-fire he had encouraged collapsed in 2003. "I was told talking to groups like Hamas was not the way to fight the war on terror," he explained.[2]

But Crooke was not a man to give up easily. Bounced out of official diplo-macy, he set up a parallel channel, establishing the independent Conflicts Forum in Lebanon. He had contacts from Beirut to Pakistan, and he wanted to challenge what he saw as Western misconceptions and misrepresentations of Islamist movements. He still hoped to bridge the widening gulf between Islam and the West.

Crooke set up his new venture on Lebanon's Green Line—the unkempt strip that had divided mainly Muslim West Beirut from the predominantly Christian East during fifteen cruel years of civil war. He found an old build-ing located next to the ruins of an abandoned snipers' post on a historic east-west demarcation. It seemed an appropriate location for what he had in mind.

Israel's invasion of Lebanon in the summer of 2006, and the reemergence of rivalries that had underpinned the old Lebanese conflict, knocked the shine off Beirut's multibillion-dollar recovery. But it drew Crooke and his Conflicts Forum to the heart of a regional showdown, in a way he could never have imagined just two years before.

Crooke prided himself on having no official contact with Washington, and he was reluctant even to acknowledge that thirty years as a British agent might have filled his Filofax with useful names and numbers. But on January 7, 2007, Crooke posted a report on the Conflicts Forum Web site that sug-gested he had eyes and ears at the most senior levels of the three arms of U.S. foreign policy—the White House, the Pentagon, and the State Department. The report, written in conjunction with a colleague, was carefully stitched together. Crooke had been told of an odd encounter a year before, involving a Palestinian business delegation to Washington shortly after the Palestinian elections in January 2006. The group had been received at the White House by the deputy national security advisor, Elliott Abrams.

Abrams was the president's policy point man on the Middle East. He had been dubbed the "democracy czar" when he was appointed in 2005,[3] but his background suggested he was more an "ends justify the means" kind of operator. Once billed as a "Reaganite villain," Abrams was seen in some quarters as an apologist for brutal dictators in El Salvador and Guatemala in the 1980s. He had pleaded guilty to lying to Congress in the Iran-Contra scandal.

The visiting Palestinian businessmen were taken aback when Abrams canvassed the need for the United States to provide guns, ammunition, and training to enable Mahmoud Abbas's Fatah forces to wrest control of the Occupied Territories from the elected government of Hamas. There had previously been indications of a campaign by Washington and Israel to "destabilize" Hamas, but it had been interpreted to mean bleeding the new government of funds—not armed revolt.[4]

Crooke's report on the Conflicts Forum Web site suggested that the Abrams strategy was already in play. The rising street violence in Gaza— which had been perceived as Fatah's frustration over its loss of power—was in fact deliberate and organized provocation. Moreover, it was being "seeded" by Elliott Abrams's push for a Palestinian civil war, Crooke reported.

Alastair Crooke's attribution of the word "coup" to Abrams in his January 7 Web post was the first time it had been used to seriously describe Washington's policy objective in the Occupied Territories. Previously it had been used more as a rhetorical flourish.

Crooke quoted anonymous administration officials said to be deeply troubled by the plan. He analyzed it in the context of regional anxieties. And he included an account of then defense secretary Donald Rumsfeld's objection to it all, and the reluctance of the Central Intelligence Agency even to having the plan parked on the CIA's docket.

President Bush, according to Crooke's sources, had warned Rumsfeld that the Palestinian brief was not within the purview of the Defense Department; it remained the responsibility of Condoleezza Rice, as part of the State Department's program for democracy in the Middle East.

Crooke's report was sensational. It put meat on the bones of regional theories that had, until then, been shot down as overblown anti-U.S. sentiment in paranoid diplomatic and news-media circles. But there was another development that strengthened the hands of those looking for proof that the United States was actively fomenting an insurrection against the elected government of the Occupied Territories. Forty-eight hours before Crooke posted his extraordinary report on the Conflicts Forum Web site, it emerged that the U.S. administration was seeking congressional approval for a security allocation of $86.4 million for the coffers of the Fatah leader and Palestinian Authority president, Mahmoud Abbas.[5] Compared with Washington's past aid offerings to the Palestinians, this was a staggering amount of money.

Two weeks elapsed between Crooke's first posting and an interview he gave to Al-Jazeera, where he acknowledged for the first time that he had relied on a leaked document. "Actually, it was a series of documents," he revealed later.[6] Describing two sets of papers he had received, he explained that one had laid out U.S.-backed deals to boost Abbas's security forces while another laid the ground for Abbas to simply dismiss the Hamas government later in the year. "This wasn't just speculation on my part, you know."

In some quarters, the effect of Crooke's report was to force a reappraisal of recent action and comment by U.S. officials. What was the real point of American and European officials inspecting a Jordan base at which Fatah loyalists were in training in the previous month?[7] Was the use of an old crisis cliché—"dismantle the infrastructure of terrorism"—in documentation on the $86.4 million security allocation for Abbas just a coded reference to Hamas?

Likewise, a rare interview given back in November to the Hebrew-language daily *Yedioth Ahronoth* by the publicity-shy Lieutenant-General Keith Dayton, who was Washington's security coordinator in the Middle East, seemed to warrant reexamination. Why had Dayton seemingly contradicted himself when, in acknowledging that he was beefing up Abbas's forces, he had insisted they were not being prepared for confrontation with Hamas? Yet, to justify his own program, the American general had argued that Iran, and possibly Syria, were funding and arming Hamas. "We must make sure that the moderate forces will not be erased," he had said.[8]

Dayton's appointment as security coordinator between Israel and the Palestinians in November 2005 was a thankless challenge for a man with little history in the region. He had joined the U.S. military in 1970 but, apart from his leadership of the failed search for Saddam Hussein's weapons of mass destruction in the aftermath of the April 2003 fall of Baghdad, this was the fifty-six-year-old officer's first Middle East assignment. Formally, his brief was to ensure that both sides lived up to their various security commitments.

Alastair Crooke's analysis might have been dismissed as flawed or partisan lobbying had not other developments run in tandem. At the regular meetings of the Middle East Quartet, Washington's envoy was Assistant Secretary of State for Near Eastern Affairs David Welch, but at times Elliott Abrams also attended. The Peruvian diplomat who served as the UN envoy, Alvaro de Soto, often found himself under pressure from the Americans to fall into line with their preferred strategy. De Soto was shocked by what he described as Washington "clearly pushing" for confrontation between Fatah and Hamas, and he detailed his concerns in a report that was later leaked to the media.

De Soto was doubly taken aback when, during an envoys' meeting in Washington in late January 2007, the American envoy Welch twice referred with great enthusiasm to the deadly friction in Gaza. "I like this violence," the U.S. envoy told his colleagues. "It means that other Palestinians are resisting Hamas."[9]

As the tailor Assad Abu Dan roused his household, deep inside Jabaliyah refugee camp, the first rays of pale light turned dawn into day over the cinderblock warrens at the northern end of Gaza.

The eldest of Assad's seven boys, Mazen, stumbled bleary-eyed to the kitchen. The twenty-one-year-old was a member of the Executive Force, Hamas's controversial new security arm. His brothers Ahmad, eighteen, and Mohammad, seventeen—both still students—soon joined him for a breakfast of bread and tea. The boy's uncle, Ismail, had stayed with them overnight. It was January 26, 2007, and they were up early to go to a nearby cemetery, to build a tombstone on the grave of the boys' recently deceased grandmother.[10]

Piling tools and materials into Ismail's small van, they set out. But as they slowed at an intersection near the entrance to the graveyard, they were set upon by masked gunmen, who forced Ismail to bring the van to a sliding halt by shooting out all four tires. Ismail and the boys were ordered to get out and then bundled into a fleet of pickups and whisked away.

Left behind, Abu Dan was shattered. As he sat in the van, wondering what to do next, another vehicle pulled up alongside. Its front passenger seat was filled with the angry bulk of a man he recognized. It was Samih Al-Madhun, a local enforcer who was a senior officer in the Preventive Security Service run by the Fatah heavy Mohammad Dahlan. Al-Madhun also doubled as a much-feared commander in the Al-Aqsa Martyrs Brigade, a militia that sprang from the ranks of Fatah during the second Intifada. He was one of the most powerful figures in the northern end of the Gaza Strip.

It was a bad day for the family to honor the boys' grandmother. They had planned their mission during a relative lull in the violence some weeks earlier, but in the last twenty-four hours the Strip had become a cauldron, with renewed clashes in Gaza City and here at the northern end. Nineteen people, eight of whom were civilian bystanders, had died. More than seventy had been injured.

The road where the family's van came to a halt was a factional flashpoint.

The previous day, an Executive Force truck had been blown up nearby, with two Hamas fighters dying and six others wounded. Overnight, Hamas had mounted retaliatory attacks on the homes of Fatah fighters, for which the thirty-two-year-old Al-Madhun now wanted his revenge. Riled by the latest clashes, he had been on local radio, reiterating the grim threats he had been issuing since unidentified gunmen had tried to kill him some weeks earlier.

In nearby Beit Lahiya, he had made a fortress of the apartment block he shared with members of his extended family. Dozens of gunmen were stationed on the rooftop terrace. Approach roads were barricaded with piles of cement blocks and mounds of earth. Now, when Al-Madhun wanted prisoners, Abu Dan and his family had chanced to be in the wrong place at the wrong time.

Abu Dan was taken to the Al-Madhun fortress, where he was marched up five flights of concrete steps to the top floor, which served as a makeshift torture chamber. About a dozen blindfolded prisoners, including his sons and his brother-in-law, were being forced to squat for long periods, at the same time as they were struck with batons and lengths of water pipe.[11] Occasionally, they were ordered to chant banal slogans in praise of local Fatah leaders—and Mohammad Dahlan in particular.

Abu Dan's torture was to be given no blindfold. He was forced to witness the abuse of his family. They were kicked and stamped upon; they were abused for their religious devotion and forced to mimic the sounds of animals—dogs, cats, and donkeys. One of Al-Madhun's men fired several shots at close range into twenty-one-year-old Mazen's lower legs.

Nearby, they could hear Samih Al-Madhun barking into his mobile phone. The Jabaliyah home of another Fatah militia commander was coming under heavy gunfire from Hamas. Al-Madhun warned that if anything untoward befell his colleague, he would shoot his captives and throw their bodies from the sixth-floor terrace.

All seemed lost. But then help came from two quarters—one family, the other factional.

When Abu Dan, his boys, and their uncle failed to return from the cemetery, others in the family had alerted Hamas. A posse was dispatched. But the even more powerful intervening force was a wild card. Samih Al-Madhun's sister was married to a cousin of Abu Dan. Suddenly she was on the phone, giving Al-Madhun a fierce tongue-lashing.

Al-Madhun was trapped. He was ready to fight Hamas, but not his sister. He agreed to separate the Abu Dan group from the other prisoners, and their abuse came to an abrupt end. At about the same time another shaky Hamas-

Fatah cease-fire came into force, requiring an exchange of prisoners. In return for the release of eighteen of its men held by Hamas, Fatah released twenty Hamas hostages, including the three boys, their father, and their uncle.

The Abu Dan group was abducted during a week when Hamas should have been celebrating the first anniversary of its stunning election victory. Instead, the level of violence was growing at an alarming rate—in the days before this abduction, more than thirty Palestinians had been killed at the hands of other Palestinians. A preacher who had criticized the killers of a Fatah security chief and seven of his bodyguards died later in a drive-by shooting as he arrived home from the mosque. The Islamic University had come under attack by Fatah forces, which set fire to three buildings. Hamas forces retaliated, overrunning three Fatah-controlled police posts in the north of Gaza.

After the cease-fire had been in place for just forty-eight hours, fierce fighting broke out at the Kerem Shalom border crossing, near where Hamas had tunneled into Israel to capture the Israeli corporal Gilad Shalit. This new fighting was sparked by the arrival from Egypt of four trucks, which, Hamas had discovered, carried American-sponsored supplies of guns, including a batch of new M14 automatic rifles, and ammunition for the Abbas forces. Fatah officials protested, claiming the convoy carried only tents, generators, and medical supplies. As Hamas's Executive Force impounded all four vehicles, one of their commanders assured Fatah it could have the "tents and pills" in due course, but not the weapons.

It was not the first such shipment. Israel was always anxious that any weapons delivered into Palestinian hands would inevitably be turned on its own forces and citizens. But at the end of December 2006, it had allowed a similar convoy from Egypt to deliver more than two thousand automatic rifles and two million bullets to the Fatah forces in Gaza. By some accounts, there had been three other such deliveries already.

Abbas's aides had tried to deny the December shipment. But they were undercut by Israeli officials who confirmed it to reporters. Previously Israel had remained silent about its aid to Abbas, on the grounds that strategically it needed to avoid diminishing him in the eyes of Palestinians, who would be furious to find their leader hand in glove with the enemy. But the strategy had changed. Information on the weapons' delivery was the sort of good news Palestinians needed to hear about their president. An Israeli spokesman had declared publicly that the arms were to reinforce Abbas against "the forces of darkness."[12]

The Palestinian president was torn. Within the Middle East Quartet, some saw him as a decent enough man who found it difficult to stand apart from a Fatah clique that encircled his office and a Washington team that drove it. During a dinner with Condoleezza Rice at his Muqata compound in Ramallah in October, nine months after the election of Hamas, Abbas had undertaken to call new elections as soon as possible, in a bid to dislodge Hamas through the same electoral process that had brought the Islamists to power.[13] But despite Rice urging him on, the Palestinian president did not have the power to call early elections, just as he did not have the power to sack the parliament.[14] Abbas's hands were tied.

Washington, however, kept up the pressure. The American consul general in Jerusalem, Jacob Walles, was dispatched to Ramallah. Armed with a sheet of talking points, which he inadvertently left behind, Walles reiterated Rice's warning: if Hamas refused to buckle to Washington's demands, the government would have to go.

Walles advised Abbas to strengthen his team with "credible figures" like Dahlan. Conscious of the deep anxiety within Fatah about a shortage of weapons and funds, Walles padded his offers of support with renewed assurances from the State Department. "If you act along these lines, we'll support you both materially and politically."[15]

Israeli intelligence analysts doubted that the expedient of more weapons could make the broken Fatah faction any more appealing to Palestinians. But they saw no alternative to bolstering Abbas. "If I have to choose between confrontation [between the Palestinian factions] and the dominance of Hamas, I choose confrontation," a senior Israeli defense official said.[16]

In mid-January, Abbas made a conciliatory gesture by traveling to Damascus to see Khalid Mishal. But the olive branch he carried had been made in the USA. The meeting was brittle, ending in deadlock after Abbas pointedly held out for recognition of the state of Israel as well as for new, early elections for the Palestinians.[17]

Dahlan, meantime, was stirring his own forces, issuing threats to Mishal and the entire Hamas leadership. Dahlan had moved into a pivotal position in Abbas's circle of power, where his uncompromising stance made him an attractive ally for the Americans. "If the leaders of Hamas think they are out of reach of our forces, they are wrong," Dahlan warned in a speech to a huge rally to mark the anniversary of the founding in 1965 of Fatah's Al-Asifa military wing.[18] When a Fatah security cordon moved in behind him, Dahlan waved them away, winning great applause as he bellowed, "Let Hamas shoot me!"[19]

In the year since the election, Egypt, Syria, Qatar, and Jordan had attempted to mediate between the factions, but with no lasting success. Now it was the turn of the regional heavyweight. Saudi Arabia managed simultaneously to be an ally of the United States, a cosmopolitan power broker by dint of its phenomenal oil wealth, and a closed society of Sunni Wahhabi fundamentalists. It was time to put its credibility on the line. Troubled by Muslim-on-Muslim bloodletting and the risk of being seen to have done nothing about it, Riyadh's King Abdullah opted to insert the Saudis' considerable diplomatic bulk between Washington and the squabbling Palestinians. He summoned the leadership of both Fatah and Hamas to the holy city of Mecca for a meeting on February 7.

Mahmoud Abbas, accustomed to saying yes to Washington, had great difficulty saying no to the Riyadh royals. There was a Saudi check for $1 billion in aid on the table and it was badly needed by both factions. To get their hands on it, they needed to reach a new agreement. Mishal held his nerve, and it was Abbas who blinked—so readily that the Israeli newspaper *Yedioth Ahronoth* headlined one of its subsequent reports on the summit, HAMAS WON THE JACKPOT.[20]

When Abbas returned to the Occupied Territories, his aides complained that he had been bullied by the Saudis. In a deal that was less advantageous to Fatah than any of the previous unity packages offered by Hamas, the Islamists' Ismail Haniyah would remain prime minister. The Executive Force, which Abbas had denounced as "murderers and gangsters," would be folded into Abbas's security forces, prompting wry speculation that the Hamas fighters would then become eligible for American paychecks.

Hamas agreed to shed control of key portfolios—including the interior, foreign, and finance ministries. The Islamists would be allowed to select an "independent" nominee for the bitterly contested interior ministry, but Abbas was given a right to vet Hamas's choice.

On the crucial Israeli and American demand that Hamas "abide" by earlier agreements, including Oslo, the language of the Mecca Accord required the new government merely to "respect" these past pacts. The accord called for an end to Palestinian-on-Palestinian violence, but neither the speeches nor the documentation made mention of Israel, the peace process, or a halt to resistance, including Palestinian rocket fire into Israel.

Abbas declared that Palestinians had arrived on the shores of peace, to which Mishal responded cheerfully, "We'll rebuild our Palestinian house on strong foundations." The deal created a unity government and presented real

possibilities that were welcomed in the Arab world and drew positive comments from Moscow and Paris—if not Washington. Hamas, with just nine of
the twenty-four ministries, would now manage the Palestinians' domestic
agenda, while Abbas and the Fatah-aligned or independent ministers would
deal with the international brief—in particular, negotiations with Israel and
the international community. Any agreement reached between Abbas and
Israel was to be put to a referendum of Palestinians, and Hamas acknowledged in advance that it would accept the outcome of such a vote.

Despite the policy gulf, Mecca had found an interfactional accommodation by which both might live. As explained by Mahmoud Abbas, ministers
of the new PA government would be obliged to honor the positions it took,
but their factions would not.[21]

For his part, Mishal explained that Hamas would retain its overarching
opposition to the state of Israel, but had accepted negotiations on a two-state
solution based on the 1967 borders. He acknowledged a pragmatic reposi-
tioning of his hard-line rhetoric. "Hamas is adopting a new political language," he said. "The Mecca agreement is a new political language [spoken
by] Hamas, and honoring the agreements is [also] a new language, because
there is a national need and we must speak a language appropriate to the
time."

Despite rejection by Israel and Washington, the unity government was
sworn in on Saturday, March 17, 2007. Abbas's circle had complained about
the president being jerked one way in Mecca, but at home he quickly demonstrated that he could be pulled the other way too. The day after the ministry
was sworn in, Abbas appointed his new national security adviser: Mohammad Dahlan, the man George W. Bush reputedly referred to as "our guy."[22]

If Abbas had searched the globe for an appointee who would most dis-
please Hamas, he could have found few more loathsome to the Islamists than
Dahlan, who, at age forty-six, was a confirmed prisoner of factional tribalism.
"I belong to Fatah and my country is Palestine—not Hamas," he said in an
interview three weeks after his appointment.[23] "It is my duty to defend the
country's interests . . . but I belong to Fatah and it is my duty to defend the
Fatah people. This is the way I understand my membership of Fatah."

As the head of Arafat's partisan Preventive Security Service in the mid-
1990s, it was Dahlan who led a heavy-handed crackdown on Hamas, rounding up activists by the thousand. Often they were held without trial. Sometimes
they were tortured. But as Islamists, the humiliation for which they always
held a grudge against Dahlan was the ritual shaving of their heads and
beards.

In giving Dahlan control of the security forces, Abbas revealed the flaw in the Mecca hoopla: the Saudis had failed to extract a workable agreement on the most burning issue in the fractured relationship between the factions. Abbas might have nodded yes to the Saudi king but, in handing the security brief to Dahlan, the president was shaking his head no to Hamas. Abbas had been a reluctant starter, but in his passive-aggressive way the president was spoiling for a fight.

The university-educated Dahlan was an elected member of the parliament. But his extraordinary influence in Gaza came in part from his control in the 1990s of the security apparatus, a force that he built from the ground up—under the tutelage of Yasser Arafat and with help from the CIA.[24] A second pillar of his power was his control of Fatah in Gaza. The Israelis had jailed him eleven times by the time he was twenty-five. They had deported him and nearly assassinated him. Abbas had twice appointed him to the PA ministry, but more recently Dahlan had come to be seen as a challenge to Abbas, who was almost thirty years his senior.

For months Dahlan had been using Fatah loyalists to goad Hamas—killing its fighters or capturing and abusing them. Now Abbas had put the fifty-thousand-plus men of his security services at Dahlan's disposal. Within Fatah, some of Dahlan's colleagues were disturbed by his "one-man show" obsessiveness. Others were troubled by the extent of the "violations" he tolerated by his followers as they went after Hamas.

Confronted in the recent past by Khalid Mishal's claim that he was a provocateur bent on *fitna*, or civil war, Dahlan responded with derision, rather than a clear-cut denial. "What coup are they talking about?" he demanded. "Is there a government we can rebel against?"[25]

In the eyes of some Palestinians, Dahlan had been given the kiss of death by President Bush when they had met at a Middle East summit in Aqaba, Jordan, in 2003. In response to a request from Bush, Dahlan had just begun to explain an aspect of security in the Occupied Territories. "Don't say any more," the president said, stopping Dahlan in his tracks. "All I wanted was to look into your eyes, and I trust you. It's exactly the way I trusted Mr. [Ariel] Sharon."[26]

It was the last thing Palestinians wanted to hear.

In Amman, no newspaper was too small to escape the net of state censorship. With a circulation of sixteen thousand copies and a small staff, Fahd Al-Rimawi's Arabic-language weekly, *Al-Majd*, indeed was small. But Al-Rimawi was an editor who knew a big story when he saw one. And, as a publisher under a repressive regime, he knew from his own bitter experience the lengths to which the Amman authorities would go to bully an editor with a big story. In April 2007, he had chanced upon an explosive document setting out a detailed plan to topple Hamas. He knew it would pit him against the authorities once again. But this was a story he planned to run.

The log of Al-Rimawi's personal run-ins with the law was a testament to courageous editing. At different times, Al-Rimawi had been forced to halt publication. He had been jailed because he had written, or was set to publish, reports that were deemed to have insulted the dignity of the king, or to have criticized the national intelligence agency, or to have offended Jordan's regional neighbors.

In 2002, Al-Rimawi was threatened with prosecution if he published reports of a rare corruption trial then being conducted under a regime-imposed media blackout. It was the trial of Samih Batikhi, formerly the all-powerful Jordanian intelligence chief from the period when Israel's Mossad had attempted to assassinate Khalid Mishal.

In 2004, Al-Rimawi's weekly made subversive use of *Plan of Attack*, a book on the Iraq war by Bob Woodward of the *Washington Post*, to support his editorial criticism of neighboring Saudi Arabia's relationship with Washington. When this was published, Al-Rimawi himself was visiting his son in America. But on his return to Amman, he was arrested as he stepped from an aircraft at Queen Alia Airport. He was jailed and his publisher's license suspended until he agreed to print an editorial that might mollify the ever-sensitive Saudis, who, after the U.S.-led invasion of Iraq in 2003, had filled the breach as Jordan's only supplier of oil.

The printing of *Al-Majd* was contracted out to a major Amman publishing house, the Jordan Press Foundation, on the capital's Queen Ranya Al-Abdullah Street. The weekly print run was too small and Al-Rimawi too poor to own his own presses. As required under the censorship regime, Al-Rimawi informed the authorities of the stories he had prepared for his April 30, 2007, edition, including his account of the plan to topple Hamas, which was scheduled to go to the presses overnight on April 29.

The page plates were ready and the presses set to roll when an agent of the General Intelligence Department phoned the pressroom, yelling that the presses were not to be started. Al-Rimawi was ordered to remove the Hamas lead story from the front page of the edition and to spike a second, much smaller item that he had placed on page two.

When Al-Rimawi refused, the security service threatened to ban the whole edition. The haggling went on for hours. When Al-Rimawi demanded an explanation, the reason proffered by the agents was an unintended compliment to his journalism. It was not that he was wrong; it was that too many of his reports were based on information from intelligence sources.

The editor held his ground. Getting nowhere, he tried to barter. If he pulled the small item on page two, reporting a visit by U.S. officials to military warehouses in the southern port city of Aqaba, might the agents allow him to keep his page-one splash? Apparently not.

They were getting nowhere. The GID men ordered the printers to remove the plates from the presses and confiscated them.

That might have been the end of the edition and the successful burial of Al-Rimawi's sensational page-one report were it not for the failure of the GID agents to grasp the wider possibilities of publishing in a modern era and, curiously, if it were not for the alertness of an anonymous Internet blogger on the other side of the world who signed himself simply as "Badger."

Badger's blog was called Missing Links, and the blogger himself was reluctant to reveal much of his biographical background. His blog featured a postcard image of two striped badgers from the Weirfield Wildlife Hospital in Lincoln, England, but information in the "about me" corner of the blog was scant. It appeared that Badger was an accountant who lived in Canada, but there was not much more. His cryptic mission statement was a one-line quote from the ancient Chinese philosopher Mencius: "I know words, and I nourish the great flowing spirit."

Badger was bilingual. His self-appointed task was to trawl Arabic news Web sites, translating into English a selection that he thought, according to a banner across the top of his spartan yet stylishly designed blog, would help "to fill in the gaps."[27] Given the effort that went into Missing Links, his readership numbers were disappointing. A dozen hits in a day was an average day.

But on May 2, 2007, when Badger uploaded his seven-page summary and English translation of Al-Rimawi's *Al-Majd* story, which the Jordanian authorities believed they had suppressed, it was the first substantive corroboration of the original Alastair Crooke report, which, since its publication in January, had gained little traction in the Western news media.

Badger's report was based on Al-Rimawi's Web site reproduction of sections of a sixteen-page document that he had acquired from one of his intelligence contacts. The first version of the document had been written in English. By the time it fell into Al-Rimawi's hands it had been translated into Arabic. Now, Badger's translation had reversed it back into English. In all that, it had lost none of its punch.

The document was a detailed set of plans for a rapid makeover of Abbas and his Fatah movement in the hope that they could be made irresistible to Palestinian voters at a new—and early—election. If the Saudis had pulled the rug from under Washington and its Quartet allies by browbeating Abbas into a unity-ticket deal with Mishal, then this was the fight-back program. The authors of the document were said by Al-Rimawi to be "Arab and American parties." It had been produced after the Mecca summit and it suggested that the Palestinians would be allowed to go through the motions of establishing their government of national unity—at least at face value. But it would be a farce.

If Elliott Abrams's talk of a "hard coup" had shocked Palestinian business-men meeting him in Washington, this was the blueprint for a "softer" coup. It could have been presented as a well-meant aid package for a long-oppressed population, but its unambiguously stated objective made it a parti-san attack on a popularly elected government. It was a declaration of war against Hamas.

Every element of the plan canvassed in the document leaked to Al-Rimawi was geared to enhancing Abbas's standing and to ensuring that his Fatah or-ganization would win a new poll. Nothing was to be left to chance—the document envisaged an early election to be called by Abbas in the autumn of 2007, less than halfway through the Hamas government's term in office.

According to the document, the key problem in the Palestinian mix was Abbas himself. By falling under the spell of the Saudis, he had lost credibility internationally. And by not insisting on the inclusion of the Middle East Quartet's conditions in the Mecca Accord, Abbas had failed to protect his own office as the center of gravity in Palestinian affairs. As a result, the docu-ment argued, international support for Abbas—and for Fatah—would be further diminished. It followed that Hamas would become stronger and all the more difficult to dislodge in the proposed early elections, the legality of which was not even addressed.

The document's authors were in a hurry. "This means avoiding the wasting of valuable time trying to alter the ideology of Hamas," they wrote. In urging financial and political support for Abbas, the objective was less about helping Palestinians generally than about striking a blow at Hamas by catering to Palestinians' needs "through the presidency and Fatah."

If Abbas and Fatah controlled security, the documents reasoned, Hamas would be deterred from any attempt at escalation. But in the place of a detailed examination of security issues, there was only a cryptic reference to earlier agreements between the American general Keith Dayton and Mohammad Dahlan.

The plan called for the World Bank and the European Union to be wheeled in behind a series of development projects that had to be guaranteed to show results that would lift Abbas's standing in the space of no more than six to nine months. All Palestinian Authority wages had to be paid through Abbas's office, to ensure that money did not fall into Hamas's hands.

Even the Israelis would be harnessed. Palestinians would be more optimistic if Abbas and Israel resumed negotiations and a schedule was set for Israeli troop withdrawals, the elimination of Israeli roadblocks and checkpoints, and the release of Palestinian prisoners.

Finally, after the plan was passed to Abbas by the head of a friendly Arab intelligence agency, the Palestinian president would be required to embrace it as his own, before going through the pretense of seeking support from the Americans and their Quartet partners, as a device to demonstrate to the Israelis and the skittish Europeans that Abbas did indeed have a concrete proposal for the future of Palestine.

Within just forty-eight hours of Badger's post at Missing Links, there was another dramatic leak. This time it was in Tel Aviv, where the Israeli daily *Haaretz* had acquired what appeared to be a companion plan to the blueprint being prepared for Abbas that had fallen into Al-Rimawi's hands. According to the *Haaretz* document, Israel would be required to approve the shipment of more weapons and ammunition to Abbas's forces. Israel also would be expected to agree to a timetable by which it would ease the checkpoint gridlock in the West Bank and allow a controlled bus service to run between Gaza and the West Bank.

It was denounced in the Israeli media as a recipe for a "terrorist bloodbath."[28] Drafted by General Dayton and reportedly approved by Secretary of State Rice, the plan was dead in the water in less than a week.

If the Israelis had been fearful, Khalid Mishal was derisory about the Dayton proposal. Swearing it was a joke, the Hamas leader wondered if the United States seriously believed that Palestinian militias would halt their rocket fire in return for the removal of just a handful of an estimated 500 Israeli roadblocks in the West Bank. "What will Washington demand in return for the removal of the other 480 roadblocks, for Israeli withdrawal and the establishment of a Palestinian state?"[29] he snorted.

Coming as it did amidst an unrelenting crisis for Ehud Olmert's government over the mismanagement of its invasion of Lebanon in the previous summer, the timing of *Haaretz*'s acquisition of the document prompted speculation that the "leak" had been orchestrated. Perhaps the deliberate intention had been to kill the plan at the same time as it allowed Washington to be portrayed in a positive light for having attempted to get a breakthrough for the Palestinians.

Abbas's aides later confirmed that American officials had been involved in the development and presentation of the plan uncovered by Alastair Crooke and by *Al-Majd*. But officials at the U.S. State Department distanced themselves from the plan, which was priced at $1.2 billion; they claimed it had been "a Jordanian initiative."[30]

When an explanation was needed, Elliott Abrams was hosting yet another delegation to the White House—this time a group of "Jewish Republicans," as the *Jerusalem Post* described them. In the same way that he had talked up the need for a "hard coup" when he had received the Palestinian businessmen a year before, Abrams reassured his latest guests that much of the administration's frenetic diplomatic activity was "process for the sake of process," merely to appease the Arabs and the Europeans.[31]

When his visitors expressed a wariness that pressure from European and Arab governments could result in Israel being boxed in, Abrams sent them away reassured. "Ultimately, the United States provides an emergency brake," members of the delegation said Abrams had told them.

The extraordinary news leaks in the first half of 2007 had revealed just how this emergency brake was to be applied. The work by Alastair Crooke in Beirut, the reports by Fahd Al-Rimawi in Amman and Badger the blogger in Canada, and then *Haaretz*'s fine scoop had sketched the substance of Washington's plan to set Fatah and Hamas on a path to civil war. On the ground, this grand design was about to become reality.

24

An Eye for an Eye

Sixteen years after the fall of the Berlin Wall, benighted Gaza had become the setting for one of the most complex global proxy wars since the end of the Cold War.

At the very heart of the matter, beyond the unceasing struggle between the Palestinians and Israel, was the wider contest between America and the Islamic theocracy in Iran. Tehran had used the decades since the ousting of the U.S.-backed shah from his Peacock Throne to build itself as a proven agent provocateur and an aspiring regional superpower.

Washington and the other powers in the area were fearful of Tehran's nuclear adventurism. Its relentless drumbeat of apocalypse for Israel had made it the wildcard in the region. The United States was desperate to neutralize Iran's proxies in the conflicts in Iraq and Lebanon, along with Hamas in the Palestinian Occupied Territories. The upshot was that Hamas, which had never struck beyond the borders of its disputed land, had been elevated to the status of a global enemy of the United States.

Regional crosscurrents imposed confusing contradictions. Riyadh's King Abdullah was exceptionally close to Washington, and yet he had thrown a lifeline to Hamas at the Mecca conference. Hamas, like the Saudi regime, was Sunni. But Hamas had its own entente cordiale with the powerful Shiite mullahs in Tehran, to say nothing of its pragmatic engagement with Syria's Al-Assad regime, which hosted the Hamas leader-in-exile, Khalid Mishal, based on their common enmity with Israel.

Washington regarded the Hamas-Fatah conflict as a clear example of the division between "moderates" and "extremists" in the region. It was by employing this simplistic dichotomy that Washington was able to put the U.S.-sponsored Fatah movement in the Occupied Territories—which had once been its sworn terrorist enemy—in the same so-called moderate camp as the U.S.-sponsored Shiite government of Iraq, which also gave Washington heartburn because of its solid relations with Tehran.

But if it was a matter of describing the various groups as "us" and "them," Riyadh's "us" were the Sunni people of Saudi Arabia, Egypt, Jordan, and the Occupied Territories. For Riyadh, the Shiite regimes in Iran and Iraq, along with Lebanon, were "them" or, as it had been dubbed by Sunni Jordan's King Abdullah II, the "Shiite Crescent." In the face of Iran's regional superpower ambitions, the Saudis wanted to pull Hamas from Iran's embrace.

From the Saudi perspective, Hamas were not Bush's extremists—they were Sunnis welcome in the Saudi capital. And for that Hamas was grateful. "The brotherhood will never be closer to Tehran than it is to Riyadh," a senior Hamas figure in Gaza explained, referring to his movement as the Palestinian branch of the Muslim Brotherhood. "Our policy is to keep a safe distance from all."[1]

Hamas made no effort to conceal its links to Tehran, one of the triumvirate of nations dubbed the "Axis of Evil" by President Bush. It was a relationship that had begun shakily enough in the aftermath of the 1979 Iranian Revolution. The ousting of the shah from Tehran had given political inspiration to Palestinians—Islamic and secular alike. But, as a Palestinian Islamist movement, Hamas was Arab and Sunni; Iran, by contrast, was Persian and Shiite.

As one of Sheikh Ahmad Yassin's older contemporaries explained, these were differences that caused initial mistrust and suspicion in the relationship. "We sent many delegations to Tehran, but we were not well received," he recalled. "We were inspired by the revolution, but there was a wall between us. We were scared of them wanting to exploit us—they wanted to export a Shiite revolution, not simply a revolution."[2]

But in time—especially in the grip of a tightening U.S.-led freeze on the transfer of funds to Hamas through the global banking system—Tehran became a vital source of financial and material support for the Palestinian movement. In the late 1980s, Washington estimated that as little as 10 percent of Hamas's funding came from Iran.[3] When aid and funds to Hamas were frozen on its election victory in January 2006, Tehran publicly pledged $250 million. After the Mecca agreement, Israel estimated the funds flow from Tehran to be about $15 million a month, all of which was directed to Hamas's fighting forces, according to Israeli and American officials.[4]

The Palestinian crisis was a central platform in Tehran's efforts to project itself over the heads of Arab leaders to their people, the so-called Arab Street—and that made Hamas an instrument of Iranian foreign policy. The Iranian leadership railed against the Jewish state and, the argument went, by encouraging violent attacks by Hamas it controlled the conflict to its own advantage.

The direct or implied charge that Hamas was a puppet of the Iranian regime made great political rhetoric in Israel and America, but the more considered view of old intelligence hands like former Mossad chief Efraim Halevy rejected this interpretation. "Hamas receives funds, support, equipment and training from Iran," he argued, "but it is not subservient to Tehran."[5]

A former senior Israeli official, who argued that Israel needed to engage Hamas, ran the same argument: "Hamas is not an Iranian tool, they're not part of the global jihad—they're nationalists; they are not Al-Qaeda—they are Palestinian patriots."

Others who still served at senior levels of the Israeli intelligence establishment agreed. There was no doubt that Khalid Mishal was the linchpin in Hamas's diplomacy and fund-raising, one of them explained, but—in contrast to the other Palestinian Islamist faction, Palestinian Islamic Jihad, which was perceived to have sold its soul to Tehran—his view was that Mishal had mastered the art of balancing the independence of Sunni Hamas with the demands of Syria and Shiite Iran.

"Islamic Jihad fell under the total control of Tehran," he said. "Hamas doesn't want that for itself. Hamas needs Tehran and Damascus, but it's a balance that Mishal manages well. He stays close to these strategic allies, but he manages to ensure that Hamas does not become an Iranian or Syrian surrogate. Sure, he consults, but Khalid Mishal makes the decisions."[6]

Mishal added flesh to this argument when he was challenged on Hamas's ties to Iran in the aftermath of the Mecca Accord. The relationship was part of Hamas's diplomacy in the Arabic and Islamic worlds, he said, producing Exhibits A and B. "We are independent, politically and organizationally," he said. "We went to Mecca—had we been part of the Iranian axis, we would not have listened to Saudi Arabia, which stands for the opposite axis." Mishal then turned to the question of Iraq, where Hamas supported the Sunni insurgency against the Iran-friendly Shiite majority. "We clearly support the [Sunnis]," he explained. "This clearly conflicts with Iranian policies. We condemned the assassination of Saddam Hussein; Iran welcomed it."[7]

Mishal and his Hamas colleagues rarely conceded any information about military aid received by Hamas from Iran. Mishal admitted to having undergone military training,[8] but he refused to disclose in which country. Iran, however, was one of a very short list of countries in which he was likely to have trained. "I can't reveal the location," he would insist later. "It was training—that's enough."

Diplomatically the Hamas leadership was like a Bedouin clan in the Arab deserts, constantly on the move. Pushed out of Kuwait, they had moved to Jordan; when time ran out in Jordan, they had regrouped in Qatar briefly, before settling in Syria. It was a precarious existence, suspended between Damascus and Tehran, which could collapse in the event of either U.S. military strikes on Iran or a breakthrough in efforts to strike a peace deal between Syria and Israel.

Mishal gave the impression that he was relaxed about the ability of his movement to read the lay of the land. "Hamas doesn't take the regional and international players at face value," he explained. "We know them quite well; we have a sense of their motives and objectives—so it's a bit hard to trick us."[9] It might have been bravado, but it had worked for many years.

Hamas had much to digest. As officials factored in the disclosures by Fahd Al-Rimawi's *Al-Majd* in Jordan and Badger's Canada-based Missing Links blog, some in the movement saw their options narrowing as they confronted a genuine identity crisis.

A halt to suicide attacks on Israel had been holding since November 2006, which meant that Hamas had ceased to function as a resistance movement. Bankrupt, under international siege and robbed of control of security in the Occupied Territories, there was little it could do as a government. For a movement like Hamas, this was double jeopardy—unable to deliver, it saw its popular support slide as Mohammad Dahlan's associates stirred the lawlessness that was to be the pretext for Dahlan and Fatah to elbow Hamas from office.

Analysts close to the Israeli defense and intelligence establishment claimed that Hamas spent much of spring 2007 copying the tactics of the highly successful Shiite Hezbollah militia of southern Lebanon. Hamas was smuggling more advanced weapons into Gaza. It was investing in efforts to improve the performance and shelf life of its rockets.[10] And it was also digging an extensive network of combat tunnels, in addition to the underground supply routes it used to bypass border crossings that were under Israeli control.

Hamas had an estimated twenty thousand men under arms in the Executive Force and in its Qassam Brigade. Mass training took place in Gaza. But since the Israeli pullout from Gaza in 2005, handpicked recruits had been smuggled out by the dozen and sent to the Iranian Revolutionary Guard in Tehran for training periods that lasted from forty-five days to six months.[11] There were other courses in Syria and Lebanon. These activities increased the movement's capacity for mass-casualty attacks on Israel, in the full expectation that the cease-fire would collapse, while also equipping them to hold the streets of Gaza—against both Fatah and Israeli forces.

The Mecca deal between Hamas and Fatah lasted just six weeks. Hani Qawasmeh, the "independent" interior minister, quit in mid-May complaining loudly that a phalanx of Fatah officers in the security agencies continually thwarted his efforts to tackle lawlessness. Each faction had attempted to bypass his office or had sought to dictate the terms by which their forces were deployed. On May 17, Dahlan made his own move to retake the streets of Gaza, deploying thousands of his men without consulting Hamas. Clashes flared as opposing forces faced off in the streets—there were twenty deaths on the first day alone.

On May 21, Israel resumed airstrikes on Hamas targets. It was responding to intensified rocket fire directed at Israeli communities on the perimeter of Gaza by Islamic Jihad. These attacks on Israel were a deliberate bid by the lesser Islamist faction to draw Israeli fire, in the hope of uniting Hamas and Fatah against their common foe. When the Israeli Air Force mounted an air strike on the Gaza home of Khalil Al-Hayya, one of Hamas's senior political leaders, he was out for the evening—but seven members of his family were killed.

The Israeli strikes forced the Hamas leadership to scatter. They were ordered to refrain from using mobile phones, which could be easily tracked, and to stay away from all Hamas buildings, which were obvious targets for Israeli aircraft. Israel's minister for public security, Avi Dichter, expressly warned Hamas's Damascus-based leadership that they were targets too. "Khalid Mishal is not immune—and he's well aware of this," Dichter said. Israel was doing Fatah a favor here, because it became more difficult for the Hamas leadership to confront Fatah when it needed to be on the run from Israeli strikes.

By Hamas's reckoning, a coup was in the making. "Fatah is following orders from the US and Israel to escalate violence," Haniyah's adviser, Ahmad Yousef, concluded.[12] For the Islamists, it had reached the point of attack—or be attacked.

Gazans stayed indoors. Gunmen were back in their rooftop nests around the city. Doctors were being singled out for attack, while education officials pleaded for a cease-fire so that seventy-thousand-plus teenagers might take their matriculation exams in peace. Leading identities on both sides were being abducted mysteriously, but each faction denied any role in the disappearances.

As the daily dead were counted, locals lost track of false-dawn cease-fires. Already there had been more than a dozen in fifteen months, some of which had lasted for just hours. Fatah claimed it was defending itself. Hamas argued it was being provoked. There were days when it became impossible to tell.

Fatah became increasingly confident as Israel and the Americans pitched in to help. About half of the $84.6 million that the Bush administration had tried to steer through Congress for training Abbas's forces earlier in the year had been approved. Training camps already operated at Jericho, in the West Bank, and in Gaza; a new facility was about to open in Jordan.[13] Egypt and Jordan had been prevailed upon to supply weapons and ammunition to Fatah. Israel again had cooperated with Abbas when it allowed five hundred Fatah fighters trained under American supervision in Egypt to enter the Strip.[14]

In the first days of June, Israel revealed that it was under pressure from Fatah to allow a fifth arms shipment to Gaza in less than eight months. This time Dahlan wanted approval for the delivery to Gaza of dozens of armored cars, hundreds of armor-piercing rockets, thousands of hand grenades, and millions of rounds of low-caliber ammunition.[15] Some Israeli officials seriously talked up the prospect of a Dahlan-led force of Fatah loyalists taking control of the northern end of the Gaza Strip, to protect Israel from rockets launched by Hamas and other Palestinian militias. They called them "Dayton's guys."[16]

Israeli intelligence was split in their estimations of Fatah's strength. The domestic agency, Shin Bet, concluded that Abbas's faction was on the verge of collapse and that a confrontation with Hamas would finish it off. Israeli military intelligence, on the other hand, believed that Fatah still might have some fight left in it.[17]

Keith Dayton had always observed a strict below-the-radar media policy, only ever agreeing to a few select interviews, which were tightly controlled. The result had been a very two-dimensional public profile. But a more robust character suddenly burst forth when the general was called to Washington to appear before the Middle East and South Asia subcommittee of the Committee on House Foreign Affairs on May 23.

There was a surreal, flashback quality to Dayton's appearance. It was like a return to the depths of the Cold War—as though the general had just stepped from a grainy, black-and-white Movietone newsreel to bring the news from Armageddon. President Abbas's "legally constituted" forces were engaged in a "battle for law and order, like never before," Dayton advised the committee. The "Fatah-loyal forces of law and order" faced "outright aggression" from Hamas militias. The paramount goal of the latter, he ventured, was the destruction of Israel, but for now they were bent on eliminating the Palestinian president's "legitimate security forces" and on creating an "extremist statelet" on Israel's border. The murkiest gray circumstances were confidently presented in black-and-white certainty.

Dayton told the subcommittee that the latest violence in Gaza could well be the start of a sustained effort by Hamas to reassert its dominance. But he intimated that Fatah was now ready to strike back hard. "There's a point where inaction—a wait-and-see attitude—is not an option." Hamas might have scored easy victories in clashes early in 2007, he asserted, but more recently the Islamist movement was being undermined and had lost the goodwill of the people.

A unit of Abbas's Presidential Guard, whose training had been supervised by the United States and funded by Europe, had fought off a determined Hamas attack in the previous week, he said. Another Abbas-loyal unit had acquitted itself well despite limited resources and the death of its battalion commander. "I fear Hamas is in this fight for keeps. We're entering a rough patch, but all is not lost,"[18] General Dayton told the committee.

Back in Gaza, Fatah security chiefs radiated even greater confidence when they were honored by President Abbas's presence in their midst. In a bid to stiffen their resolve and as a nod to Washington's demands that he "reform" his forces, Abbas had committed back in January to clearing out about 150 commanders.[19] Now, as his men crowded around him in a smoke-filled room, the Palestinian president was meeting some of the new guard who would take the fight to Hamas.

They applauded loudly as Abbas insisted that they stamp out rocket fire into Israel. "Beat them, kill them, shoot them," he insisted while at least two video cameras rolled, urging his men to pursue Hamas and the other Palestinian militants.[20] Resorting to the flowery speech-making practices of the region, one of the security chiefs assured Abbas that they were up to the challenge. "We have an army that will cover the sun!" he told his president.

Amidst all this self-congratulation, another of the men ventured to put a timeframe on Fatah's inevitable victory over Hamas. "It'll take no more than a *ghalwa*," he proclaimed. A local term for the few moments between a Turkish coffee coming to the boil and actually boiling over, a *ghalwa* was the Gaza equivalent of a nanosecond.

June 5, 2007, was the fortieth anniversary of the start of the 1967 Six-Day War, in which Israel had seized the West Bank and the Gaza Strip. Mahmoud Abbas marked the anniversary with a televised speech in which he acknowledged that perhaps his people were on the brink of civil war.

Bassam Abdul Raouf, who lived among orchards on a sandy track in Beit Hanoun, had adjusted to the new tempo of the violence. As a Fatah man, he fought with the Al-Aqsa Martyrs Brigade and on Monday, June 11, he found himself with others on rooftop guard duty at the Beit Lahiya home of Jamal Abu Jedian, one of the founders of the brigade in Gaza and a close associate of Mohammad Dahlan.

Like Samih Al-Madhun, who had abducted the Abu Dan family at the end of January, the fifty-year-old Abu Jedian ruled like a warlord over a swathe of the northern end of the Gaza Strip. Both Abu Jedian and Al-Madhun had been repeatedly targeted for assassination by hit teams from Hamas.

On this particular day, Gaza was exploding. Four days earlier, the killing of twenty-six-year-old Wael Mahmoud Wahba in the far southern district of Rafah had ignited a chain reaction of death.[21] Pleas for restraint by Egyptian security agents, who were on the ground attempting to prevent a total breakdown, went unheeded as the mayhem spread northward from Rafah.

While Abdul Raouf cradled his weapon up on Jamal Abu Jedian's rooftop, Hamas threw down the gauntlet. In a dire statement, the Islamists warned Fatah and its supporters of a peculiarly Islamic punishment: *qassas*. Lawyers at the Palestine Center for Human Rights juggled tomes on Islamic law and English dictionaries in their attempts to translate it, before they opted for a quaint, nineteenth-century Americanism—*comeuppance*—to convey the darker, deadlier meaning of this new turn in the conflict.[22]

Under the heading WE VOW COMEUPPANCE AGAINST THE KILLERS, the Hamas pamphlet began:

> Enough is enough. Self-restraint, agreements and convention are no longer fruitful with these killers. These wrongful people insist on continuing their wrong deeds and killings. Left unpunished, they would drown and make us drown with them. So they must be . . . brought to justice. But which justice?

Is it the justice of the Attorney General, the one of the judiciary or that of comeuppance?

Concluding that comeuppance was the only option, the Hamas statement argued that the crimes being committed in Gaza warranted the immediate eye-for-an-eye retribution of *qassas*, the spiritually sanctioned killing of a killer, or the injuring of an injurer, and so on. As an Islamic solution to anarchy, it was more menacing than the simpler definition of comeuppance found in the *American Heritage Dictionary*: "punishment or retribution that one deserves; one's just deserts."

In the ferocious fighting that followed, more than 160 Palestinians were killed and more than 700 wounded—a good portion of them kneecapped in calculated acts of revenge by both sides. Amidst a sickening wave of summary executions, two fighters—one Fatah, one Hamas—were hurled to their deaths from high city residential towers that became makeshift shooting platforms. Others were abducted and strapped to the top or sides of vehicles as human shields when their captors became cornered.

Four Fatah-controlled security compounds became the focus of the most sustained fighting. But as a fighting force, Fatah crumbled in disgrace. The weapons and training provided by the United States and its regional allies counted for nothing. Researchers from Raji Sourani's human rights watchdog, the Palestinian Center for Human Rights, would later document gruesome details from the battlefield as Fatah and Hamas exacted brutal vengeance, each on the other.

A Fatah-controlled television transmitter on Omar Al-Mukhtar Street was bombed. Fatah gained control of Al-Aqsa TV for a short time, during which it broadcast Fatah anthems on the Hamas satellite service. Radio stations were shut down. And the clan armies of Gaza backed in behind the faction they thought most likely to win—or the one they owed the most.

At one stage unidentified masked gunmen took over Gaza's central Shifa Hospital. "We don't know who they are or who they are fighting," Dr. Wessam Awadallah told a reporter by phone. "There will come a moment when we'll not be able to treat anyone, and [we'll] let them die."[23]

Shortly after four PM on Monday, the day Hamas warned of *qassas*, Bassam Abdul Raouf and the other Fatah fighters on Jamal Abu Jedian's rooftop received word of clashes between Hamas and members of the powerful Al-Masri clan in a nearby marketplace. The Al-Masris' alignment with Fatah had earned them the post of head of the Fatah-controlled Gaza intelligence unit for the clan's patriarch. The death toll stood at almost thirty in a blood feud started in 2005 by an Al-Masri clansman who had pulled a gun and shot a roadside fruit vendor from a rival clan when the stall holder was unable to break a twenty-shekel note for the purchase of a mango.[24]

First to die in the market exchange was Basil Daoud Kafarna, a twenty-three-year-old Hamas fighter. But in quick time three of the Al-Masri men who fought with Fatah were down too, in pools of their own blood. The Al-Masris ferried ten of their wounded to the Kamal Edwan Hospital at Beit Hanoun. As they were being treated, some of the Al-Masris threw a defensive cordon around the hospital while inside their comrades went ward to ward, searching for Hamas fighters and loyalists. Hamas fighters came after them, entering the hospital with all guns blazing.[25] "Everyone's shooting at everybody," a desperate doctor cried.[26]

Patients were terrified. Those who were mobile fled on foot; those who were confined to their beds cringed in fear as wards became battlefields. Doctors treating a badly wounded Al-Masri fighter were ordered to abandon the patient on an operating table.[27] By the time Hamas secured the hospital, three more Al-Masri men were dead—a father, his son, and one of his nephews.

On Abu Jedian's roof, Abdul Raouf and his three Fatah colleagues resisted what they believed was probing fire from another clan in the district, one aligned with Hamas. But the fighting was shifting around the neighborhood, and by eight PM they were taking blanket machine-gun fire along with the occasional rocket and mortar shell, most of it from a nearby residential block in which Hamas had made a beachhead.

"Help us," begged a woman who said she was one of more than fifty people still inside the block of six apartments, during an on-air phone call to a Fatah radio station. "They want to kill us!"[28]

Looking out from a lower level of the same building, Abdul Raouf's nineteen-year-old comrade, Thaer Obaid, estimated the Hamas forces besieging them to number in the hundreds. Nearby buildings that had been held by Fatah forces were falling to Hamas. Obaid watched in horror as Hamas fighters emerged on the next-door rooftop, where they grabbed his Fatah colleague Mahmoud Jaber Saftwai and hurled him over the parapet.

The warlord Abu Jedian was injured in a direct rocket hit on the main building. He stumbled out into the street, barely able to walk. Then a Hamas vehicle pulled up and six gunmen tumbled out. A gunshot was heard and the fifty-year-old Abu Jedian dropped to the ground with a bullet in his head.

One of the six gunmen stood on his chest, firing dozens of close-range shots into the warlord's body as others chanted: "Traitor! Collaborator! Spy!"

Thirty minutes later Abu Jedian's younger brother Majed suffered a similar fate. The battle for the family's apartment block was virtually over when Majed attempted to flee, but he was snatched back and taken in a white Mitsubishi to the Jabalya district, halfway between Beit Hanoun and Beit Lahiya. Local residents watched as he was dumped on the ground by a group of men who all wore the signature T-shirt of Hamas's Qassam Brigade. Four shots rang out.[29]

At eleven PM, Abdul Raouf had no choice but to surrender the rooftop, where he was alone and desperate. Of his three companions, one had been injured by flying shrapnel and the two others had dragged the injured man to safety. Abdul Raouf himself was wounded. Making his way down from the terrace, he came upon several terrified children huddled in the relative safety of the stairwell.

As he responded to calls from the Hamas fighters for all in the building to surrender, Abdul Raouf continued down the steps, only to collide with a wall of black-clad men moving up through the building. The personal enclave of the Fatah warlord Jamal Abu Jedian had fallen to Hamas.

Some of the Hamas men rescued the frightened children and hurried them away. Others hauled Abdul Raouf and the other three who had been on the roof into the street. As they were questioned and checked off against a written list of names of Fatah fighters, they were beaten with rifle butts. A short distance away Thaer Obaid was among four Fatah men hustled into a black pickup that drove off at high speed.

Lying on the ground, handcuffed and blindfolded, Abdul Raouf was further humiliated when his captors ordered a bystander to urinate on his head. He was manhandled into a car for a short drive, then dragged out and dumped on the roadside. Several Hamas gunmen pumped bullets into his lower legs before driving off.[30]

When he regained consciousness, he was in the Awda Hospital. But his mangled legs demanded more sophisticated treatment than could be provided by hard-pressed doctors at this local clinic. He was sent by ambulance to Gaza's central Shifa Hospital, where Fatah loyalists on the staff admitted him under a false name to conceal his identity from the Hamas squads patrolling the hospital.

Forty-eight hours later, Abdul Raouf was back in an ambulance, and rushed to the Israeli city of Ashkelon. The last he remembered was succumbing to the welcome release of a powerful sedative administered by doctors who spoke Hebrew. "I woke up and I can't find my legs," he recalled later.[31]

Late on Thursday, June 14, after eight days of unfettered bloodletting and atrocities on both sides, a car was seen driving at breakneck speed, heading south on the coast road just west of the Nusairat refugee camp. It was 6:30 PM when the driver was directed to pull over as the vehicle approached a Hamas checkpoint.

The car slowed, but as it came abreast of the checkpoint, its occupants pulled guns and opened fire. One of the Hamas fighters, twenty-three-year-old Jamal Abu Swaireh, died instantly. Two others were badly wounded. Their comrades raked the car with automatic fire, killing the driver.

Pulling two wounded passengers from the vehicle, they instantly recognized a thickset man in his early thirties. They had captured Samih Al-Madhun, one of the most violent Fatah strongmen on the Strip, making a bolt for the Egyptian border. But instead of freedom in Cairo, the man who had abducted and tortured the Abu Dan family back in January and more recently had been on the radio boasting that he had killed several Hamas leaders and torched the homes of more than twenty Hamas supporters had reached the end of the road.[32]

He was thrown into the back of one of several Mitsubishi pickups and driven under heavy guard into the teeming Nusairat refugee camp. The convoy pulled up outside the family home of Jamal Abu Swaireh.

A crowd gathered as Al-Madhun was dumped in the roadway, where he was sprayed with automatic fire. His body was strapped to the front of a vehicle, which then drove slowly, at the head of a convoy of eight Hamas pickups, through the streets and alleys of the impoverished camp. Bystanders hurled abuse and some rushed at the corpse with knives. It was a shocking spectacle of revenge, captured by video camera and aired later on Hamas's Al-Aqsa TV channel.[33]

The foreboding *qassas* warning issued by Hamas a week before had been intended to intimidate Mohammad Dahlan's Fatah fighters, and it had done that. But it had also become a license for some in the ranks of Hamas to inflict on their captives the worst of all they had heard and experienced of Fatah's methods and means of physical abuse—both real and apocryphal.

As the cool of the summer's night embraced the Nusairat camp on the evening of June 14, the battle for Gaza was over. The strange sound that settled over the coastal strip was silence.

.   .   .

In the first flush of victory, the green pennant of Hamas replaced the flag of the Palestinian Authority on government buildings in Gaza. There were claims that Gaza had been "liberated for the second time." Posters of Mahmoud Abbas and the late Yasser Arafat were trampled under foot as mobs invaded their respective Gaza residences, generating news footage that infuriated the Fatah leadership in Ramallah.

But it was not just the secular Palestinian leadership that was mocked. When Hamas briefly occupied the office of Abbas, who also was known as Abu Mazen, one of the fighters picked up a phone, making a mock call. "Hello, Condoleezza Rice?" he laughed into the handset. "You have to deal with me now—there is no Abu Mazen anymore."[34]

Previously the word most often used by Israeli and American officials in their commentary on Abbas had been "bolster"—much of what they did was geared to bolstering him in the eyes of his people. Now, having failed to bolster him, the word "legitimate" peppered the commentary—Abbas was "legitimate" and by implication Hamas was illegitimate, despite its more recent election in a popular vote.

Yet, in the face of so much condemnation, the movement had its unlikely defenders. "This is what just happened," a senior figure in the Israeli intelligence establishment said. "Washington did not want a unity government. It wanted Fatah to wreck it and it sent Dayton to create and train a force that could overthrow Hamas. When Hamas preempts it, everyone cries foul, claiming it's a military putsch by Hamas—but who did the putsch?"[35]

In *Yedioth Ahronoth*, the commentator Sever Plocker went out of his way to disagree with Hamas, before he defended its most recent performance in Gaza. The point was not that Hamas was cruel or filled with hatred for Israel, he said, so much as it had won the election. "Hamas did not 'seize control' of Gaza," he wrote. "It took the action it needed . . . disarming and destroying a militia that refused to bow to its [legitimate] authority."[36]

Fearing a Hamas uprising in the West Bank, Abbas declared a state of emergency. Finally acting on the advice he had been hearing from Washington for months, the Palestinian president sacked Hamas's Ismail Haniyah as prime minister. His choice of Salam Fayyad as the new, unelected appointee to the office of prime minister in a new, unelected regime was not exactly a masterstroke in Washington's democracy drive. As a former World Bank economist, Fayyad was widely respected in the West, but as a Palestinian he was barely known to his own people. As a candidate in the election won by

Hamas in January 2006, he had headed a slate of candidates that had garnered just 2.4 percent of the vote. Now he was the new prime minister.

Almost a week passed after the fighting stopped before a still-seething president spoke in public. Having dissolved the government, Abbas and his aides pleaded with the international community to maintain the siege of Gaza while he undertook to rule by decree. "No dialogue with those killers," Abbas declared. "These putschist assassins have no future."[37]

Abbas then ordered a roundup of key Hamas figures on the West Bank, driving much of the Islamist leadership underground as some of their institutions were torched ahead of formal orders that more than one hundred Hamas agencies must fold. "We have information they were preparing to do the same thing here as they did in Gaza," Abed Al-Salam Al-Souqi, one of Abbas's security chiefs in Jenin, claimed.[38]

The American plan to isolate Hamas had ended in a rout for Fatah and its Washington sponsors. There had been two objectives: either to starve Hamas into committing itself to the Quartet conditions, or to eject it from power. Instead, a movement that Washington had been trying to break for twenty years had taken control of 1.4 million Palestinians in a week and a day, humiliating the United States and Israel and their regional allies, Egypt and Jordan, on the way through.

As self-anointed keepers of the holy flame of Palestinian nationalism, Fatah had been humiliated twice in little more than a year. It had first tasted defeat at the ballot box in January 2006, and then again on the battlefield in Gaza eighteen months later. On top of all that, Israel now had an Islamist statelet on its doorstep.

A large block-like building—known by Gazans as "CIA House"—had been used by the Fatah forces to store weapons. It now became a symbol of the catastrophic intelligence and security failure that had just unfolded before the eyes of the world. Behind its huge gated perimeter, the walls were scorched, windows broken, and much of the furniture and fittings smashed or looted. The most serious of the looters were from Hamas. While some fighters fell to their knees in prayer, others supervised television crews filming what they said were phone-tapping and other eavesdropping equipment. Dedicated teams were assigned to sift the intelligence files, the bulk of which Fatah had failed to destroy.

A fleet of trucks and pickups was backed in to cart away much of the weaponry that Washington had organized—the same weapons that Israel had feared would end up in Hamas hands. This booty included dozens of mounted machine guns, more than seven thousand American M16 assault rifles, and eight hundred thousand rounds of ammunition. A whole convoy of new vehicles—armored personnel carriers, military jeeps, armored civilian cars, trucks with mounted water cannons and militarized bulldozers—fell into Hamas's hands.[39] Also for the taking were dozens of long-range rockets, anti-tank missiles, and tons of explosives.[40]

Hamas military leaders had anticipated a conflict that might last a month or longer. But in the same way that Saddam Hussein's overrated security edifice had collapsed with a sharp jab to the chest by invading American-led forces in 2003, Fatah's house of cards teetered almost at Hamas's first sortie. Israeli analysts had warned of the shortcomings of Dahlan's forces. But unexplained was how Washington's man on the ground, General Keith Dayton, had convinced himself that the weak and undisciplined rabble fielded by Fatah was a serious army.

Amazingly, Mohammad Dahlan had absented himself from Gaza City weeks before the June convulsion, spending his time in Europe instead, having surgery on his knees. His mansion-like home, estimated by locals to be worth in excess of $1 million, was looted and torched. The fighter who won the Hamas race to be first into Dahlan's office fired a bullet into the absent security chief's desk. "This is the fate of traitors, like the scumbag Mohammad Dahlan," he cried.[41]

Many of Dahlan's lieutenants had melted away before, or very early in the fighting. Dozens risked the Israeli naval blockade of the coast as they fled to Egypt in fishing boats. Hundreds more, who feared for their lives, were stranded for days in sweltering summer temperatures at the Erez checkpoint, pleading for Israel to reopen the crossing to allow them to get to Fatah headquarters at Ramallah.

Dahlan had had as many as fifty thousand men under his command, but many thousands decided to stay at home. "If my role in life was to be a sacrificial lamb, God would have created me as a sheep," one of them explained.[42] Others went solo, or with their commanders as they changed sides. One of these was Khalid Abu Hilal, who, in the days after the fighting, could be found in his new office, dwarfed behind a grand, Italianate desk, which he had looted from the office of Dahlan. Abu Hilal drew about one thousand fighters away from Fatah and proved to be a useful source of intelligence for Hamas on the Dahlan operation. "I told them all I knew—how Fatah thinks, how it plans its response to events," he said, revealing a mouthful of fence-post teeth.[43] "This is why I sit behind Dahlan's desk now—I have his plasma TV, his computer, and *all* his furniture."[44]

Insisting that their target had always been Dahlan, Hamas commanders claimed that they had accomplished their mission of "cleansing Fatah of a troublesome group."[45] When the fighting was done, Hamas announced that all its Fatah captives had been released. When the Hamas field commander Abu Obieda promised forgiveness—al-afu—to Fatah officials, he made a single exception. "[Dahlan] can never return," he said. "Everyone in Hamas is ready for Dahlan to return, and any of his supporters who do anything will be met with force."[46] In the end, Mohammad Dahlan had proved to be smaller than he thought he was, and not half as big as Washington had needed him to be.

Denying that it had been pursuing a political advantage, Hamas insisted it had acted in self-defense. "We had to do our own bloodletting to stop their bloodletting," Jamila Ashanti, one of Hamas's female MPs, explained.[47]

Hamas's health minister in Gaza, Bassam Naim, resorted to the same "lesser of two evils" terminology. "We were forced to choose," he insisted. Fatah had been ramping the pressure daily—with street clashes, killings, and kidnappings. "Either we did nothing and surrendered, or we responded strongly to break the enemy," he argued. "We broke the enemy and you see the result."

Refusing to accept that he had ever been deposed, Prime Minister Ismail Haniyah seemed mildly shocked, as much by the speed with which Dahlan's forces collapsed as by Hamas's total control of Gaza. "The [Damascus leadership was] as surprised as we were—there was no warning," he said some weeks later.[48] "Fatah simply fled all their positions. We weren't plotting to take over all the military operations and security compounds. But when Dahlan's men killed one of our religious scholars, we were forced to act against one of the security compounds." He described the viciousness of the fighting as simply "some unfortunate mistakes."

Isa Al-Najjar, one of the original seven who had launched Hamas from the home of Sheikh Ahmed Yassin almost twenty years earlier, explained that the in-principle decision for Hamas to retaliate had been taken by the movement's political leadership and then conveyed to the military wing for execution. "There was no control after that," he said. "There was killing everywhere and the leaders could not get to each other because of all the fighting. When it stopped, we had to take over."[49]

In Gaza, Hamas was triumphant. Its militiamen owned the streets again. Previously under threat from both Fatah and the Israelis, it had been years since they had dared to remove their camouflage ski masks in public, to visit their homes, or to take their ease in cafés. The shooting had stopped because finally one side had prevailed over the other. The streets were quiet—and for that alone, there was genuine celebration in Gaza.

As the staff of the Palestinian Center for Human Rights reconstructed the conflict, its director, Raji Sourani, laid the blame at the feet of Hamas for possibly hundreds of illegal detentions, dozens of abuse or torture cases, and a single suspected death in custody. At the same time, he defended the movement's thwarted right to govern the Occupied Territories.

"Look," he said, "ideologically or politically, I'm not a big fan of Hamas. But they're a part of us and we wanted them in the Palestinian political system."[50] Likening the Fatah clique that had refused to accept its loss of power to "some banana republic officials," he argued that Hamas had political and legal legitimacy. "But [Fatah] made life so miserable, Hamas decides to blow it up," he said. "It took them just a few days to flush away a 53,000-strong PA security apparatus which was a fourteen-year Western investment."

Sourani put some of the blame for the June atrocities on Hamas's unskilled and untrained security services, and the movement's deliberate decision to assert its authority. But who or what had sparked it all? "Provocation is Fatah's business—twenty-five hours a day," he said.

In Damascus, however, Khalid Mishal was worried. Treading more carefully than his past rhetoric had suggested, he was acutely aware that his military victory created daunting political and diplomatic challenges. Just as Arafat had discovered, it was difficult for a leader in exile to be in full control at the height of battle. He issued orders for the provocative Hamas flag to be removed from government buildings in Gaza and he appealed to both his own followers and Fatah not to allow the West Bank to erupt as Gaza had. "We are not a hobgoblin to fear," he declared.[51]

As much as Mishal wanted to placate Abbas and elements within Fatah—to avoid fanning further trouble on the ground—the questionable legality of Abbas's decisions, both to dissolve the government and to declare a state of emergency, were a new point of difference. Denying that he had just orchestrated a coup, Mishal blamed the crisis on American interference. It was the United States that had imposed what Mishal called the "two-head system" of government. When it had been displeased with Yasser Arafat as president, Washington had insisted on the creation of the office of prime minister as a competing center of power.[52]

With Hamas isolated in Gaza, it meant that Israel, Washington, and other governments were now in a position to bolster Abbas even more, at the same time as they punished Hamas, by exempting the West Bank from their regime of collective punishment for all Palestinians for having voted for Hamas in the first place. In the face of the imbroglio in Gaza, President Bush declared Abbas a "president for all Palestinians," and Washington and the EU promptly pledged to exempt the West Bank from their diplomatic and economic embargo.

Dahlan returned from his medical sojourn in time to join Abbas for a visit to the American consul general in Jerusalem, at which they were informed that the funding boycott had been lifted. The European Union followed suit.

Israel had Gaza sealed as tight as a drum, but Prime Minister Ehud Olmert announced that he would release some of the Palestinians' frozen tax receipts—which by then amounted to several hundred million dollars. Palestinians would be given the choice of carrots in the West Bank and sticks in Gaza.

Just days after the Gaza rout, Abbas revealed his appetite for even greater humiliation by telling President Bush it was time to restart talks with Israel, at the same time as he was refusing to talk to the significant proportion of his own people who were committed to Hamas.

In Ramallah, any realization that there would have to be a dialogue with Hamas would come slowly to the deflated Fatah leadership. In the short term, the more senior figures obsessed over the need for Hamas to apologize for what it had done.

Despite hints of his early misgivings, Mishal stayed on the front foot. The nearest he came to an apology was to concede that individuals on the Hamas side had made mistakes. But, he claimed, these did not compare to the activities of those who had put Palestinian security in the service of the United States and Israel.

Gazans meanwhile reveled in their newfound sense of peace and, after what they had been through in the last year, this could not be dismissed lightly. But by any one of a hundred other measures, the circumstances of the Gaza Strip were untenable.

Isa Al-Najjar volunteered that the rupture in Palestinian unity was "a gift for Israel." The Hamas MP Jamila Ashanti agreed. "This is the worst internal crisis we've had to face since 1948," she said with a rueful smile. "God help us."[53]

25

Taking the Holy Land to Court

The Earle Cabell Federal Building in Dallas evoked American history, old and new. When President John F. Kennedy was assassinated on Elm Street in Dallas as his motorcade drove through town in 1963, Earle Cabell was city mayor. The government building later named in Cabell's honor was located just a few city blocks from where Kennedy was shot. It was not an overly attractive building, but its fluted facade was reminiscent of the Twin Towers that soared over lower Manhattan until September 11, 2001. It was in a sprawling hearing room on the fifteenth floor of the Earle Cabell building that the next legal confrontation with Hamas began in the summer of 2007.

As an army of lawyers and journalists converged on the court on July 16, the country braced for an assault on the Holy Land Foundation, the most high-profile organization that Washington had put in the dock since 9/11. This was to be the showcase proof to Americans that, when it came to the forces of terror, the Bush administration was looking out for them at home just as it was doing abroad. The prosecution had more than one million pages of documents and thousands of hours of phone taps with which to build its case. In the previous fourteen years, federal agents had been dispatched all over the world—to the Middle East, Britain, Germany, and Holland—to collect evidence.

Were the men of the Holy Land Foundation, which provided charity to Palestinians, humanitarians or terrorists? Did the millions they had transferred to the Occupied Territories go to orphans and widows or to acquiring bombs and bullets? The foundation had raised more than $57 million since its founding in California in 1989, of which, according to the prosecution,

$36 million had gone to the Occupied Territories. The remainder, according to the HLF, had gone to other Muslim communities in crisis, like the victims of the war in Kosovo.

The prosecution would argue that in the Occupied Territories, the HLF was playing the role of Linda S. Hamilton to Hamas's Bernard C. Welch Jr., the "super thief" who had murdered Dr. Michael Halberstam in Washington back in 1980. Based on the legal precedent created in that case, it could be argued that a passive partner was just as guilty as the partner who wielded the gun. Washington hoped that the same legal principle would close the door on Muslim charities in America.

"In order for Hamas to achieve its ultimate . . . goal of annihilating Israel, it had to win the broad support of the Palestinian population. [HLF] set out to do just that," the prosecutor's brief said when it presented Hamas's welfare work as an adjunct to its military campaign.[1] In legal terms, it was the equivalent of Hamilton's paperwork and her fetching and carrying for her husband, the thief and murderer Welch.

In taking this approach, the prosecution stepped back from the president's stunning Rose Garden proclamation in 2001 that HLF's tax-free fund-raising in the United States had paid for murder in the Middle East—"blood money," as the chief legal officer, Attorney General John Ashcroft, had called it. Instead, the prosecution would be more nuanced, arguing that the distribution of HLF donations through an Occupied Territories network of *zakat* committees that were controlled by Hamas freed up the movement's other resources to be directed to terrorism.

As they worked up the criminal case against the Holy Land Foundation, U.S. prosecutors had been determined to improve on their scrappy track record of the 1990s. Before 9/11, the authorities had amassed a mountain of material on terrorist fund-raising—going all the way back to the secret conference of Hamas activists taped by the FBI at the Courtyard Marriot in Philadelphia in 1993. This evidence had been well trawled by the legal team that put together the civil action in the David Boim case, but it was never clear that the authorities had a fully formed idea of what to do with it.

After 9/11, the FBI had set up a powerful new Terrorist Financing Operations Section to give expert attention to terrorist money trails. One of this section's first major outings was to Texas, where it supervised the preparation of the case being held in the same city in which the Holy Land Foundation had its headquarters.[2]

As head of the Terrorist Financing Operations Section, Denis Lormel was acutely aware of the far greater challenge prosecutors would face in seeking to convince a criminal jury of the HLF defendants' intent, compared with the pedestrian ease of selling it to U.S. Treasury officials who had formulated the proposal for Bush to freeze the charity's assets and funds way back in December 2001.

The prosecutors had literally truckloads of incriminating documents after the raids on the HLF offices, and more than a decade of investigative depth behind them on this case.[3] When Lormel's experts headed to Dallas to set up their war room, their anxiety was not about what was in the documents so much as how they could be knitted into a case that a jury of ordinary Americans might grasp. "Can they [the prosecutors] get their arms around the most significant stuff?" Lormel regularly asked his man on the ground.[4] Despite the anxiety betrayed by his question, there was rising confidence as sophisticated new computer systems helped them to burrow into the raw evidence. "I felt good about the prospects for this case," Lormel later professed.[5]

The outcome of the InfoCom case in October 2006 seemed to be a good omen. In that case, a local jury had ultimately shown itself capable of grappling with some of the complex issues that would later be part of the HLF case. The El-Ashi brothers, cousins of Mousa Abu Marzook's wife, Nadia, had comprised the InfoCom executive team suspected of a range of crimes behind a money-laundering operation. They were jailed for terms of up to seven years on charges of conspiracy, money laundering, and dealing with the officially designated terrorist Abu Marzook.

Meanwhile in Chicago, the hearing of racketeering charges against Mohammad Salah and Abdel Haleem Al-Ashqar—the first man being the former Hamas bagman from Chicago and the second man being the Hamas fixer and former academic from Howard University in Washington—had unfolded in the court of Judge Amy St. Eve. This had not been without its bizarre moments.

Israel's Shin Bet had agreed that its agents could travel to Chicago to testify about their original interrogation of Salah, who had been arrested in the West Bank in 1993 with $97,000 in a bag. "Not only would the courtroom be closed, but the Israeli agents would be permitted to testify in disguises and with code names," observed Tom Durkin, a former assistant U.S. attorney in Chicago and onetime representative of Al-Ashqar. "Black crepe paper was used to cover windows in the courtroom doors and federal agents, along with a bomb-sniffing dog, barricaded the hall outside . . . two CIA-looking types in suits and headphones sat in the corner . . . with a table full of electronic equipment, supposedly scrambling any attempt by the participants in the hearing to filter information out of the courtroom."[6]

The Chicago jury went out to consider its verdict in mid-January 2007. But this time the omen was bad. After deliberating for fourteen days, the jury sent tremors through the team preparing the case against the HLF when they cleared Salah and Al-Ashqar of all the substantive charges they faced. On the evidence presented after more than a decade of investigation and litigation, the Chicago jurors did not share the views of Ashcroft, who had described the pair as a "U.S.-based terrorist recruiting and financing cell."

For all that, both Salah and Al-Ashqar had still ended up in jail—Salah for twenty-one months, for lying while being deposed in the David Boim case; Al-Ashqar for more than eleven years, for refusing to talk to the grand juries investigating Hamas. But in the hometown of Al Capone—who had famously beaten the charges relating to the Valentine's Day Massacre but ultimately went down for short-changing the taxman—the incarceration of Salah and the bespectacled Al-Ashqar on such minor charges was cold comfort for the authorities.

With two major cases concluded in Chicago—the criminal case against Salah and Al-Ashqar and the civil action taken by the Boim family—attention turned to Dallas. Hamas was now feeling the full weight of the American legal system. The Boim family's wish that their son's death not be forgotten had sustained the first salvo. But now it would be fourteen years of phone taps and surveillance that framed the onslaught on Islamist activism in America, especially on the lucrative fund-raising machine that had been set up twenty years earlier by the acolytes who had become today's Hamas leaders.

It was not surprising that the unfolding case against the Holy Land Foundation was watched closely in Damascus. But, as Khalid Mishal received his daily briefings on the goings-on in the Texas courtroom, his interest was deeply personal too. One of the defendants, the HLF's star fund-raiser Mufid Abd Al-Qadir, was his brother. Another of the defendants was to have been his cousin, Akram Mishal, the HLF's projects and grants director, but Akram Mishal had quietly slipped out of the United States three months before the trial began.

In the Damascus bunkers, Abu Marzook had a family interest too—his wife was a cousin of Ghassan El-Ashi, the HLF chairman and treasurer; and Mohammad El-Mezain, the HLF's founding chairman, was his cousin. The stakes were high, with all of the defendants facing life imprisonment.

Mufid Abd Al-Qadir most recently had been employed by day as a works supervisor at the Dallas city council. But by night he had a big Islamic following as a song-and-dance man. His star turn at community functions in cities like Orlando, Toledo, Detroit, and Chicago was a skit in which he acted out the killing of an Israeli, before donations in cash and even in chunks of gold[7] were collected. Video recordings of the stage performances by his troupe were dug up in the garden of a residence in Falls Church in northern Virginia, the area where Abu Marzook had once lived, when a new owner had attempted to landscape the property, which he had purchased from a man who, the Dallas court was told, was a Hamas activist. Khalid Mishal's brother had been fired by the city council when charges were laid in the HLF case.

In August 2007, amid extraordinary secrecy and security during the third week of evidence in the trial, reporters and spectators were cleared from the court of Judge A. Joe Fish. Washington had produced two more anonymous Israeli agents as witnesses for the prosecution. Only lawyers, jurors, and the defendants were allowed to see the faces of "Lior" and "Avi." With great certainty, the two Israelis testified that HLF was part of a global fund-raising network that financed Hamas's terrorism, and that Hamas activists controlled the vital *zakat* committees.

But "Avi" stumbled under cross-examination. He admitted that he could not really say who was in charge of any of the *zakat* committees at the particular times when HLF funds were transferred from the United States. Later, he accepted that none of the committees were among the hundreds of terrorist groups outlawed by American authorities. "Avi" was unable to tell the court how anyone, perhaps other than an Israeli intelligence official, might have been informed that specific *zakat* committees or any of their members had ties to Hamas. Likewise, he conceded, investigations in Britain and in Holland had cleared HLF-like organizations of any wrongdoing. "Clearly they didn't have my evidence," he parried lamely.

The defense countered the Shin Bet testimony with that of Edward Abington, a former number two intelligence official in the U.S. State Department. Abington told a hushed court that in all the time he had been consul general in Jerusalem in the 1990s, during which he had received daily CIA briefings, he had not once been informed that any of the HLF-funded *zakat* committees, which from time to time he had visited, were a part of Hamas.[8]

But it was the government's last witness, FBI Special Agent Lara Burns, who allowed one of the defense attorneys' better moments of courtroom theater. Burns conceded that not all "martyrs" who received assistance from the HLF were terrorists. Working with a list of Arab names that the prosecution had attempted to tie to Hamas, Defense Attorney Linda Moreno pressed Burns on the fact that these names did not appear on Washington's terrorist lists. Every time Burns conceded that an individual had not been formally designated as a terrorist, Moreno used a heavy black marker to score the name from the list of those the government was attempting to link to Hamas. After a few minutes of Moreno's questioning, virtually all of the names had been blacked out.

The lawyers' closing arguments took more than two days. "Don't get hung up on the names," Prosecutor Barry Jonas pleaded as the jury went behind closed doors to deliberate in acrimony and anger over the enormity and complexity of their task. With a total of 197 individual charges against the defendants, it sometimes took a whole day just to take a progress vote on their deliberations. Twice the jury forewoman went to the judge with complaints about conduct in the jury room and arguments that could not be resolved. There were accusations that one juror in particular regularly drifted off to sleep. "You could hear her snoring," one of her colleagues complained.

The reading of the verdict came twenty-three days later, in the fifteenth-floor courtroom crammed with spectators and some media. It was chaotic. An overflow crowd of HLF supporters spilled into a cafeteria lower in the building. But without an audio or visual feed from the court, they did not have a clue as to what was happening in the courtroom.

When the jury forewoman delivered the verdict, the prosecution was stunned. Mishal's brother Mufid was found not guilty on all charges against him.[9] Mohammad El-Mezain, and HLF's representative in New Jersey, Abdul Rahman Odeh, were acquitted on virtually all charges. In the cases of the principal defendants, Shukri Abu Baker and Ghassan El-Ashi, the jury was deadlocked. Later, it would be revealed that the panel had split down the middle on the guilt or innocence on all counts against these two.

After the call on all 197 charges, there was not a single guilty verdict. It was a comprehensive wipeout for the prosecution—and a disaster for Washington.

The media was sequestered on floor sixteen of the Earle Cabell Federal Building. They had both audio and visual feeds, but they were still almost as confused as the HLF cheer squad in the cafeteria. In the race to be first with the news, the radio and television correspondents rushed their reports to air while their newspaper colleagues were going "live" on their Web sites. But the story was changing so fast that it had raced ahead of all the reporting.

When Judge Fish polled individual jurors, to make sure each agreed with the forewoman's report, three of them sensationally leapt to their feet in the courtroom and disputed her account of their deliberations. The unidentified forewoman was in a state of shock. "I really don't understand where this is coming from," she told the court amidst great uproar. "All twelve made that decision."

Adding to the confusion, the HLF crowd in the cafeteria was behind the pace on what they thought was happening because they were relying on the media, which was itself unable to keep abreast of real-time developments in the courtroom. Sympathizers outside the building were texting messages to those in the cafeteria about what the media was reporting. But by the time each text message arrived, events had moved on in the timber-paneled court.

Flummoxed, Judge Fish had his own way of dealing with the jurors' confusion. Hoping to restore order, he sent them out yet again. Just forty minutes later they returned, pleading they could not continue. There was no way this deadlock could be broken.

Fish declared a mistrial for *all* defendants. Even the one man seemingly acquitted on all charges against him—Khalid Mishal's brother Mufid—suddenly was stripped of his brief, jury-verified innocence.

William Neal, a thirty-three-year-old art director from Dallas, was one of only two jurors to shed any light on the tortured deliberations by the panel of four men and eight women. "Overall, the [prosecution's] case was pretty weak," he said. "There really was nothing there for me, no concrete evidence." Neal suggested that he and his colleagues had been overwhelmed by the impenetrable mass of the prosecution's case—in terms of the number of charges and the mountain of evidence they were forced to climb. "I think they just put too much on us," he said. "Some of it was twenty years old. There were so many gaps; I could drive a truck through it."[10]

What remained unclear at the end of the trial was whether the government had failed in its efforts to prove its key argument—that HLF charity funds went to Hamas-controlled entities in the Occupied Territories to facilitate terrorism—or whether it had convinced the panel of its case. Some of the jurors simply were not as shocked or outraged as Washington wanted them to be.

Another juror who spoke to a reporter after the case was Nanette Scroggins, a retired insurance claims adjuster. "I kept expecting the government to come up with something, and they never did," she said. "From what I saw, this was about Muslims raising money to support Muslims, and I don't see anything wrong with that."[11]

Given the unhappiness in the jury room, it might have been risky to read too much into the self-imposed silence of the rest of the jurors in the aftermath of the trial, but none emerged to contradict William Neal's provocative commentary on the case or Nanette Scroggins's seeming endorsement of what Neal had been saying on their behalf. "The whole case was based on assumptions that were based on suspicions," Scroggins added. "If [HLF] had been a Christian or a Jewish group, I don't think [the prosecution] would have brought charges against them."

Juror Neal was particularly instructive on what had appeared to be the breaking point in the government's case. The jurors had well understood that Hamas was a designated terrorist entity and its leader Khalid Mishal personally so. But while they had been told that the FBI had concluded as early as 2001 that Hamas controlled the *zakat* committees, they understood that the combined weight of the U.S. political, legal, and lobbying machinery had failed to have these individual grassroots operations in the Occupied Territories formally declared to be terrorist organizations. This appeared to be the context in which jurors had been swayed away from guilty verdicts. "There was really only one question," Neal revealed. "Did Hamas control the *zakat* committees? There was not enough evidence [that it did]."[12]

Arab community leaders in America were ecstatic. "The government failed in Chicago; it failed in Florida; and it failed in Texas," said Nihan Awad, executive director of the Council on American Islamic Relations, as he ticked off the litany of failed prosecutions. "The reason it failed is the government does not have the facts. It has fear," he told reporters outside the court.[13]

This was to have been Washington's flagship case in the domestic fight against terrorist fund-raising. George W. Bush's personal announcement of the closure of the HLF had stamped it with the president's imprimatur. "The facts are clear—the terrorists benefit from the Holy Land Foundation," Bush had declared in 2001. "And we're not going to allow it."

Outside the Dallas court, rain came down in sheets. Shukri Abu Baker was hoisted on the shoulders of jubilant, cheering supporters. "*Allahu akbar!*" they chanted. In the finest tradition of guerrilla warfare, they had won by not losing.

In Damascus, Khalid Mishal was derisive about Washington's prosecution effort. "My brother committed no violation," he said when told of the outcome of the trial. "His only crime was to be my brother."[14]

On the October day when the government's case against the HLF fell in such a spectacular heap, Denis Lormel, the man who had headed the FBI's Terrorist Financing Operations Section at the time when the HLF case was being prepared, was attending a conference in Washington. Pausing in the lobby of the Marriot Wardman Park Hotel, Lormel conceded the daunting challenge.

"It was always going to be difficult, considering how a defendant can weave an alternate motive of humanitarian aid," he explained.[15] With the benefit of hindsight, he second-guessed the prosecution. "A couple of weeks ago, there was speculation that the Department of Justice didn't realize the difficulty of the situation they were in—I would have simplified the trial, focused on certain elements and put every exhibit into its context."

The threshold of proof in civil actions, like the Boim case, was lower than in criminal cases such as that against the HLF. And in this, there was some consolation for Lormel. Speculating on any renewed effort by the HLF to have its funds unfrozen, he explained, "That low threshold is why they have been unable to do so until now. And I would be very surprised if they were to get them unfrozen—despite the Dallas decision."[16]

This was the logic that underpinned another prediction by Lormel. In the future, he said, there would likely be more civil actions brought by victims of terrorism than criminal cases brought by the government. "Hamas has been masterful in hiding behind its *dawa* work and creating clouds of doubt [that work in its favor in criminal cases]. You know, we had the smoking gun—that was Abu Marzook's role in setting up HLF."

Lormel put a brave—and valid—spin on the disappointment in Dallas. He figured that the authorities' demonstration of intent and the resources mustered for battle on the HLF frontline would create a powerful deterrent. Donations to Muslim charities in the United States were already down significantly, because potential donors feared that merely parting with their cash might incriminate them. "This kind of case disrupts things," he said before finishing on an optimistic note. "And if the Arab Bank case gets up, every financial organization in the Middle East will be very frightened."

It made sense. If Nathan Lewin's novel theory could be used successfully in a civil action against U.S.-based Islamic fund-raisers and activists in the David Boim case in Chicago, then there had to be bigger fish to fry.

Lewin's theory had been put to work in the collapsed criminal case against HLF executives, but now it would be harnessed in a series of new high-powered civil actions. In the queue of likely defendants behind Arab Bank were the London-based National Westminster Bank and the French Credit Lyonnais, both of which were accused of working with European counterparts of the HLF to facilitate terrorism.

This, the banks responded, was nonsense. The transactions were no more than tiny electronic blips in routine international business and certainly could not be characterized as a link between a bank and any terrorist organization. In early 2008, attention turned to the big financial advisory house UBS, which found itself fending off accusations that it was an accessory to a Hamas bus bombing in Jerusalem on the grounds that it had provided financial services to a Hamas fund-raiser in Europe.[17]

Joining the attack on the Arab Bank was the celebrated South Carolina–based attorney Ron Motley, who had represented the September 11 survivors and victims' families. In that action he had built up a formidable database of more than 1.3 million pages that were of intimate relevance to the world of terrorism. Motley had made a name for himself, and a good deal of money, in beating Big Tobacco in the U.S. courts, and now almost three thousand claimants had signed on for his massive 9/11 class action.[18] He might have been thought to have had enough on his plate, but Motley could not resist the drama of the pursuit of the Arab Bank.

Based in Jordan, the bank was a venerable financial institution. With a history that spanned more than seven decades in a tumultuous corner of the globe, it had accumulated assets worth $21.5 billion. Arab Bank had a high profile in America and in Europe, and its extensive network reached across the Middle East and into North Africa. It had twenty-two branches in the Occupied Territories, which gave it the lion's share of Palestinian banking.

Ron Motley's action, on behalf of several thousand clients who mostly lived in Israel, was based in part on the provisions of a centuries-old U.S. law on piracy. Two other separate actions against Arab Bank claimed that the bank had conspired with Hamas and the other Palestinian resistance groups "by soliciting, collecting, transmitting, disbursing and providing the financial resources that allowed [them] to flourish and to engage in a campaign of terror, genocide, and crimes against humanity, in an attempt to eradicate the Israeli presence from the Middle East landscape."[19]

In a nutshell, the argument was that the bank had provided an incitement to Palestinian violence. The bank countered with a claim that the funds it processed were humanitarian aid from charities in Saudi Arabia—about two hundred thousand electronic transfers to the tune of about $90 million. But among the recipients of what the bank said were payments to hospitals and social welfare programs and help for the families of those who had been jailed, wounded, or killed, there were other families whose entitlement was based on the death of relatives who had been suicide bombers.

In rejecting the bank's motion to dismiss the case in January 2007, Judge

Nina Gershon, of the U.S. District Court sitting in Brooklyn, had raised the applicants' hopes when she wrote in her decision: "Arab Bank argues that it merely provided routine banking services . . . [but] there is nothing routine about the services the bank is alleged to have provided."[20]

Arab Bank argued that much of the documentation being marshaled against it had been obtained illegally when Israeli forces invaded its branches in the Occupied Territories years before. Israel claimed Hamas used the bank to move millions of dollars to the Occupied Territories, much of it coming via the New York branch.

Months after the civil cases were first filed in Brooklyn, the Arab Bank had suffered a badly timed blow when U.S. financial regulators moved against it following the uncovering of a Hamas account in its Beirut branch. Finding the bank's internal controls to be inadequate, the U.S. Office of the Comptroller of the Currency had fined Arab Bank $24 million in February 2005 and shut down much of its American operation, in particular its deposit-taking and money-transfer business.[21]

"This has a chilling effect," Allan Gerson, one of the lawyers acting against the bank calculated. "I don't think [any] banks are going to easily allow money to flow to terrorists if their funds are being seized."[22]

What Alyza Lewin proudly called her father's Novel Legal Theory provided an intriguing interpretation of U.S. law, but a lifetime in the legal profession was no help to Nathan Lewin when it came to identifying the flaw in the framework of antiterrorism statutes that would ultimately be the trip wire to Washington's plans to use his legal theory against Hamas.

Oddly enough, two men, who between them had more rat cunning than they had legal training, inadvertently identified the shortcomings in the law a good decade before the Holy Land Foundation case crashed to earth. They were Abu Baker and El-Ashi, whom Americans would only later come to know as the most prominent defendants in the Hamas-related trials as they unfolded in Chicago and Dallas.

It was late on an April evening in 1996 when these two HLF executives remonstrated by phone about a package of counterterrorism measures then going through the U.S. Congress. One of the measures was a bid to curb support by American citizens for foreign groups declared by Washington to be terrorists. It had the potential to wreck the HLF conduit to the Occupied Territories overnight.

When these two spoke on the evening of April 23, 1996, their conversation was recorded faithfully by one of the same FBI surveillance units that had monitored all HLF phone traffic since the fateful Philadelphia conference in 1993. However, while the transcript of this particular conversation was assessed by the authorities for its potential to damage the HLF in court[23]—and ultimately became a prosecution exhibit in the HLF case—the free legal advice from the Hamas activists contained in the twenty-page document seemingly was ignored by the high-powered U.S. prosecution lawyers.

The transcript needed to be read carefully because, as often was the case, Abu Baker and El-Ashi's revealing back-of-an-envelope analysis of the legislation was embedded in one of their interminable anti-Israel rants.

"The existing law didn't cover this angle," Abu Baker exclaimed. "That's why they've made it now [that] if you support a university, a hospital, an orphanage you expose yourself to—"

El-Ashi tried to cut in, but Abu Baker, who had a case of the sniffles, cut him off: "They will have to tell you who among the foreign organizations you are not allowed to deal with and you'll have to abide by that." Abu Baker might have expressed himself oddly, but as a bush lawyer, he was on firm ground as he declared: "The proof of the burden [*sic*] is now theirs. Without that list, I don't think they can enforce anything."

Foreshadowing the thinking of the HLF jury in 2007, the two men acknowledged that their foundation was a key target of the new laws; they even identified some of the *zakat* committees through which they distributed funds in the Occupied Territories as the bodies that needed to be individually identified and listed by the United States to give proper effect to the new law.

Canvassing what they anticipated would be the discomfort for U.S. authorities in identifying individual Palestinian charities to be denied funding, El-Ashi conjured up his own version of the legal edict that—had it been made—would have made it easier for the Dallas prosecutors to score convictions against HLF. "[If] they tell you so-and-so charitable organization which has three hundred orphans, all of whom are children of martyrs . . . [if they say] don't send them money because their parents were members of the Islamic movement"—he dropped into Arabic before continuing—"of course I'm not going to be able to transfer the money."

Washington had boxed itself in on the HLF. Six years prior to the failed prosecution in Dallas, it had enforced its will without the cost and risks of a trial—it had simply and effectively shut down the Holy Land Foundation with all the presidential fanfare that a White House Rose Garden announcement entailed. On that day Washington had achieved its objective—the Islamist fund-raiser was out of business and a very loud message had been broadcast on the risk of donating to any other charities that might slip funds to Hamas.

But the war on terror needed the theatrics of terrorists being brought to account, a show trial for the administration to demonstrate on the evening news that it was doing its job. Washington was determined that those individuals whose fund-raising machine had been smashed should be nailed individually and criminally.

Within minutes of Judge A. Fish's declaration of a mistrial against the HLF five, the lead prosecutor, James Jacks, was on his feet, voicing his expectation that Washington would go around again. He demanded a retrial. Some in the profession were dismayed. "I hope that . . . was just a reflex," said Tom Melsheimer, a distinguished defense attorney in Dallas.

Then, just when it seemed that things could not get much worse for the legal war on terror, they did. Sitting in Chicago, the Seventh U.S. Circuit Court of Appeals threw out the groundbreaking Boim decision, which had been based on the wily Nathan Lewin's Novel Legal Theory. The appeals court ruled that the bereaved parents of seventeen-year-old David Boim had failed to prove that the financial contributions to a Palestinian terrorist group had played a direct role in their son's death.

"Belief, assumption, and speculation are no substitute for evidence in a court of law," Appellate Judge Ilana Diamond Rovner wrote in the majority decision. "We must resist the temptation to gloss over error, admit spurious evidence and assume facts not adequately proved, simply to side with the face of innocence and against the face of terrorism . . . no matter how great our desire to hold someone accountable for the unspeakably evil acts that ended David Boim's life."[24]

26

The Man Who Wouldn't Die

A black Mercedes-Benz eased up to the curb, stopping momentarily to pick up a passenger before gliding back into the fumes and chaos of a Damascus afternoon. A muffled thump signaled the reactivation of the central locking system. Black curtains were drawn across tinted windows as the vehicle pulled away from the Al-Majed Hotel at the end of a downtown alley in the Syrian capital.

The driver was Miqdad. A cheerful young man dressed in Hamas black, he kept one eye on the rearview mirror as he hung loosely over the wheel. As he adjusted the audio control, the car was filled with the techno-tribal thump of Hamas anthems, which were interspersed with hectoring snatches of funda-mentalist oratory, the crack of heavy arms, and an occasional bomb blast.

Miqdad drove south away from the heart of the city, passing a rock massif on which the palatial home of Syria's leader, Bashar Al-Assad, was etched against the sky. Straight ahead, another massif was adorned by a crop of spiky communications antennae.

At first the streetscapes were uniformly drab and dull, but here and there, curved Moorish mosaics and grim, angular facades of glass and steel broke the monotony of box-like, Soviet-style architecture. Led by the purveyors of mobile phones, Syria's advertisers had run amok with garish billboards.

After about twenty minutes, Miqdad swung the Mercedes hard right, into a secured enclave that was reserved for high officials of the Damascus regime, for foreign diplomats and NGOs. This was a journey to the sanctuary of Khalid Mishal.

A United Nations agency was signposted. Diplomatic missions or residencies were identified by various national flags. But no signs pointed the way to a nondescript bunker that functioned as the headquarters of Hamas, the Islamic Resistance Movement in Palestine. The dusty four-story complex had the appearance of a residential apartment block. Festooned with swiveling security cameras, it was hard up against a broken hillside on a street at the rear of the diplomatic enclave. Through traffic was light.

The first indication that this might be the home of one of the regime's most high-security VIPs was the presence of three leather-jacketed Syrian guards who juggled firearms and walkie-talkies as they prowled the pavement outside. Less obvious but more powerful was the anti-aircraft battery concealed in a concrete shelter dug deep into the hillside, just across the street.

Miqdad had said little. But now he issued a blunt instruction for his passenger to remain in the car. Slowing the Mercedes, he jumped it onto the pavement, coming to rest under an outstretched awning that hung from the perimeter wall. House guards, moving with practiced precision, seized the loose end of two bunched canvas flaps suspended from the awning and pinned to either side of the wall. They drew them quickly out to the edge of the pavement and then along the gutter to fully envelop the car. Miqdad released the central locking only when the Mercedes was fully concealed in its anonymous canvas bubble.[1] No one saw in and no one saw out.

The arrival of an outsider was a major exercise for the attentive security detail that hovered around Khalid Mishal inside the complex. Each of his guards wore a smart suit and dark tie. They wore earpieces and all spoke into the cuffs of their jacket sleeves from time to time. Courteous enough, they applied themselves with the discipline and thoroughness of men who understood that their boss was a constant target for a determined enemy.

Visitors' cell phones were confiscated at the door. The ground-floor vestibule was filled with a walk-through metal detector and an airport-like baggage scanner, through which all bags were processed, before being taken away for a microscopic physical search—in the absence of their owner.

Up a flight of stairs that turned sharply to the right halfway up and behind a heavy, double-locked door was the sprawling first-floor room where Khalid Mishal received visitors. In the style of a traditional Arabian *diwan*, or meeting place, the long walls were lined with plump sofas and armchairs, which were upholstered in a muted Hamas green. The carpet on the floor was another shade of green. Retainers glided in with welcoming trays of muddy Turkish coffee, sweetened tea, sodas, or mineral water, and with small individual plates of Arabic sweets.

But there was more in this room than Arab hospitality. Confronting all who entered through the big double doors were portraits of about twenty Hamas "martyrs." In a mural that took up much of the space between two imposing windows, each section of a honeycomb pattern held the face of a Hamas cadre who had been liquidated in Israel's campaign of targeted assassination. A shrine to the assassinated Sheikh Ahmad Yassin was in one corner of the room. Off against the far wall, there was an elaborate scale model, in polished timber, of the Dome of the Rock, the revered Islamic shrine in the heart of Jerusalem's Old City, over which so much blood had been spilled.

Khalid Mishal was barking. Holding the whole phone in his hand, with the loudspeaker on, he was shouting in Arabic. He paced animatedly and angrily as the gaze of his aides alternated from his bulk to a television in the corner of the room. Several people, all talking at once, were on the other end of the phone line—yelling back at Mishal. The TV images were graphic, coming in from Gaza.

At a time when Hamas desperately needed to show a less violent face to the world, Al-Jazeera was broadcasting footage of battles in the streets of Gaza between Fatah crowds and a slew of Hamas fighters. It was Friday, September 7, 2007.

With some courage, the remnants of Fatah had taken to organizing Friday protests outside the bigger mosques. While prayer sessions continued inside, Fatah activists held open-air prayer meetings that doubled as anti-Hamas protest rallies outside the mosques. When prayers finished, Fatah provocateurs would taunt Hamas's forces—chanting slogans, throwing stones and tossing homemade noise grenades. Hamas's Executive Force had taken the bait.

Armed with guns and batons, the Executive Force was roughing up the crowds that ignored orders to disperse. Shots were fired in the air; rifle butts and batons left welts on flesh. Some Fatah officials were detained briefly; journalists attempting to cover the unrest had been beaten. On the phone, Mishal was laying down the law in very exact terms, trying to curb the violence. He shouted the names of Yassin and Al-Rantisi, the long-dead leaders of Hamas in Gaza.

Sprawled on a nearby couch, Hamas's old media spokesman Mohammad Nazzal nursed a fractured arm. It was the result of a traffic accident, he said. With a close-cropped beard adorning his several chins, the thickset Nazzal wore an old-style safari suit. Sotto voce, he offered advice as Mishal angrily demanded restraint by the Hamas security forces running in the streets of

Gaza. Among those on the other end of the phone was Said Siam, the interior minister in the Hamas government that had been in power in the Occupied Territories up until the appointment of the Mecca unity government in March 2007.

"I'm talking to our people to keep things calm," Mishal said with evident exasperation. "They must understand that we will not deal with Fatah as they dealt with us in the past. They put Yassin and Al-Rantisi in jail—we'll not treat them like that."

The violent clashes abated quickly enough, and Gaza, ever on a hair trigger, calmed down again. In the absence of any updates in the next hour, Mishal relaxed a fraction, claiming a degree of success. In this case, no news was good news. "Now it's like any other Friday in Gaza," he said. "Okay, so there's a bit more tension."

At age fifty-six, Khalid Mishal had lost the lean Carlos-the-Jackal look he wore in photographs appearing in the Israeli press at the time of Mossad's attempt on his life ten years earlier. In filling out physically, Mishal had taken on a burly aspect, accentuated by his height. The hair that had been Arab black a decade ago had turned silver-gray. His beard was neatly clipped.

Mishal dressed in what many Arabs referred to as "Iranian style." Usually, it was a gray or dark blue suit with an open-neck shirt—sometimes white, often a pale blue. He seemed comfortable in his solid frame, although he announced with a degree of locker-room pride that he had just shed twenty-five pounds in four months of rigorous dieting and exercise.

Ordinarily Mishal observed the Arab tradition of abandoning his shoes at the door, preferring to pad around in socks. But, as autumn set in and a chill rose through the concrete slab floor, he dispensed with custom, advising visitors to follow his lead and stay warm by keeping their shoes on.

He sat next to the portrait of Yassin and the flags of Palestine and Hamas, crossing his legs as he lounged in a big armchair. From time to time he would rise on an elbow to make a point, before folding back into the depths of his chair.

Constantly hovering around Mishal was Abu Sayf, the same strapping bodyguard who had run the Mossad hit men to ground back in 1997. Like a coiled spring, Sayf was Mishal's shadow. Jet-black hair followed the contours of his skull in a no. 3 buzz cut. As trim as he was ten years earlier, Abu Sayf now wore button-down collars, and a silver pin held his tie in place. The ubiquitous pistol was shoved into his belt.

Years of anonymity behind the facade of the Hamas political bureau had left Mishal with a one-dimensional profile in the West—that of a hard-line zealot bent on the destruction of Israel. But Hamas's election as the government of the Occupied Territories and the factional ruckus that followed had brought more studied attention to a man who had long played a shadowy role in regional affairs.

Mishal was a complex individual with a personal charm that belied the caricature and his cutthroat reputation. He had a broader interest in world affairs than his remorseless public rhetoric would suggest. The man who presided over a killing machine had the fastidious personal habits of a hospitable Arab chieftain. He would polish grapes one at a time with a tissue, or he would produce a knife to slice pieces from a ripened peach, before passing the fruit to a visitor. If the visitor's eye wandered, he would interrupt his delivery, which was principally in Arabic, and switch into English to command eye contact with the words "Excuse me!"

In fact, Mishal had a sound understanding of English. Although he was reluctant to use it, he would swiftly correct a translator on nuances of meaning, thus revealing his own keen grasp of the language. In discussing the so-called Jordan Option, by which Palestinians might be driven from the West Bank to live among their eastern neighbors, he jokingly called it the "Jordan cucumber" because the Arabic word *khiyar* translated as both "option" and "cucumber." His wordplays became political statements: "Ah! I have 'sage' in my tea; 'siege' is how the Palestinians live."

On the narrow policy spectrum within Hamas, Mishal lined up in the pragmatic center. But having observed how compromise and corruption had almost destroyed Fatah, he was hardheaded in his pragmatism, and some close observers of the movement argued that in recent years he had toughened in his policy outlook.

By the Mishal book, his championing of Hamas's participation in the political process ought to have appealed to the West. However, that endorsement never came because of his determined stand on the prime issues of the ongoing violence, of the rocket attacks, and of the cornerstone commitment in the movement's charter: its call for the destruction of Israel. Mishal had no intention of compromising on what he saw as the movement's legitimate right to resist Israel violently. Hamas might have run for election, but it did so as a resistance movement that kept its finger on a detonator.

In the aftermath of the June war between the Palestinian factions in Gaza, Mishal knew Hamas had reached a historic crossroads. Despite the strained circumstances, he was enthusiastic about the responsibility of government, but Mishal also warned that a "third Intifada" was in the cards. Hamas was open to an accommodation with Israel, but not at the movement's expense or that of the rights of the Palestinian people.

Like a chess player, Mishal stepped carefully around speculation about the circumstances in which Hamas might enter talks with Israel. If he were to acknowledge Israel, what would Israel do in return for Hamas? What might the American and European reactions be?[2] He continued to dismiss any knowledge of the cease-fire proposal Israeli sources claimed was received from Hamas in 2006. "That never happened," he insisted. "It's not correct, I'm sure. I'm the leader here—I know what's happening."

While Mishal held the muscular power in Hamas, his old rival and colleague Mousa Abu Marzook was established nearby in his own Damascus office. These two men still worked closely in the Hamas leadership team, but Abu Marzook's fortunes had taken a backseat over the years as Mishal's grip had tightened. The relationship between the two men and what it said about the shifting balance of power at the peak of Hamas was a subject of considerable interest to the United States and to Israel.

A native of Gaza, Abu Marzook was a lifelong disciple of Sheikh Ahmad Yassin. He had rebuilt the grassroots leadership of Hamas in the Occupied Territories in the early 1990s after the Israeli campaigns of mass roundups and deportation of the movement's activists. By contrast, little had emerged on Mishal's activities in the same period, which some colleagues still cryptically referred to as Mishal's "clandestine years."

Anointed by Yassin, Abu Marzook had been well positioned as the man most likely to ultimately assume the leadership of Hamas. Instead, it was Mishal—who hastily denied that his father's role as imam to a senior member of the Kuwaiti royal family had conferred any privilege on his family—who rose inexorably. During Abu Marzook's incarceration in America from 1995 to 1997, Mishal had cemented his own position in the hierarchy.

When Abu Marzook was released, he had returned to the Hamas political bureau to find he had been demoted and would serve instead as Mishal's deputy. At every opportunity in the Hamas electoral cycle, Abu Marzook had signaled his ongoing rivalry by standing as a leadership candidate—to no avail. At least three such efforts had ended in failure and the most recent of them in ignominy, when he was unable to muster the support to retain even his post as deputy, much less to dislodge Mishal from the top job.

But senior figures in Hamas explained that, in the interests of internal peace, Mishal had proposed that Abu Marzook continue to serve as an appointed deputy. "Brother Khalid carries the stick in the middle," one explained.

These days Abu Marzook worked from his hillside den above Damascus. The views were spectacular, but his accommodation had more the air of a barracks room than of the stylish, corporate headquarters he had enjoyed back in the old days in Amman in the mid-1990s. From time to time, he emerged publicly to talk to the Western media, but Abu Marzook had the look of a man who had fallen on hard times. His sagging frame carried excessive weight, and the dapper dress sense of a former chief who saw merit in color-coordinating his coffee cups with his office fittings had been surrendered to more pedestrian attire.

Outside the Hamas inner circle, some had been surprised by Mishal's effortless rise to the frontline leadership team. Observers like the Gaza-based historian and nonfactional political player Ziad Abu-Amr argued that the authority and strength of Hamas had provided the springboard for Mishal's ambition. "You must remember that sometimes a powerful and credible movement makes the leader—not the reverse," he explained.[3]

In Amman, the well-connected journalist and analyst Ranya Kadri attributed Mishal's elevation to the Israeli assassination attempt of 1997. "The day they tried to kill him was the day Mishal the leader was born," she observed later. "The man who died that day was Abu Marzook. Nobody wanted to talk to Abu Marzook after that—it was Mishal, Mishal, Mishal."[4]

Over the years there had been oblique references to a Muslim Brotherhood council of war in Amman in 1983, which had laid the foundations of Hamas.[5] But the official mythology had always pinpointed the legendary meeting on the evening of December 9, 1987, at the Gaza home of Sheikh Yassin, as the occasion on which the wheelchair-bound preacher and six others had spontaneously given birth to Hamas in an effort to channel outrage over a fluke traffic accident in which several Palestinians had died.

But by Mishal's own account, the plotting had begun much earlier—first in distant Kuwait and subsequently at the secret conference in Jordan. The plan for the creation of Hamas had been locked into the Muslim Brotherhood's strategic planning as much as four years before the fatal traffic collision, near the Erez border crossing, that heralded the onset of the first Intifada. Mishal's version suggested that the powerful imagery of the crippled Yassin, almost single-handedly working the length and breadth of the Gaza Strip in the name of Hamas, had been a clever exercise in public relations.

"It would have been impossible for the Yassin operation to succeed in Gaza and on the West Bank, without the outside project [instigated by Mishal]," a source close to the Hamas leadership said. "Even when Yassin was focused on *dawa* [as opposed to armed resistance], it was funding from the Muslim Brotherhood [outside Palestine] that kept him going."

Mishal's own explanation was that work on a new armed resistance was well on track when the Erez accident, in which a truck driven by an Israeli ploughed into oncoming traffic near the Erez crossing, killing four Palestinians, became the trigger that activated a pre-made plan. "The decision by the Gaza Seven in 1987 was not a spontaneous or momentary event happening out of context," he said. "Hamas's founders inside and outside the Occupied Territories had taken steps to prepare for the launch of the movement. Anger and rage over the traffic accident made that December the opportune moment.

"We were ready. From the outside, it might have looked like a reaction [to the accident]. But the project envisaged in 1983 was on the verge of coming to fruition, and for us this was its crowning moment. This was the appropriate environment for Hamas to come into being and to go public."

Mishal's years as an exiled Palestinian in Kuwait, seemingly intent on his new career as a physics teacher, had been an effective veil, behind which he had dreamed of another destiny. "I was a man with a mission, a cause, a project. I'd been dreaming of it since I was a kid! I'm proud that God bestowed on me the bounty of being a founder and a soldier for a project of which I've become leader. It's a position entrusted to me by my brothers. But what is personally important for me is that this is my project."

Mishal now straddled the organization, albeit from exile. By deft management or manipulation of each crisis in the organization's history—including the assassination of Yassin—he had steadily consolidated his control over an intellectually and organizationally cohesive but geographically far-flung network.

The various wings of the movement—the military and political arms; the local leadership in Gaza and the West Bank; the powerful prisoners' leadership, which managed to function inside Israel's jails; and the government team, over which Ismail Haniyah presided in Gaza—could interact only through Damascus. Mishal kept an iron grip on both the flow of funds and Hamas's extensive links with the Arab and Muslim worlds.

Mishal had the support of the more hard-line elements within the movement, particularly in Gaza. He adopted the language of violence with ease, using rhetoric and propaganda to motivate his forces and to stand Hamas apart from Fatah's checkered efforts to achieve a negotiated settlement with Israel.

But, with an eye on Western perceptions of resistance and his own role as the movement's chief diplomat, Mishal sought to play down his personal role in suicide bombings, contending that the separation of power between the military and political wings of Hamas was real. "I have not personally authorized a suicide bombing," he said. "That is the prerogative of the military wing. They're the people who authorize and plan them."

Adopting a distinction that had worked for the Irish Republican Army and Sinn Féin in Ireland in the days before September 11, Mishal explained, "The policy of the movement is to engage in resistance. The military wing decides what form it takes and it's the role of the political wing to defend and explain the resistance."

Mishal, of course, had also not deterred the suicide bombers; instead, he urged them on and had taken public satisfaction in the aftermath. But by 2004, Hamas's continued use of suicide attacks had turned international opinion decisively against the Palestinian cause. It prompted a reassessment within Hamas, in which Mishal held to his view that there was still a strategic advantage to be gained by the use of such a catastrophic weapon. By his calculation, the negative publicity was outweighed by the undermining of Israel's sense of security and the unambiguous message conveyed by each attack that the Palestinians were not giving in.

It took more than a year of intense debate within the movement, driven by Hamas's supporters in diaspora communities in the United States and in Europe, for the internal lobby against suicide missions to win the argument that there had to be another way to "make Israel bleed."[6] Mishal would not accept that the numbing violence that Palestinians and Israelis inflicted on each other had a brutalizing effect on all who were trapped in the conflict. "We don't believe that instinctively insisting on our rights dehumanizes Palestinians. He who defends himself, his people, and his country does not lose his humanity," Mishal argued, choosing to frame the decision to back away from suicide missions as a sensible exercise of the movement's *shura*, or consultative processes, and not as a personal defeat for himself. "There'll be times when I feel restrained [by the internal debate], but it doesn't limit my ability to maneuver or to come up with new ideas."

After decades of struggle that had defined not just his people, but the whole region, the Khalid Mishal who had risen through the ranks to speak with such authority on the fate of millions of people was a Palestinian enigma. It was difficult to pigeonhole him. Mishal ran a huge, complex organization.

Hamas functioned both as a government and as an army in a daunting environment. He had an international support network and a following in the Occupied Territories, which demanded that Mishal fill the roles of president, commander in chief, treasurer, and ambassador to the world.

He was branded a terrorist by the United States and the European Union. His oratory was rich in the rhetoric of jihad. But Mishal himself had never thrown a stone, much less fired a shot in combat. For him, there had been none of the resistance schooling of the prison cell or the guerrilla camaraderie of the campfire.

Mishal was a hybrid mix of the pious and the worldly. He was deeply immersed in Islam, devoting an hour a day to learning to recite the Qur'an from a *qari*, a tutor who was the last in a rare and unbroken chain of teachers that went all the way back to the Prophet Muhammad. At the same time Mishal revealed few of the traits of the stereotypical fundamentalist—the myopic, insular, and intellectually stunted extremist of Western perception. "I've met him three times now and I still have not heard him say the word 'Islam,'" an American analyst noted, almost in exasperation, after his most recent meeting with the Hamas leader.

The public Mishal projected himself as a hard man. In private he was prone to sudden, unexpected displays of emotion. Mishal indulged in misty memories of village life and the fare at his mother's table. He became morose recalling the death of Yehiya Ayyash, the master suicide bomber after whom Mishal named a son born on the day that Israeli forces assassinated Ayyash in 1996. And he shed tears when he spoke of a mystery bomb attack in Pakistan in 1989 that killed the preacher-warrior Abdullah Azzam, the mentor Mishal had shared with Osama Bin Laden. "Azzam was a great man and we owe him a lot," Mishal observed, without elaborating on the nature of the debt.

Diplomats, mediators, and analysts invariably emerged from the Damascus bunker talking more about what Khalid Mishal was not than about what he was. His critics in the West and in the Arab world were legion. They could cite a litany of his mistakes, but against the din of the rejectionist rhetoric from Washington and Jerusalem, a small but influential body of Western and Israeli support was building behind Mishal and his ability to wrestle tempest-like forces in a crisis that unfolded as a geopolitical psychodrama.

Senior analysts and former administration advisers and officials in the United States and the Middle East warned of the risk of underestimating Mishal, of denying him a seat at the table. By late 2007, it was possible to hear a former senior government adviser in Jerusalem describe Mishal as an "authentic nationalist leader," or to hear a former White House official in Washington judge him as a leader destined to play "an essential role" in the Middle East crisis.

Arab intelligence officials were troubled because Mishal was the first figure in Hamas to take control of both the political and military wings. In Israeli military intelligence, the analysis was more about the qualities that made Mishal such a formidable enemy for the Jewish state. "He understands power and the use of violence. Even if he doesn't do it himself, he understands clearly what it's about," said a former Israeli military intelligence officer who had studied Mishal from afar for fifteen years. "He steadies the Hamas boat. He's not a great ideologist and he did not invent the Hamas ideology, but he understands it and what it allows him to do. But we have to understand that Mishal is a very dangerous person. He's not crazy; he is down to earth, or at least that's what he wants us to think. Remember this—he heads a terrorist group with its bombs and rockets and with people being hurled from fifteenth-floor windows."[7]

The same caution was couched in different terms by a key Fatah activist who had observed Mishal's increasing dominance of Hamas. "He didn't win internal support for the leadership with charisma alone," he argued. "There were reasons for them deciding that Mishal would be a strong, determined leader. To get up, he had to sell the idea to Hamas and the Muslim Brotherhood that this posture of his can win important friends and neutralize significant enemies."

An Israeli agent tapped into a different, but equally potent, reservoir of resistance sentiment to define the forces driving Mishal. "He wants to be like us, like the Zionists in historic Palestine," he said. "As a homeless people, they succeeded in carving out a new state that today is home to more than 40 percent of the Jews of the world. Mishal sees himself being responsible for all Palestinians—inside *and* outside—and he wants to bring them all together in their historic home."

In an era of instant communication, Mishal kept the TV remote control handy to monitor more than half a dozen satellite news channels that fed real-time news from the Occupied Territories to the bunker in Damascus. He had a basement television studio from which his speeches were beamed back into Palestinian homes, either by Hamas's Al-Aqsa channel or by Hezbollah's Al-Manar. His principle tool of trade was the phone. He rarely touched a cell phone—the Israelis were proven masters at tampering with them. Instead, he was a creature of the old-fashioned landline. His staff handled his e-mail, but his personal connections were based on the handwritten lists he had compiled over a lifetime. When aides were unable to produce a phone number he required, one of two little black books was brought to him. Small and dog-eared, these were Mishal's who's who of the world of politics, Islam, and jihad. "It's all in here—my links to the world," he said.

Mishal had access to a secure military base in Damascus, where he could walk for exercise. More often, however, he spent an hour a day on a treadmill in the bunker. As he clocked up his daily four-mile walk on the machine, he devoured newspapers, magazines, and, sometimes, the Qur'an.

He had just finished reading the controversial memoirs of former CIA director George Tenet—*At the Center of the Storm: My Years at the CIA*—which he described as a "brave effort to open a window into the Iraq war." He was reading Jimmy Carter's *Palestine: Peace Not Apartheid* and John J. Mearsheimer and Stephen M. Walt's *The Israel Lobby and U.S. Foreign Policy*. At the same time, he was wading through the fourteenth-century Muslim intellectual Ibn Kathir's fourteen-volume history of Islam—*The Beginning and the End*. Mishal's bedside cache of reading included one of the Ibn Kathir volumes; a biography of Saladin, the Muslim warrior-king who had recaptured Jerusalem from the Crusaders in 1187; the Qur'an; and Al-Adkhar, another Islamic prayer book.

Mishal had finally curtailed his travel after years of being on the move. In an increasingly hostile environment, he remained in this shuttered bunker or in other secure locations in Damascus, which he alluded to with cryptic caution as "my other places."

"It's my destiny," he said, explaining the inevitable constraints on his household. "The family adapts. They are convinced of the nobility of the task, so they too shoulder the responsibility. It's their cause as much as mine."

Mishal's seven children attended "normal" schools and university in Damascus. At home his sons drifted in and out of his meetings, including the three who had witnessed Mossad's attempt on their father's life in 1997. Since then, most of the key figures in the Middle East crisis had moved on. Jordan's King Hussein was dead, and Samih Batikhi, his powerful intelligence chief, had been cast out by the new regime. Yasser Arafat too was dead, and Ariel Sharon was suspended in a deep coma. Bill Clinton was long gone from the White House. Of them all, it was Mishal who had been the marked man. In Hamas, they called him "the martyr who did not die."

In the aftermath of the civil war, Gaza wore two kinds of war wound. Locals could easily identify whether damage was caused by Israeli weapons or the

Palestinian factions. Where a building teetered, or had been reduced to a pile of rubble spilling into the streets, clearly it had been targeted by Israel's high-caliber, laser-guided weaponry. But a building that still stood, with its walls scorched, masonry pitted, and windows smashed, was likely to have come under small-weapons fire in the fighting between Palestinians.

For their attacks on Israel, Palestinian rocket crews were beginning to use a new targeting tool. Previously they had relied on conventional maps of their enemy's terrain, but now they cross-referenced them against satellite imagery downloaded from Google Earth,[8] a popular new eye-in-the-sky service that could be accessed with a laptop and a simple Internet connection from anywhere in the world.

On the second day of the new school year, September 2, a barrage of nine rockets was launched in the direction of Sderot, the border community that took the brunt of the rocket fire from Gaza. A dozen small children were treated for shock after one of the devices lobbed into the courtyard of an Israeli day care center.[9]

Nine days later, a Qassam rocket fired by Palestinian Islamic Jihad had the potential to take the crisis over the edge of the abyss—again. Launched in the early hours of September 11, the rocket crashed into Zikim, an IDF training base on the Gaza fringe. It hammered into an empty training tent, but dozens of young soldiers who were sleeping in adjacent tents were injured, one critically. With an additional sixty-eight injuries,[10] it was the most successful Qassam strike in the six-year campaign.

In Gaza, they expected the worst. A spokesman on Hamas Radio welcomed the strike as a "victory from God," but the leadership was rushed to safe houses and into underground bunkers. Expecting their official compounds and security complexes to be targeted, Hamas evacuated all staff. When the ministerial teams moved, they took their computers and walk-through metal detectors with them to their next, temporary quarters.

Overnight, great mounds of earth were dumped at intersections, as protection for Palestinian fighters as much as barriers that might slow an Israeli incursion. These berms appeared first in the northern communities of Beit Hanoun and Beit Lahiya, but with the passing of each day the dump trucks worked their way deeper into the Strip.

Israeli military and public opinion urged a major attack. But, still shaken by the failure of the previous summer's invasion of Lebanon and reluctant to "give Hamas what it wants," the politicians resisted.

Bracing for an onslaught, Hamas conducted nightly military exercises, which included planting explosive devices on the roads and tracks into Gaza from Israel. Senior figures in the government took heart in the knowledge that Israel was aware of Hamas's recent haul of new weapons and the fighting prowess its men had shown in routing the foreign-backed Fatah forces in June. "They don't want to push us into a corner," said Khaled Abu Hilal, the former Fatah commander who had gone over to Hamas. "It's not that we are more powerful—but they know we have nothing to lose."

The crisis over the Qassam strike on the Israeli training base collided with the euphoria of the holy month of Ramadan. It would begin on the first sighting of the new moon, which was expected two or three days after the attack on Zikim. As eyes turned heavenward, a cartoonist on the Hamas-run *Felasteen* newspaper portrayed a hapless Gazan peering into a sky in which hung not one, but two slivers of new moon—one was for Hamas, the other for Fatah.

Spying on the tableau of grim city life was Israel's own eye in the sky—a great white, unmanned spy blimp that was tethered at an altitude of about one thousand feet on the northern border of the Gaza Strip. Ordinarily during Ramadan, it was the duty of prominent figures to host and to attend *iftar*—the breaking of the daily fast—up and down the Strip. But that had become impossible because of their fear of reprisal after the Qassam rocket attack on the Israeli training camp. There was a reasonable suspicion that the blimp and drones overhead were tracking their movements.

Despite being underground, the Hamas prime minister of Gaza, Ismail Haniyah, emerged to lead prayers at the Al-Gharbi Mosque, near his home in the Shati refugee camp. Five black-clad bodyguards formed a tight cordon around the raised platform from which he spoke. Cradling AK-47s, they scanned the mosque crowd until Haniyah was finished—at which point he was hustled through a side door and back into hiding.

Like many of his senior colleagues, Haniyah spoke of the ruptured relations with Fatah as a breach that could still be remedied, despite the huge cost in blood and trust. This was the first year in four decades under Israeli occupation in which a greater number of his people had died in Palestinian-on-Palestinian violence, more than 490, than had been killed in Israeli attacks—at least 396.[11] Seven of the deaths, along with ninety woundings, took place at a huge Fatah rally in Gaza in November, after which Hamas announced that thirty-eight members of the Executive Force had been jailed, sacked, or demoted after accusations that they had indiscriminately opened fire on the Fatah crowd, which had been throwing stones and taunting them.

Others in the movement in Gaza spoke in more revolutionary terms than Haniyah, as though a line had been crossed. "This is what happens in a national power struggle," a senior figure explained. "It's not easy, but at some point you have to make decisions in the knowledge that some will not accept them—but the majority will. Go into the streets—there's not exactly a revolution against us out there! Today Iraqis are bombing each other and Lebanon has colossal problems—but here the majority is calm."

In Gaza there had been no overt or heavy-handed religious crackdown in the aftermath of the June conflict with Fatah. But, in a society that was already deeply conservative, there was a degree of self-policing. Tailors reported women requesting even lower hemlines. More men let their beards grow and the barbers of Gaza confirmed that "the sword," a thin beard running from the sideburns and along the jawline, had become a tolerable compromise between clean-shaven and the bushy undergrowth preferred by hardline Islamists.[12]

Cinemas had closed way back in the first Intifada, and the last bar to sell alcohol in Gaza had been bombed out of business in the weeks before the 2006 election. But shops selling music and DVDs, one of the first targets of fundamentalists elsewhere, were still trading in what now was derided in Israel and abroad as Hamastan.

However, the last economic lifeblood was being drained from Gaza as the Israeli and international siege entered its twentieth month. With the exception of locally grown fruit and vegetables, stores and markets were increasingly bare. Grown men almost cried for cigarettes, which were still smuggled through tunnels from Egypt, but at such a markup as to make them unaffordable for most.

Hamas did control the territory of Gaza, but it soon found that, by remote control from Ramallah, Mahmoud Abbas had at his disposal what was perhaps the most divisive weapon of the interfactional conflict. Abbas continued to pay the wages of tens of thousands of mostly Fatah public servants in Gaza, but only on condition that they did not go to work. Overnight, he had created a two-class society in Gaza.

In the absence of a formal police force, Hamas volunteers—in yellow fluorescent jackets and Hamas-green baseball caps—directed traffic. Apart from an occasional flashpoint, there were no factional gang wars, no clan feuds, no car thefts. The release of Alan Johnston, a BBC reporter held hostage for four months by a local radical group in Gaza, was celebrated with new street banners in the city. "No more threat for our foreign visitors and guests," they declared.

Essential goods were still trucked through Israeli-controlled border-crossings, but at a finely calculated, minimal rate. "After three months they have not collapsed," an Israeli intelligence figure explained. "We're letting just enough stuff through. We're Khalid Mishal's safety net—not because we like him, but because we don't want a full crisis either."[13]

Israel was between what ought to have been grand celebrations. June 2007 had marked the fortieth anniversary of the Six-Day War, in which Israel had conquered both the West Bank and Gaza in 1967. Now great planning was under way to commemorate the sixtieth anniversary of the founding of the state of Israel in May 2008. For Israelis these were meant to be great monuments to centuries of Jewish struggle and survival.

But after forty years of blood and summitry, Israel had achieved neither the security it craved nor all of the land to which its people felt entitled. By clinging to its illegal settlements, it had created the justification for the harsh security regime that encircled millions of embittered Palestinians and left many of its own citizens living a reality tinged with fear and anger. Forty years on, Israel was still fighting the last day of the Six-Day War.

Sandwiched between the two Israeli anniversaries was Hamas's twentieth anniversary. In those two decades, Hamas had withstood everything that Israel, Fatah, and the world had thrown at it. And yet the Islamist movement of late 2007 was a very different movement from the angry group that had emerged at the start of the first Intifada in 1987.

Hamas had defied the early predictions of its demise. Israel's deportation of hundreds of senior figures in 1992 did not seem even to dent Hamas's succession planning. Fatah power brokers had always claimed that the movement would splinter as pushy young militants overran the cautious old guard of the Muslim Brotherhood—but they were wrong. Israel's targeted assassinations and Arafat's crackdowns had broken neither the spine nor the spirit of Hamas. On the death of Sheikh Ahmad Yassin, Israeli commentators had insisted that there would be a leadership void, in which the young Turks would tear the movement apart. They too had been wrong.

Despite the focused strategic efforts of Israel and America, and the overwhelming impact of worldwide sanctions backed by London and Paris, Hamas had held together. "Obviously there'll be differences of governance and effective control," said a senior Fatah leader well placed to observe Hamas in the Occupied Territories. "But in Hamas it does not go to dissent or mutiny. I'm looking—and I just don't see it."

Authoritative voices in the United States had added their weight to the view of former Mossad director Efraim Halevy that Hamas needed to be brought in from the cold. They included former national security advisors Zbigniew Brezezinski and Brent Scowcroft, and former U.S. ambassador to the UN Thomas Pickering.[14] Bush's former secretary of state Colin Powell had cautiously voiced his position. "Hamas has to be engaged," he concluded. "They won the election we insisted upon having."[15]

The emphasis in the Hamas discourse had shifted subtly from jihad to *hudna*. Its territorial claims had shifted from a resumption of the land that ran from the "river to the sea" to a two-state solution based on the 1967 border. The target had become the Israeli occupation, not Judaism.

Hamas had proved it could fight, but it had also demonstrated that it could hold its fire. The movement still had a foot firmly planted in resistance, but it had stamped the other firmly in the democratic political process. Hamas refused to recognize Israel, but it had moved the bottom line. It could accept a Palestinian state adjacent to the Jewish state, and leave to future generations the question of Palestinian claims to all of the land that had become Israel.

The Hamas Charter of 1988—with its offensive language, its anti-Semitism, and its incitement to battle—had become largely redundant. However, it survived in its old form. An internal Hamas committee had spent much of 2005 working on a revision, but their work had been shelved in the aftermath of Hamas's unexpected election victory in the Occupied Territories.[16] But, until such time as the charter's call for the elimination of Israel was finally revoked, Israel and the West could point to it as Hamas's defining credo.

Mishal himself still held to the hard-line Hamas commitment to armed struggle as the only source of Palestinian power in any negotiations with Israel. He would not renounce violence in the absence of substantial concessions. Marking Hamas's twenty-year anniversary at a rally in Damascus in December 2007, he declared, "Land is only liberated by the gun."[17] It was an echo of the defiance he had displayed in an earlier BBC interview, where he warned, "Negotiation without resistance leads to surrender." The ideology might be in the process of transformation, but the rhetoric of resistance was far from dead.

There was no end to the advice Khalid Mishal received. Worried by the depth of the new Palestinian schism, his younger brother Maher had been on the phone from Amman, to insist that Hamas needed to reverse out of its newfound control of Gaza.

The next broadside came during a visit to Damascus by Mishal's old university lecturer, Asad Abdul Rahman, who warned his former student that he had to make a choice. "You can't rule a country with sermons, welfare associations, and guns," Abdul Rahman told him. "You can't be a Muslim fanatic and, at the same time, be a politician . . . especially in a modern world with gigantic enemies—the U.S. globally, Israel regionally!"[18]

The point of Abdul Rahman's lecture was that Hamas should acknowledge that the 1967 border would inevitably become the basis of a two-state solution and that, therefore, it was time for the Islamists to publicly accept the existence of the state of Israel. This likely outcome was accepted by most Arab states, he said, and many Israeli voters had come around to the belief that there should be a dialogue with Hamas. "But you have to decide," Abdul Rahman told Mishal. "You can't be half-pregnant. Either you want to engage in the peace process or not, and if you don't, there is a price to pay."

Typically, it was late at night in Damascus when Abdul Rahman unburdened himself. Mishal's enigmatic response was brief. "When the time comes," the Hamas leader replied.

Mossad had a new plan to kill Khalid Mishal. The Hamas leader's security detail was alive every day to the prospect that the next attempt might be imminent. The execution would depend on a cost-benefit analysis that was as chilling as the reckoning behind the next suicide bomb. They had tried and failed once, and Mossad's mission was to eliminate Israel's enemies. If Mishal were to present himself in the right circumstances a strike might simply be irresistible. Such were the opportunistic gambles on which wars had been won and lost. No one knew when it might come.

Mishal's predecessor and dozens of his comrades had been assassinated already by Israel, and he had been warned often enough that he remained in the crosshairs, notwithstanding the debacle a decade earlier in Amman. Hunkering in Damascus did not put the Hamas leader beyond the reach of the Israelis. Mishal had been almost nonchalant in his response to a phone call in the first week of September 2007, when he was informed that Israeli jets had penetrated deep into Syrian airspace to bomb a secret target that was alleged later to be the early stage of a suspected nuclear facility.[19]

Israel tended not to formally confirm its involvement in killings abroad, but attacks in Europe and in Amman, Tunis, and Malta in the past had demonstrated that its agencies had no regard for international borders. It had a proven track record on the ground in the Syrian capital. The Hamas operative Musbah Abou-Houwaileh had escaped certain death when his car exploded minutes after he had alighted from the vehicle with his wife and daughter in the Mazzah quarter of Damascus on December 14, 2004.[20] The bombing was widely believed to have been carried out by or on behalf of Israeli security. Syria had blamed Israel for another bomb almost three months earlier, which had exploded as the Hamas bomb maker Izz Al-Din Sheikh Khalil turned the key in the ignition of his car in the Zahraa neighborhood of Damascus.[21]

Mishal always had ready answers for questions about the attempt on his life in Amman in 1997. But when it came to the mechanics of a likely future attack, he was reluctant to speculate. He insisted that the earlier bombings in Damascus had not been directed at him personally. But he knew the Israelis were already in his backyard.

"I expect martyrdom at any time. But the decision on how and when I die is for God—not Mossad" was all he would say.

Epilogue

A spectacular car bomb in downtown Damascus in February 2008 demonstrated the ease with which Israel could liquidate its foes—as long as the operation went according to plan. Widely presumed to be the work of Mossad, this was a daring strike just miles from the Hamas bunker.

The man it killed was Imad Mugniyah, the Hezbollah terror mastermind credited with some of the worst attacks of the 1980s, including the death of more than 350 U.S. and French nationals in the bombing of a marine barracks in Beirut in 1983. It was the first attack on such a senior Hezbollah figure in sixteen years.

The leader of Hamas might just as easily have been the target. That he was not caused some to wonder. Perhaps, in the labyrinthine ways of the region, Khalid Mishal had been given a reprieve that would be understood only with the passage of time.

Throughout 2008, Hamas consolidated its grip on power in Gaza, but the job of governing became a grim exercise in crisis management.

In August the Islamists dispatched the last remnants of the Fatah-controlled security apparatus and its local proxies in a brutal clash with one of the biggest and most heavily armed of Gaza's clan militias. Hundreds of Fatah activists were rounded up and dozens of their institutions ordered to close as Fatah was subjected to the same treatment it had dealt out to Hamas over the years.

By this time, all but a handful of Gaza's factories were closed, and banks were running dangerously low on cash. The number of supply trucks passing through Israeli-controlled checkpoints was down a third from the previous year, and more than a third of Gaza's needs were smuggled from Egypt,[1] delivered through hundreds of tunnels that were managed with Hamas's signature efficiency. The Hamas Interior Ministry had a tunnel-administration unit that monitored the flow of goods by camera, and its tax collectors were stationed at every tunnel exit.[2] A fuel pipeline reportedly ran through one of the tunnels.[3] When a Rafah businessman decided he must have a zoo, his first display animals were drugged and dragged through the sandy passages from Egypt—two lions, a pair of monkeys, and three gazelles.[4]

Despite the best efforts of Mahmoud Abbas and of Israel and the Americans, Hamas from time to time managed to break out of its globally imposed isolation.

In January a series of predawn explosions demolished several sections of the border fence with Egypt. Tens of thousands of jubilant Palestinian shoppers flooded over the line and into Egyptian bazaars, where they bought up supplies of food, medicine, building materials, and livestock. Egyptian work gangs tried to rebuild, but Hamas bulldozers tore the wall down once more, keeping the border open for almost two weeks before Gazans were finally locked in again.

The short-lived carnival atmosphere this created was punctured abruptly when Hamas unleashed its first suicide squad in more than three years. A single Israeli and two Hamas bombers died in the February 4 attack, which Hamas justified as revenge for Israeli incursions and airstrikes in which more than 120 Gazans died.[5]

Talks between Israel and the Palestinian Authority, instigated by George W. Bush toward the end of 2007, made little progress. Then, after almost a year of refusing to deal with Hamas, Mahmoud Abbas reached out for talks with Hamas, as did the regime in Amman.

More sensationally, a former U.S. president, Jimmy Carter, acknowledged Mishal's leadership and authority by visiting the Damascus bunker in April—despite angry protests from Israel and Washington.[6] In June, there was another crack in the diplomatic blockade of Hamas when even Israel quietly moved through intermediaries to negotiate a cease-fire with Hamas in Gaza, but without achieving its oft-stated goal—the release of Gilad Shalit.

As 2009 approached, it seemed there would be a near clean sweep-out of the latest batch of leaders to have played a hand in this decades-old crisis. George W. Bush's second term as U.S. president would end on January 20, 2009. Mahmoud Abbas, however, was refusing to accept arguments that his own term as the elected president of the Palestinian Authority also should expire in the same month.[7]

In the face of persistent corruption allegations, Ehud Olmert agreed that he must relinquish the Israeli leadership. His foreign minister, Tzipi Livni, attempted to fill the breach, but she was unable to build sufficient support for a ruling coalition. The hapless Olmert was obliged to stay on as a lame-duck leader, pending a general election to be held early in February 2009. Riding high in opinion polls as a serious contender to be Israel's next prime minister was Benjamin Netanyahu, who had steadily rebuilt his position in Israeli politics since his fall from grace in the aftermath of the 1997 attempt on the life of Khalid Mishal.

In a Dallas courtroom in November 2008, the Bush administration finally achieved a significant victory in its seven-year legal battle to prove that the Texas-based Holy Land Foundation was a Hamas front masquerading as a charity fund-raiser. After the jury-room debacle of the first prosecution a year earlier, a new jury delivered guilty verdicts on more than one hundred charges of money laundering, tax fraud, and support for terrorism against four HLF executives and Mishal's brother Mufid Abd Al-Qadir.

In the final days of the U.S. presidential campaign, Khalid Mishal dismissed the Bush years. "If we talk about Washington's plan to uproot Hamas, well, it didn't work," he said, before firing a shot across the bow of the next American president.

"Whether it's [Barack] Obama or [John] McCain, he will find the file of the Arab-Israeli conflict on his desk, and he'll find the word 'Hamas' written on every page."[8]

Chronology

1916–1918	Great Arab Revolt: British-backed uprising against Ottoman rule.
1928	Muslim Brotherhood founded by Hasan Banna in Cairo.
1936–1939	Arab Revolt: Palestinians resist British control and Jewish settlement in historic Palestine.
May 14, 1948	Declaration of the independent state of Israel: fighting until October 1949; more than seven hundred thousand refugees displaced from historic Palestine; Jordan takes West Bank; Egypt takes Gaza Strip; Jerusalem becomes a divided city.
August 11, 1952	Hussein Bin Talal crowned king of the Hashemite Kingdom of Jordan.
1954	Yasser Arafat and other Palestinian exiles in Kuwait establish Fatah as a secular, nationalist guerrilla force to fight for a Palestinian homeland.
March 1956	Khalid Mishal born in Silwad, on the West Bank.
June 2, 1964	Palestine Liberation Organization (PLO) established to campaign for a Palestinian homeland.
1965	Sheikh Ahmad Yassin jailed by Egyptian authorities in Gaza for his Muslim Brotherhood sympathies.
June 5–10, 1967	Six-Day War: Israel overwhelms Arab armies and occupies the West Bank and East Jerusalem, the Gaza Strip and Sinai Peninsula, and Golan Heights; Khalid Mishal's family flees Silwad, resettling in Kuwait.

March 21, 1968   Battle of Karameh: Arafat is lionized in the Arab world
                        after his forces repel Israeli incursion in the Jordan Valley.

September 1970   Black September: thousands die as Arafat's and other
                        Palestinian factions are driven out of Jordan in a bitter
                        conflict with King Hussein; Arafat's forces relocate to
                        Syria and Lebanon.

September 5, 1972   Munich Massacre: Palestinian gunmen kill eleven Israeli
                        athletes at the Munich Olympics.

October 6–26, 1973   Yom Kippur War: Egypt and Syria attack Israeli forces in
                        Sinai and the Golan Heights; after initial gains, they re-
                        treat in the face of Israeli counterattacks.

October 1974   An Arab summit in Rabat anoints the Arafat-controlled
                        PLO as the sole representative of the Palestinian people.

July 4, 1976   Raid on Entebbe: Israeli commandos rescue one hundred
                        Israeli and Jewish hostages in Entebbe, Uganda, held by
                        members of Popular Front for the Liberation of Palestine
                        and the Baader Meinhof group, who had hijacked an Air
                        France Airbus.

March–June 1978   Operation Litani: Israeli forces push into southern Leba-
                        non, occupying land between the border and the Litani
                        River to protect northern Israel.

June 1978   Khalid Mishal graduates from Kuwait University and
                        starts work as a physics teacher in Kuwait.

September 1978   Camp David Accords: Egypt, Israel, and the United States
                        sign an agreement for Israel to hand back Sinai in exchange
                        for peace and normalization of relations with Cairo.

December 1979   Iranian Revolution: Ayatollah Ruhollah Khomeini be-
                        comes the supreme leader of an Islamic republic after the
                        ouster of Shah Mohammad Reza Pahlavi.

December 27, 1979   The USSR invades Afghanistan.

June 1981   Khalid Mishal marries Amal Salih, the daughter of West
                        Bank refugees in Kuwait.

October 6, 1981   Egyptian president Anwar Sadat is assassinated.

June 1982   Israel invades Lebanon and lays siege to Beirut for
                        eighty-eight days; Arafat's forces are evacuated to Tunis
                        and other Arab capitals in a U.S.-brokered deal.

September 1982   Israel-allied Christian militias enter Sabra and Shatila
                        refugee camps in Beirut and massacre approximately two

thousand unarmed Palestinians after Israel forces PLO fighters out of Lebanon.

1983   At a secret Muslim Brotherhood conference in Amman, plans are made for the establishment of Hamas.

1984   Khalid Mishal abandons his teaching career to work full-time for the Muslim Brotherhood.

June 1986   First two Muslim Brotherhood "martyrs" die in clashes with Israel.

December 8, 1987   Intifada: A traffic accident in Gaza sparks a six-year revolt in the Occupied Territories; Hamas launched; more than thirteen hundred Palestinians killed; ninety-four Israelis killed.

December 14, 1988   Yasser Arafat renounces violence and recognizes Israel. U.S. president Ronald Reagan authorizes dialogue with the PLO, in which Arafat's Fatah is the dominant faction.

1989   Sheikh Ahmad Yassin is arrested and sentenced to life imprisonment.

February 15, 1989   Soviet forces retreat from Afghanistan as the USSR begins to collapse.

August 1990–
February 1991   Gulf Crisis: Iraqi president Saddam Hussein invades Kuwait but is evicted by international forces in the American-led Operation Desert Storm.

1991   Hamas centralizes its leadership in Amman and formalizes its military wing as the Qassam Brigade.

October 1991   Madrid Peace Conference: the United States and the USSR sponsor talks among delegations from Israel, Syria, Jordan, Lebanon, and the Palestinians.

1992   Israel deports hundreds of Hamas and other Islamist leaders and activists to southern Lebanon.

January 1993   Secret Israeli-PLO talks begin in Oslo.

September 13, 1993   Arafat and Israeli prime minister Yitzhak Rabin sign an agreement based on the outcome of the Oslo talks: Israel recognizes the PLO and accepts limited autonomy in the Occupied Territories in return for peace and an end to Palestinian claims on Israeli territory.

October 1993   Secret Hamas conference at a Courtyard Marriott hotel in Philadelphia; the first series of Hamas suicide bombs kill only the bombers themselves.

February 25, 1994	Baruch Goldstein, a militant Jewish settler, massacres twenty-nine Palestinians praying at the main mosque in Hebron; Hamas retaliates with a series of deadly suicide bomb attacks.
May 4, 1994	Oslo Accords I: Israeli forces agree to withdraw from about 60 percent of the Gaza Strip and from Jericho, on the West Bank; anticipate further withdrawals and set five-year period for agreement on Jerusalem, Israeli settlements, Palestinian refugees, and borders.
July 1, 1994	Arafat returns to Gaza as the head of the new self-rule Palestinian Authority.
October 26, 1994	Israel-Jordan peace treaty.
July 25, 1995	Mousa Abu Marzook arrested at John F. Kennedy International Airport in New York.
September 28, 1995	Oslo Accords II: agreement to expand self-rule in the West Bank and Gaza and allow Palestinian elections.
November 4, 1995	Israeli prime minister Rabin assassinated by an orthodox Jewish student opposed to the peace process. Shimon Peres becomes prime minister.
January 20, 1996	Palestinian elections: Hamas refuses to participate; Fatah dominates first legislative council.
May 29, 1996	Shimon Peres loses the election to Benjamin Netanyahu, who campaigned against the Rabin-Peres peace process.
September 1996	Israel's decision to open an archaeological tunnel close to Muslim shrines in Jerusalem provokes clashes; sixty-one Arabs and fifteen Israeli soldiers are killed.
March 18, 1997	Israel starts work on a controversial settlement at Har Homa—known as Jebal Abu Ghneim by Palestinians—to complete a ring of Jewish settlements around occupied East Jerusalem.
July–September 1997	Hamas claims responsibility for a series of horrific suicide bombs in Jerusalem in which twenty-one are killed and hundreds injured.
September 25, 1997	Mossad's attempted assassination of Khalid Mishal in Amman fails; Israel forced to release Sheikh Ahmad Yassin and other Palestinian prisoners in exchange for Mossad agents held in Jordan.

October 23, 1998	Wye River Memorandum: under U.S. pressure, Netanyahu commits to further Israeli withdrawals from the West Bank.
February 7, 1999	King Hussein dies and is succeeded by his son Abdullah.
May 8, 1999	Ehud Barak replaces Netanyahu as prime minister of Israel.
August 1999	King Abdullah of Jordan shutters Hamas headquarters in Amman and deports its leadership.
December 1999	Barak puts Palestinian negotiations on hold in an effort to seek a treaty with Damascus; the effort ends in failure after a meeting in Geneva between U.S. president Bill Clinton and Syrian president Hafez Al-Assad three months later.
July 11–24, 2000	Camp David summit: under Clinton's supervision, top-level Palestinian and Israeli delegations fail to reach agreement on any of the key issues.
September 28, 2000	Al-Aqsa Intifada: also known as the second Intifada, six years of violent conflict sparked by Israeli opposition leader Ariel Sharon's controversial visit to the Temple Mount, known to Muslims as Al-Haram Al-Sharif, in Jerusalem.
December 10, 2000	Ehud Barak resigns as Israel's prime minister.
February 6, 2001	Sharon is elected prime minister.
September 11, 2001	9/11: Nearly three thousand die in Al-Qaeda attacks on New York and Washington, DC.
March 2002	Arab Initiative: Arab summit in Beirut seeks an end to the Middle East crisis, offers peace and full recognition of Israel in return for a Palestinian state based on 1967 lines of withdrawal and a "just" solution for refugees.
April 2002	Operation Defensive Shield: amid a wave of suicide bombings, Israel reoccupies much of the West Bank.
June 2002	The Sharon government decides to build a combined wall and fence to physically separate much of the West Bank from Israel; much of the wall's route is inside the West Bank.
March–April 2003	U.S.-led invasion of Iraq forces the collapse of Saddam Hussein's regime.

December 18, 2003	Sharon reveals his unilateral plan for "disengagement" from the Occupied Territories: to withdraw from all of the Gaza Strip and parts of the West Bank.
March 22, 2004	Sheikh Ahmad Yassin is assassinated in an Israeli missile strike outside a mosque in Gaza; Khalid Mishal becomes the leader of Hamas.
April 17, 2004	Abdel Azziz Al-Rantisi is assassinated in an Israeli missile strike on Gaza City.
November 11, 2004	Yasser Arafat, seventy-five, dies at Percy Military Hospital, Paris.
December 2004	A Chicago court awards the family of David Boim $156 million for his 1996 death in a Hamas gun attack north of Jerusalem; Hamas candidates stand in the first Palestinian local government elections.
March 2005	Hamas decides to contest the general election scheduled for August 2005, then rescheduled for January 2006.
August 2005	Israel carries out "disengagement" plan in Occupied Territories.
January 4, 2006	Ariel Sharon suffers a stroke and lapses into a vegetative coma; succeeded by his deputy, Ehud Olmert.
January 25, 2006	Hamas wins Palestinian election in its own right; is isolated by Israel and the West for refusing to renounce violence, recognize Israel, and abide by previous Palestinian agreements; appoints Ismail Haniyah the head of government.
June–July 2006	Palestinian militias tunnel into Israel from Gaza; their abduction of nineteen-year-old Corporal Gilad Shalit sparks mass detention of Hamas MPs and other leaders in the West Bank and a heavy military attack on the Gaza Strip, leaving government buildings, the main power station, and bridges badly damaged.
July 12, 2006	Hezbollah Shiite militia capture two Israeli soldiers in a cross-border raid from Lebanon, sparking a thirty-three-day Israeli invasion of Lebanon, killing an estimated one thousand Lebanese and destroying infrastructure and whole residential blocks of South Beirut and other communities.
June 2007	Months of factional friction in Gaza erupt into a local civil war between Hamas and Fatah; Hamas takes control of Gaza.

Notes

2: Village of the Sheikhs

1. Tom Segev, *1967: Israel, the War and the Year That Transformed the Middle East* (Metropolitan Books, 2007), 404.

2. Author interviews with Abdul Rahim Ismail Abd Al-Qadir, Amman, Jordan, August 2007.

3. Benny Morris, *Righteous Victims: A History of the Zionist-Arab Conflict, 1881–2001* (Vintage Books, 2001), 681.

4. Avi Shlaim, *The Iron Wall: Israel and the Arab World* (Penguin, 2000), 25.

5. Ziad Abu-Amar, *Islamic Fundamentalism in the West Bank and Gaza* (Indiana University Press, 1994), 2.

6. Shlaim, *Iron Wall*, 31

7. Ilan Pappe, *The Ethnic Cleansing of Palestine* (Oneworld, 2006), xii.

8. Ibid., xv.

9. David K. Shipler, *Arab and Jew: Wounded Spirits in a Promised Land* (Penguin, 2002), 16.

10. Ibid.

11. Ibid., 35.

12. Ibid.

13. Author interviews with Fatima Abdul Rahman, Amman, Jordan, August 2007.

14. Author interview with Awni Fares, Silwad, West Bank, September 2007.

15. Shlaim, *Iron Wall*, 241–45.

16. Author interviews with Fatima Abdul Rahman, Amman, Jordan, August 2007.

17. Author interviews with Ranya Kadri, journalist, Amman, Jordan, July–August 2007.

18. Author interviews with Fatima Abdul Rahman, Amman, Jordan, August 2007.

19. Segev, *1967*, 369.

20. Ibid., 429.

21. Ibid., 384.

22. Ibid., 402.

23. Ibid., 500.

24. Ibid., 576–80.

25. Ibid., 407.

26. Ibid., 532–39.

27. Ibid., 474.

28. Ibid., 404.

29. Ibid., 410.

30. Ibid., 478.

3: The Tap Dancer from Amman

1. Author interviews with Randa Habib, Amman, Jordan, June–July 2007.

2. Confidential author interview, Washington, DC, October 2007.

3. Paul McGeough, "Cultural Baggage Making Enemies Out of Friends," *Sydney Morning Herald*, March 30, 2004.

4. King Hussein, *Uneasy Lies the Head* (Bernard Geis Associates, 1962).

5. Rolland Dallas, *King Hussein: A Life on the Edge* (Fromm International, 1999), xviii.

6. Laurie A. Brand, *Palestinians in the Arab World: Institution Building and the Search for State* (Columbia University Press, 1988), 9.

7. Tony Walker and Andrew Gowers, *Arafat: The Biography* (Virgin, 2003), 48–51.

8. Ibid.

9. "Black September: Tough Negotiations," BBC News, January 1, 2001.

10. Dallas, *King Hussein*, 251.

11. Brand, *Palestinians*, 168.

12. Tom Segev, *1967: Israel, the War and the Year That Transformed the Middle East* (Metropolitan Books, 2007), 506.

13. Tim Weiner, *Legacy of Ashes: The History of the CIA* (Doubleday, 2007), 137.

14. Confidential author interview, Amman, Jordan, September 2007.

15. Weiner, *Legacy of Ashes*, 351.

16. Author interviews with Ranya Kadri, Amman, Jordan, June–November 2007.

4: The Education of a Terrorist

1. Diana Elias, "Kuwait University Separates the Sexes to Vocal Dismay of Some," Associated Press, July 17, 2002.

2. Laurie A. Brand, *Palestinians in the Arab World: Institution Building and the Search for State* (Columbia University Press, 1988), 138.

3. Author interviews with Professor Asad Abdul Rahman, Amman, Jordan, September 2007.

4. Author interviews with Mullah Abdul Qadar, Amman, Jordan, August 2007.

5. Marvin Howe, "In Kuwait, Palestinians Thrive in the Economy but Feel Bias as Aliens," *New York Times*, February 19, 1978.

6. Brand, *Palestinians*, 120.

7. Author interview with Maher Abdul Qadar, Amman, Jordan, August 2007.

8. Ibid.

9. Author interviews with Khalid Mishal, Damascus, Syria, November 2007.

10. Author interview with Azzam Tamimi, Damascus, Syria, September 2007.

11. Ibid.

12. Author interviews with Professor Asad Abdul Rahman, Amman, Jordan, September 2007.

13. Ibid.

14. Author interviews with Fatima Abdul Rahman, Amman, Jordan, August 2007.

5: "Have You Guys Lost Your Minds?"

1. Avi Shlaim, *The Iron Wall: Israel and the Arab World* (Penguin, 2001), 427.

2. Confidential author interview, Tel Aviv, Israel, November 2007.

3. David I. Fand, "Aid to Israel: Some Strings Needed," Heritage Foundation Executive Memorandum #82, April 31, 1985.

4. Confidential author interview, Tel Aviv, Israel, November 2007.

5. Author interview with Dan Kurtzer, Princeton, New Jersey, January 2008.

6. Author interview with Shalom Harari, Jerusalem, Israel, November 2007.

7. Confidential author interview, Gaza City, Occupied Territories, September 2007.

8. Ziad Abu-Amr, *Islamic Fundamentalism in the West Bank and Gaza: Muslim Brotherhood and Islamic Jihad* (Indiana University Press, 1994), 43–45.

9. Ibid., xvi.

10. David K. Shipler, *Arab and Jew: Wounded Spirits in a Promised Land* (Penguin, 2002), 156.

11. Tony Walker and Andrew Gowers, *Arafat: The Biography* (Virgin, 2003), xvi.

12. Confidential author interview, Tel Aviv, Israel, November 2007.

13. Author interview with Dan Kurtzer.

14. Ibid.

15. Ibid.

16. Ibid.

17. Ibid.

18. Ibid.

19. Ray Hanania, "Sharon's Terror Child," *CounterPunch*, January 18–19, 2003.

20. Author interview with Arnon Regular, former *Haaretz* correspondent, Jerusalem, Israel, November 2007.

21. Hanania, "Sharon's Terror Child."

22. Robert Dreyfuss, *Devil's Game: How the United States Helped Unleash Fundamentalist Islam* (Metropolitan Books, 2005), 208.

23. Ibid., 202.

24. Ibid., 209.

25. Chalmers Johnson, "The Largest Covert Operation in CIA History," History News Network, September 6, 2003.

26. Tim Weiner, *Legacy of Ashes: The History of the CIA* (Doubleday, 2007), 401.

27. Ibid., 136–37.

28. Dreyfuss, *Devil's Game*, 205.

29. Confidential author interviews, Amman, Jordan, September–November 2007.

30. Author interview with Nabil Shaath, Amman, Jordan, November 2007.

31. Author interview with Shalom Harari.

32. Ze'ev Schiff and Ehud Ya'ari, *Intifada: The Palestinian Uprising—Israel's Third Front* (Simon & Schuster, 1989), 224.

33. John Wallach and Janet Wallach, *The New Palestinians: The Emerging Generation of Leaders* (Prima Publishing, 1992), 213.

6: Arafat's Circus

1. Laurie A. Brand, *Palestinians in the Arab World: Institution Building and the Search for State* (Columbia University Press, 1988), 146.

2. Author interviews with Azzam Tamimi, Damascus, Syria, September–November 2007.

3. Author interviews with Khalid Mishal, Damascus, Syria, September–November 2007.

4. Steve Coll, *Ghost Wars: The Secret History of the CIA, Afghanistan, and Bin Laden, from Soviet Invasion to September 10, 2001* (Penguin, 2004), 142.

5. "Kuwait," Wikipedia, en.wikipedia.org/wiki/Kuwait#_note-3.

6. Brand, *Palestinians*, 144.

7. Ibid., 108.

8. Marvin Howe, "In Kuwait, Palestinians Thrive in the Economy but Feel Bias as Aliens," *New York Times*, February 19, 1978.

9. Ibid.

10. Brand, *Palestinians*, 124–25.

11. Ibid.

12. Robert Dreyfuss, *Devil's Game: How the United States Helped Unleash Fundamentalist Islam* (Metropolitan Books, 2005), 184.

13. Kristin Smith, conference paper excerpted in "Impact of 9/11 on the Middle East," *Middle East Policy* 9, no. 4 (December 2002).

14. Author interviews with Khalid Mishal.

15. Author interviews with Maher Mishal, brother of Khalid Mishal, Amman, Jordan, September 2008.

16. Author interviews with Khalid Mishal.

17. Confidential author interview, Amman, Jordan, September 2007.

18. Author interviews with Khalid Mishal.

19. Ibid.

20. Ibid.

21. Ibid.

22. Azzam Tamimi, *Hamas: Unwritten Chapters* (Hurst & Co., 2007), 44.

23. Author interviews with Khalid Mishal.

24. Author interviews with Fatima Abdul Rahman, Amman, Jordan, August 2007.

25. Author interviews with Khalid Mishal.

26. Author interview with Khalid Mishal, Damascus, Syria, November 2007.

27. Lawrence Wright, *The Looming Tower: Al-Qaeda and the Road to 9/11* (Vintage Books, 2007), 118.

28. Ibid.

29. Chris Suellentrop, "Abdullah Azzam: The Godfather of Jihad," *Slate*, April 16, 2002.

30. Author interview with Khalid Mishal, Damascus, Syria, September 2007.

31. Ibid.

32. Ibid.

33. Tamimi, *Hamas*, 300.

34. Barnett Rubin, "Arab Islamists in Afghanistan," in *Political Islam: Revolution, Radicalism, or Reform?* ed. John L. Esposito (Lynne Rienner, 1997), 194.

35. Wright, *Looming Tower*, 179.

36. Matthew Levitt, *Hamas: Politics, Charity, and Terrorism in the Service of Jihad* (Yale University Press, 2006), 150.

37. Confidential author interview, Gaza City, Occupied Territories, September 2007.

38. E-mail correspondence between author and Reuven Paz, former member of Israeli security services, February 10, 2008.

39. Tamimi, *Hamas*, 305n16.

40. Confidential author interviews, Damascus, Syria, September–November 2007.

41. Tamimi, *Hamas*, 46.

42. Author interview with Shalom Harari, Jerusalem, Israel, November 2007.

43. Tamimi, *Hamas*, 46.

7: The Palestinian Project

1. Paul McGeough, "Blood and Dust," *Good Weekend* magazine, *Sydney Morning Herald*, December 8, 1990.

2. B'Tselem, "Statistics: Fatalities in the First Intifada," http://www.btselem.org/english/Statistics/First_Intifada_Tables.asp.

3. Human Rights Watch, "Justice Undermined: Balancing Security and Human Rights in the Palestinian Justice System," November 2001.

4. Ze'ev Schiff and Ehud Ya'ari, *Intifada: The Palestinian Uprising—Israel's Third Front* (Simon & Schuster, 1989), 79.

5. Tony Walker and Andrew Gowers, *Arafat: The Biography* (Virgin, 2003), 254.

6. Schiff and Ya'ari, *Intifada*, 123.

7. Ibid.

8. Walker and Gowers, *Arafat*, 255.

9. Azzam Tamimi, *Hamas: Unwritten Chapters* (Hurst & Co., 2007), 47.

10. Ziad Abu-Amr, *Islamic Fundamentalism in the West Bank and Gaza: Muslim Brotherhood and Islamic Jihad* (Indiana University Press, 1994), 63.

11. Author interviews with Khalid Mishal, Damascus, Syria, September–November 2007.

12. Ibid.

13. Nicholas B. Tatro, "Graffiti Serves as a Guide to Political Happenings," Associated Press, March 10, 1988.

14. Author interviews with Khalid Mishal.

15. Stephen Franklin, "Fundamentalists Find Palestinian Niche," *Chicago Tribune*, August 22, 1988.

16. *U.S. v. Holy Land Foundation et al.*, Case No. 3:04-CR-240-G (N.D. Tex.), Government Exhibit 002-0022.

17. Ibid., Government Exhibit 003-0065.

18. Abu-Amr, *Islamic Fundamentalism*, 71.

19. Zaki Chehab, *Inside Hamas: The Untold Story of the Militant Islamic Movement* (Nation Books, 2007), 30.

20. Tamimi, *Hamas*, 62–63.

21. Ibid., 33.

22. Confidential author interview, Gaza City, Occupied Territories, September 2007.

23. Ibid.

24. Tamimi, *Hamas*, 67.

25. Author interview with Abdel-Salam Majali, Amman, Jordan, November 2007.

26. Confidential author interview, Gaza City, Occupied Territories, September 2007.

27. Author interview with Isa Al-Najjar, Gaza City, Occupied Territories, September 2007.

28. Ahmad Yassin, "A Witness to the Age of the Intifada," Al Jazeera, April–June 1999, trans. and quoted in Tamimi, *Hamas*.

29. Tim Weiner, *Legacy of Ashes: The History of the CIA* (Doubleday, 2007), 426–27.

30. Ibid.

31. Author interviews with Abdul Rahim Ismail Abd Al-Qadir, Amman, Jordan, August 2007.

32. Author interviews with Maher Mishal, Amman, Jordan, August 2007.

33. U.S. Library of Congress, ed., "Country Studies: Kuwait—Reconstruction Af-

ter the Persian Gulf War," www.country-studies.com/persian-gulf-states/kuwait-reconstruction-after-the-persian-gulf-war.html.

34. Author interviews with Khalid Mishal.

35. Tamimi, *Hamas*, 74.

36. Confidential author interview, Amman, Jordan, July 2007.

37. "King Hussein of Jordan—Obituary," *The Times* (London), February 8, 1999.

38. Walker and Gowers, *Arafat*, 299

39. Galia Golan, *Israel and Palestine: Peace Plans from Oslo to Disengagement* (Markus Wiener Publishers, 2007), 34.

40. *U.S. v. Holy Land Foundation et al.*, Government Exhibit 016-0025.

41. Ibid., Government Exhibit 016-0049.

42. Ibid.

43. Ibid.

44. Ibid., Government Exhibit 016-0051.

45. Ibid., Government Exhibit 016-0045.

8: The Bearded Engineer in a New York Cell

1. Executive Order 12947, "Prohibiting Transactions with Terrorists Who Threaten to Disrupt the Middle East Peace Process," White House, January 23, 1995.

2. This account of Mousa Abu Marzook's U.S. detention is reconstructed from documents filed in the U.S. District Court, Southern District of New York, in several applications regarding Israel's extradition application, case numbers 95-CIV-9799 and 97-CIV-2293—in particular, the affidavit of Joseph Hummel, "Israel's Request for Extradition of Abu Marzook," and Abu Marzook's writ of habeas corpus.

3. Confidential author interview, Amman, Jordan, August 2007.

4. Charles W. Hall and John Lancaster, "U.S. Is Asked to Turn over Terror Suspect; Israel Wants Marzook for Activities in Hamas," *Washington Post*, July 29, 1995.

4. Author interview with Dave Manners, Washington, DC, October 2007.

5. Ibid

6. Neil MacFarquhar, "Heavy Hand of the Secret Police Slows Reform in the Arab World," *New York Times*, November 14, 2005.

7. Ibid.

8. Paul McGeough, "The Making of a Human Time Bomb Primed for Endless War," *Sydney Morning Herald*, July 16, 2005.

9. Queen Noor, *Leap of Faith: Memoirs of an Unexpected Life* (Phoenix, 2003), 297.

10. Author interviews with Randa Habib, Amman, Jordan, August–September 2007.

11. Confidential author interview, Amman, Jordan, August 2007.

12. Confidential author interview, Amman, Jordan, September 2007.

13. Richard Pérez-Peña, "After Terrorist Threat, Kennedy Becomes a Wary Fortress," *New York Times*, August 14, 1995.

14. "Terrorist Threat Tightens Security at N.Y. Airports; Officials Urge Stricter Screening Nationwide," *Washington Post*, August 15, 1995.

15. Barton Gellman, "Americans Threatened in West Bank; New Group Demands U.S. Release of Detained Hamas Leader," *Washington Post*, September 24, 1995.

16. Serge Schmemann, "Israel May Seek Extradition of Arab Detained by the U.S.," *New York Times*, July 29, 1995.

17. Copy of fax in author's files.

18. Hillel Kuttler, "US Captures Top Hamas Official," *Jerusalem Post*, July 28, 1995.

19. Robin Wright, "U.S. Tries to Keep Hamas Official Out of Country Immigration," *Los Angeles Times*, July 28, 1995.

20. Kuttler, "US Captures Top Hamas Official."

21. Hall and Lancaster, "U.S. Is Asked to Turn Over Terror Suspect."

22. Ibid.

23. *U.S. v. Holy Land Foundation et al.*, Case No. 3:04-CR-240-G (N.D. Tex.), Government Exhibit 013-0104.

24. Joel Greenberg, "Israel to Ask U.S. to Yield Palestinian," *New York Times*, July 31, 1995.

25. Don Van Natta Jr., "Judge Orders Hamas Leader Extradited to Israel," *New York Times*, May 9, 1996.

26. James C. McKinley Jr., "U.S. Rejects Offer of Leader of Hamas Never to Return," *New York Times*, August 3, 1995.

27. Schmemann, "Israel May Seek Extradition of Arab Detained by the U.S."

28. Rachel Blustain, "Hamas Heavy Hires an Attorney Named Cohen, as in Controversy," *The Forward*, August 4, 1995.

29. Ibid.

30. Ibid.

31. Robert O'Harrow Jr. and Charles W. Hall, "Virginia Man Suspected of Terrorism Known for Anonymity," *Washington Post*, August 8, 1995.

32. Ibid.

33. *Mousa Mohammad Abu Marzook v. Warren Christopher et al.* (S.D. N.Y. 924 F. Supp. 565, 64 USLW 2815), affirmation of Abu Marzook, 6.

34. Ibid., 12.

35. Ibid., 16n9.

36. Author interview with Mousa Abu Marzook, Damascus, Syria, September 2007.

37. Serge Schmemann, "Israel Moves Towards Taking Hamas Figure from U.S. Custody," *New York Times*, August 2, 1995.

38. *Abu Marzook v. Christopher et al.*, "Request for the Extradition of Mousa Mohammad Abu Marzook," Israeli Ministry of Justice, 2.

39. Ibid., 3.

40. *Abu Marzook v. Christopher et al.*, affidavit of Dr. Ali A. Abbasi, 4–8.

41. Ibid.

42. *Abu Marzook v. Christopher et al.*, Judgment 31.

43. Ibid., 1.

9: Violence Is the Only Weapon

1. *Mousa Mohammad Abu Marzook v. Warren Christopher et al.*, Case No. 95-CIV-9799-KTD (S.D. N.Y.), "Israeli Request for the Extradition of Mousa Mohammad Abu Marzook," affidavits of "Nadav," September 26, 1995, and Ephraim Rabin, September 23, 1995.

2. Ibid., affidavit of Mohammad Salah, November 8, 1995, 3.

3. Amnesty International, "Under Constant Medical Supervision: Torture, Ill-Treatment and Health Professionals in Israel and the Occupied Territories," August 1996.

4. *Abu Marzook v. Christopher et al.*, Duffy judgment, 32.

5. Ibid., affidavit of Mohammad Salah, 5–6.

6. James Brooke and Elaine Sciolino, "Bread or Bullets: Money for Hamas," *New York Times*, August 16, 1995.

7. *Abu Marzook v. Christopher et al.*, affidavit of Ephraim Rabin, 1–7.

8. *U.S. v. One 1997 E35 Ford Van et al.* (N.D. Ill., E.D., 98C 3548), affidavit of Robert Wright.

9. *Abu Marzook v. Christopher et al.*, Israeli police interview with Bassam Mousa, January 30, 1993, 25.

10. Ibid., affidavit of Abu Hamed, September 25, 1995, 1–2.

11. Ibid., Israeli police interview with Salah Arouri, January 27, 1993, 10.

12. Shaul Mishal and Avraham Sela, *The Palestinian Hamas: Vision, Violence, and Coexistence* (Columbia University Press, 2000), 90.

13. Ibid.

14. Ziad Abu-Amr, *Islamic Fundamentalism in the West Bank and Gaza: Muslim Brotherhood and Islamic Jihad* (Indiana University Press, 1994), 74.

15. Confidential author interview, Washington, DC, November 2007.

16. Tony Walker and Andrew Gowers, *Arafat: The Biography* (Virgin, 2003), 365–66.

17. Amos Perlmutter, "Arafat's Police State," *Foreign Affairs*, July–August 1994.

18. Ibid., 388.

19. Amnesty International, "Trial at Midnight: Secret, Summary, Unfair Trails in Gaza," June 1, 1995, 2.

20. Walker and Gowers, *Arafat*, 389.

21. Ibid., 5–6.

22. Ibid.

23. John Kifner, "Dedicated Extremists Present Twin Threat to Mideast Peace," *New York Times*, September 15, 1993.

24. *Abu Marzook v. Christopher et al.*, affidavit of Joseph Hummel, 6.

25. Samuel M. Katz, *The Hunt for the Engineer: How Israeli Agents Tracked the Hamas Master Bomber* (Fromm International, 1999), 77.

26. Clyde Haberman, "30 Israelis Hurt by Suicide Bomber," *New York Times*, October 5, 1993.

27. "1994: Jewish Settler Kills 30 at Holy Site," *BBC On This Day*, February 25, 1994.

28. Clyde Haberman, "Suicide Bombs Kill 19 in Israel; Shadow Cast Over Peace Talks," *New York Times*, January 23, 1995.

29. Clyde Haberman, "Five Killed in Israel as Second Bomber Blows Up a Bus," *New York Times*, April 14, 1994.

30. Confidential author interview, Gaza City, Occupied Territories, September 2007.

31. Clyde Haberman, "Gazans Eject PLO Leader from Funeral," *New York Times*, November 14, 1994.

32. Confidential author interview, Ramallah, Occupied Territories, November 2007.

10: A Little Obscurity Is Good

1. Confidential author interview, Gaza City, Occupied Territories, September 2007.

2. Ibid.

3. Author interviews with Khalid Mishal, Damascus, Syria, September–November 2007.

4. Confidential author interview, Amman, Jordan, October 2007.

5. Confidential author interview, Amman, Jordan, September 2007.

6. Confidential author interview, Amman, Jordan, September 2007.

7. *Mousa Mohammad Abu Marzook v. Warren Christopher et al.*, Case No. 95-CIV-9799-KTD (S.D. N.Y.), affidavit of Yaacov Amidror, "Hamas—Organizational Structures and Decision-Making Procedure—An Expert Opinion," September 20, 1995.

8. Confidential author interviews, Amman, Jordan, August 2007.

9. Steve Rodan, "The Big Fish That Got Away," *Jerusalem Post*, October 17, 1997.

10. Tamimi, *Hamas: Unwritten Chapters* (Hurst & Co., 2007), 82.

11. Confidential author interview, Amman, Jordan, September 2007.

12. Ibid.

13. Author interview with Azzam Tamimi, Damascus, Syria, November 2007.

14. *Abu Marzook v. Christopher et al.*, writ of habeas corpus of Mousa Mohammad Abu Marzook, November 16, 1995.

15. Matthew Levitt, *Hamas: Politics, Charity, and Terrorism in the Service of Jihad* (Yale University Press, 2006), 149.

16. Ahmed Yousef, *American Muslims: A Community Under Siege* (UASR Publishing Group, 2004), 268.

17. *Abu Marzook v. Christopher et al.*, affidavit of Said Msamah, January 13, 1991.

18. Ibid., affidavit of Yaacov Amidror, "Musa Muhammad Abu Marzook—An Expert Opinion," September 20, 1995.

19. Tamimi, *Hamas*, 60–61.

20. Author interview with Wesley Egan, Washington, DC, October 2007.

21. Ibid.

22. *Abu Marzook v. Christopher et al.*, Case No. 96-CV-4107 (2nd Cir.), statement of Mousa Mohammad Abu Marzook, 3.

23. Elaine Sciolino, "To Palestinian, Israel Is Better Than U.S. Cell," *New York Times*, February 1, 1997.

24. Secret PTQ2948, U.S. State Department document, dated January 29, 1997, released to author under Freedom of Information Act request.

25. Gil Sedan, "Extradition of Hamas Leader Presents Quandary for Israel," Jewish Telegraphic Agency, May 2, 1997.

26. Serge Schmemann, "Hamas Leader May Be Spared Extradition," *New York Times*, February 20, 1997.

27. Ibid.

28. Neil MacFarquhar, "Jordan to Let Terrorist Suspect Held in U.S. into Kingdom," *New York Times*, May 1, 1997.

29. Author interviews with Randa Habib, Amman, Jordan, July–August 2007.

30. Confidential author interview, Amman, Jordan, August 2007.

31. Author interview with Wesley Egan.

32. Confidential author interview, Tel Aviv, Israel, November 2007.

33. Roger Gaess, "Interview with Mousa Abu Marzook," *Middle East Policy*, May 1, 1997.

34. John Lancaster, "Freedom Suits Hamas Leader; Fresh from U.S. Jail, Abu Marzook Minds His Step in Jordan," *Washington Post*, May 9, 1997.

35. Confidential author interview, Amman, Jordan, August 2007.

36. Ibid.

37. Ibid.

38. Confidential author interview, Damascus, Syria, September 2007.

39. Confidential author interview, Gaza City, Occupied Territories, September 2007.

40. Confidential author interview, Amman, Jordan, September 2007.

41. Gaess, "Interview with Mousa Abu Marzook."

42. Marjorie Miller, "Hamas Combat: Both Political and Mortal," *Los Angeles Times*, July 29, 1995.

43. Author interviews with Ranya Kadri, Amman, Jordan, July–November 2007.

44. Ibid., 558.

45. Avi Shlaim, *Lion of Jordan: The Life of King Hussein in War and Peace* (Penguin/Allen Lane, 2007), 567.

46. Ibid., 569.

47. Joel Greenberg, "Despite Devastation and Fear, Support for Netanyahu Seems Strong," *New York Times*, August 1, 1997.

48. Ibid.

49. Rabin Eitan and Amira Hass, "Triple Suicide Bombs Rock Jerusalem," *Haaretz*, September 5, 1997.

50. Uzi Benziman, "The Gap Between the Final Settlement and Reality," *Haaretz*, September 21, 1997.

51. Confidential author interview, Amman, Jordan, August 2007.

11: "They Used a Bizarre Instrument"

1. Author interview with Abu Sayf, Damascus, Syria, September 2007.

2. Author interview with Saad Na'im Khatib, Amman, Jordan, November 2007.

3. Smadar Perry, "Hussein Demands Mossad Fire All Involved in the Affair," *Yedioth Ahronoth*, October 10, 1997, trans. Nilly Ovnat.

4. Avi Shlaim, *Lion of Jordan: The Life of King Hussein in War and Peace* (Penguin/Allen Lane, 2007), 572.

5. Author interviews with Majali Whbee, Jerusalem, Israel, August–September 2007.

6. Author interview with Dave Manners, Washington, DC, November 2007.

12: Mishal Must Not Die

1. Smadar Perry, "Hussein Demands That Mossad Sack All Involved in the Affair," *Yedioth Ahronoth*, October 10, 1997, trans. Nilly Ovnat.

2. Author interview with Mousa Abu Marzook, Damascus, Syria, September 2007.

3. George Tenet, *At the Center of the Storm: My Years at the CIA* (HarperCollins, 2007), 41.

4. Author interview with Mousa Abu Marzook.

5. Author interviews with Bassam Akasheh, Amman, Jordan, July 2007.

6. Author interview with Mohammad Nazzal, Damascus, Syria, September 2007.

7. Perry, "Hussein Demands That Mossad Sack All Involved in the Affair."

13: "Who the Hell Is Khalid Mishal?"

1. Unless otherwise stated, this account of the entire attack and its aftermath is based on a series of confidential author interviews conducted in Amman, Jordan; Jerusalem, Israel; Tel Aviv, Israel; New York; and Washington, DC, in August–November 2007.

2. Shimon Shiffer, "Israel Reveals Formula of Secret Chemical Weapon to Jordanians," *Yedioth Ahronoth*, October 10, 1997, trans. Nilly Ovnat.

3. Gordon Thomas, *Gideon's Spies: The Secret History of the Mossad* (Thomas Dunne Books, 2005), 125.

4. Yossi Melman, "Admitting the Facts but Not the Guilt," *Haaretz*, December 18, 1997.

5. Rabin Eitan and Yossi Melman, "Other Secret Service Chiefs Kept in the Dark about Mossad Operation," *Haaretz*, October 9, 1997.

6. Kevin Sack, "Civil Rights Anniversary Points to Unfinished Tasks," *New York Times*, September 21, 1997,

7. Author phone interview with Bruce Riedel, June 9, 2007.

8. Author interview with Dave Manners, Washington, DC, October 2007.

9. Shelby Hodge, "Fertittas Host Dinner for Clinton," *Houston Chronicle*, September 29, 1997.

10. "Schedule of the President for Saturday, September 27, 1997," released by William J. Clinton Presidential Library to author under Freedom of Information Act request.

11. Author interview with Dennis Ross, Washington, DC, October 24, 2007.

12. Author phone interview with Bruce Riedel.

13. Reuters. "Hussein: 'Israel Told About Hamas Truce Before Attack,'" *Haaretz*, October 9, 1997.

14. Smadar Perry, "Hussein Demands That Mossad Fire All Involved in the Affair," *Yedioth Ahronoth*, October 10, 1997, trans. Nilly Ovnat.

15. Shimon Shiffer, "Israel Reveals Formula for Secret Chemical Weapon to Jordanians," *Yedioth Ahronoth*, October 10, 1997, trans. Nilly Ovnat.

14: Pulling a Rabbit from the King's Threadbare Hat

1. Efraim Halevy, *Man in the Shadows: Inside the Middle East Crisis with the Man Who Led the Mossad* (St. Martin's Press, 2006), 164.

2. Ibid., 166.

3. Ibid., 167.

4. Ibid.

5. Schiff Ze'ev, "A Far-Reaching Failure," *Haaretz*, October 5, 1997.

6. Halevy, *Man in the Shadows*, 170

7. Avi Shlaim, *Lion of Jordan: The Life of King Hussein in War and Peace* (Penguin/Allen Lane, 2007), 573.

8. Author interview with Sami Rababa, Amman, Jordan, July 2007.

9. Author interview with Dave Manners, Washington, DC, October 2007.

10. Narcotic Educational Foundation of America, "Designer Drugs: The Analog Game," undated, www.cnoa.org.

11. Confidential author interview, Washington, DC, October 2007.

12. Gordon Thomas, *Gideon's Spies: The Secret History of the Mossad* (Thomas Dunne Books, 2005), 128.

13. BBC, "The Moscow Theatre Siege," *Horizon*, January 15, 2004.

14. Ibid.

15. Halevy, *Man in the Shadows*, 173.

16. Ibid., 174.

17. Barton Gellman, "Botched Assassination by Israel Gives New Life to Hamas," *Washington Post*, October 6, 1997.

18. Author phone interview with Smadar Perry, January 2008.

15: The Price Bibi Paid

1. Avi Shlaim, *Lion of Jordan: The Life of King Hussein in War and Peace* (Penguin/ Allen Lane, 2007), 416, 429, 579.

2. Author interviews with Majali Whbee, Jerusalem, Israel, August–September 2007.

3. Author interviews with Khalid Mishal, Damascus, Syria, September– November 2007.

4. Author interview with Mousa Abu Marzook, Damascus, Syria, September 2007.

5. Arieh O'Sullivan, "Chronology of Events," *Jerusalem Post*, October 7, 1997.

6. Author interviews with Majali Whbee, Jerusalem, Israel, September 2007.

7. O'Sullivan, "Chronology of Events."

8. Nahum Barnea, "On a Nationalistic Background," *Yedioth Ahronoth*, October 10, 1997, trans. Nilly Ovnat.

16: The Legendary Image of Mossad

1. Gordon Thomas, *Gideon's Spies: The Secret History of the Mossad* (Thomas Dunne Books, 1995), 142–45.

2. Ibid., 74–78.

3. Uri Dan and Dennis Eisenberg, "Dig Out the Truth," *Jerusalem Post*, October 30, 1997.

4. Author phone interviews with Smadar Perry, February–April 2008.

5. Laura King, "Tactics, Not Anti-Terror Goal, Questioned in Failed Attack in Jordan," Associated Press, October 5, 1997.

6. Michael Yudelman, "Israel Conditions Yassin Return," *Jerusalem Post*, October 6, 1997.

7. Barton Gellman, "Hamas Founder Returns to Gaza Strip as a Hero; Prisoners Swapped for Israeli Agents," *Washington Post*, October 7, 1997.

8. Mike Trickey, "Israel Refuses to Apologise for Canadian Passports: Beneath Tough Talk Feds Willing to Let Episode Fade Away," *Hamilton Spectator*, October 7, 1997.

9. Leslie Susser, "A Much Tougher Fight from Now On," *Jerusalem Report*, October 30, 1997.

10. David Rudge, "Ex-Ambassador: Affair Has Damaged Relations with Jordan," *Jerusalem Post*, October 6, 1997.

11. "Ricin and the Umbrella Murder," CNN, October 23, 2003.

12. Dow Jones International News, "Netanyahu Meets with Security Chiefs over Spy Crisis," October 5, 1997.

13. Confidential author interview, Tel Aviv, Israel, September 2007.

14. Ariela Ringel-Hoffman and Guy Leshem, "Danny Yatom Is All Alone," *Yedioth Ahronoth*, October 10, 1997, trans. Nilly Ovnat.

15. Nahum Barnea, "On a Nationalistic Background," *Yedioth Ahronoth*, October 10, 1997, trans. Nilly Ovnat.

16. Thomas, *Gideon's Spies*, 327.

17. Confidential author interview, Washington, DC, October 2007.

18. Herb Keinon, "A Man of Details," *Jerusalem Post*, February 20, 1998.

19. Ibid.

20. Thomas, *Gideon's Spies*, 126.

21. Ibid.

22. Uri Dan, "Mossad's Christian Heroine Dies," *New York Post*, February 19, 2005.

23. Barry Came and Stephanie Nolen, "Canadian Passport Abuse," *Maclean's*, October 13, 1997.

24. Ibid.

25. Confidential author interview, Middle East, September 2007.

26. Bertrand Marotte, "Canadian 'Lent' Passport: Agents Used It for Two Years While Jewish Man Lived in Israel," *Hamilton Spectator*, October 6, 1997.

27. Confidential author interview, Middle East, September 2007.

28. Reuters, "Canada Confirms Jordan Attackers Not Canadian—Report," October 4, 1997.

29. Norman Spector, "Norman Spector on the Middle East, Israel and the Canadian Angle," *Globe and Mail*, October 10, 1997.

30. "Canadians at Risk from Ex-Envoy's CSIS Comments, Minister Says," *Toronto Star*, November 12, 1997.

31. Victor Ostrovsky with Claire Hoy, *By Way of Deception: The Making of a Mossad Officer* (Wilshire Press, 1990), 75, 118.

32. Confidential author interview, Middle East, September 2007.

33. Confidential author interview, Amman, Jordan, September 2007.

34. Ron Ben-Yshai, "They Did Not Check, They Did Not Consult, They Did Not Think," *Yedioth Ahronoth*, October 10, 1997, trans. Nilly Ovnat.

35. Smadar Perry, "Hussein Demands That Mossad Sacks All Involved in the Affair," *Yedioth Ahronoth*, October 10, 1997, trans Nilly Ovnat.

36. Meron Benvenisti, "Reality Is Not a Thriller," *Haaretz*, October 9, 1997.

37. Efraim Halevy, *Man in the Shadows: Inside the Middle East Crisis with the Man Who Led the Mossad* (St. Martin's Press, 2006), 166.

38. Ibid., 168.

39. Author interviews with Majali Whbee, Amman, Jordan, September–November 2007.

40. Esther Wachsman, "Three Years Too Late for Nachshon," *Jerusalem Post*, October 7, 1997.

41. Bruce Cheadle, "Don't Believe Israel, Axworthy Warned," *Hamilton Spectator*, November 5, 1998.

42. Andrew Mitrovica, "Probe of Mossad's Use of Canadian ID Halted; Intelligence Sources Say Investigation Incomplete Because Ottawa Did Not Want to Upset Israel," *Globe and Mail*, September 6, 1999.

43. Uzi Mahnaimi, "Mossad Agents Flee Bungled London Spying Mission," *Sunday Times*, March 15, 1998.

44. Uzi Mahnaimi and Andy Goldberg, "Bungling Spies," *Sunday Times*, March 1, 1998.

45. Thomas, *Gideon's Spies*, 335.

17: Brother Against Brother

1. Mouin Rabbani, "Smorgasbord of Failure: Oslo and the Al-Aqsa Intifada," in *The New Intifada: Resisting Israel's Apartheid*, ed. Roane Carey (Verso, 2001), 70.

2. "As Mideast Talks of Peace, Soft Voice Urges War," *New York Times*, August 27, 2000.

3. Confidential author interview, Washington, DC, October 2007.

4. Ibid.

5. Barton Gellman, "Hamas Founder Returns to Gaza Strip as a Hero; Prisoners Swapped for Israeli Agents," *Washington Post*, October 7, 1997.

6. Azzam Tamimi, *Hamas: Unwritten Chapters* (Hurst & Co., 2007), 189.

7. Serge Schmemann, "In Fury, Hamas Leader Masks His Intentions," *New York Times*, October 24, 1997.

8. "As Mideast Talks of Peace."

9. Gellman, "Hamas Founder Returns to Gaza Strip as a Hero."

10. Confidential author interview, Gaza City, Occupied Territories, September 2007.

11. "As Mideast Talks of Peace."

12. Nicholas B. Tatro, "Hamas Leader Calls Halt to Israeli Attacks," *Houston Chronicle*, October 20, 1997.

13. Pinhas Inbari and Ziv Hellman, "Jordan Is the Key," *Jerusalem Post*, October 17, 1997.

14. Laura King, "Hamas Founder Returns Home to Gaza Strip; Netanyahu Tries to Explain Prisoner Exchange to Israelis," *Associated Press*, October 7, 1997.

15. Associated Press, "Yassin Vows to Continue Jihad," *Haaretz*, October 24, 1997.

16. Ibid.

17. Joel Greenberg, "Freed Hamas Leader Suggests Terms for Truce," *New York Times*, October 8, 1997.

18. Jay Bushinsky, Steve Rodan, and Mohammed Najib, "Mashaal Warns of More Hamas Attacks Soon," *Jerusalem Post*, October 24, 1997.

19. Tamimi, *Hamas*, 102.

20. Author interview with Mousa Abu Marzook, Damascus, Syria, September 2007.

21. Author interviews with Khalid Mishal, Damascus, Syria, September–November 2007.

22. Khaled Abu Toameh, "Mossad Still Trying to Kill Me, Says Mashaal," *Jerusalem Report*, December 25, 1997.

23. Sheikh Ahmad Yassin, "Letter from Kfar Yona Prison to the Movement's

Leaders and Followers," *Al-Wasat*, November 12, 1993, trans. and quoted in Khaled Hroub, *Hamas: Political Thought and Practice* (Institute for Palestinian Studies, 2002), 222.

24. Author interview with Yasser Abu Hilalah, Amman, Jordan, September 2007.

25. Danny Rubinstein, "Israel's Problem Is Arafat's Nightmare," *Haaretz*, October 8, 1997.

26. Queen Noor, *Leap of Faith: Memoirs of an Unexpected Life* (Phoenix, 2004), 408.

27. Galia Golan, *Israel and Palestine: Peace Plans from Oslo to Disengagement* (Markus Wiener Publishers, 2007), 30.

28. Serge Schmemann, "After All the Talk, a Hesitant Peace," *New York Times*, October 24, 1998.

29. Dennis Ross, *The Missing Peace: The Inside Story of the Fight for Middle East Peace* (Farrar, Straus and Giroux, 2004), 448–50.

30. Joel Greenberg, "After Crackdown, Militant Group Threatens Arafat's Forces," *New York Times*, November 2, 1998.

31. Deborah Sontag, "Freed Palestinian Militant Leader Calls for Holy War Against Israel," *New York Times*, December 28, 1998.

32. Noor, *Leap of Faith*, 431.

33. Author interviews with Randa Habib, Amman, Jordan, July–August 2007.

34. Avi Shlaim, *Lion of Jordan: The Life of King Hussein in War and Peace* (Penguin/ Allen Lane, 2007), 600–606.

35. Noor, *Leap of Faith*, 441.

18: Handcuffed and Deported

1. Lee Hockstader, "A Test of Royal Will; Jordan's Crackdown on Islamic Resistance Is King's First Political, Personal Trial," *Washington Post*, October 7, 1999.

2. *U.S. v. Holy Land Foundation et al.*, Case No. 3:04-CR-240-G (N.D. Tex.), phone tap, Government Exhibit 018-0009.

3. Ibid., 5–12.

4. Lee Hockstader, "In About-Face, Jordan Cracks Down on Militant Palestinian Group," *Washington Post*, September 1, 1999.

5. Stephen Glain, *Mullahs, Merchants, and Militants: The Economic Collapse of the Arab World* (Thomas Dunne Books, 2004), 137.

6. Associated Press/Reuters/Agence France-Presse, "Jordanian Police Arrest Hamas Members in Raid; Warrants Issued for Four Leading Officials; Cooperation with Israelis, Palestinians Cited," *Globe and Mail*, August 31, 1999.

7. Hala Boncompagni, "Hamas Leaders Determined to Return Home to Jordan," Agence France-Presse, September 2, 1999.

8. Randa Habib, "Jordan Deals Heavy Blow to Hamas, Risks Alienating Islamists," Agence France-Presse, August 31, 1999.

9. Khalid Mishal interviewed by Ghassan Bin Jiddu, Al-Jazeera, September 21, 1999.

10. Randa Habib, "Jordan Has 'Proof' of Hamas Threatening New Black September," Agence France-Presse, September 23, 1999.

11. Confidential author interview, Amman, Jordan, August 2007.

12. Ibid.

13. Confidential author interview, Amman, Jordan, September 2007.

14. Azzam Tamimi, *Hamas: Unwritten Chapters* (Hurst & Co., 2007), 316–17fn.

15. *U.S. v. Holy Land Foundation et al.*, phone tap, Government Exhibit 018-0007.

16. Tamimi, *Hamas*, 133.

17. Ibid., 134.

18. Khalid Mishal interviewed by Ghassan Charbel, *Al-Hayat*, December 5, 2003.

19. Confidential author interview, Amman, Jordan, July 2007.

20. Author interviews with Khalid Mishal, Damascus, Syria, September–November 2007.

21. Avi Shlaim, *The Iron Wall: Israel and the Arab World* (Penguin, 2000), 600.

22. "Israeli Election Hinges on Attitudes Towards Netanyahu," Australian Broadcasting Corporation, May 17, 1999.

23. Ron Pundak, "From Oslo to Taba: What Went Wrong?" *Survival* 43, no. 3 (2001): 31–46.

24. Ahron Bregman, *Elusive Peace: How the Holy Land Defeated America* (Penguin, 2005), 19.

25. Ibid., 35.

26. Ibid., 47–48.

27. Deborah Sontag, "Israelis Out of Lebanon After 22 Years," *New York Times*, May 24, 2000.

28. Bregman, *Elusive Peace*, 76.

29. Dennis Ross, *Statecraft: And How to Restore America's Standing in the World* (Farrar, Straus and Giroux, 2007).

30. Hussein Agha and Robert Malley, "Camp David: The Tragedy of Errors," *New York Review of Books*, August 9, 2001.

31. Ibid.

32. Bregman, *Elusive Peace*, 121.

33. Jonathan Cook, "Targeting Haram Al-Sharif," *Al-Haram Weekly*, July 31, 2003.

34. "Sharon Tells Settlers to Grab West Bank Hilltops," Agence France-Presse, November 16, 1998.

35. Mouin Rabbani, "Smorgasbord of Failure: Oslo and the Al-Aqsa Intifada," in *The New Intifada: Resisting Israel's Apartheid*, ed. Roane Carey (Verso, 2001), 72.

36. Ibid., 76–77.

37. Institute for Palestinian Studies, "Killing Fields: Day By Day Chronology of the Second Intifada," www.leksikon.org/killingfields/.

38. Bregman, *Elusive Peace*, 77.

39. Ibid.

40. Voice of Palestine, "All Palestinian Factions Attend Leadership Meeting on Action in 'Coming Stage,'" BBC Monitoring Service—Middle East, October 10, 2000.

41. "Hamas, Arafat Discussed Ways to Step Up Uprising—Hamas Leader," Xinhua News Agency, October 8, 2000.

42. "Hamas Says It Has Discussed with Arafat Ways to Develop Unrest, Agence France-Presse, October 8, 2000.

43. "As Mideast Talks of Peace, Soft Voice Urges War," New York Times, August 27, 2000.

44. Author interview with Asad Abdul Rahman, Amman, Jordan, September 2007.

45. Tamimi, Hamas, 224, 327fn.

19: Dead Men Walking

1. Author interviews with Khalid Mishal, Damascus, Syria, September–November 2007.

2. Institute for Palestinian Studies, "Killing Fields: Day by Day Chronology of the Second Intifada," www.leksikon.org/killingfields/.

3. "Hamas Claims Responsibility for Three-Quarters of 'Zionist' Deaths," Agence France-Presse, December 3, 2001.

4. Tom Hundley, "Sharon: Israel Is at War; Retaliatory Strikes Hit Arafat's Heliport," Orlando Sentinel, December 4, 2001.

5. Mike Allen and Steven Mufson, "U.S. Seizes Assets of 3 Islamic Groups; U.S. Charity Among Institutions Accused of Funding Hamas," Washington Post, December 5, 2001.

6. "Transcript of President Bush's Dec. 4 Remarks on Financial Fight Against Terror," U.S. Newswire, December 4, 2001.

7. U.S. v. Holy Land Foundation et al., Case No. 3:04-CR-240-G (N.D. Tex.), letter from Dr. F.D. Hale, chief executive officer of Executive Protection Group, Government Exhibit 001-0195.

8. Ibid., meeting report, Government Exhibit 006-0006.

9. Ibid.

10. Alan Sipress and Dana Milbank, "Bush Demands Tough Action from Arafat over Bombings," Washington Post, December 3, 2001.

11. Trudy Rubin, "Oust Arafat? That Would Solve Little; He's a Failure but the Alternatives Are Depressing to Consider," Philadelphia Inquirer, December 5, 2001.

12. "Poll Shows 86 Percent of Palestinians Support Attacks on Settlers, Israeli Army," BBC Monitoring—Middle East, June 25, 2002.

13. Author interview with Ismail Abu Shanab, Gaza City, Occupied Territories, March 2002.

14. Deborah Sontag, "The Palestinian Conversation," New York Times Magazine, February 3, 2002.

15. Suzanne Goldenberg, "Sharon Rejects Call for Freeze on Settlements," *The Guardian*, May 23, 2001.

16. Palestine Satellite Channel TV, "Arafat Calls for End to Armed Attacks on Israelis," BBC Monitoring—Middle East, December 16, 2001.

17. Ahron Bregman, *Elusive Peace: How the Holy Land Defeated America* (Penguin, 2005), 173–74.

18. Amnesty International, "Israel: Briefing for the Committee Against Torture," AI Index No. MDE 15/075/2002, May 2002, 1–2.

19. Ibid.

20. Bregman, *Elusive Peace*, 179–80.

21. Idith Zertal and Akiva Eldar, *Lords of the Land: The War over Israel's Settlements in the Occupied Territories, 1967–2007* (Nation Books, 2007), 408.

22. Author interview with Walid Fayed, Jenin, Occupied Palestinian Territories, March 2002.

23. Author interview with Mahmoud Al-Zahar, Gaza City, Occupied Territories, March 2002.

24. Author interview with Saeb Al-Ajez, Gaza City, Occupied Territories, March 2002.

25. Amnesty International, "Israel and the Occupied Territories: Mass Detention in Cruel, Inhuman and Degrading Conditions," AI Index No. MDE 15/074/2002, May 23, 2002.

26. Matt Rees, "Streets Red with Blood," *Time*, March 18, 2002.

27. The author was in the Jenin refugee camp in the days before and immediately after the Battle for Jenin.

28. Efraim Halevy, *Man in the Shadows: Inside the Middle East Crisis with the Man Who Led the Mossad* (St. Martin's Press, 2006), 213.

29. Ibid., 214.

30. "President Bush Calls for New Palestinian Leadership," White House news release, June 24, 2002.

31. Galia Golan, *Israel and Palestine: Peace Plans from Oslo to Disengagement* (Markus Wiener Publishers, 2007), 90.

32. "Hamas Leader Mish'al Discusses Abu-Mazin's Call for Disarmament, Road Map," BBC Monitoring—Middle East, May 7, 2003.

33. Interview with Khalid Mishal on Al-Manar TV, March 12, 2003, trans. MEMRI Inquiry and Analysis Series No. 143, July 18, 2003.

34. Bregman, *Elusive Peace*, 259–61.

35. Amnesty International, "Israel and the Occupied Territories: Israel Must End Its Policy of Assassination," AI Index No. MDE 15/056/2003, July 4, 2003, 1.

36. B. Chernitsky, "The Domestic Palestinian Dispute over the Hudna," MEMRI Inquiry and Analysis Series No. 144, July 25, 2003.

37. Confidential author interview, Tel Aviv, Israel, September 2007.

38. Molly Moore and John Ward Anderson, "Israeli Jets Bomb Hamas Meeting, Injuring Spiritual Leader," *Washington Post*, September 7, 2003.

39. Amnesty International, "Israel and the Occupied Territories Surviving Under Siege: The Impact of Movement Restrictions on the Right to Work," AI Index No. MDE 15/001/2003, September 8, 2003.

40. Human Rights Watch, "Israel's 'Separation Barrier' in the Occupied West Bank: Human Rights and International Humanitarian Law Consequences," February 2004, 1–2.

41. Ibid., 4.

42. Ibid., 3.

43. Golan, *Israel and Palestine*, 119.

44. Glenn Kessler, "Bush Criticized Israeli Fence; Abbas Reminded of Need to Fight Terror," *Washington Post*, July 26, 2003.

45. Ben Lynfield, "Hamas Seeks Primacy in Gaza," *Christian Science Monitor*, March 3, 2004.

46. Ibid.

47. Paul McGeough, "At the Gates of Hell," *Sydney Morning Herald*, March 27, 2004.

48. Bregman, *Elusive Peace*, 282.

49. "Hamas May Target Israeli Prime Minister," BBC Monitoring—Middle East, March 25, 2004.

50. Ibid.

51. "Paper Cites Hamas Sources on Movement's Elections, Decision-making Process," BBC Monitoring—Middle East, March 30, 2004.

52. The author was present.

53. "Hamas Political Bureau Head Confirms Al-Rantisi Movement's Leader in Gaza," BBC Monitoring—Middle East, March 24, 2004.

50. Elisabeth Bumiller, "In Major Shift, Bush Endorses Sharon Plan and Backs Keeping Some Israeli Settlements," *New York Times*, April 15, 2004.

55. Sipress and Milbank, "Bush Demands Tough Action from Arafat over Bombings."

56. Ari Shavit, "The Big Freeze," *Haaretz*, October 8, 2004.

57. Ibid.

20: Follow the Money

1. *Elliott Jones Halberstam et al. v. Bernard C. Welch and Linda S. Hamilton*, Case No. 82-1364 (U.S. Court of Appeals, District of Columbia), Circuit Judge Wald for the court, decision.

2. Richard D. Lyons, "Escaped Felon Is Convicted of Murdering Dr. Halberstam, a Noted Washington Cardiologist," *New York Times*, April 11, 1981.

3. Associated Press, "Killer of Halberstam Given 9 Consecutive Life Terms," *New York Times*, May 23, 1981.

4. Judith Miller, "Israel Says That a Prisoner's Tale Links Arabs in the U.S. to Terrorism," *New York Times*, February 17, 1993.

5. Author interview with Nathan Lewin, Washington, DC, October 18, 2007.

6. Associated Press, "Klan Must Pay $37 Million for Inciting Church Fire," *New York Times*, July 25, 1998.

7. Frida Berrigan and William D. Hartung, "Who's Arming Israel?" *Foreign Policy in Focus*, July 26, 2006.

8. International Crisis Group, "Islamic Social Welfare—Activism in the Occupied Palestinian Territories: A Legitimate Target," *Middle East* Report No. 13, April 2, 2003, 13.

9. U.S. Treasury, "U.S. Designates Five Charities Funding Hamas and Six Senior Hamas Leaders as Terrorist Entities," news release, August 22, 2003.

10. Lee Hockstader, "Palestinians Find Heroes in Hamas; Popularity Surges for Once-Marginal Sponsor of Suicide-Bombings," *Washington Post*, August 11, 2001.

11. International Crisis Group, "Islamic Social Welfare," 11.

12. Chris McGreal, "Food Running Out in Gaza as Aid Appeal Fails," *The Guardian*, February 11, 2003.

13. *U.S. v. Holy Land Foundation et al.*, Case No. 3:04-CR-240-G (N.D. Tex.), transcript dated May 14, 2001 at 09:31:26, Government Exhibit 014-0004.

14. Dale L. Watson, "Holy Land Foundation for Relief and Development—International Emergency Economic Powers Act," FBI memorandum, November 5, 2001, 25 (hereafter "Watson Memo").

15. The author attended the meeting on March 26, 2002.

16. Intelligence and Terrorism Information Center, "Special Information Bulletin—'Charity' and Palestinian Terrorism," February 2005.

17. Intelligence and Terrorism Information Center at Centre for Special Studies, "Large Sums of Money Transferred by Saudi Arabia to the Palestinians Are Used for Financing Terror Organizations (Particularly the Hamas) and Terrorist Activities (Including Suicide Attacks Inside Israel)," www.terrorism-info.org.il/malam_multimedia//ENGLISH/SAUDI%20ARABIA/PDF/SAUDI3.PDF; Appendix C, Jamil Radaidah's letter to Colonel Jibril Al-Bakhri of the Palestinian Preventive Security Service, February 15, 2001.

18. Ibid.; Abu Mazen's letter to Salman Bo Abed Al Aziz, Captured Document E2, December 30, 2000.

19. Ibid.; Office of the President, summary of the news prepared for Yasser Arafat, Captured Document E3, January 7, 2001.

20. Don Van Natta Jr. and Timothy L. O'Brien, "Flow of Saudis' Cash to Hamas Is Scrutinized," *New York Times*, September 17, 2003.

21. Watson Memo, 15–16.

22. Mary Beth Sheridan, "Oxon Hill Development Has Ties to Terror; Hamas Leader, Man Accused of Al-Qaeda Link Invested in Barnaby Knolls," *Washington Post*, April 19, 2004.

23. Confidential author interview, Washington, DC, October 2007.

24. Steve McGonigle, "FBI Affidavit Says Dallas-Area High-Tech Firm Made Payments to Hamas Leader," *Dallas Morning News*, February 22, 2003.

25. Mike Allen, "Bush Freezes Suspected Terror Assets," *Washington Post*, December 4, 2001.

26. Author interview with Nathan Lewin.

27. John Ashcroft, "John Ashcroft Holds a Justice Department News Conference," news release, July 27, 2004.

28. "The Accused," *Chicago Sun-Times*, February 1, 2007.

29. *Mousa Mohammad Abu Marzook v. Warren Christopher et al.*, Case No. 95-CIV-9799-KTD (S.D. N.Y.), "Israeli Request for the Extradition of Mousa Mohammad Abu Marzook," transcript of Shin Bet interview with Said Msamah, January 13, 1991.

30. Michelle Mittelstadt, "U.S. Had Right to Freeze Assets of Charity Accused of Aiding Hamas, Court Rules," *Dallas Morning News*, June 20, 2003.

21: Government from the Trenches

1. Glenn Frankel, "A Quiet Ending on a Bleak Day; Few Present in Paris Dawn as Arafat's Death Is Announced," *Washington Post*, November 12, 2004.

2. Graham Usher, "'Not Red Indians,'" *Al-Ahram Weekly*, November 4–10, 2004.

3. Author interviews with Khalid Mishal, Damascus, Syria, September–November 2007.

4. Idith Zertal and Akiva Eldar, *Lords of the Land: The War over Israel's Settlements in the Occupied Territories, 1967–2007* (Nation Books, 2007), 37.

5. Margot Dudkevitch, "25 Minutes, 25 Bullets, 10 Dead," *Jerusalem Post*, March 4, 2002.

6. Matthew Gutman, "What's the IRA Doing in Ramallah," *Jerusalem Post*, July 14, 2003.

7. Amos Harel, "Sniper Who Killed 10 Israelis Arrested," *Haaretz*, October 8, 2004.

8. Ben Lynfield, "Yasser Arafat's Local Election Gambit," *Christian Science Monitor*, October 14, 2004.

9. Author interviews with Khalid Mishal.

10. Palestinian Information Centre, "Mish'al: National Leadership Is a Must at the Current Stage," BBC Monitoring—Middle East, November 22, 2004.

11. Khaled Amayreh, "Hamas Eyes Its Future Role," *Al-Ahram Weekly*, November 4–10, 2004.

12. "Israeli PM Suffers Serious Stroke," BBC, January 5, 2006.

13. Author interview with Ahmad Yousef, Gaza, Occupied Territories, September 2007.

14. Author interview with Bassam Naim, Gaza City, Occupied Territories, September 2007.

15. David Remnick, "The Democracy Game," *New Yorker*, February 27, 2006.

16. Brian Murphy, "Brother Battles Brother," Associated Press, January 20, 2006.

17. Greg Myre, "Political Sibling Rivalry: Hebron Parliamentary Race Pits Brother Against Brother," *New York Times*, January 24, 2006.

18. Murphy, "Brother Battles Brother."

19. Ibid.

20. Author interviews with Khalid Mishal.

21. International Crisis Group, "Palestinians, Israel and the Quartet: Pulling Back from the Brink," Middle East Report No. 54, June 13, 2006, 2.

22. Khalid Abu Toameh, "Fatah Activists Blame Their Leaders," *Jerusalem Post*, January 27, 2006.

23. Chris McGreal, "Palestinian Authority 'May Have Lost Billions,'" *The Guardian*, February 6, 2006.

24. Khaled Abu Toameh, "Rioting Fatah Members Turn on Abbas; PA Leader Fearing for His Life, Cancels Gaza Meeting with Hamas," *Jerusalem Post*, January 29, 2006.

25. International Crisis Group, "Palestinians, Israel and the Quartet," 10.

26. Ibid., 11.

27. Steven Weisman, "Rice Admits U.S. Underestimated Hamas Strength," *New York Times*, January 30, 2006.

28. International Crisis Group, "Palestinians, Israel and the Quartet," 32.

29. Glenn Kessler, "Push for Democracy Loses Some Energy; On Mideast Tour, Rice Focuses on Hamas," *Washington Post*, February 25, 2006.

30. Mary Curtin, "U.S. Envoy Says Palestinian Forces Unprepared for Pullout," *Los Angeles Times*, July 1, 2005.

31. "Hamas Leaders Stress Political Unity, Palestinian Rights at Gaza Celebration," Palestinian Information Center Web site, BBC Monitoring—Middle East, January 28, 2006.

32. Al-Sharq Al-Awsat, "Hamas Leader Reportedly Calls for Partnership with Palestinian Factions," BBC Monitoring—Middle East, February 13, 2006.

33. Laura King. "Hamas Faces a New Struggle," *Los Angeles Times*, January 26, 2006.

34. International Crisis Group, "Palestinians, Israel and the Quartet," 2.

35. Alastair Crooke interviewed by Ahmad Mansour, "The U.S. Campaign to Topple the Palestinian Government," Al-Jazeera, January 24, 2007, available at conflicts forum.org/2007/interview-the-us-campaign-to-topple-the-palestinian-government/.

36. Josef Federman, "Olmert: Hamas Is Not a Strategic Threat to Israel," Associated Press, February 22, 2006.

37. Sheera Claire Frenkel and Gil Hoffman, "Politicians Scramble to Spin Hamas Victory in Their Favour; Kadima, Under Fire, Declines to Comment," *Jerusalem Post*, January 27, 2006.

38. Yaakov Katz, "Red-Faced IDF Misread the 'Street'; Military Intelligence Failed to Gauge Hamas Strength," *Jerusalem Post*, January 27, 2006.

39. Al-Manar TV, "Hamas Faces No Dilemma, to Focus on Reform, Resistance—Mish'al," BBC Monitoring—Middle East, January 28, 2006.

40. Scott Wilson, "Hamas Poised to Become Insiders," *Washington Post*, January 25, 2006.

41. King, "Hamas Faces a New Struggle."

42. International Crisis Group, "Palestinians, Israel and the Quartet," 3.

43. Al-Jazeera, "Leading Palestinian Hamas Figure Discusses Participation in Government, Talks," BBC Monitoring—Middle East, January 25, 2006.

44. *Al-Safir*, "Hamas's Mishal Seeks Government of Technocrats," BBC Monitoring—Middle East, February 9, 2006.

45. Al-Hayat Al-Jadidah, "Hamas Says Ready to Negotiate with Israel on Truce Conditions," BBC Monitoring—Middle East, February 3, 2006.

46. Remnick, "The Democracy Game."

47. Associated Press, "Hamas Rejects Support of Al-Qaeda, Says Its Ideology Is Moderate Islam," March 5, 2006.

48. Bernard Wasserstein, "This May Be the 'Crack in History' That Israel Needs," *Sunday Times*, January 29, 2006.

49. Al-Manar TV, "Hamas Faces No Dilemma."

50. Lally Weymouth, "'We Do Not Wish to Throw Them into the Sea,'" *Washington Post*, February 26, 2006.

51. Henry Seigman, "Hamas: The Last Chance for Peace?" *New York Review of Books*, April 5, 2006.

52. Palestinian Information Centre, "Palestinian Hamas Chief Mish'al Interviewed During Visit to Tehran," BBC Monitoring—Middle East, February 25, 2006.

53. Associated Press, "Hamas Not Interested in 'Secret Ways' to Transfer Funds," May 5, 2006.

54. Peter Hirschberg, "Hamas Pays Workers from Suitcases Full of Dollars," Inter Press Service, June 23, 2006.

55. Khaled Abu Toameh, Yaakov Katz, and Herb Keinon, "Haniyeh Returns to Gaza, but Without His $3m in Cash; 18 Hurt as Hamas Goes on Rampage at Rafah Crossing After Israel Delays PA Premier's Reentry," *Jerusalem Post*, December 15, 2006.

56. Al-Jazeera, "Hamas Leader Mish'al Addresses Syria Rally, Vows Not to Recognise Israel," BBC Monitoring—Middle East, April 22, 2006.

57. Al-Jazeera, "Fatah, Hamas Still Trying to Contain Repercussions of Mish'al's speech," BBC Monitoring—Middle East, April 23, 2006.

58. Intelligence and Terrorism Information Center, "Rocket Threat from the Gaza Strip, 2000–2007," December 2007, 7.

59. Ibid., 74.

60. Ibid.

61. Steven Erlanger, "Hamas Fires Rockets into Israel, Ending 16-Month Truce," *New York Times*, June 11, 2006.

62. B'Tselem, "Statistics: Fatalities," www.btselem.org/English/Statistics/Casualties .asp.

63. Erlanger, "Hamas Fires Rockets into Israel."

64. Phil Zabriskie, "Death on the Beach," *Time*, June 26, 2006.

22: "No Gold Bars Left"

1. Josh Brannon et al., "IDF Poised for Gaza Offensive After Two Soldiers Killed; Army Caught by Surprise in Early Morning Cross-Border Raid," *Jerusalem Post*, June 26, 2006.

2. Ibid.

3. Conal Urquhart, "Israel Promises Revenge for Soldier Deaths," *The Guardian*, June 26, 2006.

4. Michael Matza, "Israeli Hostage: Bargaining Chip?" *Philadelphia Inquirer*, June 26, 2006.

5. Ibid.

6. Josh Brannon et al., "Captors List Demands, as IDF Braces for Gaza Incursion," *Jerusalem Post*, June 27, 2006.

7. Palestinian Information Centre, "Hamas Defends Capture of Israeli Soldier," BBC Monitoring—Middle East, June 29, 2006.

8. Associated Press. "Hamas Official Slams Abbas for Helping Israel," Dow Jones International News, June 27, 2006.

9. Ibrahim Humaydi, "Leader Mish'al Explains Hamas's 'Selective' Approach to Quartet Conditions," *Al-Hayat*, October 12, 2006, trans. BBC Monitoring—Middle East.

10. Joel Greenberg, "Palestinian Ministers Arrested; Israel Seizes Hamas Officials in W. Bank," *Chicago Tribune*, June 29, 2006.

11. Associated Press, "Syria Fires on Israeli Jets," June 28, 2006.

12. Syrian TV, "Hamas Leader Discusses Developments at July 10 Damascus News Conference," BBC Monitoring—Middle East, July 12, 2006.

13. Alvaro de Soto, "End of Mission Report," leaked in full to *The Guardian*, May 2007, available at http://image.guardian.co.uk/sys-files/Guardian/documents/2007/06/12/DeSotoReport.pdf.

14. Khaled Amayreh, "Dahlan Vows to Decimate Hamas," *Al-Ahram Weekly*, June 8, 2006.

15. Ibid.

16. Dion Nissenbaum, "Border Complex Mostly Empty," *News and Observer*, May 21, 2007.

17. Paul McGeough, "A Beach Scene That Hides the Waves of Despair," *Sydney Morning Herald*, September 2, 2006.

18. Author interview with Hamdi Basal, Gaza City, Occupied Territories, August 2006.

19. Ibid.

20. Adam Entous and Haitham Tamimi, "Hamas, Abbas Rivalry Spurs Palestinian Arms Race," Reuters, June 8, 2006.

21. Ibid.

23: Everything Is Not as It Seems

1. Alastair Crooke interviewed by Ahmad Mansour, "The U.S. Campaign to Topple the Palestinian Government," Al-Jazeera, January 24, 2007, available at conflictsforum.org/2007/interview-the-us-campaign-to-topple-the-palestinian-government/.

2. Ibid.

3. Michael Crowley, "Elliott Abrams: From Iran-Contra to Bush's Democracy Czar," *Slate*, February 17, 2005.

4. Steven Erlanger, "U.S. and Israelis Are Said to Talk of Hamas Ouster," *New York Times*, February 14, 2006.

5. Adam Entous, "U.S. to Give Abbas Forces $86 Million Amid Power Struggle," Reuters, January 5, 2007.

6. Author phone interview with Alastair Crooke, director of Conflicts Forum, June 15, 2008.

7. Adam Entous, "U.S., European Officials Visit Fatah Base in Jordan," Reuters, December 25, 2006.

8. Ari Rabinovitch, "U.S. General Says Building Up Abbas' Guard," Reuters, November 24, 2006.

9. Alvaro de Soto, "End of Mission Report," leaked in full to *The Guardian*, May 2007, available at http://image.guardian.co.uk/sys-files/Guardian/documents/2007/06/12/DeSotoReport.pdf.

10. Author interview with Assad Mousa Abu Dan, Jabalya, Gaza Strip, September 2007.

11. The author has viewed a video recording captured by Hamas of the abuse of the Abu Dan family.

12. Richard Boudreaux, "Israel Escorts Egyptian Arms Delivery to Abbas; U.S. Consents to the Shipment, Intended to Counter the Militant Hamas Movement," *Los Angeles Times*, December 29, 2006.

13. David Rose, "The Gaza Bombshell," *Vanity Fair*, April 2008.

14. Nathan J. Brown, "What Can Abu Mazin Do?" Carnegie Endowment for International Peace, June 15, 2007.

15. Rose, "The Gaza Bombshell."

16. Cam Simpson and Neil King, "Dangerous Territory: With Aid, U.S. Widens Role in Palestinian Crisis—To Undercut Hamas and Iran, Bush Pushes $86 Million Plan," *Wall Street Journal*, January 12, 2007.

17. Azzam Tamimi, *Hamas: A History from Within* (Olive Branch Press, 2007), 255.

18. "Dahlan: Any Attack on Fatah Members Will Be Met with Harsh Retaliation," *Al-Ayyam*, January 8, 2007, trans. MEMRI Inquiry and Analysis Series No. 316, January 23, 2007.

19. Associated Press, "Fatah Holds Massive Rally in Gaza Soccer Stadium," January 7, 2007.

20. Ronny Shaked, "Hamas Won the Jackpot," *Yedioth Ahronoth*, February 10, 2007.

21. *Al-Hayat Al-Jadida* (Palestinian Authority), February 27, 2007, trans. MEMRI Inquiry and Analysis Series No. 331, February 28, 2007.

22. Rose, "The Gaza Bombshell."

23. Abd-al-Ra'uf Arna'ut, "Palestinian Security Adviser Says Impartial, Professional Force Planned," *Al-Ayyam*, April 7, 2007, trans. BBC Monitoring—Middle East.

24. Palestine History.com, "Palestinian Biography—Mohammed Dahlan," www .palestinehistory.com/biography/palestine/palbio34.htm.

25. Ma'an News Agency, "Palestinian MP Dahlan Urges Government's Clear Answers Amid 'Leadership Vacuum,'" October 11, 2006, trans. BBC Monitoring—Middle East.

26. Ahron Bregman, *Elusive Peace: How the Holy Land Defeated America* (Penguin, 2005), 257.

27. "Missing Links," arablinks.blogspot.com/.

28. Evelyn Gordon, "Benchmarks for a Bloodbath," *Jerusalem Post*, May 10, 2007.

29. Nahid Hattar, "Hamas Leader Mish'al Discusses Emotional Ties with Jordan," *Al-Sabil*, May 15, 2007, trans. BBC Monitoring—Middle East.

30. Warren P. Strobel and Dion Nissenbaum, "How U.S. Policy Missteps Led to a Nasty Downfall in Gaza," McClatchy Washington Bureau, July 4, 2007.

31. Hilary Leila Krieger, "Abrams: US Trying to Appease Arabs, EU," *Jerusalem Post*, May 11, 2007.

24: An Eye for an Eye

1. Confidential author interview, Gaza City, Occupied Territories, September 2007.

2. Ibid.

3. Aaron D. Pina, "Fatah and Hamas: The New Palestinian Factional Reality," Congressional Research Service, March 3, 2006.

4. Cam Simpson, "U.S.-Iran Tension Colors Palestinian Crisis," *Wall Street Journal*, December 17, 2006.

5. Laura Rozen, "Israel's Mossad, Out of the Shadows," MotherJones.com, February 19, 2008.

6. Confidential author interview, Jerusalem, Israel, September 2007.

7. Nahid Hattar, "Hamas Leader Mish'al Discusses 'Emotional Ties' with Jordan," *Al-Sabil*, May 15, 2007, trans. BBC Monitoring—Middle East, May 17, 2007.

8. Author interviews with Khalid Mishal, Damascus, Syria, September–November 2007.

9. Ibid.

10. Intelligence and Terrorism Information Center, "Hamas' Military Build-up in the Gaza Strip," April 2008.

11. Marie Colvin, "Iran Arming and Training Hamas Force," *Sunday Times*, March 9, 2008.

12. "We Are Facing a Second Nakba," *Al-Ayyam*, May 18, 2007, trans. MEMRI Inquiry and Analysis Series No. 359, June 1, 2007.

13. Adam Entous, "Forces Loyal to Abbas Get New Bases, Training," Reuters, April 12, 2007.

14. Scott Wilson, "Fatah Troops Enter Gaza with Israeli Assent; Hundreds Were Trained in Egypt Under U.S.-Backed Program to Counter Hamas," *Washington Post*, May 18, 2007.

15. Amor Harel and Avi Issacharoff, "Fatah to Israel: Let Us Get Arms to Fight Hamas," *Haaretz*, June 7, 2007.

16. Ibid.

17. Ibid.

18. Keith Dayton, congressional testimony, May 23, 2007, *CQ* Transcriptions.

19. Khaled Abu Toameh, "PA to Retire at Least 160 Officers; Abbas Seeks to Prove to Rice He's Sincere About PA Security Reform," *Jerusalem Post*, January 11, 2007.

20. The video is now widely available in Gaza—copy in author's files.

21. Palestinian Centre for Human Rights (PCHR), "Black Pages in the Absence of Justice: Report on Bloody Fighting in the Gaza Strip from 7 to 14 June 2007," October 2007.

22. Jaber Wishah, deputy director, PCHR, e-mail to author, December 16, 2007.

23. Donald McIntyre, "Hamas Seizes Fatah Base as Bloody Battles Push Gaza Towards Civil War," *Independent on Sunday*, June 13, 2007.

24. International Crisis Group, "Inside Gaza: The Challenge of Clans and Families," Middle East Report No. 71, December 20, 2007, 7–8.

25. PCHR, "Black Pages in the Absence of Justice," 61.

26. Nidal Al-Mughrabi, "Guns Blaze in Hospital as 13 Die in Gaza Chaos," *Toronto Star*, June 12, 2007.

27. PCHR, "Black Pages in the Absence of Justice," 62.

28. Al-Mughrabi, "Guns Blaze in Hospital as 13 Die in Gaza Chaos."

29. PCHR, "Black Pages in the Absence of Justice," 33.

30. Author interview with Bassam Abdul Raouf, Beit Hanoun, Gaza Strip, Occupied Territories, September 2007; and Raouf's affidavit in PCHR, "Black Pages in the Absence of Justice," 46.

31. Author interview with Bassam Abdul Raouf.

32. Ed O'Loughlin, "Inside the Hamas Revolution," *Sunday Herald*, June 16, 2007.

33. Ibid., 39–40.

34. Conal Urquhart, Ian Black, and Mark Tran, "Hamas Takes Control of Gaza," *The Guardian*, June 15, 2007.

35. Confidential author interview, Tel Aviv, Israel, September 2007.

36. Ed O'Loughlin, "Hopeless in Gaza," *Sydney Morning Herald*, June 23, 2007.

37. Mohammed Assadi, "Abbas Assails Hamas 'Assassins,' Talks to Israel," Reuters, June 20, 2007.

38. Human Rights Watch, "Internal Fight: Palestinian Abuses in Gaza and the West Bank," July 2008, 23.

39. Aaron Klein, "Hamas Lists Seized U.S. Weapons," WorldNetDaily.com, June 20, 2007.

40. Intelligence and Terrorism Information Center, "Hamas Military Build-up in the Gaza Strip," April 2008.

41. Jeremy Bowen, "Breaking Point in the Middle East?" BBC, June 15, 2007.

42. International Crisis Group, "After Gaza," Middle East Report No. 68, August 2, 2007.

43. Author interview with Khalid Abu Hilal, Gaza City, Occupied Territories, September 2007.

44. Ibid.

45. Peter Beaumont, Mitchell Prothero, Azmi Al-Keshawi, and Sandra Jordan, "How Hamas Turned on Palestine's 'Traitors,'" *The Observer*, June 17, 2007.

46. Mitchell Prothero, "Hamas War Chief Reveals His Plans for Gaza Peace," *The Observer*, June 24, 2007.

47. Author interview with Jamila Ashanti, Gaza City, Occupied Territories, September 2007.

48. Author interview with Ismail Haniyah, Gaza City, Occupied Territories, September 2007.

49. Author interview with Isa Al-Najjar, Gaza City, Occupied Territories, September 2007.

50. Author interview with Raji Sourani, Gaza City, Occupied Territories, September 2007.

51. Khalid Mishal press conference, Damascus, Al-Manar TV, June 15, 2007.

52. "Hamas Leader Says USA Wants Calm Mideast to Prepare for New Wars," Al-Jazeera, July 17, 2007, trans. BBC Monitoring—Middle East.

53. Author interview with Jamila Ashanti, Gaza City, Occupied Territories, September 2007.

25: Taking the Holy Land to Court

1. Jack Douglas Jr., "Scrutinized for Years, Foundation Faces Trial," *Fort Worth Star-Telegram*, July 15, 2007.

2. Author interview with Dennis Lormel, former head of FBI's Terrorist Financing Operations Section, Washington, DC, October 2007.

3. Ibid.

4. Ibid.

5. Ibid.

6. Tom Durkin, "Terrorism in Our Courts," *Chicago Tribune*, February 8, 2007.

7. *U.S. v. Holy Land Foundation et al.*, Case No. 3:04-CR-240-G (N.D. Tex.),

"An Explanatory Memorandum," Government Exhibit 003-0085, 2–4 of English translation.

8. Jason Trahan, "Holy Land Defendants' Long Wait Ends as U.S. Vows to Retry Case," *Dallas Morning News*, October 23, 2007.

9. Greg Krikorian, "Mistrial in Holy Land Terrorism Financing Case," *Los Angeles Times*, October 23, 2007.

10. Trahan, "Holy Land Defendants' Long Wait Ends."

11. Greg Krikorian, "Weak Case Seen in Failed Trial of Charity," *Los Angeles Times*, November 4, 2007.

12. Trahan, "Holy Land Defendants' Long Wait Ends."

13. David Koenig, "Mistrial for Most Defendants in Muslim Charity Trial," Associated Press, October 22, 2007.

14. Author interview with Khalid Mishal, Damascus, Syria, November 2007.

15. Author interview with Dennis Lormel, former head of the FBI's Terrorist Financing Operations Section, Washington, DC, October 2007.

16. Ibid.

17. Kathianne Boniello, "Bomb Kin Sue Bank Giant," *New York Post*, February 3, 2008.

18. Jennifer Senior, "A Nation Unto Himself," *New York Times Magazine*, March 14, 2004.

19. Judge Nina Gershon, "Opinion and Order—*Oran Almog et al. v. Arab Bank*" (E.D. New York), January 29, 2007, 5.

20. Ibid., 55–56.

21. Julia Preston, "Arab Bank Is Ordered to Suspend Most Operations in U.S.," *New York Times*, February 26, 2005.

22. Amy Klein, "Waging War Against Terror, Via Courtroom," *The Record* (Bergen County, NJ), January 24, 2005.

23. *U.S. v. Holy Land Foundation et al.*, transcript dated April 23, 1996, at 21:18:50, Government Exhibit 013-0083.

24. *Boim v. Holy Land Foundation et al.*, Case Nos. 05-1815, 05-1816, 05-1821 and 05-1822 (7th Cir.), majority decision by Appellate Judge Ilana Diamond Rovner, December 28, 2007, 9.

26: The Man Who Wouldn't Die

1. The author visited the Damascus headquarters of Hamas for a series of interviews with Khalid Mishal from September 2007 to November 2007.

2. Confidential author interview, Washington, DC, October 2007.

3. Author interview with Ziad Abu Amr, Gaza City, Occupied Territories, September 2007.

4. Author interview with Ranya Kadri, Amman, Jordan, July 2007.

5. Azzam Tamimi, *Hamas: Unwritten Chapters* (Hurst & Co., 2007), 45.

6. Confidential author interview, Gaza City, Occupied Territories, September 2007.

7. Confidential author interview, Tel Aviv, Israel, September 2007.

8. Clancy Chassay and Bobbie Johnson, "Google Earth Used to Target Israel," *The Guardian*, October 25, 2007.

9. Amir Mizroch, "'Waiting for Babies to Die Is No Strategy,'" *Jerusalem Post*, September 4, 2007.

10. Yaakov Katz and Herb Keinon, "Olmert 'Won't Play into Hamas Hands' by Sending IDF into Gaza," *Jerusalem Post*, September 12, 2007.

11. Human Rights Watch, "Internal Fight: Palestinian Abuses in Gaza and the West Bank," July 2008, 18.

12. Sarah el Deeb, "Wary Gazans Adjust to Hamas Rule in Subtle Ways," Associated Press, July 1, 2007.

13. Confidential author interview, Tel Aviv, Israel, September 2007.

14. Sue Pleming, "U.S. Should Deal with Hamas, Say Ex-Officials," Reuters, October 10, 2007.

15. Colin Powell, *All Things Considered*, National Public Radio, July 18, 2007.

16. Alastair Crooke, "From Rebel Movement to Political Party: The Case of the Islamic Resistance Movement," Conflicts Forum Briefing Paper 3, undated.

17. "Hamas's Mish'al Addresses Palestinians on Movement's 20th Anniversary," Al-Aqsa Satellite TV, December 14, 2007, trans. BBC Monitoring—Middle East.

18. Author interview with Asad Abdul Rahman, Amman, Jordan, September 2007.

19. The author was present when Mishal took the call on September 6, 2007.

20. Arieh O'Sullivan, "Hamas Man Escapes Damascus Hit," *Jerusalem Post*, December 14, 2004.

21. Arieh O'Sullivan and Joseph Nasr, "Syria Blames Israel for Hamas Hit," *Jerusalem Post*, September 27, 2004.

Epilogue

1. International Crisis Group, "Round Two in Gaza," Middle East Briefing No. 24, September 11, 2008, 12–13.

2. Ibid., 14.

3. "Hamas Lays Pipeline to Supply Gaza Strip with Fuel from Egypt," UMCI News, August 31, 2008.

4. Diaa Hadid, "Drugged Lions Join Long List of Gaza Contraband," Associated Press, August 9, 2008.

5. Ahmad Yousef, "Palestinian Revenge Was Inevitable," *Haaretz*, February 12, 2008.

6. "Carter in Hamas 'Ceasefire Call,'" BBC News, April 19, 2008.

7. "Abbas Aims to Stay in Office to 2010 Despite Hamas," Reuters, September 14, 2008.

8. Alix Van Buren, "The New U.S. President Is Going to Have to Reckon with Hamas," *La Repubblica*, October 11, 2008, trans. BBC Monitoring—Middle East.

Index

Abbas, Mahmoud (Abu Mazen)
  and aftermath of civil war in Gaza, 410
  appointment as puppet prime minister,
    281–82
  blueprint for Abbas leadership, 362–63
  and Bush administration campaign to
    destabilize Hamas, 285, 339, 341–42,
    344, 346, 351–53, 362–68, 378, 381–
    82, 416–17
  Bush administration's aid to security
    forces, 351–52, 356, 370, 371
  and factional friction between Fatah and
    Hamas government, 328, 341, 348,
    355–59, 362–63, 371–72, 377–78, 382
  and Fatah leadership after Arafat's death,
    313
  and first Intifada, 64
  and Gaza civil war, 371–72, 377, 382
  and Israeli weapons shipments to Fatah,
    355, 370
  and Mecca Accord, 357–58, 357–59
  and Middle East road map, 281–82, 285
  Mishal's critique of, 281–82
  and Palestinian elections (2004–2006),
    313, 318–19, 324, 325, 326, 328
  resignation as prime minister, 285
  and Saudi charity funds during second
    Intifada, 306

  and talks between Palestinian Authority
    and Israel (2007–2008), 416–17
Abd Al-Qadir, Mufid, 38, 39, 248–49, 253,
  307, 386–89, 390
Abd Al-Qadir (Mishal's father), 5–8, 10–11,
  13–14, 31–33, 38, 39, 69
Abd El-Rahman, Ahmad, 333
Abdul Rahman, Asad, 30–31, 38, 264, 413
Abdul Raouf, Bassam, 372–76
Abdullah, Crown Prince/King (Saudi
  Arabia), 306, 357, 365
Abdullah, Prince (Jordan), 167, 244. See also
  Abdullah II, King (Jordan)
Abdullah Al-Salim Al-Sabah School
  (Kuwait), 33
Abdullah I, King (Jordan), 9, 10, 23, 27
Abdullah II, King (Jordan)
  and Arafat, 249
  and Batikhi, 255
  crackdown on Hamas in Jordan, 247–55
  as King Hussein's successor, 243–44
  and Shiite Crescent, 366
Abington, Edward, 387
Abou-Houwaileh, Musbah, 413–14
Abrams, Elliott, 350–51, 352–53, 362, 364
Abu Baker, Shukri, 76, 86–87, 253, 388, 390,
  393–94
Abu Dan, Assad, 353–55

Abu Deraa, 115

Abu Ghraib prison (Iraq), 84

Abu Hamed, 102

Abu Hanoud, Mahmoud, 268, 304

Abu Hilal, Khalid, 379, 409

Abu Hilalah, Yasser, 240

Abu Jedian, Jamal, 372, 373–75

Abu Khalid, 98

Abu Marzook, Mousa, 78–81, 84–94, 105

    arrest and jailing in New York, 78–81,
        84–94, 105, 106, 118–19, 123, 231

    and Batikhi, 80–81, 137, 150–51, 152,
        196–98, 237, 247

    and case against Holy Land Foundation,
        386

    deportation/expulsion from Jordan, 79,
        80–81, 114

    early life and career, 115–16

    FBI's Vulgar Betrayal investigation,
        307–11

    and Hamas operations in Damascus,
        401–2

    and Hamas operations in Gaza, 116–17

    and Hamas operations in U.S., 78–81, 84–
        94, 97–98, 116, 238–39, 296, 307–8

    and Hamas political bureau in Amman,
        72, 73, 74, 80–81, 111–13, 116, 122–
        24, 196, 237–40

    Israeli case against/extradition to Israel,
        85–87, 93–94, 96, 118–21

    and Israel's crackdown on Hamas, 80–81,
        96, 97–98, 99, 100, 102–3

    and Lewin's prosecution of Boim case,
        299, 308–9

    and Mishal, 79–80, 115, 123, 237–40,
        401–2

    and Mossad plot to assassinate Mishal,
        137, 145, 150–51, 152, 196–98,
        218–19

    and prospect of *hudna* (truce) with Israel,
        236–37

    release to King Hussein in Jordan, 120–25

    rivalry with Mishal over political bureau
        leadership, 237–40, 401–2

    and Yassin, 79–80, 112, 115, 125, 206–9,
        401

Abu Mazen. *See* Abbas, Mahmoud (Abu
    Mazen)

Abu Msamah, Said, 116, 310

Abu Muammar brothers, 335, 337

Abu Obieda, 380

Abu Ras, Marwan, 283

Abu Saab, 98, 101

Abu Samhadana, Jamal, 335, 336–37

Abu Sayf, Mohammad, 131–35, 150, 247,
    399

Abu Shanab, Ismail, 263, 272, 282–83

Abu Sulmiyah, Jawad, 59

Abu Swaireh, Jamal, 376

Abu Teir, Sheikh Mohammad, 65–66

Abu Zuhri, Sami, 331

Abu-Amr, Ziad, 402

Achille Lauro incident, 298–99

Afghanistan

    CIA operation to arm/train Islamic
        fundamentalists, 46, 50–51, 58, 59

    Sheikh Azzam and jihad in, 57, 58, 59

    U.S./Israel and support to Islamists in, 46

Agence France-Presse (AFP), 20, 83, 112,
    130–31, 137, 140, 144, 154–57, 194–
    95, 202, 206, 243–44, 250. *See also*
    Habib, Randa

Al-Ajez, Saeb, 276

Akasheh, Bassam, 153–54, 157, 159, 160,
    183–87

Al-Alami, Imad, 251–52, 264

Albright, Madeleine, 128, 204, 249

Amnesty International, 273

Al-Aqsa Intifada. *See* Intifada, second (Al-
    Aqsa Intifada)

Al-Aqsa Martyrs Brigade, 262, 353, 372

Al-Aqsa Mosque

    and King Abdullah assassination, 23, 27

    and Netanyahu's tunnel, 193

    Rohan's torching/repair of, 34

    Sharon's visit to Al-Haram Al-Sharif and
        second Intifada, 259, 261

Al-Aqsa TV, 373

Al-Arab Al-Yawm (newspaper), 251

Arab Bank, 391–93

Arab League, 9, 241

Arab Legion, 9

Arab Liberation Front, 303

Arab Revolt (1936–1939), 5–6, 8

"Arab Street," 367

Arafat, Yasser
  addressing UN General Assembly
    (1974), 36
  and Camp David summit (2000),
    257–59
  death of, 312–13
  driven out of Jordan (Black September),
    24–25, 254–55
  and Egyptian Muslim Brotherhood, 54
  eviction from Beirut (1982), 43–44, 50,
    259–60
  and FBI terrorist list, 91–92
  and first Intifada, 62–63, 64
  and Halevy's plan to rearrange Palestinian
    leadership, 279–80
  and Hamas suicide bombings, 108–9, 196
  and King Hussein, 24–25, 73, 106, 210,
    254–55
  and King Hussein's funeral, 245–46
  Mishal's opinion of, 52, 54, 55, 313
  and the missing Saudi contributions to
    PLO, 305–7
  and Netanyahu, 126, 127
  Nobel Peace Prize, 103–4
  Oslo peace process, 75, 92, 103–5, 127,
    225, 241, 242–43, 257–59
  Ramallah compound, 278–79
  return to Gaza as head of Palestinian
    Authority, 76, 77, 104–5
  rivalry with Yassin over control of Pales-
    tine, 231–36
  and Saddam Hussein's invasion of Kuwait,
    70, 74–75
  and second Intifada, 262–64, 271–73,
    275–80, 305–7
  security forces, 105, 214, 232, 242, 243,
    262, 358

and Sharon as prime minister, 262, 271

and Sharon's Operation Defensive Shield,
    271–73, 275–80

and Six-Day War, 12, 24

Washington's reception of, 92, 105

and Wye Memorandum, 242–43

and Yassin, 182, 210, 231–36, 241, 243,
    263, 287

Al-Armuti, Salih, 252

Arouri, Salah, 102

Ashanti, Jamila, 380, 382

Ashcroft, John, 309, 384, 386

Ashqar, Abdelhaleem, 309–10

Al-Ashqar, Abdel Haleem, 77, 385–86

Al-Assad, Bashar, 340, 396

Al-Assad, Hafez, 26, 46, 256

Attajdid (Moroccan newspaper), 268

Awad, Nihan, 390

Awadallah, Wessam, 373

Axworthy, Lloyd, 223, 225, 228

Ayyad, Sheikh Khalil, 7

Ayyash, Yehiya, 106–8, 120, 405

Al-Azhar University (Cairo), 7, 58

Azzam, Sheikh Abdullah, 57–59, 83, 405

"Badger" (anonymous Internet blogger),
    361–63

Banna, Hasan, 42

Barak, Ehud
  and aftermath of Mossad's failed assas-
    sination of Mishal, 218
  Camp David Summit (2000), 257–59,
    261
  and Netanyahu, 218, 256
  and settlements/settler housing, 261
  and Syria First strategy, 256
  withdrawal of Israeli troops from Leba-
    non, 257, 262
  and Wye Memorandum, 256

Bar-Illan, David, 235

Barnea, Nahum, 213–14, 221

Basal, Hamdi, 345

Bases of the Sheikhs (Qawaid
    Al-Shuyukh), 58

Batikhi, Samih, 103, 121, 128
and Abu Marzook, 80–81, 137, 150–51, 152, 196–98, 237, 247
corruption trial, 255, 360
King Abdullah II's regime and raids on Hamas in Jordan, 247–55
and meeting between King Hussein and Yatom, 141–43, 145–48
and Mossad's failed assassination of Mishal, 135, 137–43, 145–52, 158–60, 167–69
and negotiations following Mossad's failed assassination of Mishal, 167–69, 188–94, 196–98, 200–206, 226
BBC World Service, 12
Begin, Menachem, 14
Ben-Gurion, David, 9, 14
Bennett, Steve, 155–56, 161–62, 222–25
Berger, David, 223, 225
Berger, Sandy, 166, 172, 174–75, 176, 204
Bin Laden, Osama, 46, 58, 89, 267, 287, 307–8, 405
Bin Zeid, Prince Raad, 161–62
Bir Zeit University (West Bank), 59
Black September, 24–25, 33, 58, 251, 254–55
Blair, Tony, 245
Boim, David, 297–300, 308–9, 311, 384, 386, 395
Britain
British Mandate era, 23, 26
Palestine and Arab Revolt (1936–1939), 5–6, 7
Brzezinski, Zbigniew, 412
Buchovzeh, Herzl, 63
Burns, Lara, 387–88
Bush, George H. W., 68, 69, 74, 245
Bush, George W./Bush administration
and Abbas, 285, 339, 341–42, 344, 346, 351–53, 356, 362–68, 370, 371, 378, 381–82, 416–17
and Boim case, 297–300, 308–9, 311, 384, 386, 395
campaign to destabilize Hamas government, 285, 339, 341–42, 344, 346,
351–53, 362–68, 370–71, 378, 381–82, 416–17
commitments to Sharon campaign in the Occupied Territories, 290, 292–93
and Crooke's Conflicts Forum, 350–51
and Dahlan, 359
fight against terrorist fund-raising, 269–70, 296, 300–302, 307–11, 383–95
and Gaza civil war, 353, 364, 370–71, 377
and Hamas's win in Palestinian elections, 325–26, 327
and Israel's Operation Defensive Shield (2002), 277, 279
and Middle East peace process, 273, 275, 280–81, 285, 292–93, 331, 416–17
and Middle East road map, 280–81, 285, 292–93, 331
post-9/11 war on terror, 268–71
Rose Garden speech, 280, 309, 384, 395

Camp David summit (2000), 257–59, 261
Canada
CSIS and Mossad, 222
Embassy in Amman, 149–50, 155–56
Internet blogger "Badger," 361–62
Israeli use of Canadian passports, 221–25, 228
and Mossad's attempted assassination of Mishal, 1–3, 135, 138, 139–41, 149–51, 155–56, 161–62, 203, 222–25
Carter, Jimmy, 245, 407, 416
Castro, Fidel, 31
Central Intelligence Agency (CIA)
Counterterrorism Center, 50
covert operation in Afghanistan, 46, 50–51, 58, 59
and King Hussein's GID, 28
and Mossad plot to assassinate Mishal, 149, 166–69, 203–4
Charles, Prince, 245
Chechen guerrillas, 186–87
chemical weapons research, 184–87
Chicago Tribune, 66

Chirac, Jacques, 245, 313
Chrétien, Jean, 161, 221
Churchill, Winston, 23
Circassian Guards (Jordan), 23
civil war between Hamas and Fatah in Gaza,
    347–48, 353, 364, 369–82, 398–99,
    407–11
  and Abbas, 371–72, 377, 382
  aftermath, 377–81, 407–11, 415–16
  brutal retribution/comeuppance (*qassas*),
    372–76
  Hamas statement and start of, 372–73
  Hamas victory, 377–81
  Qassam rocket attack on Israeli training
    camp, 407–9
  Washington's plan for, 353, 364, 370–71,
    377
Clinton, Bill/Clinton administration
  and Barak, 256
  Camp David Summit and failures of,
    257–59
  conversations with King Hussein, 166,
    173–74, 177, 194
  King Hussein's funeral, 245
  and Middle East peace efforts, 92, 173,
    242–43, 249, 257–59, 272–73
  and Mossad plot to assassinate Mishal/
    negotiations following, 165–77,
    203–6
  and Syria/Barak's Syria strategy, 256
  and U.S. crackdown on Hamas, 79, 85
  Wye Memorandum, 242–43, 249
Clinton, Hillary, 165
Cohen, Stanley J., 79, 87–88, 92–93, 94, 194
Cold War, 28
Conflicts Forum Web site, 350–53
Contreras, Joe, 154–55
Council on American Islamic Relations, 390
Crooke, Alastair, 349–253

Dahabi, Mohammad, 166–67
Dahlan, Mohammad
  and friction between Fatah and elected
    Hamas government, 233, 286, 327,
    333, 342, 356, 358–59, 369, 370,
    379–80, 382
  and Preventive Security Service (PSS),
    262, 358
Dayan, Moshe, 14, 15, 16, 41–42, 246
Dayton, Keith, 352, 363, 370–71, 379
De Soto, Alvaro, 342, 352–53
Declaration of Israeli Independence, 9
Dees, Morris, 299
Defense Intelligence Agency, 46
Deif, Mohammad, 284
Democratic Front for the Liberation of
    Palestine, 265
Dhahab, Saib, 59
Dichter, Avi, 369
Al-Din Al-Najjar, Bahaa, 106
disengagement plan (Middle East road map),
    284–85, 290, 292–93, 319
DLBs ("dead-letter boxes"), 101
Doherty, Joseph, 87
Dome of the Rock, 14
Dougherty, Michael T., 79, 88–89
Dudin, Musa, 97
Duffy, Judge Kevin Thomas, 94, 96, 118–19
Durkin, Tom, 385

Egan, Wesley, 118, 120, 122, 167–69,
    172–73
Egypt
  handling of Islamists, 46, 47
  Muslim Brotherhood, 8, 53, 54
  and Six-Day War, 14
Eichmann, Adolf, 216–17
Eisencott, Gadi, 288
Eisenhower, Dwight, 46
El-Ashi, Ghassan, 86–87, 386, 388, 393–94
El-Ashi, Nadia, 78, 86–87, 89, 90–91, 115–
    16, 385
El-Mezain, Mohammad, 386, 388
Eran, Oded, 141, 175
Eretz Israel, 26
Erez, Shayke, 49
Erez border crossing accident and first
    Intifada, 63–64, 402–3

Erez terminal border crossing, 342–43, 379

Eshkol, Levi, 14, 246

Estripeau, Christian, 312

European Union, 363, 382

Ezra, Gideon, 291

Fares, Qadura, 315

Farhat, Miriam (Mother of Martyrs), 324

Fatah
  Abbas and leadership after Arafat's death, 313
  Al-Aqsa Martyrs Brigade and second Intifada, 262
  elected Hamas government and factional frictions, 326–35, 341–42, 346, 347–48, 353–64, 369–76, 415–16
  Gaza civil war with Hamas, 347–48, 353, 364, 369–82, 398–99, 407–11
  Hamas/Fatah clashes over control of community and political groups, 103
  holding salaries of government employees, 326, 332
  and Islamist Muslim Brotherhood, 31, 42–48, 52, 53–54, 58, 60
  Israeli weapons shipments to, 355, 370
  in Kuwait, 35, 36–37, 52
  Mishal's rejection of, 35, 52, 53–54
  obstructionism/refusal to relinquish power, 326, 331–32
  and Palestinian elections (2004–2006), 313–34
  training camps, 58
  See also Abbas, Mahmoud (Abu Mazen); Arafat, Yasser; Palestinian elections and Hamas/Fatah rivalry (2004–2006)

Fatah, Abdul, 13

Fayed, Walid, 276

Fayyad, Salam, 377–78

fedayeen, 24

Federal Bureau of Investigation (FBI)
  Abu Marzook interrogation, 79, 86–94
  Counterterrorism Task Force and Vulgar Betrayal investigation, 307–11
  investigations of Hamas operations in U.S., 77, 86–94, 97, 100, 248, 301–2, 307–11
  and secret Hamas conference at Courtyard Marriott in Philadelphia (1993), 77, 86
  surveillance of Holy Land Foundation, 75, 86, 301–2
  Terrorist Financing Operations Section, 384–85, 390–91

Feisal I, King (Iraq), 23

Felasteen (Hamas-run newspaper), 409

fentanyl derivatives, 2, 184–87

Fertitta, Tilman, 169–70

Fish, A. Joe, 387, 388–89, 395

Florman, Carole, 86

Ford, Gerald, 245

Franklin, Stephen, 66

Gadhafi, Muammar, 296

Gaess, Roger, 122–23

Gaza
  civil war between Hamas and Fatah, 347–48, 353, 364, 369–82, 398, 407–11, 415–16
  Erez border crossing traffic accident, 63–64, 402–3
  Erez terminal border crossing, 342–43, 379
  first Intifada, 61–64, 402–3
  Hamas/Palestinian tunnel, 336–37
  hardships of life under elected Hamas government, 342–48, 370, 410, 415–16
  Islamic revival against Israeli occupation (1980s), 41–48, 51
  Israel's airstrikes against, 334–35, 346–47, 369
  and Israel's assassination of Yassin, 286–88
  Israel's cross-border raid (abduction of Abu Muammar brothers), 334–35, 337
  Jabaliyah refugee camp, 63
  and Palestinian Authority, 76, 104–5
  Al-Rantisi as new Hamas leader, 288–90

and reinstatement of Abu Marzook to
political bureau, 238–39
Sheikh Yassin's release/return to, 207–9,
213–14, 230–36
and Six-Day War, 14
Yassin's Islamic Center and Muslim
Brotherhood activity, 42–43, 60
Gaza Center for Rights and Law, 105
Gellman, Barton, 201
General Intelligence Department (GID)
(Jordan), 22, 28, 55, 80–82, 84, 138–
39, 360–61
General Union of Palestinian Students
(GUPS), 52–53
Geneva Conventions, 15, 273
Gershon, Nina, 393
Gerson, Allan, 393
Ghalia family, 334, 344
Gharaybeh, Adnan, 18–20
Ghosheh, Ibrahim, 127, 249, 252–54,
265–66
Gillad, Roy, 154
Gillon, Carmi, 120
Golan Heights, 14
Goldstein, Baruch, 107–8
Goren, Shmuel, 41, 44–47, 64
Great Arab Revolt (1916–1918), 23
Green Line, 285, 290, 319
Gur, Mordechai, 15

Haaretz (Israeli newspaper), 218, 292,
363–64
Habash, George, 33, 89–90
Habib, Randa, 17–20, 83–84, 112, 129–31
interviews with King Hussein, 17–20, 83,
121, 243–44
and Jordan's GID, 84
and King Abdullah II's crackdown on
Hamas, 250
Radio Monte Carlo radio reports, 83–84,
131, 137, 194
and release of Mossad agents, 211–13
reporting Mossad plot to assassinate
Mishal, 129–31, 137–44, 151–52, 154–

57, 176, 187–88, 194–95, 202, 206,
227–28
and Yassin's release, 209, 211–13
Al-Hadath (Jordanian periodical), 255
Haganah (Zionist fighting force), 8
Hakim, Nasser Abdel, 324
Halberstam, Michael, 295, 299, 384
Halevy, Efraim, 292, 367, 412
as head of Mossad, 229, 279–80
and King Hussein's truce offer to Netanyahu, 225–26
and Middle East road map, 280–81
negotiations following Mossad's failed
assassination of Mishal, 178–80,
181–83, 188–91, 199
scheme to rearrange Palestinian leadership, 279–81
Hamas
changes during 1980s and 1990s, 234
charities/fund-raising, 101–2, 269–70,
296, 300–302, 307–11
Clinton administration's crackdown on,
79, 85
communication via DLBs, 101
creation of (1987), 64–69, 402–3
first charter, 65, 330, 412
and first Intifada, 64–66, 402–3
first mention in foreign media (1988), 65
first weapons/early bombing missions, 67
hudna (truce) talks with Israel, 128, 141,
146, 225–26, 236–37
in Iraqi-occupied Kuwait, 70–71
King Abdullah II's crackdown on Jordan
operations, 247–55
layers of authority in, 112–13
Majlis Shura (advisory council), 112–13,
251–52, 270
name of, 64
network of HLF-funded zakat committees, 384, 387, 390, 394
operations in Doha, Qatar, 253–55,
264–66
Oslo and Wye Memorandum, 242–43,
249

Hamas (*cont.*)
  and Oslo peace process, 103–5, 231–32,
    242–43
  post-Yassin era, 288–93
  and second Intifada, 263–64, 268–70,
    300–302
  second Intifada and economic crisis in
    Occupied Territories, 300–302, 305–7
  secret meeting at Courtyard Marriott in
    Philadelphia, 75–77, 86
  shura principle and decision making, 113
  twentieth anniversary/longevity of,
    411–12
  Yassin and creation of, 64–66, 67, 68–69,
    402–3
  and Yassin's death, 287–89
  and Yassin's return to Gaza, 234–38
  See also Hamas and use of violence;
    Hamas government; Hamas operations
    in Amman, Jordan; Hamas operations
    in Damascus, Syria; Hamas operations
    in U.S.; Palestinian elections and
    Hamas/Fatah rivalry (2004–2006)
Hamas and use of violence, 104, 327, 404,
    412
  and Al-Rantisi, 289
  Mishal and, 404, 412
  and Palestinian elections, 322
  post-Oslo, 105–8
  second Intifada, 268–69, 271–75, 282–83,
    285, 288
  suicide bombings, 106–8, 106–9, 120,
    126–27, 163, 196, 268–69, 271–75,
    285, 322, 404
  See also suicide bombings by Hamas
Hamas government
  post-election/aftermath, 324–35
  abandonment of cease-fire, 334, 338
  Al-Rimawi's 2007 report of plan to top-
    ple, 359–64
  and anti-Semitic Hamas charter, 330, 412
  Bush administration's aid to Abbas, 339,
    341–42, 344, 346, 351–53, 362–64,
    365–68, 378, 381–82
  Bush administration's campaign destabi-
    lize, 285, 339, 341–42, 344, 346,
    351–53, 362–68, 378, 381–82, 417
  and changed tone, 329–33
  civil war with Fatah in Gaza, 347–48, 353,
    364, 369–82, 398–99, 407–11
  and Crooke's Conflicts Forum report,
    351–53, 361, 364
  Executive Force, 341, 353, 354, 357,
    368–69, 398, 409
  factional friction with Fatah, 326–35,
    341–42, 346, 347–48, 353–64, 369–76,
    415–16
  Fatah's obstructionism/refusal to relin-
    quish power, 326, 331–32
  finances and currency smuggling for cash,
    331
  finances frozen/aid blocked to, 327, 331,
    366
  and hardships of life in Gaza, 342–48,
    370, 410, 415–16
  international efforts to topple/destabilize,
    327–28, 331, 339, 341–42, 344, 346,
    351–53, 359–68, 378, 417
  and Islamic law (Sharia), 330
  and Israel, 327, 329–40, 346–47, 355,
    369–70, 400–401, 412–13
  links to Iranian regime, 365–68
  Mecca Summit and Accord, 357–59, 362,
    365, 367
  and Middle East Quartet, 341–42, 344,
    352–53, 362
  military training activities, 368–69
  and Mishal, 326–33, 339, 348, 358,
    367–68, 400–402
  and Netanyahu, 327–28
  refusal to recognize Israel, 329–31, 412–13
  tunnel into Israel/capture of Shalit, 336–40
  the unity government, 358
Hamas operations in Amman, Jordan,
    71–74, 247–55
  and Abu Marzook's political bureau, 72,
    73, 74, 80–81, 111–13, 116, 122–24,
    196, 237–40

King Abdullah II's crackdown on, 247–55
and King Hussein, 72–74, 81–83, 117–18, 121–25, 237
King Hussein's plan to reform, 121–25, 237
and Kuwait crisis (1991), 74–75
Mishal as leader of political bureau, 111–15, 116, 121, 123–24, 128, 237–40
move from Kuwait/centralizing of leadership, 71–74
rivalry over leadership of political bureau, 123–24, 237–40, 401–2
See also Mishal, Khalid (Mossad's 1997 plot to assassinate)
Hamas operations in Damascus, Syria, 264–70, 396–407, 413–14, 416
Hamas operations in U.S.
and Abu Marzook, 78–81, 84–94, 97–98, 116, 238–39, 296, 307–8
Bush administration fight against terrorist fund-raising, 269–70, 296, 300–302, 307–11, 383–91, 393–95
Clinton administration crackdown on, 79, 85
FBI investigations, 77, 86–94, 97, 100, 248, 301–2, 307–11
recruitments by Salah, 98
Hamdan, Osama, 338
Hamed, Ibrahim, 315
Hamed, Taleb, 316
Hamed, Thaer, 316
Hamilton, Linda S., 294–95, 299, 384
Hanegbi, Tzachi, 119
Haniyah, Ismail, 284, 291, 340, 357, 377
and civil war between Hamas and Fatah in Gaza, 347–48, 380, 409–10
and Hamas's refusal to recognize Israel, 330–31
on Palestinian elections, 318, 329
Al-Haram Al-Sharif, 257, 259–62
Harari, Shalom, 41–42, 45, 47–48, 60, 65, 329
Hashash, Ghanem, 101
Hassan, Crown Prince, 149, 169, 180

and negotiations following Mossad failed assassination of Mishal, 188–89, 192–94, 200, 201–6
passed over as King Hussein's successor, 244–45
and Yassin's release, 210
Hatch, Orrin, 85
Havel, Vaclav, 245
Al-Hayat Al-Jadidah (Palestinian newspaper), 329–30
Al-Hayya, Khalil, 369
Hebron Protocol (1997), 260
Herbert, Emmanuel, 27
Hezbollah, 41
cross-border raid into Israel (2006), 340–41
and deportation of Hamas leaders to Lebanon, 68
and Hamas government, 368
and Mossad attack in Damascus (2008), 415
and Mossad surveillance, 229
and withdrawal of Israeli troops from Lebanon, 257, 262, 288
Holy Land Foundation (HLF), 116, 253, 383–91
and Bush administration fight against Hamas fund-raising, 269–70, 296, 300–302, 307–11, 383–91, 393–95
FBI monitoring of, 75, 86, 301–2
and Lewin's prosecution of Boim case, 300, 309, 311
and network of zakat committees, 384, 387, 390, 394
prosecution of (2007), 383–91
and secret Hamas meeting at Courtyard Marriott in Philadelphia (1993), 75–77, 86, 296
Human Rights Watch, 284
Hummel, Joseph, 79, 88–93, 106
Hussein, King (Jordan), 17–29
and Arafat, 24–25, 73, 106, 210, 254–55
and Clinton, 166, 173–74, 177, 194
decision to anoint Prince Abdullah his successor, 243–44

Hussein, King (Jordan) (*cont.*)
  driving Arafat and PLO out of Jordan,
    24–25, 26
  funeral, 245–46
  and Hamas operations in Amman,
    72–74, 81–83, 117–18, 121–25, 237
  and Hashemite Kingdom, 15, 23, 26
  and *hudna* (truce) talks between Hamas
    and Israel, 128, 141, 146, 225–26,
    236–37
  illness and death, 242–46
  and Jordan's 1994 treaty with Israel, 106,
    137, 146–47, 168, 173–74, 178–79,
    180, 192, 193, 197, 199
  and Kuwait crisis (1991), 72, 74–75
  and Mossad's failed assassination of Mishal,
    3, 140, 141–43, 145–48, 152, 160, 167–
    80, 189–94, 198–203, 206, 224
  and Muslim Brotherhood in Jordan,
    25–26, 47, 82, 122
  and Oslo peace process, 105–6, 121,
    173–74, 242–43
  and Palestinian refugee situation, 25
  personal characteristics, 21–22
  Randa Habib's interviews with, 17–20, 83,
    121, 244
  reaction to Rabin's assassination, 121
  relations with Israel, 27, 29, 81
  relations with Netanyahu, 125–28, 139,
    160, 168–69, 203
  relations with U.S./Washington,
    27–28, 29
  release of Abu Marzook to Jordan,
    120–25
  royal palaces, 22–23
  and Six-Day War, 23–24, 26
  and West Bank plans, 15, 19, 28–29
Hussein, Mohammad, 345
Hussein Bin Talal. *See* Hussein, King (Jordan)
Al-Husseini, Abd Al-Qadir, 8

Ibn Kathir, 407
Ibrahimi Mosque in Hebron, Goldstein's
  1994 massacre of Palestinians at, 107–8

"Ikhwan Al-Muslimun." *See* Muslim
  Brotherhood
Ikhwan project, 53–54
Immigration and Naturalization Service
  (INS), 78, 85–86, 87
Indyk, Martin, 117, 119, 120, 172, 256
InfoCom Corp., 307–8, 309, 385
Intercontinental Hotel in Amman, Jordan,
  1–3, 17–19, 158
Intifada, first (1987–1993), 61–66, 347, 402–3
Intifada, second (Al-Aqsa Intifada), 256,
    259–64, 268–93, 300–307, 317, 319
  Abbas's appointment as puppet prime
    minister, 281–82
  Arafat's leadership under, 262–64, 271–
    73, 305–7
  cease-fire negotiations, 272–73, 282–83,
    319
  and charity donations/contributions to
    Palestinians, 301, 305–7
  Halevy's scheme to rearrange Palestinian
    leadership, 279–81
  Hamas and economic crisis/budget in
    Occupied Territories, 300–302, 305–7
  Hamas suicide bombings, 268–69, 271–
    75, 282–83, 285, 288
  Israeli settlements, 290, 292–93
  Israel's assassinations of Hamas leaders,
    276, 282–83, 286–88, 290–91
  Israel's attack on Jenin, 275–78
  and Middle East road map, 280–82, 284–
    85, 290, 292–93
  Palestinian death toll, 273, 284, 319
  and Palestinian elections (2004–2006),
    317, 319
  post-Yassin era, 288–93
  and Al-Rantisi, 288–91
  rapprochement and release of Hamas
    operatives from Palestinian prisons,
    263–64
  and right of refugee return, 290, 292–93
  and Sharon, 259–62, 271–73, 275–80
  Sharon's Operation Defensive Shield,
    276–80, 304

Sharon's plan for unilateral disengagement from Occupied Territories, 284–85, 290, 292–93, 319

Sharon's visit to Al-Haram Al-Sharif, 259–62

Sharon's "war on terror" against Palestinians, 271–73, 275–80, 284–85, 292

siege at Arafat's Ramallah compound, 278–79

the West Bank wall, 271, 284–85, 319

Iran

and Hamas government, 365–68

the 1979 revolution, 41, 366

and U.S. manipulation of Hamas-Fatah conflict, 365–68

Iraq, 69–71, 366, 367

Irgun, 7

Irish Republican Army (IRA), 67, 87, 315–16, 404

Islamic Association for Palestine, 53, 59, 76, 116, 300, 307

Islamic Association of Palestinian Students, 52–53

Islamic Jihad, 333

Islamic Resistance Movement (Harakat Al-Muqawamah Al-Islamiyah), 64. *See also* Hamas

Israel

airstrikes against Gaza, 334–35, 346–47, 369

crackdowns on Hamas in Occupied Territories, 67–69, 93, 95–103, 117, 125–28

cross-border raid (abduction of Abu Muammar brothers), 334–35, 337

early arrests of Hamas leaders (1988), 67–69

and the elected Hamas government, 327, 329–40, 346–47, 355, 369–70

and emerging Islamism in occupied Gaza (1980s), 41–48, 51

extradition of Abu Marzook, 85–87, 93–94, 96, 118–21

Hamas government's refusal to recognize, 329–31, 412–13

Hezbollah's cross-border raid/retaliatory invasion (2006), 340–41

invasion of Lebanon (1982), 40

and Islamists in Afghanistan, 46

jailing of Yassin, 68–69, 112, 117, 126

planning sixtieth anniversary of state founding, 411

weapons shipments to Fatah/Abbas, 355, 370

West Bank raid and capture of Hamas officials, 339–40

See also Intifada, second (Al-Aqsa Intifada)

Israel Defense Forces (IDF), 63

Israel's War of Independence (1948), 8, 9–10

Itzik, Dalia, 218

Jabari, Sheikh Muhammad Ali, 15–16

Jacks, James, 395

Janssen Pharmaceutica, 184–86

Al-Jazeera (satellite TV network), 83, 249–50, 254, 267, 278, 284, 290, 333, 352, 398

Jenin camp, 275–78

Jerusalem Post, 86, 194–95, 222, 226, 364

JFK airport (New York City), 78–79, 84–85

Jibril, Ahmad, 64, 90

Jihaz Filastin (Palestine Apparatus), 56, 114

Johnson, Lyndon, 14

Johnson & Johnson, 184

Johnston, Alan, 410

Jonas, Barry, 388

Jones, Elliott, 295

Jordan

annexation of West Bank, 10

censorship regime and Al-Rimawi's *Al-Majd*, 360–61

deportation of Abu Marzook, 79, 80–81, 114

General Intelligence Department (GID), 22, 28, 55, 80–82, 84, 138–39, 360–61

Hamas operations in, 72–74, 81–83, 117–18, 121–25, 237, 247–55

Jordan (*cont.*)
    Hamas political bureau, 72–74, 80–81,
        111–16, 121, 122–25, 128, 196, 237–40
    Israeli Embassy in Amman, 137, 139–40,
        141–42, 163, 165, 189
    King Abdullah II's regime and Hamas,
        247–55
    King Hussein's funeral, 245–46
    Muslim Brotherhood in, 25–26, 55–56,
        72–73, 82, 122, 156, 252
    Palestinian refugees in, 25, 72
    riots in Ma'an (1989), 83–84
    treaty with Israel, 106, 137, 146–47, 168,
        173–74, 178–79, 180, 192, 193, 197,
        199
    See also Hussein, King (Jordan); Mishal,
        Khalid (Mossad's 1997 plot to assas-
        sinate)
Jordan Option, 27, 28–29, 400

Kadri, Ranya, 110–12, 154–55, 201–2, 402
Kafarna, Basil Daoud, 374
Kamel, Hussein, 118
Kaplinsky, Moshe, 280
Karameh, Battle of (1968), 24, 33, 42
Karmi, Raed, 273
Kather, Sami, 249
Kessler, Martha, 46
Khair, Saed, 202
Khalaf, Salah, 33
Khalil, Izz Al-Din Sheikh, 414
Khater, Sami, 128, 145, 155
Khatib, Fathi, 273–74
Khatib, Saad Na'im, 134–35
Al-Khatib, Abd Al-Ilah, 254
Al-Khatib, Nasser, 100
Khomeini, Ayatollah Ruhollah, 41, 230
Kibbutz Kerem Shalom, 336–37
Kimelman, Marnie, 67
King Hussein Medical City (KHMC)
    Mishal's hospitalization at, 149, 152–54,
        155, 157–60, 183, 206, 240
    and Yassin, 209, 210–11
Klinghoffer, Leon, 298

Kohn, Irit, 93
Kurtzer, Dan, 41, 44, 45–46
Kuwait
    Hamas/Mishal in, 70–71, 113–14
    Muslim Brotherhood in, 34–38, 51–52
    Palestinian refugees in, 31–32, 51–52,
        69–71
    Saddam Hussein's invasion (1990), 69–71,
        74–75
    Silwadi men going to work in (1950s), 11
Kuwait University, 30–31, 37–39

Lapid, Ephraim, 220
LaSalle Talman Bank (Chicago), 95, 100
Lebanese Civil War, 37
Lebanon
    Barak's withdrawal of Israeli troops from,
        257, 262
    Crooke's Conflicts Forum, 350
    deportation of Hamas leaders to, 68
    Hezbollah's cross-border raid into Israel/
        Israel's invasion (2006), 340–41
    Sharon's invasion/siege of the PLO in
        Beirut (1982), 43, 45, 50, 259–60
Levy, David, 179
Lewin, Alyza, 297, 393
Lewin, Nathan
    Boim case, 297–300, 308–9, 311, 395
    and civil actions against Hamas, 295–300,
        307–11, 391, 393
    and Klinghoffer law, 298–300, 309, 311
    legal career, 297–98
    "Novel Legal Theory," 297, 391, 393, 395
Lewis, Leslie, 228
Livni, Tzipi, 417
Lormel, Dennis, 385, 390–91

Al-Madhun, Samih, 353–55, 372, 376
Maghawri, Haitham, 77
Al-Mahmoud, Ahmad Abdullah, 254
Majali, Abdel-Salam, 68
Al-Majd (Jordanian periodical), 255, 359–61
Majlis Shura (Hamas advisory council), 112–
    13, 251–52, 270

Malchin, Zvi, 217
Malley, Robert, 258–59
Mandela, Nelson, 230
Manners, Dave, 81, 166–69, 203, 205
Al-Maqdisi, Abu Mohammad, 83
Markov, Georgi, 219
Al-Masri clan, 373–74
Mearsheimer, John J., 407
Mecca Accord, 357–59, 362, 365, 367
Mecca Investments, 92
Meir, Gideon, 283
Meir, Golda, 27
Melsheimer, Tom, 395
Meron, Theodore, 14–15
Middle East road map, 280–82, 284–85, 290,
    292–93, 331
Mirvat, Sister, 302
Mishal, Abd Al-Qadir (Mishal's father), 5–8,
    10–11, 13–14, 31–33, 38, 39, 69
Mishal, Abdul, 13
Mishal, Akram, 302, 307, 386
Mishal, Amal, 50, 56–57, 70, 131–32, 144,
    188, 228, 248
Mishal, Fatima (mother of Mishal), 4–7,
    10–14, 31, 32, 38, 39, 69, 144
    and assassination attempt on Mishal, 144,
        151, 153, 157
Mishal, Hashim, 34, 38
Mishal, Khalid, 49–60
    and Abu Marzook, 79–80, 115, 123,
        237–40, 401–2
    and Arafat (opinion of), 52, 54, 55, 313
    arrest at Amman airport and detention/
        tribunal, 252–53
    childhood and family in Silwad, 4–7,
        10–14, 16, 32
    control of Hamas political/military wings,
        406
    and creation of Hamas, 64–65, 402–3
    critique of Abbas, 281–82
    deportation to Doha, Qatar, 253–55
    early rejection of Fatah, 35, 52, 53–54
    and elected Hamas government, 326–33,
        339, 348, 358, 367–68, 400–402

family's settling as refugees in Kuwait, 31
graduation from university, 49
and Hamas operations in Damascus,
    Syria, 264–65, 267–70, 396–407,
    413–14, 416
and Hamas's capture of Shalit, 338–40
and Hamas's links to Iranian regime,
    367–68
and Hamas's victory in Gaza civil war,
    381, 382
introduction to political Islamism/
    Palestinian nationalism, 30–39, 49,
    52–53
and Islam, 405
Israeli recognition of, 405–6
and King Abdullah's 1999 crackdown on
    Hamas in Jordan, 247–55, 265
in Kuwait, 70–71, 113–14, 403
Kuwait University studies/activism,
    30–31, 37
as leader of Hamas political bureau in
    Jordan, 111–15, 116, 121, 123–25, 128,
    237–40
marriage, 49–50, 56–57
and Mecca Accord, 358, 367
name change, 115
as new leadership of Hamas (changes to
    Hamas), 234
and Palestinian elections, 316–18, 323,
    326–27, 328, 329–30
Palestinian Project (1980s), 52–60
personal characteristics, 399–400, 405
and post-Oslo landscape, 105
power as Hamas leader, 114–15, 124,
    288–89, 291, 398–407
reading material, 34, 36, 407
religious education/observance, 33, 34, 36
and student branch of Muslim Brother-
    hood, 34–37, 38, 49, 52–53
U.S. recognition of, 405–6
and U.S. case against his brother Mufid
    and HLF, 386, 390
Yassin meeting, 206–7
and Yassin's death, 287

Mishal, Khalid (Mossad's 1997 plot to
    assassinate), 1–3, 128, 129–98
  and Abu Marzook, 196–98
  Bab Al-Salam palace meeting between
    King Hussein and Yatom, 141–43,
    145–48
  and Batikhi, 135, 137–43, 145–52, 158–
    60, 167–69, 180, 188–94, 196–98, 200–
    206, 226
  the "Canadian" assailants, 1–3, 135, 138,
    139–41, 149–51, 155–56, 161–62, 203,
    222–25
  and Clinton administration, 165–77,
    203–6
  and Halevy, 178–80, 181–83, 188–91,
    199
  and Israeli cabinet, 176, 191
  and Israeli Embassy in Amman, 137,
    139–40, 141–42, 163, 165, 189
  Israeli media coverage, 217–18
  and King Hussein, 3, 140, 141–43, 145–
    48, 152, 160, 167–80, 189–94, 198–
    203, 206, 224
  Mishal's hospitalization, 145, 147, 149,
    152–54, 155, 157–60, 183, 206, 240
  Mishal's interviews, 215
  and Mossad's tarnished image, 215–21,
    228–29
  negotiations regarding prisoner release,
    188–94, 196–98, 201–2, 206–14
  negotiations regarding the poison anti-
    dote, 158–60, 164, 169, 170–77, 183
  and Netanyahu, 139, 141, 148, 160, 163,
    168–79, 182–83, 191–94, 199, 205,
    215–21
  the original plan, 163–65
  the poisoning, 2, 144–45, 146, 147–48,
    151–60, 164–65, 172, 175–77, 183–87,
    219
  Randa Habib's reporting on, 129–31,
    137–44, 151–52, 154–57, 176, 187–88,
    194–95, 202, 206, 227–28
  and Sharon, 176, 191, 199–201, 211, 226
  the street attack, 131–37, 139–40, 164

  and Yassin's release, 180–83, 189–90, 197–
    98, 201, 206–14
  and Yatom (Mossad director), 139,
    141–43, 145–48, 158, 163–65, 178,
    193, 205, 231
Mishal, Maher, 5, 34, 38, 70, 412
Mishal, Miriam, 10, 13
Mishal, Mithqal, 248–49
Mishal, Safiyah, 10, 13
Missing Links (blog), 361–62, 363
Mitchell, George, 272
Mobutu Sese Seko, 28
Mofaz, Shaul, 287
Molloy, Mike, 223–25
Mordechai, Yitzhak, 176
Moreno, Linda, 388
Morocco, Arab summit in (1974), 26, 47
Mossad
  capture of Eichmann in Buenos Aires,
    216
  and Jordan's GID, 138–39
  the legendary image/mystique of, 216
  retaliation for Munich Massacre, 221
  Thunderbolt rescue mission at Entebbe
    (1976), 216
Mossad's 1997 plot to assassinate Mishal
  acquisition of poison/fentanyl, 184–86
  criticism of mission, 215–21, 228–29
  Israeli investigative commission report on,
    228–29
  later assassination plans, 413–14, 415
  Mossad-Canada relations and Canadian
    passports, 221–25, 228
  and Yatom, 139, 141–43, 145–48, 158,
    163–65, 178, 193, 205, 215–21,
    228–29, 231
  See also Mishal, Khalid (Mossad's 1997
    plot to assassinate)
Motley, Ron, 392
Muammar, Fares, 101–2
Mubarak, Hosni, 89
Mugniyah, Imad, 415
Muheiddin, Nasouh, 137–38, 139, 141
Munich Olympics Massacre (1972), 221

Musa, Bassam, 100–103
Muslim Brotherhood
  Egyptian, 8, 53, 54
  and Fatah, 31, 42–48, 52, 53–54, 58, 60
  in Jordan, 25–26, 55–56, 72–73, 82, 122,
    156, 252
  in Kuwait, 34–38, 51–55
  and Mishal's claim for historic roots of
    armed resistance, 53–54
  Mishal's global Islamist Palestine project
    (1980s), 52–60
  and Mishal's introduction to Islamism/
    Palestinian nationalism, 34–37, 38, 49,
    52–53
  and mujahideen war in Afghanistan, 46,
    50–51, 57, 58, 59
  and Saudi Arabia, 51
  secret Amman conference (1983),
    55–56, 59
  Syria's massacre/suppression of 1982
    uprising, 46, 265
  Yassin's Islamic Center in Gaza, 42–43, 60
Mustafa, Riyad, 323
Mutawi, Samir, 140

Naim, Bassam, 320, 380
Najah University in Nablus, 43
Al-Najjar, Isa, 68, 380, 382
Al-Nakhba, 9, 36. See also Israel's War of
    Independence (1948)
Narkis, Uzi, 14, 16
Nasrallah, Hassan, 257
Nasser, Gamal Abdel, 47
Naveh, Danny, 178
Nazzal, Mohammad, 74, 128, 215, 398–99
  and King Abdullah II's crackdown on
    Hamas in Jordan, 247, 249, 251
  and Mossad plot to assassinate Mishal,
    129–31, 136–39, 144–45, 151–52, 155,
    156, 160
  and Yassin's release, 207, 212
Neal, William, 389, 390
Netanyahu, Benjamin
  and Arafat, 126, 127

challenge to Sharon's leadership of Likud
    Party, 261
  end of term as prime minister, 256
  and Hamas suicide bombings, 126–27,
    163, 218
  and Israeli case against Abu Marzook,
    120, 121, 122
  and Israel's crackdown on Hamas, 125–28
  and King Hussein, 125–28, 139, 160,
    168–69, 191–93, 203, 245–46
  and King Hussein's plan to reform Hamas
    in Jordan, 122
  and Mossad plot to assassinate Mishal,
    139, 141, 148, 160, 163, 168–79,
    182–83, 191–94, 199, 205, 215–21
  and Oslo peace process, 127, 241, 242
  and Palestinian elections, 327–28
  rebuilt position in Israeli politics, 417
  and tunnel under Al-Aqsa Mosque, 193
  and Yatom, 220–21
Netanyahu, Yonatan, 216
New York Times, 119, 195
Newsweek, 154
Nezavisimaya Gazeta (Russian newspaper),
    331
9/11 terrorist attacks, 267–70
Noor, Queen, 83, 143, 242, 244, 245
Noriega, Manuel, 28
Nusseibeh, Sari, 98

Obaid, Thaer, 374, 375
Ocalan, Abdullah, 265
Odeh, Abdul Rahman, 388
Odeh, Kamal Bani, 107
Odeh, Mohammad, 273–74
Oklahoma City bombing (1995), 85
Olmert, Ehud, 417
  and Hamas government, 330–31, 340,
    341, 382
  mismanaged invasion of Lebanon,
    340–41, 363–64
  succeeding Sharon as prime minister, 320
Operation Defensive Shield (2002), 275–80,
    304

Oslo Declaration of Principles, 260
Oslo peace process
    and Arafat, 75, 92, 103–5, 127, 225, 241,
        242–43, 257–59
    Camp David summit (2000), 257–59, 261
    and Clinton administration, 92, 173, 242–
        43, 249, 257–59, 272–73
    and failed Mossad assassination of
        Mishal, 173–74
    Hebron Protocol (1997), 260
    and Jewish settlements, 75, 261
    and Jordan's 1994 treaty with Israel, 106,
        137, 147, 168, 173–74
    and King Hussein, 105–6, 121, 173–74,
        242–43
    Oslo Declaration of Principles, 260
    Oslo II (1995), 260
    Palestinian concession of land, 258
    and Palestinian elections (2004–2006),
        317
    and Rabin's assassination, 121
    and secret Hamas conference at Court-
        yard Marriott in Philadelphia (1993),
        75–77
    Sharm Al-Sheikh Agreement (1999), 260
    Sharon's opinion of, 262
    Wye River Memorandum (1998), 242–43,
        249, 256, 260
Ostrovsky, Victor, 223
Ottoman Empire, 6, 21, 28

Palestine Liberation Organization (PLO)
    and creation of Hamas, 66
    driven out of Jordan (Black September),
        24–25, 254–55
    eviction from Beirut (1982), 43–44, 50,
        259–60
    and first Intifada, 62–63, 64
    guerrilla hijacking of passenger jets, 25
    Hamas's attempt to destabilize (1993),
        106
    and Islamist Muslim Brotherhood, 43, 54
    Oslo Accords and the negotiated settle-
        ment, 75

    rivalry between Arafat and Yassin over
        control of Palestine, 231–36
    second Intifada and rapprochement
        between Arafat and Hamas, 263–64
    See also Arafat, Yasser; Fatah
Palestinian American Research Center,
    260
Palestinian Authority, 76, 77, 104–5
    Abbas and talks with Israel (2007–2008),
        416–17
    Arafat's security forces, 105, 242, 243
    and King Abdullah II, 249
    and Netanyahu's changes, 127
    second Intifada and economic crisis, 300–
        302, 305–7
Palestinian Center for Human Rights, 372,
    373, 381
Palestinian Center for Policy and Survey
    Research, 124
Palestinian elections and Hamas/Fatah
    rivalry (2004–2006), 313–34
    and Abbas, 313, 318–19, 324, 325, 326,
        328
    campaign issues, 322
    and family unity/divisions, 320–22, 323
    Fatah humiliation/recriminations, 324,
        327, 328–29
    Fatah parliament seats, 324
    Hamas candidates, 316–17
    and Hamas cease-fire (March 2005), 318,
        330, 334
    Hamas parliament seats, 323–24
    Hamas seeking opposition role, 318, 323
    local municipal elections in Occupied
        Territories, 314–16, 318
    and Mishal, 316–18, 323, 326–27, 328,
        329–30
    Mishal victory rally in Khan Younis,
        326–27
    post-election/aftermath, 324–35
    reactions in Washington/Bush adminis-
        tration, 318, 322–23, 325–26, 327
    reactions of Israel, 318, 322–23, 327, 329,
        330

renewed Fatah/Hamas rivalry, 326–35
See also Hamas government
Palestinian Islamic Jihad, 54–55, 265, 282, 367, 408
Palestinian Liberation Army (PLA), 134, 135
Palestinian nationalism
and Arab Revolt, 5–6, 7, 8
and Kuwait refugee communities, 32, 33–34, 51–52
Mishal's introduction to, 30–39, 49, 52–53
and Muslim Brotherhood, 34–37, 38, 49, 52–53
Zionist campaign post–World War II, 7–8
Palestinian refugees
and first Intifada/Jabaliyah refugee camp in Gaza, 63
and Israel's War of Independence (Al-Nakhba), 9–10
in Jordan, 25, 72
in Kuwait, 31–32, 51–52, 69–71
and Palestinian nationalism, 32, 33–34, 51–52
"Plan D" and forced migrations, 8–9
regional issue of, 21
Sabra and Shatila massacre (1982), 260
second Intifada and right of return, 290, 292–93
and Sharon, 260
and Six-Day War, 4–5, 13–16
Pan Am Flight 103 bombing (1988), 296
Pappe, Ilan, 8
Peres, Shimon, 40, 44, 87, 104, 125, 218, 219
Perry, Smadar, 194–95, 217
Philadelphia meeting of Hamas (1993), 75–77, 86, 296
Pickering, Thomas, 412
"Plan D," 8–9
Plan of Attack (Woodward), 360
PLO Radio, 64
Plocker, Sever, 377
Popular Front for the Liberation of Palestine, 89–90, 265

Popular Front for the Liberation of Palestine—General Command, 64, 90
Popular Resistance Committees, 335, 337
Powell, Colin, 280, 292, 412
Preventive Security Service (PSS), 347
Arafat's, 214, 232, 262, 358
and Dahlan, 262, 358

Al-Qaeda terror network, 46, 58, 267–70
Qassam, Izzadin, 5
Qassam Brigade (military wing of Hamas)
and Ayyash's campaign of suicide bombings, 107–8
creation and first recruits, 67
and Hamas capture of Shalit, 338
and Israel's crackdown on Hamas operations in Occupied Territories, 101, 102–3
and Khalid Mishal, 114
and Yassin's funeral in Gaza, 287
Qatar
Hamas operations in Doha, 253–55, 264–66
Mishal's deportation to, 253–55
Qawasmeh, Hani, 369
Qudah, Sameer, 82
Quranic Literacy Institute, 300
Qussos, Yousef, 151
Qutb, Sayyid, 42

Rababa, Sami, 153–54, 157, 160, 183–84
Rabat (Morocco), Arab summit in (1974), 26, 47
Rabbani, Mouin, 260, 261
Rabin, Yitzhak, 8–9, 40, 44, 92, 106
and Abu Marzook's extradition, 87
assassination, 121
and Hamas suicide bombings, 108
negotiated peace settlement with Jordan, 103–4, 199
Radaidah, Hisham, 305
Radaidah, Ziad Zaud Ahmed, 305
Radio Cairo, 12, 13
Radio Monte Carlo (RMC), 83, 131, 137, 194

Rajoub, Jibril, 321, 323, 333–34

Rajoub, Nayef, 321–22, 323

Rajoub family of Hebron, 320–22, 323, 333–34

Al-Rantisi, Abdel Azziz, 126, 234, 241, 276, 282, 284, 288–91

Raphael, Sylvia, 221

Rashid, Nathir, 161

Red Crescent Association, 103

Reno, Janet, 84–85, 87

Rice, Condoleezza, 280, 292, 325–26, 351, 356, 363

Riedel, Bruce, 166, 173, 174, 204, 205, 207, 255

Al-Rimawi, Fahd, 255, 359–62

Al-Rishiq, Izzat, 249

Robinson, Aubrey E., Jr., 295

Roed-Larsen, Terje, 278

Rohan, Michael Dennis, 34

Ross, Dennis, 170–72, 174, 207, 210, 225, 257–58

Rovner, Ilana Diamond, 395

Rubinstein, Elyakim, 176, 178, 191

Rumsfeld, Donald, 280, 351

Russia's chemical weapons research, 186–87

Sa'adon, Ilan, 99

Al-Sabah, Sheikh Jaber, 51

Sabra and Shatila massacre (1982), 260

Sadat, Anwar, 37, 41, 46, 52, 256

Saddam Hussein
    contributions to Occupied Territories during second Intifada, 301, 302–3
    Kuwait invasion (1990), 69–71, 74–75
    and Randa Habib, 84

Saftwai, Mahmoud Jaber, 374

Sakal, Shlomo, 63

Salah, Azita, 100

Salah, Mohammad
    FBI's Vulgar Betrayal investigation, 307, 309
    interrogation and confession about Hamas operations, 95–100, 296

and Lewin's prosecution of Boim case, 299–300
    racketeering charges, 385–86

Salam, Rakad, 303

Al-Salam Al-Souqi, Abed, 378

Salameh, Ali Hassan, 221

Al-Saleh, Mussid, 51

Salem, Abdel, 76

Samia, Yom Tov, 209

Saudi Arabia
    contributions to Palestinians during second Intifada, 301, 305–7
    and Hamas's links to Iranian regime, 365–66
    handling of Islamists, 47, 51
    Mecca Accord/mediation between Fatah and Hamas government, 357–59, 362, 365, 367

Sawalha, Mohammad Hassan, 43

Schroeder, Gerhard, 245

Scowcroft, Brent, 412

Scroggins, Nanette, 389–90

Segev, Yitzhak, 43

Selassie, Haile, 22

settlements
    after Six-Day War, 14–15
    and Barak, 261
    first Intifada and "transfer" plans, 63
    near Silwad village on West Bank, 314–15
    Netanyahu's promises to King Hussein, 193
    and Oslo peace process, 75, 261
    and second Intifada, 290, 292–93
    and Sharon, 260, 272, 290, 292–93, 319–20

Shaath, Nabil, 47, 345–46

Shalit, Gilad, 337–41, 416

Shamir, Shimon, 218

Shapira, Shimon, 178–79

Shara, Farouk, 256

Sharm Al-Sheikh Agreement (1999), 260

Sharon, Ariel
    and Arafat, 262, 269, 271, 278–79
    and assassination of Yassin, 287

and Bush administration, 290, 292–93

invasion of Lebanon/siege of PLO in
Beirut (1982), 43, 45, 50, 199, 259–60

and Middle East road map, 281–82,
284–85, 292–93, 319, 331

negotiations following Mossad plot to
assassinate Mishal, 176, 191, 199–201,
226

Operation Defensive Shield, 276–80, 304

opinion of Oslo process, 262

plan for unilateral disengagement from
Occupied Territories, 284–85, 290,
292–93, 319

and second Intifada, 259–62, 271–73,
275–80

and settlements, 260, 272, 290, 292–93,
319–20

stroke, 320

visit to Al-Haram Al-Sharif, 259–62

"war on terror" against Palestinians,
271–73, 275–80, 284–85, 292

and West Bank wall, 271, 284, 319

Al-Sharuf, Ahmad Mohammad Abdullah,
305

Shehadeh, Salah, 283

Shevchenko, Yuri, 186

Shiite Muslim regimes, 365–66

Shikaki, Khalil, 124

Shin Bet, 95–96, 232, 336, 370, 385

Shubaylat, Layth, 22

Shukri, Ali
meeting at King Hussein's palace, 145–46
meetings with Canadian diplomats, 162,
223–24
meetings with CIA's Manners, 167, 203
and Mossad plot to assassinate Mishal,
145–46, 148, 151, 153, 154, 158–60,
162, 167, 172–73, 175, 180, 183,
191–92, 203, 223–24
move of Mishal to KHMC, 153
and the poisoning/antidote, 148, 151, 154,
158–60, 183

Siam, Said, 399

Silberg, David, 128

Silwad (village in West Bank), 5–7, 10–14,
16, 31, 32, 314–16

Sinai, 14

Six-Day War (June 1967), 4–5, 11–16,
23–24, 411

Skolnik, Avinoam, 274

Sourani, Raji, 105, 373, 381

Spector, Norman, 222–23

St. Eve, Amy, 385

Stern Gang, 7

Subhi, Fathi, 102

Sudan, 89

suicide bombings by Hamas, 106–8, 126–27,
163, 271–75, 404
and Ayyash, 106–8, 120
charity donations to martyrs' families,
302–4
Jerusalem and Haifa bombings (2001),
268–69, 271–73
Jerusalem bombings (1997), 126–27, 163
Matza bombing, 275–76
and Mishal, 404
and Palestinian elections, 322
Passover Massacre at Netanya's Park
Hotel, 273–75
second Intifada, 268–69, 271–75, 282–83,
285, 288
Tel Aviv bombing and Fatah, 333

Sunni Muslim regimes, 365–66

Symmes, Harrison, 27

Syria
Barak's Syria First strategy, 256
Hamas operations in Damascus, 264–70,
396–407, 413–14, 416
and Israel's retaliation against Hamas, 340
massacre of Muslim Brotherhood sympathizers, 46, 265
Palestinian "rejectionist" factions in, 265

Al-Tadhamun Society in Nablus, 304

Tal, Ron, 63

Tamimi, Azzam, 35–37, 49

Tamimi, Kamal, 302

Tannun, Hassan, 35–36

Tenet, George, 149, 203–4, 272, 407
terrorist fund-raising, Bush administration
    fight against
    Arab Bank case, 391–93
    Holy Land Foundation investigation/
        prosecution, 269–70, 296, 300–302,
        307–11, 383–91, 393–95
Thunderbolt rescue mission at Entebbe
    (1976), 216
Tubasi, Shadi, 275–76, 277
Al-Turabi, Hasan, 89
Turkey, 265

Union of Arab Journalists, 209
United Nations Convention Against Torture,
    273
United Nations Relief and Works Agency,
    301, 346
United Nations Resolution 181, 8, 9–10
United States. *See* Bush, George W./Bush
    administration; Clinton, Bill/Clinton
    administration; Hamas operations
    in U.S.
Usher, Graham, 313

Village Leagues, 45
Vulgar Betrayal investigation (FBI), 307–11

Wachsman, Esther, 226–27
Wachsman, Nachshon, 226–27
Wahba, Wael Mahmoud, 372
wall in West Bank, 271, 284–85, 319
Walles, Jacob, 356
Walt, Stephen M., 407
War of the Knives, 67
Washington Post, 85, 90, 201, 360
Al-Watan (newspaper), 51
Weisglass, Dov, 292–93
Welch, Bernard C., Jr., 294–95, 299, 384
Welch, David, 172, 352–53
West Bank
    first Jewish settlements, 14–15
    Israel's raid/capture of Hamas officials,
        339–40

Jordan's annexation, 10
    Rajoub family of Hebron, 320–22
    and Sharon's Operation Defensive Shield,
        275–78
    and Sharon's wall, 271, 284–85, 319
    and Six-Day War, 12, 14
Whbee, Majali, 142, 199–201, 202, 211, 213,
    226
Wilcox, Philip, 45–46
Wilson, Walter, 159–60
Wood, Kimba M., 94
Woodward, Bob, 360
World Bank, 363
World Trade Center bombing (1993), 85
World War I, 6, 21
World War II, 7–8
Wright, Robert, 100, 307
Wye River Memorandum (1998), 242–43,
    249, 256, 260

Ya'alon, Moshe, 287
Yassin, Sheikh Ahmad, 41–43
    and Abu Marzook, 79–80, 112, 115, 125,
        206–9, 401
    and Arafat, 182, 210, 231–36, 241, 243,
        263, 287
    assassination of, 283–84, 286–88
    and cease-fire negotiations, 282
    changes to Hamas after return to Gaza,
        234–36
    and creation of Hamas, 64–66, 67, 68–69,
        402–3
    first arrest in Israel (1984), 60, 64
    Islamic Center in Gaza and Muslim
        Brotherhood, 42–43, 60
    meeting Mishal, 206–7
    and PLO ruling council, 241
    and prospect of *hudna* (truce) with Israel,
        236
    radical anti-occupation views, 41–43
    release following Mossad's failed assas-
        sination of Mishal, 180–83, 189–90,
        197–98, 201, 206–14, 226–28
    return to Gaza, 207–9, 213–14, 230–36

second arrest/jailing in Israel (1989),
68–69, 112, 117, 126
and Sharon's Operation Defensive Shield,
276
Yatom, Danny (Mossad director), 139,
141–43, 163–65, 178, 225
criticism of role at Mossad, 219–21, 228–29
meeting with King Hussein, 141–43,
145–48
and Mossad legend/mystique, 216
and Netanyahu, 220–21
original plan to assassinate Mishal,
163–65, 231
and poisoning of Mishal, 146, 147–48, 158
resignation, 229

Yedioth Ahronoth (Tel Aviv–based daily), 194,
213–14, 217, 352, 357, 377
Yehiya, Omar Ahmad, 77
Yeltsin, Boris, 245
Yom Kippur War, 26–27
Yousef, Ahmad Mohammad, 89, 320,
369

Al-Zahar, Mahmoud, 276, 289, 322, 331
zakat committees, 384, 387, 390, 394
Al-Zarqawi, Abu Musab, 83, 115
Al-Zawahiri, Ayman, 330
Zein, Abdullah, 229
Zinni, Anthony, 275
Zionists, 7–9